MW00719129

Handbook of Forensic Assessment

Psychological and Psychiatric Perspectives

Eric Y. Drogin

Frank M. Dattilio

Robert L. Sadoff

Thomas G. Gutheil

WILEY

John Wiley & Sons, Inc.

Library of Congress Cataloging-in-Publication Data:
    Handbook of forensic assessment : psychological and psychiatric perspectives/[edited by] Eric Y. Drogin . . . [et al.].
        p.; cm.
    Includes bibliographical references and index.
    ISBN 978-0-470-48405-0 (cloth: alk. paper); 978-1-118-02799-8 (eMobi); 978-1-118-02800-1 (ePub); 978-1-118-02798-1 (ePDF); 978-1-118-09339-9 (Wiley online library)
    1. Forensic psychiatry—Handbooks, manuals, etc. 2. Capacity and disability—Handbooks, manuals, etc. 3. Informed consent (Medical law)—Handbooks, manuals, etc. I. Drogin, Eric York.
    [DNLM: 1. Forensic Psychiatry—methods—United States. 2. Mental Competency—United States. 3. Mental Disorders—diagnosis—United States. 4. Mental Disorders—psychology—United States. 5. Psychological Tests—United States. W 740]
    RA1151.H245 2011
    614'.15—dc22
                                                                                        2010048922

Printed in the United States of America

10 9 8 7 6 5 4 3 2 1

Contents

Foreword

T HE PSYCHOLOGICAL AND psychiatric assessment of individuals involved in legal proceedings have significantly advanced during the past decade. In part, this reflects the increasing maturity of the fields of forensic psychiatry and forensic psychology, accompanied by the influence of increased focus on evidence-based practice seen more broadly in medicine and mental health. Courts are increasingly receptive to mental health expert input, and ever larger numbers of general psychologists and psychiatrists have entered the realm of forensic practice. Legislators, intentionally or otherwise, have enacted additional statutes that necessitate expert mental health information and testimony. Forensic psychology and psychiatry are increasingly informed by an empirical foundation, and research-based testimony is increasingly possible. The present book, involving an unusual and close collaboration between forensic psychologists and forensic psychiatrists, provides ample illustration of many of these advances.

But it is worth noting that the chapters in this excellent book go well beyond the general description of advances and summary of the "state of the field" that we often see in broadly based edited volumes. Indeed, there are three unusual features to *Handbook of Forensic Assessment* that, taken together, make it a unique contribution to the literature.

The first involves the collaboration between psychiatry and psychology that is evident in the coauthorship of almost all chapters by a forensic psychologist and a forensic psychiatrist. These specializations each draw considerably on their respective disciplines, yet share much of the relevant law, science, ethics, and practice that guide the best practice of forensic mental health assessment. It is refreshing to see this acknowledged in the kind of collaboration that is evident in these chapters.

A second significant feature of the volume is the focus on foundational principles that are important across various legal questions in forensic psychiatry and forensic psychology. These principles have been discussed in some detail during the last decade (Heilbrun, 2001; Heilbrun, Grisso, & Goldstein, 2009) and appear to have the potential for providing a general framework within which empirically supported practice in forensic mental health can be more easily applied. Nonetheless, there clearly remains a good deal of work—conceptual, empirical, and applied—that must be done before such principles can be said to have substantial influence on most of the mental health assessments performed for courts and attorneys. Books like *Handbook of Forensic Assessment* can move the field meaningfully toward the larger goal of best practice guided by foundational principles.

The third significant feature of the work, related to the second, is the specific focus on the quality of forensic evaluations conducted by mental health professionals. Much of the evidence gathered in the 1990s suggested generally that the quality of evaluations conducted for courts and attorneys was not what it could have been. This may be changing, however, with the increased research and professional focus on evaluation quality, and the potential for using quality improvement approaches to make the forensic evaluations and reports submitted to courts more legally relevant, scientifically supported, ethically guided, and consistent with standards of practice (see Wettstein, 2005).

Eric Y. Drogin, Frank M. Dattilio, Robert L. Sadoff, and Thomas G. Gutheil are to be congratulated for assembling a group of contributors whose work, taken together, advances the fields of forensic psychiatry and forensic psychology several steps. We anticipate that a wide variety of mental health professionals, even at different levels of forensic experience, will find the book to be a valuable addition to their libraries. The quality and usefulness of information provided by forensic practitioners to the courts should thereby be enhanced.

Kirk Heilbrun, PhD
Robert M. Wettstein, MD

REFERENCES

Heilbrun, K. (2001). *Principles of forensic mental health assessment*. New York, NY: Kluwer Academic/Plenum Press.

Heilbrun, K., Grisso, T., & Goldstein, A. (2009). *Foundations of forensic mental health assessment*. New York, NY: Oxford.

Wettstein, R. M. (2005). Quality and quality improvement in forensic mental health evaluations. *Journal of the American Academy of Psychiatry and the Law, 33*, 158–175.

Preface

AS AVID COLLECTORS of books on forensic mental health assessment for more decades than we may care to admit, we remain perplexed by two recurrent features of the genre: (1) an emphasis on research-based justification of forensic evaluations—at the expense of informing the reader how one actually conducts them; and (2) a discipline-specific focus on either psychology or psychiatry—at the expense of identifying the other's unique and complementary contributions.

By contrast, John Wiley & Son's *Handbook of Forensic Assessment: Psychological and Psychiatric Perspectives* adopts an overtly practice-focused and inclusive approach. For a comprehensive range of forensic applications in both criminal and civil cases, the reader will learn in each instance how the forensic evaluator engages in "preparation," "data collection," "data interpretation," and finally "communication" of the results. Many will recognize these as the four broad stages encompassed by Professor Kirk Heilbrun's well-established "Principles of Forensic Mental Health Assessment." By addressing each of these stages in sequence on a chapter-by-chapter basis, we respond to the question we hear most often from forensic clinicians at every stage of professional development: "How do I do this?"

Each chapter is written by both a psychologist and a psychiatrist in order to capture both disciplines' goals and methodologies simultaneously. In the appendices, the reader will find several aids to making the most of this combined perspective, including a scientific glossary, a compendium of psychological tests, and examples of how a psychologist and a psychiatrist might address the same forensic inquiry either separately or in the context of a coauthored report. A glossary of legal terms is also provided.

To enhance further the reader's incorporation of evaluation-specific guidance, we include additional chapters to address such matters as developing and operating a forensic practice, conducting one's practice across jurisdictional lines, conceptualizing and assessing malingering in various contexts, and accommodating transcultural considerations.

We are greatly indebted to Professors Kirk Heilbrun and Robert Wettstein for their foreword to this *Handbook*, and to all of our colleagues who labored so long and patiently to bring you their up-to-date perspectives on forensic mental health assessment. We hope that this resource serves you well in your own practices, and trust that you share our sense of fascination with the evolving contributions of psychology and psychiatry to the legal system.

Eric Y. Drogin, JD, PhD, ABPP
Frank M. Dattilio, PhD, ABPP
Robert L. Sadoff, MD
Thomas G. Gutheil, MD

Contributors

Elliot L. Atkins, EdD
Independent Practice
Marlton, New Jersey

Curtis L. Barrett, PhD, ABPP
University of Louisville School
   of Medicine
Louisville, Kentucky

Gillian Blair, PhD, LLM
Independent Practice
Narberth, Pennsylvania

Henry R. Bleier, MD, MBA
University of Pennsylvania
   School of Medicine
Philadelphia, Pennsylvania

John M. W. Bradford, MD
University of Ottawa
Ottawa, Ontario

Stanley L. Brodsky, PhD
The University of Alabama
Tuscaloosa, Alabama

Harold J. Bursztajn, MD
Harvard Medical School
Boston, Massachusetts

Mary Connell, EdD, ABPP
Independent Practice
Fort Worth, Texas

Gerald Cooke, PhD, ABPP
Independent Practice
Plymouth Meeting,
   Pennsylvania

Frank M. Dattilio, PhD, ABPP
Harvard Medical School
Boston, Massachusetts

**Eric Y. Drogin, JD, PhD,
ABPP**
Harvard Medical School
Boston, Massachusetts

Albert M. Drukteinis, MD, JD
New England Psychodiagnostics
Manchester, New Hampshire

Amanda M. Fanniff, PhD
University of South Florida
Tampa, Florida

Nicole Foubister, MD
NYU Medical School
New York, New York

Laurentine Fromm, MD
University of Pennsylvania
  School of Medicine
Philadelphia, Pennsylvania

Seema Garg, PhD
Independent Practice
Boston, Massachusetts

Liza H. Gold, MD
Georgetown University
  School of Medicine
Washington, District
  of Columbia

Alan M. Goldstein, PhD, ABPP
Independent Practice
Hartsdale, New York

Robert P. Granacher, Jr., MD, MBA
University of Kentucky College
  of Medicine
Lexington, Kentucky

Thomas G. Gutheil, MD
Harvard Medical School
Boston, Massachusetts

Mark J. Hauser, MD
Harvard Medical School
Boston, Massachusetts

Kirk Heilbrun, PhD, ABPP
Drexel University
Philadelphia, Pennsylvania

Dawn M. Hughes, PhD, ABPP
Weill Cornell Medical College
New York, New York

Richard F. Limoges, MD
University of Pennsylvania
  School of Medicine
Philadelphia, Pennsylvania

Donald J. Meyer, MD
Harvard Medical School
Boston, Massachusetts

Pietro Miazzo, MD
Temple University School
  of Medicine
Philadelphia, Pennsylvania

Timothy J. Michals, MD
Independent Practice
Philadelphia, Pennsylvania

Laurence Miller, PhD
Independent Practice
Boca Raton, Florida

David F. Mrad, PhD, ABPP
School of Professional
  Psychology at Forest
  Institute
Springfield, Missouri

Donna M. Norris, MD
Harvard Medical School
Boston, Massachusetts

Aderonke Oguntoye, MD
Harvard Medical School
Boston, Massachusetts

Randy K. Otto, PhD, ABPP
University of South Florida
Tampa, Florida

Lisa Drago Piechowski, PhD, ABPP
Independent Practice
Glastonbury, Connecticut

Robert F. Putnam PhD, BCBA-D
May Institute
Randolph, Massachusetts

Urrooj Rehman, MD
Harvard Medical School
Boston, Massachusetts

William H. Reid, MD, MPH
Independent Practice
Horseshoe Bay, Texas

Carla Rodgers, MD
University of Pennsylvania
    School of Medicine
Philadelphia, Pennsylvania

Richard Rogers, PhD, ABPP
University of North Texas
Denton, Texas

Robert L. Sadoff, MD
University of Pennsylvania
    School of Medicine
Philadelphia, Pennsylvania

Steven E. Samuel, PhD
Independent Practice
Philadelphia, Pennsylvania

Mark Siegert, PhD
William Alanson White Institute
New York, New York

Kathleen P. Stafford, PhD, ABPP
Louis Stokes Cleveland Veterans
    Affairs Medical Center
Cleveland, Ohio

Annie G. Steinberg, MD
University of Pennsylvania
    School of Medicine
Philadelphia, Pennsylvania

William J. Stejskal, PhD
Independent Practice
Woodbridge, Virginia

Kenneth Tardiff, MD, MPH
Weill Cornell Medical College
New York, New York

Clarence Watson, JD, MD
University of Pennsylvania
    School of Medicine
Philadelphia, Pennsylvania

Kenneth J. Weiss, MD
University of Pennsylvania
    School of Medicine
Philadelphia, Pennsylvania

Philip H. Witt, PhD, ABPP
Associates in Psychological
    Services, P.A.
Somerville, New Jersey

Gregory I. Young, MS
Northeastern University
Boston, Massachusetts

PART 1

CRIMINAL MATTERS

CHAPTER 1

Competence to Stand Trial

KATHLEEN P. STAFFORD and ROBERT L. SADOFF

INTRODUCTION

Competence to stand trial has long been recognized as "the most significant mental health inquiry pursued in the system of criminal law" (Stone, 1975, p. 200), reflecting both the prevalence of court-ordered competency evaluations, and the concern regarding trial competence reflected in the body of case law on this subject.

Hoge, Bonnie, Poythress, and Monahan (1992) estimated that pretrial competence evaluations are sought in 2% to 8% of all felony cases. LaFortune and Nicholson (1995) reported that judges and attorneys estimate that competency is a legitimate issue in approximately 5% of criminal cases, although only two-thirds of these defendants whose competency is questionable are actually referred for formal competency evaluations. Stafford and Wygant (2005) found that nearly all defendants referred for competency evaluation by a mental health court in misdemeanor cases were found incompetent to proceed, and remained incompetent after 60 days of hospitalization.

Trial Competence Defined

The Supreme Court of the United States, in *Dusky v. U.S.* (1960), established the minimal constitutional standard for competency to stand trial as whether the defendant "has sufficient present ability to consult with his lawyer with a reasonable degree of rational

3

understanding—and whether he has a rational as well as factual understanding of the proceedings against him" (p. 789).

In the case of *Wieter v. Settle* (1961), the Court outlined functional criteria for competence, noting that mental illness does not necessarily mean that a defendant lacks the mental faculties required to stand trial. According to *Wieter*, defendants should have the mental capacity:

1. To appreciate their presence in relation to time, place, and things.
2. To appreciate that they are in a court of justice, charged with a criminal offense, with a judge on the bench, a prosecutor who will try to convict them of a criminal charge, and a lawyer who will undertake to defend them against that charge.
3. To appreciate that they will be expected to tell their lawyer to the best of their mental ability the circumstances, the facts surrounding them at the time and place where the offense is alleged to have been committed.
4. To appreciate that there is, or will be, a jury present to pass upon evidence adduced as to their guilt or innocence.
5. For memory sufficient to relate those things in their own personal manner. (pp. 321–322)

BASIS FOR RAISING THE ISSUE OF COMPETENCE

In *Pate v. Robinson* (1966), the Supreme Court of the United States held that a trial judge must raise the issue of competency if either the court's own evidence, or that presented by the prosecution or defense, raises a "bona fide doubt" about the defendant's competency. In *Drope v. Missouri* (1975), the Court clarified that evidence of the defendant's irrational behavior, demeanor at trial, and any prior medical opinion on competence to stand trial are relevant to determine whether further inquiry is required during the course of the proceedings.

AMNESIA AND COMPETENCE

In *Wilson v. U.S.* (1968), a federal appellate court upheld the conviction of a man who had sustained head injuries in the course of a high-speed chase by police and was therefore amnesic for the offenses. However, the court remanded the case for more extensive posttrial findings on the issue of whether amnesia deprived the defendant of a fair trial and effective assistance of counsel. Six factors were articulated to assist the trial court in determining whether the fairness and accuracy of the proceedings had been compromised and the conviction should be vacated:

1. The extent to which the amnesia affected the defendant's ability to consult with and assist his lawyer.
2. The extent to which the amnesia affected the defendant's ability to testify in his own behalf.
3. The extent to which the evidence in suit could be extrinsically reconstructed in view of the defendant's amnesia (such evidence would include evidence relating to the crime itself as well as any reasonably possible alibi).
4. The extent to which the prosecution assisted the defendant and his counsel in that reconstruction.
5. The strength of the prosecution's case.
6. Any other facts and circumstances that would indicate whether or not the defendant had a fair trial. (pp. 463–464)

COMPETENCE TO PLEAD GUILTY

Over 90% of criminal cases in the United States are resolved by pleas of guilty, often the result of plea bargaining. The competency of defendants to plead guilty involves the waiver of the right to a jury trial, of the right to confront one's accusers, and of the privilege against self-incrimination. The majority of the circuits have concluded that the standard of incompetence to plead is the same as that of incompetence to stand trial (*Allard v. Hedgemoe*, 1978). The *Allard* court agreed that the waiver of rights and the plea of guilty need to be closely examined, but suggested that the capacity to make such decisions be considered part of the *Dusky* standard.

In an earlier decision (*North Carolina v. Alford*, 1970), the Supreme Court of the United States had ruled in a capital case that defendants may waive their right to trial and plead guilty even if they deny their guilt. The court focused on the logic of the defendant's reasoning in choosing to plead guilty to a murder he stated he did not commit.

Competence to Refuse the Insanity Defense

The prevailing view by federal appeals courts is that a trial judge may not impose a defense of insanity over the defendant's objections if a competent defendant intelligently and voluntarily decides to forgo a defense of insanity (*Frendak v. U.S.*, 1979). An earlier case, *Whalem v. U.S.* (1965), did provide that a trial judge may impose an insanity defense when the defense would be likely to succeed, but it was overturned by *U.S. v. Marble* (1991) and is not followed in most jurisdictions. If it appears that competency to waive an insanity defense may be an issue in a given case, it is prudent for the evaluator to address it as part of the trial competency evaluation.

Competence to Waive Counsel

The Supreme Court of the United States ruled in *Westbrook v. Arizona* (1966) that a competency to stand trial hearing was not sufficient to determine competence to waive constitutional rights to the assistance of counsel and to conduct one's own defense. In *Faretta v. California* (1975), the Court noted that waiver of counsel must be knowing and intelligent, but that defendants' ability to represent themselves has no bearing on their competence to choose self-representation. In *Godinez v. Moran* (1993), the Court held that the competency standard for pleading guilty or waiving the right to counsel is the same as the *Dusky* standard for competency to stand trial, reasoning that "the defendant has to make a number of complicated decisions during the course of a trial, and that a trial court must in addition satisfy itself that the waiver of his constitutional rights is knowing and voluntary. . . . In this sense, there *is* a heightened standard for pleading guilty and for waiving the right to counsel, but it is not a heightened standard of *competence*" (pp. 400–401).

The concurring opinion in *Godinez* suggests that the *Dusky* competence standard should not be viewed too narrowly, as a defendant must be competent throughout the proceedings, from arraignment to pleading, trial, conviction, and sentencing, and whenever the defendant must make a variety of decisions during the course of the proceedings. In this regard, Melton et al. (2007) noted that to ensure that defendants are competent to stand trial, it is important to ask every defendant about his or her understanding of the rights that are waived by a plea of guilty.

In *Indiana v. Edwards* (2008), the Court considered the issue of competence to waive counsel in the case of a mentally ill defendant who intended to represent himself at trial, rather than to plead guilty. Mr. Edwards disagreed with counsel's defense strategy, lack of intent, and instead wished to claim self-defense. The Court ruled that the Constitution does not preclude states from adopting a higher standard for competency to waive counsel than for competency to stand trial. For the examiner conducting competency evaluations, this finding implies that the capacity to waive counsel, as well as the capacity to make decisions about trial strategy, is a consideration in conducting a competency evaluation in such cases. Input from defense counsel, always important in conducting competency evaluations, would be critical in terms of understanding the basis of the defendant's preferences. Morris and Frierson (2008) articulate the challenge of addressing the individual's unique abilities and limitations without addressing legal abilities or points of law beyond the experience of most forensic psychologists and psychiatrists.

DECISIONAL COMPETENCE

In *U.S. v. Duhon* (2000), a federal district court emphasized the ability to make decisions in rejecting the opinion of hospital forensic examiners that a mentally retarded defendant was competent to stand trial. The court ruled that the defendant's factual understanding of the proceedings, after hospital staff taught him to memorize and retain some information, was insufficient. Rather, the defendant lacked the ability to consult with an attorney with a reasonable degree of rational understanding, to otherwise assist in his defense, and to have a rational understanding of the proceedings.

THE STANDARD OF PROOF

In *Cooper v. Oklahoma* (1996), the Supreme Court of the United States ruled unanimously that Oklahoma, in imposing the higher standard of clear and convincing evidence for a defendant to prove incompetence (rather than the lower standard of preponderance of the evidence) violated due process by allowing "the State to put to trial a defendant who is more likely than not incompetent" (p. 369). The Court termed the consequences of an erroneous competency determination *dire*, impinging on the defendant's right to a fair trial. In contrast, the consequence to the state of an erroneous finding of incompetence when a defendant is malingering was termed *modest*, as it is unlikely that even an accomplished malingerer could "feign incompetence successfully for a period of time while under professional care" (p. 365). The Court added that "the defendant's fundamental right to be tried only while competent outweighs the State's interest in the efficient operation of its criminal justice system" (p. 367).

LENGTH OF TREATMENT FOR INCOMPETENCE TO STAND TRIAL

In *Jackson v. Indiana* (1972), regarding a hearing-impaired defendant who could not speak, and whom treatment staff did not believe would ever learn the communication skills necessary to stand trial, the Supreme Court of the United States ruled that incompetent defendants can be hospitalized only for the "reasonable" period of time necessary to determine whether there is a substantial probability that competency can be attained in the foreseeable future. The Court held that continued commitment could be justified only on the basis of progress toward the goal of competency restoration. Otherwise, the alternatives would be release of the defendant or initiation of civil commitment proceedings.

Similarly, in the above-referenced *U.S. v. Duhon* (2000), a federal district court ordered the release of a mentally retarded defendant who was not dangerous to any persons or property and would never achieve trial competency.

INVOLUNTARY MEDICATION

The issue of involuntary medication of defendants during trial was addressed by a federal appellate court in *U.S. v. Charters* (1987). In this case, the court held that forced administration of psychotropic medication to an incompetent defendant requires a separate judicial decision, using the substituted judgment/best interests standard. One year later, the court endorsed a reasonable professional judgment standard with the availability of judicial review (*U.S. v. Charters*, 1988). The *Charters* cases were not appealed to the Supreme Court of the United States in light of the Court's 1990 decision in *Washington v. Harper* (1990). In this prison case, the Court held that the reasonable professional judgment review of involuntary medication in the treatment of prisoners was constitutional.

In *Riggins v. Nevada* (1992), the Supreme Court considered the issue of involuntary administration of psychotropic medication of pretrial detainees. The trial court had found Riggins competent and denied his motion to suspend administration of psychotropic medication during his murder trial in order to show the jurors his true mental state as part of his insanity defense. He was subsequently convicted and sentenced to death. Riggins argued that involuntary medication had infringed on his freedom, and that the effects on his mental state during trial denied him due process in presenting his insanity defense. The Court reversed Riggins's conviction and extended the *Washington v. Harper* (1990) ruling on the right to refuse medication to pretrial detainees, absent an "overriding justification and a determination of medical appropriateness" (p. 135). Once the defendant stated that he wanted his medication discontinued, the state had to "establish the need for Mellaril and the medical appropriateness of the drug," which could have been established by showing that the medication was essential for the defendant's safety or the safety of others, or that the state could not obtain an adjudication of "guilt or innocence by using less intrusive means" (p. 135).

In *Sell v. U.S.* (2003), the Court ruled that before ordering forced medication to restore competence, trial courts must find that important governmental interests are at stake in bringing the defendant to trial; that the proposed medication would be substantially likely to render the defendant competent without causing side effects that would interfere with his ability to work with his attorney; that involuntary medication is necessary to further governmental interests and that alternative, less intrusive treatments are unlikely to restore the defendant's competence; and that the proposed involuntary medication is in the patient's best medical interest in light of his medical condition.

PREPARATION

Doubts about competency to stand trial may be raised by defense or prosecution, or by the court on its own motion. Psychologists and psychiatrists generally conduct competency evaluations upon the order of the court, whether the defense, prosecution, or the court itself raises the issue. However, defense counsel may also retain an examiner to conduct a competency evaluation under attorney–client privilege. Defense counsel would generally disclose the results of this consultative evaluation only if they raise or support concerns about the defendant's competency. The ultimate finding of competence or incompetence to stand trial is always made by the court.

There are a number of steps to take in preparing for, and conducting, a trial competency evaluation. Throughout the process, ethical issues specific to forensic practice are likely to surface. Although the steps enumerated here consider these issues, it is recommended that the examiner refer to relevant practice guidelines and ethical standards, listed in the reference section, for guidance when specific issues arise.

In response to a referral for evaluation of competence to stand trial, we recommend that the psychologist or psychiatrist:

- Consider whether he or she has relevant training and expertise to conduct the evaluation.
- Determine whether this particular case raises any ethical issues, such as multiple relationships with the defendant, the referring party, the court, or the victim, that would preclude objective involvement in the matter.
- Review the relevant case law regarding competence to stand trial.
- Review the competency standard for the jurisdiction in which the case is to be heard.
- Establish the source of the referral—defense attorney, or the court upon its own motion or upon the motion of defense or prosecution—through either a retainer letter by counsel or a court order to conduct the evaluation.
- Clarify how and to whom the results of the evaluation are to be communicated.
- Ask the referral source to describe any specific concerns or doubts about the defendant's competence regarding the case at issue.
- Ask defense counsel what is likely to be required of the defendant in order to assist counsel in this case (occasionally, inclusion

of the attorney in part of the evaluation may be helpful in observing or understanding the defendant's difficulty in assisting counsel).

- Review relevant court case information, such as the complaint or indictment, the definition and potential sentence of the charges, and criminal investigation reports of the alleged offenses, obtained from defense counsel, the prosecutor, or the court.
- Consider whether it would be appropriate or disruptive to include a third-party observer in the evaluation, such as defense counsel, or psychiatry residents or psychology interns.
- Weigh the advantages and disadvantages of recording the evaluation (if psychological testing is to be administered, taping might be discontinued at that point of the evaluation to avoid deviation from standard administration and test security problems).
- Ensure that the evaluation can be scheduled in a quiet setting, relatively free of distractions, for an adequate period of time (this can be a challenge when the defendant must be seen in a jail or detention facility).

In preparing to conduct the competency evaluation, the issue of third-party observers is sometimes raised. Evaluations are often completed in settings that provide training to psychology or psychiatry interns, residents, or fellows. Although this is standard professional practice, the impact of a second professional on the forensic assessment of defendants must be considered, particularly with defendants who are overly anxious, suspicious, or delusional.

Defense counsel might be involved at the beginning of the assessment, to inform the defendant of the purpose of the evaluation and encourage cooperation, or to illustrate the difficulty he or she is having in working with the defendant, but the presence of defense counsel throughout a competency evaluation is not standard practice. Guidelines for dealing with the presence of third party observers are provided by sources that also raise concerns about test validity and security when nonclinical observers wish to be present (American Academy of Clinical Neuropsychology, 2001; Committee on Psychological Tests and Assessment, 2007; National Academy of Neuropsychology, 2000).

DATA COLLECTION

GENERAL STEPS FOR PROCEEDING

There are general, comprehensive references regarding competency to stand trial, as well as recent, detailed guidelines published for conducting competency to stand trial evaluations, by both psychologists (Stafford, 2003; Zapf & Roesch, 2009) and psychiatrists (Miller, 2004; Mossman et al., 2007). The following steps reflect general professional consensus on conducting a competency evaluation:

1. Provide the defendant a verbal and written explanation of the purpose of the evaluation, and how and to whom the results will be communicated, at a level the defendant is likely to understand.
2. Seek the defendant's verbal and written assent or consent to the evaluation.
3. Conduct a targeted clinical interview of the defendant, including relevant history and a structured mental status examination.
4. Administer psychological tests, as needed, to assess for intellectual functioning, literacy, neurocognitive deficits, psychopathology, and malingering.
5. Use structured competency assessment instruments when appropriate.
6. Review relevant third-party information, such as school, employment, and military records; medical and mental health treatment records; and legal history, witness statements, and investigation of the alleged offenses.
7. Interview third parties, if necessary, to clarify history and level of functioning.

THIRD-PARTY INFORMATION

Interviews of third parties, written documents, computer records, laboratory data, and multimedia information are often obtained in the process of investigating and prosecuting offenses. The indictment and court docket of events in cases are increasingly available online in many jurisdictions. Criminal investigation materials can sometimes be obtained through access to the prosecutor's file, or through information provided by the prosecutor to the defense attorney in the process of discovery. Access to such information is helpful in determining whether defendants understand the basis for the charges and how realistic they are in appraising the strength of the case and the attorney's defense options.

Input from the defense attorney, who generally raises the issue of competency to stand trial, is essential in understanding counsel's concerns about the defendant's competence, counsel's experience in meeting with the defendant (including time spent in a private setting), and what the defendant needs to be able to do so that the attorney can resolve the case in a reasonable fashion. Grisso (2002) lists potential case-related demands that could be reviewed with defense counsel. Zapf and Roesch (2009) provide a questionnaire that may be sent to an attorney to complete, or used as an interview guide, to determine the attorney's specific concerns about the defendant's competency. These guides do not include questions about the quantity and quality of time the attorney has been able to spend with the defendant, often a critical factor in serious cases and with defendants who are suspicious or distressed or have other emotional or cognitive limitations.

Educational and treatment records, interviews with family members and treatment providers, and behavioral observations by correctional staff are often helpful in identifying factors that could affect competency to stand trial. This information can help to clarify issues of malingering, versus genuine symptoms or impairment, in considering ability to proceed. For individuals with a major mental disorder, information about the defendant's current access to, and compliance with, psychotropic medications and therapeutic support is important in determining whether the defendant is likely to remain stable enough over the course of the proceedings to resolve the case in a reasonable manner, or whether the defendant's mental state is precarious and likely to deteriorate with the stress of court proceedings.

The forensic clinician must ultimately consider the reliability and objectivity of third-party information in determining the weight it is accorded in assessment of trial competency. When the clinician personally conducts interviews of third parties, the clinician's role and purpose in seeking the information, and the potential for the disclosure of the information and its source in a report or testimony, must be conveyed to the third party at the outset of the contact. Heilbrun, Warren, and Picarello (2003) address the use of third-party information in forensic assessment in greater detail.

COMPETENCE ASSESSMENT INSTRUMENTS

Several instruments have been developed for the purpose of structuring and informing trial competence evaluations.

- *Competency Screening Test (CST).* The CST (Laboratory of Community Psychiatry, 1973) employs hypothetical situations in a sentence completion format to identify defendants who might require a fuller, hospital-based competency evaluation. However, studies of the CST found problems in terms of classification accuracy and utility (Nicholson, Robertson, Johnson, & Jensen, 1988; Roesch & Golding, 1980). The last major research published on the CST (Bagby, Nicholson, Rogers, and Nussbaum, 1992) found that there was little stability in factor structure across studies for the CST, making it difficult to determine just what aspects of competency this instrument measures.
- *Competency to Stand Trial Assessment Instrument (CAI).* The CAI, a rating scale of 13 functions derived from the legal literature and clinical/courtroom experience, has generally been used as an interview guide rather than as a psychometric instrument (Schreiber, 1978). Studies indicated high levels of interrater reliability among trained examiners (0.87 to 0.90) and significant correlations between competency status and CAI ratings (Nicholson & Kugler, 1991). Like the CST, this instrument served an important function in training mental health professionals about the concept of competency to stand trial, but is infrequently used now, as other measures have been developed to reflect changes in case law about decisional competence.
- *Interdisciplinary Fitness Interview (IFI).* Golding, Roesch, and Schreiber (1984) developed the IFI to assess symptoms of psychopathology and assess understanding of legal concepts/functions through a structured, joint interview by a psychologist and a lawyer. The potential strength of the instrument lies in its attempt to assess the defendant's functioning in the context of the anticipated demands of his or her particular legal situation. Preliminary data found 95% agreement among the IFI interviewers on opinions regarding competence, and substantial interrater reliability on most of the psychopathology items. Golding (1993) updated the instrument

(Interdisciplinary Fitness Interview—Revised [IFI-R]) in the context of new case law, and a study of competency reports (Skeem, Golding, Cohn, & Berge, 1998). Empirical studies of the IFI-R have not been published. The IFI-R is a promising interview guide that tailors the assessment to the individual case, ensures lawyer input, and highlights the connection between psychopathology and psycholegal impairment.

- *Georgia Court Competency Test (GCCT)*. The GCCT (Wildman et al., 1978) is a screening instrument that uses a courtroom drawing as a reference point for 12 questions about the physical positions and functional roles of court participants in a trial. It also consists of five questions about the defendant's charge(s) and defense. Nicholson et al. (1988) created the Mississippi State Hospital version (GCCT–MSH) by adding four questions about knowledge of courtroom proceedings and changing the weights of some items. They reported excellent interscorer reliability ($r = -0.95$) and classification accuracy of 81.8%. The false-positive rate was high, in that 67.7% of individuals rated as incompetent by the test were considered competent by a hospital evaluation, but the false-negative rate was low, as 3.8% of defendants considered competent by the test were evaluated as incompetent at the hospital. Nicholson and Johnson (1991) found that the GCCT or GCCT-MSH was the strongest predictor of competency decisions on an inpatient unit, and that the GCCT did not correlate highly with diagnosis. A factor analytic study (Bagby et al., 1992) confirmed the finding of Nicholson et al. that the GCCT-MSH yielded stable, independent factors: general knowledge, courtroom layout, and specific legal knowledge. This screening instrument does not address ability to make decisions in consultation with counsel, and to assist in one's defense.
- *Fitness Interview Test (FIT)*. Roesch, Webster, and Eaves (1984) developed the FIT, a Canadian interview schedule focused on legal issues and assessment of psychopathology. McDonald, Nussbaum, and Bagby (1991) reported a high degree of correspondence between FIT ratings and legal decisions about competence, but the legal decisions were made with knowledge of the FIT ratings. Bagby et al. (1992) found that factor analyses of the FIT legal items failed to yield a stable factor structure

across samples, most likely due to the uniformity of item content. The Fitness Interview Test—Revised (FIT-R) was subsequently developed for use in both Canada (Roesch, Zapf, Eaves & Webster, 1998) and the United States (Roesch, Zapf & Eaves, 2006) as a screening instrument that focuses on legal issues. The authors recommend its use in conjunction with a structured clinical interview of psychopathology, such as the Brief Psychiatric Rating Scale (Overall & Gorham, 1962) or the Structured Clinical Interview for DSM-III-R, Patient Edition (Spitzer, Williams, Gibbons, & First, 1990). They report that the FIT-R is a promising screening measure to determine whether an inpatient competency evaluation is required (Zapf, Roesch & Viljoen, 2001). However, in jurisdictions where thorough competency evaluations are routinely completed outside of a hospital setting, the utility of a screening measure is limited.

- *Competence Assessment for Standing Trial for Defendants with Mental Retardation (CAST-MR).* The CAST-MR (Everington & Luckasson, 1992) consists of three scales developed to assist in evaluation of competency to stand trial of mentally retarded defendants, including Basic Legal Concepts (multiple-choice items addressing essential courtroom notions); Skills to Assist Defense (multiple-choice items about hypothetical situations the defendant may face in working with his or her attorney); and Understanding Case Events (open-ended questions tapping understanding of aspects of case events in his or her own court case). Everington, Notario-Smull, and Horton (2007) instructed adjudicated criminal defendants with mental retardation to try to pretend that they did not know the answers to the CAST-MR, even though they did. These persons scored significantly lower than mentally retarded individuals who took the test under standard instructions. The authors maintained that these results demonstrated that defendants with mental retardation are able to lower their scores when told to do so; however, such results do not establish that these defendants would malinger under standard instructions, as mentally retarded individuals tend to be acquiescent and strive to do their best under standard instructions on most tasks.

- *MacArthur Competence Assessment Tool—Criminal Adjudication (MacCAT-CA).* The MacCAT-CA (Otto et al., 1998) is an abbreviated, clinical version of a more extensive research instrument designed to assess distinct competence-related abilities, rather than merely current knowledge. It attempts to measure the ability to *understand* information related to law and adjudicatory proceedings, and the ability to *reason* about specific choices that confront a defendant in the course of adjudication. The Understanding and the Reasoning scales each contain eight items that are based on a hypothetical legal scenario. The Appreciation scale taps the ability to *appreciate* the meaning and consequences of the proceedings in the defendant's own case, through six items that refer to the specific legal situation. The authors noted that the MacCAT-CA does not include measures of response set, that the possibility of malingering needs to be assessed through other methods, and that the MacCAT-CA should be employed in the context of a comprehensive competency evaluation.

- *Evaluation of Competency to Stand Trial—Revised (ECST-R).* Rogers, Tillbrook, and Sewell (2004) developed the ECST-R to assess aspects of the *Dusky* standard in the defendant's own case, and to assess feigned incompetency in a standardized manner. The ECST-R contains scales tapping Factual Understanding of the Courtroom Proceedings, and Overall Rational Ability (combined measures of Rational Understanding of the Courtroom Proceedings, and Consult With Counsel). The ECST-R also contains a measure of response style comprised of items tapping realistic, psychotic and nonpsychotic, and impairment types of items. The scales are reported to have high internal consistency and interrater reliability. It is a promising guide to systematically assessing competency to stand trial.

OTHER PSYCHOLOGICAL TESTS

Psychological tests that assess cognitive abilities, psychopathology, and/or malingering provide measures relevant to considering actual lack of *capacity* to understand and participate in court proceedings, when defendants appear to have *functional* deficits on the face valid measures of understanding the proceedings or assisting counsel in their defense. They may also be useful in assuring the judge, attorney, and prosecutor that defendants' histories of mental disorder have been carefully considered in nevertheless reaching the opinion that they are able to proceed, particularly in serious cases.

DATA INTERPRETATION

The process of data interpretation involves integration of multiple sources of data. These include information regarding legal concerns about the defendant's competence; the likely demands of the case, defense strategy, and the attorney–client relationship; third-party information from legal and mental health records; mental status and behavioral observations; structured assessment of relevant aspects of trial competency through interview and assessment instruments; targeted psychological testing; and consideration of treatment needs and current response to medication.

Experienced examiners often note that, particularly in complex or serious cases, or with defendants who have limitations, they are not sure of their opinion regarding competency until all of this information is summarized in a report, the strength of converging and diverging sources of information is weighed, inconsistencies are noted and resolved, and a thoughtful opinion is reached. Opinions in complex cases may often include conditions, noting, for example, the need for a possible updated evaluation should a mentally ill defendant's condition deteriorate, or treatment is refused, prior to resolution of the proceedings, or for defense counsel to be afforded extra time and a private space to work with the defendant in preparing for court.

COMMUNICATION

Reports and testimony regarding trial competency should convey, to the extent relevant in a particular case, the following components:

- Disclosure to the defendant of the purpose and limited confidentiality of the evaluation.
- Legal criteria for competence to stand trial in the jurisdiction in question.
- Consideration of the demands of the defendant's own case and other input from defense counsel.
- The defendant's appreciation of the charges and proceedings.

- Discussion of decisional abilities, particularly the waiver of constitutional rights, such as the right to counsel, the right to a jury trial, the right to testify, and implications of a guilty plea, given the prevalence of resolution of criminal cases through plea bargaining.
- Documentation of other decisional capacities that were directly assessed, such as the ability to make a knowing and intelligent decision about the insanity defense, and the level of ability the defendant displayed in considering those specific decisions.
- Results of competency assessment instruments, if used, and their implications for this defendant and his or her case.
- A summary of relevant treatment, educational, and other third-party information.
- Discussion of psychological test results in terms of malingering and indications of mental conditions that could impair the defendant's psycholegal functioning.
- Substantiation of diagnosis, including the possibility of malingering.
- The linkage between any psycholegal deficits and symptoms of psychopathology or cognitive impairment.
- Discussion of medication issues, such as need for medication, the defendant's compliance, the effect of the medication on the defendant's demeanor and awareness, and changes in mental state from his or her mental state at the time of the offense as the result of treatment with psychotropic medication.

Because the forensic psychologist or psychiatrist provides an expert opinion and does not make the ultimate decision about trial competency, it is essential to provide elucidated reasoning in support of forensic conclusions. Reports and testimony should provide an accurate and understandable presentation of the defendant's psychopathology, specific psycholegal abilities and impairments, and the relationship, if any, between psychopathology and competence deficits. Experts should integrate information from multiple sources and include the facts and reasoning underlying the opinion in detail sufficient for the court to understand the basis for the opinion and to make an independent finding. They must also be prepared to answer questions about the opinion through testimony in a straightforward, factual, and understandable manner.

REFERENCES

Allard v. Hedgemoe, 572 F.2d 1 (1st Cir. 1978).

American Academy of Clinical Neuropsychology. (2001). Policy statement on the presence of third party observers in neuropsychological assessments. *The Clinical Neuropsychologist, 15*, 433–439.

Bagby, R., Nicholson, R., Rogers, R., & Nussbaum, D. (1992). Domains of competency to stand trial: A factor analytic study. *Law and Human Behavior, 16*, 491–507.

Committee on Psychological Tests and Assessment. (2007). *Statement on third party observers in psychological testing and assessment: A framework for decision making.* Washington, DC: American Psychological Association.

Cooper v. Oklahoma, 517 U.S. 348 (1996).

Drope v. Missouri, 420 U.S. 162 (1975).

Dusky v. U.S., 362 U.S. 402 (1960).

Everington, C., & Luckasson, R. (1992). *Competence assessment to stand trial for defendants with mental retardation (CAST-MR).* Worthington, OH: International Diagnostic Services.

Everington, C., Notario-Smull, H., & Horton, M. L. (2007). Can defendants with mental retardation successfully fake their performance on a test of competence to stand trial? *Behavioral Sciences and the Law, 25*, 545–560.

Faretta v. California, 422 U.S. 806 (1975).

Frendak v U.S., 408 A.2d 364 (D.C. 1979).

Godinez v. Moran, 509 U.S. 389 (1993).

Golding, S. L. (1993). *Interdisciplinary Fitness Interview—Revised.* Training manual and instrument available from the author at the University of Utah, Department of Psychology, Salt Lake City, UT 84112.

Golding, S., Roesch, R., & Schreiber, J. (1984). Assessment and conceptualization of competency to stand trial: Preliminary data on the Interdisciplinary Fitness Interview. *Law and Human Behavior, 8*, 321–334.

Grisso, T. (2002). *Evaluating competencies: Forensic assessments and instruments* (2nd ed.). New York, NY: Plenum Press.

Heilbrun, K., Warren, J., & Picarello, K. (2003). Third party information in forensic assessment. In A. M. Goldstein (Ed.), *Handbook of psychology: Forensic psychology*, Vol. 11 (pp. 69–86). Hoboken, NJ: John Wiley & Sons.

Hoge, S. K., Bonnie, R. J., Poythress, N., & Monahan, J. (1992). Attorney-client decision-making in criminal cases: Client competence and participation as perceived by their attorneys. *Behavioral Sciences and the Law, 10*, 385–394.

Indiana v. Edwards, 554 U.S. 164 (2008).

Jackson v. Indiana, 406 U.S. 715 (1972).

Laboratory of Community Psychiatry, Harvard Medical School. (1973). *Competency to stand trial and mental illness* (DHEW Publication No. ADM-77–103). Rockville, MD: Department of Health, Education, and Welfare.

LaFortune, K., & Nicholson, R. (1995). How adequate are Oklahoma's mental health evaluations for determining competency in criminal proceedings? The bench and the bar respond. *Journal of Psychiatry and Law, 23*, 231–262.

McDonald, A., Nussbaum, D., & Bagby, R. (1991). Reliability, validity and utility of the Fitness Interview Test. *Canadian Journal of Psychiatry, 36*, 480–484.

Melton, G. B., Petrila, J., Poythress, N. G., & Slobogin, C. (2007). *Psychological evaluations for the courts: A handbook for mental health professionals and lawyers*. New York, NY: Guilford Press.

Miller, R. D. (2004). Criminal competency. In R. Rosner (Ed.). *Principles and practice of forensic psychiatry* (pp. 186–212). New York, NY: Chapman & Hall.

Morris, D. R., & Frierson, R. L. (2008). Pro se competence in the aftermath of *Indiana v. Edwards*. *Journal of the Academy of Psychiatry and the Law, 36*, 551–557.

Mossman, D., Noffsinger, S. G., Ash, P., Frierson, R. L., Gerbasi, J., & Hackett, M. (2007). AAPL practice guideline for the forensic psychiatric evaluation of competence to stand trial. *Journal of the American Academy of Psychiatry and the Law, 35*(4), S3–S72.

National Academy of Neuropsychology. (2000). Presence of third party observers during neuropsychological testing. *Archives of Clinical Neuropsychology, 15*, 379–380.

Nicholson, R. A., & Johnson, W. (1991). Prediction of competency to stand trial: Contribution of demographics, type of offense, clinical characteristics to psycholegal ability. *International Journal of Law and Psychiatry, 14*, 287–297.

Nicholson, R. A., & Kugler, K. E. (1991). Competent and incompetent criminal defendants: A quantitative review of comparative research. *Psychological Bulletin, 109*, 355–370.

Nicholson, R., Robertson, H., Johnson, W., & Jensen, G. (1988). A comparison of instruments for assessing competency to stand trial. *Law and Human Behavior, 2*, 313–321.

North Carolina v. Alford, 400 U.S. 25 (1970).

Otto, R. K., Poythress, N., Nicholson, R., Edens, R., Monahan, J., Bonnie, R., . . . Eisenberg, M. (1998). Psychometric properties of the MacArthur Competence Assessment Tool—Criminal Adjudication. *Psychological Assessment, 10*, 435–443.

Overall, J. E., & Gorham, D. R. (1962). The brief psychiatric rating scale. *Psychological Reports, 10,* 799–812.

Pate v. Robinson, 383 U.S. 375 (1966).

Riggins v. Nevada, 504 U.S. 127 (1992).

Roesch, R., & Golding, S. (1980). *Competency to stand trial.* Urbana-Champaign: University of Illinois Press.

Roesch, R., Webster, C. D., & Eaves, D. (1984). *The Fitness Interview Test: A method for examining fitness to stand trial.* Toronto, Ontario, Canada: University of Toronto Centre of Criminology.

Roesch, R., Zapf, P. A., & Eaves, D. (2006). *Fitness Interview Test: A structured interview for assessing competency to stand trial.* Sarasota, FL: Professional Resource Press.

Roesch, R., Zapf, P. A., Eaves, D., & Webster, C.D. (1998). *The Fitness Interview Test* (Revised edition). Burnaby, BC: Mental Health, Law, and Policy Institute, Simon Fraser University.

Rogers, R., Tillbrook, C. E., & Sewell, K. W. (2004). *Evaluation of Competency to Stand Trial—Revised (ECST-R).* Odessa, FL: Psychological Assessment Resources.

Schreiber, J. (1978). Assessing competency to stand trial: A case study of technology diffusion in four states. *Bulletin of the American Academy of Psychiatry and the Law, 6,* 439–457.

Sell v. U.S., 539 U.S. 166 (2003).

Skeem, J., Golding, S., Cohn, N., & Berge, G. (1998). Logic and reliability of evaluations of competence to stand trial. *Law and Human Behavior, 22,* 519–547.

Spitzer, R. L., Williams, J. B., Gibbons, M., & First, M. B. (1990). *Structured clinical interview for the DSM-IIIR.* Washington, DC: American Psychiatric Press.

Stafford, K. P. (2003). Assessment of competence to stand trial. In I. B. Weiner (Series Ed.) & A. M. Goldstein (Vol. Ed.), *Comprehensive handbook of psychology: Vol. 11. Forensic psychology* (pp. 359–380). Hoboken, NJ: John Wiley & Sons.

Stafford, K. P., & Wygant, D. B. (2005). The role of competency to stand trial in mental health courts. *Behavioral Sciences and the Law, 23*(2), 245–258.

Stone, A. (1975). *Mental health and law: A system in transition.* Rockville, MD: National Institute of Mental Health.

U.S. v. Charters, 829 F.2d 479 (4th Cir. 1987).

U.S. v. Charters, 863 F.2d 302 (4th Cir. 1988).

U.S. v. Duhon, 104 F. Supp. 2d 663 (W.D. La. 2000).

U.S. v. Marble, 940 F.2d 1543 (D.C. Cir. 1991).

Washington v. Harper, 494 U.S. 210, 110 S.Ct. 1028 (1990).

Westbrook v. Arizona, 384 U.S. 150 (1966).

Whalem v. U.S., 346 F.2d 812 (D.C. Cir. 1965).

Wildman, R. W., Batchelor, E. S., Thompson, L., Nelson, F. R., Moore, J. T., Patterson, M. E., & deLaosa, M. (1978). *The Georgia Court Competency Test: An attempt to develop a rapid, quantitative measure of fitness for trial.* Unpublished manuscript, Forensic Services Division, Central State Hospital, Milledgeville, GA.

Wieter v. Settle, 193 F. Supp. 318 (W.D. Mo. 1961).

Wilson v. U.S., 391 F.2d 460 (D.C. Cir. 1968).

Zapf, P. A., & Roesch, R. (2009). *Evaluation of competence to stand trial.* New York, NY: Oxford University Press.

Zapf, P. A., Roesch, R., & Viljoen, J. L. (2001) Assessing fitness to stand trial: The utility of the Fitness Interview Test (revised edition). *Canadian Journal of Psychiatry, 46*, 426–432.

CHAPTER 2

Competency to Waive
Miranda Rights

ELLIOT L. ATKINS and KENNETH J. WEISS

INTRODUCTION

Criminal suspects in custody are protected against forced extraction of information and against prosecution without representation. These rights were enunciated in the famous Supreme Court of the United States decision *Miranda v. Arizona* (1966). Following *Miranda*, all states are required to have procedures in place to ensure that suspects are apprised of the following prior to giving a statement: the right to remain silent; that what they say will be used against them; that they have a right to a lawyer; that they can request that a lawyer be present before they say anything; and that they can stop the questioning at any time. The process and timing of transmitting the content of these rights and of the waiver may be subject to procedural challenges without specific reference to mental state. The capacity to waive *Miranda* rights refers to the ability of a criminal suspect to waive rights to due process and against self-incrimination *knowingly*, *intelligently*, and *voluntarily*. Federal jurisdiction judges the reliability of a confession on a balancing test that takes in the "totality of circumstances," pursuant to *Dickerson v. U.S.* (2000).

Though it may be difficult to understand why an innocent person would confess to a crime, it has long been known that there are many and varied dynamics contributing to decisions during custodial interrogations. A defendant's confession may be the prosecution's sole link to the crime. Thus, it is essential that the mental state of the defendant be examined when there is a question of state of mind during the interrogation. Embedded in the analysis are two related issues: the capacity of the suspect during the early stage of the interrogation when *Miranda* rights typically are read, and the mental state of the suspect during questioning, which may have become altered or weakened, thus giving rise to a false confession from an otherwise competent person. To a degree they coexist, since disorientation, fear, intimidation, and psychopathology may play a role in *why* a suspect would agree to speak with police after being told, "Whatever you say will be used against you"—the same dynamics that would be at work in the false-confession scenario. This chapter focuses on the first issue and acknowledges the substantial and important literature on the second.

The reliability and voluntariness of a confession can be cornerstones of criminal prosecutions, especially when other forms of evidence are weak. Prosecutors have an ethical responsibility to ensure that incriminating statements are properly obtained. Defense attorneys often are faced with clients who cannot account for why they waived constitutional rights and acted against interest. Among the many and varied dynamics within the interrogation–confession process, psychiatric and psychological factors are prominent. Though judges, at the pretrial stage, are reluctant to suppress confession evidence, occasions for expert testimony may also arise at trial.

Admissible and reliable testimony is more likely if the forensic psychologist/psychiatrist considers the following recommendations:

- Conduct a personal examination of the defendant and utilize appropriate psychometrics.
- Utilize as comprehensive a set of materials as is possible, including recordings of the confession in any media and collateral sources regarding the defendant's condition.
- Know the standards, statutes, and case law governing suppression of a custodial confession.
- Document mental status findings and historical diagnoses that shed light on the defendant's mental capacity at the time of the confession.
- Describe in detail how the measured or observed deficits interfered with the defendant's capacity during the interrogation.

PREPARATION

In preparation for a psychological/psychiatric analysis of a confession, evaluators must be aware of several domains of information: the prevailing statutory and case law governing suppression of evidence; the manner in which testimony may be used (for example, at a pretrial hearing versus during trial); the circumstances surrounding the interrogation (physical and psychological); wherever possible, a video or audio recording of the interrogation; an examination of the defendant to explore memory and subjective factors that gave rise to the confession; and a complete set of school and mental health records that may shed light on vulnerabilities explaining a false confession.

THE REFERRAL

The referral usually involves a request to evaluate a criminal defendant who claims to either have given a false confession, that he/she did not understand the right to remain silent, or both. The defendant may be looking for an expert witness to support a claim of incompetence, or the referral may come as a request from a prosecutor for a second opinion on such a claim.

A waiver of *Miranda* rights, to be competent, must be given *knowingly, intelligently,* and *voluntarily.* It is important early on to understand exactly the position of the defendant. For example, a defendant who did not possess the requisite capacity to understand the rights in question due to mental subnormality may not satisfy the *knowing* component. One who had a mental illness or medical condition present during the confession that interfered with the capacity to weigh the risks and benefits of a confession may not satisfy the *intelligent* component. And the defendant whose will was overborne by police conduct or the physical circumstances of the interrogation may not have confessed *voluntarily.*

FOCUS AND SCOPE OF THE EVALUATION

It is important to remember that the court is not asking the expert witness whether an incriminating statement is, in fact, false. Questions of *fact* are left to the judge (in a pretrial or bench trial situation) or the jury (weighing the statement in light of other evidence). The defendant is asserting it, but the expert witness can do no more than to link identifiable psychopathology to self-incriminating behavior and to explain to the court whether the defendant possessed or lacked certain capacities. It is not self-evident that *anyone* who confesses and regrets it later was mentally impaired at the time. The focus of the evaluation, then, is to examine the causal nexus, if any, between a person's mental state and/or predispositions and the production of a confession that is now being challenged. The scope of the analysis may include the defendant's intellectual capacity, emotional predispositions and state at the time in question, how a reasonable person might act under similar circumstances, and what is known about the conduct of the detectives who administered the *Miranda* rights and waiver.

TIMING

Since the retrospective analysis of a specific capacity may relate to psychological conditions no longer present, the examiner must be careful to state how inferences are made. In the case of mental retardation or brain injury, there are enduring cognitive character-istics that may be inferred from a present examination bolstered by a review of preincident records. The examiner must also be careful to appreciate that the defendant may have learned much between the time of the statement and that of the examination. This phenomenon is especially important in assessing individuals with subnormal intellect, since they are likely to want to display what they know. In addition, defendants whose first language is not English may learn subsequently that they did not understand their rights, though they may have possessed the capacity to have known them if discussed in their native language. This may be the case even if a translator is present because of the various differences with dialect and so on.

Other defendants learn about their rights while they are incarcer-ated. The examiner must remember that the analysis of competency to waive *Miranda* rights is a retrospective one, unlike the examina-tion for present-state trial competency.

The defendant's memory may also be an issue. Accordingly, the interview portion of the evaluation may have to include a line-by-line review of the statement with the defendant. It is common for defendants to respond with, "I didn't say that" or "I would never say that." Yet, it is important that the defendant come to terms with the facts that the prosecution will use as evidence. Whenever possible, the defendant should have access to the transcript or media recording, so that memory, as unreliable as it is, can be enhanced. The same issue may hold true for interviews with detectives and police officers, who, by the time your evaluation takes place, may have interrogated hundreds of other suspects. Yet, these law enforcement agents will be the ones delivering the prosecution's evidence in court, where their recollection of procedures, circumstances, and behaviors may be tarnished by the passage of time.

COLLATERAL INFORMATION

Two types of collateral information may inform the evaluation of a confession: (1) observations by individuals who can document the defendant's mental state at or around the time of the statement (or at least historically); and (2) interviews with the interrogating detectives. Such information is especially important when the defendant is claiming a mental disorder that interfered with the ability to form clear memories of the interrogation session—psychological trauma, psychosis, a drug-induced or withdrawal state, dissociation, and so forth. It is key for the examiner to be aware that the validity of a waiver of rights and a statement is judged by a "totality of circumstances" analysis. Thus, for example, when the defendant claims he/she did not understand *Miranda* warnings due to lack of intellect or under the influence of some substance, but it is apparent that this was one of a dozen arrests, a judge is likely to say that intellectual capacity is overridden by experience and repetition. However, when the defendant's relatives inform the examiner that the defendant always obeys authority, it sheds a different light on the process.

Obtaining collateral information from a police officer or detective may, at first blush, seem obvious, given his/her firsthand view of the situation. However, one must recognize that this individual may be the prosecution's key witness. That is, the detective will testify for the prosecution and read into the record (likely play an audio or videotape) the defendant's statement, which usually includes a repeat of the *Miranda* warnings. There are two important reasons that a detective's collateral information is less than useful to the forensic examiner. First, a detective may close ranks with the prosecutor. Because both parties are aiming to convict the defendant, it is highly unlikely that a detective would suggest coercion, poor treatment of the suspect, improper reading of rights, or any overt "clinical" signs of the suspect's impairment. Second, if the evaluator is working for the defense, interviewing the detective may have the unintended consequence of telegraphing the defense strategy to the prosecution. While working for the prosecution, it is also unlikely that a detective would intimate that there had been any problems with the interrogation—either procedurally or with the suspect's mental capacity. Therefore, the evaluator must carefully think through, with counsel, the risk–benefit ratio of interviewing detectives. Detectives are likely to say, "We did everything by the book" and "We didn't notice anything wrong with the suspect." As a final word of caution to the neophyte forensic professional, if such a collateral interview is conducted—especially for the prosecution—the evaluator is urged not to be unduly influenced, and to conclude that the defendant must be malingering.

Obtaining collateral information about the defendant's mental state can be done via family members, friends, and health professionals. Because individuals with mental disorders may be "poor historians," the evaluator would want to obtain information about the defendant's behavior, habits, substance use, general functioning, literacy, and adaptability to stress. Examples include: "He was high / intoxicated more than usual that day"; "She was off her medication and starting to hear voices again"; "He has always been deathly afraid of police"; "He can't read, or didn't have his glasses, so he just signed his name to whatever was put in front of him"; and "She thinks when the police talk to you, you have to answer." Collateral information is most important when obtaining a history of developmental disability or when there has been traumatic brain injury, about which the defendant cannot report with authority.

ETHICAL ISSUES

The ethical issues associated with capacity to waive *Miranda* rights pertain mainly to the nature and extent of the expert opinions in the context of the reliability of the data. In the case of a defendant with mental retardation, the claim that the capacity to waive *Miranda* rights was lacking is readily testable by ordinary psychometrics, school records, and examination. The nature of the report and testimony will be similar to other situations in which a specific capacity is tested—with the understanding that there is a retrospective element here.

Where the claim is a transitory state, such as medical or mental illness or intoxication, it is generally not an ethical issue to establish capacity, so long as the opinion reaches a reasonable degree of scientific certainty or probability (depending on which term is favored by the jurisdiction in question). In the scenario in which the defendant claims coercion or torture, and there is some objective basis for it, expert testimony on the effects of the external force is generally unnecessary. The question of *internal* compulsion to confess, which the Supreme Court took up in *Colorado v. Connelly* (1987), is a more delicate matter. Here, the jurisdictional variations may or may not support the use of expert testimony, since the state cannot be held responsible for a suspect's hallucinations.

In the typical situation in which a defendant has a mental illness or personality disorder and becomes anxious in the interrogation—without coercion—there is a question of reliability of expert testimony. The ethical consideration is whether an opinion about the relationship between a given mental state and the reliability of a confession is valid. Depending on jurisdiction, admissibility of testimony may undergo scrutiny at the pretrial level via a *Frye* (1973) or *Daubert* (1993) hearing. The witness would have an ethical obligation to disclose the internal logic of the opinion and the scientific basis for making the causal connection. Our reading of the emerging literature is that testimony based on clinical findings is often more acceptable than that based on general social psychological literature on how people behave in interrogation situations.

An additional ethical burden falls on the examiner working for the prosecution, namely, not to stress the defendant unduly. By the time the evaluator interviews the defendant, there should already be an idea of whether the defense argument is about a *state* or a *trait* issue. That is, if it is about a transitory *state* of mind (intoxication or drug withdrawal), there is less concern about the defendant's being caught off-guard. In the intermediate zone is an individual who may have been suffering from active psychotic symptoms during the interrogation. Here, the examiner must be more careful not to take advantage of someone who may have a residual thought disorder. At the far end of the continuum is the individual with a developmental *trait* such as mental retardation, learning disability, or Asperger's disorder. As with any forensic examination performed for an adverse party, here the evaluator must be sure that the defendant understands the nature and purpose of the examination and, not ironically, that the results may be used against him/her. It would be unethical for a forensic examiner working for the prosecution to obtain incriminating information and intentionally pass it on to the prosecutor. Such a view would be in keeping with the Supreme Court of the United States holding in *Estelle v. Smith* (1981). In that case, it was not permissible for information obtained during a competency evaluation to be used against the defendant in a death-penalty trial. Depending on jurisdiction, the defendant's attorney or expert witness may have the right to sit in on the examination. In our view, this is not a bad thing, as it is in the spirit of openness and is only slightly more intrusive than being asked to make a video recording of the examination. It should be noted that any attorney or expert observing must not interfere with the examination in any way.

DATA COLLECTION

INTERVIEWING THE EXAMINEE

As with any retrospective evaluation of mental capacity (e.g., criminal responsibility), the criminal defendant's capacity must be *inferred* from available information. The psychiatric and psychological interviews are necessary and integral to understanding the basis for the defendant's claim that he/she lacked capacity to waive constitutional rights and/or that the confession was false. The principal importance of the interview is to provide the examiner with the defendant's recollection and subjective response to the interrogation and to fill in the gaps left by an incomplete recording and detective statement. A simple example is underscored by the aphorism attributed to Elvin Semrad, that "the autonomic nervous system doesn't lie," and Semrad's full quotation is even more illuminating: "If you feel like crying, you cry. You see, there's one thing you can depend on, and that's the autonomic nervous system. It never lies. It's so far from the head it doesn't even know there is a head" (Rako & Mazer, 1980, p. 27). Similar to interviewing traumatized patients, discussing an interrogation may be vividly reminiscent in a way that is apparent in body language, fear, tearfulness, and so forth. The examiner must be cautioned not to overinterpret such reactions as representing *objective* truth; but they can form the basis of an inference about the defendant's subjective state at the time in question. The following is a list of subjects the examiner may want to address during the open-ended examination:

- *Identifying information.* The defendant may or may not have experience with mental health professionals. Moreover, there may be residual hypersensitivity to being questioned, if the interrogation itself was traumatic. Beginning the session with lightweight, easy questions is a good way to gauge the examinee's responses and to begin an informal mental status examination.
- *Current mental status.* In the event that the claim of an unreliable confession is due to mental retardation or dementia (traumatic or neurodegenerative), the present examination of orientation and general capacity may be indicative of the defendant's specific capacity at the time in question. This is especially true in the evaluation of capacity to waive rights, since the interrogation situation is inherently stressful—both by design and in its novelty for many suspects—and may give rise to impaired decision making. Though neither mental status nor psychometric testing is entirely dispositive of the question of capacity, the examiner must carefully document findings that convey a sense of how the individual was functioning at the time in question.

  Other current mental status findings may serve to bolster a defendant's claim of mental illness during interrogation. Thus, if the examiner were to find clinical evidence of psychosis, for example, thought disorder, or apparent hallucinations, if there is an antecedent history of schizophrenia, one could infer the presence of active symptoms during the *Miranda* waiver.
- *Education.* In addition to obtaining school records (see below), attention to the defendant's educational level is another window into how he/she may have been functioning during the interrogation. Do not assume that a defendant is literate—even with a high school diploma—due to the possibility of "social promotion" in some school districts. Take first the *Miranda*

warnings ("You have the right to remain silent" and so forth). Greenfield, Dougherty, Jackson, Podboy, and Zimmermann (2001) conducted reading-level analyses of the *Miranda* cards read by police in the 21 counties of New Jersey, finding that the verbiage used varied from fourth grade to college levels. A few words of caution: Reading level of a *Miranda* card does not, by itself, indicate whether a particular suspect understood the rights. In addition, experienced suspects may have enough "street smarts" to understand the meaning. However, there are many individuals with functional illiteracy, mental retardation, or borderline intellectual functioning who, by way of lifetime adaptation, never expose their deficits. Such individuals not only fail to grasp the meaning of the rights implied under *Miranda*; they cheerfully go along with waivers and incriminate themselves as a means of *acquiescence*. As will be discussed later, a simple index of comprehension, such as the Wide Range Achievement Test, Fourth Edition (WRAT4; Wilkinson & Robertson, 2006) may reveal the basis for an inference about the defendant's capacity to have understood abstract rights—even while the defendant is seen on the tape acquiescing to the rights as read by the detective.

- *Mental health and medical histories.* It is essential to determine the life history of the defendant's medical and mental conditions, to see what, if any, of them may have been operating at the time of the confession. Any assertions by the defendant that the confession took place during an active-symptom phase of an illness should be verified, whenever possible, with collateral history and contemporaneous clinical documentation from treaters. The examiner should also look at the police reports of the underlying incident for evidence of disorganized behavior that may support the claim of an incompetent confession.

- *Recollection of the interrogation.* Ideally, there will be a videotape of the interrogation against which to understand the defendant's reactions. However, while gross evidence of coercion or abuse may be needed for the defendant to argue that the statement was invalid, the types of cases that come before psychologists and psychiatrists are usually subtler. Additionally, police often begin the official recording after the suspect has already acquiesced to making a statement. In that case, the

recording will show a rote mirandization followed by an emo-
tionless recitation of the version of the story that had been
negotiated by the detective and suspect. Thus, evidence for the
suspect's subjective state may not be apparent on the recording,
as is usually the case with written transcripts. The examination,
then, will rely in part on the defendant's recollection of events
surrounding and during the interrogation session. We recommend as full a discussion of the details of the interrogation as
the defendant is able to provide—especially when there is a
false-confession claim made.

- *Open-ended discussion of Miranda rights.* The examiner will want
  to have an estimate, if not a quantitative analysis, of the
  defendant's ability to understand and apply *Miranda* rights.
  The open-ended interview, accordingly, should cover the subject of understanding the concept of *rights* and how such rights
  might have been employed during the interrogation. This can be
  brief if it is the examiner's intent to pursue a formalized
  assessment of capacity, such as outlined by Grisso (1998b).
  This part of the examination must be understood in the context
  that it conveys a sense of the defendant's capacity at the time of
  the examination, which may or may not be identical to the
  capacity at the time in question. Because there are transitory as
  well as fixed-deficit conditions that may be in play during an
  interrogation (Weiss, 2003), the analysis of competency at the
  remote time may be complicated by the passage of time, subsequent learning, and improvement in clinical state.

- *Review of transcript/recording.* As noted, the police, if they have
  discretion, may begin the formal recording at the end of the
  interrogation. Because the responses to the *Miranda* procedure
  tend to be "Yes," at this stage, little can be inferred regarding
  capacity. That is, though the prosecutor may use the presence of
  these responses to argue that the police discharged their duty
  and that the suspect clearly understood the rights in question,
  it would not be scientifically acceptable to conclude that the
  suspect's affirmative responses were proof of a knowing, intelligent, and voluntary statement.

- *Discussion of false-confession dynamics.* Part of the analysis of
  capacity may include the dynamics of the suspect's emotional
  state and motivation during the interrogation. In a false-

confession claim, the key to understanding it may be the type of compliance, acquiescence, internalization, or response to coercion discussed in the social science literature (Gudjonsson, 2003). However, because the literature merely categorizes these dynamics, the examiner will have to state specifically how the suspect's psychological vulnerabilities gave rise to a statement against interest. That is, the expert witness will have to spell out how the dynamics of the interrogation caused or did not cause the suspect to waive rights and make an incriminating statement. Though it is self-evident, for example, that torture or direct threats may alter a suspect's behavior, most situations are subtler and involve cognitive and affective changes not readily visible on a recording. Accordingly, the examination should include a discussion with the defendant about how his or her motivations, attitudes, and stress responses changed over the course of the interrogation.

PSYCHOLOGICAL TESTING

The use of psychological testing in any forensic evaluation is dictated by the functional areas being assessed that are relevant to the legal question being posed. Consequently, it is hard to envision an assessment of the capacity of a defendant to waive *Miranda* rights that would not include psychological testing to assess abilities related to comprehension. Therefore, it should be standard practice for such an assessment to incorporate some measure of intellectual ability and educational achievement. As an adjunct to these tests, consideration should be given to the use of forensic assessment instruments specifically designed to measure abilities related to the legal issues at hand. In addition to the assessment of the specific, relevant functional abilities of intelligence, achievement, memory, and reading and listening comprehension, a comprehensive evaluation of one's capacity to waive *Miranda* rights should include an assessment of psychopathology and personality structure. The use of objective psychological instruments to assess these areas will also allow for comparison to a normative group. If indicated, an assessment of the defendant's response style should also be undertaken.

The Wechsler Adult Intelligence Scale (now WAIS-IV) is the most widely utilized and generally accepted measure of general intelligence and of specific intellectual strengths and weaknesses (Wechsler, 2008a). The reliability and validity of the WAIS in its various iterations has been firmly established, and, therefore, its use as part of a forensic assessment is supported by the literature (Heilbrun, Marczyk & DeMatteo, 2002; Wechsler, 2008b). Such an instrument would provide information that could have an influence on determining whether a waiver was knowing and intelligent. Fulero and Everington (1995) found that individuals with mental retardation scored significantly lower on the Instruments for Assessing Understanding and Appreciation of *Miranda* Rights (Grisso, 1998a) than individuals without mental retardation. Other research has demonstrated similar findings using alternative assessment instruments (Cloud, Shepherd, Barkoff & Shur, 2002). Furthermore, the WAIS-IV may provide important information regarding an individual's ability to comprehend information presented during an interrogation. For example, the Verbal Comprehension Index (VCI) measures an individual's verbal acquired knowledge and verbal reasoning. The items of the subtests that comprise this index are presented verbally, and the examinee must articulate the responses. As the attentional/working memory subtests are not included in the VCI, the index may be conceptualized as a more refined, "purer" measure of verbal comprehension (Wechsler, 2008b). Obviously, this skill would have a direct bearing on the legal question being addressed here.

Like the WAIS-IV, instruments such as the WRAT4 can provide information relevant to one's ability to make a knowing and intelligent waiver (Wilkinson & Robertson, 2006). The WRAT4 is one of the more widely utilized measures of basic academic skills critical to the comprehension of both written and orally presented materials (Wilkinson & Robertson, 2006). The use of the Wide Range Achievement Test for the assessment of capacity to waive *Miranda* rights has been supported by the literature (e.g., DeClue, 2005b; Heilbrun et al., 2002; Oberlander, Goldstein, & Goldstein, 2003). These studies were based on the previous version of the Wide Range Achievement Test, the WRAT3. Unlike the WRAT3, the WRAT4 includes a measure of sentence comprehension, a skill directly related to the legal issue at hand. The WRAT4 is a psychometrically sound instrument with well-established reliability and validity that also allows for a comparison to a normative sample (Wilkinson & Robertson, 2006). Other measures of academic skills include the Nelson Denny Reading Test and Gray Oral Reading Tests, Fourth Edition (GORT-4; Wiederholt & Bryant, 2001) and the Wechsler Individual Achievement Test-III (WIAT-III; Wechsler, 2009).

Results from the preceding instruments will provide the evaluator with information relevant to the defendant's overall intellectual abilities and academic achievement, as well as information specifically relevant to his or her ability to comprehend information of the type presented in the *Miranda* warnings. Though essential to such an evaluation, this information, in and of itself, tells only part of the story. There is no *direct* correlation between either intellectual ability (or academic achievement) with the capacity to comprehend *Miranda* rights. Individuals with intelligence quotients (IQs) in the mentally deficient range may be capable of comprehending these rights, as may those with significantly depressed achievement levels. Similarly, and particularly relevant to many *Miranda* assessments, is the fact that average or better intellectual and/or academic functioning does not necessarily ensure that an individual has the capacity to comprehend and/or to waive *Miranda* rights.

While intellectual and academic achievement levels may be static over time, other factors may have influenced the defendant at the time of the waiver. With this in mind, forensic tools have been developed to assist forensic psychologists and psychiatrists in determining the ability to understand and appreciate the content of the *Miranda* warnings at the time of the psychological/psychiatric evaluation. By incorporating this information with the other aspects of the evaluation as described above, a more complete picture can be constructed of the defendant's capacity to waive *Miranda* rights at the time of the interrogation. The most widely recognized and utilized of such tools is the Instruments for Assessing Understanding and Appreciation of *Miranda* Rights (Grisso, 1998a). The Grisso instruments are consistently regarded as forensic tools representing a critical component of a comprehensive evaluation of capacity to waive *Miranda* rights (DeClue, 2005a; Heilbrun et al., 2002; Melton, Petrila, Poythress & Slobogin, 2007; Oberlander et al., 2003). Furthermore, the use of the Grisso tools as part of such an evaluation complies with professional and legal guidelines for the use of psychological tests (see Heilbrun et al., 2002), as well as the guidelines promulgated by Heilbrun (1992) for using such tests as part of forensic mental health assessment.

The Grisso instruments consist of four sections:

1. The Comprehension of *Miranda* Rights (CMR) instrument provides an overall assessment of the individual's understanding of *Miranda* rights by asking the evaluee to interpret and summarize each component of the *Miranda* warnings.
2. The Comprehension of *Miranda* Rights—Recognition (CMR-R) is an instrument that can assist in determining whether an individual understands each *Miranda* right. The instrument is comprised of true–false statements that determine the individual's ability to recognize statements that are similar to, or contrary to, the components of the *Miranda* warnings.
3. The Comprehension of *Miranda* Vocabulary (CMV) asks the individual to define six of the critical words—*consult, attorney, interrogation, appoint, entitled,* and *right*—used in most *Miranda* warnings. This instrument can assist in determining whether the lack of comprehension of the vocabulary used in the *Miranda* warnings may have contributed to an individual's misunderstanding of the warnings.
4. The Function of Rights in Interrogation (FRI) is an instrument used to assess whether a defendant understands the rights functionally, as applied to circumstances involving arrest and interrogation by the police. The instrument uses vignettes involving hypothetical situations, together with pictures depicting police interrogations.

Essential in any analysis of an individual's comprehension of *Miranda* rights is the determination of the reading level required for the warning's comprehension. There is no standard or established universal wording of the *Miranda* warnings provided to defendants (DeClue, 2005a). In fact, the actual wording of the *Miranda* warnings varies among police agencies and jurisdictions (Greenfield et al., 2001). The Grisso tools, for example, utilize wording based on the *Miranda* warnings given by police in St. Louis County, Missouri. DeClue (2005a) suggests that forensic clinicians supplement the data provided by using the structured Grisso tools with a similar analysis of the relevant capacities using the exact wording of the *Miranda* warnings provided by the local jurisdiction from which the referral came.

However, as DeClue (2005a) observed, the Grisso tools, while directly relevant to the legal question, are not *tests* of the legal question. Grisso (1998a, 1998b, 2003) made it clear that the tools were never intended to be dispositive of whether an individual understood the *Miranda* warnings at the time of questioning. Moreover, he makes no claim that the instruments can be used to determine the validity of the waiver, a determination that involves the totality of the circumstances surrounding the waiver, not just the capacity of the individual to make a knowing, intelligent, and voluntary waiver. Most significantly, the author advocates for the use of the tools as part of a comprehensive assessment of the legal question. The capacity of an individual to waive *Miranda* rights should never be based solely on performance on the Grisso tools or any single measure (DeClue, 2005a; Grisso, 1998a, 1998b, 2003; Heilbrun, 1992; Heilbrun et al., 2002). This is a concept essential to the forensic clinician in assembling the components that will be utilized in the assessment. It is also important to keep in mind the fact that the legal question is whether the defendant waived *Miranda* rights *prior* to questioning by the police. An analysis of an individual's capacity to waive *Miranda* rights is a retrospective analysis. It is important to recognize that the forensic psychological or psychiatric expert is being asked to offer an opinion about one's capacity to waive these rights at some time in the past. The evaluation is an assessment undertaken at a later time and in a different situation—a forensic evaluation, as opposed to an interrogation.

In order to preserve the clinical utility of the Grisso tools, the instruments are currently undergoing revision as well as new validation studies (see Grisso, Vincent, & Seagrave, 2005). The new version of the instruments will be titled the Miranda Rights Comprehension Instruments-II (MRCI-II). According to Grisso et al., research is currently being conducted to provide normative data with various populations, including juvenile offenders, adult offenders, adult offenders with serious mental illness, and adults with mental retardation.

If neuropsychological or neurological impairment is suggested, additional testing in these areas is usually necessary. To further assess the need for additional testing, a neuropsychological screening test may be administered. Instruments to be considered might include the Bender-Gestalt, Rey 15-Item Memorization Test, Symbol

Digit Modalities Test, and/or the Screening Test for the Luria-Nebraska Neuropsychological Battery (LNNB-ST).

Additional psychological testing may also be warranted based on the information obtained from historical data, documents provided, clinical interview, and the results of the above-referenced testing. An objective measure of psychological functioning and personality structure, such as the Minnesota Multiphasic Personality Inventory, 2nd Edition (MMPI-2) (Butcher, Dahlstrom, Graham, Tellegen, & Kaemmer, 1989) can be used when information is needed for determining the extent of any psychopathology or personality factors that may have influenced the defendant's ability to make a knowing, intelligent, and voluntary waiver. Other objective measures of psychological functioning and personality structure include Personality Assessment Inventory (PAI) and the Millon Clinical Multiaxial Inventory-III (MCMI-III). Such instruments also provide an assessment of the defendant's response style that may warrant an assessment of the defendant's self-presentation, defensiveness, and/or malingering. Whether or not objective personality testing suggests such an assessment, a properly conducted and thorough forensic evaluation should incorporate an assessment of malingering. It is not uncommon for a defendant to feign an intellectual deficiency, cognitive impairment, organic brain disorder, or mental illness in an attempt to convince a forensic examiner that he or she did not understand the *Miranda* warnings.

Among the forensic instruments more commonly utilized for assessing malingering are the Validity Indicator Profile, the Structured Interview of Reported Symptoms (SIRS), and the Test of Memory Malingering (TOMM). The Validity Indicator Profile (VIP; Frederick, 1997) is an instrument used to identify malingering of a cognitive deficit, such as mental retardation (Oberlander et al., 2003). Use of the VIP as part of a test battery for the assessment of competence to confess (Gamache, 2009; Oberlander et al., 2003), other forensic issues (Rogers, 2008), and as a general screening tool when forensic psychologists are assessing cognitive impairment relative to the forensic issue (van Gorp, 2007), is supported by the literature. The VIP has been shown to be a valid and reliable measure of malingering (Drwal, 2005; Rogers, 2008; Rogers & Shuman, 2005).

The SIRS (Rogers, Bagby, & Dickens, 1992) is used to assess malingering of mental illness and, more specifically, of psychotic symptoms. Though someone with psychosis may claim their symptoms interfered with their ability to understand the *Miranda* warnings, research has shown that psychosis, in and of itself, is not a significant predictor of a lack of comprehension (Viljoen, Roesch, & Zapf, 2002). The validity and reliability of the SIRS is well established (Heinze, 2003; Rogers, Payne, Berry, & Granacher, 2009; Rogers et al., 1992), and its use in forensic evaluations is well supported by the literature (DeClue, 2005a, 2005b; Lally, 2003; Oberlander et al., 2003; Rogers, 2008).

The TOMM (Tombaugh, 1996) is a 50-item visual recognition test specifically designed to help psychologists and psychiatrists discriminate between malingered and true memory impairments. The TOMM has firmly established validity and reliability data (Haber & Fichtenberg, 2006; Rees, Tombaugh, Gansler, & Moczynski, 1998; Tombaugh, 1996, 1997) and its use in forensic evaluations is supported by the literature (DeClue, 2005a, 2005b; Oberlander et al., 2003; Tombaugh, 2002).

DATA INTERPRETATION

It is the forensics professional's duty to present reliable and scientifically supportable reports and testimony. The evaluation of a possible false-confession case does not begin at a neutral point. Rather, it arises out of the defendant's claim either that his/her statement was based on lack of capacity to understand constitutional rights or that due to certain medical/social/psychological factors there was a false admission of guilt. The expert witness will then have to use the available data to reconstruct, if possible, the state of mind of the individual and, without speculating, assess the reliability of the confession. Surely, there will be many antisocial defendants who will brag about a crime to detectives and try to recant later, saying they were confused, coerced, and so forth. For this reason alone, the expert witness must not rely too heavily of the defendant's manifest claims.

CAPACITY TO WAIVE *MIRANDA* RIGHTS

Psychologists and psychiatrists may be permitted to infer an individual's mental capacity from a variety of sources. Indeed, various capacities can be assessed in living or regarding deceased individuals, most famously testamentary capacity. The interpretation of data in a confession case must adhere to basic principles: (1) the data should be objective and not rely excessively on the perceived mental state of the defendant; (2) the examiner must rely on a variety of sources to yield information about an individual's characteristics and behavior; and (3) the interpretation itself must bridge the conceptual gap between the social science literature and the specifics of the individual at a particular place and time. All told, the examiner will be expected to have an opinion within a reasonable degree of scientific certainty about whether *this* defendant on *this* occasion had the mental capacity to understand his or her *Miranda* rights and, if so, whether the waiver of rights was *knowing, intelligent,* and *voluntary*.

FACTORS REDUCING RELIABILITY OF A CONFESSION

There are many factors that bear on motivation, cognitive capacity, impulse control, and judgment—any of which may be in play during the extreme stress of a custodial confession (Weiss, 2003). This, by itself, tells us nothing about *why* a defendant confessed falsely, let alone *whether* the confession was true or false. The question of *whether* is the domain of the judge or jury. Therefore, there is an ethical requirement that the witness adhere to the scientific basis for suggesting that the defendant was behaving in an impaired manner during the interrogation. Even so, prosecutors and judges are skeptical of opinions that appear to cross the line of being prejudicial. In interpreting the data of clinical factors affecting the reliability of a confession, the examiner must be circumspect and conservative; otherwise, opinions that invade the province of the fact finder will not be admitted.

SOCIAL SCIENCE INPUT

As noted earlier, there is a substantial and growing literature on the response of humans to stress, coercion, suggestion, and so forth (Gudjonsson, 2003). Much of it claims to apply to the real-world situation of the custodial confession. While the application of social psychology to criminal justice has much intuitive appeal, it is not enough for expert witnesses to opine that people with certain characteristics make bad choices, that the defendant has those characteristics, and that his/her confession would not have been reliable. The interpretation of the data can be bolstered by the literature on human behavior, but to rely on it to the exclusion of clinical data would be to have the tail wag the dog—an admissibility issue.

COMMUNICATION

REPORT ORGANIZATION

The report ideally will contain the following essential elements:

- A statement of the legal question
- The agency (defense attorney or prosecutor to whom the consultation is directed)
- The governing legal standards (statute or case law)
- Description of all sources upon which the opinion relies (examinations, collateral interviews, records, testing)
- An explanation of the methodology, including the setting and format of the interview and the essentials of the psychometrics
- Statement on confidentiality that was issued to the evaluee
- The findings as they relate to the requisite capacities
- Diagnosis, if applicable
- The opinion, expressed within reasonable scientific certainty, indexed to the legal question and standard
- Recommendations for remediation, if applicable

THE REPORT

The written work product must clearly state how the data support the conclusion, and the conclusion, in turn, must be stated with reasonable scientific certainty (more likely than not). In addition to covering the required elements listed earlier, it is essential that the expert be aware of the need to "connect the dots" between clinical and psychometric findings and the defendant's capacity at the time in question. Though it is common for the prosecution to have the burden of proof that a confession is valid, defense experts must provide a cogent and transparently reasoned document. The clinical findings must state whether the waiver of rights was knowing, intelligent, and voluntary. In the event that lack of voluntariness was due to the suspect's will being overborne either by active police conduct or the circumstances of the interrogation, the report should include specific examples from the transcript or recording. A sample report is found in DeClue's (2005a) handbook. As in DeClue's example, when psychological testing is used, the expert should provide the rationale for the use of the test, information about the test and its scoring, the results, and the significance of the results for the specific legal question. It must be emphasized that, because it is conducted after the interrogation, testing may or may not reflect the defendant's state at the relevant time. Experts must keep in mind that a defendant who appears competent now may have been in a markedly different—and possibly impaired—state of mind during the stressful interrogation.

Admissibility of medical or psychological testimony is not automatic—especially when the judge does not perceive the opinion as helpful; or worse, that the opinion may be prejudicial to a jury. There may be a challenge to the admissibility of testimony about a confession, though in our experience it is more likely to happen when there is a false-confession claim, rather than an incompetent-waiver claim. It is nearly always required that the expert witness support opinions with clinical data obtained through firsthand examination, in contrast with opinions derived from psychological studies of human behavior. The literature supports use of social science testimony when used in conjunction with an individualized examination and clinical correlation with the prevailing standard (Quintieri & Weiss, 2005; Watson, Weiss, & Pouncey, in press).

REFERENCES

Butcher, J. N., Dahlstrom, W. G., Graham, J. R., Tellegen, A. M., & Kaemmer, B. (1989). *MMPI-2: Manual for administration and scoring*. Minneapolis, MN: University of Minnesota Press.

Cloud, M., Shepherd, G. B., Barkoff, A. N., & Shur, J. V. (2002). Words without meaning: The constitution, confessions, and mentally retarded suspects. *University of Chicago Law Review, 69*, 495–624.

Colorado v. Connelly, 479 U.S. 157 (1987).

Daubert v. Merrell Dow Pharmaceuticals, Inc., 509 U.S. 579 (1993).

DeClue, G. (2005a). *Interrogations and disputed confessions: A manual for forensic psychological practice*. Sarasota, FL: Professional Resource Press.

DeClue, G. (2005b). Psychological consultation in cases involving interrogations and confessions. *Journal of Psychiatry & Law, 33*, 313–358.

Dickerson v. U.S., 530 U.S. 428 (2000).

Drwal, W. (2005). The use of the Validity Indicator Profile with a 15- to 18-year-old population. *Dissertation Abstracts International: Section B: The Sciences and Engineering, 66*(2-B), 1166.

Estelle v. Smith 451 U.S. 454 (1981).

Frederick, R. I. (1997). *VIP (Validity Indicator Profile) manual.* Minneapolis, MN: NCS Pearson.

Frye v. United States, 293 F. 1013 (D.C. Cir., 1973).

Fulero, S. M., & Everington, C. (1995). Assessing competency to waive *Miranda* rights in defendants with mental retardation. *Law and Human Behavior, 19*, 533–543.

Gamache, M.(2009). *VIP Validity Indicator Profile: Review of a new instrument to assess response style.* Retrieved January 8, 2009, from http://www.pearsonassessments.com/resources/vipreview.htm

Greenfield, D. P., Dougherty, E. J., Jackson, R. M., Podboy, J. W., & Zimmermann, M. L. (2001). Retrospective evaluation of *Miranda* reading levels and waiver competency. *American Journal of Forensic Psychiatry, 19*, 75–86.

Grisso, T. (1998a). *Instruments for assessing understanding and appreciation of Miranda rights.* Sarasota, FL: Professional Resource Press.

Grisso, T. (1998b). *Assessing understanding and appreciation of Miranda rights: Manual and materials* (3rd ed.). Sarasota, FL: Professional Resources Press.

Grisso, T. (2003). *Evaluating competencies: Forensic assessments and instruments* (2nd ed.). New York, NY: Plenum Press.

Grisso, T., Vincent, G., & Seagrave, D. (2005). *Mental health screening and assessment in juvenile justice.* New York, NY: Guilford Press.

Gudjonsson, G. H. (2003). *The psychology of interrogations and confessions: A handbook.* West Sussex, UK: John Wiley & Sons.

Haber, A. H., & Fichtenberg, N. L. (2006). Replication of the Test of Memory Malingering (TOMM) in a traumatic brain injury and head trauma sample. *Clinical Neuropsychologist, 20*, 524–532.

Heilbrun, K. (1992). The role of psychological testing in forensic assessment. *Law and Human Behavior, 16*, 257–272.

Heilbrun, K., Marczyk, G., & DeMatteo, D. (2002). *Forensic mental health assessment: A casebook.* New York, NY: Oxford University Press.

Heinze, M. (2003). Developing sensitivity to distortion: Utility of psychological tests in differentiating malingering and psychopathology in criminal defendants. *Journal of Forensic Psychiatry & Psychology, 14*, 151–177.

Lally, S. (2003). What tests are acceptable for use in forensic evaluations? A survey of experts. *Professional Psychology: Research and Practice, 34*, 491–498.

Melton, G. B., Petrila, J., Poythress, N. G., & Slobogin, C. (2007) *Psychological evaluations for the courts* (3rd ed.). New York, NY: Guilford Press.

Miranda v. Arizona, 384 U.S. 436 (1966).

Oberlander, L., Goldstein, N. E., & Goldstein, A. M. (2003). Competence to confess: Evaluating the validity of Miranda waivers and trustworthiness of confessions. In A. M. Goldstein (Ed.), *Handbook of Psychology: Volume 11, Forensic psychology* (pp. 335–357). Hoboken, NJ: John Wiley & Sons.

Quintieri, P., & Weiss, K. J. (2005). Admissibility of false-confession testimony: Know thy standard. *Journal of the American Academy of Psychiatry and the Law, 33*, 535–538.

Rako, S., & Mazer, H. (1980). *Semrad: The heart of a therapist*. New York, NY: Aronson.

Rees, L. M., Tombaugh, T. N., Gansler, D. A., & Moczynski, N. P. (1998). Five validation experiments of the Test of Memory Malingering (TOMM). *Psychological Assessment, 10*, 10–20.

Rogers, R. (2008). *Clinical assessment of malingering and deception* (3rd ed.). New York, NY: Guilford Press.

Rogers, R., Bagby, R. M., & Dickens, S. E. (1992). *Structured Interview of Reported Symptoms professional manual*. Lutz, FL: Psychological Assessment Resources.

Rogers, R., Payne, J., Berry, D., & Granacher, R. (2009). Use of the SIRS in compensation cases: An examination of its validity and generalizability. *Law and Human Behavior, 33*, 213–224.

Rogers, R., & Shuman, D. (2005). *Fundamentals of forensic practice: Mental health and criminal law*. New York, NY: Springer.

Tombaugh, T. N. (1996). *Test of Memory Malingering (TOMM)*. North Tonawanda, NY: Multi-Health Systems.

Tombaugh, T. N. (1997). The Test of Memory Malingering (TOMM): Normative data from cognitively intact and cognitively impaired individuals. *Psychological Assessment, 9*, 260–268.

Tombaugh, T. N. (2002). The Test of Memory Malingering (TOMM) in forensic psychology. *Journal of Forensic Neuropsychology, 2*, 69–96.

van Gorp, W. (2007). Neuropsychology for the forensic psychologist. In A. M. Goldstein (Ed.), *Forensic psychology: Emerging topics and expanding roles* (pp. 154–168). Hoboken, NJ: John Wiley & Sons.

Viljoen, J. L., Roesch, R., & Zapf, P. A. (2002). An examination of the relationship between competency to stand trial, competency to waive interrogation rights and psychopathology. *Law and Human Behavior, 26*, 481–506.

Watson, C., Weiss, K. J., & Pouncey, C. (in press). False confessions, expert testimony and admissibility. *Journal of the American Academy of Psychiatry and the Law*.

Wechsler, D. (2008a). *Wechsler Adult Intelligence Scale, Fourth Edition: Administration and scoring manual*. San Antonio, TX: Psychological Corporation.

Wechsler, D. (2008b). *Wechsler Adult Intelligence Scale, Fourth Edition: Technical manual*. San Antonio, TX: Psychological Corporation.

Wechsler, D. (2009). *Wechsler Individual Achievement Test—Third Edition (WIAT-III) manual*. San Antonio, TX: Psychological Corporation.

Weiss, K. J. (2003). Confessions and expert testimony. *Journal of the American Academy of Psychiatry and the Law, 31*, 451–458.

Wiederholt, J. L., & Bryant, B. R. (2001). *Gray Oral Reading Test—Fourth Edition (CORT-4) manual*. San Antonio, TX: Psychological Corporation.

Wilkinson, G. S., & Robertson, G. J. (2006). *Wide Range Achievement Test, Fourth Edition: Professional manual*. Lutz, FL: Psychological Assessment Resources.

CHAPTER 3

Sentencing

ELLIOT L. ATKINS and CLARENCE WATSON

INTRODUCTION

Sentencing is the fundamental process for administering punishment to individuals convicted of crimes. Clinicians may be asked to participate in the sentencing process to ensure that various factors are considered, which could influence a defendant's ultimate sentence, such as mental illness or risk of future dangerousness. This chapter reviews the role of the clinician in the sentencing process and offers an approach to issues often faced by clinicians in that setting.

The principles underlying judicial sentencing of criminal offenders in the United States derive directly from the four traditional theories of punishment: retribution, deterrence, rehabilitation, and incapacitation (Huigens, 2005). Retribution addresses the "eye for an eye" concept regarding the culpability of a criminal offender against the harm inflicted on society. The principle of deterrence relates to two overall objectives. The first objective is to discourage the individual offender from engaging in future criminal activities (specific deterrence). The second objective is to discourage other citizens from engaging in criminal activities as a consequence of punishing an offender (general deterrence). The principle of rehabilitation relates to efforts to reform criminal offenders, so that their choices align more with socially acceptable behaviors. Incapacitation serves the purpose of physically preventing an offender from committing future criminal acts.

In addition to these traditional theories, three other principles relate to criminal sentencing (Simons, 2009). First, criminal sentences should be uniform. Accordingly, similarly situated criminal offenders who engage in similar criminal acts should receive similar punishment. Second, criminal sentences should be proportional to the gravity of the offense. Therefore, more serious criminal acts should receive more punishment than less serious criminal acts. Finally, criminal sentences should not be excessive. Criminal offenders, then, should not receive more punishment than is necessary to meet the underlying traditional principles of punishment. Taking these principles together, federal and state courts manage the daunting task of administering equitable criminal sentences for a wide range of criminal behaviors within the context of society's "evolving standards of decency" (*Trop v. Dulles*, 1958). Depending on the criminal offense, convicted defendants may face a wide range of sentences that are aimed at upholding the principles of punishment. During the sentencing phase, the prosecutor presents aggravating factors, such as ongoing dangerousness or lack of remorse, to demonstrate that the defendant deserves the maximum sentence allowable under the law. In opposition, defense counsel presents mitigating factors to humanize the defendant and offer explanations for the defendant's behaviors in an effort to obtain leniency in sentencing. Accordingly, the sentencing process allows for individualized punishment of offenders.

RANGE OF SENTENCES

The range of available sentences may vary depending on the type of offense, the severity of the crime, and the jurisdiction in which the sentence is to be served. Historically, sentencing judges had broad discretion in tailoring individualized punishment for the particular needs of each offender with a goal toward rehabilitation (Reitz, 2000). This approach, called *indeterminate sentencing*, faced criticism for disparities in sentencing practices, and accordingly, federal and some state jurisdictions moved toward *determinate sentencing* (Berman, 2005). Under determinate sentencing, specific minimum and maximum sentences for particular offenses were outlined, including allowable alternatives to incarceration. Incarceration allows the physical detention of individuals in prison for a specified period and essentially prevents the offender from reoffending. However, the presence of various offender characteristics (e.g., age or mental illness) or the presence of societal pressures (e.g., prison overcrowding) has made alternatives to incarceration desirable in some cases.

One alternative to incarceration is pretrial diversion programs, such as Pretrial Intervention (PTI) or Accelerated Rehabilitative Disposition (ARD) programs. These programs generally allow first-time offenders with minor charges who are amenable to rehabilitation and treatment to avoid trial, conviction, and sentencing. Successful completion of these programs usually results in the criminal charges being dropped. For defendants who are convicted, there are other alternatives to incarceration. For example, offenders may receive a suspended sentence to be placed on probation. As a result, the offender may avoid incarceration contingent on specified conditions of probation, such as avoiding additional criminal acts and compliance with mental health or substance abuse treatment. Violation of the probation conditions may result in incarceration following the revocation of probation.

While on probation, some offenders may be subjected to the condition of home confinement or house arrest. Home confinement serves as an alternative to incarceration while restricting the offender's freedom in the community. This alternative allows the offender to serve his sentence at his home, while being monitored electronically for movement outside of authorized locations. Offenders may also be sentenced to perform community service, which requires the performance of unpaid community work as repayment to society. Eligible offenders who have been incarcerated for a period of time or offenders under home confinement may be allowed to participate in community work-release programs. Work-release programs allow eligible offenders to engage in paid employment in the community, but require the offender to return to a halfway house or to home confinement at the end of the workday.

While there may be some alternatives to incarceration, depending on the criminal offense involved, clearly certain criminal offenses would not be eligible for such alternatives. Specifically, there are some offenses that not only require incarceration as a sentence, but in cases involving capital offenses, such as murder, a defendant may be sentenced to death. Currently, the federal government and 35 states allow eligible offenders to be sentenced to death in the United States (Death Penalty Information Center, 2009). The Supreme Court of the United States has required courts to weigh both aggravating and mitigating factors of the crime and the defendant prior to sentencing a defendant to death (*Lockett v. Ohio*, 1978).

PREPARATION

PREEXAMINATION CONSULTATION WITH COUNSEL

Mental health experts are often used during the sentencing phase to help establish aggravating or mitigating factors related to the criminal offense in both noncapital and capital criminal cases. Mental health experts retained by either the prosecution or defense counsel may provide opinions related to a defendant's amenability to treatment, personal background, or the presence of mental disorders that may have influenced the criminal act. Regardless of whether the prosecution or the defense retains the expert, mental health experts must bear in mind their ethical obligation to strive for objectivity prior to examining the defendant (American Academy of Psychiatry and the Law, 2005).

It is critical that the expert consult with the retaining attorney prior to examining the defendant for the purpose of sentencing. Such consultation will allow the expert to be apprised of all aspects of the offense leading to conviction. The attorney will also be able to communicate his/her view of the potential aggravating or mitigating factors in the matter to the expert. If the expert is satisfied that the matter contains issues upon which he/she is qualified to opine, he/she should request all available records necessary to formulate his/her opinion (Sadoff, 2003). The expert may need to direct the attorney in obtaining the type of records required for presentence evaluations. The records required for such an evaluation are often extensive and may often require a subpoena (i.e., prison and probation/parole records, etc.). Evaluators need to review all relevant documentation regarding the defendant's life. This must be communicated to the retaining attorney. In addition, the expert should also convey the importance of personally interviewing collateral sources of information, such as family and friends, previous employers, school teachers, and the like, who may shed light on various personal characteristics of the defendant.

RECORD REVIEW

A thorough review of all available records reflecting various aspects of a defendant's life is critical in order to piece together factors that may have influenced his or her criminal behavior or may indicate the likelihood of successful rehabilitation. Personal historical information, including events in early childhood, may impact the defendant's perceived level of culpability and the ultimate sentence. Such information is required to counterbalance any proposed aggravating factors, such as the egregiousness of the crime (Tomes, 1997). The following records should be reviewed when preparing these evaluations:

- *Medical records.* Medical records, including birth records, if available, may shed light on physical and cognitive disorders suffered by the defendant prior to the criminal act. For example, birth records may document difficulties during delivery that may have caused an anoxic brain injury and a resulting developmental disorder, such as fetal alcohol syndrome. As a mitigating factor, the presence of such a disorder may help lower the defendant's level of culpability due to a decreased capacity to fully appreciate the nature of the criminal act. A similar approach may be utilized if medical records indicate that the defendant suffered a traumatic brain injury in the past. Medical records establishing the neurological consequences of such an injury, including permanence of the injury, personality changes, and impulsivity, will be relevant during a presentence evaluation.
- *School records.* School records may be useful in several ways during these evaluations. These records may offer mitigating information such as learning disorders and mental retardation. Prior intelligence quotient (IQ) testing may establish a record of low intelligence and form the basis of a diagnosis of mental retardation. This point is particularly important in capital cases, given the Supreme Court's ban on the execution of mentally retarded individuals (*Atkins v. Virginia*, 2002). Even in the absence of formal IQ testing, the defendant's academic curriculum (e.g., special education courses) may provide an indication of the defendant's prior level of intellectual functioning.

Further, evidence of academic excellence and involvement in extracurricular activities may personalize the defendant and suggest the potential benefit of rehabilitative efforts instead of harsh sentencing. However, the records may provide evidence of aggravating factors. For example, a defendant with an extensive history of disciplinary problems may find it difficult to persuade the sentencing authority to hand down a more favorable sentence, unless this can be linked to nonvolitional stimuli in the individual's home environment. Evidence of multiple suspensions or expulsions, truancy, difficulty with authority figures, and ineffective disciplinary interventions may adversely impact the defendant during the sentencing phase.

School records may also contain observations made by teachers about such issues as the defendant's dressing, grooming, mood, and so forth. This information ultimately may be weighed as mitigating factors.

- *Mental health records.* The review of the defendant's mental health history is fundamental in presentence evaluations. Mental illness has historically been considered a mitigating factor in sentencing. Some states have specifically listed mental illness as a mitigating factor in their death penalty statutes (Sondheimer, 1990). The presence of mental illness has been viewed as a factor that reduces the criminal culpability of defendants and justification for leniency during sentencing. Accordingly, mental health records documenting a history of psychiatric disorders that may have influenced the defendant's behavior at the time of the crime must be considered. The existence of such records may bolster any assertions of extreme emotional distress during the criminal act.

It must be noted that while mental illness is generally considered a mitigating factor, it has been interpreted as an aggravating factor in some situations (Edersheim & Beck, 2005). Mental illness may be improperly equated with an ongoing threat to society, especially in cases where previous treatment has been unsuccessful. Previous episodes of psychiatric symptom exacerbation may have coincided with dangerous behaviors, and therefore may adversely impact sentencing, although they may also be used to make the case for why a defendant should be sentenced to life without parole as opposed to death.

- *Substance abuse records.* Just as the review of the defendant's mental health history is necessary in these evaluations, a review of substance abuse records is equally important. These records may reveal that substance abuse played a significant role in the defendant's life prior to the crime and may illustrate that the defendant's need for drug treatment outweighs the need for harsh punishment. Depending on the circumstances, the defendant may be viewed as unlikely to have engaged in criminal activity but for drug addiction. This may be the case especially if there is documentation of the defendant's attempts to cease drug use, despite being unsuccessful. A careful review of the substance abuse history, including the age of onset and how the defendant was initially introduced to illicit substances, may further affect mitigation, along with a history of such abuse with the defendant's parents or relatives. For instance, a defendant who had been introduced to illicit substances as an adolescent by family members may be viewed as having an abusive upbringing and deserving of rehabilitative interventions in lieu of incarceration. A loose case may also be made for genetic propensity for addiction.
- *Criminal records.* The existence of a criminal record will receive much attention during the sentencing process, and therefore, it is critical that the expert review these records for details regarding previous offenses. Of course, the absence of a criminal record will represent a mitigating factor for the defendant. When a criminal record does exist, the nature and severity of previous criminal offenses will certainly influence whether it represents mitigating or aggravating factors. For example, a pattern of criminal acts occurring only with episodes of psychiatric symptom exacerbation may be considered a mitigating factor. However, a pattern of callous criminal behaviors will certainly represent an aggravating factor, unless the nonvolitional explanation of antisocial personality is used in a way to explain the defendant's behaviors as a result of the general fabric of his/her environment.

OTHER COLLATERAL SOURCES

Because it is important to explore and understand the nature of the defendant's character in preparation for the sentencing phase, all aspects of the defendant's life must be considered. However, it is rare that all major events of a defendant's life have been fully documented for the expert to review. Therefore, preparing the defendant and the defendant's family and friends to discuss all known aspects of the defendant's life is essential, regardless of the level of personal sensitivity. Interviews of persons who played a major role in the defendant's life and know the defendant best are critical, especially when preparing for sentencing in capital cases. Such information may offer the judge and jury a glimpse at the defendant's character that is absent from the available records and offer some explanation for the defendant's criminal behavior.

It is important to note that initially it may be difficult to obtain potentially mitigating information from defendants and their families. Defendants and their families may feel ashamed and embarrassed by events in the defendant's life, even when they understand why these issues are being explored (Sadoff & Dattilio, 2008). Families may feel that information previously considered "family secrets" will now be discussed openly in the courtroom or that they could be blamed for the defendant's poor upbringing and considered indirectly responsible for the defendant's behavior. Issues related to childhood physical or sexual abuse and family history of mental illness or substance abuse should be investigated to determine their impact on the defendant's behaviors. It is vital to carefully explain to defendants and their families the importance of full disclosure in this regard in order to adequately identify mitigating factors.

SCHEDULING THE EVALUATION

As the vast majority of these evaluations occur in the correctional setting, scheduling often requires coordination with the retaining attorney to obtain the court's authorization to permit the expert to examine the defendant within the correctional facility. Some jurisdictions have established mental health court clinics where the defendant may be transported by court order for such evaluations. Regardless of the location, the setting should allow for unimpeded dialogue in a quiet setting with minimal distractions. Bearing that issue in mind, it remains important that adequate measures have been considered in order to ensure the safety of the expert during the evaluation.

DATA COLLECTION

CLINICAL INTERVIEW

Regardless of the type of sentencing evaluation being completed, any clinical interview should begin with informing the examinee of the interview's purpose and the limitations of confidentiality. The referral question and the specific issues that follow will guide the remainder of the interview. Independent background information, such as school records, medical records, and/or third-party interviews, are not always available, making the clinical interview the central focus of the evaluation in those cases. Therefore, a structured or semistructured interview should be utilized to ensure thorough and accurate data collection. With capital cases, much of this background information may be gathered through the reports of mitigation experts' (specialists) reports. Recent Supreme Court decisions in addition to the 2003 edition of the American Bar Association's *Guideline for the Appointment and Performance of Defense Counsel in Death Penalty Cases* recommend that the capital defense team should include two attorneys, a mitigation specialist, and an investigator (Dattilio & Sadoff, 2007, p. 262).

There are two types of questions that should be asked: (1) general content areas that should be addressed in every interview and (2) questions specific to the type of sentencing evaluation being conducted. The general content areas include the client's family history, psychiatric and medical history, criminal history, and facts surrounding the current offense. The evaluator should be familiar with the relevant statute or legal standard in his or her jurisdiction and ask specific questions accordingly. For example, questions regarding the client's mental capacity at the time of the offense and relevant treatment needs should be explored during a federal sentencing evaluation (see below). If a sex offender evaluation is being conducted, relevant risk factors and factors related to likelihood of rehabilitation should be covered (see Chapter 5, Sex Offender Evaluations).

It is important to consider the type of information that will be collected before beginning any interview. Some content areas may be uncomfortable or painful for the client to discuss (e.g., past sexual abuse, witnessing family violence, a history of foster care). This is especially the case with capital sentencing evaluations where psychologists and psychiatrists can be asked to present any and all possible mitigating evidence. When conducting such evaluations, it may be beneficial (or even necessary) for the forensic mental health practitioner to meet with the client and have rapport-building sessions before beginning the actual interview. This can be facilitated by having representing counsel present for this initial meeting.

PSYCHOLOGICAL TESTING

There are a number of psychological assessments available for use in sentencing evaluations. The forensic mental health practitioner may choose a standardized academic achievement or intelligence test, such as the Wide Range Achievement Test, Fourth Edition (WRAT4; Wilkinson & Robertson, 2006) or Wechsler Adult Intelligence Scale—Fourth Edition (WAIS-IV; Wechsler, 2008). If an issue regarding memory arises, such measures as the Wechsler Memory Scales IV (WMS-IV) should be employed. The WRAT4 is commonly used to assess current academic functioning in a number of specific areas and will assist the evaluator in determining deficits in functioning and future treatment needs. The WAIS-IV is a measure of general intelligence with sound psychometric properties. It is therefore commonly used in forensic assessments to help determine mental retardation, learning disabilities, and other mitigating evidence. When assessing for mental retardation, the evaluator may choose to administer an adaptive functioning test such as the Vineland Adaptive Behavior Scales (Sparrow, Cicchetti, & Balla, 1984). Adaptive functioning is also useful in determining the treatment needs of the client.

Measures of psychopathology, personality functioning, and response style are also useful in sentencing evaluations. The Minnesota Multiphasic Personality Inventory, 2nd Edition (MMPI-2; Butcher, Dahlstrom, Graham, Tellegen, & Kaemmer, 1989) is a standard objective measure of adult psychopathology and personality structure that can be used to assess a number of issues related to sentencing. The MMPI-2 may assist in determining the extent to which psychopathology or personality factors affected the client's mental state at the time of the offense (see federal sentencing statute below), the client's current mental state (see relevant capital sentencing statute), and the client's treatment needs and/or amenability to treatment. Similar measures include the Personality Assessment Inventory (PAI) and the Millon Clinical Multiaxial Inventory-III (MCMI-III). Further, the MMPI-2 has built-in validity scales that are useful in assessing a client's response style. Assessing response style is particularly useful when the prosecution and defense retain different psychologists and/or psychiatrists. The psychological/ psychiatric evaluations in these situations tend to produce conflicting conclusions, and a "battle of the experts" may result. Accurately assessing response style will help confirm or disprove evaluators' hypotheses by determining the likelihood that a client is malingering or a psychological condition is being feigned.

The forensic mental health practitioner should determine if the referral question, or clinical interview, suggests that a more thorough evaluation of psychopathology is necessary. For example, if mental capacity is being assessed (see federal sentencing statute), it will be important to determine what, if any, psychological symptoms may have reduced the client's decision-making abilities at the time of the offense. Further, a comprehensive mitigation review is required in capital cases (*Wiggins v. Smith*, 2003), which includes both past and current psychopathology. Whatever instrument is administered, it should produce diagnostic information that relates to conventional diagnostic criteria, such as the *Diagnostic and Statistical Manual of Mental Disorders*, 4th ed., Text Revision (DSM-IV-TR; American Psychiatric Association, 2000) diagnoses (Melton, Petrilla, Poythress, & Slobogin, 2007). In some cases, a neuropsychological evaluation may be necessary to rule out the existence of brain damage.

As a last note of caution, the assessment instruments utilized should be client appropriate. The client should have the requisite skills to complete the instruments' tasks, such as the minimum reading level as listed in the administration manual. Further, if the client is a juvenile, the evaluator should be familiar with and, subsequently, utilize age-appropriate measures. For a more thorough review of instruments developed for use with juveniles, see Grisso, Vincent, and Seagrave's (2005) *Mental Health Screening and*

Assessment in Juvenile Justice. In the same vein, culturally appropriate measures should be used with defendants from different cultures (see Chapter 30, Transcultural Considerations).

ACTUARIAL MEASURES

When a forensic mental health practitioner is asked to perform a risk assessment (i.e., future risk of violence prediction or identifying risk factors and recommending how to reduce such risks), he/she can increase the evaluation's accuracy by administering an actuarial measure (Heilbrun, Marczyk, & DeMatteo, 2002). Actuarial measures assist the evaluator in preparing a sound risk assessment based on an empirically supported foundation. Such instruments provide a way for the evaluator to collect and organize findings based on known risk factors. The research identifies two classes of risk factors: (1) static factors are those that cannot be changed with intervention (e.g., criminal history, history of childhood maladjustment); and (2) dynamic factors are those that can potentially change (e.g., current adjustment, psychological symptoms) and predict recidivism. In deciding which instrument to administer, the evaluator must consider the population on which the instrument was developed (e.g., general offenders, psychiatric offenders, sexual offenders) and the type of outcomes the instrument has been found to predict (e.g., violent reoffending, sexual reoffending) to ensure that the instrument is relevant to the referral question (Heilbrun et al.). The following are commonly used specialized risk-assessment instruments:

- *Level of Service/Case Management Inventory (LS/CMI).* The LS/CMI is a standard objective measure of risks and needs information relevant to offender treatment planning and determining appropriate levels of freedom and supervision (Andrews, Bonta, & Wormith, 2004). The LS/CMI is the latest version of the Level of Service Inventory—Revised (LSI-R) and includes additional domains to document specific responsivity factors and includes a case management section. This risk/assessment instrument is theoretically driven and although static risk factors are included, it was designed to accurately measure dynamic risk factors. The LS/CMI was primarily developed with, and subsequent research has focused on, probation and general inmate populations. It can be used to aid in the prediction of general (as compared to specialized) reoffending, violent reoffending (Wormith, Olver, Stevenson, & Girard, 2007), and can aid in decision making regarding supervision requirements (Andrews et al., 2004).

- *Hare Psychopathy Check List—Revised, 2nd Edition (PCL-R).* The PCL-R is a well-validated, semistructured interview consisting of 20 clinician-rated items and is intended for use with an offender population, particularly in prison and forensic mental health facilities (Hare, 2003). The PCL-R is not a risk-assessment instrument per se, but rather a measure of personality traits and behaviors related to psychopathy (e.g., criminal behavior, callousness, lack of remorse) that has been shown to predict violence in offender populations. Research assessing the PCL-R has focused on special offender populations (i.e., sexual offenders, forensic patients, mentally disordered offenders) and the prediction of specialized outcomes (i.e., violent reoffending and sexual reoffending) (Wormith et al., 2007). The PCL-R has since been modified into two additional versions: the Hare Psychopathy Checklist: Screening Version (PCL-SV) and the Hare Psychopathy Checklist: Youth Version (PCL-YV). Further, it has been incorporated into other risk assessment instruments (see the following).

  The PCL-R has been used in a number of sentencing evaluations, including sexually violent predator (SVP) classifications, in assessing future dangerousness in the context of parole or probation appropriateness, general sentencing evaluations, and capital sentencing evaluations (DeMatteo & Edens, 2006). As a note of caution, the use of the PCL-R has been challenged in a number of cases, and courts have excluded PCL-R evidence when it provided little probative value or was prejudicial (i.e., improperly emphasizing defendant's potential for future dangerousness in capital case) (see DeMatteo & Edens). Finally, the term *psychopath* may have an unintended impact on the jury; therefore, the consequences of using the PCL-R in any psychological/psychiatric evaluation should be thoroughly considered.

- *Violence Risk Appraisal Guide (VRAG).* The VRAG is an actuarial tool that includes the Hare PCL-R (as discussed above) as one of its measures (Harris, Rice, & Quinsey, 1993; Quinsey, Harris, Rice, & Cormier, 1998). The VRAG was originally developed to evaluate violent recidivism among mentally disordered offenders and has since been shown to predict violent recidivism, general recidivism, and institutional misconduct in non-psychiatric incarcerated males (Kroner & Mills, 2001). It is made up of 12 items that sample the areas of personality disorders, early school maladjustment, age, marital status, criminal history, schizophrenia, and victim injury (Quinsey et al., 1998). Two limitations to consider are that the VRAG contains only static risk factors and, therefore, cannot be used to measure change, and it is designed only to be used with individuals who are 18 years of age or older.

- *Historical/Clinical/Risk Management-20 (HCR-20: Version 2)*. Although the HCR-20 is not a pure actuarial instrument, it does provide information regarding static and dynamic risk factors that is intended to help guide clinical decision making (Webster, Douglas, Eaves, & Hart, 1997). It does not produce norm- or criterion-referenced scores but does include empirically supported items, including the Hare PCL-R (discussed above). The HCR-20 consists of 10 static historical items (e.g., first violent incident, substance abuse problems, psychopathy, early maladjustment), 5 dynamic clinician-rated items (e.g., negative attitudes, impulsivity, unresponsiveness to treatment), and 5 risk management items (e.g., lack of personal support, stress). It is intended for use with forensic, criminal justice, and civil psychiatric populations.

    Sex offender–specific instruments. (a) The Rapid Risk Assessment for Sex Offense Recidivism (RRASOR; Hanson, 1997); (b) The Static-99 (Hanson & Thornton, 1999); and (c) The Sex Offender Risk Appraisal Guide (SORAG; Quinsey et al., 1998). See Chapter 5, Sex Offender Evaluations, for more instruments.

COLLATERAL CONTACTS

Third-party information is essential to any forensic psychological/psychiatric evaluation (Melton et al., 2007). Independently corroborating evidence should be incorporated throughout the written report and referred to during expert witness testimony to support the evaluator's findings. The presentation of independent supporting evidence will likely decrease jurors' skepticism of expert witnesses and increase the likelihood that they accept the evaluator's conclusions (Atkins, Podboy, Larson, & Schenker, 2007). Whenever possible, an evaluator should interview collateral sources in addition to reviewing the collateral records he/she is provided.

If an evaluator is not provided with third-party contact information, from the referral source, for example, he/she should ask the client who the client believes would be helpful in obtaining such information. If feasible, collateral interviews should be conducted in person. When there are a number of interviews to conduct in a short period of time, it may be more practical to conduct the interviews by telephone. The collateral contacts should be those people who will provide the most useful and relevant information concerning the referral question. Common third-party collaterals include family members (e.g., spouses, parents, or siblings), people with whom the client spends meaningful time (e.g., coworkers, superiors, or friends), people who have witnessed the client's current behaviors (e.g., people who live in the client's household or institutional staff), and past or current treatment providers.

DATA INTERPRETATION

In order to adequately weigh potential mitigating and aggravating factors relevant to sentencing, the expert must pull together various dimensions of the defendant's background to determine how that background collectively influenced the defendant's behavior. Accordingly, there are important questions that the expert will need to address for the sentencing judge or jury. Why did the defendant commit the criminal act? Is the defendant likely to commit similar criminal acts in the future? Is the defendant the type of person who would respond to treatment? Does the defendant have compelling characteristics or background that alters the perception of the criminal act? The various aspects of the defendant's life prior to the criminal behavior and the nature of the criminal act are taken together and weighed during the sentencing process. Accordingly, the information obtained about the defendant must be placed into the context of other variables, such as the defendant's cultural and socioeconomic background.

FACTORS RELEVANT TO SENTENCING

- *Cultural factors.* While reviewing the defendant's personal and family history, the expert should also consider the values, attitudes, and beliefs of the defendant's specific cultural group. Such factors may play a strong role in the defendant's character and behaviors, and offer an explanation for the defendant's criminal act. Issues such as the defendant's level of acculturation, language fluency, and cultural belief system must be explored. It is important to note that psychological testing must be used with caution and may be unreliable with certain cultures, since standard tests have not been validated in every immigrant group (Boehnlein, Schaefer, & Bloom, 2005). Nonetheless, the cultural background of the defendant is one critical element that must be considered during the assessment for sentencing.
- *Military experience.* While history of military experience may not directly relate to the specific crime for which the defendant is being sentenced, it has been used by courts as a mitigating factor (Hessick, 2008). Military service falls into the category of prior good acts that may be indicative of the good character of a defendant, and therefore deserving of leniency during sentencing. Hessick cites several studies that concluded that military veterans have significantly lower rates of recidivism than other offenders (Hessick, p. 1139). Prior military experience, honorable discharge from the military, military honors, and service in combat may demonstrate a defendant's previous service to society and may be relevant at sentencing.
- *Gang involvement.* Because of the association between gangs, violence, and other criminal acts, gang involvement is usually considered an aggravating factor. The degree of a defendant's gang involvement may be used by prosecutors to show the defendant's bad character and the risk of future dangerousness.
- *Socioeconomic status.* Mitigating evidence of poor socioeconomic status may support the defendant's assertions of extreme

childhood deprivation, neglect, and inability to take advantage of educational opportunities. Associated features such as regularly witnessing violence or suffering physical violence may also serve as mitigating evidence. While not necessarily providing insight into the character of the defendant, this information may be useful in explaining why the defendant committed the crime.

- *Offense-related factors.* Two factors that may impact sentencing are the defendant's motive for the crime and his/her role in the offense. Motive describes the reasons why a defendant may have committed a criminal act and may serve as either aggravating or mitigating evidence during the sentencing phase (Hessick, 2006). Aggravating motives include a desire for financial gain or a desire to inflict pain (Hessick, p. 102). Mitigating motives include a desire to help a family member or the belief that his/her actions were guided by moral justification (Hessick, p. 107). The defendant's role in the offense may also serve as either an aggravating or mitigating factor. Evidence that the defendant played a minor part in a crime may lower the sentence, while a more active role may suggest that the defendant deserves a more severe sentence.
- *Defendant's character.* In addition to various defendant characteristics described previously, other factors may influence the perception of the defendant's character. Factors such as the defendant's cooperation with law enforcement, expressions of remorse, and requests for treatment for addiction or psychiatric disorders may reflect the defendant's willingness to accept responsibility for his/her criminal behaviors. Regarding expressions of remorse, while some critics argue against its use as a mitigating factor during sentencing, courts have traditionally allowed it, viewing the remorseful defendant as more likely to benefit from rehabilitation efforts (Ward, 2006). A defendant's lack of remorse for his/her actions has been traditionally considered an aggravating factor.

The diagnosis of a maladaptive personality disorder may adversely impact the defendant during sentencing. For example, a defendant diagnosed with antisocial personality disorder may be viewed as lacking remorse, an ongoing threat to society, and not amenable to rehabilitation (Fabian, 2003). While such a diagnosis may intuitively be viewed as an aggravating factor, it may also be used to illustrate the consequence of a deprived background (Fabian, 2003). The age of the defendant may also impact sentencing. As the Supreme Court of the United States stated in *Eddings v. Oklahoma* (1982), age operates as a mitigating factor because children and adolescents are "less mature and responsible than adults" (p. 116). This view was again illustrated by the U.S. Supreme Court's prohibition of the execution of minors in *Roper v. Simmons* (2005).

- *Victim-related variables.* The characteristics of the defendant may also be considered in the light of the victim's behavior at the time of the crime. Evidence demonstrating that the victim's misconduct provoked the defendant's actions may be considered during sentencing. While not operating as an excuse for the defendant's criminal behavior, victim provocation may lower the defendant's level of culpability and mitigate the sentence (Kirchmeier, 2004). Victims and their families may also influence sentencing by providing victim impact statements to courts (Mulholland, 1995). Accordingly, victims may testify regarding the psychological, emotional, and financial effects that have resulted from the defendant's crime. In *Payne v. Tennessee* (1991), the U.S. Supreme Court held that survivors of a victim in a death penalty case may also provide impact statements regarding the effect of the murder on their lives.

COMMUNICATION

REPORT WRITING—SPECIAL ISSUES

Writing reports for sentencing evaluations should follow the same principles as discussed elsewhere. For the purpose of this chapter, we will be focusing on special issues related to specific types of sentencing evaluations:

- *Federal sentencing.* The Supreme Court of the United States in *U.S. v. Booker* (2005) held that the federal sentencing guidelines are constitutional only if they are advisory, rather than mandatory. As a result, judges have more discretion to consider psychological/psychiatric reports and testimony in making federal sentencing determinations. The federal sentencing guidelines provide a sentencing range based on the severity of the defendant's offense (convicted criminal conduct and offense specifics) and the defendant's criminal history (United States Sentencing Commission, 2008). Judges can depart from the given sentencing range only by providing an explicit rationale. The guidelines recognize a number of characteristics and circumstances that provide a rationale for departure (downward and upward), many of which are areas where a psychological/ psychiatric evaluation would be relevant (U.S.S.G. § 5K2.0). These include victim conduct (§ 5K2.10), lesser harms (e.g., in an assisted suicide context; § 5K2.11), coercion and distress (§ 5K2.12), and diminished capacity (§ 5K2.13).

The evaluator's federal sentencing report should include the relevant section of the federal sentencing guidelines in the report and relate all conclusions to this legal standard. Further, it is important that the evaluator does not address legal issues outside his/her expertise as a psychologist or psychiatrist. For example, section 5K2.13 provides:

> A downward departure may be warranted if (1) the defendant committed the offense while suffering from a significantly reduced mental capacity; and (2) the significantly reduced mental capacity contributed substantially to the commission of the offense. Similarly, if a departure is warranted under this policy statement, the extent of the departure should reflect the extent to which the reduced mental capacity contributed to the commission of the offense. However, the court may not depart below the applicable guideline range if (1) the significantly reduced mental capacity was caused by the voluntary use of drugs or other intoxicants; (2) the facts and circumstances of the defendant's offense indicate a need to protect the public because the offense involved actual violence or a serious threat of violence; (3) the defendant's criminal history indicates a need to incarcerate the defendant to protect the public; or (4) the defendant has been convicted of an offense under chapter 71, 109A, 110, or 117, of title 18, United States Code.

It is within the scope, and competence, of a forensic psychological/psychiatric evaluation to assess whether the defendant was suffering from "significantly reduced mental capacity" at the time of the offense. Such expertise can also be used to assess the manner and degree to which these impairments may have contributed to the commission of the offense. Conversely, such evaluations cannot address whether "the facts and circumstances of the defendant's offense" or the "defendant's criminal history indicate a need to incarcerate the defendant to protect the public" (§ 5K2.13).

- *Capital sentencing.* The evaluator may want to discuss the specific areas of mitigation with the referral source before conducting a capital sentencing evaluation. Even if the evaluator is not given such direction, he/she should consider all available mitigating evidence when compiling the report. The Supreme Court of the United States has required that mitigation investigations include all efforts to discover "all reasonably available" mitigating evidence (*Wiggins v. Smith*, 2003). Further, the jury must be able to consider all possible mitigating factors (i.e., a state cannot limit the possible mitigating factors) when determining whether an offender should receive a death sentence.

  The report should focus on the following areas, when applicable: (1) social and cultural factors that may have impacted the defendant's development, (2) the defendant's prison experience, (3) factors surrounding the offense (e.g., diminished capacity, moral justification), (4) favorable defendant characteristics (e.g., young age, lack of criminal history), and (5) victim-related variables, including the victim's support of a life sentence (Atkins et al., 2007). Further, the report should specifically address the jurisdiction's statutory mitigating factors, as well as any mitigating factors that are not statutorily enumerated. As discussed earlier, the evaluator must be sure to firmly support his or her findings with independent corroborating evidence. Finally, the evaluator should keep in mind the goals of mitigation when writing the report and testifying in court: to humanize the client to the jury and save the client's life (Atkins et al., 2007).

- *Sexual offenses.* An evaluator writing a sex offender sentencing report, for either a postadjudication/presentencing evaluation or an SVP civil commitment evaluation, must be sure to include any legal requirements specific to his/her jurisdiction. Further, if the evaluator is unable to meet with the offender, the report should thoroughly review the collateral sources and incorporate these data into the evaluator's recommendations. See Chapter 5 for a more complete discussion of sexual offender evaluations.

- *Parole.* At times, the forensic mental health practitioner is called upon to provide information in anticipation of an upcoming parole hearing. At issue is the degree to which the client has been "rehabilitated" and whether he/she would present as a danger to his/her community upon release. The parole panel must determine whether he/she has achieved concrete gains in rehabilitating him/herself.

Forensic mental health practitioners are in the position to work with defense counsel in bringing information regarding such successful rehabilitative efforts as grounds for early release before the parole board. In their discussion of forensic psychological consultation in death penalty cases, Atkins et al. (2007) discussed the areas of focus for a mitigation evaluation and included three areas germane to the issue of parole: issues related to the defendant's prison experience, factors related to the offense itself, and the defendant's character. Aspects of the defendant's character and personality makeup consistent with the potential for genuine remorse and the aberrant nature of his/her offense-related behavior should also be addressed.

Galegher and Carroll (1985) reviewed the development of modern parole guidelines and referenced the four criteria listed in the model penal code in 1962 as offense severity, participation in programs, institutional discipline, and certainty of favorable parole outcome. They referenced the primary concerns as (1) ensuring that offenders are punished in proportion to the seriousness of their offenses, and (2) protecting the community from offenders who are unlikely to perform favorably on parole. Galegher & Carroll (1985) spoke of the issue of recidivism and commented:

> The fact that the dimensions used in the construction of the parole guidelines embodied normative decision goals means that there are external criteria against which the correctness of the decisions can be measured. This is most apparent in the case of the parole prognosis dimension. Because the probability of

recidivism is used as a basis for parole release decisions, and because recidivism is a measurable outcome, one can observe whether the predictive outcomes do occur. (p. 110)

In their discussion of the federal sentencing guidelines, Ruback and Wroblewski (2001) discussed actuarial methods for predicting recidivism, stating that "in virtually all cases of complex decision making, statistical prediction is superior to clinical judgment, regardless of what people believe" (p. 757). Implications for forensic mental health consultants include the recommendation that actuarial instruments be included in their efforts to predict a defendant's appropriateness for early release. The authors describe the integration of clinical judgment with actuarial assessment techniques as a "bootstrapping model" and describe such a methodology as superior to clinical judgment alone. For a list of common actuarial measures, see the "Actuarial Measures" section earlier in this chapter. A further discussion of the construction and use of actuarial instruments for the prediction of recidivism is beyond the scope of this chapter. Such a discussion of actuarial instruments and their use can be found in Chapters 5 and 15.

Parry and Drogin (2000) discussed the issue of the assessment of future dangerousness and addressed the "common errors" related to risk assessment:

> First, as with risk assessments generally, there is the danger that experts and the courts will arrive at opinions or draw conclusions without properly relating the individual's characteristics or behavior to the "statistical prevalence for particular behavior over a set period of time." For instance, common sense would suggest that the more serious the crime that the defendant has committed, the more dangerous the defendant is likely to be in the future. Unfortunately, this commonsense opinion may actually be false, or only true in certain circumstances. Moreover, even though clinicians may believe that they have observed this phenomenon to be generally true, it still needs to be measured empirically and viewed in the context of a particular defendant. (p. 214)

Also relevant to the forensic mental health consultant is the authors' underscoring of the importance for the forensic mental health consultant to account for the defendant's age, "since studies indicate that as people become more elderly, there is a diminishing of criminal and violent activities" (Parry & Drogin, 2000, p. 215).

Hemingway and Hinton (2009), in their discussion of post-sentencing rehabilitation, discussed specific examples of such rehabilitation that might be relevant to the issue of parole. These include the defendant's tutoring inmates in prison, serving as a prison chaplain's assistant, evidence of defendant's change in attitude, age, medical condition, extreme remorse, extreme acceptance of responsibility, and extraordinary mental and emotional condition.

- *Prosecution.* While the prosecution is more likely to engage the services of a forensic mental health practitioner to rebut the testimony of a similarly trained professional in an affirmative defense (e.g., insanity or diminished capacity), it will also engage the services of such professionals in an effort to respond to proffered testimony regarding the defendant at the time of sentencing. When defense experts proffer opinions regarding the defendant's mental health, dangerousness, remorse, acceptance of responsibility, or institutional adjustment, the prosecution can engage forensic psychiatrists or psychologists to rebut these opinions as well as to address the issue of malingering.

  Similarly, while aggravating factors are typically not the province of the forensic mental health professional, the prosecutor might utilize such services in rebutting mental health testimony regarding mitigating factors. Depending on the nature of the crime, mitigation evidence is often viewed skeptically by the fact finder and will certainly be challenged by the prosecution. It is within this context that the forensic mental health professional is in the position to address findings of psychological mitigation that are not firmly supported by independent corroborating evidence.

  Winick (1999) observed that defense arguments based on client rehabilitation, for example, may be met by a degree of cynicism. He also addressed the use of forensic mental health testimony by either side "where the question is raised as to whether participation in rehabilitation or the making of an apology has not been genuine" (p. 1051). At such times, consideration might be given to the use of an expert witness on malingering. The fields of both psychiatry and psychology have developed an ever-increasing ability to detect deception and malingering as well as a variety of psychometric instruments for this purpose.

Parry and Drogin (2000) discussed the issue of testimony regarding a defendant's institutional adjustment. Consultants for the prosecution are in the position to present evidence indicating that the prediction of the defendant's future dangerousness based on his/her behavior in prison can often be misleading. The authors observed:

> Institutional circumstances are very different from those found in normal society. In particular, rates of violence in prison and in the community are markedly different depending on the type and severity of violence. Thus, when courts draw conclusions about the defendant's violence in the future, it is important to take into consideration the milieu in which the violent behavior would likely occur, the type of violence at issue and it's severity. (p. 215)

CONSULTATION

In addition to, or in lieu of, their role as an expert witness at the time of sentencing, forensic practitioners are often called upon to serve as consultants to the defending attorney. An example of the consultative role of the forensic mental health professional is found in the American Bar Association's (ABA) *Guidelines for the Appointment and Performance of Defense Counsel in Death Penalty Cases* (2003). The Guidelines recommend the utilization of a forensic mental health professional who possesses:

> clinical and information-gathering skills and training that most lawyers simply do not have. They have the time and the ability to elicit sensitive, embarrassing and often humiliating evidence that the defendant may have never disclosed. They have the clinical skills to recognize such things as congenital, mental or neurological conditions, to understand how these conditions may have affected a defendant's development and behavior and to identify the most

appropriate experts to examine the defendant or testify on his behalf. (p. 33)

Atkins et al. (2007) in their discussion of sentencing in death penalty cases, addressed the role of the forensic mental health professional:

While psychologists are usually called upon to evaluate whether mitigators are present, it is important to recognize that the psychologist may be called upon to fill different roles depending on the circumstances. In many cases, the psychologist is seen and employed as an independent evaluator and expert witness. As an independent evaluator, he or she will obtain and review evidence relevant to mitigation, provide a written report of a diagnosis or findings and testify before the jury regarding his or her findings. In addition to the role of independent evaluator, the psychologist may also serve as a consultant to counsel. In this role, based upon the understanding that the consultant has developed of the defendant, the psychologist may assist counsel. For example, he or she may aid in devising communication strategies to reach and aid the defendant in making the difficult choices that arise in capital litigation, such as accepting a plea to a life sentence in order to avoid a death sentence. (p. 8)

As a consultant, the forensic mental health practitioner is in the position of advising counsel of the contextual, as well as the substantive, issues at hand. Atkins et al. (2007) observed:

It can be argued that the requirement of mitigation evidence in the sentencing decision is of little moment if not properly presented to, or adequately considered by, the jury. Thus, mitigation evidence should be developed with an eye towards the system in which it will be presented. . . . The early development of psychological mitigation evidence is critical to decision making and the effect of representation of . . . defendants. First, identifying jurors who may not be willing to consider the type of psychological mitigation that will be offered and, second, determining at what point psychological mitigation evidence will be presented to the jury. . . . To consider psychological mitigation as merely a diagnosis to be expressed to the jury at the last stage of the trial process greatly underestimates the impact that the psychological can have and limits his/her role in the process. In this partnership between the disciplines of psychology and law, it is imperative that there be a full recognition by both partners of how the information developed is best used. (pp. 10–12)

This consultative role is consistent with the therapeutic jurisprudence/preventive law model discussed by Winick (1999). This model views the law, and the way in which it is applied, as having "inevitable consequences" for the psychological well-being of the defendant, particularly at the time of sentencing. Winick observed:

It is a mental health approach to law and the way it is applied, suggesting the need for law makers and law appliers to be sensitive to law's impact on psychological health and to perform their roles with an awareness of basic principles of psychology. (p. 1039)

The forensic mental health consultant is in a position to facilitate the enlightenment and development of such psychologically minded attorneys who would be sensitive to the emotional climate of the attorney–client relationship. According to Winick (1999), such an attorney would have:

a heightened sensitivity to the psychological dimensions of the attorney–client relationship and (would use) insights from psychology in interviewing and counseling clients. . . . When the behavior that resulted in criminal charges is related to substance abuse, mental illness, or psychologically maladaptive behavior patterns, confronting the existence of such a problem and coming to terms with a need to deal with it can produce considerable psychological distress. Dealing with the issue of rehabilitation and relapse prevention in the context of plea bargaining or sentencing thus may be regarded within the terminology of therapeutic jurisprudence/preventive law as a psycholegal soft spot. . . . Attorneys who ignore the emotional dimensions of dealing with clients in these contexts risk a serious loss of effectiveness in representing them at plea bargaining and sentencing. (pp. 1040–1041)

The forensic mental health consultant can work with counsel toward a better understanding of all aspects of the defendant, not simply his/her legal problems. The consultant is also in the position to familiarize counsel with the full range of rehabilitative opportunities that might be available as well as the conditions for eligibility into these programs.

TESTIMONY

Any time a psychological/psychiatric evaluation is conducted as part of judicial proceedings, the evaluator must be prepared to be called as an expert witness. Conducting a sentencing evaluation, regardless of the specific referral question, is no different. With that said, there are several possible points during the postconviction process when an evaluator may be called upon to testify. Depending on the type of sentencing evaluation conducted, a forensic mental health practitioner may be called during the defendant's original sentencing hearing, during a reconsideration hearing, or during an evidentiary hearing on/during postconviction relief. If testimony is required, the evaluator should follow the same principles he/she followed while writing the report. This includes only answering the referral question, addressing each part of the necessary legal standard, not giving an opinion on the ultimate legal question directly, being prepared for possible direct examination and cross-examination questions, and providing a complete description of the evaluation's findings during direct examination (Heilbrun et al., 2002). Although the procedure for gathering information may differ, depending on when in the legal process the evaluation is conducted, the same principles apply to testimony regardless of whether it is during the original sentencing hearing, a reconsideration hearing, or an evidentiary hearing during postconviction.

REFERENCES

American Academy of Psychiatry and the Law. (2005). *Ethics guidelines for the practice of forensic psychiatry.* Bloomfield, CT: Author.
American Bar Association. (2003). *Guidelines for the appointment and performance of defense counsel in death penalty cases.* Washington, DC: Author.

American Psychiatric Association. (2000). *Diagnostic and statistical manual of mental disorders* (4th ed., Text Revision). Washington, DC: Author.

Andrews, D., Bonta, J., & Wormith, J. S. (2004). *The Level of Service/Case Management Inventory*. Toronto, ON: Multi-Health Systems.

Atkins v. Virginia, 536 U.S. 304 (2002).

Atkins, E. L., Podboy, J., Larson, K., & Schenker, N. (2007). Forensic psychological consultation in U.S. death penalty cases in state and federal courts. *American Journal of Forensic Psychology*, 25(3), 7–20.

Berman, D. A. (2005). Punishment and crime: Reconceptualizing sentencing. *University of Chicago Legal Forum, 2005*, 1–53.

Boehnlein, J. K., Schaefer, M. N., & Bloom, J. D. (2005). Cultural considerations in the criminal law: The sentencing process. *Journal of the American Academy of Psychiatry and the Law, 33*, 335–341.

Butcher, J., Dahlstrom, W., Graham, J., Tellegen, A., & Kaemmer, B. (1989). *MMPI-2: Manual for administration and scoring*. Minneapolis, MN: University of Minnesota Press.

Dattilio, F. M., & Sadoff, R. L. (2007). *Mental health experts: Roles and qualifications for court* (2nd ed.). Mechanicsburg, PA: PBI Press.

Death Penalty Information Center. (2009). Retrieved November 29, 2009, from http://www.deathpenaltyinfo.org

DeMatteo, D., & Edens, J. F. (2006). The role and relevance of the Psychopathy Checklist—Revised in court: A case law survey of U.S. courts (1991–2004). *Psychology, Public Policy, and Law, 12*(2), 214–241.

Eddings v. Oklahoma, 455 U.S. 104 (1982).

Edersheim, J. G., & Beck, J. C. (2005). Commentary: Expert testimony as a potential asset in defense of capital sentencing cases. *Journal of the American Academy of Psychiatry and the Law, 33*, 519–522.

Fabian, J. M. (2003). Death penalty mitigation and the role of the forensic psychologist. *Law and Psychology Review, 27*, 73–120.

Galegher, J., & Carroll, J. S. (1985). Sentencing guidelines: Construction and utilization. In C. P. Ewing (Ed.), *Psychology, psychiatry, and the law: A clinical and forensic handbook* (pp. 95–127). New York, NY: Professional Resource Exchange.

Grisso, T., Vincent, G., & Seagrave, D. (2005). *Mental health screening and assessment in juveniles*. New York: Guilford Press.

Hanson, R. (1997). *The development of a brief actuarial risk scale for sexual offense recidivism*. Ottawa, Ontario: Department of the Solicitor General of Canada.

Hanson, R., & Thornton, D. (1999). *Static 99: Improving actuarial risk assessments for sex offenders*. Ottawa, Ontario: Department of the Solicitor General of Canada.

Hare, R. D. (2003). *The Hare Psychopathy Checklist—Revised* (2nd ed.). Toronto, ON: Multi-Health Systems.

Harris, G. T., Rice, M. E., & Quinsey, V. L. (1993). Violent recidivism of mentally disordered offenders: The development of a statistical prediction instrument. *Criminal Justice and Behavior, 20*, 315–335.

Heilbrun, K., Marczyk, G., & DeMatteo, D. (2002). *Forensic mental health assessment: A casebook.* New York, NY: Oxford University Press.

Hemingway, D., & Hinton, J. (2009). *Departures.* A. B. Evans (Ed.). Unpublished manuscript.

Hessick, C. B. (2006). Motive's role in criminal punishment. *Southern California Law Review, 80*, 89–150.

Hessick, C. B. (2008). Why are only bad acts good sentencing factors? *Boston University Law Review, 88*, 1109–1164.

Huigens, K. (2005). Punishment and crime: On commonplace punishment theory. *University of Chicago Legal Forum, 2005*, 437–457.

Kirchmeier, J. L. (2004). A tear in the eye of the law: Mitigating factors and the progression towards a disease theory of criminal justice. *Oregon Law Review, 83*, 631–730.

Kroner, D. G., & Mills, J. F. (2001). The accuracy of five risk appraisal instruments in predicting institutional misconduct and new convictions. *Criminal Justice and Behavior, 28*(4), 471–489.

Lockett v. Ohio, 438 U.S. 586 (1978).

Melton, G. B., Petrilla, J., Poythress, N. G., & Slobogin, C. (2007). *Psychological evaluations for the courts: A handbook for mental health professionals and lawyers* (3rd ed.). New York, NY: Guilford Press.

Mulholland, C. L. (1995). Sentencing criminals: The constitutionality of victim impact statements. *Missouri Law Review, 60*, 731–748.

Parry, J. W., & Drogin, E. Y. (2000). *Criminal law handbook on psychiatric and psychological evidence and testimony.* Washington, DC: American Bar Association.

Payne v. Tennessee, 501 U.S. 808 (1991).

Quinsey, V. L., Harris, G. T., Rice, M. E., & Cormier, C. A. (1998). *Violent offenders: Appraising and managing risk.* Washington, DC: American Psychological Association.

Reitz, K. R. (2000). Sentencing. In M. Tonry (Ed.), *The handbook of crime and punishment* (pp. 542–562). New York, NY: Oxford University Press.

Roper v. Simmons, 543 U.S. 551 (2005).

Ruback, R. B., & Wroblewski, J. (2001). The federal sentencing guidelines: Psychological and policy reasons for simplification, *Psychology, Public Policy, and Law, 7*(4), 739–775.

Sadoff, R. L. (2003). Practical issues in forensic psychiatric practice. In R. Rosner (Ed.), *Principles of Forensic Practice* (2nd ed., pp. 45–51). New York, NY: Arnold.

Sadoff, R. L., & Dattilio, F. M. (2008). *Crime and mental illness: A guide to courtroom practice.* Mechanicsburg, PA: PBI Press.

Simons, M. A. (2009). Prosecutors as punishment theorists: Seeking sentencing justice. *George Mason Law Review, 16*, 303–355.

Sondheimer, J. N. (1990). A continuing source of aggravation: The improper consideration of mitigating factors in death penalty sentencing. *Hastings Law Journal, 41*, 409–446.

Sparrow, S. S., Cicchetti, D. V., & Balla, D. A. (1984). *Vineland Adaptive Behavior Scales.* Bloomington, MN: Pearson Assessments.

Tomes, J. P. (1997). Damned if you do, damned if you don't: The use of mitigation experts in death penalty litigation. *American Journal of Criminal Law, 24*, 359–399.

Trop v. Dulles, 356 U.S. 86 (1958).

U.S. v. Booker, 543 U.S. 220 (2005).

United States Sentencing Commission. (2008). *The federal sentencing guidelines manual.* Washington, DC: Thompson/West.

U.S.S.G. §§ 5K2, 18 U.S.C.

Ward, B. H. (2006). Sentencing without remorse. *Loyola University Chicago Law Journal, 38*, 131–167.

Webster, C. D., Douglas, K. S., Eaves, D., & Hart, S. D. (1997). *HCR-20: Assessing risk for violence (version 2).* Vancouver: Mental Health Law & Policy Institute, Simon Fraser University.

Wechsler, D. (2008) *WAIS-IV administration and scoring manual.* San Antonio, TX: Psychological Corporation.

Wiggins v. Smith, 539 U.S. 510 (2003).

Wilkinson, G. S., & Robertson, G. J. (2006). *Wide Range Achievement Test—Fourth Edition.* Lutz, FL: Psychological Assessment Resources.

Winick, B. J. (1999). Redefining the role of the criminal defense lawyer at plea bargaining and sentencing: A therapeutic jurisprudence/ preventive law model, *Psychology, Public Policy, and the Law, 5*(4), 1034–1083.

Wormith, J. S., Olver, M. E., Stevenson, H. E., & Girard, L. (2007). The long-term prediction of offender recidivism using diagnostic, personality, and risk/need approaches to offender assessment. *Psychological Services, 4*(4), 287–305.

CHAPTER 4

Competency Restoration

STEVEN E. SAMUEL and TIMOTHY J. MICHALS

INTRODUCTION

Like many legal concepts, competence to stand trial (CST; see Chapter 1 in this volume) seems reasonably clear in its definition, yet considerably more vague in its application and understanding by the public and by forensic examiners (Gutheil, 1999). As noted by the Supreme Court of the United States in *Godinez v. Moran* (1993), "while the decision to plead guilty is undeniably a profound one, it is no more complicated than the sum total of decisions that a defendant may be called upon to make during the course of a trial" (p. 398). How, then, when defendants have initially been determined incompetent to stand trial, are they optimally restored to competency?

The answer to this question lies in recognizing and addressing the psychiatric conditions and other personal circumstances underlying this forensic disability. Trial incompetency is strongly associated with psychosis and the presence of more severe psychopathology, including disorientation, hallucinations, impaired memory, and impaired thought and communication (Nicholson & Kugler, 1991). A defendant's competency may be impaired by other factors, including mental retardation, neurocognitive disorders, the effects of substance abuse, and physical illness. CST is a multidimensional construct, and it varies depending on the content, the person, and the task that is the subject of the evaluation (Freckelton, 2009); defendants are seldom globally impaired or equally functional across all realms of competence.

Several discrete considerations inform the forensic evaluator's approach to competency restoration. First, judges typically place a high value on CST assessments. Cruise and Rogers (1998) estimated that the court agreed with clinicians' conclusions 90% or more of the time. Second, the threshold for competency is low and is constituted of minimal criteria (*Wieter v. Settle*, 1961). Third, statutory law defines patient competence in terms of an open norm, and the legal, psychological, and ethical literature reveals myriad different, often mutually incompatible definitions, approaches, and criteria. Furthermore, empirical research has shown that in the practice of health care, explicit assessments of patients' competence are hardly ever made. The meaning of *competence to stand trial* is generally considered to be contextual; it is often in the eye of the beholder.

Pendleton (1980) concluded that defendants who are committed to psychiatric hospitals for competency restoration after being found incompetent make up the largest group of psychiatric patients who are hospitalized via the criminal justice system. McGarry and Curran (1973) estimated that there were 25,000 to 36,000 such defendants yearly. Winick (1977) concluded that approximately 15,000 criminal defendants were hospitalized at any particular time in the United States after being adjudicated incompetent to stand trial. Steadman, Monahan, Hartstone, Davis, and Robbins (1982) stated that nearly one-third of all admissions of mentally disordered criminal offenders to state and federal mental health facilities are for incompetence to stand trial; this figure translates to approximately 25,000 defendants nationally each year.

Davis (1985) determined that as many as 9,000 inpatient beds were reserved nationwide for individuals who have been adjudicated incompetent to stand trial, with the most common reason for deficits in pretrial competency abilities being psychotic symptoms and mental retardation. Subsequently obtained data showed that in 1986 approximately 3,200 incompetent defendants in the United States were utilizing a forensic mental health bed in one day, and that many more were utilizing other psychiatric resources (Way, Dvoskin, & Steadman, 1991).

Melton, Petrila, Poythress, and Slobogin (2007) describe various research studies indicating that approximately 30% of defendants for a competency evaluation are ultimately deemed incompetent. Of these individuals, psychotic disorders are the most common Axis I diagnosis. Other research indicates that between 45% and 65% of defendants evaluated for competency who have schizophrenia or other psychotic illnesses are found to be incompetent to stand trial (Nicholson & Kugler, 1991; Reich & Wells, 1985; Roesch, Eaves, Sollner, Normandin, & Glackman, 1981; Warren, Fitch, Dietz, & Rosenfeld, 1991).

A MacArthur Foundation Research Network study on Mental Health and the Law (Hoge et al., 1997) concluded that 65% of defendants hospitalized as incompetent to stand trial had a diagnosis of schizophrenia. Goldstein and Burd (1990); Otto et al. (1998); and James, Duffield, Blizard, & Hamilton (2001) likewise concluded that active psychotic symptoms are strongly correlated with impairments in trial-related abilities.

PREPARATION

While the focus of this chapter is on restoration of incompetent defendants to stand trial, we understand that for some defendants the issue is not resurrecting something lost but rather achieving something new. We also recognize that the notion of a surgical separation between competent and noncompetent defendants advanced by evaluators and galvanized by a court's ruling is more a matter of resolving cognitive dissonance than an accurate reflection of clinical realities. In actuality, there is commonly some type of overlap between these conditions; competency, therefore, in our view, is not an absolute condition.

Competency restoration is not a simple construct. Neither is it a process designed to train a criminal defendant to think or act like a lawyer. *Restoration* refers to restoration of abilities generally associated with competency to stand trial, following a finding of incompetence.

The individuals assigned to the task of restoring competency to incompetent defendants face a number of challenges from scientific, legal, and mental health forums, and potential countertransference reactions that result from having to weigh pride in one's clinical efforts against ethical tensions created from knowing that successful treatment may culminate in the individual's successful prosecution. Consider as well the ethical conflicts faced by the competency restoration staff regarding how, and in what ways, information could be obtained from a defendant that might not be in the defendant's best interests.

The goal of restoration of incompetent defendants to stand trial in general terms is to expand and correct the legal knowledge base of defendants, to help defendants manage symptoms of their mental disorder and cognitive impairments, and to educate defendants about the courtroom participants and legal process. Appelbaum (1994) noted that clinicians who provide specific educational training efforts to defendants with mental retardation may feel that they are serving the interests of the criminal justice system rather than those of their patients. His solution to this dilemna is to obtain informed consent from defense attorneys and defendants or their surrogate decision makers before beginning competency training, because "in the absence of consent, rehabilitation aimed at enhancing competence to stand trial introduces risk of further abuse of an already victimized group of people" (pp. 232–324).

RESEARCH WITH PARTICULAR RELEVANCE TO PREPARATION

The early literature on forensic hospitals that offered restoration of competency programming for incompetent defendants indicates that the programs, with few exceptions nationwide, offered very little specialized training and used medication treatment as the sole intervention. Only a handful of articles, mostly descriptive in nature, discuss psycholegal programming designed to restore competence in defendants in forensic inpatient settings.

Early research studies examining the effects of competency restoration training were descriptive, with small sample sizes assessed within a relatively short study period; very few individuals were described as successfully restored. McGarry (1969) outlined the pertinent issues related to restoration of competency. McGarry (1971) reported a study of 204 defendants deemed incompetent to stand trial who were committed indefinitely to Bridgewater State Hospital in Massachusetts as of 1963. Steadman's (1979) monograph described his prospective study of 539 incompetent to stand trial defendants in New York State. Grisso (1992); Cooper and Grisso (1997); and Mumley, Tillbrook, and Grisso (2003) reviewed evolving studies on competence to stand trial for approximately two decades at 5-year intervals.

Pinals's (2005) review of research-based and descriptive literature represents a significant contribution to developing a perspective on the history and complexities of competency restoration programming, including programming for mentally retarded defendants and juvenile defendants. Her review considers juvenile defendants, restoration rates, and the effectiveness of competency restoration programs, the latter of which "has often been measured in the literature by an ultimate clinical recommendation to the court that the defendant has regained or attained competence, and/or whether the courts have adjudicated the defendants as competent" (p. 97).

Among the studies reviewed by Pinals (2005) were Pendleton's (1980) frequently cited research on training-based treatment of persons found incompetent to stand trial that was completed at Atascadero State Hospital; Davis's (1985) clinical treatise describing a multidisciplinary treatment approach, which prioritized competency restoration for patients whose reason for hospitalization was incompetence to stand trial and focused on cognitive facets of competence and treatment that was tailor-made for specific psychiatric complaints; Brown's (1992) study of didactic programming taking place 5 days a week for 30- to 40-minute periods and focused on improving functioning related to the criminal justice process; and Noffsinger's (2001) research on a 40-bed competency restoration unit, consisting of 15 hours of weekly contact with staff, mock trials, videotaped role-playing, and individualized treatment programming. While further details are beyond the scope of this chapter, those preparing to provide restoration services are well advised to seek out this review and also the component studies in their original contexts.

Nelson (1989) evaluated the effects of a one-day didactic workshop on levels of competency based on results of the Competency Screening Test. The study found no statistical differences between pretest and post-test data for the experimental and control groups.

Siegel and Elwork (1990) reported that 21 patients determined incompetent to stand trial were assigned to an experimental group or a control group. Each group received 1 hour of training three times weekly for 3 weeks. Patients in the experimental group received an admixture of education regarding legal concepts, videotape rehearsals, discussions of the roles of courtroom personnel, mental health treatment, and cognitive–behavioral programming that focused on their particular types of incompetence. The control group received mental health treatment only. More from the experimental treatment group than the standard treatment group were ultimately deemed to be competent.

Siegel and Elwork's (1990) research also included data from a questionnaire they sent to 128 directors of forensic facilities around the United States, asking them to report on the prevalence of their different approaches to treating incompetence to stand trial. Approximately one-half of the recipients responded. The data indicated that only 43% of the facilities reported that patients adjudicated incompetent to stand trial underwent a different form of treatment from other patients; 57% of the respondents stated that they did not treat these individuals differently from other patients. The responding facilities stated that they placed a stronger emphasis on treating the underlying mental illness than on treating the particular symptoms that legally substantiated incompetence to stand trial.

Miller's (2003) survey of forensic mental health program directors, while not focusing on programming per se, determined that most restoration of competence to stand trial occurs in inpatient hospital settings within the time period allotted for such restoration and is primarily dictated by statute. This study concluded that incompetent defendants are a prominent fixture within the larger pool of patients admitted to state forensic mental health hospitals.

Anderson and Hewitt (2002) investigated the reevaluations of CST of 75 criminal defendants with mental retardation who were originally found incompetent and who were referred for treatment and the effect of competency restoration training. The defendants were administered the CST Education Program (Fritsch & Moseley, 1982), an educational program consisting of a series of seven 1-hour classes composed of 4 to 10 defendants led primarily by social workers; however, the qualifications of the individuals leading the program varied according to the facility. The participants were administered a pretest consisting of 21 true/false questions to assess their knowledge of legal issues. The investigation concluded that, for the most part, competency training for defendants with mental retardation was questionably effective. The investigation also concluded that higher intelligence quotient (IQ) and being African American rather than Caucasian were predictive of restoration.

Bertsch, Younglove, and Kerr (2002), in response to a California statute, conducted a limited evaluation of the Porterville, California, Developmental Center Court Competency Training program. The participants in the program were developmentally delayed criminal defendants who were not mentally ill.

Results showed that individuals who were adjudged as incompetent to stand trial due to developmental disability and enrolled for 6 months in the training program demonstrated significant gain in Competency Assessment Instrument (CAI) score. The same gain was not evidenced by developmentally delayed Porterville residents who were not criminal defendants and not enrolled in the training program.

Bertman (2003) utilized a random/matched assessment research design to assign individuals to one of three treatment programs for restoration of competency. Group 1 ($n = 8$) received weekly 45-minute group legal concept sessions for four weeks. Group 2 ($n = 10$) received six weekly 45-minute sessions that focused on deficit remediation and legal rights education using a Legal Rights Study Guide Protocol in addition to four weekly 45-minute group sessions. Group 3 ($n = 8$) received four weekly 45-minute group sessions in addition to six individual sessions that focused on cognitive impairments specific to each group member. Bertman reported that there were no significant baseline differences among the groups, and concluded that all groups differed significantly on competency measures obtained before and after testing, and that the deficit-focused remediation and the legal rights education groups (Groups 2 and 3) demonstrated significantly higher posttreatment scores on competency compared to the standard hospital treatment group (Group 1). The deficit-focused remediation and legal rights group (Group 2) also demonstrated approximately 50% greater improvement on the competency measures than the standard hospital treatment group (Group 1), indicating that education on legal rights issue was a valuable undertaking in this regard. This study did not make clear whether the positive results of Group 3 were due to the nature of the treatment or to the greater number of treatment sessions.

Wall, Krupp, and Guilmette (2003) developed and implemented a formal training tool, the Slater Method, for restoration of competency in clients with mental retardation who were judged to be incompetent to stand trial. The Slater Method was designed to consider the needs of a population otherwise ignored or not explicitly addressed by competency restoration programs, and assesses certain capacities related to competence to stand trial. It was not designed to be a formal competency assessment instrument, but rather a detailed training program using various strategies to improve the organizational and cognitive skills of mentally retarded defendants so that they may return to the criminal justice system and have their charges adjudicated. The Slater Method is based on four areas: the teaching ability of the trainer, the content of the material to be presented to the defendant, the manner in which the material is presented, and the usefulness to legal counsel of restoration methods.

Schouten (2003), in a commentary on the Slater Method, raises the reasonable concern that defendants whose participation in the program may attain the "technical standard for competence to stand trial (CST) without developing the level of understanding necessary to be an informed participant in the trial process" (p. 202). He questioned whether the Slater Method can properly prepare a mentally retarded defendant to withstand a typical prosecutor's scrutiny, and whether "such training results in technical fulfillment of a legal definition but a failure of justice" (p. 204).

Mueller (2004) surveyed 151 state hospitals listed by the National Association of State Mental Health Program Directors regarding incompetent defendants in forensic mental health beds. Seventy-five out of 94 hospitals reported that they work with clients who are incompetent to stand trial. A majority of the responding programs used medication treatment. However, 88% reported using some type of didactic or psychoeducational group intervention for competency restoration; 41% stated that they utilized competency restoration manuals; and 67% stated that their staff participated in competency training.

Mueller and Wylie (2007) evaluated the effectiveness of the "Fitness Game" (Cuneo & Owen, 1990), a board game used to teach individuals about the legal system according to the eight criteria for competency outlined by *Wieter v. Settle* (1961). Research participants consisted of 38 individuals admitted to the Hawaii State Hospital between August 2002 and May 2003 who met a number of criteria, including incompetence to stand trial. The participants were randomly assigned to a competency restoration group ($n = 21$) and a control group ($n = 17$). The competency restoration group was exposed to the Fitness Game, while the control group engaged in a different measure that focused on generally healthy behaviors. Results identified that both groups demonstrated significant pretest to posttest improvements, calling the isolated effectiveness of the Fitness Game into question.

Schwalbe and Medalia (2007) identified psychopathology, demographics, and degree of cognitive impairment as the three ways in which competent and incompetent defendants were seen to differ. Hubbard, Zapf, and Ronan (2003) examined the competency evaluation reports of 468 defendants evaluated for CST. Incompetent defendants significantly differed from competent defendants with regard to age, employment status, ethnicity, criminal charges, and psychiatric diagnosis. This study also concluded that few significant differences existed between defendants predicted to be restorable and those predicted not to be restorable by mental health examiners.

After analyzing a sample of 351 inpatient pretrial defendants who underwent competency restoration at a state psychiatric hospital from 1995 to 1999, Mossman et al. (2007) concluded that a reduced probability of restoration was associated with nine variables: misdemeanor charge; longer cumulative length of hospitalization intended to restore competency; number of previous admissions to state hospitals; non–African American ethnicity; substance abuse; mental retardation; schizophrenia and schizoaffective disorder diagnoses; older age; and diagnoses of mental retardation. The research concluded that the overall rate of successful restoration for felony defendants was 75%. The study also concluded that there were two types of incompetent evaluees who had well below average probabilities of being restored: chronically psychotic defendants with histories of lengthy inpatient hospitalizations, and defendants whose incompetence was the result of mental retardation and other cognitive disorders not subject to remediation.

Morris and Parker (2008) reviewed a database of defendants in Indiana State Hospitals who participated in restoration of competence between 1988 and 2005. Analysis of 1,475 restoration of competence admissions identified that there was an increase in annual admissions over the study period, that the forensic units restored a higher percentage of individuals compared to non-forensic Indiana State Hospitals, and that the percentage of defendants successfully restored to competence decreased over time in all hospitals. The authors concluded that factors associated with an increased likelihood of successful restoration to competence included admission to the forensic hospital, female gender, and mood disorder diagnosis, whereas older age, mental retardation, and psychotic disorder diagnosis were associated with decreased likelihood of restoration.

HOPES FOR AN EVOLVING STANDARD OF PRACTICE

We would be remiss in failing to acknowledge that one can by no means simply assume the existence a uniformly observed standard of practice in the area of competency restoration. Our own pilot research study may be illustrative in this regard. It is our sincere hope that the standard of practice soon exceeds what we found reflected in the following results.

From 2003 to 2004, we contacted by mail 27 programs from various locations in the United States that were identified by a forensic state hospital database as administering competency restoration programming to criminal defendants. Eleven programs agreed to participate in a telephone interview. The questions we posed were developed by reviewing the literature on competency and competency restoration drawn from a computerized MEDLINE literature search that identified approximately 400 articles under the heading "competency."

Our interviews revealed the following: 78% of the individuals attending competency restoration programming were returned to court as competent within 3 months; 20% were returned as competent from 3 to 12 months; and 2% remained at the hospital for more than 1 year. The programs could not provide an opinion regarding the average number of sessions an individual attended before competency was restored. The respondents were unable to state whether an individual or group treatment format was more productive. The respondents were also unable to conclude which kinds of patients benefited from each type of mental health treatment approach.

The clinicians who administered the competency restoration programming, with two exceptions, did not receive competency restoration training. The two programs that provided training to staff who led the restoration of competency classes did so through workshops and educational handouts. The remaining nine programs used word-of-mouth as the means of educating their staff. Nine of the 11 programs stated that the competency restoration staff's work was not videotaped, observed, or routinely supervised.

All 11 programs reported that judges agreed with their recommendations 90% of the time. The programs stated that judges appear to rely solely upon their reports. The programs did not have a consensus regarding how best to predict which of their patients could be successfully restored.

We asked the programs to describe specific aspects of their restoration of competency programming. Two programs were described as well-organized with ongoing research, whereas the remaining nine programs characterized themselves as not having a set time for the restoration programming to occur. The two programs that described themselves as "more organized" distributed instructional handouts on a regular basis. Three of the 11 programs utilized a competency evaluation instrument. Three of the 11 programs consulted with their patients' attorneys; however, all programs stated that it would be of "great importance" for them to talk with their patients' attorneys.

Nine of the 11 programs indicated that a majority of staff who administer competency restoration training do not do so on an assigned daily basis. This meant that a staff member who leads a group one day would not likely lead the group the next day. Finally, 9 of the 11 programs relied entirely or significantly upon psychological and cognitive testing results as the basis for determining competency status, rather than on the results of competency assessment instruments administered (Borum and Grisso, 1995).

DATA COLLECTION

Standardized Competency Tests

Supplementing appropriately structured clinical and forensic interviews, there are number of standardized competency assessment measures—for additional details, see Chapter 1 in this volume—that objectively measure a defendant's potentially restored abilities in this regard. Most of these instruments can be administered within 45 minutes to 1 hour. Of the measures described in detail in Grisso's (2003) review, we recommend the following for use in restoration evaluations.

1. MacArthur Competence Assessment Tool—Criminal Adjudication (MacCAT-CA; Hoge, Bonnie, Poythress, & Monahan, 1999).
2. Evaluation of Competency to Stand Trial—Revised (ECST-R; Rogers, Tillbrook, & Sewell, 2004).
3. Fitness Interview Test—Revised (FIT-R; Roesch, Zapf, Eaves, & Webster, 1998).
4. Competency to Stand Trial Assessment Instrument (CAI; McGarry & Curran, 1973).
5. Competency Screening Test (CST; Laboratory of Community Psychiatry, 1973).
6. Georgia Court Competency Test (GCCT; Wildman et al., 1978).
7. Competency Assessment to Stand Trial for Defendants With Mental Retardation (CAST-MR; Everington & Luckasson, 1992).

DATA INTERPRETATION

RESEARCH-BASED CONSIDERATIONS

A review of core literature concerning competency restoration (Anderson & Hewitt, 2002; Bertman 2003; Davis, 1985; Hubbard et al., 2003; Morris, 2009; Mueller & Wylie, 2007; Pendleton, 1980; Rogers, Gillis, McMain, & Dickens, 1988; Siegel & Elwork, 1990; Wall, Krupp, & Guilmette, 2003) identifies the following findings with relevance to interpreting—particularly in regard to prognosis—data collected in this context.

1. Overall, 80% to 90% of defendants with mental illness can be restored to competence, typically within a period of less than 6 months.
2. Across the nation, competency restoration programs apply a plethora of competency restoration training techniques. It appears that most do not utilize standardized competency

assessment instruments to evaluate pre- and postlearning status; nor do they educate hospital staff using standardized protocols.

3. Sample sizes evaluated for competency restoration research are typically small, and their results are not easily generalized.
4. Few studies specifically focus on CST in elderly and demented defendants. There are fewer still studies on juveniles (Viljoen and Grisso, 2007; Grisso, 1998; Grisso, 2003).
5. Studies describing competency restoration programs frequently neglect to describe both medication and nonmedication aspects of treatment, despite their often simultaneous utilization.
6. The success rates of competency restoration for defendants with mental retardation are low, with only one-third to one-half being able to attain competency, and when competency is achieved, this takes longer to realize than for other individuals.
7. There are as yet no clearly established means to predict with accuracy which competency restoration candidates are restorable and which are not.
8. Defendants with psychotic disorders and nonpsychotic major disorders are more likely to be judged incompetent, while incompetent defendants with a diagnosis of nonpsychotic minor disorders are more likely to be predicted restorable.
9. Incompetent defendants are less likely to be diagnosed with a personality disorder than are competent defendants.

COMMUNICATION

CONVEYING APPROPRIATE PROCEDURES

When communicating the results of attempts to restore pretrial defendants to competency, it is worthwhile to (1) reflect on the following notions; (2) determine the extent to which the notions are reflected in the reports and testimony that resulted in an initial adjudication of incompetency; and (3) be prepared to describe how these notions informed one's own forensic work product.

- *Assessment.* Were standardized, objective assessment of competency instruments administered to all participants prior to and at the conclusion of restoration of competency programming?

- *Programming.* Was restoration of competency programming multimodal, including a combination of group and individual mental health treatment, medication treatment when indicated, legal concept education, cognitive rehabilitation, role playing, and participation in mock courtroom competency proceedings?
- *Staffing.* Were specific staff assigned, educated, and supervised in providing restoration of competency programming?
- *Ethics.* Were ethical issues related to restoration of competency a component of staff training?
- *Remediation.* Neuropsychological deficits inherent to major psychiatric disorders compromise an individual's ability to understand and recall information necessary to be found competent. Studies have identified a relationship between cognitive deficits and incompetency and nonrestorability (Schwalbe & Medalia, 2007). There is a body of research literature supporting the conclusion that cognitive deficits of psychotic patients, a group most likely to be refractive to restoration of competency, can be treated with cognitive remediation. Was this type of intervention utilized?

REFERENCES

Anderson, S. D., & Hewitt, J. (2002). The effect of competency restoration training on defendants with mental retardation found not competent to proceed. *Law and Human Behavior, 26,* 343–351.

Appelbaum, K. L. (1994). Assessment of criminal justice related competencies in defendants with mental retardation. *Journal of Psychiatry and Law, 22,* 311–327.

Bertman, L. J. (2003). Effect of an individualized treatment protocol on restoration of competency in pretrial forensic inpatients. *Journal of the American Academy of Psychiatry and the Law, 31,* 27–35.

Bertsch, J., Younglove, J., & Kerr, M. (2002). A Pilot Study of the Porterville Developmental Center's Court Competency Training Program. *Criminal Justice Policy Review, 13*(1), 65–77.

Borum, R., & Grisso, T. (1995). Psychological test use in criminal forensic evaluations. *Professional Psychology: Research and Practice, 26,* 465–473.

Brown, D. (1992). A didactic group program for persons found unfit to stand trial. *Hospital and Community Psychiatry, 43,* 732–733.

Cooper, D. K., & Grisso, T. (1997). Five-year research update (1991–1995): Evaluations for competence to stand trial (adjudicative competence). *Behavioral Sciences and the Law, 15,* 347–364.

Cruise, K., & Rogers, R. (1998). An analysis of competency to stand trial: An integration of case law and clinical knowledge. *Behavioral Sciences and the Law, 16*, 35–50.

Cuneo, D., & Owen, B. (1990). *The fitness game.* Chicago: Illinois Department of Human Services.

Davis, D. (1985). Treatment planning for the patient who is incompetent to stand trial. *Hospital and Community Psychiatry, 36*, 268–271.

Everington, C., & Luckasson, R. (1992). *Competence assessment for standing trial for defendants with mental retardation (CAST-MR).* Worthington, OH: IDS Publishing Corp.

Freckelton, I. (2009). Book review. Competence in the law from legal theory to clinical application by M. L. Perlin, P. Champine, H.A. Dlugacz, and M. Connell. *Psychiatry, Psychology and Law, 16*, 152–154.

Fritsch, F., & Moseley, D. (1982). Competency education program. Unpublished manuscript, Fulton State Hospital, Fulton, MO.

Godinez v. Moran, 506 U.S. 389 (1993).

Goldstein, A., & Burd, M. (1990). Role of delusions in trial competency evaluations: Case law and implications for forensic practice. *Forensic Reports, 3*, 361–386.

Grisso, T. (1992). Five-year research update (1986–1990): Evaluations for competence to stand trial (adjudicative competence). *Behavioral Sciences and the Law, 10*, 353–369.

Grisso, T. (1998). Forensic evaluation of juveniles. Juvenile's competence to stand trial. Sarasota, FL: Professional Resource Press, 83–126.

Grisso, T. (2003). *Evaluating competencies: Forensic assessments and instruments* (2nd ed.). New York, NY: Kluwer Academic/Plenum Press.

Grisso, T., Steinberg, L., Woolard, J., Cauffman, E., Scott, E., Graham, S., . . . Schwartz, R. (2003). Juveniles' competence to stand trial: A comparison of adolescents' and adults' capacities as trial defendants. *Law and Human Behavior, 27*(4), 333–363.

Gutheil, T. (1999). A confusion of tongues: Competency, insanity, psychiatry and the law. *Psychiatric Services, 50*, 767–773.

Hoge, S. K., Bonnie, R. J., Poythress, N. G., & Monahan, J. (1999). *The MacArthur Competence Assessment Tool—Criminal Adjudication.* Odessa, FL: Professional Assessment Resources.

Hoge, S. K., Poythress, N., Bonnie, R. J., Monahan, J., Eisenberg, M., & Feucht-Haviar, T. (1997). The MacArthur adjudicative competence study: Diagnosis, psychopathology, and competence-related abilities. *Behavioral Sciences and the Law, 15*, 329–345.

Hubbard, K. L., Zapf, P. A., & Ronan, K. A. (2003). Competency restoration: An examination of the differences between defendants predicted restorable and not restorable to competency. *Law and Human Behavior,* *27,* 127–139.

James, D. V., Duffield, G., Blizard, R., & Hamilton, L.W. (2001). Fitness to plead: A prospective study of the interrelationships between expert opinion, legal criteria and specific symptomatology. *Psychological Medicine, 31,* 139–150.

Laboratory of Community Psychiatry, Harvard Medical School (1973). *Competency to stand trial and mental illness* (DHEW Publication No. ADM-77-103). Rockville, MD: Department of Health, Education, and Welfare.

McGarry, A. L. (1969). Restoration and research in competency for trial and mental illness: Review and preview. *Boston University Law Review, 49,* 46–61.

McGarry, A. L (1971). The fate of psychotic offenders returned for trial. *American Journal of Psychiatry, 127,* 1181–1184.

McGarry, A. L., & Curran, W. J. (1973). *Competency to stand trial and mental illness.* Rockville, MD: National Institute of Mental Health.

Melton, G. B., Petrila, J., Poythress, N., & Slobogin, C. (2007). *Psychological evaluations for the courts* (3rd ed.). New York, NY: Guilford Press.

Miller, R. (2003). Hospitalization of criminal defendants for evaluation of competence to stand trial or for restoration of competence: Clinical and legal issues. *Behavioral Sciences & the Law, 21,* 369–391.

Morris, D. R., & Parker, G. F. (2008). Jackson's Indiana: State hospital competence restoration in Indiana. *Journal of the American Academy of Psychiatry and the Law, 36,* 522–534.

Mossman, D., Noffsinger, S. G., Ash, P., Frierson, R. L., Gerbasi, J., Hackett, M., . . . Zonana, H. V. (2007). AAPL practice guideline for the forensic psychiatric evaluation of competence to stand trial. *Journal of the American Academy of Psychiatry and the Law,* S3–S72.

Mueller, C. (2004). 1st Forensic Mail Survey Results Summary. Unpublished results obtained from data from the State of Hawaii Dept. of Health, Adult Mental Health Division.

Mueller, C., & Wylie, A. (2007). Examining the effectiveness of an intervention designed for the restoration of competency to stand trial. *Behavioral Sciences and the Law, 25,* 891–900.

Mumley, D. L., Tillbrook, C. B., & Grisso, T. (2003). Five-year research update (1996–2000): Evaluations for competence to stand trial (adjudicative competence). *Behavioral Sciences and the Law, 21,* 329–350.

Nelson, K. T. (1989). The patient-litigant's knowledge of the law: Importance in treatment to restore sanity and in competency proceedings. *American Journal of Forensic Psychology, 7*(3), 29–41.

Nicholson, R., & Kugler, K. (1991). Competent and incompetent criminal defendants: A quantitative review of comparative research. *Psychological Bulletin, 109,* 355–370.

Noffsinger, S. G. (2001). Restoration to competency practice guidelines. *International Journal of Offender Therapy and Comparative Criminology, 45,* 356–362.

Otto, R., Poythress, N. G., Nicholson, R., Edens, J. F., Monahan, J., Bonnie, R. J., . . . Eisenberg, M. (1998). Psychometric properties of the MacArthur Competence Tool—Criminal Adjudication. *Psychological Assessment, 10,* 435–443.

Pendleton, L. (1980). Treatment of persons found incompetent to stand trial. *American Journal of Forensic Psychology, 137,* 1098–1100.

Pinals, D. A. (2005). Where two roads meet: Restoration of competence to stand trial from a clinical perspective. *New England Journal on Criminal and Civil Confinement, 31,* 81–108.

Reich, J., & Wells, J. (1985). Psychiatric diagnosis and competency to stand trial. *Comprehensive Psychiatry, 26,* 421–432.

Roesch, R., Eaves, D., Sollner, R., Normandin, M., & Glackman, W. (1981). Evaluating fitness to stand trial: A comparative analysis of fit and unfit defendants. *International Journal of Law and Psychiatry, 4,* 145–157.

Roesch, R., Zapf, P. A., Eaves, D., & Webster, C. D. (1998). *Fitness Interview Test—Revised.* Burnaby, BC: Simon Fraser University.

Rogers, R., Gillis, J. R., McMain, S., & Dickens, S. E. (1988). Fitness evaluations: A retrospective study of clinical, legal, and sociodemographic variables. *Canadian Journal of Behavioral Science, 20,* 192–200.

Rogers, R., Tillbrook, C., & Sewell, K. (2004). *Evaluation of Competency to Stand Trial—Revised.* Lutz, FL: Professional Assessment Resources.

Schouten, R. (2003). Commentary: Training for competence: Form or substance? *Journal of the American Academy of Psychiatry and Law, 31,* 202–204.

Schwalbe, E., & Medalia, A. (2007). Cognitive dysfunction and competency restoration: Using cognitive remediation to help restore the unrestorable. *Journal of the American Academy of Psychiatry and the Law, 35,* 518–525.

Siegel, A. M., & Elwork, A. (1990). Treating incompetence to stand trial. *Law and Human Behavior, 14,* 57–65.

Steadman, H. (1979). *Beating a rap? Defendants found incompetent to stand trial.* Chicago, IL: University of Chicago Press.

Steadman, H. J., Monahan, J., Hartstone, E., Davis, S. K., & Robbins, P. (1982). Mentally disordered offenders: A national survey of patients and facilities. *Law and Human Behavior, 6,* 31–38.

Viljoen, J. L., & Grisso, T. (2007). Prospects for remediating juveniles' adjudicative incompetence. *Psychology, Public Policy, and Law, 13*, 87–114.

Wall, B. W., Krupp, B. H., & Guilmette, T. (2003). Restoration of competency to stand trial: A training program for persons with mental retardation. *Journal of the American Academy of Psychiatry and the Law, 31*, 189–201.

Warren, J. I., Fitch, W. L., Dietz, P. E., & Rosenfeld, B. D. (1991). Criminal offense, psychiatric diagnosis, and psycholegal opinion: An analysis of 894 pretrial referrals. *Bulletin of the American Academy of Psychiatry and the Law, 19*, 63–69.

Way, B. B., Dvoskin, J. A., & Steadman, H. J. (1991). Forensic psychiatric inpatients served in the United States: Regional and system differences. *Bulletin of the American Academy of Psychiatry and the Law, 19*, 405–412.

Wieter v. Settle, 193 F.Supp. 318 (W.D. Mo. 1961).

Wildman, R. W., Batchelor, E. S., Thompson, L., Nelson, F. R., Moore, J. T., Patterson, M. E., & deLaosa, M. (1978). *The Georgia Court Competency Test: An attempt to develop a rapid, quantitative measure of fitness for trial.* Unpublished manuscript, Forensic Services Division, Central State Hospital, Milledgeville, GA.

Winick, B. (1977). Psychotropic medication and competence to stand trial. *American Bar Association Research Journal, 3*, 769–816.

CHAPTER 5

Sex Offender Evaluations

PHILIP H. WITT, FRANK M. DATTILIO, and JOHN M. W. BRADFORD

INTRODUCTION

Sex offenses raise strong feelings among the general public. Hardly a day passes when one does not read media accounts of heinous sex crimes and hear calls for increased penalties for sex offenders. Many states and even municipalities have passed legislation placing special restrictions or conditions on sex offenders, such as residency restrictions or community notification requirements. At present, 20 states have special civil commitment statutes designed specifically for sex offenders (cf. discussions in Melton, Petrila, Poythress, & Slobogin, 2007, pp. 280–284; Witt & Conroy, 2009, pp. 3–14).

Laws targeted at sex offenders date to the mid-1930s, when they were termed *sexual psychopath laws* (Melton et al., 2007). In the 1980s, as the pendulum in managing criminals shifted away from a rehabilitation model toward a punishment/just desserts approach, many of these specialized sex offender laws were repealed. However, during the past decade, such sex offender–targeted laws have proliferated, at both the state and the federal level, mainly due to the public disgust about the nature of such offenses.

The increase in special statutes directed at sex offenders has resulted in an increased need for forensic mental health evaluations of such individuals. These forensic evaluations can occur in a number of legal contexts (see Witt & Conroy, 2009).

Preadjudication

Initially, an evaluation can be requested at the outset of a sex offender case once a criminal investigation has begun or at the time that the individual is formally charged, but well prior to adjudication. The referring source in such cases is usually a defense attorney, who is hoping to use the evaluation results in negotiating a more favorable plea, particularly if the evaluation is favorable to the client. The defense attorney typically wants to know what risk the individual presents to the community and whether they are amenable to treatment rehabilitation. It is also important to know whether any special sentencing laws are likely to apply to that individual. Most commonly, the evaluator will address whether the individual's level of risk is such that he/she could be managed as an outpatient and what treatment and risk management plan might be most suitable for the individual. Such a risk management plan could include a variety of elements: psychotherapy focusing on the criminogenic needs (Andrews & Bonta, 2003) found in the evaluation; psychotropic medication, if a psychiatric condition contributes to the individual's risk; and cooperation between monitoring agencies while the individual is under any legal supervision, such as bail. There may not be any specific statutory guidance for preadjudication evaluations, unless one's jurisdiction has specific statutory or case law guidance regarding suitability for bail or regarding criteria for any special sentencing provisions.

One question that the evaluator cannot address in preadjudication evaluations is whether the individual committed the alleged offense if that individual denies having done so. Some attorneys and other criminal justice professionals still hold the outdated belief that it is possible to determine whether an individual meets some personality profile that all sex offenders are presumed to share, such as with the "mental abnormality" prong under Pennsylvania's Megan's Law that is believed to be a lifelong congenital disorder for which there is no cure (42 Pa. C.S.A. §§ 9791–9799.9). Not only is there no such profile, but it would be unethical to perform an evaluation of an alleged sex offender to determine guilt or innocence. For instance, the practice guidelines for the Association for the Treatment of Sexual Abusers (ATSA; 2005) state: "Evaluators do not offer conclusions regarding whether an individual has or has not committed a specific act of sexual abuse" (p. 11).

POSTADJUDICATION, PRESENTENCING

Some states have specialized sentencing statutes for sex offenders, which may well have criteria for which forensic mental health evaluations are relevant. For example, the state of New Jersey requires an evaluation of individuals convicted of certain enumerated sex offenses after conviction, but prior to sentencing to determine whether they are repetitive and compulsive (Witt & Barone, 2004), in which case they may be sentenced to a specialized treatment facility within the department of corrections. In Pennsylvania, convicted sex offenders found to meet certain criteria may be given enhanced sentences. In both cases, there is statutory and case law guidance regarding the contours of the evaluation, and forensic mental health issues, such as the risk of recidivism or level of compulsivity, are relevant.

REGISTRATION AND COMMUNITY NOTIFICATION

All states and the District of Columbia presently have sex offender registration and community notification laws, and many, although not all, of these states determine the extent of community notification based on an assessment of the individual's risk. Although in some jurisdictions, such as the state of New Jersey, the risk assessments are initially done by prosecutors or other criminal justice professionals, forensic mental health evaluations may also be requested by either the prosecution or defense in difficult or contested cases. Some communities have passed residency restriction laws, preventing sex offenders from living within a certain distance of, for example, a school zone or playgrounds, and forensic mental health evaluations may well be relevant to an assessment of the individual's risk in determining eligibility for such a restriction.

SEXUALLY VIOLENT PREDATOR (SVP) CIVIL COMMITMENT

Prior to release from incarceration (or in some states also prior to release from a mental institution if found not guilty by reason of insanity or incompetent to stand trial), in roughly 20 states a sex offender will be evaluated to determine whether he meets criteria for civil commitment under the jurisdiction's sexually violent predator

(SVP) statute (see Witt & Conroy, 2009). These evaluations focus on three related criteria:

1. Whether the individual has a mental disorder
2. Whether the mental disorder results in volitional impairment
3. Whether 1 and 2 render the individual likely to commit another sex offense if released to the community

Although these evaluations, and the resulting civil commitments, are technically civil, not criminal, the result is nonetheless continued confinement for the committed individual. There has been voluminous case law published on the criteria for SVP commitment, beginning with *Kansas v. Hendricks* (1997) and *Kansas v. Crane* (2002). Evaluators would be wise to become familiar with the guiding case law and statutes in his or her jurisdiction.

PREPARATION

THE REFERRAL

The importance of determining exactly what the court, referring agency, or the retaining attorney is asking the evaluator to do in a sex offender case cannot be emphasized enough. The evaluator should have a reasonable familiarity with the various legal contexts in which sex offender evaluations are needed and the parameters surrounding each of those contexts. At times, the referring attorney or agency may be unclear with their referral question, and in such cases, the evaluator's first task is to clarify the specific referral question and what points need to be addressed in the evaluation. It may be that the initial referral question is unrealistic (e.g., if the referral source wishes to know whether an alleged, but denying, sex offender actually committed or is capable of committing the alleged sex offense). In other cases, even after some preliminary telephone consultation with the referral source, it may be evident that an evaluation is not likely to provide the referral source with the result it desires (such as a defense attorney who is hoping for a preadjudication evaluation result indicating that the defendant is low risk, when the defendant has numerous prior sexual and nonsexual offense convictions). It is always best practice to be straightforward with referral sources. Although it is the attorney's role to advocate for his/her client, that is not the appropriate role for an evaluator. It is important that referral sources have realistic expectations regarding the evaluation and that you educate them as to the limits and boundaries or your role as an expert.

DETERMINING THE PROPER FOCUS AND SCOPE OF THE EVALUATION

Prior to beginning the evaluation, the evaluator should develop a plan. What information will be needed? What instruments is the evaluator likely to use? How much corroboration will be useful or necessary? What third-party sources should be contacted, if any? This may or may not include the victims and/or their families. Depending on the referral question and the legal context of the evaluation, the evaluator may have available varying types of information. For example, for preadjudication evaluations, especially those that occur prior to indictment, there may be little or no discovery materials available. Therefore, the evaluation may be mostly dependent on the individual's self-report, with all its inherent limitations. By contrast, when evaluating individuals for SVP civil commitment, the file frequently can be voluminous, with extensive documentation of the individual's entire life history. In any event, prior to beginning the evaluation, the evaluator should determine what information is needed and how to structure the evaluation to answer the referral question. The evaluator always wants to avoid receiving such missing information after he or she has taken the witness stand.

COLLATERAL INFORMATION

According to Otto, Slobogin, and Greenberg (2007), collateral information is useful because "forensic examinees may be deliberately or inadvertently less than candid in their presentation," "information from third parties is not only ethical, but necessary for administration of a number of forensically relevant instruments," and "information from collateral sources enhances the face validity of the examination and the competence of the expert in the eyes of the legal decision maker" (p. 191). This advice is particularly germane in evaluating sex offenders, given that obvious legal incentives (as well as understandable feelings of shame for those who have committed sex offenses) result in the distinct possibility of minimization. However, the evaluator should be aware that his/her role is not that of an investigator, and so should exercise some judgment regarding the extent of the collateral information needed.

ETHICAL ISSUES

Certain ethical issues surface routinely in performing evaluations of sex offenders. First, the evaluator should be competently trained in conducting sex offender evaluations, familiar with both the relevant mental health literature and the legal context. In some jurisdictions, sex offender evaluators may be professionals other than psychologists/psychiatrists (e.g., social workers) (Dattilio & Sadoff, 2007). For both psychologists and psychiatrists, one major ethical principle involves practicing within one's area of competency. The *Ethical Principles of Psychologists and Code of Conduct* (American Psychological Association, 2002) that "when assuming forensic roles, psychologists are or become reasonably familiar with the judicial or administrative rules governing their roles" (p. 1064). Similarly, according to the *Specialty Guidelines for Forensic Psychologists* (SGFP; Committee on Ethical Guidelines for Forensic Psychologists, 1991, currently under revision), "forensic psychologists are responsible for a fundamental and reasonable level of knowledge and understanding of the legal and professional standards that govern their participation as experts in legal proceedings" (p. 658). Similarly, the *Ethics Guidelines for the Practice of Forensic Psychiatry,* provided by American Academy of Psychiatry and the Law (AAPL, 2005) requires psychiatrists to know "the appropriate laws of the jurisdiction" (p. 2), whereas the American Psychiatric Association's *Principles of Medical Ethics with Annotations Especially Applicable to Psychiatry* (American Psychiatric Association, 2009) identify a need to understand "local laws governing medical practice" (p. 6).

Second, the evaluator should obtain informed consent or assent from the examinee. The SGFP (1991), indicate that the evaluator should inform the examinee regarding the use to which the evaluation will be used and that they will not be in a treating role. For psychiatrists, the AAPL Guidelines (2005) state that "at the outset of a face-to-face evaluation, notice should be given" of "the nature and purpose of the evaluation and the limits of its confidentiality" (p. 2). Finally according to the *Principles of Medical Ethics* (American Psychiatric Association, 2009), forensic evaluations require that psychiatrists "fully describe the nature and purpose and lack of confidentiality of the examination to the examinee at the beginning of the examination" (p. 7). The evaluator should disclose only information relevant to the evaluation referral question. The SGFP (1991) maintains that "in situations where the right of the client or party to confidentiality is limited, the forensic psychologist makes every effort to maintain confidentiality with regard to any information that does not bear directly upon the legal purpose of the evaluation" (p. 660). According to the AAPL Guidelines (2005), psychiatrists are charged with maintaining confidentiality "to the extent possible, given the legal context" (p. 1). The *Principles of Medical Ethics* add that "in the event that the necessity for legal disclosure is demonstrated by the court, the psychiatrist may request the right of disclosure of only that information which is relevant to the legal question at hand" (p. 7), and "may disclose only that information which is relevant to a given situation" (p. 6).

DATA COLLECTION

FILE REVIEW

Prior to interviewing the individual, the evaluator should review the file, if available. As noted previously, in preadjudication cases, no file or discovery materials may yet exist. In postadjudication cases, however, normally a file exists, and reviewing the file will help orient the evaluator to the case. In most postadjudication cases, a presentence investigation report has been completed, and this can serve as a useful starting point for obtaining an overview of the individual's history. In other legal contexts, such as SVP commitment or community notification cases, there may well be a legal petition by the state, with supporting documentation. In SVP commitment cases, the examinee will have an institutional file as well, possibly including treatment and housing unit reports. Reviewing the individual's background before interviewing him can help guide the interview, raising issues into which the evaluator wishes to inquire, as well as helping in selection of assessment instruments, depending on what issues need to be clarified. In some contexts, such as SVP commitment evaluations, the examinee may decline to cooperate with an interview, and the evaluator may need to rely more heavily on archival data. In some cases, it may also be necessary for the representing attorney to obtain a court order for records that have been refused or are not yet available.

INTERVIEWING THE EXAMINEE

At the outset of the interview, as discussed previously, the evaluator should inform the examinee of the purpose and the limitations of confidentiality. The remainder of the interview should be guided by the specific referral question, in particular, what psycholegal question is to be answered. Given that most sex offender evaluations involve an assessment of the individual's risk or likelihood for rehabilitation, information relevant to risk and potential rehabilitation is essential. Consequently, the evaluator should be familiar with the literature on sex offender risk and sample areas of the individual's history relevant to risk. Two broad sex offense risk factors, common to most if not all instruments designed to assess this area, are sexual deviance and general criminality (or in its more extreme variant, psychopathy) (Doren, 2004; Witt & Conroy, 2009). Consequently, a structured interview or risk assessment scale that focuses on these areas—such as the Hare Psychopathy Checklist—Revised (PCL-R; Hare, 2003) or SVR-20 (Boer, Hart, Kropp, & Webster, 1997)—can be helpful.

Moreover, risk assessment instruments also sample two forms of risk factors: static, historical risk factors (i.e., those that don't change with the passage of time) and dynamic risk factors (such as current and recent adjustment). Therefore, the use of an instrument or instruments that focus on both static and dynamic risk is important. Although we recommend that the evaluator assess dynamic risk factors, this recommendation is not meant to be a carte blanche suggestion that unstructured clinical opinions form the basis for one's assessment of this area. A long history of research indicates that unstructured clinical opinions are generally less accurate than other methods of assessing risk (cf. Meehl, 1954/1996), and a recent meta-analysis of a combined sample of over 45,000 sex offenders corroborates this position (Hanson & Morton-Bourgon, 2009).

The evaluator should be aware if his/her jurisdiction has any specific requirements concerning what needs to be addressed in the particular legal context. For instance, in SVP commitment cases, Texas requires an assessment of psychopathy (Witt & Conroy, 2009), and California has a list of content areas that the report must address (California Department of Mental Health, 2004, p. 20), including:

- Brief developmental history
- Psychiatric history
- Substance abuse history
- Juvenile and adult criminal history
- Parole history
- Institutional history
- Psychosexual history
- Relationship history
- Mental status examination, behavioral observations
- Psychiatric diagnosis on Axis I and II
- Explanation and justification of psychiatric diagnoses

Witt and Conroy (2009, p. 110) suggest sampling the following areas in assessing the presence of a paraphilia:

- Early sexual experiences and interests
- Number and context of sexual partners
- Paraphilic sexual behavior
- Indicators of sexual self-control difficulties (e.g., extensive pornography use, prostitute use)
- History of illegal sexual activity, charged or otherwise

In some cases, the examinee will decline to provide information regarding the areas of most relevance, specifically history of antisocial acts or paraphilic sexual interests. In such cases, the evaluator will again need to rely more heavily on historical markers for these areas, such as juvenile criminal record, school disciplinary history, and prior arrests and convictions.

COLLATERAL CONTACTS

In some cases, such as SVP civil commitment evaluations, it is not feasible to interview collateral sources. The offense itself in such cases is likely to have taken place years before, and the evaluator is unlikely to have access to witnesses. In such cases, the primary source of collateral information will be the individual's file. However, the evaluator must make a concerted effort to obtain any victim impact statements that may have been used at sentencing.

In other cases, especially those in which the examinee still resides in the community, interviews of collateral sources, even if by telephone, may well be helpful. For instance, the evaluator may wish to interview the examinee's wife, parent, or parole/probation officer to obtain another perspective on the individual's history or recent community adjustment. Third-party information, here specifically collateral interviews, are predicated on the assumption that in forensic evaluations (unlike in treatment), the most accurate information may not actually come from the examinee, but from other sources of information (Heilbrun, Warren, & Picarello, 2003).

PSYCHOLOGICAL TESTING

Even though there is no specific test to determine if someone is a sex offender, psychological testing in general in sex offense evaluations may serve several purposes. First, it is helpful to obtain a standardized measure of the examinee's response style, and many psychological tests, such as the Minnesota Multiphasic Personality Inventory, 2nd Edition (MMPI-2; Butcher, Dahlstrom, Graham, Tellegen, & Kaemmer, 1989) and the Millon Clinical Multiaxial Inventory-III (MCMI-III; Millon, 1997) include scales that assess response style, termed validity scales. Second, the use of well-validated psychological tests can assist in assessing whether a mental disorder is present. The MMPI-2, for example, is considered to be the test of choice for sexual deviation in the state of California (Lanyon, 1993).

However, the evaluator must be realistic in his/her expectations for psychological testing. Most such tests in common use, such as the two noted above, are self-report inventories, and are therefore highly dependent on the examinee's candor when taking the test.

Moreover, there is no consistent empirical literature that relates any specific psychological test pattern to increased risk of sex offending, so one should not expect to obtain such information from administering a psychological test, but it does speak to their amenability to respond to sex offender treatment.

PHYSIOLOGICAL ASSESSMENT

Deviant sexual preference drives deviant sexual behavior. The objective measurement of sexual arousal measured in a laboratory setting provides the measurement of sexual preference independent of the reported sexual preference by the sexual offender or persons suffering from a paraphilia.

Three methods of physiological assessment have come into common use with sex offenders: phallometry, polygraphy, and viewing time analysis. The method with perhaps the longest history of use with sex offenders is perhaps phallometry, made possible by the measurement of penile tumescence in a laboratory setting as an objective measure of sexual preference (Fedoroff, Kuban, & Bradford, 2009). The physiological measurement of sexual arousal has been described by various names such as phallometry (Freund, 1963); penile tumescence testing (PTT; Karacan et al., 1974); and penile plethysmography (PPG; McConaghy, 1974). Regardless of whatever name is used, the methodology used is the measurement of sexual arousal based on physiological changes in blood flow in the penis in response to various stimulus modalities that depict normal and deviant sexual behavior. It is established over 40 years ago that increased penile blood flow is strongly associated with sexual arousal (Bancroft, Jones, & Pullan, 1966). The most commonly used method is changes in the circumference of the penis while in some centers volumetric measurements are used (Fedoroff et al., 2009). Various comprehensive reviews of penile tumescence testing have been published (Barbaree, 1990; Marshall & Fernandez, 2000a, 2000b; Marshall & Fernandez, 2003).

There are some legal contexts in which it would be unusual (if not unheard of) to see such a physiological assessment performed. For example, in SVP commitment hearings, a recent survey indicates that 70% of evaluators in SVP commitment cases had never used phallometric assessment in that context and that 0% use phallometric assessment always or most of the time (Jackson & Hess, 2007). However, anecdotal evidence indicates that the use of phallometry to assess sexual interest is common among outpatient treatment programs. Similarly, we know of no evaluators who use polygraphy in the context of SVP civil commitment evaluations, and, in fact, a recent text on SVP evaluations recommends against its use in this context (Witt & Conroy, 2009). However, polygraph examinations are common among outpatient sex offender treat- ment programs, typically to monitor treatment compliance, and such use of polygraphy is supported by the ATSA practice guide- lines (2005, p. 43), with two purposes:

1. To generate information beyond what can be obtained from simple self-report
2. To increase compliance with supervision conditions and treat- ment procedures

The use of viewing time as a measure of sexual interest is more controversial. Although one method of assessing viewing time has come into common use, that being the Abel Assessment of Sexual Interest (AASI; Abel, Huffman, Warberg, & Holland, 1998), results from outside Abel's laboratory have not been encouraging regarding its classification efficiency (e.g., Fischer & Smith, 1999; Smith & Fischer, 1999). Moreover, in a widely discussed opinion, one court, the Massachusetts Court of Appeals opined in *Ready v. Commonwealth* (2005), that the AASI did not meet *Daubert* standards of admissibility.

DATA INTERPRETATION

At this point, the evaluator will have amassed a wide array of data, possibly including file review, interviews of the examinee, interviews of collaterals, psychological testing, and physiological assessment. The particular set of information, of course, varies from case to case, depending on availability and relevance. It is the evaluator's job now to integrate the disparate sources of information into a coherent whole that clearly addresses the refer- ral question. We recommend that the evaluator consider what aspects of the examinee's life history are relevant to the referral question. The referral source is not necessarily interested in every detail of the examinee's life, just in obtaining an answer to the referral question.

GENERAL CONSIDERATIONS

We recommend that the evaluator approach interpretation as a form of hypothesis testing. That is, the evaluator should form a series of hypotheses about the examinee and systematically use the available data to test these hypotheses. In the ideal case, there will be a close fit between a hypothesis (or hypotheses) and the data. However, this may not always be the case for a few reasons (see Witt & Conroy, 2009, pp. 127–132, for a more extensive discussion). First, it is possible that there are extensive data, but that the data do not clearly support one hypothesis over the others. For instance, there may be aspects of the examinee's history that to some extent support diagnoses of both antisocial personality disorder and a paraphilia, but with insufficient clarity to definitively make either diagnosis. Second, the data themselves may be incomplete. For instance, there may be no information in the records (or from self-report) about the presence of any adolescent antisocial behavior, thereby making a diagnosis of antisocial personality disorder difficult, even if suspected. Third, the facts themselves might be contested, with unproven (and denied) allegations listed in the records. One option is to make a conditional interpretation. That is, the evaluator can indicate that a given hypothesis would be supported if certain facts are true (or assumed), allowing an appropriate finder of fact, such as the court, to determine what facts are credible.

Heilbrun, Marczyk, and DeMatteo (2002) suggest the following steps for translating legal constructs into mental health constructs in the context of an evaluation:

- Identify the relevant legal construct by reviewing the relevant statutory and case law, as well as commentary.
- Operationalize the legal constructs, determining what areas to assess and how these areas could be assessed.
- Sample the relevant domains to assess these constructs.

ANTISOCIAL LIFESTYLE AND PERSONALITY

As noted above, one relevant aspect of the examinee's life is the extent to which he has antisocial personality characteristics. It is common practice for evaluators to determine the extent to which an examinee generally violates the rights of others and breaks laws. Such characteristics increase the likelihood of criminal activity generally. The *Diagnostic and Statistical Manual of Mental Disorders,* 4th edition, Text Revision (DSM-IV-TR) diagnostic criteria for Antisocial Personality Disorder, involving "a pervasive pattern of disregard for and violation of the rights of others . . ." is a useful guide in this respect (American Psychiatric Association, 2000, p. 701).

Perhaps the most widely known, expedient, and best researched instrument for assessing antisocial characteristics is the PCL-R (Hare, 2003). The PCL-R has two broad factors:

- Factor 1: callous, egocentric personality style
- Factor 2: impulsive, antisocial lifestyle

Factor 2 PCL-R criteria generally parallel DSM-IV-TR antisocial personality disorder criteria, focusing on an impulsive, antisocial lifestyle. A high PCL-R score (30 or greater) has been found to be related to higher rates of sex offending, although some studies have found the PCL-R to better predict general offending than sex offending (Quinsey, Rice, & Harris, 1995) and to better predict sex offending in rapists than in child molesters (Hare, 2003; Rice & Harris, 1997).

AGE

Perhaps the most robust finding of criminology has been what is called the "age invariance effect" (Hirschi & Gottfredson, 1983)— that is, that above the teenage years, crimes of all kinds increase through an individual's 20s, and decline steadily thereafter, as the individual ages. With regard to sex offenses specifically, the highest rate of offending occurs in males between the ages of 18 and 30 years old; particularly in men over 60, the base rate of sex offending is extremely low (Hanson, 2002). Therefore, simply knowing the examinee's age can at least give one a start as to the base rate of sex offending in his age cohort.

SEXUAL DEVIANCE

The evaluator will almost certainly want to offer an opinion as to the extent of sexual deviance present in the examinee. In SVP commitment hearings, given that a mental disorder, broadly construed, is required to commit the individual, an actual diagnosis of a paraphilia is common (Doren, 2002; Levenson, 2004). Not surprisingly, a history of illegal sexual behavior is perhaps the best predictor of future illegal sexual behavior. Virtually every sex offender risk assessment scale in use today includes this variable. In fact, the Static-99, the scale that is generally considered the gold standard for assessing historical risk factors, assigns multiple risk points for prior sex offense charges or convictions (Hanson & Thornton, 1999), the only one of the Static-99 criteria that has more than one point assigned in scoring.

In some cases, simply considering the nature of the victim can give some indication of extent of deviant sexual interests. Research indicates that individuals who sexually molest related victims have lower recidivism rates than those who molest unrelated victims (Hanson & Morton-Bourgon, 2004).

Seto and Lalumière (2001) developed a screening scale for pedophilia, the Screening Scale for Pedophilic Interests (SSPI), which has a strong positive relationship with phallometry results. The SSPI consists of four items, all focusing on victim characteristics:

1. Male victim
2. More than one victim
3. Victim aged 11 or younger
4. Stranger victim

STATIC RISK FACTORS

Many of the preceding indicators—such as history of sexual deviance, antisocial behavior history, age, victim characteristics—are termed *static risk factors*. These are risk indicators that do not change over time (or in the case of age, change very slowly). Most authorities agree that a risk assessment should be anchored in static risk factors. These are the risk factors that have the highest predictive validity (Hanson & Morton-Bourgon, 2009; Quinsey, Rice, & Harris, 1995). Use of an actuarial scale to organize and interpret one's findings concerning static risk is useful, and we recommend using such an actuarial scale as a foundation for one's opinion. Commonly used scales include the Static-99 (Hanson & Thornton, 1999) and the Minnesota Sex Offender Screening Tool—Revised (MnSOST-R; Epperson, Hesselton, & Kaul, 1999). Both scales focus heavily on static risk factors—the Static-99 entirely so. Use of an actuarial scale allows the evaluator to base his or her assessment of risk on an empirically supported foundation.

However, an assessment of risk should not begin and end with a static risk factor actuarial scale. Even the one of the authors of the Static-99 acknowledges its limitations (and generally the limitations of actuarial scales) (Helmus & Hanson, 2007, no page number): "Despite its success, it [the Static-99] is far from ideal. The predictive accuracy is only moderate and the scores have no intrinsic meanings. The items were selected based on their ease of administration and association with recidivism."

DYNAMIC RISK FACTORS

In recent years, there has been increased research on dynamic risk factors. Common sense (and the research) indicates that all else equal, an individual whose life is well managed presents less risk than an individual whose life is in disarray. Studies indicate that the following dynamic risk factors are relevant in assessing sex offending risk (Hanson & Morton-Bourgon, 2004, 2005; Witt & Conroy, 2009):

- Quality of social supports
- Emotional congruence of preoccupation with children
- Attitudes tolerance of sexual abuse
- Antisocial lifestyle
- Poor self-management
- Hostility, particularly toward women
- Substance abuse
- Poor cooperation with supervision
- General sexual preoccupation

There are a number of ways to assess dynamic risk factors, but, again, one way we do not recommend is by unstructured clinical opinion. Although unstructured clinical opinion was the method of choice perhaps two decades ago, there are now available structured methods of assessing dynamic risk factors.

One method is use of a risk assessment scale specifically designed to assess dynamic risk factors. Two related scales with empirical support are the Stable-2007 and Acute-2007 (Hanson, Harris, Scott, & Helmus, 2007). The Stable-2007 assesses characteristics that can change, but only with time and effort. These include many of the above listed dynamic risk factors, with a sampling period of the previous 12 months. The Acute-2007 measures immediate adjustment issues, such as victim access, sexual preoccupation, rejection of supervision, collapse of social supports, and emotional collapse, all sampled at the present time. Hanson et al. (2007) provide prediction tables that allow integration of the results from a Static-99, Stable-2007, and Acute-2007, thereby combining static and dynamic risk factors in a systematic manner.

STRUCTURED PROFESSIONAL JUDGMENT

Although actuarial risk assessment tools are useful, structured professional judgment (SPJ) tools have been developed to assess sex offender risk. Such tools can be useful in sex offender evaluations in helping the evaluator move beyond unstructured clinical impressions, while still allowing assessment of idiographic data for the examinee (Sadoff & Dattilio, 2008). SPJs are based on a rational review of the empirical and theoretical literature; however, the most commonly used SPJs for sex offenders, such as the SVR-20 (Boer et al., 1997), have been empirically validated and shown to have a positive relationship to sex offender risk. SPJs are particularly useful for organizing one's findings and ensuring that one has sampled all the relevant domains. The SVR-20, for example, has 20 criteria distributed among three areas: social adjustment (e.g., sexual deviation, drug abuse history, relationship problems, employment problems); sex offense characteristics (e.g., high-density, harm to victim, use of weapon); and future plans (e.g., lack of realistic plans, negative attitude toward supervision).

COMMUNICATION

Report Organization

The report is where the forensic evaluator organizes his or her thoughts and commits opinions to paper. There is no one format for a psychological or psychiatric evaluation of a sex offender. In fact, in some jurisdictions or legal contexts, the format may be dictated by local requirements. However, unless in letter form, reports typically begin with a listing of identifying information, such as name, age, date of evaluation, and referring party. Following should be the reason for referral—the question that the evaluation must address. The reason for referral should be clearly articulated, and any psycholegal issue made clear. Some potential referral questions, such as an assessment of risk, are relevant to virtually all sex offender evaluations, whereas other questions are specific to the legal context of the referral. The report should contain information regarding the referral source, the purpose, and any legal authority for the evaluation (if relevant). Reports generally include a list of the sources of information—interviews, records reviewed, collateral sources, testing, and any specialized forensic assessment tools (such as risk assessment scales). Informed consent or assent is typically documented in the report.

Although all reports include a psychosocial history, the extent of this history varies among evaluators, contexts, and jurisdictions. Some evaluators take the position that an extensive history is always required, whereas other evaluators streamline the history section, focusing only on areas directly relevant to the referral question. The same holds true for the observations and interview section. Some evaluators follow a traditional and comprehensive approach to this area, including a mental status examination, and others focus the interview and observations sections only on issues related to the referral question. On occasion, the report may be limited to a records review only, especially in SVP cases in which a prosecutor's expert was denied access to interview the defendant personally.

If psychological testing was administered, the specific tests used should be listed. Some evaluators even provide a brief description of each report in the initial section of the report regarding sources of information. If any difficulties were incurred during the administration of any instruments, that should be discussed here. We recommend strongly against relying heavily on computerized test narratives, given that one frequently does not know the decision rules or algorithms that generated the interpretive paragraphs. Moreover, we have seen use of the computerized narratives become a crutch for evaluators who are unwilling to do the work necessary to interpret the instruments properly, a failing that can be embarrassing under cross examination. The psychological testing section would include any relevant test interpretations and the data upon which these interpretations are based. There are some who believe that the computer scoring of the profile alone on the MMPI-2 helps to ensure accuracy of hand scoring and can be used in tandem.

Many sex offender reports have a section specifically titled "Risk Assessment." In this section, the evaluator reports the findings of any specialized risk assessment tools used and interprets the results. If an SPJ instrument is used, some evaluators create a template that reviews the results of the SPJ instrument criterion by criterion. In this section, the evaluator interprets the risk instrument results and integrates the findings from the different instruments, if more than one was used.

In the final section of the report, the evaluator integrates the findings and offers recommendations. This section frequently involves a brief overview of the relevant data, and then indicates how the evaluator is drawing inferences from those data. As we have noted previously, we recommend that the evaluator follow a hypothesis-testing model, indicating what data are consistent with and inconsistent with the various hypotheses. The evaluator should then describe how he or she is determining which hypothesis provides the best fit to the data.

Recommendations in sex offense cases tend to be of two types:

1. A recommendation (essentially an opinion) regarding a psycholegal referral question (such as whether an examinee meets criteria for SVP commitment)
2. A risk management strategy for handling the offender

TESTIMONIAL ISSUES

Not every sex offender case leads to testimony. Certainly, preadjudication cases are far less likely to lead to testimony than are SVP commitment cases. However, the evaluator should always be pre-pared to testify upon his or her finds, given that it is not always possible to predict which evaluation will lead to testimony. Drogin (2000) has proposed the following "checklist for preparing an expert mental health witness for courtroom testimony" (p. 308):

1. Relevance
2. Admissibility
3. Pertinence
4. Consistency
5. Ethicality
6. Accuracy
7. Authoritativeness
8. Supportability
9. Comfortableness
10. Orientation

When testifying, the evaluator should be aware that he/she is essentially a teacher. Courts are unfamiliar with constructs and procedures that may be second nature to the forensic evaluator in sex offense cases, for example, predictive validity, sensitivity, positive predictive power, and hormonal assay results. It is the evaluator's job to explain these matters clearly in simple language that is accessible to the nonspecialist, yet in an appropriate manner that is not misconstrued as "preaching to the court."

REFERENCES

Abel, G. G., Huffman, J., Warberg, B., & Holland, C. L. (1998). Visual reaction time and plethysmography as measures of sexual interest in child molesters. *Sexual Abuse: A Journal of Research and Treatment, 10,* 81–95.

American Academy of Psychiatry and the Law. (2005). *Ethics guidelines for the practice of forensic psychiatry.* Bloomfield, CT: Author.

American Psychiatric Association. (2000). *Diagnostic and Statistical Manual of Mental Disorders* (4th ed., Text Revision). Washington, DC: Author.

American Psychiatric Association. (2009). *The principles of medical ethics with annotations especially applicable to psychiatry.* Arlington, VA: Author.

American Psychological Association. (2002). Ethical principles of psychologists and code of conduct. *American Psychologist, 57,* 1060–1073.

Andrews, D. A., & Bonta, J. (2003). *The psychology of criminal conduct* (3rd ed.). Cincinnati, OH: Anderson Press.

Association for the Treatment of Sexual Abusers. (2005). *Practice standards and guidelines for the evaluation, treatment, and management of adult male sexual abusers.* Beaverton, OR: Author.

Bancroft, J. H., Jones, H. G., & Pullan, B. R. (1966). A simple transducer for measuring penile erection with comments on its use in the treatment of sexual disorders. *Behavior Research and Therapy, 4,* 239–241.

Barbaree, H. (1990). Stimulus control of sexual arousal. Its role in sexual assault. In W. L. Marshall, D. R. Laws, & H. E. Barbaree (Eds.), *Handbook of sexual assault: Issues, theories, and treatment of the offender* (pp. 115–142). New York, NY: Plenum Press.

Boer, D., Hart, S., Kropp, R., & Webster, C. (1997). *Manual for the Sexual Violence Risk-20.* Burnaby, British Columbia: Simon Fraser University.

Butcher, J., Dahlstrom, W., Graham, J., Tellegen, A., & Kaemmer, B. (1989). *MMPI-2: Manual for administration and scoring.* Minneapolis: University of Minnesota Press.

California Department of Mental Health. (2004). *Clinical evaluator handbook and standardized assessment protocol.* Sacramento, CA: Author.

Committee on Ethical Guidelines for Forensic Psychologists. (1991). Specialty guidelines for forensic psychologists. *Law and Human Behavior, 15,* 655–665.

Dattilio, F. M., & Sadoff, R. L. (2007). *Mental health experts: Roles and qualifications for court* (2nd ed.). Mechanicsburg, PA: Pennsylvania Bar Institute.

Doren, D. M. (2002). *Evaluating sex offenders: A manual for civil commitment and beyond.* Thousand Oaks, CA: Sage.

Doren, D. M. (2004). Toward a multidimensional model for sexual recidivism risk. *Journal of Interpersonal Violence, 19,* 835–856.

Drogin, E. Y. (2000). Evidence and expert mental health witnesses: A jurisprudent therapy perspective. In E. Pierson (Ed.), *New developments in personal injury litigation* (pp. 295–333). New York, NY: Aspen.

Epperson, D. L., Hesselton, D., & Kaul, J. D. (1999). *Minnesota Sex Offender Screening Tool—Revised (MnSOST-R): Development, performance, and recommended risk level cut scores.* Minneapolis, MN: Minnesota Department of Corrections.

Fedoroff, J., Kuban, M., & Bradford, J. (2009). Laboratory measurement of penile response in the assessment of sexual interests. In F. M. Saleh,

A. J. Grudzinkas, J. M. Bradford, & D. J. Brodsky (Eds.), *Sex Offenders: Identification, risk assessment, treatment and legal issues* (pp. 89–100). New York, NY: Oxford University Press.

Fischer, L., & Smith, G. (1999). Statistical adequacy of the Abel Assessment for Interest in Paraphilias. *Sexual Abuse: A Journal of Research and Treatment, 11*, 195–205.

Freund, K. (1963). A laboratory method for diagnosing predominance of homo- or heteroerotic interest in males. *Behavior Research and Therapy, 1*, 85–93.

Hanson, R. K. (2002). Recidivism and age: Follow-up data from 4,673 sexual offenders. *Journal of Interpersonal Violence, 17*, 1046–1062.

Hanson, R. K., Harris, A. J., Scott, T., & Helmus. L. (2007). *Assessing the risk of sexual offenders on community supervision: The dynamic supervision project.* Ottawa, ON: Public Safety and Emergency Preparedness Canada.

Hanson, R. K., & Morton-Bourgon, K.E. (2004). *Predictors of sexual recidivism: An updated meta-analysis.* (Research Rep. No. 2004-02). Ottawa, ON: Public Safety and Emergency Preparedness Canada.

Hanson, R. K., & Morton-Bourgon, K. (2005). The characteristics of persistent sexual offenders: A meta-analysis of recidivism studies. *Journal of Consulting and Clinical Psychology, 73*, 1154–1163.

Hanson, R. K., & Morton-Bourgon, K. E. (2009). The accuracy of recidivism risk predictions for sex offenders: a meta-analysis of 118 prediction studies. *Psychological Assessment, 21*, 1–21.

Hanson, R. K., & Thornton, D. (1999). *Static-99: Improving actuarial risk assessments for sex offenders.* (User Report 99-02). Ottawa, ON: Department of the Solicitor General of Canada.

Hare, R. D. (2003). *Hare Psychopathy Checklist—Revised (PCL-R)* (2nd ed.). Toronto, ON: Multi-Health Systems.

Heilbrun, K., Marczyk, G. R., & DeMatteo, D. (2002). *Forensic mental health assessment: A casebook.* New York, NY: Oxford University Press.

Heilbrun, K., Warren, J., & Picarello, K. (2003). Third party information in forensic assessment. In A. M. Goldstein & I. B. Weiner (Eds.), *Handbook of psychology, volume 11, forensic psychology* (pp. 69–86). Hoboken, NJ: John Wiley & Sons.

Helmus, L. M., & Hanson, R. K. (2007). *Predictive validity of the Static-99 and Static-2002 for sex offenders on community supervision.* Retrieved March 24, 2009, from http://www.sexual-offender-treatment.org/60.html

Hirschi, T., & Gottfredson, M. (1983). Age and the explanation of crime. *American Journal of Sociology, 89*, 552–584.

Jackson, R. L., & Hess, D. T. (2007). Evaluation for civil commitment of sex offenders: A survey of experts. *Sexual Abuse: A Journal of Research and Treatment, 19*, 425–448.

Kansas v. Hendricks, 521 U.S. 346 (1997).

Kansas v. Crane, 534 U.S. 407 (2002).

Karacan, I., Williams, R. L., Guerrero, M. W., Salis, P. J., Thornby, J. I., & Hursch, C. J. (1974). Nocturnal penile tumescence and sleep of convicted rapists and other prisoners. *Archives of Sexual Behavior, 3*, 19–26.

Lanyon, R. I. (1993). Validity of MMPI sex offender scales with admitters and nonadmitters. *Psychological Assessment, 5*, 302–306.

Levenson, J. S. (2004). Sexual predator civil commitment: A comparison of selected and released offenders. *International Journal of Offender Therapy and Comparative Criminology, 48*, 638–648.

Marshall, W. F., & Fernandez, Y. M. (2000a). Phallometric testing with sexual offenders: Limits to its value. *Clinical Psychological Review, 20*, 807–822.

Marshall, W. F., & Fernandez, Y. M. (2000b). Phallometry in forensic practice. *Journal of Forensic Psychological Practice, 1*, 77–87.

Marshall W. L., & Fernandez, Y. M. (2003). *Phallometric Testing With Sexual Offenders. Theory, Research and Practice*. Brandon, VT: Safer Society Press.

McConaghy, N. (1974). Measurements of change in penile dimensions. *Archives of Sexual Behavior, 3*, 381–388.

Meehl, P. E. (1996). *Clinical versus statistical prediction: A theoretical analysis and review of the literature*. Northvale, NJ: Jason Aronson (original work published in 1954).

Melton, G. B., Petrila, P., Poythress, N. G., & Slobogin, C. (2007). *Psychological evaluations for the courts: A handbook for mental health professionals and lawyers* (3rd ed.). New York, NY: Guilford Press.

Millon, T. (1997). *MCMI-III manual* (2nd ed.). Minneapolis, MN: Pearson Assessments.

Otto, R. K., Slobogin, C., & Greenburg, S. A. (2007). Legal and ethical issues in accessing and utilizing third-party information. In A. M. Goldstein (Ed.), *Forensic psychology: Emerging topics and expanding roles* (pp. 190–205). Hoboken, NJ: John Wiley & Sons.

Quinsey, V. L., Rice, M. E., & Harris, G. T. (1995). Actuarial prediction of sexual recidivism. *Journal of Interpersonal Violence, 10*, 85–105.

Ready v. Commonwealth, 824 N.E.2d 474 (Mass. Ct. App. 2005).

Rice, M. E., & Harris, G. T. (1997). Cross validation and extension of the Violence Risk Appraisal Guide for child molesters and rapists. *Law and Human Behavior, 21*, 231–241.

Sadoff, R. L. & Dattilio, F. M. (2008). *Crime and mental illness*. Mechanicsburg, PA: Pennsylvania Bar Institute.

Seto, M. C., & Lalumière, M. L. (2001). A brief screening scale to identify pedophilic interests among child molesters. *Sexual Abuse: A Journal of Research and Treatment, 13,* 15–25.

Smith G., & Fischer L. (1999). Assessment of juvenile sexual offenders: Reliability and validity of the Abel Assessment for interest in paraphilias. *Sexual Abuse: A Journal of Research and Treatment, 11,* 207–216.

Witt, P. H., & Barone, N. M. (2004). Assessing sex offender risk: New Jersey's methods. *Federal Sentencing Reporter, 16,* 170–175.

Witt, P. H., & Conroy, M. A. (2009). *Evaluation of sexually violent predators.* New York, NY: Oxford University Press.

CHAPTER 6

Criminal Responsibility

ROBERT L. SADOFF and FRANK M. DATTILIO

INTRODUCTION

The assessment of criminal responsibility (or insanity) is one of the major functions of the forensic psychiatrist and psychologist. The concept of relief from criminal responsibility dates to biblical times when those who committed criminal behavior were exonerated if they were deemed to be insane. The concept of insanity or lack of criminal responsibility has roots in Talmudic Law, Greek writings, including Aristotle in his *Nichomachean Ethics.* Perlin (1989) notes, "The insanity defense's 'modern roots' has been a major component of the Anglo-American common law for over 700 years." He states that the fore-runners to insanity can "actually be traced back over 3,000 years." Perlin cites the sixth century code of Justinian that explicitly recognized that the "insane were not responsible for their acts," and also articulated the early roots of the temporary insanity and diminished capacity doctrines. Perlin also refers to a case dated 1505 that is determined to be the first recorded jury verdict of insanity, "but it is clear that even prior to that case juries considered 'acquittal to be the appropriate result' in certain insanity defense cases" (pp. 283–284).

In England, the history of the development of the insanity defense is presented by Whitlock (1963), who states that "little note was taken in English law of the criminal acts of the insane until the beginning of the 17th century, when Sir Edward Coke's observations drew attention to the subject" (p. 13) and notes that Shakespeare presented cases of insanity in his writings.

Bracton, a Roman cleric and judge, commented on insanity in civil law by equating persons with madness with wild brutes "who are without reason" (Whitlock, 1963, p. 13). In the early English *Beverly's Case* (1604), Lord Coke ruled that no felony or murder can be committed without a felonious intent or purpose. He states, "If a person was so deprived of reason that he resembled a beast rather than a man he could have no felonious intent and therefore could not be convicted of crime" (p. 123b). Coke delineated four types of insanity as follows:

1. Non compos mentis
2. The idiot or fool
3. He who was of good and sound memory and by the visitation of God has lost it
4. A person rendered non compos mentis by his own act as a drunkard (Whitlock, 1963)

Sir Matthew Hale attempted to distinguish between "perfect and partial insanity" (Whitlock, 1963, p. 14). By this he meant total versus partial insanity, the latter of which provided no excuse in the criminal law. Partial insanity included cases where people held delusions about one particular subject, but were sane in all other matters.

English history is replete with cases in the 18th and 19th centuries that focused on mental state and resulted in insanity determinations and subsequent rules for insanity. *Arnold's Case* (1724) is a prime example in which Arnold was arraigned for attempting to murder Lord Onslow. Arnold had a delusion that Lord Onslow was responsible for all the problems in the country and for devils that were plaguing Arnold. Tracey, the judge in the case, summarized as follows:

> It is not every kind of frantic humour or something unaccountable in a man's actions that points him out to be such a madman as is exempted from punishment; it must be a man that is totally deprived of his understanding and memory, and doth not know what he is doing no more than an infant, than a brute, or a wild beast. Such a one is never the object of punishment. (pp. 764–765)

Maudsley (1896) later referred to this distinction as "the Wild Beast form of knowledge test" (p. 92).

Perhaps one of the most celebrated cases in England occurred in 1800, when Hadfield shot at King George III, in Drury Lane. Erskine, the attorney who defended Hadfield, argued that Hadfield was insane because he had a delusion that he had to sacrifice his life in order to save the world. Because he was religious, he did not wish to kill himself as that was a sin, so he thought of a crime that would carry the death penalty and by his death the world would be spared. Hadfield had incurred head injuries during the war and his delusions and hallucinations, as well as his behavior, were not only argued by Erskine but observed by his friends and relatives during the day he assaulted the king. Erskine argued when commenting on the concepts of Coke and Hale, "If total deprivation of memory was intended by these great lawyers to be taken in the literal sense of the words. . . . If it was meant that, to protect a man from punishment, he must be in such a state of prostrated intellect as not to know his name, nor his condition, nor his relation towards others . . . then no such madness ever existed in the world. It is idiocy alone which places a man in this helpless condition" (p. 1312). Hadfield was acquitted on the basis of what was later to be termed the "delusion test of insanity." As a result of Hadfield's acquittal, Parliament passed the Criminal Lunatics Act of 1800 regulating the disposition of persons found insane or not guilty by reason of insanity (Whitlock, 1963).

The next major case in England came in the early 19th century when Bellingham shot at Prime Minister Spencer Perceval and was tried, sentenced, and executed within a week of the killing, despite evidence that he was paranoid and deluded. Apparently, the experts could not arrive in time to present his mental illness to the court (*Bellingham's Case*, 1812).

Oxford, an 18-year-old barman, shot at Queen Victoria and her Prince Consort. At his trial, there was sufficient evidence that he had delusional insanity (à la *Hadfield*). The judge in that case, Lord Denman, stated, "A person may commit a criminal act and not be responsible. If some contributory disease was in truth, the acting power within him which he could not resist, he would not be responsible" (*R. v. Oxford*, 1840, p. 525).

McNaughten Case

Perhaps the most celebrated case in England was *R. v. McNaughten* (1843). Daniel McNaughten, who had a paranoid delusion of persecution by the Tory Party, attempted to kill Sir Robert Peel, then prime minister of England, but instead killed his private secretary, Edward Drummond. The defense attorney, Mr. Cockburn, presented McNaughten's history of delusions and related them clearly to the crime at hand. He was acquitted on the basis of his insanity. Cockburn alluded to the Doctrine of Partial Insanity promulgated by two prominent psychiatrists, Esquirol and Isaac Ray under the concept of "monomania." As a result of his acquittal, coupled with that of the Oxford case 3 years earlier, Queen Victoria prevailed upon the House of Lords to ask the judiciary certain questions about insanity and crime (Whitlock, 1963). The replies given by the judiciary became known as the *McNaughten* Rules, which can be summarized as follows: "To establish a defense on the ground of insanity, it must be clearly proved that, at the time of committing the act, the party accused was laboring under such a defect of reason, from disease of the mind, as not to know the nature and quality of the act he was doing or, if he did know it, that he did not know he was doing what was wrong" (*R. v. McNaughten*, 1843, p. 722).

The two issues raised by the *McNaughten* case, which is extant in most states of the United States and many countries of the world, are the definitions of "nature and quality" of the act and "wrong." In Pennsylvania, the Supreme Court has declared that the meaning of "nature and quality" is not separate and distinct, but means "Did he know what he was doing?" The issue of wrongfulness has been debated as to whether or not there is a difference between legal wrong and moral wrong. Cases have been turned on the basis of whether the defendant knew there was a law against killing at the time of the act.

It should be noted that questions are often erroneously asked whether the defendant knew "right from wrong." That is not the *McNaughten* Test, nor is it the test in any jurisdiction as far as we know. The test is whether the defendant knew what he was doing at the time of the act and whether he knew that what he was doing was wrong. It has nothing to do with the philosophical concept of rightness versus wrongness. It is a specific test that asks the question whether a particular person knew, at a particular time, that his particular act was wrong. Thus, it is time limited and event limited. For example, a defendant may know clearly that killing another person is against the law and morally wrong, but could not know that killing the person that he killed at the time was wrong because his delusional beliefs told him that the individual being killed was the devil and the devil was going to kill him if he didn't kill the devil first.

Following *McNaughten*, there had been several attempts at modifying the insanity definition in various jurisdictions. One of the earlier modifications occurred in New Hampshire following the correspondence between Chief Justice Charles Doe and Dr. Isaac Ray (often referred to as the Doe-Ray correspondence). Chief Justice Doe, in *State v. Pike* (1870) and *State v. Jones* (1871) declared that an accused would not be criminally responsible if his criminal behavior was the offspring of his mental illness. That case led, many decades later, to *Durham v. United States* (1954) in which Judge Bazelon rejected both *McNaughten* and the Irresistible Impulse Test and came to a broader test that he felt was appropriate and more in keeping with psychiatric theory and testimony. He declared that an accused would not be criminally responsible if his "unlawful act was the product of mental disease or mental defect." That test lasted for 18 years, until the *United States v. Brawner* decision (1972) that adopted the American Law Institute Model Penal Code which declared that a defendant would not be criminally responsible if "as a result of mental disease or defect, he lacked substantial capacity either to appreciate the criminality of his conduct or to conform his conduct to the requirements of law" (p. 981). This formulation included the cognitive, affective, and volitional aspects of mental makeup. The test was propounded by a select group of lawyers and mental health experts in order to incorporate all aspects of 20th century theory of the mind and its functions.

Following the shooting of President Ronald Reagan by John W. Hinckley, Jr., Congress passed the Comprehensive Crime Control Act of 1984 (1984), which returns to the concept of total lack of mental ability when declaring that a person would be held not criminally responsible (not insane) if at the time of the commission of the act in question, the person suffers from a mental defect such that he could not appreciate the criminality of his behavior. The act removes the volitional test but maintains the conative aspect with the word *appreciate*, which substitutes for the cognitive concept of *know*. Nevertheless, following highly publicized insanity cases that are successful for the defense, legislatures have always attempted to tighten the rules to either prevent or limit the success of future insanity defenses. Take, for example, the *McNaughten* case in 1843, which limited the delusion test to a cognitive test and the Comprehensive Crime Control

Act of 1984 that limited insanity to a total rather than partial loss of mental ability and removed the volitional arm.

It should be noted that this act is effective in federal jurisdictions only and that various states have their own insanity rules, including some that have maintained the volitional arm; for example, Wisconsin (Wis. Stat. § 971.15(1)).

GUILTY BUT MENTALLY ILL

Another consequence of the Hinckley acquittal was the increased number of states adopting guilty but mentally ill statutes (Perlin, 1989). This concept is a compromise for the jury between total acquittal by reason of insanity and finding of guilty without the concept of mental illness. The issue has been debated in a number of legislatures, rejected by some, and adopted by few. The concept involves the recognition that a person may not be totally insane but should be given some consideration for his mental illness that affected his judgment and behavior. Thus, the Pennsylvania standard for guilty but mentally ill is that the defendant had a mental defect that caused him to behave according to the standards of the ALI Model Penal Code Test (that he lacked substantial capacity either to conform his conduct to the requirements of law or to appreciate the criminality of his behavior). Note that the wording of "lacking substantial capacity" is not a total loss, but a substantial loss.

IRRESISTIBLE IMPULSE

Another concept that needs to be considered is irresistible impulse. That is an early attempt at including the volitional arm, but was not successful after its initial attempt (*Parsons v. State*, 1886) by the Alabama State Supreme Court, because it was difficult for expert witnesses to distinguish between an irresistible impulse and an unresisted impulse. The utilization of the "policeman at the elbow test" proved unsatisfactory.

DIMINISHED CAPACITY

Another attempt at aiding the mentally ill charged with crimes is the concept of diminished capacity that began in California with Dr. Bernard Diamond in the cases of *People v. Wells* (1949) and *People v. Gorshen* (1959). It is clear that diminished capacity was developed in murder cases to avoid the death penalty by raising the question of the defendant's mental state even when insanity was not a viable defense.

The history and development of the insanity defense is presented in greater detail in many books and articles, but is summarized here as a prelude to the discussion of forensic psychiatric and psychological assessment. It is essential for the mental health expert to know and understand the specific insanity test in the jurisdiction in which he is working. It is also essential for the mental health expert to be able to develop clinical evidence to support any opinion or conclusion (within reasonable medical or psychological certainty) that the defendant was insane according to the test in that jurisdiction at the time of the commission of the crime.

DATA COLLECTION

Initially, the mental health expert is requested by a defense attorney, a prosecutor, or the judge to conduct a thorough and comprehensive assessment to determine whether or not the defendant, at the time of the commission of the act in question, met the legal test of insanity. To accomplish his mission, the expert must conduct a thorough face-to-face psychiatric, psychological interview and examination that may take several hours. Prior to the examination, it is helpful and often essential to have comprehensive records to aid in the examination. These records must include the official charges, the police investigation reports, the discovery (although it is understood that in some jurisdictions the defense attorney does not get discovery until the first day of trial), medical records, school records, work records, and other records that may impact on the mental state of the defendant. If there has been a confession or a statement made to the police, it should be reviewed, as well as the circumstances that led to the statement. There may be either audiotape or videotape of the interrogation that led to the statement. Collateral statements by witnesses and others are also important as well as the notes of testimony at the preliminary hearing, the arraignment or other legal hearings prior to trial. Clearly, any psychiatric or psychological records of prior treatment or assessment must be obtained.

It should be noted that assessing criminal responsibility is different from assessing competency to stand trial. That assessment is contemporaneous, that is, an assessment of present state of mind. Criminal responsibility is an assessment at some prior time that one needs to extrapolate from earlier and subsequent data.

Obtaining statements from people who knew the defendant and were with him prior to the act in question and those with him following the act would be extremely helpful in the overall evaluation and the extrapolation to an opinion of mental state at a previous time. The examination itself offers the expert an opportunity to question the defendant about his motivation, his orientation, his delusional system if present, whether any hallucinations influenced or affected his behavior and whether or not he acted alone or in concert or conspiracy with others.

Clearly, a thorough and comprehensive history of family, developmental records, and school behavior and performance, as well as work records, aid in the total assessment. It is important to correlate and compare what the defendant says in the examination with the actual records. For example, one defendant told a mental health examiner that he accidentally fired his gun as he was running out the door of the store that he was robbing. The police investigation reports that "the witnesses and victims indicated that there were several shots, many aimed at the security guard and at the proprietor." How does one correlate these two very different statements? What does it mean in the assessment of a person's state of mind at the time of the commission of the act in question?

It is also important to have crime scene evidence, autopsy reports (if relevant), and other forensic science investigative reports. There may be, for example, a question of who wrote a particular document, the presence of forensic odontology to correlate with the dentation of the defendant or the victim, a forensic fire marshal or arson expert or a toxicologist, in some cases, all of which depends upon the circumstances of the crime charged.

It is not unknown that a defendant will learn what to say to the mental health expert from other prisoners in order to be seen as someone who has a bona fide mental illness. It is unlikely that the voices or visions began only after the crime or only relevant to the crime itself. This would be too convenient with no precrime symptoms that led up to the behavior in question.

It may be necessary to have a full battery of psychological tests, neuropsychological tests, and others in order to substantiate or negate what is said in the course of the examination. In one case, two prior psychologists had opined that the defendant was severely mentally retarded and autistic. The examination by a neutral forensic examiner showed a very high level of vocabulary, excellent memory, and it was unlikely that the defendant was mentally retarded. The appropriate psychological testing confirmed there was no autism and the intelligence quotient (IQ) was closer to average than it was to retarded.

PSYCHOLOGICAL TESTING AND APPRAISALS

Psychological testing and appraisals are used to provide the examiner with information about the defendant's functioning at the time the tests are administered. They do not necessarily provide information about the defendant's behavior at the time of the crime and, therefore, inferences have to be drawn in order to make this determination. Psychological test results may provide investigators with information on intellectual, neurological, and psychological characteristics, as well as traits that are relevant to developing an understanding of one's general functioning and those factors that may have contributed to the individual's behavior in the instant offense.

There is a wide variety of psychological tests and appraisals that may be employed for this purpose. Ethically, certain standards should be maintained when choosing psychological test instruments and appraisals according to the Standards for Educational and Psychological Testing (American Educational Research Association, American Psychological Association, and National Council on Measurement in Education, 1999). Traditionally, clinical tests, such as the Minnesota Multiphasic Personality Inventory-2 (MMPI-2), have been used in determining psychopathology and personality assessment. The MMPI-2 is one of the most widely used personality inventories in forensic settings. An enormous amount of empirical research exists on the MMPI-2. It is readily available through handbooks and other publications and indicates the validity of satisfactorily assessing psychopathology in a raw sense (Butcher & Williams, 1992; Graham, 2000). There are a number of general psychological characteristics that may be assessed with the use of the MMPI-2 that can be useful in the evaluation of criminal responsibility. These include formal psychopathology such as thought disorder or depression; personality disorders such as narcissistic and antisocial, which may be related to impulsivity and potential for acting out under stress; family problems; alcohol and substance abuse; and abnormal health concerns. From much of these data, important hypotheses can be formulated.

Another personality inventory includes the Millon Clinical Multi-axial Inventory-III (MCMI-III). This is primarily a diagnostic instrument for the assessment of personality disorders (Millon, 1994; Millon, 1996). It is popular with many psychologists, particularly in matters of criminal responsibility because it is a shorter alternative to the MMPI-2 and also tends to focus more on Axis II content, namely personality disorders.

Other measures may involve some forensic assessment appraisals such as the Rogers Criminal Responsibility Assessment Inventory (Rogers, 1984), as well as the Rogers Criminal Responsibility Assessment Scales (Rogers), and forensically related tests, such as the Structured Interview of Reported Symptoms (Rogers, Sewell, & Gillard, 2010), Validity Indicator Profile (Frederick, 1997), and the Hare Psychopathy Checklist—Revised (PCL-R; Hare, 1991). All of these appraisals can provide important information in helping the clinician make a determination of criminal responsibility.

There is some controversy in the literature suggesting that some believe that psychological tests and appraisals of any type are rarely, if ever valid, for legal purposes and that using them constitutes a waste of time and resources, particularly in matters of criminal responsibility (Goldstein, Morse, & Shapiro, 2003). The vast majority of experts, however, truly believe that when used in an appropriate manner, these tests and appraisals can be very helpful to forensic examiners.

Another psychological test measure is the Wechsler Adult Intelligence Scale-IV (WAIS-IV), as well as the Wechsler Memory Scales-III (WMS-III). These are measures of intelligence quotients and memory, but may also provide information with regard to cognitive and memory deficits, as well as any potential brain damage. They may also help detect malingering and deception, which must be ruled out in forensic assessments. There are more specific tests used for malingering, such as the Malingering Probability Scales (MPS; Silverton & Gruber, 1998) and the Structured Interview of Reported Symptoms (SIRS-2; Rogers et al., 2010). Measures such as these may aid in disclosing malingering or inconsistencies when defendants claim or demonstrate symptoms of serious mental illness.[1] It is also helpful to determine whether or not the defendant has a diagnosis of schizophrenia or bipolar illness. The Validity Indicator Profile (Frederick, 1997) may also be appropriate if a defendant contends to have cognitive impairment, including symptoms of mental retardation or mental disturbances.

Measures such as the Rogers Criminal Responsibility Assessment Scale (R-CRAS; Rogers, 1984) may often be helpful with regard to determining malingering. This scale contains 25 variables in which the clinician rates the reliability of the defendant's presentation and possible malingering, the presence or absence of organic impairment, mental retardation, and various symptoms of mental illness. It is also helpful to determine whether or not there is evidence of either cognitive impairment or loss of behavioral control at the time of the instant offense. This is a particularly helpful assessment tool because it provides criteria-based decision models that the forensic expert can complete to address the issue of criminal responsibility for the American Law Institute, and *McNaughten* standards for insanity or for the guilty but mentally ill (GBMI) standard.

DATA INTERPRETATION

Following a full examination and interview, with review of records, the expert may still not be certain about either the diagnosis or the final opinion of insanity. It may be necessary to interview collateral individuals and/or to see the defendant a second or even a third time. Sometimes, information is obtained by use of psychological testing that did not become apparent during clinical examination. The psychiatrist may wish to reexamine after the psychologist has uncovered various conflicts and information gleaned from the testing. Occasionally, special testing is required, such as neuropsychological testing, magnetic resonance imaging (MRI), computerized axial tomography (CAT), or positron emission tomography (PET) through neuroimaging to determine specific deficits in the brain.

---

1. Readers are cautioned about drawing a clear distinction between true malingering and inconsistency in examinee's responses.

AMNESIA

Very often, the defendant will declare that he or she does not remember what happened at the time of the act in question. There are a number of procedures that one might perform in order to obtain this memory if the defense attorney is willing. Sometimes, the concern is that the memories may be so inculpatory that it is not in the defendant's best interest to uncover the lost memory. Occasionally, the memories are there, but the defendant consciously wishes to conceal them, so it is not amnesia, but deception.

In the course of uncovering lost memory, one may utilize a polygraph or neuroimaging to determine whether the defendant is truthful about his loss of memory. If it is determined that there is a bona fide amnesia, the expert may resort either to the use of sodium amytal interview or hypnosis to help uncover the memories that were lost.

In one case, a woman who had killed her husband by battering him with a baseball bat because she believed he was sexually assaulting their son had been reminded of the sexual abuse she encountered at the hands of her stepfather. She totally repressed the memory of her violent assault on her husband. Hypnosis was able to uncover the regression she experienced when she became a 10-year-old, again victimized by her stepfather, but this time acting out her impotent rage that had dwelled within her for several years. The whole procedure was videotaped; the prosecution experts viewing the regression under hypnosis and the reason for the violent outburst agreed with the insanity plea, and the defendant was hospitalized, treated successfully, and is currently in the community raising her family. In addition to hypnosis, some mental health experts utilize sodium amytal or sodium pentothal interviews, but that modality has diminished considerably in forensic cases.

It should be noted that, generally, the insanity defense is a rare defense in criminal cases. It is usually not successful when contested; that is, about 10% of the contested cases are successful. Mostly, the insanity defense is successful if both experts for the defense and the prosecution agree.

One such case involved a woman in her 60s who killed her 90-year-old parents because she had the delusional belief that they wanted her to do so in the most humane way as they were suffering from debilitating physical illnesses. When she described the delusions and hallucinations that she had about her parents and the behavior she encountered for 5 days after the killing, it was clear to all concerned that she was psychotic, deluded, and, in fact, met the test of insanity for that *McNaughten* jurisdiction. She was found to be legally insane, hospitalized and treated, and is currently released to the community after 12 years.

Assessment techniques vary depending on the individual and for whom he is working. The defense chooses to focus on the mental illness, the craziness, the psychosis, the delusions that a person may have that impact on his or her behavior, especially with respect to the crimes charged. However, the prosecution chooses to focus on the behavior of the defendant to indicate or demonstrate what the defendant knew and whether he knew what he was doing was wrong.

There are a number of cases that could illustrate such distinction. However, in reviewing the popular literature, we note the example utilized by Robert Tanenbaum (2009), a former New York district attorney and legal expert, in his fictional book entitled *Escape.* In that book, Tanenbaum presents a case of a woman who killed her three children because God told her to do so. She had had postpartum depression and postpartum psychosis in the past. Her children were 6, 3, and 1 year of age, and she had planned to drown them. Prior to carrying out "God's Will," she purchased items to implement her plan. Tanenbaum's protagonist, New York District Attorney Butch Karp, recognized that the defendant who was charged in the killing of her children was seriously mentally ill but that she did not meet the specific test for insanity (the *McNaughten* Test), that is, that he could prove she knew what she was doing at the time and knew that it was against the law and was wrong. Karp proved that in court, beyond a reasonable doubt, to the jury by presenting her behavior demonstrating her intent and her knowledge, despite her continued and consistent claim that she was acting under God's orders. She told her husband and the police that the children were "with God" and that she had carried out His instructions and His orders. However, she had prepared for the event and she covered up her behavior by drowning the children in a river far from the New York area so the bodies would not be found.

The defense would argue that she had to have the implements in order to carry out God's Will and that she hid the bodies in the river far from New York because she wanted to protect her children and not have them discovered and have God's Will attacked. However, the behavior was clear that she had some knowledge that what she was doing would be frowned upon by others who would consider it to be wrong. At some point, she herself was reluctant to carry out the act.

This case, which is fictional, is beautifully written by Tanenbaum and demonstrates the tension between the defense expert and the prosecution expert in presenting data to the jury for consideration of insanity. As a tactical matter, Karp chose not to present an expert to rebut the testimony of a very weak defense expert, one who stumbled in her presentation to the jury. Rather, he chose to utilize effective cross-examination of the defense expert and to present the evidence demonstrating her knowledge of what she was doing and that it was wrong.

In addition, this case demonstrates the difficulties the defense has in presenting evidence for insanity. Despite the fact that the insanity defense gets much news print, the insanity defense is rarely used and rarely successful, especially if it is effectively rebutted by the prosecution. The prosecution expert may readily agree with the diagnosis of mental illness, but will argue that despite the diagnosis, the defendant still knew what she was doing and knew that it was wrong.

OTHER DISORDERS QUALIFYING FOR THE INSANITY DEFENSE

There are a number of nonpsychotic conditions, nonorganic brain syndromes, that have been considered for insanity by various professionals: Fink (2008), for example, presents the relationship between dissociative events and criminal responsibility. He points to the concept of multiple personality disorder (MPD), now called dissociative identity disorder (DID) for consideration in insanity cases. Even if the condition were proven (and in many cases it is conjecture or speculative, according to a number of critics of the diagnosis), it may not rise to the level of insanity. An example is that of a young man in New York who had been charged with killing a classmate. It was determined, after intensive evaluation and assessment, that indeed he had a valid diagnosis of DID. The prosecutor insisted on being present and videotaping the examination to bring out the alters. Five alters emerged, one confessing to the crime, proving the diagnosis, but not absolving the host personality from criminal responsibility. Instead, the prosecutor agreed to a plea negotiation and a lower sentence so the defendant could be placed in a correctional facility that had the means to treat his DID. Most cases of DID diminish responsibility and allow for plea negotiation to a lesser charge or a lighter sentence rather than full exculpation by reason of insanity.

Saks (1995) notes that because MPD is more frequently diagnosed today than in the past, it is likely that more multiples will plead insanity. She states that "the courts are in a state of disarray as to how best to respond to these pleas" (p.119), noting that either they are different people, they are different personalities, or they are parts of one complex, deeply divided personality. Saks further opines that "on all three theories, multiples are nonresponsible" (p. 119). Saks cites the third alternative, the broadest, which is found, she states in the recent case of *United States v. Denny-Schaffer* (1993), which holds that a multiple is insane if her host personality was unaware of and did not participate in the crime. She also notes a similar case in which the court noted that the host personality was not responsible because it was not she who committed the crime but another alter: "It was Pam Lease, not Pat Parker, who conducted the check 'kiting' scheme and Pat Parker had no control, knowledge or responsibility for what Pam Lease did. However, Pat Parker was served the sentence, not Pam Lease" (*Parker v. State,* 1980, p. 587).

Saks's concept is important in the assessment of defendants in insanity cases. It points to a thorough evaluation of the defendant to determine whether, in fact, MPD or DID is relevant to her defense. It is more likely that the defendant having DID would be found less culpable rather than legally insane. She may get a lesser sentence or serve it in a treatment facility rather than in a correctional institution.

Although not a particular diagnosis, the concept of being provoked could lead to violent behavior and possible insanity. Mitchell (1995) presents the notion of "provoked violence, capacity, and criminal responsibility" and asks "was the person provoked, was he forced, and how voluntary was his action—how much control did he have in his behavior?" (p. 291).

Posttraumatic Stress Disorder

Posttraumatic stress disorder (PTSD) is another condition that may be utilized in determining criminal responsibility. This is a timely topic because many of our military personnel, returning from Iraq and Afghanistan, have been diagnosed with PTSD. Some have become suicidal, and others violent. Friel, White, and Hull (2008) relate PTSD to violent behavior and the possibility of an insanity defense. They refer to the concept of "flashback associated violence" (p. 73), which has been successful in insanity pleas where the diagnosis has been proven. In this regard, the authors cite Silva, Derecho, Leong, Weinstock, and Ferrari (2001), who presented five case studies involving flashback experiences that led to dissociation from consciousness, causing misidentification. They also consider the concept of sleep disturbance and mood lability associated with violence. It is important to note that those who do have PTSD and become violent are not necessarily legally insane. Friel et al. note that "the use of PTSD in criminal law, either as a defense or as a mitigating factor, has always been controversial" (p. 76). They also cite Sparr and Atkinson (1986), who highlighted many of the difficulties, including the subjective, often nonspecific, nature of the symptoms and the need to prove a causal link between the symptoms and the stressor as well as a causal link between PTSD and the criminal act. "The subjective nature of the symptoms means that the possibility of a factitious disorder needs consideration" (Friel et al., p. 76).

Friel et al. (2008) also consider the diagnosis of PTSD and automatism, which may be a valid defense for insanity in the United Kingdom, and cite a study by Appelbaum and colleagues (1993) who correlated the data of insanity pleas in eight states in America between 1980 and 1986 and found only 0.3% of those pleading not guilty by reason of insanity to have a primary diagnosis of PTSD.

One case by one of the authors (RLS) involved a veteran of Vietnam who had been charged with the killing of a 10-year-old girl coming out of the YMCA in a small town in central Pennsylvania in the late 1970s. The circumstances of the killing involved a dollar bill stuffed in the mouth of a Coke bottle and a knife used to slash the throat of the young girl. The defendant was not familiar with this girl and had no relationship with her; he indicated to the forensic examiner that he had been in Vietnam and had a flashback of an experience that he had there in which he was on guard duty, defending a tank. He found a young Vietcong soldier coming up with a Molotov cocktail, that is, gasoline in a Coke bottle with a dollar bill as the wick to blow up the tank. He caught the assailant and slashed his throat only to find that the Vietcong was a young girl. He had had nightmares and flashback phenomena of the killing since that time and had been discharged from the service with a serious psychiatric condition. The young girl in Pennsylvania was found with a Coke bottle and a dollar bill near the central monument, which was a tank in the center of town. The plea of insanity was successful in that particular case.

More likely, the diagnosis of PTSD would be used to diminish responsibility or decrease the sentence rather than to resolve it in a successful insanity plea. Friel et al. (2008) note that

> when assessing PTSD it is important to establish the presence of the core symptoms—i.e., intrusive phenomena, symptoms associated with avoidance and emotional numbing, and symptoms suggestive of hyper arousal. As always, this should be done through careful history and mental state examination, although the process can be aided by the use of some of the structured assessment tools available. (p. 81)

TRAUMATIC BRAIN INJURY AND DYSFUNCTION

Another diagnosis that is often used in insanity pleas is that of traumatic brain injury or brain dysfunction. Kroeber (2007) has presented his concept of brain research, free will, and legal responsibility. He notes that "the debate leads to the conclusion that human behavior cannot be described adequately in physical terms of cause and effect. The psychological approach to describe reasons, motives, and intentions is substantially more appropriate" (p. 251), and reaches five conclusions, three of which are:

1. Every adult person usually has strong motives and good reasons for his deeds.
2. His motives and reasons are originated, influenced, and limited by the physical status of each person, especially by the structure of his brain and the patterns of his thinking.
3. A person is legally responsible if she is able to act according to her reasons, which are not forced on to her by acute mental illness (p. 260).

ASPERGER'S DISORDER

Another diagnosis that has been connected with legal insanity is that of Asperger's disorder. Haskins and Silva (2006) comment on this condition and its relation to criminal responsibility. They refer to the higher functioning autism spectrum disorders (hfASDs). They state, "Preliminary findings indicate that hfASDs are over represented in criminal populations relative to their prevalence in the general population. However, more comprehensive studies are needed to confirm these findings" (p. 382), and conclude that "as forensic clinicians become more aware of the complex biopsychosocial nature of hfASDs, our ability to describe the contribution of autistic psychopathology to criminal conduct will expand" (p. 383).

The authors assessed a young man who was charged with sexually abusing young boys at a camp. He was in his mid-40s and had a clear case of Asperger's disorder that was brought to the surface only after his mother alerted the experts to his history and the likelihood that he carried this diagnosis. Since the utilization of Asperger's in insanity cases is relatively rare, the authors decided to call upon one of the experts in this disorder to serve as the expert witness in the case. Despite her excellent background and experience and her exemplary presentation in court, the jury found the defendant guilty, but the court did take his diagnosis into consideration during sentencing.

CHILDHOOD AND ADOLESCENCE

Childhood and adolescence have sometimes been utilized as a condition, though not a clinical diagnosis, when determining judgment and criminal responsibility. Goldstein et al. (2003) give an excellent example of 4-year-old Peter Gordon, who, after watching an episode of *Peter Pan* with his parents, went to bed. Two hours later, he entered his parents' bedroom highly agitated and anxious and informed them that he had taken his infant sister, Karen, out of her crib and, as a result of being influenced by the movie, insisted she could fly by opening a window and holding her outside and letting her go. Upon hearing this, the parents checked and found the infant dead in the bushes beneath the window. As a result of a police investigation of homicide, Peter was not charged. It was determined that his state of mind was such that he had not intended to cause her death; rather, he actually believed that his sister would take flight as he had witnessed in the movie *Peter Pan* (p. 381). The authors go on to state that there is good empirical evidence to suggest that 4-year-old children do not cognitively understand the concept of death as the complete biological termination of life. Thus, there is question concerning whether any child of this age can genuinely intend to cause death. In essence, Peter was not a morally responsible agent. Causal and moral responsibilities are clearly distinct. Moral responsibility depends on the mental state with which an individual acts.

Fried and Reppucci (2001) note, "There are some age-based effects on both the standardized measures of the psychological factors and measures of judgment," that "age was related to perceptions of culpability. Younger adolescents were more likely to think that they would be punished more harshly in adult criminal court and more likely to think they should be transferred to adult criminal court," and that "it is possible that as adolescents mature, they are better able to equate punishment with criminal responsibility and see immaturity as a mitigating factor in the assignment of punishment" (p. 570). The authors conclude that "if adolescents have less developed decision-making capabilities, then the rationale for a juvenile justice system that holds adolescents to adult-like standards of criminal responsibility, and culpability is challenged" (p. 58). The authors also attribute to Feld (1999) the notion that "it may be reasonable to consider age as a mitigating factor in all criminal situations" (p. 60).

Psychopathy

The next consideration is that of psychopathy with respect to criminal responsibility on sexual predators. Schopp and Slain (2000) present "exculpatory arguments from impaired capacity or character defect" (p. 251). They argue that those with character defects may be eligible for insanity considerations. They also present the issue of DID and psychopathic states of consciousness. These issues are included because in the interest of accurate and comprehensive assessments, proper diagnoses must be made. The authors consider psychopathy to be a defect in moral emotionality.

Schopp and Slain (2000) further maintain that

> a critic might object that psychopaths lack moral motive generally while the ordinary criminal only lacks sufficient moral motive to refrain from some crimes in some circumstances. The critic might also respond that psychopaths do not qualify as accountable agents

because they lack the capacity for moral motivation and not merely because they lack moral motive regarding a specific crime. (p. 266)

The authors relate the concept of psychopathy to the sexual psychopath statutes or the sexually violent predator (SVP) statutes, but these concepts do not usually result in insanity findings.

VOLUNTARY INTOXICATION

Another consideration for insanity is that of voluntary intoxication as proposed by Marlowe, Lambert, and Thompson (1999). They consider the laws in various jurisdictions that govern the use of intoxication evidence to negate *mens rea*, that is, to establish diminished capacity to support an insanity defense and to mitigate criminal sentencing. The authors state that "in the case of *Montana v. Egelhoff* (1996), the U.S. Supreme Court held that a criminal defendant does not have a fundamental right to introduce evidence of voluntary intoxication in his or her defense," but that, however, the use of "evidence of voluntary intoxication continues to be received in the majority of jurisdictions, particularly on issues related to *mens rea* and sentencing mitigation," while "a number of jurisdictions are developing 'drug courts' and other alternative correctional programs to divert non-violent, non-recidivist substance abusing offenders from the jurisdiction of the criminal court" (p. 210).

Marlowe et al. (1999) note that it is rare to use voluntary intoxication to negate criminal responsibility. They criticize forensic assessors or evaluators for not following up "negative responses to their questions" and for tending to be overly broad, giving potentially misleading diagnoses such as "polysubstance abuse or mixed substance abuse," although

substance abuse is the most common behavioral syndrome in forensic and correctional settings. Indeed, the shared variance between substance abuse and crime is so high that, from a purely statistical standpoint, there may even be little justification for treating them as wholly distinct phenomena. Forensic experts must therefore be more sensitized to substance abuse issues. At a minimum, it should be clear that one cannot perform a competent clinical forensic examination without closely attending to these matters. (p. 210)

Berman and Coccaro (1998) relate neurotransmitter functioning and violent behavior in citing the literature to support the notion that neurotransmitter functioning is related to human aggressive behavior. They present a case study in which neurotransmitter functioning was introduced as evidence to support an insanity defense. Despite the detailed information given about the neurotransmitter defect on the impulsive aggressive behavior, the court was not persuaded that the defendant met the state's legal test for not guilty by reason of insanity. The defendant was found guilty of murder in the first degree, and the court subsequently sentenced him to death.

The authors discuss neurotransmitter deficits and the insanity defense, and state that "the schizophrenic defendant who raises an insanity plea will generally argue that his or her cognitive functioning or behavioral self-regulation was severely impaired. Presence of delusional beliefs or hallucinatory experiences directly related to the commission of the instant offense is extremely relevant to the success of the plea. Courts will likely view testimony regarding the prevalence of violence in schizophrenics and the potential underlying biological substrates for the disorder, as less relevant to the ultimate issue," and that "neurobiological evidence may be more compelling if presented within a cogent theoretical framework, especially if hypotheses derived from the theory have withstood adequate testing" (p. 313). Thus, it is important for the comprehensive assessment of the defendant in a criminal case to determine criminal responsibility by the presence or the absence of neurotransmitter defects.

Morse (1999), a prominent psychologist and law professor, addresses why mental disorder is relevant to criminal responsibility. He provides a theoretical account of responsibility and excuse in general. He then examines why mental disorder can sometimes produce either a complete or a partial excusing condition such as legal insanity or "partial responsibility." He argues that mental disorder rarely negates *mens rea*, but in those cases in which a plausible claim for negation could be made, defendants should be allowed to make this claim. Professor Morse concludes that "if criminal responsibility is properly understood, it becomes clear that mental disorder *per se* is not an exculpating condition, but it may produce genuine excusing conditions in some cases and in some cases may negate *mens rea*" (p. 164).

COMMUNICATION

The forensic examiner should attempt to summarize findings in a proper *Diagnostic and Statistical Manual of Mental Disorders*, 4th edition, Text Revision (DSM-IV-TR; American Psychiatric Association, 2000) formulation on the five axes. The reason for this is that in most jurisdictions, insanity would not be allowed or admissible if the diagnosis is depression, anxiety, antisocial personality disorder, or some other Axis II diagnosis. In most jurisdictions, one must have a psychosis or organic brain syndrome or severe mental retardation. Schizophrenia and bipolar disorder are acceptable, but generalized anxiety disorder or even obsessive–compulsive disorder would not qualify. Use of chemicals, drugs, or alcohol may mitigate the sentence, but would not lead to insanity *per se*. These would be seen as self-administered drugs that the individual could not be rewarded for taking to diminish his ability to know what he was doing.

REFERENCES

American Educational Research Association; American Psychological Association; & National Council on Measurement in Education. (1999). *Standards for educational and psychological testing* (3rd ed.). Washington, DC: American Educational Research Association.

American Law Institute. (1962). *Model penal code*. Washington, DC: Author.

American Psychiatric Association. (2000). *Diagnostic and statistical manual of mental disorders* (4th ed., Text Revision). Washington, DC: American Psychiatric Publishing.

Appelbaum, P. S., Jick, R. Z., Grisso, T., Givelber, D., Silver, E., & Steadman, H. J. (1993). Use of post-traumatic stress disorder to support an insanity defense. *American Journal of Psychiatry, 150*, 229–234.

Arnold's Case, 16 State Tr. 695 (1724).

Bellingham's Case, 1 Collinson on Lunacy (1812).

Berman, M. B., & Coccaro, B. F. (1998). Neurobiologic correlates of violence: Relevance to criminal responsibility. *Behavioral Sciences & the Law, 16*, 303–318.

Beverly's Case, 4 Coke's Rep. 123b (1604).

Butcher, J. N., & Williams, C. L. (1992). *Essentials of MMPI-2 and MMPI-A interpretation*. Minneapolis, MN: University of Minnesota Press.

Comprehensive Crime Control Act of 1984, 18 U.S.C. §17 (1984).

Durham v. United States, 214 F.2d 862 (D.C. Cir. 1954).

Feld, B. (1999). *Bad kids*. New York, NY: Oxford University Press.

Fink, D. L. (2008). *Dissociation and criminal responsibility*. Paper presented in Forensic Psychiatric Seminar, University of Pennsylvania, Philadelphia, PA.

Frederick, R. (1997). *Validity Indicator Profile*. Minneapolis, MN: National Computer Systems.

Fried, C. S., & Reppucci, N. D. (2001). Criminal decision making: The development of adolescent judgment, criminal responsibility, and culpability. *Law and Human Behavior, 25*, 45–61.

Friel, A., White, T., & Hull, A. (2008). Posttraumatic stress disorder and criminal responsibility. *Journal of Forensic Psychiatry and Psychology, 19*, 64–85.

Goldstein, A. M., Morse, S. J., & Shapiro, D. L. (2003). Evaluation of criminal responsibility. In I. B. Weiner (Series Ed.) & A. M. Goldstein (Vol. Ed.), *Comprehensive handbook of psychology: Vol. 11. Forensic psychology* (pp. 407–436). Hoboken, NJ: John Wiley & Sons.

Graham, J. R. (2000). *MMPI-2: Assessing personality and psychopathology* (3rd ed.). New York, NY: Oxford University Press.

Hare, R. D. (1991). *The Hare Psychopathy Checklist—Revised*. Toronto, ON: Multi-Health Systems.

Haskins, B. G., & Silva, J. A. (2006). Asperger's disorder and criminal behavior: Forensic-psychiatric considerations. *Journal of the American Academy of Psychiatry and the Law, 34*, 374–384.

Kroeber, H. L. (2007). The historical debate on brain and legal responsibility—revisited. *Behavioral Sciences and the Law, 25*, 251–261.

Marlowe, D. B., Lambert, J. B., & Thompson, R. G. (1999). Voluntary intoxication and criminal responsibility. *Behavioral Sciences & the Law, 17*, 195–217.

Maudsley, H. (1896). *Responsibility in mental disease*. New York, NY: D. Appleton & Co.

Millon, T. (1994). *The Millon Clinical Multiaxial Inventory-III manual*. Minneapolis, MN: National Computer Systems.

Millon, T. (1996). *Disorders of personality* (2nd ed.). New York, NY: John Wiley & Sons.

Mitchell, B. (1995). Provoked violence, capacity and criminal responsibility. *Psychology, Crime and Law, 1*, 291–300.

Morse, S. J. (1999). Craziness and criminal responsibility. *Behavioral Sciences & the Law, 17*, 147–164.

Parker v. State, 597 S.W. 2nd 586, 587 (Ark. 1980).

Parsons v. State, 2 So. 854 (Ala. 1886).

People v. Gorshen, 336 P.2d 492 (Cal. Super. 1959).

People v. Wells, 202 P.2d 53 (Cal. Super. 1949).

Perlin, M. (1989). *Mental disability law: Civil and criminal* (Vol. 3) Charlottesville, VA: Michie.

R. v. Hadfield, 27 State Tr. 1281 (1800).

R. v. McNaughten, 8 Eng. Rep. 718 (1843).

R. v. Oxford, 9 Car. & P. 525 (1840).

Rogers, R. (1984). *Rogers Criminal Responsibility Assessment Scales (R-CRAS) and test manual*. Odessa, FL: Psychological Assessment Resources.

Rogers, R., Sewell, K. W., & Gillard, N. (2010). *Structured Interview of Reported Symptoms-2 (SIRS-2) and professional manual*. Lutz, FL: Psychological Assessment Resources.

Saks, E. R. (1995). The criminal responsibility of people with multiple personality disorder. *Psychiatric Quarterly*, *66*, 119–131.

Schopp, R. F., & Slain, A. J. (2000). Psychopathy, criminal responsibility, and civil commitment as a sexual predator. *Behavioral Sciences & the Law*, *18*, 247–274.

Silva, J. A., Derecho, D. V., Leong, G. B., Weinstock, R., & Ferrari, M. (2001). A classification of psychological factors leading to violent behavior and post-traumatic stress disorder. *Journal of Forensic Sciences*, *46*, 309–316.

Silverton, L., & Gruber, C. (1998). *Malingering Probability Scale (MPS)*. Los Angeles, CA: Western Psychological Services.

Sparr, L. F., & Atkinson, R. M. (1986). Posttraumatic stress disorder as an insanity defense: Medical legal quicksand. *American Journal of Psychiatry*, *143*, 608–612.

State v. Jones, 50 N.H. 369 (1871).

State v. Pike, 49 N.H. 399, 442 (1870).

Tanenbaum, R. K. (2009). *Escape*. New York, NY: Vanguard Press.

United States v. Brawner, 471 F.2d 969, 981 (D.C. Cir. 1972).

United States v. Denny-Schaffer, 2 F.3d 999 (1993).

Whitlock, F. A. (1963). *Criminal responsibility and mental illness*. London, UK: Butterworth.

Wis. Stat. § 971.15(1).

CHAPTER 7

Capital Litigation: Special Considerations

ALAN M. GOLDSTEIN and HAROLD J. BURSZTAJN

INTRODUCTION

From biblical times onward, a fundamental principle of proportion-ality, to prevent excessive punishment, has informed criminal liability (i.e., that the punishment should fit the crime.) In its original form, this principle was presented as *lex talionis*, or the law of reciprocal justice (e.g., an eye for an eye). Today, to establish guilt, it must be proven not only that the defendant actually committed the prohibited act (*actus reas*), the conduct element of the crime, but that when the act was committed, the defendant acted with the required state of mind (*mens rea*), the mental state element required, to be held responsible for that offense (Bursztajn, Scherr, & Brodsky, 1994; Goldstein, Morse, & Shapiro, 2003). For example, a defendant takes the life of another person, typically referred to as a homicide. The law provides that the defendant's state of mind at the time of the killing will determine the punishment he is to receive. *Mens rea* may serve as a reflection of the "evilness" of the act, and more evil acts are likely to receive more severe sentences. The defendant may have been insane at the time of the crime (see Chapter 6), unaware of the nature of his action or its wrongfulness; as such, he may be found to be not criminally responsible for his conduct and no punishment will be forthcoming. He may have genuinely, but mistakenly, believed that his life was in danger and acted in self-defense, and could be convicted of a lesser offense such as criminally negligent homicide. The defendant may have gotten into an argument with the victim, lost his temper, and struck the victim, who then fell, hitting his head on the pavement, which caused the victim's death. Under such circumstances, the defendant may be found guilty of manslaughter, a crime bringing with it a long sentence, but one less than that associated with murder. To be found guilty of murder, most states require that taking of the victim's life was fueled by a conscious intent to purposefully or knowingly cause the victim's death. In all cases, someone has died at the hands of the defendant, but the *mens rea* associated with each crime has been different, affecting the punishment the defendant could receive.

A special category of murder involves those in which the circumstances of the crime or the defendant's *mens rea* is viewed as so evil or wicked that a sentence of life without the possibility of parole is perceived to be inadequate punishment for the act. In such cases, federal statutes and the statutes of 35 states (as of December 2, 2009) allow for the death penalty (Death Penalty Information Center, 2009). The death penalty is also potential punishment in U.S. Military Court.

The Death Penalty Information Center, an anti–death penalty organization that maintains a comprehensive website (www.death penaltyinfo.org) reporting facts about capital punishment and updates case law in this area, reports (www.deathpenaltyinfo.org) that at the start of 2009, 3,297 inmates were held on death rows in the United States. As of December 2, 2009, 1,185 executions were performed. The most common means of execution in the United States is lethal injection, followed by electrocution, the gas chamber, hanging, and firing squad (only in Utah). This organization notes that since 1973, over 130 inmates awaiting execution were released from death rows, based on evidence of their actual innocence.

Obviously, the stakes are high when experts conduct evaluations of defendants who are facing trials for capital offenses. In *Woodson v. North Carolina* (1976), the Supreme Court of the United States emphasized that a sentence of death is qualitatively different from any other punishment a defendant might receive. It is irrevocable and, as such, before "the ultimate punishment of death" is imposed, deliberations require guided case-by-case consideration of "relevant facts of the character and record of the individual offender or the circumstances of the particular offense." The caution noted in

Woodson that "there is the need for reliability in the determination that the death penalty is the appropriate punishment in a specific case" clearly applies to forensic mental health experts called upon to conduct capital litigation assessments.

If courts and jurors are to rely on the testimony of experts in their deliberations on this life-versus-death issue, the opinions of the expert must be based on best practice standards in this area of forensic assessment (see Heilbrun, Grisso, & Goldstein, 2009; Heilbrun, DeMatteo, Marczyk, & Goldstein, 2009, for a discussion of the elements of the standard of practice in forensic mental health assessment; see Cunningham, 2010, for specific information on the best practice standard in assessing capital cases).

At times, experts are called upon to conduct assessments related to competence to be executed or to review the work of another forensic mental health expert who evaluated a defendant whose case ended with a sentence of death and who is appealing that conviction. Although this chapter focuses on the assessment of defendants who are to be tried for capital murder and how these evaluations are conducted, the same principles apply in performing these assessments. In this chapter, we consider the need to rely on multiple sources of relevant data; information that is reliably interpreted; and communicating findings and opinions in an organized, objective manner, consistent with the ethical codes of the expert's profession.

PREPARATION

An expert involved in a death penalty case must understand the structure of a capital trial, how a capital trial is conducted, and the criteria for capital sentencing in the jurisdiction in question.

Capital trials are bifurcated; that is, they consist of the trial phase in which the trier of fact, the judge or jury, decides whether the defendant is guilty of capital murder, is guilty of some lesser offense, is fully acquitted of the charges, or if another defense such as insanity or self-defense is established. If the defendant is found guilty of a capital murder, then the case proceeds to the sentencing or death penalty phase. While forensics experts may be called to testify during the trial phase on matters related to insanity or other mental state (at the time of offense) defenses (or at pretrial hearings involving trial competency or the capacity to understand and appreciate

Miranda rights), this chapter focuses on the role of the expert during the sentencing phase of the trial.

In *Gregg v. Georgia* (1976), the Supreme Court of the United States acknowledged that Georgia's newly legislated death penalty act was constitutional. This statute called for a two-part or bifurcated trial to avoid the prejudicial effects that the introduction of possibly incendiary details about the circumstances of the offense, the offender, or the victim might have on the outcome of the trial. It established a set of mitigating and aggravating circumstances, factors a jury could consider during the penalty phase of the trial when deciding whether the penalty of death was appropriate. *Gregg* indicated that the trier of fact should be informed of "any mitigating circumstances or aggravating circumstances otherwise authorized by law and any of the [10] statutory aggravating circumstances which may be supported by the evidence" (p. 164). The jury is instructed to weigh those aggravating circumstances they believe exist against the mitigating circumstances they believe were established in deciding the punishment the defendant is to receive.

The attorney should provide the black letter of the law that governs the sentencing phase in the specific capital case. This includes those aggravating factors that the prosecution intends to establish at trial, along with the jurisdiction's list of possible mitigating factors. Mitigating factors, especially, often fall within the province of forensic mental health evaluation. In New Hampshire, for example, along with five mitigating factors that are largely matters for factual determination, there are four that call for forensic mental health evaluation (New Hampshire Criminal Code 630:5.VI):

1. The defendant's capacity to appreciate the wrongfulness of his conduct or to conform his conduct to the requirements of law was significantly impaired, regardless of whether the capacity was so impaired as to constitute a defense to the charge.
2. The defendant was under unusual and substantial duress, regardless of whether the duress was of such a degree as to constitute a defense to the charge.
3. The defendant committed the offense under severe mental or emotional disturbance.
4. Other factors in the defendant's background or character mitigate against imposition of the death sentence.

The fourth of these criteria allows defense counsel to offer case-specific mitigating factors not covered by the other three categories. Based on a U.S. Supreme Court case, *Lockett v. Ohio* (1978), the court affirmed the obvious, that death is qualitatively different from all other sentences and that capital defendants can offer as mitigation any information about the defendant's background, history, or circumstances of the offense. These might include such factors as a history of childhood trauma, exposure to family or neighborhood violence, undiagnosed or misdiagnosed conditions such as mental retardation or emotional disorder, the presence of a learning disability or attention deficit/hyperactivity disorder (ADHD), gang or cult membership, the minor role played by the defendant in the crime, or tendencies to acquiesce to authority or to suggestions from others as a factor in the crime. Most recently, ineffectiveness of counsel was cited by the Court in a decision calling for a new death penalty trial for a convicted defendant based on his attorney's failure to introduce evidence of a prior history of posttraumatic stress disorder associated with military service during the Korean War (*Porter v. McCollum*, 2009). Other states and the federal government have similar lists of mitigating factors. A forensic evaluator, whether retained by the defense or prosecution, must be prepared to undertake an objective, thorough evaluation of any mitigation that might exist.

Aggravating factors may also be susceptible to forensic mental health analysis. In New Hampshire, for example, along with three statutory aggravating factors having to do with previous criminal convictions, there are seven that potentially, at least in part, fall within the scope of forensic mental health evaluation (New Hampshire Criminal Code 630:5.VII):

a. The defendant:
  1. purposely killed the victim;
  2. purposely inflicted serious bodily injury which resulted in the death of the victim;
  3. purposely engaged in conduct which:
    A. the defendant knew would create a grave risk of death to a person, other than one of the participants in the offense; and
    B. resulted in the death of the victim.
b. In the commission of the offense of capital murder, the defendant knowingly created a grave risk of death to one or more persons in addition to the victims of the offense.

c. The defendant committed the offense after substantial planning and premeditation.
d. The victim was particularly vulnerable due to old age, youth, or infirmity.
e. The defendant committed the offense in an especially heinous, cruel, or depraved manner in that it involved torture or serious physical abuse to the victim.
f. The murder was committed for pecuniary gain.
g. The murder was committed for the purpose of avoiding or preventing a lawful arrest or effecting an escape from lawful custody.

These statutory aggravating factors are similar to those considered by a number of states and the federal government in their death penalty statutes. In addition, either the defense or prosecuting attorney may raise questions regarding the likelihood that the defendant will commit acts of serious violence in the future if a sentence of less than death is entered. As such, these evaluations may include a violence risk assessment (see Chapter 15 in this volume), testimony found to be admissible according to *Barefoot v. Estelle* (1983). Whether retained by the defense or the prosecution, experts in most cases should address issues related to the presence or absence of aggravating factors in their evaluations.

THE REFERRAL AND FOCUS OF THE ASSESSMENT

When contacted by the attorney, it is essential to clarify the precise nature of the referral. Obtaining an overall background history of the defendant, potential areas of assessment that the expert should focus on (i.e., possible mental retardation, abuse as a child, presence of psychosis, childhood trauma, risk assessment) will alert the expert as to the methods that might be employed in the assessment, the records needed, and who else, in addition to the defendant, should be interviewed. It is important to obtain a timetable from the attorney of various legal filing dates, hearings, and the approximate trial date to ensure that a report, if requested, can be submitted on time.

At times, if retained by a defense attorney, the expert may be asked to refrain from interviewing the defendant about the offense itself. Certainly, the defendant has a constitutional right not to discuss the crime with the expert. However, the attorney should be informed that without specific information about the crime, it may not be possible to relate any mitigating factors that may be found to the crime itself. That is, although a defendant may be found to be intellectually challenged, it may be difficult to offer this limitation as an "explanation" or contributing factor to the crime. Although the expert can describe the defendant's intellectual limitations, the inability to relate these findings to the murder itself may limit the impact of any potential testimony. Likewise, an expert retained by the prosecution may need to create an atmosphere otherwise conducive to free and open communication by the defendant despite limits on the scope of the interview imposed by the defense attorney.

Attorneys may ask the expert to review records without ever interviewing the defendant. In such cases, if the expert has an opinion, testimony may be of a somewhat academic nature, based on what has been learned from the records and the relationship of this information to the professional literature. The attorney should be informed of this limitation at the time of the referral. For example, the expert learns that records show that the defendant was severely neglected and abused as a child, witnessed his mother being battered on a regular basis, and was expected to break into apartments in his building, starting at age 5, to steal food and money for his family. Although the literature on the effects of these childhood experiences on neurological growth, on the development of a moral sense, on self-image, and on the likelihood of violently acting out as an adult may be the subject of testimony, it can be questioned as a relevant finding for the *specific* case in question. If this or *any* limitations imposed by the attorney appear to limit the data made available sufficiently to prevent the expert from formulating an informed opinion, the expert should decline the case.

Timing

Because of the harshness of the potential punishment, the unlimited nature of possible mitigating factors, and the need to address aggravating factors in the assessment, adequate funding and time are needed to conduct these assessments. Fortunately, requests to conduct a forensic mental health assessment in a capital case typically are made early in the history of the case. Experienced defense attorneys often believe that the best time for them to "win" a capital case is *before* it is officially declared to be a death penalty case. There is usually a window of time granted to the defense to convince the prosecutor that either the chances that a jury will return a sentence of death are slim or that the death penalty is not appropriate given the findings of the expert. As such, there is usually sufficient time to obtain records, schedule evaluation sessions, conduct interviews, and prepare a report.

In individual cases, there may be the need to visit the scene of the crime (if permitted) and the defendant's living quarters before he was incarcerated. In one case, a forensic psychiatrist found aluminum foil with which the defendant had covered his windows and walls to protect himself from threatening intrusions, in the expert's opinion, an indicator (together with other data) of psychosis. Whereas this defendant's mother had kept his room just as he had left it, many defendants, once incarcerated, do not have family members to maintain their homes for subsequent inspection.

ETHICAL ISSUES

Forensic mental health evaluations in capital litigation are guided by the same ethical principles as any other forensic context (see, e.g., Committee on Ethical Guidelines for Forensic Psychologists, 1991; American Academy of Psychiatry and the Law [AAPL], 2005).

- *Competence of the expert.* The American Psychological Association's *Code of Ethics* (2002a, Section 2.01) states that psychologists must practice within their areas of expertise. Before accepting a case involving death penalty litigation, the psychologist should consider the criteria used to consider competence as stated in the *Code*: "education, training, supervised experience, consultation, study, or professional experience" (p. 1063). The *Specialty Guidelines for Forensic Psychologists* (Committee on Ethical Guidelines for Forensic Psychologists, 1991) cautions that expertise in specific areas of forensic practice requires a "fundamental and reasonable level of knowledge and understanding of the legal and professional standards, which govern their participation as experts in the legal proceedings" (p. 658). Similarly, the *Ethics Guidelines for the Practice of Forensic Psychiatry*, authored by AAPL (2005), indicate that before conducting any forensic evaluation, the psychiatrist must possess an understanding of "the appropriate laws of the jurisdiction" (p. 2).

There is an overrepresentation of minority defendants for whom the death penalty is under consideration and for whom a verdict of death has already been rendered (Cunningham, 2010; Cunningham & Goldstein, 2003; Death Penalty Information Center, December 2, 2009; Eisenberg, 2004). Experts should possess specific knowledge or have specific training or experience in working with those from culturally, racially, and ethnically diverse populations when asked to conduct assessments of those from such populations (American Psychological Association, 2002b). Before embarking on a death penalty evaluation, the forensic mental health evaluator must be competent to practice in this specific area. At the same time, the evaluator needs to be careful to avoid using culture either as an excuse or as a stigma.

- *Informed consent.* Of special concern is the need to obtain informed consent for the examination. *Estelle v. Smith* (1981), a landmark Supreme Court of the United States case emphasizing the need to obtain informed consent when conducting forensic mental health assessments, in fact arose in the context of a capital case. This informed consent process includes giving the defendant the "*Lamb* warning" (*Commonwealth v. Lamb*, 1974), which makes clear that the examination does not constitute medical treatment or psychotherapy, does not create a doctor–patient relationship, and is not confidential. Some have loosely analogized the *Lamb* warning to the *Miranda* warning to given to suspects when they are apprehended by the police. The examiner informs the defendant which party has retained the examiner and that what the defendant communicates may be used in the judicial proceedings to the defendant's advantage or disadvantage. The defendant may choose not to answer specific questions, but such refusal may be noted in the examiner's report and testimony. As in nonforensic clinical situations, the examiner is responsible for assessing the defendant's capacity to consent to the examination.

- *Avoiding bias.* The expert must resist any temptation to use the forensic evaluation as a platform for promoting moral, religious, or policy positions about the death penalty—whether for or against. Whatever one's views as a private citizen, to participate appropriately in the legal process, one must be able to perform an honest evaluation in which one strives for objectivity, as in any other type of forensic evaluation (AAPL, 2005). An evaluator should not use a forensic mental health evaluation as an occasion to protest against or endorse the death penalty. If you wish to promote a political position or feel incapable of objectivity in a capital sentencing evaluation, it is best to excuse yourself from capital cases. Retention as an expert in such cases is elective; no one is required to conduct such evaluations.

- *The team approach.* The need to be objective and to avoid bias in forensic evaluation is even more pronounced in capital cases. As described by Goldstein (2001), Cunningham and Goldstein (2003), and Eisenberg (2004), attorneys may refer to the expert as a member of the "defense team." This concept may be used in discussions with the expert or in introducing the expert to the defendant. It is important for the expert to directly, but politely, clarify the role that is to be served: not as a member of a "team," whose purpose is to help one side win, but rather as an educator, whose job to inform the lawyer of all of the findings and have the lawyer decide whether, as a whole, the findings will be of benefit to the defendant. Although the use of the word *team* may seem innocent, its subtle meaning distorts the expert's role and violates ethical principles: experts are not advocates for the side that retained them in capital or any other cases. Thus, the evaluation (like any other forensic evaluation) needs to be performed on a noncontingency basis. One is paid for one's time and skills, not for one's opinion.

- *The ultimate issue.* It is helpful to keep in mind that the evaluator's expert opinion does not directly determine whether the death sentence is imposed. Rather, the evaluator addresses questions that are within the province of forensic psychiatry or psychology, exploration of which can help the jury to determine sentence under the law of the jurisdiction. It is inappropriate, unless ordered by the court, to offer an ultimate opinion in a forensic evaluation. For example, opinions that a defendant was unable to validly waive *Miranda* rights or that a defendant was insane at the time of offense are legal, moral judgments, outside the scope of the forensic mental health expert's expertise. Fortunately, in capital cases, the ultimate opinion is obviously so "out of bounds" for experts (i.e., "In my opinion, the aggravating factors outweigh the mitigating factors and I believe the defendant should be put to death"), this issue is unlikely to present a problem.

DATA COLLECTION

An effective and cost-effective forensic mental health examination is built on a foundation of review and analysis of a wide range of data sources (Appelbaum & Gutheil, 2007; Bursztajn et al., 1994; Goldstein, 2003; Grisso, 1986, 2003; Heilbrun, 2001; Heilbrun, Grisso, & Goldstein, 2009; Melton, Petrila, Poythress, & Slobogin, 2007).

COLLATERAL DATA

Unlike nonforensic clinical assessments in which there is no reason to question the veracity of the client's answers to questions during interviews and the client's responses to tests, in forensic mental health assessments there is a readily identifiable reason for defendants to provide misleading or false information. In death penalty assessments, the defendant may exaggerate, malinger, or withhold damaging information to avoid execution. Therefore, experts rely on corroborative information, including the review of records and interviews of third parties, in forming opinions (Heilbrun, Warren, & Picarello, 2003; Otto, Slobogin, & Greenberg, 2007). The evaluator should review police, court, medical, mental health, and prison records as well as school, employment, and military records. Collateral witnesses, including family members and other close associates of the defendant, may be interviewed by the expert. Depending on cost and time constraints and other factors, some of these interviews may be conducted by a mitigation specialist, usually a social worker trained in conducting third-party interviews in capital cases.

Reviewing records prior to the first evaluation session may serve to focus the interview on relevant areas that should be covered. In addition, a review of written documents may assist the expert in selecting appropriate tests for the defendant. Record review may indicate a need for psychological or neuropsychological testing, medical laboratory testing (e.g., for nutritional deficiencies, blood disorders, or liver dysfunction), or for visual or audiological evaluation.

A visit to the defendant's residence may be of value as in the case previously discussed of the defendant who papered his walls and windows with aluminum foil. Critical data can emerge from a site visit. Likewise, visiting the scene of a crime might aid in reconstructing the motivational dynamics of the individuals involved, including the defendant and the victim or victims.

INTERVIEWING THE EXAMINEE

Forensic interviewing is a specialized application of clinical interviewing and requires specialized knowledge. The interview focuses on the specific psycholegal issues in question: mitigating and aggravating circumstances and, possibly, the assessment of violence risk. Forensic mental health experts must be familiar with the aggravating factors the prosecution will attempt to establish. They must recognize that mitigating factors are not limited to those that are included the jurisdiction's death penalty statute, but, because of *Lockett v. Ohio* (1978), these may include anything relevant to the defendant's background, character, or circumstances of the offense, and thus can be considered as mitigating evidence a jury is entitled to consider. Consequently, because of the almost unlimited scope of the information the expert is expected to consider, multiple interview sessions may be required.

- *Scope of the interviews.* Forensic interviews serve a number of purposes. As described by Goldstein and Goldstein (2010), forensic interviews include the following goals:
  - Acquire a detailed background history from the defendant.
  - Evaluate the defendant's mental status.
  - Identify sources of corroborative information, including records and people to interview.
  - Observe the defendant's demeanor, affect, behavior, and approach to tasks.
  - Assess the defendant's reliability as a historian in terms of accuracy, openness, delusional systems, and honesty when reporting historical information that can be corroborated through record review.

  The interview may provide information that might contribute to a formal psychiatric diagnosis. The interview may provide suggestions regarding the defendant's motivational dynamics, placing the offense within intrapsychic, interpersonal, social, and situational contexts. The interview may also provide information regarding the defendant's capacity to communicate, anticipate, reflect, and plan, all elements of *mens rea* (Bursztajn et al., 1994). Thus, the forensic interview may also suggest the presence of intellectual deficits and neurological conditions that may require neuropsychological testing. In cases where the expert is asked to conduct a risk assessment, the interview may provide information about "triggers" that have, in the past, led to violent actions and that may be set off by hidden but powerful delusions (Day & Manschreck, 1988). Finally, certain areas of exploration may be off limits in the interview. As discussed previously, counsel may have instructed the defendant not to speak about the crime to avoid revealing potentially self-incriminating information beyond that already known to the prosecutor.

- *Logistics of examination in prison.* The retaining attorney must arrange for the examiner to be given access to a correctional facility and must communicate any restrictions on what the expert may bring into the prison (e.g., a laptop, a recording device, psychological tests) and whether the expert can work through lunch or the institution's prisoner "count."

- *Limitations on normal examination procedure.* Prison examinations, especially in the case of inmates charged with capital crimes, may impose constraints on the expert's accustomed procedures. The defendant may be physically constrained; for example, an inmate the staff views as dangerous may be expected to participate in psychological testing while wearing handcuffs. If testing may be compromised because of this requirement (i.e., some tests are timed and the defendant's responses would be affected), the expert can ask the attorney to contact correctional authorities and explore a mutually agreeable solution to this problem. There may be a requirement that a corrections officer remain in the room during the course of the examination or that the assessment be observed by correctional staff through a one-way window. Each of these constraints may inhibit the defendant from revealing highly personal or potentially damaging information.

The presence of the defendant's attorney may be unavoidable because of a court order or a request that the lawyer be present when the expert is evaluating the defendant for the prosecution.

Research findings and a consensus among forensic mental health examiners suggest that the presence of a third party can interfere with the interview, perhaps calling into question the reliability of the examination findings (Cramer & Brodsky, 2007; Shealy, Cramer, & Pirelli, 2008; Simon, 1996). Professional organizations such as the American Academy of Clinical Neuropsychology (2001) have issued policy statements discouraging the participation of third-party observers in forensic examinations. If an attorney must be present, it must be only to observe, not to participate or interrupt the evaluation. If an attorney's initial presence is mandated, it can be helpful (where permitted) for the attorney to leave the room as soon as possible (e.g., following the introductions and the *Lamb* warning) or to sit as unobtrusively as possible behind the examinee so as not to communicate even nonverbal cues. For guidelines for minimizing distraction and maintaining reliability in the face of demands for third-party presence during evaluation sessions, see Shealy et al. and Simon. If the examiner cannot exclude the attorney, it is both prudent and informative to take into account the potentially distorting effects when reporting on the examination.

Likewise, audio or video recording has been shown to have potentially distorting effects on a forensic mental health examination (Constantinou, Ashendorf, & McCaffery, 2002). A long history of research establishes that recording clinical psychotherapeutic interviews changes the nature of the interaction from what it is intended to be (see Zinberg, 1985). In a forensic examination, recording equipment can inhibit the examinee's ability to keep an open mind, use insight, and communicate potentially conflictual, non–socially normative or previously unvoiced thoughts, feelings, memories, and attributions. Depending on the circumstances, taping can either exacerbate the perceived adversarial nature of an examination or give the defendant a "stage" on which to recite a prepared "script." These drawbacks should be weighed against the potential benefit of preventing subsequent claims of distortion or misrepre, entation of what was said in the interchange.

- *Situational stressors and "normalizing" factors.* The defendant's presentation is not likely to reflect accurately his or her mental or physical condition at the time of the offense. First, determine what medications the examinee is taking, as compared with the medications (or absence of medications), alcohol, and/or street drugs taken prior to incarceration. Medication may mask underlying impairments, contributing to an appearance of normality that may not reflect the defendant's state of mind when the offense was committed. Sedating medications may exacerbate some cognitive impairments, thereby reducing energy, alertness, and task concentration. It is important to remember that it is not only psychotropic medications that can have psychotropic effects, and that treated or untreated medical conditions may also play a role in mitigation. In the absence of prison contraband, the examinee will not manifest the effects of alcohol or illegal drugs, possible factors in shaping the defendant's mental state at the time of the crime and thus possible statutory mitigation arguing against the death penalty. Moreover, good medical treatment or good nutrition in prison may mask a systemic condition such as diabetes that may have impaired the defendant's decision making at the time of the offense. It should also be recalled that the defendant may manifest agitation precipitated by conflicts with or threats by other inmates or correction officers, as well as depression and anxiety resulting from the fact that the defendant is facing the death penalty. These emotional states may not have been present at the time the crime was committed.

- *What to look for.* The following categories of information may suggest possible mitigation: medical conditions; brain damage; history of alcohol or drug abuse; cognitive impairment, including the presence of a thought disorder or a delusional system; affective symptoms, which can impair judgment and decision making even in a person with otherwise unimpaired cognitive capacities (Bursztajn, Harding, Gutheil, & Brodsky, 1991; Gutheil & Bursztajn, 1986); personality traits and disorders; effects of prior traumas on current functioning; overuse or failure to use prescribed medications at the time of the offense; and side effects of prescribed medications. This is not meant to be an all-inclusive list, which is impossible because *Lockett* indicates that mitigating factors will vary on a case-by-case basis. In addition, information revealed during the interview and observations of the defendant's behavior across multiple sessions may provide data regarding the simulation of deficits and impairments. Information and observations acquired through interviews may also serve to contradict a defendant's claims of psychiatric or neurological symptoms or mental retardation, and may thereby provide data consistent with exaggerating or malingering. At the other extreme, even a capital defendant who would rather appear bad than mad may simulate sanity (Diamond, 1994). At the same time, the examiner should be careful not to overlook the often guarded, yet malignantly narcissistic or sociopathic traits that may be expressed in exuberance about or "bragging rights" to the homicide once the defendant lets his guard down. As discussed above, any impressions arising from the interviews are to be confirmed through an examination of other sources of information.

PSYCHOLOGICAL TESTING

Psychological testing is typically considered a component of any death penalty assessment. Tests are typically administered, scored, and interpreted by a licensed psychologist, whose training includes expertise in test administration and interpretation. Occasionally, psychiatrists may have completed training in the administration, scoring, and interpretation of psychological tests, and, under such circumstances, they may perform testing in the course of these assessments. Although a number of structured personality tests can be scored and interpreted by computer, the expert is expected to be as familiar with that test's norms, reliability, and validity as if the expert had scored and interpreted the test himself.

The Role of Psychological Testing in Capital Litigation Cases   Testing serves as a potential corroborative source of information. The use of objective psychological tests adds an element of objectivity to the assessment because scores are based on norms rather than subjective opinion or professional experience. In the case of computer-generated reports based on test results, the interpretation of the test data is independent of the expert, and statements in the report that corroborate other, less objective data may serve to provide convergent validity for the opinions that are reached. "Blind" interpretation by a computer-generated protocol may also provide a check to counter claims of bias and misinterpretation by the examiner.

The forensic expert should administer a comprehensive battery of tests to the defendant, appropriate to each defendant's history and demographic background and related to information acquired during the interviews and to data contained in records (i.e., suggesting intellectual limitations, neurological impairment, emotional or psychotic states).

Because of the *Lockett* decision, the expert should consider administering psychological tests to confirm the presence of or to detect previously undiagnosed conditions, including those that might have produced intellectual, cognitive, neurological, and emotional impairments. The selection of specific tests will vary from case to case, based on the issues in question (including the aggravating circumstances and the suspected mitigating factors for the case), the demographics of the defendant, and the preferences of the examiner.

To assess intellectual functioning and to address the possibility of an underlying neurological disorder, the Wechsler Adult Intelligence Scale-IV (WAIS-IV) can be administered (Wechsler, 2008). In capital cases, substituting the Wechsler Abbreviated Scale of Intelligence (WASI; Wechsler, 1999) should not be done; the savings in time and effort come at the sacrifice of potentially valuable data, a trade-off that is inappropriate when the defendant's life is at risk. Tests that measure academically oriented abilities may be of value as well. These may include the Wide Range Achievement Test, 4th Edition (WRAT4; Wilkinson & Robertson, 2006) and the Wechsler Individual Achievement Test-III (WIAT-III; Wechsler, 2009). Screening tests for neurological brain damage such as the Symbol Digit Modalities Test (Smith, 1982) and the Stroop Neuropsychological Screening Test (Trenerry, Crosson, DeBoe, & Leber, 1989) should be included as well. If these tests suggest brain damage, then more specific neuropsychological instruments can be administered. If this area of practice is not within the forensic examiner's expertise, a referral should be made to a qualified, board-certified neuropsychologist.

Personality tests should be selected in terms of their objective nature, their reading level, the demographics of the defendant, and their appropriateness to the case. Structured personality tests used in capital cases include the Minnesota Multiphasic Personality Inventory, 2nd Edition (MMPI-2; Butcher, Dahlstrom, Graham, Tellegen, & Kaemmer, 2001) and the Personality Assessment Inventory (PAI; Morey, 1991). If there are questions regarding the defendant's risk of future violence, a violence risk assessment can be conducted. There is a range of actuarial instruments available for this purpose (see Chapter 15).

In addition, because of the possibility of malingering and exaggeration, a factor to be considered in any forensic mental health examination, tests designed to assess malingered impairments should be included in the battery. If there are symptoms of memory loss reported or claimed during the interviews, a test such as the Test of Memory Malingering (TOMM) should be administered (Tombaugh, 1996). If symptoms associated with schizophrenia are demonstrated or found on measures of intelligence, personality, or other aspects of cognitive functioning, the Structured Interview of Reported Symptoms (SIRS; Rogers, Bagby, & Dickens, 1992) should be given. If there are claims of intellectual deficits during the interview or found on intelligence tests, the Validity Indicator Profile (VIP; Frederick, 1997) should be considered.

DATA INTERPRETATION

The expert is now ready to make sense of the data that have been collected from a range of sources of information. The data are now analyzed and interpreted, focusing on the relevant legal issues that prompted the referral in the first place: the mitigating and aggravating circumstances that a jury should be made aware of when it deliberates on the appropriateness of the death penalty and, possibly, the issue of violence risk.

GENERAL CONSIDERATIONS

As indicated by Goldstein and Goldstein (2010), a "forensic opinion on this or on any psycholegal question is only as good as the data upon which it is based" (p. 149).

That is, it is assumed that an appropriate interview was conducted; a battery of tests relevant to this psycholegal question was validly administered; the tests were valid and reliable; the tests were rescored to check for errors; sufficient information was provided by the defendant during the interviews related to this referral question; and relevant medical and legal records were reviewed and appropriate third parties were interviewed.

The cornerstone of data interpretation is the consistency of reliable information across sources of information. "That is, in examining and interpreting the data, what consistent patterns or themes emerge that bear directly on the referral question?" (Goldstein & Goldstein, 2010, p. 149). The content of the report and the testimony to be offered are directly related to this stage of the evaluation process. Hypothesis testing, comparing possible interpretation from one source of information against similar data from other sources, is the process by which opinions evolve. As such, it is essential to keep in mind Heilbrun's statement that: "Independently obtained information on a second measure about the same construct can be used to support (or refute) hypotheses that may have been generated by the results of the first measure," such that "impressions from a psychological test in the forensic context are most appropriately treated as hypotheses subject to verification through other psychological tests, history, medical tests, and third party observations" (Heilbrun, 1992, p. 267).

INTERPRETIVE FOCUS

Grisso (1986) discussed a number of criticisms of forensic evaluations. He wrote that in general, these criticisms could be broken down to three categories: "(1) *ignorance and irrelevance* in courtroom testimony; (2) *psychiatric or psychological intrusion* into essentially legal matters; and (3) *insufficiency and incredibility* of information provided to the courts" (p. 8). Keeping these criticisms in mind, when interpreting the data, experts should: (1) focus data examination, analysis, and interpretation on the relevant issue in death penalty evaluations—mitigating and aggravating circumstances and, possibly, the assessment of violence risk; (2) not interpret the data to the level of ultimate opinions; and (3) limit interpretation to those opinions for which there are sufficient, reliable data.

Cunningham (2010) has identified areas to be addressed in examining and interpreting the data. Among the broad categories he emphasizes are those related to *adverse factors* such as: (1) neurodevelopmental factors, including neurological traumas, neuroendocrine disorders, developmental disorder and delay, intellectual limitations; academic difficulties; and genetic predispositions (to substance abuse and psychological disorder); (2) parenting issues involving quality and continuity, parental inadequacy (i.e., substance abuse; maltreatment, poor modeling, lack of supervision) and deprivation and poverty; and (3) family influences involving negative sources of influence, problems with sexual boundaries, and other forms of victimization. Cunningham indicates that data should be examined for difficulties related to *community issues*, including: (1) poverty, illegal street activity such as drug trafficking and prostitution, and inadequate schooling; and (2) witnessing community violence, hearing gunfire, and having friends who have been victims of violent crime. In addition, data should be examined for consistent, reliable information related to *trajectory*: (1) nature of peer relationships; (2) school and employment difficulties; (3) romantic and sexual history; (4) substance abuse; (5) presence of and treatment for psychological disorders; and (6) criminal records as a juvenile and adult, including incarceration history. If the assessment includes a request to conduct a violence risk evaluation, Cunningham indicates that data should be examined with reference to base rates of violence, especially for those who were sentenced to death and those who received lesser sentences than the death penalty (see also Cunningham & Goldstein, 2003). It is important, with any risk factor that is identified as a potential causal factor, to conduct a causation analysis to distinguish a contributing cause from a passive and convenient focus or an incidental finding (Bursztajn, Feinbloom, Hamm, & Brodsky, 1990). Simple co-occurrence or correlation should not be overlooked, but it is not sufficient to establish causation.

COMMUNICATION

A report in a death penalty case typically serves a number of purposes. Using a model described by Goldstein and Goldstein (2010) related to reports focusing on the validity of *Miranda* rights assessments, a report in a death penalty case serves to:

- Organize massive amounts of data into a logical, orderly summary
- Structure direct examination testimony
- Provide an available reference or "prompt" when asked questions during testimony
- Function as a document that can be reviewed by the trier of fact during deliberations
- Fulfill some jurisdictional requirements that a report or "proffer" of testimony be submitted prior to testimony

In addition, a defense attorney may request a report long before testimony is scheduled. The report may serve as a vehicle to convince the prosecutor's office that the death penalty is not appropriate or cannot be achieved in the specific case. Similarly, the defense attorney may use the report as part of an attempt to reach a pretrial agreement for a sentence less than death in exchange for the client's guilty plea.

A report of a forensic mental health evaluation with respect to capital sentencing is essentially similar to the reports prepared in other forensic mental health contexts. Typically, it consists of components such as the following:

- Identification of the legal and factual background and the questions to be addressed
- Qualifications of the examiner (highlighting those pertinent to the case at hand)
- Basis of the opinion (list of all data reviewed and analyzed, including the interview, psychological testing, records reviewed, others interviewed, and relevant literature)
- Formulation of the opinion, supported by detailed discussion showing how the data were analyzed
- Statement allowing for supplementation of the opinion through review and analysis of additional data

Reports should follow the general principles of the ethics of the profession and conform to the standard of practice in the field (Cunningham, 2010; Heilbrun, Grisso, & Goldstein, 2009). The expert's opinion should be formulated so as not to be vulnerable to a *Daubert/Kumho* challenge (Bursztajn, Pulde, Pirakitikulr, & Perlin, 2006).

Given this overall structure, the following considerations can be helpful to keep in mind, both for effective communication of forensic evaluations generally and as they apply specifically to capital sentencing evaluations.

AVOIDING RIGIDITY OF FORMAT

Avoid the reality or appearance of generic reports. In an area of evaluation such as this, where dynamic observation and analysis are essential, no two reports can be the same. The structure of the report needs to flow from the presentation and analysis of data rather than be imposed a priori.

STATUTORY CRITERIA FOR SENTENCING DETERMINATIONS

Include reference to the statutory criteria (mitigating factors, aggravating factors, and any others) that were considered. Indicate which of those criteria the forensic mental health evaluation will address. In formulating the opinion, make clear whether the defendant has been found to meet each of the applicable criteria.

FRAMING THE OPINION

It is important to frame the opinion with a clear summary statement at the beginning of the report and—especially when the analysis is long and complex—at the end. Attorneys and judges may lose the forest for the trees, and it can be very helpful to pull together the main themes of the analysis in a paragraph that can be readily understood as a whole.

AVOIDING OVERRELIANCE ON THE DSM

DSM-IV diagnoses may appear as applicable (in some cases as required) in the report; often, they are better woven into than superimposed on the analysis of data. Even in clinical diagnostics, the DSM is most useful for identifying symptom patterns on an aggregate rather than individual basis, and for taking diagnostic "snapshots" rather than understanding the developmental processes and personal narratives that lead up to the commission of a capital crime. The authors of the DSM have made clear in the introduction to the manual that the application of its diagnostic categories to forensic questions is fraught with uncertainties, which are amplified by the diverse cultural backgrounds of the defendants to be evaluated. Moreover, some of the major diagnostic categories have been created by panels on which clinicians with ties to pharmaceutical companies have been heavily represented (Cosgrove & Bursztajn, 2009). For these reasons, the mechanistic use of DSM categories risks obscuring more than it illuminates.

DOCUMENTING ANALYTICAL REASONING

Avoid offering *ipse dixit* opinions (i.e., those that take the form "It is so because I say it is so") (Gutheil & Bursztajn, 2003). In a methodologically reliable evaluation, the data are documented and the analysis is set forth so that other evaluators can accept or take issue with the reasoning on which the opinion is based. A report that clearly and carefully presents the kinds of observation, contextual interpretation, and convergent validity that this chapter has attempted to illustrate is one that can increase the likelihood of a just outcome in capital litigation.

REFERENCES

American Academy of Clinical Neuropsychology. (2001). Policy statement on the presence of third-party observers in neuropsychological assessments. *Clinical Neuropsychologist, 15,* 433–439.

American Academy of Psychiatry and the Law. (2005). *Ethics guidelines for the practice of forensic psychiatry.* Bloomfield, CT: Author.

American Psychological Association. (2002a). Ethical principles of psychologists and code of conduct. *American Psychologist, 57,* 1060–1073.

American Psychological Association. (2002b). *Guidelines on multicultural education, training, research, practice, and organizational change for psychologists.* Washington, DC: Author.

Appelbaum, P. S., & Gutheil, T. G. (2007). *Clinical handbook of psychiatry and the law* (4th ed.). Philadelphia, PA: Lippincott Williams & Wilkins.

Barefoot v. Estelle, 463 U.S. 880 (1983).

Bursztajn, H. J., Feinbloom, R. I., Hamm, R. M., & Brodsky, A. (1990). *Medical choices, medical chances: How patients, families, and physicians can cope with uncertainty.* New York, NY: Routledge.

Bursztajn, H. J., Harding, H. P., Gutheil, T. G., & Brodsky, A. (1991). Beyond cognition: The role of disordered affective states in impairing competence to consent to treatment. *Bulletin of the American Academy of Psychiatry and the Law, 19,* 383–388.

Bursztajn, H. J., Pulde, M. F., Pirakitikulr, D., & Perlin, M. (2006). *Kumho* for clinicians in the courtroom: Inconsistency in the trial courts. *Medical Malpractice Law & Strategy, 24*(2), 1–7.

Bursztajn, H. J., Scherr, A. E., & Brodsky, A. (1994). The rebirth of forensic psychiatry in light of recent historical trends in criminal responsibility. *Psychiatric Clinics of North America, 17,* 611–635.

Butcher, J. N., Dahlstrom, N. G., Graham, J. R., Tellegen, A., & Kaemmer, B. (2001). *MMPI-2: Manual for administration and scoring* (2nd ed.). Minneapolis, MN: University of Minnesota Press.

Committee on Ethical Guidelines for Forensic Psychologists. (1991). Specialty guidelines for forensic psychologists. *Law and Human Behavior, 15,* 655–665.

Commonwealth v. Lamb, 365 Mass. 265 (1974).

Constantinou, M., Ashendorf, L., & McCaffery, R. (2002). When the third-party observer of a neuropsychological evaluation is an audio-recorder. *Clinical Neuropsychologist, 16*, 407–412.

Cosgrove, L., & Bursztajn, H. J. (2009). Towards credible conflict of interest policies in clinical psychiatry. *Psychiatric Times, 26*, 40–41.

Cramer, R. J., & Brodsky, S. L. (2007). Undue influence or ensuring rights? Attorney presence during forensic psychology evaluations. *Ethics & Behavior, 17*, 51–60.

Cunningham, M. D. (2010). *Best practices in forensic mental health assessment: Evaluations for capital sentencing.* New York, NY: Oxford University Press.

Cunningham, M. D., & Goldstein, A. M. (2003). Sentencing determinations in death penalty cases. In I. B. Weiner (Series Ed.) & A. M. Goldstein (Vol. Ed.), *Comprehensive handbook of psychology: Vol. 11. Forensic psychology* (pp. 407–436). Hoboken, NJ: John Wiley & Sons.

Day, M., & Manschreck, T. C. (1988). Delusional (paranoid) disorders. In A. M. Nicholi, Jr. (Ed.), *The new Harvard guide to psychiatry* (pp. 296–308). Cambridge, MA: Belknap Press of Harvard University Press.

Death Penalty Information Center (2009, December 2). Available from www.deathpenaltyinfo.org.

Diamond, B. L. (1994). The simulation of sanity. In J. M. Quen (Ed.), *The psychiatrist in the courtroom: Selected papers of Bernard L. Diamond, M.D.* (pp. 157–167). Hillsdale, NJ: Analytic Press.

Eisenberg, J. R. (2004). *Law, psychology, and death penalty litigation.* Sarasota, FL: Professional Resource Press.

Estelle v. Smith, 451 U.S. 454 (1981).

Frederick, R. I. (1997). *The Validity Indicator Profile.* Minneapolis, MN: National Computer Systems.

Goldstein, A. M. (2001). Objectivity in capital cases. *American Psychology-Law Society News Letter, 21*, 8–9, 14.

Goldstein, A. M. (Ed.). (2003). *Comprehensive handbook of psychology: Vol. 11. Forensic psychology.* Hoboken, NJ: John Wiley & Sons.

Goldstein, A. M. (Ed.). (2007). *Forensic psychology: Emerging psychology: Emerging topics and expanding roles.* Hoboken, NJ: John Wiley & Sons.

Goldstein, A. M., & Goldstein, N. E. S. (2010). *Best practices in evaluating capacity to waive Miranda rights.* New York, NY: Oxford University Press.

Goldstein, A. M., Morse, S. J., & Shapiro, D. L. (2003). Evaluation of criminal responsibility. In I. B. Weiner (Series Ed.) & A. M. Goldstein (Vol. Ed.), *Comprehensive handbook of psychology: Vol. 11. Forensic psychology* (pp. 381–406). Hoboken, NJ: John Wiley & Sons.

Gregg v. Georgia, 428 U.S. 153 (1976).

Grisso, T. (1986). *Evaluating competencies: Forensic assessments and instruments*. New York, NY: Plenum Press.

Grisso, T. (2003). *Evaluating competencies: Forensic assessments and instruments* (2nd ed.). New York, NY: Plenum Press.

Gutheil, T. G., & Bursztajn, H. J. (1986). Clinicians' guidelines for assessing and presenting subtle forms of patient incompetence in legal settings. *American Journal of Psychiatry, 143*, 1020–1023.

Gutheil, T. G., & Bursztajn, H. J. (2003). Avoiding ipse dixit mislabeling. *Journal of the American Academy of Psychiatry and the Law, 31*, 205–210.

Heilbrun, K. (1992). The role of psychological testing in forensic assessment. *Law and Human Behavior, 16*, 257–272.

Heilbrun, K. (2001). *Principles of forensic mental health assessment*. New York, NY: Kluwer Academic/Plenum Press.

Heilbrun, K., DeMatteo, D., Marczyk, G., & Goldstein, A. M. (2009). Standards in practice and care in forensic mental health assessments: Legal, professional and principles-based considerations. *Psychology, Public Policy and Law, 14*, 1–26.

Heilbrun, K., Grisso, T., & Goldstein, A. M. (2009). *Foundations of mental health assessment*. New York, NY: Oxford University Press.

Heilbrun, K., Warren, J., & Picarello, K. (2003). Third party information in forensic assessment. In I. B. Weiner (Series Ed.) & A. M. Goldstein (Vol. Ed.), *Comprehensive handbook of psychology: Vol. 11. Forensic psychology* (pp. 69–86). Hoboken, NJ: John Wiley & Sons.

Lockett v. Ohio, 438 U.S. 586 (1978).

Melton, G., Petrila, J., Poythress, N., & Slobogin, C. (2007). *Psychological evaluations for the courts: A handbook for mental health professionals and lawyers* (3rd ed.). New York, NY: Guilford Press.

Morey, L. C. (1991). *The Personality Assessment Inventory professional manual*. Odessa, FL: Professional Assessment Resources.

New Hampshire Crim. Code 630: 5VI.

Otto, R. K., Slobogin, C., & Greenberg, S. A. (2007). Legal and ethical issues in accessing and utilizing third-party information. In Goldstein, A. M. (Ed.), *Forensic psychology: Emerging topics and expanding roles* (pp. 190–208). Hoboken, NJ: John Wiley & Sons.

Porter v. McCollum, 558 U.S. (2009).

Rogers, R., Bagby, R. M., & Dickens, S. E. (1992). *Structured Interview of Reported Symptoms (SIRS) and professional manual*. Odessa, FL: Professional Assessment Resources.

Shealy, C., Cramer, R. J., & Pirelli, G. (2008). Third party presence during criminal forensic evaluations: Psychologists' opinions, attitudes, and practices. *Professional Psychology: Research and Practice, 39*, 561–569.

Simon, R. I. (1996). "Three's a crowd": The presence of third parties during the forensic psychiatric examination. *Journal of Psychiatry & Law, 24*, 3–25.

Smith, A. (1982). *Symbol Digit Modalities Test manual*. Los Angeles, CA: Western Psychological Services.

Tombaugh, T. N. (1996). *TOMM: The Test of Memory Malingering*. North Tonawanda, NY: Multi-Health Systems.

Trenerry, M. R., Crosson, B., DeBoe, J., & Leber, W. R. (1989). *Stroop Neuropsychological Screening Test manual*. Odessa, FL: Psychological Assessment Resources.

Wechsler, D. (1999). *WASI manual*. San Antonio, TX: Harcourt Assessments.

Wechsler, D. (2008). *WAIS-IV: Administration and scoring manual*. San Antonio, TX: Pearson.

Wechsler, D. (2009). *Wechsler Individual Achievement Test—Third Edition (WIAT-III) manual*. San Antonio, TX: Psychological Corporation.

Wilkinson, G. S., & Robertson, G. J. (2006). *Wide Range Achievement Test-4 professional manual*. Lutz, FL: Professional Assessment Resources.

Woodson v. North Carolina, 428 U.S. 280 (1976).

Zinberg, N. E. (1985). The private versus the public psychiatric interview. *American Journal of Psychiatry, 142*, 889–894.

CHAPTER 8

Diminished Capacity in Federal Sentencing

GERALD COOKE and HENRY R. BLEIER

INTRODUCTION

Section 5K2.13 of the United States Sentencing Guidelines (USSG; United States Sentencing Commission, 1987) allows for a sentence below the applicable guideline range if the defendant committed the offense while suffering from a significantly reduced mental capacity. The phrase "significantly reduced mental capacity" is further defined as: "means the defendant, although convicted, has a significantly impaired ability to a) understand the wrongfulness of the behavior comprising the offense or to exercise the power of reason; or b) control behavior that the defendant knows is wrongful." Such a departure below the applicable guideline range is known as a "diminished capacity" departure.

Initially, such a departure was limited to "nonviolent offenses," but after November 1, 1998, 5K2.13 no longer made reference to a "nonviolent offense," allowing for the possible inclusion of violent offenses. However, 5K2.13 does have exceptions: "the Court may not depart below the applicable guideline range if (1) the significantly reduced mental capacity was caused by the voluntary use of drugs or other intoxicants, (2) the facts and circumstances of the defendant's offense indicate a need to protect the public because the offense involved actual violence or a serious threat of violence, or (3) the defendant's criminal history indicates a need to incarcerate the defendant to

171

protect the public." Also, the extent of the departure should reflect the extent to which the reduced mental capacity contributed to the commission of the offense.

The guidelines were formulated to deal with disparity in sentencing. This disparity existed across geographic regions, jurisdictions, and characteristics of defendants (e.g., gender, race, ethnic origin). The disparity resulted in markedly different sentences for defendants committing similar criminal acts. A grid was developed based on offense level and criminal history points, which defined a range in months of imprisonment. For example, for an offense level of 15 and 0–1 criminal history points, the range is 18 to 24 months. However, for the same offense level, if the defendant fell in the highest criminal history category (13 or more points) the sentence range is 41 to 51 months.

The guidelines were meant to be mandatory, with judicial discretion limited to the range unless the judge presented an explicit rationale for an upward or downward departure from the guidelines. Appeals of such cases led to a gradual move away from the guidelines being mandatory, to the current situation in which the guidelines are "advisory" (*Apprendi v. New Jersey*, 2000; *Blakely v. Washington*, 2004; *United States v. Booker and Fanfan*, 2005). Thus, the sentencing court must consider the guidelines, but can tailor the sentence in light of other factors as well. This takes into consideration individual factors, but also can be grouped into categories.

Interestingly, a starting point is the collection of "prohibited or discouraged departures" in Chapter 5H of the guidelines, which are no longer prohibited. These include the age of the defendant; mental and emotional conditions; physical condition, including drug and alcohol addictions; family ties and responsibilities; military, civic, charitable, and public service; lack of guidance as a youth; and similar circumstances. In addition, the guidelines recognize downward departure for criminal behavior that deviates markedly from the defendant's previous behavior (5K2.20). This is known as an "aberrant behavior" departure. However, to qualify for this departure, not only must there be a "marked deviation" from an otherwise law-abiding life, but also the crime must have been committed without significant planning and must have involved limited duration.

Another category that is a basis for downward departure is for "coercion and duress" (5K2.12). Under this standard, departure is warranted if the criminal act was committed because the defendant was threatened with physical injury or damage to personal property, but did not rise to the level of a complete defense at the guilt phase of the trial. However, this section specifically prohibits financial incentives as a means of coercion. Another basis for downward departure is "extraordinary post offense rehabilitation efforts." This provides for those persons who have pursued treatment for a mental disorder, including drug and sexual addictions and, typically, have demonstrated both determination and progress in treatment. There is also a catch-all phrase in the guidelines "... mitigating circumstance of a kind or to a degree that was not adequately taken into consideration by the Sentencing Commission." This opens the door to admit anything from history and testing.

Forensic mental health experts have played a role in federal downward departure cases both when the guidelines were mandatory and since they have become advisory (Krauss & Goldstein, 2007). For some types of departure criteria, such as offering an opinion that there is a mental disorder that resulted in a significantly reduced mental capacity, the use of a mental health expert is obvious. Similarly, where "postoffense rehabilitation efforts" are the issue, the value of testimony by the treating mental health professional is obvious, but experts have been used in other, less obvious areas as well. For example, in cases where the issues of family ties and responsibilities have been raised, the expert can testify to the parenting behaviors and capacities of the defendant, the strength of the parent–child(ren) bond(s), and the impact on the family of a lengthy sentence of imprisonment. Similarly, where the issue is "coercion and duress" a personality profile of the defendant may explain how this individual's psychological makeup made him or her more susceptible to coercion and duress.

PREPARATION

The Referral

The referral for a forensic mental health evaluation in a diminished capacity case typically comes from the defendant's attorney or federal public defender. However, the evaluation may be requested by the assistant United States attorney (AUSA) prosecuting the case in anticipation that the defense will raise the issue. The process differs somewhat depending on whether the source of the referral is defense or prosecution. The typical situation is a defense referral, so that will be discussed in more detail later. If the referral is from the prosecution, and the defense has already had an evaluation performed, it is necessary to obtain the report and raw test data of the defense evaluator before conducting a prosecution evaluation. This enables the forensics expert for the prosecution to assess the basis of the downward departure opinion and to determine whether it follows from the interview, history, and test information. The evaluator for the prosecution should also have all the records that were made available to the defense evaluator.

When the referral comes from the defense attorney or federal defender, it is necessary for the forensics expert, in discussion with the attorney, to determine the presumed basis for the downward departure so that the evaluator can choose the appropriate test instruments and/or interview format so that the relevant issues will be thoroughly assessed. The offenses for which a downward departure motion is made vary somewhat. Among the most frequent categories are drug possession and possession with intent to distribute, possession and/or distribution of child pornography, and embezzlement and fraud.

TIMING

Typically, the diminished capacity issue is not raised until after the defendant has decided to plead guilty or has taken the case to trial and been found guilty. Thus, guilt is assumed and the evaluation focuses only on sentencing issues. When possible, the evaluation should not take place until after a Post Sentencing Investigation Report (PSR) has been compiled by the U.S. Probation Office. These reports include not only offense information but also criminal record and personal history information. It is important to have this in hand so that if there are discrepancies between what the defendant tells the evaluator and what is in the PSR, these can be addressed as part of the interview. If the PSR is not yet available, and discrepancies are apparent when it is received, it may be necessary to reinterview the defendant.

As with any forensic evaluation, there may or may not be significant time constraints. Some defense attorneys contact the forensic expert well in advance. Unfortunately, others do not do so until a sentencing date has already been set and time is short. When the defendant is incarcerated at a federal detention center (FDC) or a county facility that contracts to house federal defendants, the attorney must notify the facility in writing (with a copy to the forensic expert) of the planned date for evaluation. Facilities vary in terms of how much advance notice they require. This ranges from a few days to as much as 3 weeks. Also, FDCs require that each forensic expert submit an application yearly to be allowed entry, and approval of these usually requires at least 3 weeks. Thus, unless the forensic expert is already approved for the facility, this time requirement also has to be considered.

DETERMINING THE PROPER FOCUS AND SCOPE OF THE EVALUATION

Determining the focus and scope depends on the presumptive basis for the downward departure. A thorough history regarding childhood is always important, in and of itself, as well as related to any one of the specific reasons for downward departure. Any evidence of childhood emotional abuse, physical abuse, sexual abuse, and/or neglect, and how this related to the development of the defendant's personality, and possibly to involvement in the offense, is often considered by the court.

If the basis of the downward departure motion is based on mental illness, then this requires not only review of past treatment records, interviewing about the dates, length, and type of treatment, but also psychological testing (specific recommendations for testing will be included in the "Data Collection" section of this chapter). If physical condition is a factor, then medical records will be needed. If family ties and responsibilities are a factor, then the evaluation should include not only the defendant, but also his/her spouse and children. Any records, such as parent–teacher conference reports, that document involvement in school and other child-related activities should be obtained. If public service or similar issues are a factor, then any records (e.g., awards) and character reference letters should be obtained.

A criminal history record should always be obtained (and is always part of the PSR), and is particularly relevant to establish the "aberrant behavior" departure. Work records, character references, and so on can be used to establish the prior prosocial lifestyle required for this departure. For "coercion and duress" psychological testing, as well as an exploration of the history of the relationship with the codefendants, is needed. If the issue is postoffense rehabilitative efforts, treatment records and letters from treating professionals may be needed.

COLLATERAL INFORMATION

The need for various records, depending on the nature of the downward departure motion, has been addressed. These would include the PSR or other official version of the offense such as the indictment, criminal investigation records of both the local jurisdictions and the FBI (known as 302s), transcripts of Internet chats, and so on. The forensics expert should also obtain, where possible and relevant, mental health treatment records, school records, Children and Youth Service records, work records, and character reference letters. Often, the attorney will obtain these directly. If not, the defendant may have to sign a release for the forensics expert to obtain them. Collateral information is crucial in these cases, as in all forensics cases, because of the potential for the defendant to misrepresent the past history to be more favorable to the case (Otto, Slobogin, & Greenberg, 2007).

ETHICAL ISSUES

Both the American Academy of Psychiatry and the Law (AAPL, 2005) and the American Psychological Association (APA, 2002) have ethics codes that apply to forensic as well as other cases. Forensic psychologists are also guided by the Specialty Guidelines for Forensic Psychologists (Committee on Ethical Guidelines for Forensic Psychologists, 1991). Some aspects of the ethical issues are worthy of particular emphasis. If the evaluation is being conducted at the request of the defense attorney, then it is protected by the attorney–client privilege, since the forensics expert is an agent of the attorney, and the client should be informed of this. In the forensics context, the doctor–patient privilege does not apply. If the evaluation is being conducted at the request of the AUSA, then there is no privilege or confidentiality. The defendant must be informed of this and told that all information will be provided to the AUSA. Defendants should also be informed that this is an evaluation and they are not being seen for treatment purposes. This "psychological *Miranda* warning" also serves to cover informed-consent issues.

An issue that has become increasingly important as general clinicians attempt to move into the forensics arena is the examiner's competency. "Forensics experts" obtain that title by virtue of special training and/or experience. In addition, as in any forensics case, competency to practice involves a knowledge of the applicable legal standards. These standards evolve with federal case law. Thus, the forensics expert should request of the attorney copies of the most recent cases having to do with the specific downward departure issue.

DATA COLLECTION

INTERVIEWING THE DEFENDANT

The forensics expert needs to obtain basic identifying information. The interview then moves on to exploration of background history that includes, but is not limited to, family background (including perception of relationships with parents, siblings, the presence of any abuse, etc.), educational history, occupational history, social history, substance abuse, current medication, prior arrest history, medical history, and psychiatric/psychological treatment history. The interviewer then explores the offense-related behavior. Future plans for treatment, both during incarceration and after, as well as plans upon eventual release, should also be discussed. Though in some cases this may be years off, it can provide helpful information regarding how appropriate and realistic such plans are, and may also help to address the issue of potential for recidivism.

The examiner should complete a formal mental status examination to include: a description of the examinee's appearance, attitude and manner, form and content of speech, with reference to the presence or absence of formal thought disorder, distorted or false beliefs, and false perceptions in any domain. The examinee's mood should be identified and the range of affects displayed during the interview, commenting on their congruence or lack of it with the content and themes of the narrative. The presence of any suicidal or violent ideation should be noted, with reference to the degree of intent expressed and the presence or absence of any plans. Examinees' personal perspectives on the motivation for their behavior and the implications of their actions for themselves or others should be solicited to assess insight and judgment. Cognitive performance may be assessed as described below.

The standard evaluation of mental status includes an assessment of the examinee's "decision-making capacity." Its determination is of critical importance in the medical setting, where this cognitive function must be confirmed by the physician as a prerequisite element for the receipt of informed consent to proceed with tests and/or procedures. If deficient or absent, a surrogate decision maker must be identified to provide substituted consent.

The elements of decision-making capacity include appreciation, reasoning, and the ability to express a preference. Appreciation is demonstrated by the patient's being able to communicate an understanding of the fact that he/she is suffering from a particular illness, the risks and benefits associated with various treatment options, and the likely outcome of the illness without treatment.

Reasoning is demonstrated by the patient's ability to rationally manipulate the information available to him/her and to integrate this material with his/her attitudes, preferences, and personal values in the service of deciding what to do. Ability to express a preference is demonstrated by the patient's ability to communicate his/her decision. Clinicians often refer to a "sliding scale of capacity" to advert to the fact that decisions about care may be more or less "weighty," and that the higher the risks associated with a given intervention and the less likely the probability of benefit, the more "capacity" is required to make the decision (Appelbaum & Grisso, 1988).

In this context, the determination of "diminished capacity" is a bedside judgment made by the examiner. However, this model can also be applied to diminished capacity in federal sentencing. Here, as in the medical setting, the clinician must assess how any deficits in reasoning or decision-making capacity contributed to the commission of the offense.

PSYCHOLOGICAL TESTING

There are hundreds of psychological tests and most psychologists have a favored battery. This chapter identifies one example while acknowledging that there are numerous alternatives.

If the issue for downward departure involves mental retardation, it usually arises when one of the codefendants in a federal drug conspiracy case is a "mule" who is recruited only to follow simple instructions involving delivering drugs and returning with money. The most recent version of the Wechsler Adult Intelligence Scale (WAIS) is the WAIS-IV (Wechsler, 2008). Mental retardation is partially defined as an intelligence quotient (IQ) below 70. The Peabody Picture Vocabulary Test-IV (PPVT-IV; Dunn & Dunn, 2007) is also useful because it does not require a verbal response and provides age equivalents.

The other prong of the definition involves impairment in at least two of the following areas of adaptive behavior: communication, self-care, home living, social/interpersonal skills, use of community resources, self-direction, functional academic skills, work, leisure, health, and safety. Some of the information relevant to adaptive impairment can be obtained from interview and records. For academic skills, an optimal measure is the Wide Range Achievement Test, Fourth Edition (WRAT4; Wilkinson & Robertson, 2006). This generates percentiles and grade and educational level equivalents in word reading, spelling, sentence comprehension, and math computation. The Vineland Adaptive Behavior Scales-II (Sparrow, Balla, & Cicchetti, 2005) or similar measures can be used to assess adaptive functioning in communication, social skills, self-care, and other areas.

Often at issue in diminished capacity testimony is the defendant's potential for recidivism, also known as risk assessment. A useful actuarial measure is the Psychopathy Checklist—Revised (PCL-R; Hare, 2003). This measure of psychopathy has been found to be predictive of risk of future sexual and/or aggressive acting out. The Inventory of Offender Risk, Needs and Strengths (IORNS; Miller, 2006) compares the defendant's risk of criminal and violent behavior to other offenders. The particular strength of this measure is that in addition to static historical risk factors, which have been the main focus of prior actuarial measures, it also evaluates dynamic needs (e.g., criminal orientation and attitudes, alcohol and drug problems, aggression, etc.) and protective strengths, which are characteristics related to protection from crime involvement (better decision making, improved anger control, training and education that aids in employment), and support from friends and family.

Personality testing is often a critical component of a diminished capacity evaluation. There are many objective personality tests available, but the two most widely used are the Minnesota Multiphasic Personality Inventory-2 (MMPI-2; Butcher, Graham, Ben-Porath, Tellegen, & Dahlstrom, 2001) and the Minnesota Multiphasic Personality Inventory-2 Restructured Form (MMPI-2-RF; Ben-Porath &

Tellegen, 2008). Both tests provide validity scales to assess the consistency of responding and test-taking attitude, that is, over- or underreporting of pathology. There are also basic clinical scales and additional special scales to assess a wide range of psychopathology and personality dynamics. Many of the profiles relate to potential for acting out of impulses as compared to inhibition and control of impulses. Thus, information can be provided to the court regarding how this defendant's personality structure developed, the contribution of psychopathology to the offense, amenability to treatment, and the potential for criminal behavior and for future aggressive and/or sexual acting out.

Many individuals who end up in the legal system have experienced numerous traumatic events in their lives such as child sexual abuse or physical abuse. Some have developed symptoms of posttraumatic stress disorder. A measure specific to this is the Detailed Assessment of Posttraumatic Stress (DAPS; Briere, 2001).

Projective personality testing—as opposed to the objective personality testing discussed above—has both strengths and weaknesses. The Rorschach Inkblot Technique has been used by many clinicians since the 1920s. The Exner System (Exner, 2005) was developed to aid in its interpretation. However, in recent years a body of literature has been developed (Wood, Nezworski, Lilienfeld, & Garb, 2003) that questions the validity of this system. Thus, the Rorschach must be used with caution. However, because it is unstructured and ambiguous, it will sometimes reveal information about the defendant's functioning that is missed by the structured personality tests. Similarly, the Incomplete Sentences Blank (Rotter, 1977) may generate additional information regarding needs, fears, attitudes, and perception of interpersonal relationships.

DATA INTERPRETATION

Establishing a mental disorder is a necessary but not sufficient condition for addressing the issue of a significantly reduced mental capacity for a diminished capacity defense. Thus, the first step in data interpretation is to integrate the history, interview, mental status examination, record review, and testing in order to establish one or more diagnoses utilizing the criteria from the *Diagnostic and Statistical Manual of Mental Disorders*, 4th edition, Text Revision

(DSM-IV-TR; American Psychiatric Association, 2000). While Axis II (personality disorders) is not ruled out as a basis for reduced mental capacity, it is rare that a diminished capacity defense is success-ful unless an Axis I mental disorder can be established. Cases have found significantly reduced mental capacity in the context of bipolar disorder, schizophrenic disorder, major depressive disorder, obsessive–compulsive disorder, posttraumatic stress disorder, and even just "psychological problems" (Ellis, 1999).

The next and crucial step is to analyze how this disorder con-tributed to the commission of the offense. Specifically, the analysis has to spell out how the illness impacted on either or both of the criteria, that is, for the first prong, how the illness impaired the defendant's ability to understand the wrongfulness of the behavior comprising the offense or to exercise the power of reason. Several cases (e.g., *United States v. McBroom*, 1998) provide further guidance on addressing this criterion: the analysis has to address whether the person is unable to absorb information in the usual way or to exercise the power of reason. For the second prong, "a significantly impaired ability . . . to control behavior that the defendant knows is wrongful," the analysis has to demonstrate that the mental illness compromised the defendant's ability to control his behavior. Unless the link between the mental illness and the offense behavior is established, the diminished-capacity defense is not likely to succeed.

The issue of drug use is complicated because, under the guide-lines, a diminished-capacity downward departure is excluded if the significantly reduced mental capacity was caused by the voluntary use of drugs or other intoxicants. If the *only* diagnosis that can be established is drug dependence/abuse or alcohol dependence/ abuse, then the criteria for diminished capacity is not met. However, many defendants use drugs and/or alcohol to self-medicate for an underlying illness. If the underlying illness can be established, then the drug/alcohol use does not preclude the defense.

COMMUNICATION

REPORT ORGANIZATION

While different mental health professionals approach report organi-zation somewhat differently, there are certain elements that must be presented. Generally, the report begins with an explanation of why the evaluation is being conducted and for what legal purposes. The next paragraph addresses when and where the defendant was seen and what procedures were utilized; for example, "In addition to a clinical interview and history, the following tests were administered. . . . " It is helpful for the reader of the report if the mental health professional provides for each of the tests a capsule definition of the purpose of the test, though not at this point the findings specific to the defendant.

Some evaluators list what records were reviewed at this point in the report. Others proceed to the findings and list the records near the end of the report just before the conclusions. In either case, in addition to listing the records reviewed, it is important to summarize the content of each record, particularly when related to the issue of significantly reduced mental capacity. For example, if a prior mental health record documented a diagnosis relevant to that issue, it should be indicated here.

Typically, the next paragraph addresses behavioral observations and mental status. This should include the degree of cooperation, observations about dress and hygiene, and any clinical evidence of depression, anxiety, anger, thought disorder, and/or psychosis. Here or elsewhere should be a statement to the effect that the evaluator explained the limits of confidentiality and privilege to the defendant and that these were understood.

The next paragraph addresses the defendant's history. This is generally broken down into a number of subcategories, including childhood and family history (including any physical, sexual, or emotional abuse or neglect as a child), education, occupation, social history, substance abuse, arrest history, medical history, and psychiatric/psychological treatment history. The latter should include an account of past and present medication.

The next portion of the report may address the circumstances and events leading up to the defendant's offense behavior, though this is not always included in the report. Since the defendant has already announced his/her intention to plead guilty or has been found guilty at trial, some attorneys prefer that the offense behavior be omitted, as it may raise legal implications if it is not consistent with the terms of the guilty plea agreement. However, in most cases, this information does not have to be included in order to establish the context for demonstrating how the mental illness contributed to the commission of the offense.

The report then presents test results. Typically, this is broken down into three sections. The first section addresses the intellectual findings. Special attention needs to be given to covering problems with attention, concentration, memory, reasoning, judgment, and problem solving, as these may be directly related to the issue of the defendant's ability to reason and absorb information. The second section deals with the actuarial measures. While risk assessment is not technically part of the criteria for diminished capacity, judges almost inevitably want to know the defendant's potential for recidivism, as it does relate to the exclusionary factor of whether the defendant's functioning indicates a need to protect the public. The next section presents the results of the personality testing. The most widely used personality tests have validity scales. There should be a statement about how the defendant approached the testing, for example, whether he/she was candid and straightforward or whether there was evidence of overreporting of symptoms (malingering, exaggeration) or underreporting of symptoms (guardedness, defensiveness). Information about personality functioning should not be presented test by test; rather, there should be an integrated analysis of the defendant's personality structure, personality dynamics, and symptoms. Where these factors are directly relevant to the criteria, they should be described in detail.

The next portion presents the diagnoses that follow from the interview, history, and testing, and discusses how they relate to the forensic referral question. This is where the mental health professional ties together the mental illness, its relationship to the commission of the offense, and specifically how it impacts on one or both of the prongs.

While recommendations for treatment are not directly relevant to the referral issue, they are important in terms of risk of future dangerousness. This may include a recommendation for individual or group therapy, drug or alcohol rehabilitation, anger management, and so on. If the individual poses a risk of suicidal or aggressive behavior, this should be addressed here as well. The extent to which that treatment will affect future functioning should also be included.

Either at the beginning or end of the report, a statement should be made that the findings and conclusions are held to a reasonable degree of psychiatric/psychological/scientific certainty.

TESTIMONIAL ISSUES

Typically, the defense attorney will determine whether the report is sufficient or whether the mental health professional will need to testify in person. This will depend on whether the AUSA agrees that the report can be admitted, and essentially waives the right to cross-examine the expert. It may also depend on the judge and whether the expert is known to the judge. Some judges feel that since they have the report, the testimony is redundant. However, others want the opportunity for the AUSA to cross-examine the expert, and still others have questions they wish to ask of the examiner. Also, the attorney will make a judgment whether live testimony may be more compelling than just submitting the written report.

If testimony is required, it is essential that the attorney and the expert prepare so that the expert knows what questions the attorney will be asking and in what order, and the attorney knows what the expert's responses will be. The attorney and the expert should also prepare together for anticipated areas of cross-examination.

Many texts, chapters, and articles have discussed the role of the expert witness on the witness stand (e.g., Hess, 2006). A detailed presentation of issues related to testimony is beyond the scope of this chapter. However, in testifying about diminished capacity, as in other areas of testimony, the witness must approach the role as that of an educator of the court, rather than an advocate for the defendant, and present information in a candid and honest manner.

REFERENCES

American Academy of Psychiatry and the Law. (2005). Ethics guidelines for the practice of forensic psychiatry. Bloomfield, CT: Author.

American Psychiatric Association. (2000). *Diagnostic and statistical manual of mental disorders* (4th ed., Text Revision). Washington, DC: Author.

American Psychological Association. (2002). Ethical principles and code of conduct. *American Psychologist, 57,* 1060–1073.

Appelbaum, P. S., & Grisso, T. (1988). Assessing patients' capacities to consent to treatment. *New England Journal of Medicine, 319,* 1635–1638.

Apprendi v. New Jersey, 530 U.S. 466 (2000).

Ben-Porath Y. S., & Tellegen, A. (2008). *Minnesota Multiphasic Personality Inventory-2 Restructured Form (MMPI-2-RF).* Minneapolis, MN: NCS Pearson.

Blakely v. Washington, 542 U.S. 296 (2004).

Briere, J. (2001). *Detailed Assessment of Posttraumatic Stress (DAPS).* Odessa, FL: Professional Assessment Resources.

Butcher, J. N., Graham, J. R., Ben-Porath, Y. S., Tellegen, A., & Dahlstrom, W. G. (2001). *Minnesota Multiphasic Personality Inventory-2 (MMPI-2).* Minneapolis, MN: NCS Pearson.

Committee on Ethical Guidelines for Forensic Psychologists. (1991). Specialty guidelines for forensic psychologists. *Law and Human Behavior, 15,* 655–665.

Dunn, L. M., & Dunn, D. M. (2007). *Peabody Picture Vocabulary Test-IV (PPVT-IV).* Minneapolis, MN: Pearson.

Ellis, A. (1999). Answering the "why" question: The powerful departure ground of diminished capacity, aberrant behavior, and post-offense rehabilitation. *Federal Sentencing Reporter, 11,* 322–327.

Exner, J. E. (2005). *The Rorschach: A comprehensive system.* San Francisco, CA: John Wiley & Sons.

Hare, R. D. (2003). *Psychopathy Checklist—Revised (2nd ed.) (PCL-R).* North Tonawanda, NY: Multi-Health Systems.

Hess, A. K. (2006). Serving as an expert witness. In A. K. Hess & I. B. Weiner (Eds.), *Handbook of forensic psychology* (3rd ed., pp. 652–697). Hoboken, NJ: John Wiley & Sons.

Krauss, D. A., and Goldstein, A. M. (2007). The role of forensic mental health experts in federal sentencing proceedings. In A. M. Goldstein (Ed.), *Forensic psychology: Emerging topics and expanding roles* (pp. 359–384). Hoboken, NJ: John Wiley & Sons.

Miller, H. A. (2006). *Inventory of Offender Risk, Needs and Strengths (IORNS).* Lutz, FL: Professional Assessment Resources.

Otto, R., Slobogin, C., & Greenberg, S. A. (2007). Legal and ethical issues in assessing and utilizing third party information. In A.M. Goldstein (Ed.), *Forensic psychology: Emerging topics and expanding roles* (pp. 190–205). Hoboken, NJ: John Wiley & Sons.

Rotter, J. (1977). *Incomplete Sentences Blank.* San Antonio, TX: Psychological Corporation.

Sparrow, S. S., Balla, D. A., & Cicchetti, D. V. (2005). *Vineland Adaptive Behavioral Scale-II.* Bloomington, MN: Pearson Assessments.

United States v. Booker and Fanfan, 543 U.S. 220 (2005).

United States v. McBroom, 991 F. Supp 445 (D.N.J. 1998).

United States Sentencing Commission. (1987). *Federal sentencing guidelines manual*. Eagan, MN: WestGroup.

Wechsler, D. (2008). *Wechsler Adult Intelligence Scale—Fourth Edition (WAIS-IV)*. San Antonio, TX: NCS Pearson.

Wilkinson, G. S., & Robertson, G. J. (2006). *Wide Range Achievement Test* (4th ed.). Lutz, FL: Professional Assessment Resources.

Wood, J. M., Nezworski, T. M., Lilienfeld, S. O., & Garb, H. N. (2003). *What's wrong with the Rorschach?* San Francisco, CA: Jossey-Bass.

CHAPTER 9

Testimonial Capacity

RANDY K. OTTO, ROBERT L. SADOFF, and AMANDA M. FANNIFF

INTRODUCTION

COMMON LAW

Testimonial capacity—also referred to as competence to testify—references an individual's ability to provide sworn testimony in a civil or legal proceeding. Historically, questions about testimonial capacity were typically raised with respect to children or persons with mental disorders or substance abuse problems, sometimes referred to in statutes and case law as being impaired by *immaturity, insanity, idiocy, lunacy,* or *drunkenness* (see, e.g., Code of Alabama 12-121-162-165). Questions about the capacity of these groups stemmed from concerns that juries had little ability to assess the accuracy of statements made by such persons (Strong et al., 1999). When the issue of a particular witness's capacity to testify was raised, courts typically considered one or more of the following factors: whether the proffered witness (1) was able to incorporate and make sense of what transpired at the time of the event about which he or she was to testify, (2) possessed an adequate memory of the events in question at the time he or she was to testify, (3) was able to relay that information in a coherent manner at the time he or she was to testify, and (4) appreciated the significance of the oath and associated requirement to tell the truth at the time he or she was to testify. "The principle . . . is that the child shall be sufficiently mature to receive correct impressions by her senses, to recollect and narrate intelligently, and to appreciate the moral duty to tell the truth" (*State v. Segerberg*, 1945; also see Strong et al., 1999, for an expanded discussion).

FEDERAL LAW

Federal Rule of Evidence (FRE) 601 directs that, "Every person is competent to be a witness except as otherwise provided in these rules. However, in civil actions and proceedings, with respect to an element of a claim or defense as to which State law supplies the rule of decision, the competency of a witness shall be determined in accordance with State law." This rule essentially eliminated all grounds for barring a potential witness on the basis of incapacity, except in a subset of civil cases in which state law impacts the legal claim—in which case state law regarding witness competence controls.

There are, of course, a number of FREs that go toward limiting the testimony of proffered witnesses. For example, FRE 602 directs that the witness must have personal knowledge of matters about which he or she will testify, FRE 401 directs that all evidence— including testimony—be relevant, and FREs 605 and 606, in barring judges and jurors from testifying in cases in which they are involved, refer to their "competency." These rules and associated exclusions do not involve the capacity or ability of witnesses to testify, but rather, their knowledge regarding the matters about which they will testify, the relevance of what they know, or their independence. Rule 602 can be applied in such a manner as to exclude the testimony of potential witnesses if there is a disruption in their perception or memory of the events in question, and rules regarding relevancy and the oath can also be utilized to exclude witnesses despite a presumption of competency (Colquitt & Gamble, 1995).

The rationale for the general presumption included in the FREs is laid out in the accompanying Notes of the Advisory Committee:

> Standards of mental capacity have proved elusive in actual application. . . . Discretion is regularly exercised in favor of allowing the testimony. A witness wholly without capacity is difficult to imagine. The question is one particularly suited to the jury as one

of weight and credibility, subject to judicial authority to review the sufficiency of the evidence.

The adoption of FRE 601 and its equivalent at the state level has been described as "the culmination of an historical trend in the law toward permitting virtually all witnesses to testify" (Colquitt & Gamble, 1995, p. 157).

The thrust of FRE 601 is that—at least in all federal criminal proceedings and some federal civil proceedings—all proffered witnesses are permitted to testify and concerns about capacity, when raised, go to the credibility or weight of their testimony (e.g., *U.S. v. Allen*, 1997; *U.S. v. Raineri*, 1980). In some jurisdictions, statutes specifically governing the testimony of children have also been enacted to ensure that their testimony is almost always allowed[1] (e.g., 18 U.S.C. § 3509.c; Valenti-Hein & Schwartz, 1993). This being said, it is possible that a mental health professional could be called to testify in a federal proceeding about the impairments that a particular witness might have and how that could affect the capacity to form, remember, and relate impressions of what is being testified to, or the capacity to understand and appreciate the significance of the oath (see, e.g., *Isler v. Dewey*, 1876; *State v. Armstrong*, 1950). Such testimony might also occur in a state that, like the federal courts, does not allow challenges to testimonial capacity. In these cases, however, expert testimony would not serve to inform a decision about testimonial capacity since all witnesses are permitted to testify, but rather, would provide the legal decision maker with information so that it can make a more informed decision about the weight the witness's testimony should be accorded.

STATE LAW

As is always the case, there is some variability in the law across states, and practitioners should be familiar with the law of the jurisdiction in which they practice. Consistent with the spirit of

---

1. Special conditions applied to enable the testimony of children, such as the use of closed circuit testimony, and evaluations conducted to inform the application of such conditions are beyond the scope of the current chapter, as these determinations are made based on the potential for harm or trauma to a child witness rather than concerns about the child's testimonial capacity.

FRE 601, some states allow all proffered witnesses to testify assuming basic requirements like relevance and personal knowledge are met (see, e.g., Maryland Rules of Evidence 5-601, Illinois Compiled Statutes 735, Article VII, Part 1). A number of states, however, while presuming the competence of all witnesses, allow for this presumption to be overcome and their proffered testimony to be barred based upon certain proof. As summarized in Table 9.1, factors most commonly considered by the court include the person's ability to appreciate the significance of the oath and relay information in a way that is understandable. The rules of Kentucky and Pennsylvania, which are the most comprehensive, are offered for consideration.

> Every person is competent to be a witness except as otherwise provided in these rules or by statute. A person is disqualified to testify as a witness if the trial court determines that he: (1) Lacks the capacity to perceive accurately the matters about which he proposes to testify; (2) Lacks the capacity to recollect facts; (3) Lacks the capacity to express himself so as to be understood, either directly or through an interpreter; or (4) Lacks the capacity to understand the obligation of a witness to tell the truth. (Kentucky Rules of Evidence 601)

> Every person is competent to be a witness except as otherwise provided by statute or in these Rules. A person is incompetent to testify if the Court finds that because of a mental condition or immaturity the person: (1) is, or was, at any relevant time, incapable of perceiving accurately; (2) is unable to express himself or herself so as to be understood either directly or through an interpreter; (3) has an impaired memory; or (4) does not sufficiently understand the duty to tell the truth. (Pennsylvania Code Title 225 Article VI, Rule 601)

PREPARATION FOR THE EVALUATION

COMPETENCE

When conducting any type of forensic evaluation mental health professionals must have an adequate understanding of the legal rule or test, identify those psychological factors that are relevant, and determine how to best assess them (Grisso, 1986, 2003). As indicated

Table 9.1

State Laws Regarding Testimonial Capacity

State	Identified Psycholegal Capacities					Identified Predicates		
	Competence With No Identified Psycholegal Exceptions	Ability to Form Impressions of Events	Ability to Form Memories of Events	Ability to Relay Impressions at Trial	Appreciation of Oath at Trial	Age	Mental Disorder	Substance Abuse
Alabama					✓	✓	✓	✓
Alaska					✓			
Arizona[i]		✓		✓		✓	✓	
Arkansas	✓							
California				✓	✓			
Colorado	✓							
Connecticut		✓	✓	✓	✓			
Delaware	✓							
D.C.	✓							
Florida				✓	✓			
Georgia					✓	✓	✓	✓
Hawaii				✓	✓			
Idaho		✓		✓	✓	✓	✓	
Illinois	✓							
Indiana							✓	
Iowa	✓							
Kansas				✓	✓			

(continued)

Table 9.1
(Continued)

State	Identified Psycholegal Capacities					Identified Predicates		
	Competence With No Identified Psycholegal Exceptions	Ability to Form Impressions of Events	Ability to Form Memories of Events	Ability to Relay Impressions at Trial	Appreciation of Oath at Trial	Age	Mental Disorder	Substance Abuse
Kentucky		✓	✓	✓	✓			
Louisiana	✓							
Maine		✓	✓	✓	✓			
Maryland	✓							
Massachusetts	✓							
Michigan			✓	✓	✓			
Minnesota			✓	✓	✓	✓	✓	✓
Mississippi	✓							
Missouri		✓		✓	✓	✓	✓	
Montana				✓	✓			
Nebraska	✓							
Nevada	✓							
New Hampshire		✓	✓	✓	✓			
New Jersey				✓	✓			
New Mexico	✓							
New York[ii]				✓	✓	✓	✓	
North Carolina				✓	✓			
North Dakota	✓							

State						
Ohio			✓			
Oklahoma	✓		✓		✓	
Oregon	✓		✓		✓	
Pennsylvania	✓	✓	✓	✓	✓	
Rhode Island	✓			✓		
South Carolina	✓		✓	✓		
South Dakota	✓					
Tennessee	✓		✓			
Texas	✓		✓		✓	
Utah	✓	✓	✓		✓	
Vermont	✓		✓			
Virginia	✓		✓			
Washington	✓		✓		✓	✓
West Virginia	✓					
Wisconsin	✓					
Wyoming	✓					

Note: In some cases, the general rule of competency has been enacted in state Rules of Evidence subsequent to the passage of statutes excluding witnesses in the manner noted above. In such instances, the Rules of Evidence create a presumption of competence (e.g., Alabama; see Colquitt & Gamble, 1995, for a discussion). Also, case law may clarify the competency requirements in each state, but a case law review is beyond the scope of this chapter. Finally, examiners should always familiarize themselves with the specific law in their jurisdiction.

[i]Arizona's rules regarding witnesses differ for criminal and civil trials. According to ARS §13-4061: "In any criminal trial every person is competent to be a witness." According to ARS §12-2202: "The following shall not be witnesses in a civil action: 1. Persons who are of unsound mind at the time they are called to testify. 2. Children under ten years of age who appear incapable of receiving just impressions of the facts respecting which they are to testify, or of relating them truly."

[ii]New York's Rules of Criminal Procedure (§ 60.20.2) direct that if a witness is unable to understand the nature of an oath either due to mental disease or defect or due to young age (under 9), they may provide "unsworn evidence if the court is satisfied that the witness possesses sufficient intelligence and capacity to justify the reception thereof."

earlier, such evaluations are typically precipitated by allegations that the proffered witness has some impairment (e.g., limitations associated with youth, symptoms of mental disorder, intellectual limitations) that limits his/her ability to provide helpful testimony. Thus, before taking on such an evaluation, the examiner should make sure that he/she has an adequate understanding of the disorder or deficit that is considered to impair the person's capacity. For example, a psychiatrist not skilled in working with children might turn down a referral for evaluation of a child whose developmental limitations are thought to impair testimonial capacity, or a psychologist who knows little about dementia and its manifestations might choose not to evaluate a proffered witness whose capacity to testify might be impaired by such.

ACCESSING COLLATERAL INFORMATION

One of the many ways in which forensic mental health evaluations differ from therapeutic pursuits is in the examiners' reliance on collateral information or third-party documentation (Heilbrun, Warren, & Picarello, 2003; Melton et al., 2007; Otto, Slobogin, & Greenberg, 2007). Mental health professionals who have the opportunity to review collateral information that describes aspects of the examinees' emotional, behavioral, and cognitive functioning that may be relevant to the psycholegal issues at hand can conduct more focused and presumably more complete evaluations than those who do not. Although the retaining attorney will sometimes provide relevant documents or materials, in other cases the examiner may have to request collateral information because its relevance is not obvious to the attorney. Although review of these supplemental sources of information before the evaluation is probably ideal, in some cases their existence and/or potential relevance may only be discovered during or after evaluation of the proffered witness. In such cases, they should be accessed and reviewed afterwards, with follow-up contact with the examinee occurring if necessary.

The different types of records that may contain, or third parties who may provide, information that is helpful to forming judgments about the examinee's capacity to testify are varied. A helpful rule of thumb is that examiners should consider any collateral information that provides data about aspects of the examinee's emotional, behavioral, and cognitive functioning that can impact relevant testimonial capacities—with a particular focus on disorders or impairments and specific aspects of testimonial capacity that have been raised as concerns by the referral source or others.

DATA COLLECTION AND INTERPRETATION

GATHERING RELEVANT HISTORY

We suggest that, after informing the examinee about the nature and purpose of the evaluation, the examiner gather a complete history that addresses *relevant* aspects of the examinee's developmental, family, social, educational, vocational, medical, psychological/psychiatric, and legal histories. Beginning the evaluation with this inquiry may assist in reducing the examinee's anxiety and establishing rapport. Furthermore, this inquiry may help identify aspects of the examinee's emotional, behavioral, and cognitive functioning that can affect testimonial capacity and are therefore deserving of more focused inquiry and assessment.

ASSESSING PAST AND CURRENT EMOTIONAL, BEHAVIORAL, AND COGNITIVE FUNCTIONING

The forensic examiner's task, put most simply, is to assess and describe the examinee's testimonial capacity (as defined by the law of the particular jurisdiction) and identify the cause of or basis for any limitations or impairments. Thus, accurate assessment of the examinee's current and past emotional, behavioral, and cognitive functioning is necessary, when deficits in testimonial capacity are observed, in order to identify the cause and, in some cases, recommend interventions that may remedy or attenuate the limitations.

As is the case in all forensic and therapeutic evaluations, mental health professionals should use a variety of assessment strategies including gathering a relevant history (see earlier discussion) and clinical assessment. Psychological, medical, or neurological testing may prove of value in some cases, largely depending on the emotional, behavioral, cognitive, or other factors that may affect the examinee's capacity to testify. For example, if it is alleged that the proffered witness's capacity to understand and appreciate the significance of the oath is impaired by intellectual deficits, then administering measures of intelligence and adaptive behavior may be helpful. Alternatively, if concerns are raised regarding the proffered witness's vulnerability to suggestive questioning, then administration of measures that address this issue (e.g., the Gudjonsson Suggestibility Scale) (Gudjonsson, 1992) may prove valuable.

Two primary cautions are indicated given the potential for the misuse of testing. First, psychological, medical, or neurological testing can provide information only about the conditions or functioning that may be responsible for any observed deficits. No psychological, medical, or neurological test provides any data about the specific abilities that are relevant to the capacity to testify. An examiner can conclude little about an examinee's appreciation of the oath and associated responsibilities simply based on an obtained full-scale intelligence quotient (IQ) estimate of 79. Similarly, test results indicating that a potential witness has enlarged ventricles or an "abnormal EEG" reflect nothing about her ability to accurately remember and recount what occurred on the evening in question. Second, given the many ways in which proffered witnesses may differ with respect to their capacity to testify, along with the multitude of conditions or concerns that might impair testimonial capacity, we do not believe that a particular set or "battery" of tests or measures should be employed routinely when evaluating a person's testimonial capacity. Rather, decisions about test administration should be made based on case-specific factors.

Next to address is the examinee's capacity to testify. This inquiry, of course, is largely shaped by the law in the jurisdiction in which the evaluation takes place. In this section, we discuss strategies for the clinical assessment and interpretation of four primary psycholegal capacities that are considered in various jurisdictions when the issue of testimonial capacity is raised.

CAPACITY TO INCORPORATE AND UNDERSTAND WHAT TRANSPIRED

Assessing the examinee's ability to observe and make sense of what occurred may be the most challenging capacity to assess since this inquiry focuses on the examinee's ability at a prior point in time (i.e., when the event in question occurred). In some cases, it may be alleged that the examinee's capacity was impaired as the result of a more enduring or static factor (e.g., limited intelligence, developmental "limitations" associated with age). In these circumstances, assessment of the examinee's *current* capacity to incorporate and make sense of events may provide information relevant to drawing conclusions about his or her capacity at the earlier point in time—particularly in those cases in which (1) not much time has transpired between the incident in question and the evaluation or (2) there is no reason to believe that the underlying impairment and associated limitations have changed over time. In other cases, the impairment cited as responsible for limited capacity may be more acute or dynamic (e.g., intoxication, acute psychotic symptoms). In these cases, assessment of the examinee's *current* capacity to incorporate and make sense of events may not provide much information helpful to drawing conclusions about his/her abilities when the events of interest occurred.

In some cases, collateral information may prove helpful with respect to informing the examiner about the examinee's functioning and adjustment at and around the time of the incident in question. For example, arrest reports, hospital emergency department records, or witness statements might provide relevant information about the proffered witness's level of intoxication, whereas, in other cases, health care records or accounts offered by treating mental health professionals may provide information that goes toward understanding the severity of psychiatric symptoms experienced by the proffered witness at and around the time of the relevant event.

Memory for the Event in Question and Capacity to Relay the Experience Coherently

At the risk of oversimplifying matters, memory is complicated (Wells & Loftus, 2003). Accurate depiction of past events requires adequate perception, integration, encoding, retrieval, and recitation. Interference or disruption at any stage can affect the person's ability to offer an accurate recounting of what occurred. Although one's memory for the event in question and the ability to recount it in a way that is understandable to others are clearly separate phenomena, because it is difficult to tease them apart for purposes of assessment, they are discussed together here.

Assessment of these two components is focused on the examinee's current mental state. Although impairment at and around the time of the event is relevant to memory integration and encoding, any memory deficits are likely to present similarly in an evaluation regardless of whether the memory problem relates to early-stage (e.g., encoding) or later-stage (e.g., retrieval) disruptions.

In all cases, the examiner should discuss with the examinee his/ her understanding of and memory for the events that transpired, with an eye toward assessing the examinee's ability to offer a coherent and logical recitation of the events. The examiner should begin by asking the examinee to offer a recounting of the event at issue, and then follow this with nonleading questions that encourage elaboration (since essentially all testimony is facilitated by questions that are presented during direct examination and cross-examination). When making this inquiry, it is important to determine whether, in the period between when the event occurred and when the evaluation takes place, the examinee has discussed and considered the matter with others, including attorneys, law enforcement officers, social service professionals, friends, family members, and other mental health professionals. This is because what the examinee reports as his/her understanding can be shaped by such interactions. Perhaps the best example of this is in the case of child witnesses who have undergone repeated interviews. In cases in which the child has been repeatedly interviewed about the event in question (e.g., by parents, law enforcement officers, attorneys, protective service investigators), it may be difficult to ascertain how much of what he/she offers has been affected by such.

As noted above, concerns are sometimes raised about the person's ability to offer a coherent account of the relevant events that transpired due to "developmental limitations" associated with age or current psychiatric or cognitive impairments. Opinions about the proferred witness's capacities can be formed primarily by assessing his/her ability to relate an organized account of what occurred to, and answer questions presented by, the examiner. The examiner, however, must realize that there may be important differences between the examination room and courtroom. For example, the examiner—as a result of his/her expertise, knowledge, and style— may interact with the examinee in ways that facilitate communication, and are different from attorneys' behavior during direct examination and cross-examination. Similarly, the examinee may feel less anxious during the examination than he/she would during actual testimony (much like the examiner). As a result, the examiner should begin by asking the individual to provide a description of the events of interest, followed by providing questions designed to facilitate the examinee's description (akin to what might occur during both direct examination and cross-examination). Then, the examiner can consider implementing strategies designed to make the assessment setting approximate more closely the feel of testifying in court via direct examination and cross-examination (e.g., asking questions in a more challenging manner, demonstrating some skepticism of what is offered by the examinee, asking compound questions). Finally, if the examiner does note some limitations when the examinee is questioned in a more adversarial manner, he/she can provide strategies that the attorneys and court could use to facilitate the proffered witness's capacity (e.g., asking noncompound questions, using age-appropriate vocabulary, ensuring that the witness is acquainted with the courtroom and process of testifying before the trial or hearing).

Concerns may be raised about the proffered witness's acquiescence or suggestibility. In such cases, most important is that the examiner determine whether the examinee previously discussed the matter with others (also see above). In cases in which discussions between the proffered witness and a third party have been documented (e.g., by way of a recorded interview or deposition), review of the interchange may also prove helpful insofar as the examiner can determine the degree to which previous interviewers may have contaminated the witness's recollection. Concerns about susceptibility to suggestibility are often raised when the proffered witness is a child who is to testify about abuse or neglect that he/she is alleged to have endured. A summary of the extensive literature regarding the ability of children to recount and testify about past events, their vulnerabilities, and the best ways to question them is well beyond the scope of this chapter. (The interested reader is directed to Lyon, in press; Goodman & Melinder, 2007; Ceci & Bruck, 1999; and Goodman & Bottoms, 1993, for review and commentary regarding this topic.)

The examiner can also gather information relevant to, and form opinions about, matters of acquiescence and suggestibility by assessing the examinee's general level of susceptibility. For example, with some persuasion, can the examinee be convinced that he takes a medication that he does not, or had an experience that the examiner knows did not occur (e.g., a trip to Hollywood the preceding year)? If so, then the examinee's susceptibility to suggestive questioning around the issues of interest may be of concern—either during the course of investigations by third parties or while on the witness stand. It is important that the examiner, when "testing the limits" of suggestibility or acquiescence, *not* discuss matters related to the event of interest given that such a tactic could affect the examinee's memory for and understanding of the event in question.

CAPACITY TO APPRECIATE THE SIGNIFICANCE OF THE OATH AND THE REQUIREMENT TO TELL THE TRUTH

Many states identify the ability to appreciate the significance of the oath and resulting requirement to tell the truth as necessary to testify. This, obviously, is a present-mental-state issue and can be affected both by static (e.g., age, intellectual disability) and dynamic (acute psychiatric symptomatology) factors. Although the other capacities are all focused, in some way, on the examinee's abilities as they relate to understanding, remembering, and recounting the event at issue, this capacity is not related to case-specific factors, but rather, the examinee's understanding and appreciation of one important and narrow aspect of the legal process.

Assessment of this capacity may be the most straightforward of all. The examiner should begin by asking the proffered witness if he or she is familiar with the oath and its significance. If the examinee reports having no knowledge or understanding of the oath, it is important to provide this information since ignorance does not necessarily reflect incapacity. The inquiry should focus on the examinee's (1) ability to discern telling the truth from telling a falsehood (including appreciation of the concept of intentionality), (2) understanding and appreciation of the oath and the duty it imparts to tell the truth, and (3) appreciation of the ramifications of not testifying truthfully. The examiner can provide the examinee with statements that are accurate along with statements that are inaccurate, with different reasons for the inaccuracy (i.e., intention to deceive versus a mistaken fact) and assess his/her descriptions of them as truthful, untruthful, or mistakes/errors. The examiner can also consider the examinee's ability to make these distinctions after gaining an understanding of the potential witness's testimony, and then asking him/her questions about such. For example, the examiner can ask if it would be the truth, a lie, or a mistake if the witness testified that the assailant had a gun when he knew that the assailant did not, or it would be the truth, a lie, or mistake if the witness who was examined by a nurse testified that she was examined by a doctor because she was confused about such.

The examiner can also assess the witness's appreciation of the oath and related issues by inquiring about what the witness would be willing to do to obtain a desired case outcome. For example, would the witness be willing to lie when testifying about what time she remembers hearing her murdered spouse scream if it would ensure the defendant's conviction? This being said, it is important to note that lying while under oath—or a willingness to lie while under oath—does not *necessarily* reflect a lack of appreciation of the oath and the associated duty to testify truthfully. That is, there are certainly some witnesses who, although they appreciate the legal duty to tell the truth while testifying, choose not to do so. These persons who indicate a willingness to commit perjury should not be considered to lack capacity.

It is also important to consider the proffered witness's understanding of the implications of lying. Typically, this can be addressed by assessing the examinee's appreciation of the significance of the proceedings and the outcomes or penalties for perjury. As previously indicated, ignorance does not necessarily reflect incapacity. Accordingly, if the examinee is ignorant about the sanctions for perjury, the examiner should provide this information and then assess the examinee's understanding and appreciation of this matter further.

COMMUNICATING FINDINGS AND OPINIONS

Of course, general principles that apply to all forensic evaluation practices control in these evaluations as well (see, e.g., American Academy of Psychiatry and the Law, 2005; Committee on Ethical Guidelines for Forensic Psychologists, 1991). Examiners should (1) document their work carefully, with the expectation that it will be scrutinized by others (e.g., attorneys, the court, other experts); (2) offer a complete account of sources of information they considered when conducting the evaluation; (3) richly describe aspects of the examinee's emotional, behavioral, and cognitive functioning that may impact the relevant psycholegal capacities; (4) provide a detailed account of the examinee's relevant psycholegal capacities; and (5) in cases in which some limitations in capacity are observed, identify the basis or cause, as well as whether any type of treatment, intervention, or accommodation by officers of the court (e.g., use of non-compound questions, non-leading questions, or basic vocabulary) could remedy or attenuate the observed deficits.

Finally, because it is ultimately a legal issue, examiners should avoid offering opinions about whether the examinee does or does not have the capacity to testify. Rather, in order to be most helpful to the court, examiners should offer the rich descriptions referenced here so that the judge can reach an informed decision about the examinee's capacities, based on an understanding of the legal standard in combination with the particular abilities of the proffered witness.

REFERENCES

American Academy of Psychiatry and the Law. (2005). *Ethics guidelines for the practice of forensic psychiatry*. Bloomfield, CT: Author.

Ceci, S. J., & Bruck, M. (1999). *Jeopardy in the courtroom: A scientific analysis of children's testimony*. Washington, DC: American Psychological Association.

Colquitt, J. A., & Gamble, C. W. (1995). From incompetency to weight and credibility: The next step in an historic trend. *Alabama Law Review, 47*, 145–176.

Committee on Ethical Guidelines for Forensic Psychologists. (1991). Specialty guidelines for forensic psychologists. *Law and Human Behavior, 15*, 655–665.

Goodman, G. S., & Bottoms, B. L. (1993). *Child victims, child witnesses: Understanding and improving testimony*. New York, NY: Guilford Press.

Goodman, G. S., & Melinder, A. (2007). Child witness research and forensic interviews of young children: A review. *Legal and Criminological Psychology, 21*, 1–19.

Grisso, T. (1986). *Evaluating competencies: Forensic assessments and instruments*. New York, NY: Plenum.

Grisso, T. (2003). *Evaluating competencies: Forensic assessments and instruments* (2nd ed). New York, NY: Kluwer Academic/Plenum Press.

Gudjonsson, G. (1992). *The psychology of interrogations, confessions, and testimony.* New York, NY: Wiley.

Heilbrun, K. H., Warren, J., & Picarello, K. (2003). Use of third party information in forensic assessment. In A. Goldstein (Ed.), *Forensic psychology* (pp. 69–86). Hoboken, NJ: John Wiley & Sons.

Isler v. Dewey, 75 N.C. 466 (1876).

Lyon, T. D. (in press). Investigative interviewing of the child. In D. N. Duquette & A. M. Haralambie (Eds.), *Child welfare law and practice* (2nd ed.). Denver, CO: Bradford.

Melton, G. B., Petrila, P., Poythress, N. G., Slobogin, C., Lyons, P., & Otto, R. K. (2007). *Psychological evaluations for the courts: A handbook for mental health professionals and lawyers* (3rd ed.). New York, NY: Guilford Press.

Otto, R. K., Slobogin, C., & Greenberg, S. A. (2007). Legal and ethical issues in accessing and utilizing third-party information. In A. M. Goldstein (Ed.), *Forensic psychology: Emerging topics and expanding roles* (pp. 190–205). Hoboken, NJ: John Wiley & Sons.

State v. Armstrong, 62 S.E.2d 50 (1950).

State v. Segerberg, 41 A.2d 101 (1945).

Strong, J. W., Brown, K. S., Dix, G. E., Imwinkelried, E. J., Kaye, D. H., Mosteller, R. P., & Roberts, E. F. (1999). *McCormick on evidence.* St. Paul, MN: West Group.

U.S. v. Allen J., 127 F.3d 1292 (10th Cir. 1997).

U.S. v. Raineri, 91 F.R.D. 159 (W.D. Wis. 1980).

Valenti-Hein, D. C., & Schwartz, L. D. (1993). Witness competency in people with mental retardation: Implications for prosecution of sexual abuse. *Sexuality and Disability, 11,* 287–294.

Wells, G. L., & Loftus, E. F. (2003). Eyewitness memory for people and events. In I. B. Weiner (Series Ed.) & A. M. Goldstein (Vol. Ed.), *Comprehensive handbook of psychology: Vol. 11. Forensic psychology* (pp. 149–160). Hoboken, NJ: John Wiley & Sons.

CHAPTER 10

Postconviction Proceedings

ADERONKE OGUNTOYE and ERIC Y. DROGIN

INTRODUCTION

Postconviction proceedings address "the full range of issues regarding persons who have been found guilty of—or have pled guilty to—state or federal criminal charges" (Drogin, 2007, p. 385). According to King and Hoffman (2008), this lengthy and often confusing process may involve (1) "a direct appeal, which can include multiple proceedings in several different courts that are all considering the same questions"; (2) "state postconviction proceedings, where again, the same questions may be considered several times by several different courts"; and (3) "federal *habeas corpus* review, where constitutional questions are raised in the district court, then in the federal court of appeals, and often in yet another certiorari petition to the U.S. Supreme Court" (pp. 433–434).

At the center of this three-ring (or more) procedural circus may be the postconviction evaluator and his/her opinions on the defendant's likely mental state—both currently and at various points in the past. Did the defendant receive proper treatment and evaluations prior to trial, such that the court was properly informed on such issues as trial competency, criminal responsibility, diminished capacity, or the competency to confess? Have proper accommodations been made for identified learning disabilities in the course of prison-based programs to address anger management or sexual offense recidivism? Under what circumstances and conditions will the release of an insanity acquittee or parole be appropriate? What of competency to confess for someone who may be diagnosable with mental retardation or severe mental illness?

For a new trial to be granted, "the defendant must show that counsel's performance was deficient," and must further demonstrate that "counsel's errors were so serious as to deprive the defendant of a fair trial" (*Strickland v. Washington*, 1984, p. 687). One error counsel is charged with avoiding is the failure to conduct a proper review of mental health issues at the pretrial level (*Rompilla v. Beard*, 2005). A number of resources exist to guide counsel in this regard, including the American Bar Association's *Criminal Justice Mental Health Standards* (1989) and *Guidelines for the Appointment and Performance of Defense Counsel in Death Penalty Cases* (2003), and the National Legal Aid and Defender Association's *Performance Guidelines for Criminal Defense Representation* (1995). The postconviction evaluator's opinion on the adequacy of the mental health records in question will assist the courts in determining whether counsel's review should have led to a different approach prior to or during trial (Poortinga & Guyer, 2006).

It will come as no surprise that such proceedings are hotly contested. "The postconviction world is a complex and important one" (Taslitz, 2009, p. 4), in which prosecutors who have won a favorable decision in a criminal matter "fear that opposing counsel's performance will be characterized, mistakenly or inaccurately, as ineffective assistance," and that "an unclear record will not expose the defendant's self-serving mischaracterization of his attorney's work" (Kreeger & Weiss, 2004, p. 18), while bearing a heavy and very public burden of prosecutorial discretion in these matters (Green & Yaroshefsky, 2009). Defense attorneys, already informed that "indigent defense in this country is in a state of crisis" (Primus, 2009, p. 6), and concerned that incompetent defendants may be waiving postconviction relief inappropriately (Ellis & Bussert, 2010; Larson & Gruzdinskas, 2008; Shapiro, 2008) or denied an effective review outright (Miller, 2008), may be encouraged to consider their own postconviction roles "indispensible" (Kilborn, 2010, p. 315) and may feel that when a motion for a new trial is granted they should at least be "thankful for small favors" (Mogin, 2003, p. 26). The postconviction evaluator will find many ways to be useful to counsel on either side of the aisle.

PREPARATION

Buttressed by a thorough review of pertinent statutes, case law, regulations, and ethical guidelines—in addition to sufficient discussion with current counsel (Gutheil & Simon, 2002)—the best preparation for engaging in a postconviction evaluation depends on identifying, locating, and engaging with the components of two broad sources of information: records and interviewees. The manner in which such preparation is conducted can have very significant legal and ethical implications (Otto, Slobogin, & Greenberg, 2007). Drogin (2006, pp. 30–32) has outlined these components as updated and encapsulated next.

RECORDS

Records originate from a dauntingly diverse array of sources, and gathering such materials in the context of postconviction evaluation is further complicated by the fact that the sole existing copy of a document may now reside in the files of any of a number of prior experts—some of whom may be hostile or even unknown to current counsel. Following is a detailed description of various classes of records frequently sought in this context.

- *Legal records.* In addition to reviewing all pertinent pretrial and other legal records, the postconviction evaluator should determine the extent to which such records were utilized by counsel or by a retained mental health expert either prior to or during the sentencing phase. Did prior counsel obtain—or attempt to obtain—evaluations of trial competency, criminal responsibility, or diminished capacity where applicable?
- *Educational records.* School records may contain such elements as academic grades, program placement reviews, and disciplinary files, in addition to reports of counseling sessions, cognitive testing, and personality assessment. When it comes to postconviction assessment of malingering, school records may become particularly relevant as the court is encouraged to consider how likely it is that currently claimed disorders have been "faked" since childhood.

- *Treatment records.* These documents are created for different reasons and with a different mindset than forensic evaluation records, which adds to their credibility when it can be established that they were not developed in contemplation of litigation. Treatment providers will not serve as forensic experts but may nonetheless be featured as informative and persuasive fact witnesses concerning the criminal defendant's condition during a specified period of time.
- *General medical records.* Medical records may provide evidence that can support, or refute claims made elsewhere. There is often documentation of learning disabilities, physical disabilities, or brain injuries that could affect decision-making capability. There may also be documentation of claims of abuse and employment history as well as relevant family history. As with treatment records, these documents were also likely created independent of forensic evaluation.
- *Military records.* Military records may be among the most difficult to obtain, due to bureaucratic hurdles and that the fact that such documents are often condensed or discarded with an ease not found in civilian practice. One obvious context for reviewing these records is in cases featuring allegations of post-traumatic stress disorder. In some cases, the defendant may have been characterized as unfit or only marginally fit for duty, either at induction or later.
- *Forensic records.* Records generated by other forensic evaluators can help to confirm or disconfirm one's own hypotheses, and the adequacy of these documents and the forensic work they reflect are often the substantial focus of postconviction proceedings. To what extent may identified errors in test administration or test scoring contribute to faulty pretrial forensic conclusions, to challengeable legal rulings, and eventually to postconviction relief?
- *Discovery.* Postconviction evaluators may question the utility of sifting through hundreds or even thousands of pages of pretrial discovery material—including, for example, dozens of pictures of the footpath leading to scene of the crime. There is considerable value in gaining a fuller understanding of the overall case—in addition to the ability to represent that one reviewed the entire file, and not just those portions identified by counsel as potentially relevant.

- *Work product.* Postconviction evaluations are best conducted on the basis of immersion in how the case in question actually "worked." Counsel will naturally be concerned with the extent to which this might somehow serve to impair the privilege that prevents the compelled disclosure of certain materials. It is important to reach a preliminary understanding with counsel concerning the potential ramifications of reviewing materials not typically considered to be "discoverable."

INTERVIEWEES

A criminal defendant's personal profile does not spring to life solely from a battery of psychological tests; in fact, reliance on such a strategy by experts at trial may be the reason that postconviction relief was sought in the first place. Multiple valuable sources of insight may have been passed over, and some will be ready—even eager—to share what they know about the defendant. Following is a detailed description of various categories of potential interviewees.

- *Teachers.* In many cases, teachers have served as virtual surrogate parents for criminal defendants—particularly when abuse histories wind up playing a pivotal role in understanding how matters have come to their current pass. Teacher recollections may wind up being the most important source of information concerning an individual's academic struggles and achievements, in situations in which school records are no longer accessible.
- *Family.* Family members are a rich source of interview data for the criminal defendant over the full course of his/her life. Such data may include developmental milestones, childhood injuries and diseases, sibling relationships, and family histories for both genetically and environmentally influenced medical and psychological conditions. Family members may also possess diaries, school records, photographs, and other forms of useful documentation.
- *Friends.* A criminal defendant's childhood, adolescent, and adult peer relationships can provide valuable insight into behavioral inclinations, lifestyle preferences, emotional needs, and stated desires. It may be that the enlistment of friends will encourage and enable the criminal defendant to take a

more active role in the postconviction process, as a result of behavioral modeling and a desire to reopen or affirm personal connections.

- *Police.* The arresting or interrogating officer may possess the most accurate, detailed, and compelling recollections of an exculpatory as well as inculpatory nature. The results may be among the most critical for as accurate a *post hoc* assessment of criminal responsibility as may be possible some years after the incident in question. To what extent was this information sought out, reviewed, and reported by the pretrial forensic examiner?
- *Jailers.* These persons may be the only reason why the criminal defendant is still alive. Close and meaningful personal contacts are often developed between jail personnel and the persons under their care and direction. Correctional staff persons also may have developed voluminous records concerning mental status and emotional functioning that would not have made their way into trial counsel's file without a specific request or a court order for production.
- *Witnesses.* Years after the fact, these persons may still possess vivid memories of crime scene incidents that were insufficiently tapped by investigators and even overlooked entirely. Permission should be sought from counsel or the courts before undertaking to interview witnesses, particularly those who may still have an active role to play in postconviction proceedings, and great care should be taken that questioning is not perceived as intimidating.

DATA COLLECTION

THE POSTCONVICTION EXAMINATION

In some cases, the postconviction evaluator will conduct one or more clinical forensic examinations. This may be because no examinations were performed during the pretrial phase of legal proceedings, or because postconviction counsel has perceived a need to challenge—or to enshrine—the results of earlier examinations. A fresh look at the examinee may consist of any combination of three different components: interview, observation, and psychological testing (Parry & Drogin, 2000).

- *Interview.* The postconviction evaluator should bear in mind that the examinee may have been through multiple prior interviews and thus may approach this latest task with a mixture of frustration on the one hand and hard-won savvy on the other. Under these circumstances, it is often useful to inquire of the examinee just what he or she remembers from earlier clinical and forensic encounters. How long were the prior examinations? What did they cover? What tests were administered? Did the examiner merely rely on tests and answers to some competency oriented questions, or was a full personal history taken? (Mason, 2004). Interviews conducted without the benefit of prior reports are likely to require additional time so that relevant states of mind at earlier intervals can be queried.
- *Observation.* Prior evaluations may or may not reflect detailed descriptions of what the examinee's demeanor, appearance, or exhibited behaviors comprised at earlier junctures (Parry & Drogin, 2007). To what extent do current observations comport with—or contradict—what existing records have documented? Is it possible that any differences are attributable—for better or for worse—to the examinee's current conditions of confinement? It may be that the incarcerated examinee is now free of a substance abuse or dependence condition that was exerting a marked effect upon his or her earlier presentation. The experienced postconviction evaluator is, of course, aware that substance abuse may occur within correctional facilities. If introductions are made by postconviction counsel, how does the examinee interact with his/her current attorney?
- *Psychological testing.* The decision of what measures to administer—or to avoid—for these examinations is fraught with competing considerations. On the one hand, will current results from tests administered earlier now run afoul of the "practice effect," involving "gains in scores on cognitive tests that occur when a person is retested on the same instrument, or tested more than once on very similar ones"? (Kaufman, 1994, p. 828). On the other hand, it may be that it is just the scores previously obtained using instruments that are the specific focus of postconviction proceedings. In the latter instance, if suitable alternative measures are not available to address the same cognitive constructs, a review of the original test's technical manual and

related literature will help in determining just how long any "practice effect" is predicted to endure.

RELEASES, SUBPOENAS, COURT ORDERS, AND HIPAA

Many postconviction evaluations focus primarily or even exclusively upon the work—or lack thereof—performed by prior clinical and forensic practitioners. In such cases, records that until now may have been important suddenly become critical. These are obtained in different ways in different legal situations.

- *Releases.* This may be the simplest and least burdensome way to obtain records. Postconviction counsel typically presents his or her client with a number of generic releases during the very first meeting, and these often suffice for obtaining general clinical records and even some records of prior forensic evaluations. Upon consultation with counsel, the postconviction evaluator may want to proffer releases of his or her own for signature. It is important for counsel to consider the potential impact upon the litigant of having executed such a release—and for counsel to advise the postconviction evaluator accordingly. Is the release truly valid when the examinee may not be competent to execute it? Will a presumption that the examinee possessed this competency be exploited by the other side in the eventual course of these proceedings?
- *Subpoenas.* The use of a subpoena may prompt decisive action on the part of a records custodian; however, it may be that such action could be the opposite of what the requesting party intended. As a subpoena for production of records is typically considered to be more formal than a mere release, it may alert the recipient to the serious and possibly consequence-laden nature of production, and also trigger a reflexive reaction on the part of institutional counsel to have the subpoena quashed. This could result in considerable delay and perhaps place some records out of reach that might otherwise have been obtained without fanfare. Depending on the way they are drafted, subpoenas may also wind up prematurely drawing to the court's attention the identity of the postconviction evaluator, contrary to counsel's overall litigation plan.

- *Court orders and the Health Insurance Portability and Accountability Act of 1996 (HIPAA).* If postconviction counsel is confident that the court will endorse the validity of a request for records, and is also unconcerned by the prospect of revealing the identity of the postconviction evaluator, counsel may wish to move beyond the use of a subpoena to obtaining the court's direct order that identified records be sent directly to a specified party and location. This may lead to quicker production of documents and may also serve to underscore in a positive fashion for everyone's benefit that the results of prior evaluations and treatment are of central importance to current legal proceedings. Institutional counsel may at times balk at complying with the court's order for fear that this would somehow run afoul of HIPAA rules; however, HIPAA (1996) makes it clear that a judge's order trumps these considerations.

RECORDS RETENTION AND "SPOLIATION"

- *Records retention.* The original version of American Psychological Association's *Record Keeping Guidelines* (1993) offered succinct guidance for the retention of clinical and forensic records:

  > The psychologist is aware of relevant federal, state, and local laws and regulations governing record retention. Such laws and regulations supersede the requirements of these guidelines. In the absence of such law and regulations, complete records are maintained for a minimum of 3 years after the last contact with the client. Records, or a summary, are then maintained for an additional 12 years before disposal. If the client is a minor, the record period is extended until 3 years after the age of majority. (p. 985)

  The recently revised version of the *Record Keeping Guidelines* (American Psychological Association, 2007) adopts the looser, nondirective stance typical of the APA's modern practice guidelines:

  > In the absence of a superseding requirement, psychologists may consider retaining full records until 7 years after the last date of service delivery for adults or until 3 years after a minor reaches the age of majority, whichever is later. In some circumstances,

the psychologist may wish to keep records for a longer period, weighing the risks associated with obsolete or outdated information, or privacy loss, versus the potential benefits associated with preserving the records. (p. 999)

Drogin, Connell, Foote, and Sturm (2010) maintain that the latter recommendation "stands in striking contrast to the one found in the original," particularly since "despite the revised RKG's description of factors that psychologists are free to take into account, its 'may consider' paradigm means that no psychologist can be penalized for running afoul of it," with additional portions of the revised document indicating that "retention under some circumstances is actually being discouraged."

What this means for the postconviction evaluator is that time is of the essence in requesting and securing psychological records generated in prior clinical and forensic contexts. No comparable freestanding guideline exists for psychiatrists—a circumstance suggesting that swift action on the part of evaluator is the wisest course of action concerning this source of documentation as well.

- *"Spoliation."* This legal term addresses "the destruction or significant alteration of evidence, or the failure to retain property for another's use as evidence in pending or future litigation" (Durrant, 2005). Here, the focus is less upon evidence that no longer exists because a mental health professional innocently—if ineptly—disposed of files without consideration for possible future production requests, and more upon those situations in which trial is looming and files are destroyed, perhaps due either to a fear of exposure of one's clinical work or to a desire to influence the outcome of legal proceedings.

  Although "prosecutors and former counsel may not destroy evidence that may be relevant to [for example] a capital defendant's appeals or post-conviction proceedings" (Kessler, 2005, p. 14), spoliation by clinical and forensic practitioners is rarely if ever conducted at counsel's direction. As noted in the recently revised version of the *Record Keeping Guidelines* (American Psychological Association, 2007):

  Many statutes, regulations, and rules of evidence prohibit the alteration or removal of information once a record has been made.

In the context of litigation, addition or removal of information from a record that has been subpoenaed or requested by court order may create liability for the psychologist. Psychologists may wish to seek consultation regarding relevant state and federal law before changing an existing record. It is recommended that later additions to a record be documented as such. (p. 996)

Counsel may be blissfully unaware of the existence of records not present in trial counsel's file and the specter of spoliation in the narrow context of clinical and forensic mental health documentation. The postconviction evaluator will do well to remind counsel of this notion and to encourage all parties to bear these issues in mind as records are requested from practitioners of all disciplines.

DATA INTERPRETATION

ETHICAL ISSUES: CLINICAL

The American Psychiatric Association provides *The Principles of Medical Ethics with Annotations Especially Applicable to Psychiatry* ("Principles of Medical Ethics"; 2009) while the American Psychological Association provides the *Ethical Principles of Psychologists and Code of Conduct* ("Ethics Code"; 2002). These sources of guidance apply to forensic as well as mainstream clinical practice, but our focus in this section is primarily on the latter. Following are a few representative examples of how each document addresses issues frequently encountered in postconviction cases.

- *Institutional discrimination.* Prior evaluations or treatment may have failed to take into account the unique characteristics of the examinee, resulting in either deliberate or inadvertent discrimination, perhaps as a part of a codified institutional approach to mental health services. According to the Principles of Medical Ethics (2009), "a psychiatrist should not be a party to any type of policy that excludes, segregates, or demeans the dignity of any patient because of ethnic origin, race, sex, creed, age, socio-economic status, or sexual orientation" (p. 3). Similarly, the psychologists' Ethics Code (2002) indicate that if "the demands of an organization with which psychologists are affiliated or for whom they are working" conflict with nondiscrimination re-quirements, psychologists have various obligations for address-ing this situation (p. 1063).

- *Professional impairment.* Postconviction cases occasionally focus upon trial counsel's incapacity, based upon any of a host of issues that include senility, addiction, and other forms of phys-ical or mental illness. Impairment on the part of prior evaluators and treatment providers may be equally relevant to a given legal matter. The Principles of Medical Ethics (2009) make reference to those psychiatrists "who, because of mental illness, jeopardize the welfare of their patients and their own reputa-tions and practices," while the psychologists' Ethics Code (2002) direct that when psychologists "become aware" of such diffi-culties they "take appropriate measures, such as obtaining professional consultation or assistance" and also "determine whether they should limit, suspend, or terminate their work-related duties" (p. 1064).

- *Overdisclosure and speculation.* Statements in clinical or forensic reports that stray beyond the referral question or focus of treatment, or that lack proper substantiation, may reflect poorly upon the doctor's professionalism and also may prove mislead-ing in the subsequent context of postconviction proceedings. According to the Principles of Medical Ethics, "the psychiatrist may disclose the information which is relevant to a given situation," in addition to which "he or she should avoid offering speculation as fact" (p. 6). Similarly, the psychologists' Ethics Code indicates that "psychologists include in written and oral reports and consultations, only information germane to the purpose for which the communication is made" and "disclose information only to the extent necessary to achieve the purposes of the consultation" (p. 1066).

- *Boundaries of competence.* According to the Principles of Medical Ethics (2009), "a psychiatrist who regularly practices outside of his or her area of professional competence should be considered unethical" (p. 5). The psychologists' Ethics Code (2002) adopts a somewhat stricter stance in stating that "psychologists provide services, teach, and conduct research with populations and in areas only within the boundaries of their competence, based on their education, training, supervised experience, consultation, study, or professional experience" (p. 1063), although there is also a provision for venturing—in "emergencies"—into activities for which they may not possess the "necessary training," with the understanding that such activities will be "discontinued as soon as the emergency has ended" (p. 1064).

ETHICAL ISSUES: FORENSIC

The American Academy of Psychiatry and the Law provides *Ethics Guidelines for the Practice of Forensic Psychiatry* ("AAPL Guidelines"; 2005) while the Committee on Ethical Guidelines for Forensic Psychologists (a joint undertaking of the American Psychology-Law Society and the American Academy of Forensic Psychology) provides the *Specialty Guidelines for Forensic Psychologists* ("AP-LS Guidelines"; 1991). Following are a few representative examples of how each document addresses common issues in postconviction cases.

- *Confidentiality.* Evaluations and treatment conducted in the forensic context may have unintended consequences that merit evaluation during the postconviction phase of legal proceedings. Relevant to such situations, the AAPL Guidelines (2005) indicate that "at the beginning of a forensic evaluation, care should be taken to explicitly inform the evaluee that the psychiatrist is not the evaluee's 'doctor,'" and should "take precautions to ensure that they do not release confidential information to unauthorized persons" (p. 2). The AP-LS Guidelines (1991) state that "forensic psychologists inform their clients of the limits to the confidentiality of their services and their products" and extend "every effort to maintain confidentiality with regard to any information that does not bear directly on the legal purpose of the evaluation" (p. 660). One example of relevant case law is *Commonwealth v. Lamb* (1974), which ultimately led in Massachusetts to the mandatory provision of a "*Lamb* warning" at the inception of forensic evaluations, analogous to the "*Miranda* warning" given by law enforcement personnel.
- *Honesty and objectivity.* According to the AAPL Guidelines (2005), psychiatrists functioning as experts "should adhere to the principle of honesty and strive for objectivity," and "although they may be retained by one party to a . . . criminal

matter, psychologists should adhere to these principles when conducting evaluations, applying clinical data to legal criteria, and expressing opinions" (p. 3). Similarly, the AP-LS Guidelines (1991) direct that "when testifying, forensic psychologists have an obligation to all parties to a legal proceeding to present their findings, conclusions, evidence, or other products in a fair manner," although "this principle does not preclude forceful representation of the data and reasoning upon which a conclusion or professional product is based" (p. 664).

- *Qualifications.* Postconviction proceedings often focus on the specific qualifications of prior evaluators, by way of establishing that such professionals were—or were not—suited to the forensic tasks they saw fit to undertake. The AAPL Guidelines (2005) indicate that "expertise in the practice of forensic psychiatry should be claimed only in areas of actual knowledge, skills, training, and experience," with reference to "areas of special expertise, such as the evaluation of children, persons of foreign cultures, or prisoners" (p. 4). According the AP-LS Guidelines (1991), "forensic psychologists provide services only in areas of psychology in which they have specialized knowledge, skill, experience, and education," and that they are obligated to present "the factual bases . . . for their qualification as an expert" (p. 658).

SPECIALIZED APPLICATIONS

Drogin (2007) addressed a series of "specialized applications" for evaluations in this context, including criminal responsibility, competency to stand trial, prison programming, parole board review, release of insanity acquittees, competency to confess, and competency to be executed (pp. 405–408). Such topics are, of course, addressed in greater detail in other chapters of this book. Here, each of these previously explored applications is encapsulated and updated for the specific purpose of describing how it may pertain to the postconviction phase of legal proceedings.

- *Criminal responsibility.* A considerable amount of time can pass between the alleged commission of a crime and those periods during which a defendant is evaluated, tried, and convicted (Simon & Shuman, 2002). Postconviction evaluations may occur still years later, but such inquiries may benefit from the presence of jail or prison records that provide ongoing documentation of the examinee's recent condition. Such indicia of chronic, ongoing mental illness—or the lack thereof—may be of considerable assistance in determining whether the course of an examinee's psychiatric complications comports with the diagnoses that were earlier alleged as the basis of his or her criminal behavior. Care should be taken to determine the extent to which current diagnostic criteria (American Psychiatric Association, 2000) are similar to those that would have been utilized when psychiatric conditions were first ascribed.

- *Competency to stand trial.* Although the passage of time between pretrial representation and postconviction proceedings is of course less than that which has elapsed since the commission of the crime itself, many of the same temporal issues clouding *post hoc* determinations of criminal responsibility are also present in similar analyses of prior trial competency. One advantage that the postconviction evaluator may possess in comparison to the original forensic experts charged with addressing competency is that additional pretrial documentation may be revealed that has lost its former privileged status. Similarly, it may be that trial counsel is available not only as a sworn witness but also as a participant in interviews about the examinee's capacity to participate rationally in his or her own defense and to comprehend the nature and consequences of pretrial proceedings. Trial counsel, whose earlier performance is now being subjected to especial scrutiny, should not automatically be assumed to be biased in favor of the defendant's perspective.

- *Prison programming.* The seminal case in this area is *Pennsylvania Department of Corrections v. Yeskey* (1998), in which the Supreme Court of the United States determined that a person denied participation in an early release program was a victim of prohibited discrimination under the Americans with Disabilities Act (1990), because that denial was based on a treatable medical condition. To what extent do postconviction examinees possess psychiatric diagnoses—be these learning disabilities, psychotic illnesses, or other conditions—that may constitute unfair bases for exclusion from prison programming? It may be, for example, that a convicted felon has been prevented from enrolling in an anger management class—the timely and successful completion of which could mean a reduced custodial sentence—because of a sixth-grade reading level, where prison authorities have determined that failure to master the program's written content calls for exclusion without recourse to a reasonable accommodation such as oral presentation of the materials in question.

- *Parole board review.* Since no one is "entitled" to parole under any cognizable constitutional principle (Palmer, 2010), there is typically little state or federal funding available to support the work of postconviction evaluators in this context; however, privately funded cases do exist and are a frequent practice focus for forensic psychiatrists and psychologists, reflecting the fact that there are currently over 5 million offenders now under community supervision (Glaze & Bonczar, 2009). Topics addressed in this context may include substance abuse relapse, sexual offense relapse, amenability to supervision, availability and efficacy of family support, reintegration into society (Meffert & Chamberlain, 2009), and—in particular—risk of dangerousness, for which it remains axiomatic that "a reasonable predictor of future violence is a history of violent behavior, especially an ongoing pattern of aggressive acts" (Felthous, 2010, p. 540). The work of the parole board is highly complex and fraught with policy implications (Morris, Longmire, Buffington-Vollum, & Vollum, 2010). What documentation is the parole board going to review? Familiarity with those particular sources of information is likely to impact the board's decision-making process. On what issues has this particular board previously been relevant in making its determinations? What are the specific reasons for which the inmate currently being considered for parole may have been rejected in the past?

- *Release of insanity acquittees.* For the postconviction evaluator, there are several ways in which this process differs from that of parole board review proceedings. For one thing, there exists an obligation to make a determination, based on clear and convincing evidence, that the examinee remains dangerous and possesses a condition that constitutes a suitable basis for ongoing restriction of civil liberties (*Foucha v. Louisiana*, 1992; *U.S. v. Comstock*, 2010), which in turn means significantly greater availability of public funding for this purpose. For another, release hearings possess more of the contours of traditional trial settings with which all forensic evaluators tend to be more familiar, including observance of standard due process. Proffers of evidence, deliberations, and eventual decisions from the bench are very similar to those observed in cases of involuntary civil commitment.

- *Competency to confess.* The postconviction evaluator has a wealth of issues to explore concerning confession competency that may or may not have been addressed during the pretrial phase. Were examinations of any sort conducted? Did these evaluations include the administration of standardized cognitive testing to determine oral vocabulary and reading levels? To what extent did the specific vocabulary and phrasing utilized in the actual *Miranda* warnings administered to the defendant wind up being the ones to which his or her language skills were compared? Did pretrial analysis proceed from a written transcript, an audio recording, or a video recording? If more than one of these modalities was employed, were they cross-checked for consistency? In such cases, "the outcome of lengthy and highly complex legal proceedings can turn literally on the presence or absence of a single word" (Rogers, Shuman, & Drogin, 2008, p. 5). At the postconviction stage of legal proceedings, the evaluator should bear in mind that it becomes even more likely that the examinee has become sensitized to the content and import of a warning in question *subsequent* to its initial application.

- *Competency to be executed.* According to the Supreme Court of the United States in *Ford v. Wainwright* (1986)—and as it affirmed in *Panetti v. Quarterman* (2007)—capital punishment cannot be visited upon persons whose mental illness prevents them "from comprehending the reasons for the penalty or its implications" (*Ford v. Wainwright*, p. 417). The Court has further ruled that persons with mental retardation are "ineligible for the death penalty" (*Atkins v. Virginia*, 2002, p. 320). Both of these are substantially "here-and-now" determinations of current mental conditions, such that the postconviction evaluator is freed from much of the guesswork attending assessments of criminal responsibility and competency to stand trial—although difficulties in substantiating the "onset . . . before age 18 years" component

(American Psychiatric Association, 2000, p. 49) reflected in many statutory definitions of mental retardation will often lead to a paper chase for decades-old documentation. An "Interview Checklist for Evaluations of Competency for Execution" (Melton, Petrila, Poythress, & Slobogin, 2007; Zapf, Boccaccini, & Brodsky, 2002) is now available to assist in these cases.

COMMUNICATION

Reports and testimony are conveyed by postconviction evaluators in much the same fashion as they would have been on respective topics during pretrial hearings or at trial, with one important distinction: Typically, the postconviction evaluator is being called to describe not only what *is* being done, but also what *has* been done and what *should have* been done. This role calls for demonstration of a level of expertise and an attention to detail that establishes the report writer or witness as an authority on "expertise" itself. Errors, vacillations, and "waffling" in documents or on the stand (Gutheil, 2007) will be even more damaging than usual to counsel's attempts to convey a legal argument based on the postconviction evaluator's opinions.

Forensic reports often proceed from the following checklist of considerations (Appelbaum & Gutheil, 2007):

1. Plan (or outline) the structure and content of the report well in advance.
2. Include all materials and information to support each of your conclusions.
3. Ensure that the report can stand alone, without additional appendices.
4. List all documents and resources reviewed as the database, including interviews.
5. Describe the reason for your role in the legal proceeding.
6. Present your conclusion, clearly identified, in the relevant statutory language.
7. Describe the supporting data that validate each of your conclusions.
8. Proffer any alternative scenarios that derive from contested facts.

9. Identify any constraints on your evaluation and resulting limitations on your data.
10. Consider presenting opposing views and rebuttals.
11. Refrain from writing a report if none is requested or if instructed not to do so.
12. Discuss changes in the wording of the report with the attorney (p. 308).

Concerning the expert's testimonial demeanor, Gutheil (2009) has recommended that for expert witnesses:

> Your identity on the stand is that of a teacher. Be clear; get interested in what you have to say and stay interested. Make your point because it matters, it is important, and you want the jury to understand it. An expert who doesn't seem to care about his or her own testimony has probably irreversibly lost the jury; why should they care if the expert doesn't? (p. 78)

Postconviction evaluations often address issues for which resolution is fairly practical and concrete—*e.g.*, scoring errors committed by experts in pretrial evaluations. It may be, however, that with the passage of time and the contradictory nature of various sources of information the answers are anything but clear. Such shortcomings should be acknowledged as they arise, and in fact the candor associated with this approach winds up reinforcing the credibility of the witness. In order to approach these and other situations with confidence, "preparation with your retaining attorney is very helpful to identify what concerns you have about cross-examination lines of attack and to design in collaboration ways of addressing them on direct." (Gutheil & Dattilio, 2008, p. 57)

REFERENCES

American Academy of Psychiatry and the Law. (2005). *Ethics guidelines for the practice of forensic psychiatry*. Bloomfield, CT: Author.

American Bar Association. (2003). ABA guidelines for the appointment and performance of counsel in death penalty cases (revised edition). *Hofstra Law Review, 31*, 913–1090.

American Bar Association Criminal Justice Standards Committee. (1989). *ABA criminal justice mental health standards*. Washington, DC: American Bar Association.

American Psychiatric Association. (2000). *Diagnostic and statistical manual of mental disorders* (4th ed., Text Revision). Washington, DC: Author.

American Psychiatric Association. (2009). *The principles of medical ethics with annotations especially applicable to psychiatry.* Arlington, VA: Author.

American Psychological Association. (1993). Record keeping guidelines. *American Psychologist, 48,* 984–986.

American Psychological Association. (2002). Ethical principles of psychologists and code of conduct. *American Psychologist, 57,* 1060–1073.

American Psychological Association. (2007). Record keeping guidelines. *American Psychologist, 62,* 993–1004.

Americans with Disabilities Act of 1990, 42 U.S.C. §12101 et seq. (1990).

Appelbaum, P. S., & Gutheil, T. G. (2007). *Clinical handbook of psychiatry and the law* (4th ed.). Philadelphia, PA: Lippincott Williams & Wilkins.

Atkins v. Virginia, 536 U.S. 304 (2002).

Committee on Ethical Guidelines for Forensic Psychologists. (1991). Specialty guidelines for forensic psychologists. *Law and Human Behavior, 15,* 655–665.

Commonwealth v. Lamb, 311 N.E.2d 47 (Mass. 1974).

Drogin, E. Y. (2006). Psychological assessments in postconviction proceedings. *Criminal Justice, 21*(3), 26–33.

Drogin, E. Y. (2007). Postconviction assessment. In A. M. Goldstein (Ed.), *Forensic psychology: Emerging topics and expanding roles* (pp. 385–417). Hoboken, NJ: John Wiley & Sons.

Drogin, E. Y., Connell, M., Foote, W. E., & Sturm, C. A. (2010). The American Psychological Association's revised "Record Keeping Guidelines": Implications for the practitioner. *Professional Psychology: Research and Practice, 41,* 236–243.

Durrant, R. (2005). Spoliation of discoverable electronic evidence. *Loyola of Los Angeles Law Review, 38,* 1803–1834.

Ellis, A., & Bussert, T. (2010). Stemming the tide of postconviction waivers. *Criminal Justice, 25*(1), 28–30.

Felthous, A. R. (2010). Personal violence. In R. I. Simon & L. H. Gold (Eds.), *Textbook of forensic psychiatry* (2nd ed., pp. 529–561). Arlington, VA: American Psychiatric Publishing.

Ford v. Wainwright, 447 U.S. 399 (1986).

Foucha v. Louisiana, 504 U.S. 71 (1992).

Glaze, L. E., & Bonczar, T. P. (2009). *Probation and parole in the United States, 2008.* Washington, DC: U.S. Department of Justice.

Green, B. A., & Yaroshefsky, E. (2009). Prosecutorial discretion and postconviction evidence of innocence. *Ohio State Journal of Criminal Law, 6,* 467–517.

Gutheil, T. G. (2007). The problem of evasive testimony: The expert "waffle." *Journal of the American Academy of Psychiatry and the Law, 35*, 112–117.

Gutheil, T. G. (2009). *The psychiatrist as expert witness* (2nd ed.). Arlington, VA: American Psychiatric Publishing.

Gutheil, T. G., & Dattilio, F. M. (2008). *Practical approaches to forensic mental health testimony.* Philadelphia, PA: Lippincott Williams & Wilkins.

Gutheil, T. G. & Simon, R. I. (2002). *Mastering forensic psychiatric practice: Advanced strategies for the expert witness.* Washington, DC: American Psychiatric Publishing.

Health Insurance Portability and Accountability Act of 1996 (HIPAA), Pub. L. No. 104-191, 110 stat. 1936.

Kaufman, A. A. (1994). Practice effects. In R. J. Sternberg (Ed.), *Encyclopedia of human intelligence* (pp. 828–833). New York, NY: Macmillan.

Kessler, D. J. (2005, September/October). Spoliation in capital post-conviction proceedings: Theory of spoliation in habeas corpus—Part I. *The Champion,* pp. 14–19.

Kilborn, J. H. (2010). Convicted but innocent: Why post-conviction lawyers are indispensable. *Louisiana Bar Journal, 57,* 314–316.

King, N. J., & Hoffman, J. L. (2008). Envisioning post-conviction review for the twenty-first century. *Mississippi Law Journal, 78,* 433–451.

Kreeger, L., & Weiss, D. (2004, March/April). Preparing for post-conviction challenges. *Prosecutor,* pp. 18–21.

Larson, K. A., & Gruzdinskas, A. J. (2008). Waiver of postconviction relief (PCR) and PCR counsel. (2008). *Journal of the American Academy of Psychiatry and the Law, 36,* 402–404.

Mason, J. (2004). Personal narratives, relational selves: Residential histories in the living and telling. *Sociological Review, 52,* 162–179.

Meffert, S. M., & Chamberlain, J. (2009). Expansion of liberty interests under parole conditions: Beyond antipsychotics. *Journal of the American Academy of Psychiatry and the Law, 37,* 264–266.

Melton, G. B., Petrila, P., Poythress, N. G., & Slobogin, C. (2007). *Psychological evaluations for the courts: A handbook for mental health professionals and lawyers* (3rd ed.). New York, NY: Guilford Press.

Miller, H. R. (2008). "A meaningless ritual": How the lack of a postconviction competency standard deprives the mentally ill of effective habeas review in Texas. *Texas Law Review, 87,* 267–298.

Mogin, P. (2003, September/October). Using new evidence of a constitutional violation to get a new trial. *The Champion,* pp. 26–28.

Morris, R. G., Longmire, D. R., Buffington-Vollum, J., & Vollum, S. (2010). Institutional misconduct and differential parole eligibility among capital inmates. *Criminal Justice and Behavior, 37,* 417–438.

National Legal Aid and Defender Association. (1995). *Performance guidelines for criminal defense representation.* Washington, DC: Author.

Otto, R. K., Slobogin, C., & Greenberg, S. A. (2007). Legal and ethical issues in accessing and utilizing third-party information. In A. M. Goldstein (Ed.), *Forensic psychology: Emerging topics and expanding roles* (pp. 190–205). Hoboken, NJ: John Wiley & Sons.

Palmer, J. W. (2010). *Constitutional rights of prisoners* (9th ed.). Cincinnati, OH: Anderson.

Panetti v. Quarterman, 551 U.S. 930 (2007).

Parry, J. W., & Drogin, E. Y. (2000). *Criminal law handbook on psychiatric and psychological evidence and testimony.* Washington, DC: American Bar Association.

Parry, J. W., & Drogin, E. Y. (2007). *Mental disability law, evidence and testimony: A comprehensive reference manual for lawyers, judges and mental disability professionals.* Washington, DC: American Bar Association.

Pennsylvania Department of Corrections v. Yeskey, 524 U.S. 206 (1998).

Poortinga, E., & Guyer, M. (2006). Quantum of evidence of mental retardation required of a defendant in application seeking postconviction relief. *Journal of the American Academy of Psychiatry and the Law,* 34, 112–114.

Primus, E. B. (2009). Procedural obstacles to reviewing ineffective assistance of trial counsel claims in state and federal postconviction proceedings. *Criminal Justice,* 24(3), 6–13.

Rogers, R., Shuman, D. W., & Drogin, E. Y. (2008). *Miranda* rights . . . and wrongs: Myths, methods, and model solutions. *Criminal Justice,* 23(2), 4–9.

Rompilla v. Beard, 545 U.S. 374 (2005).

Shapiro, P. (2008). Are we executing mentally incompetent inmates because they volunteer to die? A look at various states' implementation of standards of competency to waive post-conviction review. *Catholic University Law Review,* 57, 567–604.

Simon, R. I., & Shuman, D. W. (Eds.). (2002). *Retrospective assessment of mental states in litigation: Predicting the past.* Arlington, VA: American Psychiatric Publishing.

Strickland v. Washington, 466 U.S. 668 (1984).

Taslitz, A. E. (2009). Priming postconviction representation. *Criminal Justice,* 24(3), 4.

U.S. v. Comstock, 560 U.S. (2010).

Zapf, P. A., Boccaccini, M. T., & Brodsky, S. L. (2002). Assessment of competency for execution: Professional guidelines and an evaluation checklist. *Behavioral Sciences and the Law,* 21, 103–120.

CHAPTER 11

Juvenile Delinquency and Decertification

FRANK M. DATTILIO and LAURENTINE FROMM

INTRODUCTION

HISTORY AND IMPORTANT CONCEPTS

Adjusting penalties for crimes committed by youths has been known for hundreds of years, as exemplified by the 10th century statute of Anglo-Saxon king Aethelstan, which provides that no person younger than 15 years should be slain [for robbery], "except he should make resistance or flee." Further, the miscreant would not be imprisoned if the family would assure that he would "evermore desist from every kind of evil" (Sanders, 1970). Similarly, the reform era in the United States in the 1800s and early 1900s saw legislation intended to protect dependent and delinquent youth brought before the court system. Since Colonial times, children under the age of 7 had been exempt from criminal prosecution in the belief that their young age excused them from responsibility, and in the 19th century the Illinois legislature raised the minimum age to form criminal intent to 17 (Grisso, 1998a). Juvenile courts, first established by the Illinois Juvenile Court Act in 1899 and existing in all but two states by 1925, were designed to rehabilitate, rather than punish, juveniles brought before the court (Benedek & Schetky, 2002). The reader is referred to a number of comprehensive sources for additional historical information on this topic, namely Stapleton and Teitelbaum (1972), Grisso (1998a), and Benedek and Schetky (2002).

The rehabilitative and confidentiality provisions in these juvenile court procedures were found to result in the lack of legal protections for youth that are constitutionally required for adult defendants. The lack of these constitutional safeguards eventually gave rise to major reforms within the juvenile court system, two of which are reflected in Supreme Court of the United States decisions in the 1960s: *Kent v. U.S.* (1966) and *In re Gault* (1967). *Kent* held that youths faced with hearings that might lead to their transfer to criminal court should have many of the same procedural due process rights as adults in criminal proceedings, and listed factors that were to be considered in the decision to waive the juvenile offender to adult court, including the violence of the offense and the likelihood that the juvenile could be rehabilitated. *In re Gault* held that youths should have the same rights to avoid self-incrimination, to consult legal counsel when questioned by police, and to be informed of those rights [rights affirmed for adults in *Miranda v. Arizona* (1966)]. The Supreme Court extended these rights by requiring the state to prove allegations in delinquency cases beyond a reasonable doubt (*In re Winship*, 1970) to justify the deprivation of liberty associated with the court's assumption of custody of youths adjudicated delinquent.

Media coverage of juvenile violence, particularly mass shootings at schools, contributes to society's current view that juvenile crime is out of control. The U.S. Department of Justice reports that, as of April 2009, 2.18 million arrests were made in the previous decade of persons under the age of 18, and that juveniles accounted for 16% of all violent crimes (U.S. Department of Justice, 2009). The level of juvenile crime increased steadily from the 1970s through the 1990s and resulted in increased referrals of juveniles to the court system (Marczyk, Heilbrun, Lander, & DeMatteo, 2005). In the late 1990s, states enacted legislation allowing for what is variously termed *transfer*, *bind over*, *waiver*, or *certification* of juveniles charged with serious crimes to adult court. More stringent statutes call for juveniles charged with certain serious crimes, particularly homicide, to be automatically handled in adult court, unless they are shown to be amenable to rehabilitation in the juvenile justice system, or *decertified*.

The continuing debate over appropriate punishments of juveniles convicted of serious crimes is evident in the U.S. Supreme Court case *Roper v. Simmons* (2005), in which the Court ruled that the death penalty for crimes committed by juveniles under age 18 violated the Eighth Amendment prohibition of cruel and unusual punishment. In *Graham v. Florida* (2010), the Supreme Court has ruled that the imposition of life without parole for juveniles convicted of non-homicide offenses violates the Eighth Amendment's prohibition of cruel and unusual punishment, affecting laws in 37 states and the District of Columbia. Life without parole had been a sentencing option 90% of the states had deliberately retained to deal with serious juvenile violence (Brief for the States of Louisiana et al., 2010).

The recent movement of states toward decertification of juveniles, particularly older juveniles, charged with violent crimes means that most jurisdictions now allow 14-year-old juveniles automatically to be tried in (adult) criminal court (Heilbrun, Leheny, Thomas, & Huneycutt, 1997), unless they are individually shown to be amenable to rehabilitation in the juvenile system. In many cases where clinicians in the past were asked to "certify" a juvenile to adult court, they are now asked to "decertify" the juvenile: that is, while in the past the question was whether a juvenile was *not* amenable to rehabilitation in the juvenile system, the question has become whether he or she *is* amenable to rehabilitation in that system, and thus eligible to be handled in juvenile court.

Methods for Charging Juveniles as Adults

There are three ways that juvenile offenders may be charged as adults. The first is by *legislative waiver*, or "mandatory waiver," in which a state identifies specific offenses that will automatically lead to a juvenile at or over a certain age being charged as an adult. This typically involves cases of murder/homicide. *Prosecutorial waiver* gives the prosecutor discretion to present to a judge the reasons it believes that a particular youth should be tried as an adult. In *judicial waiver*, the most common method of transfer, the juvenile court judge uses his/her discretionary authority to transfer a case to adult court (Flesch, 2004). Waiver depends on the seriousness of the crime, the risks the juvenile poses to the community, and his or her amenability to rehabilitation within the juvenile system prior to the age of 21.

Forensic psychologists and psychiatrists play a significant role in evaluating juveniles for the court system, for competence to waive *Miranda* rights (Grisso, 1980), and competence to stand trial

(Grisso, 1988), as well as for certification to or decertification from adult court. Each of these evaluations will be discussed in the following sections.

PREPARATION

Before starting an evaluation, the clinician should understand the goal of the evaluation, whether for waiver of *Miranda* rights, competence to stand trial, or certification/decertification. In each case, the evaluator should also have a clear idea of the specific question that prompted the referral. If the evaluation has not been ordered by the court, consent for the evaluation should be obtained from the parent or legal guardian of any minor child; assent from the juvenile should be sought. The purpose of the evaluation and the limits of its confidentiality should be explained to the juvenile evaluee, as well as to any collateral informants, such as family, teachers, or therapists. The evaluator should explain whether or not there will be a treatment relationship with the evaluator. These points should be recorded in the written report (see "Communication" later in this chapter).

WAIVER OF MIRANDA RIGHTS

Much has been written in recent years about the validity of confessions that juveniles make to police and other law enforcement agents (Grisso, 1981; Grisso, 1998b; Gudjonsson, 1984b). The question has been raised as to the capability of a juvenile "voluntarily, knowingly, and intelligently" to waive his/her rights to remain silent and to have counsel present during questioning, upon being mirandized by authorities. The effect on juvenile interrogations of the Supreme Court decision that a detainee waives the right to remain silent by making an uncoerced statement to the police (*Berghuis v. Thompkins*, 2010) remains to be seen.

Grisso and colleagues (2003) have conducted research on the issue of whether juveniles are competent to waive their rights "voluntarily, knowingly, and intelligently" based on their level of maturity. The research has been mixed, showing that many are not competent to understand fully the meaning of "waive your rights." The issue of developmental maturity of juveniles has been elaborated on elsewhere in the professional literature (Scott & Steinberg, 2008; Steinberg & Cauffman, 1996, 1999;). This issue was first addressed in the California Supreme Court case of *People v. Lara* (1967) and was affirmed by the U.S. Supreme Court in *Fare v. Michael C.* (1979). The mere fact that a defendant is a juvenile does not necessarily invalidate a waiver of rights. However, psychiatric disorder, limited level of intelligence, and social/emotional immaturity may all impede the juvenile's capacity to understand and waive rights, and the evaluator should bear these factors in mind. Although this issue is often raised by criminal defense attorneys long after the juvenile's confession, the evaluator needs to explore the characteristics of the juvenile at the time the confession was made, as well as the circumstances of the interrogation itself, and the nature of the offense.

Grisso (1986) outlines the essential components of evaluation of all legal competencies: functional abilities, interactive and judgmental abilities, and causal explanations. *Functional abilities* encompasses whether juveniles comprehend the *Miranda* warnings and the significance of the rights to be waived, and have the ability to process information adequately to decide to waive these rights. *Interactional and judgmental abilities* encompass the match or mismatch between the juvenile's abilities and the demands of the situation. *Causal explanations* refers to explaining the reasons for identified deficits in abilities, such as cognitive impairment, developmental delay, intellectual deficit, mental disorder or malingering (Grisso, 1998a). Typically, the more serious the crime, the higher the level of functional ability required to competently waive these rights.

COMPETENCE TO STAND TRIAL

Forensic psychologists and psychiatrists may be asked to provide an evaluation of a juvenile's competence to stand trial, whether the trial is in adult or juvenile court. Every jurisdiction employs a legal definition of *competence* patterned after that stated by the Supreme Court of the United States in *Dusky v. U.S.* (1960), which indicates that a defendant must have sufficient present ability to consult with an attorney, a reasonable degree of rational understanding of the charges, and a rational, as well as factual, understanding of the proceedings against him. Relevant deficiencies must be due specifically to mental illness or the result of mental retardation. Defendants are presumed competent to stand trial unless the question is raised by the defense counsel, prosecution, or the court. It is often defense counsel who first notices that a defendant has difficulty understanding the charges or trial process or in cooperating in preparation of a defense.

Grisso, Miller, and Sales (1987) suggest that the question of a juvenile's competence to stand trial should be raised in cases involving any of the following: age 12 years or younger; prior diagnosis/ treatment of a mental illness or mental retardation; borderline level of intellectual functioning, or any history of learning disability; pretrial observations by others suggesting deficits in memory, attention, or interpretation of reality. A clear understanding of the specific concern of the defense attorney, the prosecutor, or the court that prompted the referral for competency evaluation focuses the evaluation, and should be elicited by the clinician before the evaluation is begun.

The first objective of an evaluation of competence is to formulate the juvenile's understanding of the charges, the trial process, and potential consequences, as well as his/her ability to cooperate with an attorney in a defense and to participate appropriately in court proceedings. The next objective is to identify causes of any errors in understanding or impairments of abilities. A clear connection must be demonstrated between any identified deficits and impairment of competence abilities. The deficits must be considered in light of the specific demands of the criminal or juvenile court proceedings at hand. This is particularly important when there is a complex legal defense or plea bargaining. When a trial process is expected to be lengthy, the clinician should form an opinion as to the likelihood of any fluctuation in level of competence-related abilities during the court process.

EVALUATIONS FOR CERTIFICATION TO OR DECERTIFICATION FROM CRIMINAL COURT

Nearly every state jurisdiction in the United States has mechanisms for waiver of certain types of cases involving juveniles from juvenile to adult court. As noted above, this can be done by judicial waiver, in which the juvenile court judge makes the decision to transfer the case to adult court. Transfer by *statutory exclusion* requires certain cases involving youths above a certain age (either 13 or 14 years) who are charged with very serious crimes to be automatically charged as adults. Transfer by *prosecutor direct file* allows prosecutors discretion to file charges against youths in either juvenile or criminal court for certain types of offenses. When this occurs, *judicial waiver* by juvenile courts may occur (Grisso, 1998a).

In a number of states, criminal courts receiving transferred youths by statutory exclusion or prosecutor direct file have the option of transferring them to juvenile court by reverse transfer, or decertification. Criminal defense attorneys may file a petition to decertify, in which the criminal court judge may waive jurisdiction and remand to juvenile court a particular youth who is considered immature, amenable to rehabilitation, or otherwise more appropriately handled in the juvenile justice system. Such decertification needs to be determined on the basis of whether the individual youth meets certain legal standards for the waiver decision. The courts have relied on forensic psychologists and psychiatrists to provide information related to the decertification decision. This decision is particularly important when the offense is serious, such as in cases of murder, rape, involuntary deviant sexual intercourse, aggravated assault, kidnapping, voluntary manslaughter, or use of a deadly weapon during the commission of a crime. Recent legislative changes in many states have removed enumerated offenses from the definition of *delinquent act,* thus allowing a youth to be tried in adult criminal court for some serious offenses. The definition of the term *serious* is now more broadly defined than in the past, when it was limited to murder (Cauffman, Piquero, Kimonis, Steinberg, Chassin, & Fagan, 2007).

A youth may request that his/her case be transferred from the adult criminal system to the juvenile system when he/she is charged with one of the enumerated offenses excluded from delinquent acts, including the crime of murder. However, the youth is required to establish by a preponderance of the evidence that transfer will serve the public interest. The burden of proof is on the youth to show by a preponderance of the evidence that he/she is amenable to treatment in the juvenile system prior to the age of 21. The petition to transfer from criminal to juvenile court typically needs to list the factors that would allow the court to find that such a transfer would serve both the public interest and benefit the youth charged with the offense.

When transfer is sought from juvenile court to adult criminal court, a hearing on whether the transfer should be made is held. Notice in writing of the time, place, and purpose of the hearing is given to the youth and his/her parents, guardian, or other custodian several days before the hearing. The court must find that there is a *prima facie* case that the youth committed the alleged delinquent act and that the delinquent act would be considered a felony if committed by an adult.

DISCRETIONARY CERTIFICATION TO ADULT COURT

Clinicians may be requested by juvenile probation officers or the court to assess whether a juvenile should be discretionarily certified to adult court. For example, cases in which the juvenile did not commit a violent or serious crime with a deadly weapon, but has already had rehabilitation attempts in facilities and/or programs within the juvenile system may be considered for handling in adult court. There are several adult correctional facilities in the country that offer juvenile programs. These facilities have separate juvenile programs, and some of these youth are transferred to the adult population after treatment. These youth are handled in the adult system, but are considered amenable for treatment in a juvenile program within the adult correctional system. Examiners need to bear in mind the risks to the juvenile of incarceration in an adult correctional facility, such as increased risks of victimization and of recidivism, as well as the stigma of establishing a criminal record. Recommendations for such certification typically are not made until resources within the juvenile system have been exhausted.

DATA COLLECTION

An extensive clinical interview on more than one occasion is typically necessary in order to appreciate the juvenile's view of his/her own goals and motivations, as well as his/her background and psychological makeup to see patterns of interaction that elucidate behavior and thinking. All evaluations should include collateral information such as school records, mental health evaluations, medical records, delinquency and placement records, and police investigative reports, as well as comprehensive interviews with parents and family members, or other individuals who know the juvenile well. Each of these pieces of information enhances the evaluator's understanding of the juvenile from a variety of perspectives (Sadoff & Dattilio, 2008).

Psychological assessments may be used as adjuncts to the clinical evaluation. General intelligence testing may be used to assess overall intellectual functioning. Specific cognitive testing, such as the Instrument for Assessing, Understanding, and Appreciation of *Miranda* (Grisso, 1981) assesses a juvenile's understanding of the components of the *Miranda* warning itself. It is normatively based on 400 juveniles in detention centers and addresses the following areas:

- Comprehension of *Miranda* Rights (CMR)
- Comprehension of *Miranda* Rights—Recognition (CMR-R)
- Comprehension of the *Miranda* Vocabulary (CMV)
- Function of Rights in Interrogation (FRI)

Other measures of general cognitive ability may be used, such as the Wechsler Intelligence Scale for Children-IV (WISC-IV), Wechsler Individual Achievement Test (WIAT), or the Wide Range Achievement Test, 4th (Jastak, Wilkinson, & Jastak, 1984). Other objective personality measures might include the Millon Adolescent Personality Inventory (Millon, Green, & Meagher, 1982), the Millon Adolescent Clinical Inventory (Millon, 1993), or the Minnesota Multiphasic Personality Inventory—Adolescents (Butcher et al., 1992). The Gudjonsson Suggestibility Scale (Gudjonsson, 1984a & b, 1992) is a standardized measure for determining the acquiescence and the potential for youths to "cave in" during a *Miranda* warning.

As in any evaluation, clinicians need to be concerned about malingering of cognitive or neuropsychological deficits. Measures for malingering are incorporated into some of the instruments described, although there are also specific tests such as the Test of Malingered Memory (TOMM; Ashendorf, Constantinou, & McCaffrey, 2004) to screen for malingering and deception.

The specific competency assessment involves one or more clinical interviews with the juvenile, a mental status examination, and may include psychological testing. Psychological testing might involve cognitive assessments (i.e., intelligence testing), as well as specific assessments for competency to stand trial, such as the Competency

Assessment Interview (CAI) developed by McGarry (1973) and the Fitness Interview Test—Revised (FIT-R) (Roesch, Webster, & Eaves, 1994; Zapf & Roesch, 1997). A more recent instrument is the MacArthur Competence Assessment Tool—Criminal Adjudication (MacCAT-CA) (Hoge et al., 1997). Lipsitt, Lelos, and McGarry (1971) introduced the Competency Screening Test (CST), which can be used for individuals with an intellectual level above the borderline range. In addition, the Georgia Court Competency Test—Mississippi State Hospital (GCCT-MSH; Nicholson, Robertson, Johnson, & Jensen, 1988) is a popular measure. In situations in which the juvenile may be mentally retarded or challenged, the Competency Assessment to Stand Trial—Mental Retardation (CAST-MR) (Everington, 1990) is strongly recommended to the extent normed on the relevant juvenile population.

RISK ASSESSMENT

In addition to the clinical interview of the juvenile, collateral information, including social history from parents or guardians, academic, psychological, psychiatric, and medical records and information, as well as past legal involvement, is desirable. Specific information about the current offense, including police reports, should also be reviewed.

Reviewing multiple sources of information allows for a more thorough risk assessment evaluation, especially regarding dangerousness, sophistication, maturity, and amenability to treatment (Salekin, Rogers, & Ustad, 2001). Reports from a variety of observers provide background information from multiple perspectives. If such reports corroborate the examiner's observations, the examiner's impressions are supported and validated. Records from probation officers or psychotherapists may give a longitudinal view of the youth's functioning. Reports from law enforcement and other agencies, as well as rap sheets, provide information about prior contacts with the justice system. Disciplinary records from schools and admission records from juvenile facilities/psychiatric hospitals are particularly useful since institutions and/or hospitals provide a day-to-day record of the youth's observed interactions in a confined or semiconfined setting. Unfortunately, these sources are not always available and the clinician must work with less collateral information.

THE CLINICAL INTERVIEW

No report should lack the clinical interview of the youth by the examiner. Engaging youths to discuss past delinquencies and aggressive behaviors can be challenging, and may require more than one clinical interview. Questions about the youth's own views of his/her aggressive behavior may more likely be answered by asking about what helps to control behavior rather than what has caused problems. This gives the examiner the opportunity to assess the youth's temperament and existing coping skills, as well as the extent of his/her interest in and capacity for learning new strategies to manage aggressive feelings.

Where the forensic psychologist may rely more heavily on structured instruments such as psychological testing, the forensic psychiatrist may rely more heavily on the clinical interview, including the mental status examination. The clinical assessment of the youth should incorporate observation of the way in which the youth relates to the examiner, as well as the content of his/her answers to historical and mental status examination questions. Review of writings by the youth, such as diaries, journals, web logs, and electronic networking sites, may reveal attitudes that the youth does not readily disclose in a face-to-face interview. Inquiry into recreational interests, including behavior with pets, as well as types of movies and video games enjoyed, may illuminate particular fantasy interests.

PSYCHOLOGICAL TESTS AND MEASURES

Unfortunately, there is no specific psychological test that serves to determine risk for violence among youths. However, there are a number of psychological measures and appraisals that may help forensic psychologists and psychiatrists to make a better determination. One of these measures is the Minnesota Multiphasic Personality Inventory—Adolescent version (MMPI-A) (Butcher et al., 1992). The MMPI-A has excellent validity and reliability and is one of the most widely used instruments in forensic settings. Another personality assessment is the Millon Adolescent Clinical Inventory (Millon, 1993). These are empirically validated measures that have a history of accuracy in assessing youths. Evaluators may also consider employing the Jesness Behavior Checklist (Jesness, 1996), as well as the Youth Behavior Checklist (Achenbach, 1991). Other appraisals include the Violence Risk Assessment-HCR 20 (Webster, Douglas, Eaves, & Hart, 1997) and the Violence Risk Appraisal Guide (VRAG; Harris, Rice, & Quincey, 1993), as well as the adolescent version of the Hare Psychopathy Checklist (Frick et al., 1994), or other measures of aggression, temperament, and psychopathology. Not all of these measures constitute psychological tests *per se*; some function essentially as appraisals or screening devices.

MALINGERING AND DISSIMULATION

Malingering and deception among juveniles has been addressed in the professional literature (McCann, 1998; Grisso, 1998a; Oldershaw & Bagby, 1997). The forensic psychologist has a number of instruments available, as indicated previously, that have indicators for malingering and either exaggeration or suppression of traits. The MMPI-A and the Millon Adolescent Clinical Inventory are two that were previously discussed that may help to detect such activity. In addition, Rogers, Bagby, and Dickens (1992) introduced the Structured Interview of Reported Symptoms (SIRS), which provides scores to indicate signs or suggestion of the probability of malingering. SIRS norms for juveniles between the ages of 14–17 have been subsequently established for this specific purpose (Rogers, Hinds, & Sewell, 1996). Although there is now a new SIRS-2, at the time of its publication the authors noted that this latest version "lacks sufficient data on effect sizes and cut scores to be employed with younger adolescents"; practitioners were advised to look for "forthcoming studies on the clinical applications of the SIRS-2 with adolescents younger than 18 years" (Rogers, Sewell, & Gillard, 2010, p. 14). It is essential that the evaluator always consider the likelihood of malingering and deception, particularly as an aspect of an antisocial behavior pattern.

TEAM VERSUS SOLO APPROACHES

It is likely that the most thorough evaluation of the juvenile is accomplished when a team approach is used. In that case, the psychiatrist, psychologist, and a social worker cooperate in gathering background information, use a multidisciplinary approach to diagnostic formulation and risk assessment, and confer to synthesize impressions and make dispositional recommendations.

However, when the psychologist or psychiatrist is solely responsible for the evaluation, common principles apply equally:

- Careful interview of the juvenile
- Collateral information from caregivers
- Review of pertinent treatment, legal, and school records
- Administration of appropriate measures or testing instruments in which the clinician is trained
- Correlation of testing results with clinical findings
- Identification of psychiatric disorders, if any, and potential risks to the youth and to the community
- Recommendations to the court for treatment and rehabilitation, keeping in mind the time and facilities available for treatment

The juvenile waiver process is one of the most important aspects of the handling of juvenile offenders in the courts. Careful diagnostic evaluation and risk assessment, together with knowledge of the treatment options available in the relevant justice settings and thoughtful dispositional recommendations assist the court in making appropriate disposition and improve the chances of successful rehabilitation of youth brought before the court. The thorough forensic psychiatric/psychological evaluation therefore plays an important role in this phase of the justice process.

DATA INTERPRETATION

As in the case of competency to waive *Miranda* rights, the standard for meeting competency to stand trial is higher for the more serious crimes.

FACTORS AFFECTING TRANSFER

The evaluation for certification to adult court, or decertification from adult court, includes community safety factors (risk of future violence in the community); individual developmental factors (psychosocial maturity/immaturity); intelligence level (presence or absence of mental retardation); social or family factors which influence the juvenile's adjustment (poverty, victimization); psychiatric disorders or psychological problems; and characteristics of the offense. There must also be reasonable grounds to believe that the public interest is better served by the transfer of the case either for adjudication in the juvenile system or for criminal prosecution.

The impact of the juvenile's offense on the victim or victims involved is important, particularly whether harm caused is permanent or longstanding. Any hardship that the act may have caused, particularly in precipitating violent or dysfunctional behaviors on the part of the victim, relates to the impact that the offense has on the community at large and the effect on crime and vigilance among community members.

The nature and circumstances of the alleged offense are considered, particularly whether the youth acted alone or together with others. The specific influence that others may have had on the youth as opposed to the influence the youth exercised on others is considered. The degree of culpability and how much responsibility is taken by the youth for the delinquent act are also considered in determining amenability to rehabilitation.

The adequacy and duration of dispositional alternatives available under the juvenile justice system and the adult criminal justice system are weighed. Is the youth likely to benefit from placement in a juvenile facility for a period of time prior to the age of 21? Does the juvenile pose a threat to public safety if released to the jurisdiction of juvenile court? Both the availability of appropriate resources, and whether the youth is likely to benefit are considered. The clinician should review any prior placement under the juvenile system, and if there was failure to adjust or whether the youth did well and benefited from the treatment program. Prior success or failure is an indicator of the chance of future success in a juvenile rehabilitative setting.

Age and maturity are important for amenability to treatment, as is intellectual capacity. Typically, juveniles functioning in or above the "below average" range of intelligence are more likely to process and assimilate new information and, consequently, to benefit from cognitively based treatments than are those functioning at or below "borderline" intellectual levels. Youth in the mentally retarded range are less likely to benefit from cognitive treatments, because of limitations in the ability to acquire and use new information. Even for youth with intelligence in the normal range, immature ability to use that intelligence in sound decision-making and realistic risk appraisal contribute to the increased incidence of delinquent behaviors (Scott & Steinberg, 2008).

The specific role of the youth in the act (as gathered from a variety of sources) and the degree of criminal sophistication exhibited are considered: whether the youth was the originator of the delinquent act, whether there was premeditation, and whether an attitude of callousness was evident. The nature and extent of any prior delinquent history, as well as success or failure of any previous rehabilitation is reviewed. How they did on juvenile probation and institutional reports are also important factors.

This may involve the clinician interviewing family members, friends, teachers, probation officers, police officers, physicians, counselors, and school personnel, to develop a more complete picture of the youth's pattern of behavior. Medical records may also elucidate the issue of amenability to treatment in the juvenile system. This is particularly important when working with older juveniles who may be close to the age of 18. If a juvenile commits an offense shortly before age 18, he/she may be close to 19 years of age before the process of decertification is considered, allowing little time for rehabilitation before age 21, which must be considered in the decertification evaluation.

VIOLENCE RISK ASSESSMENT

A major aspect of the juvenile offender assessment is the degree of "dangerousness" or the "risk of harm" posed by the juvenile to the community. The evaluating clinician can assist the court by identifying the potential risk factors for any particular youth. Such risk factors include both attributes of the youth as well as the youth's past and future social environments. Known risk factors for an individual youthful offender include: male gender; school failure; age at first violent behavior (younger age at first episode correlates with higher risk); frequency and variety of past assaultive behavior; level of volatility; substance abuse; exposure to violence; availability of weapons; gang involvement; fire setting; and animal cruelty. A higher number of risk factors may indicate a greater risk to public safety and the need for a more secure environment for pretrial detention as well as for rehabilitation. Included in this assessment, of course, is the degree of threat to self, as well as to others (Kruh & Brodsky, 1997).

The opinion regarding risk of future violence recognizes that social context affects behavior. A youth who acted out in a less structured or chaotic social environment may show more prosocial behavior when confined in a more structured placement (Witt & Dyer, 1997). For example, a youth from a home life in which there is a tumultuous relationship with the parents may be less likely to escalate in a structured, supportive placement. The assessment should be made relative to demographically similar youth. The clinician can then estimate future risk, based on the number of risk factors identified, as high, medium, or low.

Although known risk factors may be identified, there is no universal pattern. For example, even though youths who commit homicide often have violent histories, they are just as likely to have no prior record of delinquent behavior (Grisso, 1998a). It should be noted that research indicates that delinquent behavior increases from ages 13 through 18, and then usually subsides (Gottfredson & Hirschi, 1990).

Grisso outlines risk factors in *Forensic Evaluation of Juveniles* (Grisso, 1998a), which are adapted and addressed in greater detail below.

PAST BEHAVIOR

Although it is often said that one can predict future behavior by looking at past behavior, a youth may have a blameless past and still engage in risky behavior. However, past behavior should be examined for patterns. The chronicity, dangerousness, and emotional context of past violent behavior should be considered individually. *Chronicity* refers to the frequency and duration of such past behavior. How recently the youth has engaged in violent behaviors should also be assessed. The *dangerousness* of the behavior refers to the severity of the violence and the seriousness of the actual or potential harm. The *specific emotional context* of the behavior, whether impulsive and mood driven (affective) or planned, targeted, and exploitative (predatory) (Meloy, 2006), should be determined. Did the risky behavior occur only in the context of an episode of treatable psychiatric disorder? Does past risky behavior constitute a pattern rising to the level of a diagnosis of conduct disorder (the diagnostic prerequisite for antisocial personality disorder in adulthood)?

Behavior of more chronicity and higher dangerousness, which is exploitative in character, poses a higher risk for future antisocial acting out. Behavior of lower chronicity and less seriousness, which is mood or illness driven, is more apt to respond to treatment and potentially less risky for future social adjustment.

SUBSTANCE USE

Another risk factor is abuse of drugs or alcohol, whether or not the behavior occurred while the individual was under the influence. Some individuals act out only when under the influence of substances or alcohol. While the abuse of drugs or alcohol is not an excuse for such behavior, it may help to explain certain acts, particularly if the acts occur only while under the specific influence. The youth who abuses substances may demonstrate certain maladaptive thinking patterns (Twersky, 1997) which impair adaptive social behavior, and which need to be addressed in cognitively oriented therapy.

PEERS AND COMMUNITY

How often a youth's aggressive behaviors are committed with peers or as part of a gang is also important. The social influence may serve as a predictor. Again, whether or not the youth acts out when alone as opposed to in response to the influence of others may provide insight into behavior patterns. Research (Frick et al., 1994; Otto, 1992) underscores the notion of peer influence and change in behaviors that is vital to understanding peers' influence with delinquent behavior. Gang or peer group–associated violence is a risk factor.

FAMILY CONFLICTS AND AGGRESSION

If aggressive and destructive behaviors have been modeled by the family of origin, then the youth may be at increased risk. A juvenile's history of direct victimization by abuse or neglect by a parent or caretaker, as well as a history of having witnessed domestic violence against a parent, is a risk factor (Widom, 1989; Widom &

Maxfield, 1996). Having a parent or caretaker who has been diagnosed with antisocial personality disorder or who has a history of juvenile delinquency also increases risk. Although such a diagnosis may not be known to the evaluating clinician, it may be possible to ascertain whether a parent is or has been incarcerated.

SOCIAL STRESSORS AND EXTERNAL SUPPORT

Youth with poor social support and weakened family ties are at increased risk. The lack of such support, and poor social skills, lessen a youth's capacity to resist peer pressure and intimidation.

PERSONALITY TRAITS

Although personality *disorders* are not ordinarily diagnosed before age 18, certain personality *traits* are associated with increased future risk. Stable, maladaptive patterns of behavior, including deceitfulness, difficulty handling anger, and the inability to display empathy, have all been identified as contributing to future risk. Conduct disorder, thought to be the juvenile antecedent of antisocial personality disorder, when diagnosed in the juvenile justice setting may prompt care staff to neglect more treatable psychiatric disorders (Wills, 2009) and should, therefore, be diagnosed with caution and not to the neglect of other psychiatric disorders.

MENTAL ILLNESS

Serious mental illness, especially if occurring together with other risk factors, is a major risk factor for future aggressive behavior if left untreated. Physiologic predisposition to serious psychiatric disorders such as bipolar or the schizoaffective disorders, together with barriers to medication compliance and appropriate supports in the community, predispose individuals with these disorders to relapse in the community setting. Other psychiatric illnesses, such as depression, attention deficit/hyperactivity disorder, posttraumatic stress disorder, or traumatic brain injury, also jeopardize adjustment in the community. If they are diagnosed in the assessment, appropriately designed treatments can be recommended.

OPPORTUNITIES TO OFFEND

Environmental conditions that increase frequency and dangerousness of violent acting out should be minimized if possible, including
the youth's access to substances of abuse and firearms.

FUTURE RESIDENCE

It has been said that removing the juvenile from the environment
in which the delinquent act occurred reduces risk (Steinberg &
Cauffman, 1996). Assessment should consider, therefore, whether
a return to the setting in which the delinquent act occurred will
increase the risk of recurrence. As stated earlier, the degree of security
(emotional security as well as physical safety) in that environment
will also have an impact on the reduction of future risk.

FACTORS INVOLVING RESILIENCY

The resiliency of families of origin or caretakers should be considered. Youth who have come from environments with "good
resiliency factors" (i.e., family cohesiveness, good communication,
etc.) are more likely to avoid future delinquency. Those who have
fewer resiliency factors are less likely to do well.

USE OF PSYCHOLOGICAL TESTING INSTRUMENTS

Some psychological testing instruments and measures have limits
on who can employ them. The evaluator should be familiar with
the validity and reliability factors of each measure used, as well as
the specific qualifications required for its administration. Forensic
psychologists who are licensed and properly trained are usually
the most appropriate to use such measures. However, other mental health professionals may use certain appraisals if they have
the specific appropriate training (Dattilio & Sadoff, 2007; Dattilio,
Tresco, & Siegel, 2007). In the risk assessment, the results of such
measures should specify a juvenile's potential for violent behavior toward him/herself and to others, reflecting the potentials
in particular settings (home versus structured residence versus
hospitalization).

MALINGERING AND DISSIMULATION

Evaluators need to be aware that a youth may malinger or attempt to convince the court to retain or waive him/her to juvenile court in order to avoid prosecution in the adult system. Being adjudicated in the juvenile system offers the offender the benefit of an age limit to judicial control (21), as well as what are likely to be seen as less severe sentences than those imposed in adult court. Therefore, the motivation for deception and dissimulation may be great. Juveniles often believe that they are less likely to be waived to criminal court if they are perceived as seriously mentally ill and, therefore, may feign an illness or exaggerate an existing illness. Alternatively, a juvenile with a genuine psychiatric disorder may believe that acting "more normal" will improve the chance of remaining in the juvenile system.

COMMUNICATION

In most cases, documentation of the clinician's findings and opinion will be requested in report form. Testimony may also be required. A written report should include labeled sections: the type of evaluation and the question that gave rise to the evaluation; court order under which the evaluation was conducted; consents obtained (if necessary); confidentiality disclosures made to the evaluee and collateral informants; whether there is or will be a treatment relationship with the evaluee; listing of sources of information and clinical interviews completed; psychological tests or measures administered and their results; clinical impressions; opinion and reasoning; and dispositional recommendations. The "opinion and reasoning" section distinguishes the forensic report from a clinical treatment record. In it, the evaluator elucidates for the court the findings of the evaluation including the specific causal links between the conclusions of the opinion and any identified deficits, citing the evidence supporting the deficits, whether in the records reviewed, collateral information, clinical interview, or psychological test results. To the extent possible, the clinician should avoid professional jargon, and explain findings in terms understandable to the educated non–mental health professional. When medical or psychological terminology is necessary, such as a medication or a psychological symptom pattern, it should be explained briefly.

A carefully reasoned report may obviate the need for testimony. If testimony is required, a report in which the clinician's reasoning is clearly documented puts the clinician at ease by eliminating the need to "think on one's feet." It aids the clarity of testimony by serving to refresh the clinician's memory about the evidence used to support the opinion.

The clinician's opinion as to the juvenile's competence, whether to waive *Miranda* rights, or to stand trial, should reflect the specific abilities required by statute, taking into consideration the seriousness of the offense and whether the matter is to be adjudicated in juvenile court or tried in adult court. The manner in which clinical or developmental disorders affect the competence functions should be described.

In anticipation of the possibility that the juvenile may be found incompetent to stand trial, the clinician is expected to address whether competency is "restorable": whether the conditions responsible for the incompetence can be rectified within a reasonable period of time. This involves identifying specific deficiencies, what particular treatment options are available to address them, and whether specific deficits can be ameliorated sufficiently to allow for competent participation in the trial process. If specific incapacities are due to developmental immaturity, rather than to remediable educational deficits or treatable psychiatric disorder, competency restoration may not be achievable within a reasonable period of time, and this should be included in opinions transmitted to the court.

VIOLENCE RISK ASSESSMENT

The assessment of risk is an important part of the certification/decertification assessment, and includes developmental and constitutional (individual), environmental, and situational factors. The seriousness of the instant offense is always taken into consideration. The ability of clinicians to determine who will and will not enact violence in the future is limited (Otto, 1992; Rogers, 2000), and the evaluating clinician often educates the court about the predictive limitations of the risk assessment. A risk assessment is appropriately expressed in relative, not absolute, terms and is necessarily limited. For example, a clinician might state, "It is not clear whether this youth will or will not engage in violent behavior. However, his/her risk of future violence is greater (or less) than risk posed by other youths in the same type of setting." While judges or other personnel might prefer a more specific prediction, it is important that we state that it is within our ethical boundaries to indicate the limits on prediction consistent with current science. This distinction is also helpful when forensic psychologists or psychiatrists are cross-examined and need to support testimony with evidence.

The report or testimony regarding the risk evaluation often addresses the following dispositional questions: whether secure detention prior to trial is necessary; whether the juvenile offender presents too great a danger to be handled in the juvenile justice system; and, if adjudicated delinquent in juvenile court, whether rehabilitation will require a secure setting.

RECOMMENDATIONS TO THE COURT

It is useful to the court for the evaluator to make specific recommendations for the juvenile's rehabilitation. Beyer (2006) points out the need for evaluators to address the juvenile's disabilities, recovery from trauma, and maturation of thinking in the process of rehabilitation. Specific recommendations for rehabilitation make it easier for the court to match the juvenile with the appropriate placement and treatment.

The question of whether the evaluator should address the youth's culpability may arise when a preadjudicatory evaluation is requested in which the court also requests dispositional recommendations. In that case, the evaluator is advised to avoid making a judgment, which is the proper purview of the finder of fact, and to make the requested recommendations in the conditional—in other words, to write "*If* the court adjudicates Jane Doe delinquent, appropriate disposition *would* include. . . ."

In any evaluation, all opinions should be rendered to a reasonable degree of psychological or medical certainty or probability. Questions asked to which the evaluator is not able to give an opinion with a reasonable degree of psychological or medical certainty should be identified.

REFERENCES

Achenbach, T. (1991). *Manual for the Youth Self-Report and 1991 Profile.* Burlington, VT: University of Vermont Department of Psychiatry.

Ashendorf, L., Constantinou, M., & McCaffrey, R. J. (2004). The effect of depression and anxiety of the TOMM in community dwelling older adults. *Archives of Clinical Neuropsychology, 19,* 125–130.

Benedek, E., & Schetky, D. (2002). *Principles and practice of child and adolescent forensic psychiatry.* Washington, DC: American Psychiatric Publishing.

Berghuis v. Thompkins, 130 S.Ct. 2250 (2010).

Beyer, M. (2006). Fifty delinquents in juvenile and adult court. *American Journal of Orthopsychiatry, 76,* 206–214.

Brief for the States of Louisiana, et al., as Amici Curiae in Support of Respondent, *Graham v. Florida,* U.S. (2010). (No. 08-7412); *Sullivan v. Florida,* U.S. (2010) (No. 08-7621).

Butcher, J., Williams, C., Graham, J., Archer, R., Tellegen, R., Ben-Porath, Y., & Kaemmer, B. (1992). *MMPI-A: Manual for administration scoring and interpretation.* Minneapolis, MN: University of Minnesota Press.

Cauffman, E., Piquero, A. R., Kimonis, E., Steinberg, L., Chassin, L., & Fagan, J. (2007). Legal, individual, and environmental predictors of court disposition in a sample of serious adolescent offenders. *Law and Human Behavior, 31,* 519–535.

Dattilio, F. M., & Sadoff, R. L. (2007). *Mental health experts: Roles and qualifications for court* (2nd ed.). Mechanicsburg, PA: Pennsylvania Bar Institute.

Dattilio, F. M., Tresco, K., & Siegel, A. (2007). An empirical survey of psychological testing and the use of the term "psychological": Turf battles or clinical necessity? *Professional Psychology: Research and Practice, 38,* 682–689.

Dusky v. U.S., 362 U.S. 402 (1960).

Everington, C. (1990). *The Competence Assessment for Standing Trial for Defendants with Mental Retardation (CAST-MR). Criminal Justice and Behavior, 17,* 147–168.

Fare v. Michael C., 442 U.S. 707 (1979).

Flesch, L. M. (2004). Juvenile crime and why waiver is not the answer. *Family Court Review, 42,* 583–596.

Frick, P., O'Brien, H., Wootton, J., & McBurnett, K. (1994). Psychopathy and conduct problems in children. *Journal of Abnormal Psychology, 103,* 700–707.

Gottfredson, M., & Hirschi, T. (1990). *A general theory of crime.* Stanford, CA: Stanford University Press.

Graham v. Florida, 130 S.Ct. 2011 (2010).

Grisso, T. (1980). Juveniles' capacities to waive *Miranda* rights: An empirical analysis. *California Law Review, 68,* 1134–1166.

Grisso, T. (1981). *Juveniles' waiver of rights: Legal and psychological competence.* New York, NY: Plenum Press.

Grisso, T. (1986). *Evaluating competencies: Forensic assessments and instruments.* New York, NY: Plenum Press.

Grisso, T. (1988). *Competency to stand trial evaluations: A manual for practice.* Sarasota, FL: Professional Resource Press.

Grisso, T. (1998a). *Forensic evaluation of juveniles.* Sarasota, FL: Professional Resource Press.

Grisso, T. (1998b). *Instruments for assessing understanding and appreciation of Miranda rights.* Sarasota, FL: Professional Resource Press.

Grisso, T., Miller, M., & Sales, B. (1987). Competency to stand trial in juvenile court. *International Journal of Law and Psychiatry, 10,* 1–20.

Grisso, T., Steinberg, L., Woolard, J., Cauffman, E., Scott, E., Graham, S., . . . Schwartz, R. (2003). Juveniles' competence to stand trial: A comparison of adolescents' and adults' capacities as trial defendants. *Law and Human Behavior, 27,* 333–363.

Gudjonsson, G. (1984a). *Gudjonsson Suggestibility Scale.* London: Psychology Press.

Gudjonsson, G. (1984b). A new scale of interrogative suggestibility. *Personality and Individual Differences, 5,* 303–314.

Gudjonsson, G. (1992). *The psychology of interrogations, confessions and testimony.* New York, NY: John Wiley & Sons.

Harris, G. T., Rice, M. E., & Quinsey, V. L. (1993). Violent recidivism of mentally disordered offenders: The development of a statistical prediction instrument. *Criminal Justice and Behavior, 20,* 315–335.

Heilbrun, K., Leheny, C., Thomas, L., Huneycutt, D. (1997). A national survey of U.S. statutes on juvenile transfer: implications for policy and practice. *Behavioral Sciences and the Law, 15,* 125–149.

Hoge, S., Poythress, N., Bonnie, R., Monahan, J., Eisenberg, M., & Feicht-Haviar, T. (1997). The MacArthur adjudication competence study: Diagnosis, psychopathology, and adjudicative competence-related abilities. *Behavioral Sciences and the Law, 15,* 329–345.

In re Gault, 387 U.S. 1 (1967).

In re Winship 397 U.S. 358 (1970).

Jastak, S., Wilkinson, G., & Jastak, J. (1984). *Wide Range Achievement Test—Revised.* Wilmington, DE: Jastak Associates.

Jesness, C. F. (1996). *The Jesness Inventory manual.* Toronto, ON: Multi-Health Systems.

Kent v. U.S., 383 U.S. 541 (1966).

Kruh, I. P., & Brodsky, S. I. (1997). Clinical evaluations for transfer of juveniles to criminal court: Current practices and future research. *Behavioral Science and the Law, 15*, 151–165.

Lipsitt, P., Lelos, D., & McGarry, A. L. (1971). Competency for trial: A screening instrument. *American Journal of Psychiatry, 128*, 105–109.

Marczyk, G. R., Heilbrun, K., Lander, T., & DeMatteo, D. (2005). Juvenile decertification: Developing a model for classification and prediction. *Criminal Justice and Behavior, 32*, 278–301.

McCann, J. (1998). *Malingering and deception in adolescents: Assessing credibility in clinical and forensic settings.* Washington, DC: American Psychological Association.

McGarry, L. (1973). *Competency to stand trial and mental illness.* Rockville, MD: Department of Health, Education, and Welfare.

Meloy, J. R. (2006). Empirical basis and forensic application of affective and predatory violence. *Australian and New Zealand Journal of Psychiatry, 40*, 539–547.

Millon, T. (1993). *Millon Adolescent Clinical Inventory.* Minneapolis, MN: National Computer Systems.

Millon, T., Green, C., & Meagher, R. (1982). *Millon Adolescent Personality Inventory.* Minneapolis, MN: National Computer Systems.

Miranda v. Arizona, 384 U.S. 436 (1966).

Nicholson, R., Robertson, H., Johnson, W., & Jensen, G. (1988). A comparison of instruments for assessing competency to stand trial. *Law and Human Behavior, 12*, 313–321.

Oldershaw, L. & Bagby, R. M. (1997). Children and deception. In R. Rogers (Ed.), *Clinical assessment of malingering and deception* (pp. 153–166). New York, NY: Guilford Press.

Otto, R. (1992). Prediction of dangerous behavior: A review and analysis of "second-generation" research. *Forensic Reports, 5*, 103–113.

People v. Lara, 432 P.2d 202 (Cal. 1967).

Roesch, R., Webster, C., & Eaves, D. (1994). *The Fitness Interview Test-Revised: A method for examining fitness to stand trial.* Burnaby, BC: Department of Psychology, Simon Fraser University.

Rogers, R. (2000). The uncritical acceptance of risk assessment in forensic practice. *Law and Human Behavior, 24*, 595–605.

Rogers, R. (2008). (Ed.). *Clinical assessment and malingering and deception* (3rd ed.). New York, NY: Guilford Press.

Rogers, R., Bagby, R., and Dickens, S. (1992). *Structured interview of reported symptoms: Professional manual.* Odessa, FL: Psychological Assessment Resources.

Rogers, R., Hinds, J., & Sewell, K. (1996). Feigning psychopathology among adolescent offenders: Validation of the SIRS, MMPI-A, and SIMS. *Journal of Personality Assessment, 67,* 244–257.

Rogers, R., Sewell, K. W., & Gillard, N. D. (2010). *Structured Interview of Reported Symptoms, 2nd Edition: Professional manual.* Lutz, FL: Psychological Assessment Resources.

Roper v. Simmons, 543 U.S. 551 (2005).

Sadoff, R. L., & Dattilio, F. M. (2008). *Crime and mental illness: A guide to courtroom practice.* Mechanicsburg, PA: Pennsylvania Bar Institute.

Salekin, R. T., Rogers, R., & Ustad, K. L. (2001). Juvenile waiver to adult criminal court: Prototypes for dangerousness, sophistication, maturity, and amenability to treatment. *Psychology, Public Policy and Law, 7,* 381–408.

Sanders, W. (Ed). (1970). *Juvenile offenders for a thousand years.* Chapel Hill, NC: University of North Carolina Press.

Scott, E. S., & Steinberg, L. (2008). *Rethinking juvenile justice.* Cambridge, MA: Harvard University Press.

Stapleton, W., & Teitelbaum, L. (1972). *In defense of youth.* New York, NY: Russell Sage.

Steinberg, L., & Cauffman, E. (1996). Juvenile transfer cases: Risk assessment and risk management. *The Journal of Psychiatry and Law, 25,* 581–614.

Steinberg, L., & Cauffman, E. (1999). Maturity of judgment in adolescence: Psychosocial factors in adolescent decision-making. *Law and Human Behavior, 20,* 249–272.

Twersky, A. J. (1997). *Addictive thinking.* Center City, MN: Hazelden Foundation.

U.S. Department of Justice, Office of Juvenile Justice and Delinquency Prevention (OJJDP). (2009). *Juvenile arrests 2007 (OJJDP) No. 2007-JF-FX-K003.* Washington, DC: Author.

Webster, C. D., Douglas, K. S., Eaves, D., & Hart, S. D. (1997). *HCR-20: Assessing Risk for Violence (Version 2).* Burnaby, BC: Mental Health, Law and Policy Institute, Simon Fraser University.

Widom, C. (1989). Does violence beget violence? A critical examination of the literature. *Psychological Bulletin, 106,* 3–28.

Widom, C., & Maxfield, M. (1996). A prospective examination of risk for violence among abused and neglected children. In C. Ferris & T. Grisso (Eds.), *Understanding aggressive behavior in children* (pp. 224–237). New York, NY: Annals of the New York Academy of Sciences.

Wills, C. (2009). Psychiatry site visit report. In *S. H. v. Stickrath,* United States District Court Southern District of Ohio Eastern Division, Case No. 2:04-cv-1206, class action suit settled in May, 2008, as per www.dys.ohio.gov

Witt, P. H., & Dyer, F. J. (1997). Juvenile transfer cases: Risk assessment and risk management. *Journal of Psychiatry and Law, 25,* 581–614.

Zapf, P., & Roesch, R. (1997). Assessing fitness to stand trial: A comparison of institution-based evaluations and a brief screening interview. *Canadian Journal of Community Mental Health, 16,* 53–66.

CHAPTER 12

Addictions

CURTIS L. BARRETT and RICHARD F. LIMOGES

INTRODUCTION

Roman citizens could not be sold into slavery to resolve their unpaid debts or other offenses, but they could be subjected to indentured servitude by an "assignment in service to their creditors" (Webster, 1848, p. 14). There persons became *ad dicted* ("spoken over"), with the result that their freedom of action was rendered inoperative. Like that of slaves, their will became subservient to something outside themselves.

Given that "addiction" has to do with loss of will, we may consider what effect this has on the circumstances of criminal defendants. Will exists on a continuum, as does the need to exercise that will. For example, while a significant degree of will might be required to pilot an airplane, little or no will is required to be a comatose patient following a stroke. Thus, an impairment of will in criminal proceedings does not exist independent of tasks requiring a specified level of competence.

Terms such as *will, freedom of choice,* or *mind* may be accepted uncritically by juries or other finders of fact, but not by some scientists. Pinker (1997) famously stated—in reference to a notion prevalent in medical science for decades—that "mind is what the brain does" (p. 21). Anything that impairs the brain must also impair the mind, and will is almost unquestionably a function of mind. Recognition of this basic notion will help evaluators to avoid distraction by a host of scientific and philosophical arguments that lack direct relevance to the forensic assessment of addictions.

According to the Office of National Drug Control Policy (2000), persons engaging in illicit drug use within the past year were "about 16 times more likely than nonusers to report being arrested and booked for larceny or theft," and "more than nine times more likely to be arrested and booked on an assault charge" (pp. 1–2). Overall, it was recently asserted that "about half of the nation's 2.2 million jail inmates meet clinical criteria for drug or alcohol dependence, while the majority of state or federal inmates regularly used drugs prior to their incarceration" (Aldhous, 2006, p. 6). Addictions constitute an inescapable aspect of forensic psychiatry and psychology in criminal cases.

PREPARATION

TRAINING AND CERTIFICATION

Substance Dependence   For psychiatrists, there can be no substitute for the perspective offered by advanced training in addiction medicine and, in particular, addiction psychiatry (Ries, Fiellen, Miller, & Saitz, 2009). Both the American Society of Addiction Medicine (ASAM; www.asam.org) and the American Academy of Addiction Psychiatry (AAAP; www2.aaap.org) are invaluable resources in this regard.

For psychologists, similar training can be obtained in the course of qualifying for the Certificate of Proficiency in the Treatment of Alcohol and Other Psychoactive Substance Use Disorders, which is offered by the American Psychological Association Practice Organization's College of Professional Psychology (www.apaprac ticecentral.org). This particular credential reflects a more restricted area of knowledge than is available from addiction medicine and addiction psychiatry sources, as it focuses more on knowledge of studies that meet scientific standards than it does on clinical lore or perspectives from various self-help groups. Thus, we recommend that psychologists seek out additional training experiences in order to establish competency in this specialty area. Such experiences may include attending open meetings of Narcotics Anonymous, Alcoholics Anonymous, and Gamblers Anonymous as well as seeking out continuing education programs primarily designed for certified alcohol and drug counselors. Overall, it is important to state and list qualifications that are valid and trustworthy, and to distinguish these from those that are in effect purchased and perhaps even bogus (Dattilio & Sadoff, 2007).

Addictions Without Substance   Psychiatrists and psychologists alike will need specific preparation in order to assess the "addictions without substance" (AWS; Barrett & Drogin, 2000). These conditions include pathological gambling (American Psychiatric Association, 2000) and sexual addiction (Levine, 2010). The AWS—identified on occasion as "process addictions" (Hagedorn, 2009)—are given little, if any, emphasis in professional training programs that address substance dependence. A valuable source of training in this area is the National Council on Problem Gambling (NCPG; www.npcgambling .org) and its state-level affiliates.

EMBRACING THE LEGAL PERSPECTIVE

Preparation for the forensic assessment of an individual with an addictive disorder includes developing an in-depth appreciation of the legal context in which one's work will be judged and—perhaps—utilized. In the criminal justice system, these include responsibility for forbidden acts and the identification—or lack thereof—of mitigating circumstances. Persons who embezzled company funds might argue that pathological gambling robbed them of their will to resist this behavior. Perhaps they and their victims will best be served by focusing on restitution rather than punishment. If an addictive disorder is appropriately clinically managed, does the pathological gambler offer a tangible threat to anyone? How will the results of a forensic evaluation support or negate the legal arguments that are being made in these cases? Further, which aspects of these results will be persuasive to the trier of fact?

   The concept of identifying—as opposed, of course, to manufacturing—"persuasive evidence" has become central to the thinking of the psychologist author of this chapter. In one capital case, the defendant presented evidence that the onset of his alcoholism occurred when he was no more than 5 years of age. It was clearly established that he had become severely addicted by the time he became a teenager. After his conviction of murder, the defendant refused to exercise his right to an appeal, so the appeal was made against his wishes, and the evaluator was posed several intriguing questions. For example, was the defendant's original use of alcohol voluntary, and his addiction thus something that he brought on himself? Were his later refusals of a defense against a charge of murder voluntary and rational, or were they aspects of his alcoholism (e.g., chronic depression, seeking approval)?

It was undisputed that the defendant first encountered alcohol when, as a mere child, he was first fed whiskey by his father. Was this a voluntary act on his part, or instead the reaction of a genetically vulnerable minor to the normal influence of a parent, reflecting a stress-diathesis model of addictions (Healy & Tranter, 1999) that incorporates both biological factors and life experience? Regardless of how he became addicted, how—if at all—was this condition related to the defendant's subsequent acts? What responsibility did the defendant have for what he did under the influence of an unintended alcoholism—if that is what it was—including his refusal of an appeal?

In this case, the judge ruled that the defendant's behavior was due to sociopathy and nothing else, and stated that he found the prosecution psychiatrist's arguments "more persuasive" than those of the senior author. The defendant was subsequently executed. In retrospect, we are left with the question of what counsel might have done to make the senior author's findings "more persuasive." What opportunities for persuasion were missed?

EXPERT COLLABORATION AND RECORD REVIEW

The forensic assessment of addictive disorders in criminal cases is optimally styled as a multidisciplinary endeavor, with the psychiatrist and psychologist assuming appropriate responsibility for respective medically and behaviorally focused roles. It may be that budgetary, evidentiary, or other considerations will result in the appointment of a single evaluator, in which case that professional will be all the more intent on reviewing relevant records in order to provide as clinically global a perspective as possible. A review of all available records will be optimal, particularly when one source purports to quote another verbatim. All too often, original reports are inaccurately or incompletely quoted—or even deliberately distorted—by subsequent reporters. Overall, it is advisable to leave to counsel the task of obtaining and distributing requested records.

In these matters, perhaps more than in any other criminal law evaluation, there will be a need to supplement the defendant's self-report with information gained from collateral sources including specific medical documentation. While psychiatrists and psychologists may know a great deal about the general effects that certain frequently abused chemicals have on the mind, other factors will be critical in establishing the relevant nature and degree of intoxication for the incident in question. What concentrations of various substances were acknowledged at the time of the arrest, or verified on the basis of breath analyses, blood levels, or hair samples? What were the documented chronicity and cycling of the defendant's addictive process? What were the defendant's weight, nutrition, hydration, and associated medical conditions?

With regard to gambling addiction, for instance, similar questions will be asked. It may appear that the powerful effect of modeling (Bandura & Kupers, 1964; Malone, 2002) could well account for the onset of pathological gambling. For example, consider the case of a boy of 5 who was exposed to the role of wagering on "numbers" in the context of his father's and his uncle's gambling. This exposure was no more voluntary than was that of the 5-year-old who was fed whiskey by his father. The boy was taken to the scene of a highly charged gambling event, learned the ropes, practiced, and then became addicted as a teen. Collateral sources are invaluable in establishing—or disproving—the veracity of such arguably compelling circumstances.

There are two kinds of gambling, both of which can lead to financial improprieties of a criminal nature. It may be useful to distinguish between the thrill-seeking nature of roulette, blackjack, craps, and chemin de fer, and the mindless, repetitive, numbing nature of slot machines, where the very opposite of acute awareness and acuity is sought. In both, however, the person seeks to escape the real world.

In preparing to assess the degree of an individual's addiction-based impairment and the voluntariness of the addiction in question, the forensic evaluator will often need to determine in advance whether the addiction was to an illegal substance or behavior—or whether it occurred in a broader illegal context. For example, even a relatively mild addiction may be related to a most serious legal circumstance if developed while selling or distributing cocaine. Addiction to gambling may also involve association with organized crime or even taking the "enforcer role" in order to earn the money needed to sustain an addiction.

AGENCY ISSUES

Skilled forensic examiners know that the first thing to be established is for whom they are working—that is, whose agent are they? Private practitioners will know ahead of time which lawyer or governmental agency has retained them, and in criminal matters it will be clear whether one is working with the prosecution or with the defense. Who ultimately becomes entitled to sensitive addiction-related information obtained during the examination is an essential issue that must be made clear from the beginning. It must also be established that such results are not part of a typical "medical record" and that the services by which they are derived are not "treatment." These and other forensic evaluations do not establish a doctor–patient relationship (Gutheil & Simon, 2002).

On the one hand, examinees may court sympathy and longer-term involvement, seeing evaluators as persons who can help them in various ways. On the other hand, examinees may be defensive, suspicious, and withholding, in fear of the short-term consequences of the forensic evaluation. It is essential for evaluators to make clear for whom they are working, to whom evaluation results will be conveyed, and that there is no "confidentiality" to speak of in these transactions.

While this is standard forensic practice, with addictions there is another dynamic in play, raising the stakes dramatically. While persons with addictive disorders may want help with the consequences of their conditions, they also want to protect their ability to perpetuate their maladaptive patterns of behavior. The evaluator must be wary of becoming the agent of the addiction itself. Rescue fantasies can be engendered even in the most skilled of evaluators, particularly if one does not examine or treat many persons with addictive disorders. Evaluators may also find themselves subject to punitive inclinations, particularly if there are injured parties who also engender sympathy for being the victims of the examinee's intemperate behavior. Viewing the examinee as lacking will power or moral fiber can produce subtle partisanship on behalf of the alleged victim.

DATA COLLECTION

INITIAL CONSIDERATIONS

Data collection begins as one revisits and confirms the stated purpose of the assessment that is to be conducted. Forensic evaluators often assume that the referring attorney will have determined the ultimate purpose of the referral, but this may not be the case, reflecting to some degree the notion that mental health defenses are typically defenses of last resort. Just as likely is the possibility that the referring attorney has very limited knowledge of and experience with utilizing mental health professionals—particularly those doctors specializing in addictive disorders. Counsel may not have detected, in the initial legal workup of a case, how mental health factors such as addiction will be featured in a defense or its prosecutorial rebuttal. Is this "data collection"? Experience has led us to believe that it is. Overall, one must assume that part of the task, when accepting a referral in such cases, is to educate counsel and to gently and diplomatically convey what counsel may not know—with particular attention to those beliefs counsel may hold about addiction that simply are not valid.

Evidence from various forms of brain scanning is increasingly available; however, absent dramatic indicia of readily observable damage, the legal admissibility of such material is highly variable on a jurisdiction-by-jurisdiction basis (Samson, 2007). For that reason, the forensic evaluator remains largely dependent on verbal reports, collateral source reports, psychometric testing, and observations of behavior in order to determine the degree to which the examinee's will has become impaired.

INTERVIEW PRESENTATION

Narratives supplied by addicted criminal defendants may be incomplete, superficial, full of blame for others, and replete with all manner of excuses designed to minimize and justify behavior. When this occurs, the effect on the unwitting forensic evaluator can be to engender pity, protective feelings, and a desire to "save" examinees from the consequences of their unfortunate circumstances—in effect, a form of *forensic countertransference* (Gutheil & Simon, 2002, pp. 86–88) with all of the labyrinthine complexity that the term implies (Sattar, Pinals, & Gutheil, 2004). Unless examiners possess a sound understanding of the interrelated processes of denial, self-deception, and other manifestations of "addictive thinking" (Twerski, 1997), they may be dragooned into protecting examinees from various outcomes necessary for gaining an appreciation of the adverse consequences of addiction.

The forensic interview—extending perhaps over several hours or sessions—should include an extensive and thorough family history of addictive diathesis. It will often prove useful to ask about other addicts in the family, who may be "heavy drinkers," "pill takers," gamblers, hard-core addicts, sexual compulsives, or any number of other types of familial "black sheep" who are rarely mentioned or who have disappeared from the family narrative. It is important to establish this history because of the genetics of addiction, in which one may discover a whole line of addicts running through one or both sides of the family of origin.

In addition, the evaluator may need to establish how a given cultural unit such as this family might encourage addictive behavior as normative, with this being all they have ever known, and with the examinee consequently convinced that "everyone behaves this way." Surprisingly, evaluators often neglect to determine whether the examinee was adopted. If so, then a genetic history may take a different course, and inquiry into the reason for the adoption could be useful.

Data collection through interview of the client—or the often critically important consultation of collateral informants (Otto, Slobogin, & Greenberg, 2007)—should consider that addictive disorders are likely to be minimized by the examinee, unless the examinee is well into recovery (e.g., participating in a self-help group for addicts or significant others). Even those who admit to ingestion of alcohol far above normal limits will characterize their intake as "social drinking," buttressed by such observations as "I work hard, and I play hard." These assertions may also be made by a collateral informant, especially if codependency (Dear, Roberts, & Lange, 2005) is involved. Interview-based data collection should be conducted with a clear-eyed recognition that denial mechanisms are likely to be at work.

It is important, if possible, to interview at least one other person with direct knowledge of the examinee. If one can speak with several persons, then this may be even better, bearing in mind that the evaluator will always need to confirm a collateral interview strategy with retaining counsel. Collateral sources of information are critical to ensuring that the examinee's narrative is valid and that one's report has probity. The evaluator will strive to avoid producing a report based only on an examinee's "dictation" or a report that appears in any way partisan.

In addition, it cannot be stressed enough that timing is a critical issue in these cases. As noted by Drogin (2000) in advice to criminal law practitioners:

> Often the substance-dependent defendant is first encountered in the throes of withdrawal from chronic intoxication. The best strategy is to reschedule planned interviews, seeking a continuance on this basis if necessary. Not only will questioning at this juncture provide questionably reliable information and planning; it may also engender considerable resentment on the part of clients who will find it difficult to forget that defense team members chose such an inopportune time to put them through their paces. (p. 31)

PHYSICAL EXAMINATION

Data collection through a physical examination is the responsibility of the psychiatrist as a physician. In addition to accepted medical criteria for that function, there are considerations specific to data collection in addiction cases.

The examination proper should begin with careful observation of the examinee. It may be wise to insist on a physical examination from an internist or general physician. When first meeting examinees, one observes their gait. Are they unsteady; do they step firmly? Next, one shakes their hand. Are their palms sweaty; is their grip adequate? What is the body habitus, that is, their build or physique? Are the arms thin; is the abdomen prominent? Do the hands shake? What color is the skin? One looks closely at their faces. Are there signs of the rosacea of chronic drinking? Are the eyeballs yellow? Are the pupils dilated or constricted? Is there involuntary mouth movement that may be due to chronic use of amphetamines? Much can be learned before the first word is spoken.

The evaluator will want to ask specifically about tattoos and request to see them. What is the story behind each tattoo? Are the tattoos hiding injection sites? It is important to ask examinees to roll up their sleeves so that one may check for needle marks or tracks. Examinees should be informed at the beginning of the examination—but not before—that there will be urine sampling to check for drugs. One might also consider using a saliva test and obtaining a hair sample that can be sent off for chemical testing.

PSYCHOLOGICAL TESTING

Just as physical examination is the purview of the psychiatrist as physician, psychometric assessment will be conducted by the psychologist. According to Drogin & Barrett (1998), "many popular, standardized, and objective personality tests employ scales designed to identify and characterize patterns of addictive behavior" (p. 70).

For example, as analyzed in detail by Miller, Shields, Campfield, Wallace, and Weiss (2007), the Minnesota Multiphasic Personality Inventory (MMPI-2) includes the MacAndrew Alcoholism Scale—Revised (MAC-R), the Addiction Acknowledgment Scale (AAS), and the Addiction Potential Scale (APS), while similar scales exist for the adolescent version of this measure (MMPI-A; Weed, Butcher, & Williams, 1994). The Millon Clinical Multiaxial Inventory (MCMI-III) contains Alcohol Dependence (Scale B) and Drug Dependence (Scale T) measures (Vanem, Krog, & Hartmann, 2008), and the adolescent form of this test possesses similar scales as well (MACI; Millon, 1993). The Personality Assessment Inventory (PAI) includes the Alcohol Problems Scale (ALC; Ruiz, Dickinson, & Pincus, 2002).

Free-standing addiction tests are also available, including the Alcohol Use Inventory (AUI; Chang, Lapham, & Wanberg, 2001), the Michigan Alcoholism Screening Test (MAST; Laux, Newman, & Brown, 2004), and the Substance Abuse Subtle Screening Inventory-3 (SASSI-3; Lazowski, Miller, Boye, & Miller, 1998), the South Oaks Gambling Screen (SOGS; Cox, Enns, & Michaud, 2004). In addition, standardized cognitive measures such as the Wechsler Adult Intelligence Scale—Fourth Edition (WAIS-IV; Wechsler, 2008) the Shipley Institute of Living Scale-2 (SILS-2; Shipley, Gruber, Martin, & Klein, 2009) can be analyzed to determine what sorts of functional impairment and even organic damage may have occurred as a product of chronic substance abuse.

Forensic evaluators should bear in mind that testing truly comes into its own in these matters when analyzed in the context of interview and available third-party documentation. Testing is of little utility when reviewed outside of this context.

COLLABORATIVE ASSESSMENT

For cases in which both a psychiatrist and a psychologist have been retained, we believe that it is proper for these parties to meet and consult once their respective examinations have been conducted. This does not remove the responsibility for the collaborators to arrive at individual opinions in the case—they should. It will be important, however, to attempt to resolve any substantive differences of opinion on the nature of the information that has been obtained. The potential for generating distinct and occasionally conflicting databases—and therefore differing opinions—in addiction-related criminal cases is substantial.

SPECIAL CONSIDERATIONS FOR ADDICTIONS WITHOUT SUBSTANCE

While substance dependence involves the effect of an externally introduced chemical agent, the AWS reflect the effect of such natural stimuli as the action associated with wagering (Suurvali, Hodgins, & Cunningham, 2010) or the release of endorphins triggered by sexual activity (Serra, Collu, & Gessa, 1988). Psychopharmacology is among the most relevant areas of expertise in the former situation, while learning theory is among the most relevant areas of expertise in the latter. At the present time, clinical lore and scientific findings on the AWS are in relative infancy when compared with those of alcohol and other substance abuse. Practitioners who conduct forensic assessment of addictions will do well to keep a weather eye out for this evidence.

Of particular relevance when it comes to pathological gambling is the part money plays. Defendants being assessed in this context will rarely have enough money for a proper evaluation; indeed, they are likely to be destitute. In addition, there may be little opportunity to establish forensically relevant clinical findings as long as defendants have enough money to prolong their activities. They are typically firm in their belief that they will soon win enough to erase all their misfortune. Also of note is that all of the depression, despair, hopelessness, and defeat may seem magically to vanish as soon as defendants find enough money to repay their debts and are free once again to resume gambling. Has the defendant ever participated in a program such as Gamblers Anonymous (Toneatto, 2008) and gained at least some initial insight in this regard?

DATA INTERPRETATION

Having determined to their satisfaction that all of the necessary data in a case have been obtained, forensic evaluators will be ready to proceed to data interpretation. Data interpretation per se will be guided by three major perspectives. First and foremost, data interpretation will be guided by the referral question that the attorney in the case indicates it should be. This is in the purview of the attorney who, after all, bears the ultimate responsibility of representing his or her client. Second, data interpretation will be guided by the evaluator's perspective on the nature of the examinee. Third, data interpretation will be guided by the concept of addiction that the evaluator brings to the case.

There may be an assumption that a particular drinking pattern equals alcoholism, or that regular and steady ingestion of controlled medications means that a person has an addiction. Such assumptions are particularly problematic when the examinee is being treated with maintenance controlled substances for such conditions as anxiety, hyperactivity, sleep apnea, or chronic pain. Throughout the data interpretation process, it will be important to consider the examinee's particular personal circumstances.

In the criminal forensic context, it is also critical to bear in mind that addiction is not sociopathy, and that sociopathy is not addiction, although some acts that are the product of addiction can be seen as sociopathic. They are more likely illegal because of the laws that pertain to drug possession, distribution, or use. Sociopathy cannot definitively be ascribed while defendants remain in an actively addicted state, unless the behavior in question predated the addiction.

THE EXAMINEE IN CONTEXT

We know of no better perspective on the examinee in context than that espoused by the late Wayne Oates, who suggested that we human beings are best seen as biological, psychological, sociological, and spiritual entities. This has been termed, by some, as the *biopsychosocial/spiritual* approach (Bullis & Cherry, 1994). Those who are familiar with the history of the mental health professions will readily recognize that this view is deeply rooted in the "common sense psychiatry" of Adolf Meyer (Lief, 1948; Roback, 1961).

Ideally, forensic evaluators will develop an understanding of how each aspect of the biopsychosocial/spiritual approach operates in the addicted examinee. By way of illustration, a defendant whose life has been dominated by the biological fact of a genetic anomaly will certainly differ from one who has always fallen into the "normal" range on most measurable dimensions. As we noted above, a client who was exposed to social learning that emphasized illegal gambling will present quite differently from one who was always taught that such activities were sinful, but who has deviated from recommended behavior—and, of course, those raised with the notion of a vengeful deity controlling behavior through guilt will view addiction far differently than will someone whose faith tradition emphasizes forgiveness and deific love.

This inclusive analytic approach not only has heuristic value for forensic data interpretation, but can be developed in each case with an eye toward its eventual utility as a framework for communicating with triers of fact—in particular, juries. It is, after all, rooted in "common sense" and not psychiatric or psychological jargon that can prove so distracting in the context of courtroom testimony.

INTEGRATION OF DATA WITH THE CONCEPT OF ADDICTION

Forensic evaluators—working alone or in tandem—must reach agreement on the concept of addiction that they accept. Whether the underlying etiology of a given case is primarily biochemical or instead rooted in social learning, effective data interpretation requires recognition that it is the impairment of will that justifies raising addiction in the context of criminal proceedings. Interpretation of the available data with regard to such questions as voluntariness of ingestion, voluntariness of exposure to addictive situations, and the like can be critical. The available data, during the interpretation phase, are to be woven into a credible accounting of the circumstances that a jury must assess. The trier of fact will eventually seek a comprehensive and persuasive narrative. Data interpretation is the path to providing it—a path that cannot be developed without a unifying notion of addiction.

FALSE DICHOTOMIES OF ADDICTION

In interpreting data, we recommend planning to assist the trier of fact by recognizing that almost every aspect of addiction occurs on a continuum, such that very little is dichotomously "all or none." Evaluators will rarely find that legal dispositions rest solely upon whether someone is either "addicted" or "not addicted." Persons with these conditions will be found to be addicted to one degree or another. Similarly, ingestion of psychoactive chemicals will not usually be an "all-or-none" situation—particularly when it is discovered that what the client *intended* to ingest was not ingested after all. For example, an examinee who intended to drink alcohol heavily at a party may actually have ingested a powerful hallucinogen. What impairment of his or her will was accountable for subsequently actionable behavior? In practice, examinees have seldom ingested anything like a chemical that was as pure as the one used in evaluating drug effects on the brain, and therefore, on the will of the examinee.

PRESCRIBED MEDICATION

The use of prescribed psychoactive chemicals should be explored. Treatment providers often have no knowledge of a patient's chemical dependence, and the patient is careful not to reveal it. There are medical specialists who focus so narrowly on a particular condition and its treatment that they may fail to consider other aspects of the patient's general health. There also exist doctors who will prescribe virtually any chemical that their patients request. Forensic evaluators sometimes discover that a defendant has been receiving the same medications from several different physicians. One way to investigate this possibility is to request pharmacy records and to consult centralized registries for prescribed narcotics.

CONSIDERING THE NOTION OF CONSEQUENCES

In criminal matters involving addictions, one must remain aware of the paradox that punishing addicted persons does little or nothing to change the nature of the disorder; however, actuality of consequences—including punishment or the loss of valued status, privileges, possessions, or relationships—is frequently the only motivator sufficient to spur efforts toward recovery and sobriety. Thus, invoking the presence of an addictive disorder or defect in order to deflect all consequences ultimately constitutes a disservice to the addicted defendant. It may be that neither the prosecutor's goal of punishment nor defense counsel's notion of absolution will ultimately serve the medical and psychological needs of the person with an addictive disorder.

CONCLUDING THE DATA INTERPRETATION PROCESS

Simply put, the evaluator communicates to the referring attorney what the data potentially make possible. For example, it may be that the data speak poorly to the issue of criminal responsibility—even though that may have been the focus of the initial referral question—while making a strong case for the client's not being *presently* competent to stand trial. The permutations and combinations of potential referral questions and available data generate a huge number of possibilities in any case. The attorney is the person who must choose after weighing all of the evidence made available. Mature forensic evaluators will respect that unique attorney role and not question it. The time to have taken issue with the referral question was at the inception of the evaluation, and not on the eve of—or during—trial.

COMMUNICATION

It goes without saying that communication through forensic report writing should be a skill emphasized and continually developed by every forensic evaluator. There is, of course, a vast difference between what is required in a traditional clinical report and what must be generated in response to an attorney's referral. This is particularly true regarding forensic aspects of addictions, as each jurisdiction—indeed, each individual criminal court—will have its own grasp of scientific jargon, its own tolerance for exculpatory theories of intoxication, and its own case law and local custom to accommodate.

In writing the forensic report, it is imperative to go beyond a mere recitation of facts, test results, and data and to try to convey the patient's narrative in a realistic and balanced fashion—conveying the defendant's humanity, but not, by doing so, pleading the cause of either side. One must take care to leave the law to the lawyers and to remember the task of the forensic evaluator: to apply clinical data and knowledge to a legal question.

We recommend that forensic evaluators—particularly those who anticipate referrals stemming from newly posited addictive disorders—pay the price of consulting with a qualified attorney, independent of any specific case, to determine the rules under which mental health experts are likely to be working when it comes to forensic report writing and courtroom testimony. It will be well worth the price of such consultation.

The late Father Joseph Martin wrote in his very well known *Chalk Talks About Alcohol* (Martin, 1989) of an emergency room nurse he knew who reflected that whenever an intoxicated person appeared in her hospital, she said to herself, "That's my Uncle Ray." What this nurse meant was that, for her, alcoholism equated to what she had learned by observing this uncle and his behaviors, family-wide. Forensic evaluators must be prepared to communicate with persons who have had a wide variety of experiences with addicts and addiction, and must take care to avoid providing any bases for misunderstanding.

Communicating on the topic of AWS presents a particularly difficult problem in this regard. It is safe to say that almost everyone has experienced the effects of chemicals on human pain or perception. Experience in the dentist's chair provides a convenient vehicle for making this point. Who has not lost the ability to experience normal pain and exercise a normal judgment (avoid pain) after receiving a common anesthetic? Who has not witnessed, or experienced, behavioral changes in themselves or another person following a few shots of tequila? Most people have even experienced the clear distortions of perception that accompany loss of the ability to perceive dental pain. Almost all of us know that we can look in a mirror and see a normal face, while experiencing (with numbness) much thickened lips and inability to speak clearly. Yet, we can observe no physical change in our look. One's tongue can feel huge without changing volume at all! This is the common experience that the forensic evaluator will encounter when talking about the effects of alcohol and other drugs.

With gambling disorders, for example, it is much different and more difficult. Gambling addicts do not stagger, they show no injection tracks on their arms, and their breath does not smell of lottery cards or poker chips. When experts opine that such persons are addicted and that their will has become impaired, judges and juries may wonder just how that can possibly be true. Thus, the assessor must expect that his or her narrative about a gambling-addicted defendant is unlikely to find, initially, a receptive listener among triers of fact. Part of the task of communication in such cases will be determining, in collaboration with counsel, a way to explain just what AWS are and how they work.

Overall, what the legal system wants to learn from forensic evaluators is what effect an addictive substance or behavior had on the defendant's executive functioning—that is, how it affected his or her "mind" and thus "will." Judges and juries are far less interested in how knowledgeable the forensic evaluator is about addictions in general than in what the expert knows that may be relevant to what the trier of fact must ultimately decide.

REFERENCES

Aldhous, P. (2006, July 29). Breaking the cycle of drug addiction and crime. *New Scientist*, 6–7.

American Psychiatric Association. (2000). *Diagnostic and statistical manual of mental disorders* (4th ed., Text Revision). Washington, DC: Author.

Bandura, A., & Kupers, C. J. (1964). Transmission of patterns of self-reinforcement through modeling. *Journal of Abnormal and Social Psychology, 69,* 1–9.

Barrett, C. L., & Drogin, E. Y. (2000). Gambling, pathological addiction without substance. In C. D. Bryant (Series Ed.) & C. E. Faupel & P. M. Roman (Vol. Eds.), *Encyclopedia of criminology and deviant behavior: Vol. 4. Self destructive behavior and disvalued identity* (pp. 344–346). Philadelphia, PA: Taylor & Francis.

Bullis, R. K., & Cherry, A. D. (1994). Pastoral care for the head-injured: A biopsychosocial/spiritual perspective. *Pastoral Psychology, 42,* 321–333.

Chang, I., Lapham, S. C., & Wanberg, K. W. (2001). Alcohol Use Inventory: Screening and assessment of first-time driving while impaired offenders. *Alcohol and Alcoholism, 36,* 112–121.

Cox, B., Enns, M. W., & Michaud, V. (2004). Comparisons between the South Oaks Gambling Screen and a DSM-IV-based interview in a community survey of problem gambling. *Canadian Journal of Psychiatry, 49,* 258–264.

Dattilio, F. M., & Sadoff, R. L. (2007). *Mental health experts: Roles and qualifications for court* (2nd ed.). Mechanicsburg, PA: PBI Press.

Dear, G. E., Roberts, C. M., & Lange, L. (2005). Defining codependency: A thematic analysis of published definitions. In S. P. Shohov (Ed.), *Advances in psychology research* (pp. 189–205). Hauppauge, NY: Nova Science.

Drogin, E. Y. (2000). Breaking through: Communicating and collaborating with the mentally ill defendant. *The Advocate, 22*(4), 27–34.

Drogin, E. Y., & Barrett, C. L. (1998). Addictions and family law. In E. Pierson (Ed.), *1998 Wiley family law series* (pp. 61–106). New York, NY: John Wiley & Sons.

Gutheil, T. G., & Simon, R. I. (2002). *Mastering forensic psychiatric practice.* Washington, DC: American Psychiatric Publishing.

Hagedorn, W. B. (2009). The call for a new *Diagnostic and Statistical Manual of Mental Disorders* diagnosis: Addictive disorders. *Journal of Addictions and Offender Counseling, 29,* 110–127.

Healy, D., & Tranter, R. (1999). Pharmacological stress diathesis syndromes. *Journal of Psychopharmacology, 13,* 287–290.

Laux, J. M., Newman, I., & Brown, R. (2004). The Michigan Alcoholism Screening Test (MAST): A statistical validation analysis. *Measurement and Evaluation in Counseling & Development, 36,* 209–225.

Lazowski, L. E., Miller, F. G., Boye, M. W., & Miller, G. M. (1998). Efficacy of the Substance Abuse Subtle Screening Inventory-3 (SASSI-3) in identifying substance dependence disorders in clinical settings. *Journal of Personality Assessment, 71*(1), 114–128.

Levine, S. B. (2010). What is sexual addiction? *Journal of Sex & Marital Therapy, 36*, 261–275.

Lief, A. (1948). *The common sense psychiatry of Adolf Meyer.* New York, NY: McGraw-Hill.

Malone, Y. (2002). Social cognitive theory and choice theory: A compatibility analysis. *International Journal of Reality Therapy, 22*, 10–13.

Martin, J. C. (1989). *Chalk talks about alcohol.* New York, NY: Harper & Row.

Miller, C. S., Shields, A. L., Campfield, D., Wallace, K. A., & Weiss, R. D. (2007). Substance use scales of the Minnesota Multiphasic Personality Inventory: An exploration of score reliability via meta-analysis. *Educational and Psychological Measurement, 67*, 1052–1065.

Millon, T. (1993). *Millon Adolescent Clinical Inventory.* Minneapolis, MN: National Computer Systems.

Office of National Drug Control Policy. (2000). *Drug-related crime.* Washington, DC: Author.

Otto, R. K., Slobogin, C., & Greenberg, S. A. (2007). Legal and ethical issues in accessing and utilizing third-party information. In A. M. Goldstein (Ed.), *Forensic psychology: Emerging topics and expanding roles* (pp. 190–205). Hoboken, NJ: John Wiley & Sons.

Pinker, S. (1997). *How the mind works.* New York: Norton.

Ries, R. K., Fiellin, D. A., Miller, S. C., & Saitz, R. (2009). *Principles of addiction medicine* (4th ed.). Philadelphia, PA: Lippincott, Williams & Wilkins.

Roback, A. A. (1961). *History of psychology and psychiatry.* Secaucus, NJ: Citadel Press.

Ruiz, M. A., Dickinson, K. A., & Pincus, A. L. (2002). The validity of the Personality Assessment Inventory Alcohol Problems (ALC) Scale in a college student sample. *Assessment, 9*, 261–270.

Samson, K. (2007, April 3). Brain scans gain momentum as forensic evidence, but jury is still out on its relevance. *Neurology Today, 1*, 12, 14.

Sattar, S. P., Pinals, D. A., & Gutheil, T. G. (2004). Countering countertransference, II: Beyond evaluation to cross-examination. *Journal of the American Academy of Psychiatry and the Law, 32*, 148–154.

Serra, G., Collu, M., & Gessa, G. L. (1988). Endorphins and sexual behaviour. In R. J. Rodgers & S. J. Cooper (Eds.), *Endorphins, opiates and behavioural processes* (pp. 237–247). Oxford, UK: John Wiley & Sons.

Shipley, W. C., Gruber, C. P., Martin, T. A., & Klein, A. M. (2009). *Shipley-2 manual.* Los Angeles: Western Psychological Services.

Suurvali, H., Hodgins, D. C., & Cunningham, J. A. (2010). Motivators for resolving or seeking help for gambling problems: A review of the empirical literature. *Journal of Gambling Studies, 26*, 1–33.

Toneatto, G. (2008). A cognitive-behavioral analysis of Gamblers Anonymous. *Journal of Gambling Issues, 21,* 68–79.

Twerski, A. J. (1997). *Addictive thinking: Understanding self-deception* (2nd ed.). Center City, MN: Hazelden.

Vanem, P., Krog, D., & Hartmann, E. (2008). Assessment of substance abusers on the MCMI-III and the Rorschach. *Scandinavian Journal of Psychology, 49,* 83–91.

Webster, N. (1848). *An American dictionary of the English language.* New York, NY: Harper & Bros.

Wechsler, D. (2008). *Wechsler Adult Intelligence Scale—Fourth Edition (WAIS-IV).* San Antonio, TX: NCS Pearson.

Weed, N. C., Butcher, J. N., & Williams, C. L. (1994). Development of MMPI-A alcohol/drug problem scales. *Journal of Studies on Alcohol, 55,* 296–302.

PART 2

CIVIL MATTERS

Personal Injury: The Independent Medical Examination in Psychology and Psychiatry

LAURENCE MILLER, ROBERT L. SADOFF, and FRANK M. DATTILIO

INTRODUCTION

The typical *independent medical examination* (IME) is often a misnomer. That is, it is not truly "independent" if it is conducted by a mental health professional selected by either the plaintiff or the defense in a civil case. A true IME is one that is conducted by an expert either selected by the judge or agreed upon by both plaintiff and defense attorneys. The former is unusual, and the latter is fairly rare. However, there are mental health professionals who are seen as unbiased and fair in their assessments, and a judge may appoint a mental health expert in cases in which there is disagreement on the part of the plaintiff's expert and the defense expert or where the judge seeks a third opinion. Generally, court-appointed experts are far more common in the criminal law arena than in civil lawsuits (Miller, 2001b, 2008a; Posey & Wrightsman, 2005), although, as the role of mental functioning becomes more recognized as a component of civil matters, the use of experts has grown more popular.

APPLICATIONS OF PSYCHOLOGY TO PERSONAL INJURY LITIGATION

Psychologists and psychiatrists are generally retained as experts in civil cases that have been referred to as *traumatic disability syndromes*

(Miller, 1993a, 1993c, 1998c, 1999a, 1999b, 2007c; O'Donnell, Creamer, Bryant, Schnyder, & Shalev, 2003; Rosen & Taylor, 2007; Simon, 1995). These typically fall into three main categories:

1. *Neuropsychology.* A patron of an amusement park sustains a closed head injury when a roller-coaster car breaks loose and falls to the ground. Although there was no significant loss of consciousness at the scene, a year later he reports being unable to work due to impaired memory, dizziness, and fatigue. He also experiences repeated flashbacks about the details of the accident.
2. *Chronic pain.* Another rider twists her back in the accident and sustains a lumbar disk injury. She reports being unable to work or care for her family because of excruciating pain and also develops a reactive depression.
3. *Psychological injury.* A third rider, terrified that he would be killed, reports being so traumatized that he can no longer ride in any vehicle or be in crowds, and has become a virtual recluse in his home.

It is also not uncommon for these traumatic disability syndromes to co-occur in the same claimant: An electrician working on the ceiling of a big box store falls off an insecurely mounted scaffold, striking his head on the tile floor, injuring his left shoulder, and terrifying him because "I just knew I was a dead man when I hit that floor." Six months later, he cannot work because of difficulty concentrating, chronic back pain, and fear of heights.

Other such personal injury cases include workplace violence or harassment, medical malpractice, "toxic torts," or civil lawsuits filed in the wake of criminal acts (Miller, 1993a, 1993b, 1995, 1997a, 2001b, 2001c, 2007a, 2007b, 2008b). Any and all of these cases can also constitute a crisis in the individual's life (Dattilio & Freeman, 2007).

In these cases, plaintiff's counsel will usually retain experts to document the impairment caused by the injury and to attribute those impairments to the injury in question. As part of the *discovery* process, by which each side gathers information about the case, defense counsel, retained either by a private defendant (such as a corporation in a toxic tort or defective product lawsuit) or an insurance company (as in a motor vehicle, medical malpractice, or workers' compensation claim), will almost always retain their own expert. His/her job will be to examine the plaintiff in order to attempt to refute the plaintiff expert's claims as to the nature of the injury and/or its relationship to the *index event* (the event which injured the plaintiff). Where all or part of the claim for damages involves compensation for psychological or neuropsychological injury, mental health experts, usually either psychologists or psychiatrists, may be among the experts called.

PREPARATION

Not every psychologist or psychiatrist will make an effective expert witness, and practitioners who are clinical maestros in their consulting room may find themselves tone deaf in a forensic setting. That is because the forensic mental health evaluator's role is typically more like that of a detective than a healer. His/her job is to get the facts; interpret those findings in light of the present case; arrive at an objective conclusion as to the nature, extent, causes, and future implications of the index injury; and communicate these conclusions effectively to the trier of fact (Barton, 1990; Gutheil & Dattilio, 2008; Miller, 1990, 1996b; Mogil, 1989; Stone, 1984; Taylor, 1997; Varney, 1990; Vinson & Davis, 1993). This typically requires the evaluator to assume an adversarial role with the claimant, which is anathema to the helper role adopted in most clinical treatment settings.

That said, there may be times when a treating clinician is called to testify or has his/her records subpoenaed by either side in a case. However, in such cases, there would be no expectation that the treating clinician is an *independent* expert, because it would be understood that one of the roles of a treating therapist is to be (within reason) an advocate for his/her patient.

CREDENTIALS AND QUALIFICATIONS

For purposes of being an expert evaluator and witness, a doctoral degree, typically an MD, DO, PhD, or PsyD, sometimes an EdD or equivalent degree, is usually desirable to establish basic professional credibility, although other qualified professionals may occasionally testify under special circumstances (Dattilio & Sadoff, 2007). You should be licensed to practice in your state and preferably board certified by a reputable and respected credentialing body (Dattilio, Sadoff, & Gutheil, 2003). Degrees from prestigious universities are always impressive but not crucial if other qualifications are appropriate. Honors, awards, professional publications, and the like are also impressive, as long as they complement the more basic qualifications of clinical expertise and experience. Publications in your field, although not essential, are usually a plus because they speak of an expert who remains abreast of the professional literature in the field and is capable of making scholarly contributions to his/her own field of knowledge, which, in turn, implies that he/she keeps current with new developments. Holding a faculty position may be important for two reasons. First, it reinforces your depth and breadth of knowledge in training others and, second, it gives you good experience for testifying, that is, comfort in public speaking before groups and the ability to boil down technical subjects for a lay audience.

Be prepared for attorneys to ask questions about your practice, your credentials, your experience, and the kinds of cases you've worked on and testified in. Always have an updated curriculum vitae ready to upload or mail. In fact, be suspicious of any new attorney who seems willing to hire you on the spot without taking the due diligence to vet you properly. They may want you to cut corners and bend rules later on.

FEES AND CONTRACTS

The noble pursuit of justice may be one of many reasons a personal injury attorney is pursuing a case, but the big factor is money: this is how they make their living. Most personal injury plaintiff's attorneys work on contingency, that is, they get paid a percentage of what they collect for their client: the bigger the settlement or award, the larger their cut. Defense attorneys are typically paid at an hourly rate by their retaining agency, often an insurance company: How much they make is therefore a function of the number of billable hours they generate. Attorneys are intent on winning, and there is often a huge financial stake riding on the case. Accordingly, once you begin working with your retaining attorney, you'll be asked to do a lot of work that may lead to a large fee. Accept it graciously and without guilt or shame.

After a brief discussion in which you agree to sign on to the case, send the attorney a written contract that specifies what types of services you will and will not perform, your hourly fee for clinical evaluation, review of records (which may consist of anything from a few pages to a stack of cartons), attorney conferences (live or by phone), and testimony at deposition and trial. Because it is so time and labor intensive, many expert witnesses charge more for deposition or trial testimony than for other services. If you're unsure of what to charge, do some research as to fee schedules of similar experts in your area and decide how your credentials and experience stack up to theirs. In general, try not to charge the lowest amount nor the highest (unless you are in high demand).

Experienced experts have developed an intuitive or actuarial sense of how much time they typically spend on a particular type of case, or at least of the typical minimum time investment, which determines the amount of their *retainer*, which is an advance payment they receive upon opening a case. As you keep track of professional time, you subtract your hourly rate from the retainer until it is consumed. If there are additional charges (retainers usually cover evaluative services, not testimony), bill your attorney in a timely fashion and expect to be paid accordingly; don't let big unpaid bills pile up. If an attorney initially gives you any grief about fees and billing, politely decline the case because this person is likely to be trouble to work with from day one. Discuss the fee issues early, so you can use all your energy to concentrate on the case.

DATA COLLECTION

The conduct of your IME examination will be reflected in the structure of your report, which is why the latter is considered prospectively throughout this section (Barton, 1990; Miller, 1990; 1996b, 1999b, Taylor, 1997).

STRUCTURE OF THE PSYCHOLOGICAL IME

Time and Place of the Clinical Interview and Examination   While, ideally, the IME examination should take place in the mental health expert's office, a variety of venues may be utilized, depending on the special circumstances of the claimant. For example, claimants who are too disabled to travel may be evaluated in their place of residence or a treatment facility, or in a neutral office close to the claimant's home.

Once the time and place of the examination has been established, the examiner then meets with the plaintiff at the designated location and time. Introduce yourself to the plaintiff and explain the nature and purposes of the evaluation and the rights and limitations on confidentiality. This includes telling the plaintiff who you are (a psychiatrist, a psychologist), whom you represent (the defense if this is an IME), and what you will do with the information you obtain from the plaintiff (prepare a report that you will send to the defense attorney, who will then forward it to the plaintiff's attorney). Also explain what the claimant will be asked to do during the evaluation (answer questions, perform tasks) and emphasize the importance of best effort and honest responding.

Length of Examination The length of the examination depends mainly on the type of case. With proper background and familiarization with the case from record review, an average clinical interview takes about an hour or two, although in complex cases this can take many hours. In brain injury cases, a typical neuropsychological test battery can take anywhere from 4 to 8 hours to administer and may have to be split between different days. In fact, when one is exposing claimants to so much stimuli (i.e., multiple measures and psychological tests), it may be prudent to see them on more than one occasion. Following the IME, the examiner reviews the data and may come up with some follow-up questions that he/she can explore through obtaining additional records, scheduling a reexamination of the claimant, or through a few brief phone follow-up interviews.

Site Visits Occasionally, your psychiatric/psychological investigation may take you out of the office to do a little on-site detective work. This is especially likely to be the case in matters involving workplace injury. In one case (RLS), a woman argued that she had been the victim of sexual harassment and abuse at certain locations at her workplace, but when the medical expert visited the site, it was noted that the physical layout of the building made it impossible for those events to have transpired as described by the plaintiff.

Video Surveillance   Not uncommonly, insurance companies hire videographers to follow the claimant around secretly and document any discrepancies between their claimed disability ("I can't remember how to drive, and my severe back pain makes it hard to even get out of bed") and the realities of their daily life (claimant is filmed loading his pickup truck with building supplies, driving home, and constructing a shed in his back yard). Not surprisingly, plaintiffs almost always are outraged at being "spied on" in this way when it finally comes to their attention.

In cases of egregious inconsistencies (one of LM's cases claimed blindness and was filmed dancing inconsistently with that condition at a club), the case may end the moment the plaintiff and his/her attorney are confronted by the damning evidence; in some cases, the plaintiff may even be sued by the insurance company for filing a false claim. In more subtle cases, you, as an expert examiner and witness, may be called upon to opine whether the actions seen on the tape—for example, bending over the open hood of a car with a group of friends (a past case of LM's)—is truly inconsistent with the claimant's post–brain injury report of losing the ability to perform mechanical tasks (in this case, all I could determine was that the claimant was looking at the engine; I couldn't honestly declare that he was actually making a repair or doing anything mechanical).

In another case, I (RLS) had examined a woman who claimed she had been injured on an airplane landing in a large metropolitan city. She claimed the emotional damage was so bad that she could not fly and that she was anxious even about traveling from her home. Her presentation of her condition was so convincing to me as the IME, that I agreed that she did have significant emotional damage as a result of the incident on the airplane. The defense attorney was not upset with my call, as he had information that he gained subsequent to my examination that he would use in cross-examining me when the plaintiff's attorney called me as their expert. The defense attorney found evidence that the plaintiff had indeed flown several times since the incident and had left her home on several occasions that he had videotaped. It was clear that he could get more information from me on cross-examination than he could on direct examination. When the evidence of her misrepresentation was presented to me in court, I had no alternative but to change my opinion of her condition.

Establishing Rapport Any kind of productive human interaction requires some degree of interpersonal engagement. It is advisable to prepare the plaintiff for the fact that you may have to ask potentially embarrassing or disturbing personal questions as part of the IME. Nothing is to be gained by trying to trick, trap, or shock the subject into giving you information, except to alienate him/her from further cooperation and possibly compromise the validity of your findings.

Remember what every police detective knows: even in a legally adversarial setting, the establishment of good interview rapport is a powerful tool for getting what you want, otherwise known as the "catching more flies with honey" principle. Adversarial does not have to mean confrontational. Be neither intimidatingly hostile nor seductively ingratiating, but rather act firm, polite, and business-like in your interactions with the claimant. Treat your subject with reasonable respect and expect to be treated the same in return.

The Presence of Third Parties or Recording Devices at the Examination Perhaps because of past experiences with browbeating examiners, some plaintiff's attorneys will request or demand that they be allowed to be present during the IME, ostensibly to protect the rights of their client and guard against any perceived misuse of the evaluation. This question is still controversial and has not been completely settled in all jurisdictions (Goldstein, 1988; National Academy of Neuropsychology, 2000; Rachlin & Schwartz, 1988; Simon, 1996). Bear in mind that this can also be an intimidation tactic: some experts may be unnerved by the prospect of an adversarial attorney glaring at them and taking notes during the evaluation. And, not incidentally, the attorney is billing for this time. Generally, if you decide to accede to this request, make sure you inform the attorney that, in order for the examination to be valid, counsel should be there as an observer only and make him/herself as unobtrusive as possible, for example, by sitting out of direct sight of either examiner or examinee and being quiet. In fact, in some states it is against the law for counsel to utter one word during an IME.

Sometimes, the presence of third parties at the examination can be helpful, even crucial. Examinees with mental retardation, brain injury, dementia, or serious mental illness may become confused, disoriented, and frightened without the presence of a familiar caretaker or advocate. The same goes for children. One of us (LM) has had overzealous spouses insist on remaining in the room with their husband or wife during an interview. Another (RLS) was glad to have a trusted third party in the room during an evaluation of a borderline patient in order to deflect charges of inappropriate behavior. Finally, for non–English speakers, a competent interpreter is essential, even when the examiner speaks the language. This may ensure that the communication is clear.

Usually, after an initial awkward few minutes, the third party blends into the background. After an hour or so, many of these observers, not realizing what they were getting into, find themselves becoming excruciatingly bored. Some will start to fidget and disturb the examinee. I've (LM) had at least two observers doze off during a prolonged testing session; one actually snored loud enough for the plaintiff herself to ask him to leave. Others will take out books or other reading matter, or play with their cell phones, or even click away on their laptop computers, further disturbing the scene. Some initially take notes, but then seem to lose interest. A few excuse themselves for a bathroom break and never come back. In general, remember that anything that makes the examinee more comfortable is likely to result in more useful information. Ultimately, it may boil down to the examiner's own comfort level, as well.

With regard to recording devices (audio or videotaping), in most cases a court order is needed, but again, how this affects the examination depends on the personality of the examiner and examinee. You may use your own recording as well. As with live observers, it is surprising how easily this recording hardware diffuses out of consciousness as the examination proceeds. Some attorneys will get an order for a court reporter to record the entire examination as if it were a deposition or trial testimony. And I've (LM) conducted at least one evaluation where there was a videographer, a court reporter, *and* an attorney present (happily, everybody was on their best behavior).

CORE COMPONENTS OF THE PSYCHOLOGICAL IME

Although the purposes of a personal injury psychological IME evaluation may vary from case to case—for example, posttraumatic stress disorder following a transportation accident or criminal assault, postconcussion syndrome following a closed head injury, chronic pain and depression following a work-related injury—the basic structure of the examination and report should include the following components, although not necessarily involving these exact categories or in this exact order. Most experienced experts have evolved their own protocol, which is most comfortable for them.

Reason for Evaluation—Case Background How was this examinee referred to you? What were the circumstances of the injury or other cause of action? What does the examinee report? What do the records say? Be as specific as possible as to the time line of events and to where the information comes from (i.e., subject's self-report, clinical records, collateral interviews, etc.).

Review of Records Depending on the individual case, the volume of pertinent records can range from a few sparse sheets to literally cartons of documents (this is an occupational hazard for any forensics expert). Not all of these records may be directly relevant to the present case, but the examiner won't know that until he or she has sorted through them. For most experts, distilling this raw data down to a few paragraphs or pages that will summarize the main points and then integrating this with the information gained from the clinical interview and test findings, is one of the most time-consuming and cognitively demanding aspects of report writing. Be clear about the sources of the records you cite: you may be expected to justify every statement you make at a subsequent deposition or trial.

The expert should initially obtain all available medical and legal records and documents. Specifically, you should have a copy of the plaintiff's legal filing alleging mental or emotional damage as a result of an accident, an incident at work, or other civil traumatic event. Other documents include records of evaluation and treatment of the index injury, police reports if any, past medical and psychiatric records, prior school and work records if available, and reports of any collateral interviews or examinations that were conducted by the plaintiff's expert.

Clinical Interview and Behavioral Observations Basic points of information to be gathered during the clinical interview include the following:

- How is the examinee doing now, at the time of the evaluation?
- What effects has the injury had, immediately following and throughout the past time interval?
- What are the findings of your clinical examination and how do they relate to the injury in question?
- What are your mental status and behavioral observations of the subject?
- What clinical signs does the claimant show and what clinical symptoms does he/she report?

Emphasizing the importance of speech content, voice tone, eye contact, body language, and general appearance, much useful information can be gleaned about a subject from a good, face-to-face clinical interview. How the subject answers questions—cooperatively, defensively, impulsively, evasively, effortfully, sarcastically, overenthusiastically, ramblingly, dramatically—is just as important as what he/she says. Clinical status—anxious, depressed, manic, delusional, angry, intoxicated, hung-over, guilty, lackadaisical, cognitively impaired—can be determined most accurately only by a one-on-one interpersonal interaction between the examiner and the subject. Another important benefit of this interaction is to develop a rapport with the examinee sufficient to allow accuracy of responding and test taking.

Clinical History There's an old joke about the injured patient who asks his physician, "Doc, will I be able to play the violin again?" Doctor: "Sure you will, sir." Patient: "Great—because I never could before!" In other words, what was this examinee's life like before the injury? What was his/her medical history? Family history? Highest level of education and vocational history? Prior injuries of this type or other types? Prior involvement with the legal system—civil litigation or criminal justice system? Skill set and areas of deficiency? Emotional and interpersonal functioning? Essentially, you're putting the current clinical findings into the context of the claimant's past and present life. For example, a validly obtained intelligence quotient (IQ) score of 93 in a former surgeon, engineering professor, or corporate CEO may well reflect a loss of cognitive ability following a brain injury, but what about in a waiter or cross-country trucker? Remember that, with few exceptions, no clinical finding or test score interprets itself: context is essential.

Test Findings For psychologists, these usually mean psychological test findings, such as personality testing, neuropsychological testing, pain inventories, structured assessments for posttraumatic stress disorder, tests and scales for malingering, and so on. For psychiatrists, testing may include blood panels, imaging, electrophysiology, and other studies. Many psychiatrists tend to rely on an extensive clinical interview and some may subcontract out cognitive and personality testing to psychologists. It should be noted that psychiatrists are typically not permitted to conduct psychological testing unless they have formal training to do so and that it is also within the scope of their professional licensure/certification (see Dattilio, Tresco, & Siegel, 2007).

Testing may consist of just a few short rating scales (otherwise known as appraisals) completed by the claimant in the waiting room, or involve an extensive psychological and/or neuro-psychological test battery spanning hours or days. Bear in mind that more is not necessarily better. While there is no universally agreed upon psychological test battery for most forensic psychological evaluations, and each psychologist has his/her preferences, there do exist certain standards as to what types of basic diagnostic issues should be addressed by these instruments. Some psychological tests are specifically designed for forensic assessments, while others are general tests of psychological functioning that can be adapted to the IME setting. The basic areas that should be covered by these measures include general intelligence, cognitive functioning (attention, concentration, memory, reasoning), personality profile, assessment of mood (anxiety, depression), and screening for psychotic symptoms (delusions or hallucinations). IME psychologists typically insert specific measures for malingering to gauge if the subject is being truthful in his/her reports and test item responses (see below).

Collateral Interviews Collateral interviews are interviews—in person, by phone, through e-mail, or by written accounts—with other people who have information that is relevant to the case. These may include family members (the most common), medical treaters (police and EMS responders, emergency room doctors, hospital and rehab staff), supervisors, employees, coworkers, family members, neighbors, and others. Special sensitivity should be exercised to maintain the maximum degree of confidentiality possible for both the collateral sources and the examinee.

Diagnostic Impression—Conclusions and Discussion This is where you put it all together and carefully explain your interpretation of the findings in terms of how they relate to the injury in question. This section should be a succinct summary of the main points relevant to the referral question(s), with documentation of your reasoning on each point. As a defense IME expert, you may conclude that there is no significant injury, that there is an injury but that it will resolve spontaneously or with treatment, that the claimant's signs and symptoms are due to a preexisting or coexisting condition not related to the index injury, or that the claimant is a "thin eggshell" whose level of injury-related disability is contributed to by a preexisting or coexisting condition. Here is also where you state whether the signs and symptoms are veridical or influenced by unconscious amplification or deliberate malingering (see below).

Diagnoses In some cases, a formal diagnosis will not be required or may not be possible, based on the available information. But in most cases, clinical credibility is enhanced by rendering clinical DSM diagnoses (American Psychiatric Association [APA], 2000, or latest version), supported by appropriate diagnostic criteria. The same rigorous standards of practice used in clinical evaluation and diagnosis of a patient for treatment should be applied to diagnosis of a litigant in a personal injury lawsuit, whether for plaintiff or defense.

Recommendations There is a common misconception that forensic evaluators are not supposed to make treatment recommendations. It is true that the evaluating expert is almost never the treatment provider him/herself (except in cases where a prior clinical relationship has existed and the doctor is testifying as a *treating expert*). However, it is usually of vital importance to the case for the forensic expert to specify what kind, and how much psychiatric or psychological treatment or accommodation of disability the claimant will require. This is perhaps the most challenging section of the report, because here the psychiatrist or psychologist has to distill his/her findings down to specific recommendations that will affect this claimant's future life (Miller, 1992).

For plaintiffs' experts, this usually involves carefully delineating any and all possible treatment needs to cover any and all possible consequences of the injury that may arise in the short term or in the distant future following the injury. These data are typically combined with other sources by an expert *rehabilitation consultant* and/or *medical economist*, who then develops a painstakingly detailed *life care plan* for the claimant that spells out the dollars-and-cents costs of compensating the claimant for the rest of his life. This sum will then become part of the supporting data package accompanying the *demand letter* that the plaintiff's attorney presents to the defendant.

For defense experts, the task becomes one of providing a "reality check" to the putatively inflated projection of future medical and rehabilitative needs presented by the plaintiff. As a result of his alleged injury-related severe traumatic brain injury and post-traumatic stress disorder, the plaintiff may be asking for millions to compensate him for months out of every year, for the next 30 years, to undergo expensive inpatient psychiatric treatment, as well as total loss of his ability to work for the rest of his natural life. As the defense expert, you may conclude that his mild postconcussion syndrome and adjustment disorder with simple phobia can be successfully treated with a prescription for a mood stabilizing medication and 6 months of outpatient cognitive–behavioral psychotherapy, with a minor modification of work schedule for the first four weeks back on the job.

In making this counterrecommendation as the IME psychiatrist, you may be expected to spell out exactly what medication you're recommending, the dosage and timing of administration, over what period of time, with how many follow-up visits, and the expected cost per session and for total treatment. Likewise, the IME psychologist will be expected to explain what kind of therapy is recommended, how many times a week, and how much will the cost be per session times total number of sessions. Mental health professionals who are used to a more flexible and empirical style of clinical decision making may be uncomfortable being asked to generate these cut-and-dried projections, but in a civil lawsuit, money is fighting money, and part of your job is to load the ammunition. In fact, at some point in your involvement in the case, you may be asked by your retaining attorney to do a line-by-line refutation of relevant sections of the plaintiff's life care plan and to testify to that effect.

For example, in one of my (RLS) cases, a psychiatrist had been accused of sexually abusing his borderline personality–disordered patient. He was found guilty of the charges and agreed, in the civil case, to pay damages. The plaintiff argued that the doctor's misbehavior was so psychologically damaging that the plaintiff required 5 years of treatment, which included 2 years in a hospital and 3 years of outpatient treatment. That would be the ideal treatment for the borderline personality disorder patient who has serious difficulties with psychotic thinking and disturbed behavior. However, the psychiatrist did not cause her to have borderline personality disorder—his behavior merely aggravated her condition. After a thorough IME was conducted, the recommendation was that the damages include 1 year of hospitalization and 1 year of outpatient treatment rather than the full 5 years that was requested. The court agreed to the diminished damages on the basis of the logic of the IME evaluator's report.

Summary Although not essential, for the sake of clarity, I (LM) typically like to give a brief, one- or two-sentence summary statement at the end of the report that makes the essential conclusions of my evaluation available at a glance, for example:

> Thirty-three-year-old, right-handed, white, married, female retail store manager with mild-moderate postconcussion syndrome, moderate chronic back and shoulder pain, and moderate-severe residual posttraumatic stress disorder caused by physical and psychological injuries sustained in a robbery and attempted sexual assault at her place of business.

REVISING THE REPORT

Bear in mind that the final document you submit will be clucked over and microanalyzed by multiple parties, so rewrite and self-edit your report as many times as you think is necessary to make your points as clear as possible before submitting it to your retaining attorney. Not infrequently, however, your attorney will read your carefully prepared report and ask you to make certain changes and revisions. Legally, since any extant records are fair game for the discovery process, your initial report will at this stage likely be considered an *attorney work product,* not subject to discovery. In other cases, if opposing counsel gets wind of your initial report, they may insist on the right to examine it. In such cases, your retaining attorney will label it a "draft" or "attorney work product," implying that this document is not necessarily the final expression of the expert's conclusions. You, the expert, may then be asked to make changes, a request that usually comes as a shock to doctors who are not used to having their clinical reports "graded" and corrected. Some experts feel that clinicians should never revise their reports in response to such attorney requests for fear of compromising clinical credibility. While this is generally true, there may be some exceptions.

First, new data may have come in since the first draft of the report. In such cases, a revised report can be generated, incorporating this new information, without affecting credibility: Indeed, changes in conclusions and recommendations in response to new data is a recognized standard of care in clinical treatment. The second situation is trickier and involves the attorney's asking you to make changes in the wording, organization, and or content of your report (typically still at the attorney work product stage), perhaps expanding on certain topics and downplaying others. Before automatically saying no, a general guideline that might prove helpful is to regard an attorney's attempt to "edit" your report as similar to a real editor who suggests changes in a manuscript that you're submitting for publication. That is, if you honestly feel that the requested changes will highlight and clarify the points you're trying to make, *without compromising the content and substance of your findings and conclusions,* then consider making the revisions: After all, brilliant clinicians are not always skilled expository writers, so be willing to accept this help if it is warranted.

But if you suspect that the attorney is subtly or overtly trying to skew your conclusions in a direction that you're not prepared to go, then politely but firmly decline. Also, bear in mind that opposing counsel will often ask you flat out at a deposition or trial if "you made any changes in your report since you wrote the first draft and, if so, why," so make sure you're able to justify your answer on legitimate clinical grounds. In general, for purposes of transparency and credibility (see earlier), always retain a copy of your initial report and be prepared to offer a credible reason for any changes made in the final draft.

DATA INTERPRETATION

Often, certain features of both the clinical and forensic aspects of a case may complicate the expert evaluator's data collection and data interpretation, with predictable effect on one's attempt to provide the appropriate communication in terms of report writing and testimony.

THIN EGGSHELLS

Thin eggshell basically refers to a preexisting vulnerability that makes the claimant more susceptible to the disabling effects of the index injury than the average person (Barton, 1990; Miller, 1999b; Taylor, 1997). Too bad, says the law: If the plaintiff is truly negligent and liable for the injury, then he/she "takes the victim as he/she finds him/her." Quite commonly, in fact, individuals who report seeming disproportionately disabling psychological trauma from apparently minor injury events frequently have histories of prior traumatic events and show psychological and psychophysiological indices of heightened emotional vulnerability. Where this may become relevant in mitigating damages is where it can be demonstrated that the preexisting vulnerability is wholly or partially self-induced (voluntary substance abuse or willful failure to follow medical treatment; Miller, 1997b), or where the vulnerability overlaps with multiple causation (see below).

MULTIPLE CAUSATION

It is probably more common than not that an index event will result in more than one type of injury. This is especially true in auto accident, workplace injury, and criminal assault cases (Miller, 1998a). In many of these cases, a plaintiff may complain of cognitive impairment, chronic pain, and posttraumatic distress—the "big three" of personal injury cases (Miller, 1998a, 1999b). Here, the IME expert's job is to delicately tease apart the causative factors for a given disability (e.g., is the claimant's dizziness and inability to concentrate due to postconcussion syndrome, whiplash neck injury, or posttraumatic anxiety—or some combination?). When this is compounded by a history of past injuries, the task becomes all the more complex.

MALINGERING AND ITS ALTERNATIVES

By definition, plaintiffs have something to prove and something they want to get, whether validation of their martyred victimhood or a generous cash settlement. Accordingly, every good IME psychological/psychiatric evaluation will include some clinical and/or psychometric measures of malingering. Just as important for clinical credibility, however, is that the expert be able to diagnose other syndromes of nonveridicality that do not necessarily involve deliberate malingering per se (Binder, 1992; Heilbronner, Sweet, Morgan, Larrabee, & Millis, 2009; Miller, 1996a, 1998b, 2001a, 2002; Nies & Sweet, 1994; Parker, 1994; Travin & Potter, 1984; Trimble, 1981).

In fact, *malingering* is not classified as a true psychiatric disorder, but rather is defined as the conscious and intentional simulation of illness or impairment for the purpose of obtaining financial compensation or other reward; evading duty, responsibility, obligation; or exculpation or mitigation for the consequences of criminal or other illicit behavior (APA, 2000).

Based on a topology by Lipman (1962), malingering can be categorized into four main categories, which I (Miller, 1998b, 2002) have summarized by the mnemonic acronym, FEEM:

1. *Fabrication.* The patient has no symptoms or impairments resulting from the injury, but fraudulently represents that he has. Symptoms may be atypical, inconsistent, or bizarre, or they may be perfect "textbook" replicas of real syndromes. In common litigation practice, this wholesale invention of an impairment syndrome is the rarest form of malingering.
2. *Exaggeration.* The patient has true symptoms or impairments caused by the injury, but represents them to be worse than they are. This is probably the commonest form of malingering in clinical and forensic practice.
3. *Extension.* The patient has experienced symptoms or impairments caused by the injury, and these have now recovered or improved, but he falsely represents them as continuing unabated, or even as having worsened over time.
4. *Misattribution.* The patient has symptoms or impairments that preceded, postdated, or were otherwise unrelated to the index injury, but he fraudulently attributes them to that injury.

In forensic personal injury settings, exaggeration of existing symptoms is generally more frequent than pure malingering of totally nonexistent illnesses or injuries.

Other syndromes commonly seen in a personal injury context include the somatoform disorders and factitious disorder (Miller, 1999b; 2002). Note that these do *not* represent conscious malingering and *are* considered bona fide mental disorders: hence, if they can be attributed to the index injury, they may represent additional compensable psychological disabilities in and of themselves.

Somatoform Disorders   The common feature of the *somatoform disorders* is the presence of subjective physical symptoms that suggest a medical illness or syndrome, but are not fully explainable by, or attributable to, a general medical condition, substance abuse, or other type of mental disorder. In the current classification (APA, 2000), somatoform disorders include several subtypes.

- *Somatization disorder.* This involves a history of multiple unexplained physical symptoms and complaints, beginning before age 30, and often traced to childhood and adolescence. Outbreaks of numerous and varied symptoms may occur in clusters that wax and wane over time, often in response to interpersonal, vocational, and other stressors. Associated features include anxiety, depression, impulsivity, relationship problems, psychosocial discord, and substance abuse. Symptoms in somatization disorder may closely mimic standard syndromic clusters associated with traumatic disability syndromes or they may be atypical or frankly bizarre in quality, location, or duration. The underlying motivation is frequently inferred to be a quest for support, reassurance, manipulation of the affection of a significant other, and/or the satisfaction of dependency needs by reliance on caretakers or the protective role of medical authority.
- *Conversion disorder.* Here, the essential feature is the presence of sensory or motor deficits that appear to suggest a neurological or medical illness or injury. The unconscious motivation typically involves the attempted resolution of psychological conflicts, such as dependency wishes, by channeling them into physical impairment. Alternatively, there may be an actual symbolic "conversion" of a particular psychological conflict

into a representative somatic expression, and exacerbations are typically precipitated by psychosocial stresses related to job or family, or the stress of the accident itself, with resultant financial and legal hassles.

- *Pain disorder.* The essential feature of this condition is chronic pain that causes significant distress or impairment in social, occupational, or other important areas of functioning, and in which psychological factors are judged to play a significant role in the onset, severity, exacerbation, or maintenance of the pain. The pain is not intentionally produced or feigned as in malingering or factitious disorder, but rather expresses, represents, or disguises an unconscious need, fear, or conflict, closer to somatization disorder.

- *Hypochondriasis.* This is the conviction that one has a serious illness or injury, in the face of numerous medical pronouncements to the contrary. Unlike somatization disorder, hypochondriacs tend to focus on one or a few chosen symptoms and remain preoccupied with them, although the focus may shift over time from one symptom or disorder to another (e.g. from memory impairment to headaches to dizziness to limb weakness). Unlike conversion disorder, there may be no actual observed or experienced impairment per se: It is the *fear* of dire impairment that is the problem. Often, the unconscious motivation involves a deflection of anxiety away from issues of broader psychosocial concern, such as career or relationships, with a focus on a more delimited, and hence "controllable" source of concern in the form of somatic symptoms and fear of further injury.

- *Body dysmorphic disorder.* This involves a preoccupation with imagined or exaggerated defects in appearance or function. Unconsciously, the motivation may involve deep-seated and long-standing feelings of self-loathing that are now projected onto a more objectifiable physical or mental impairment following the index injury.

- *Factitious Disorder.* This is diagnostically separated from the somatoform disorders, and is defined as the deliberate production, manipulation, or feigning of physical or psychological signs and symptoms. Because the intentionality of symptom production is conscious and deliberate, it is not classified as a somatoform disorder; however, unlike malingering, where a utilitarian motive for the deception can usually be discerned (e.g. money), the motive in factitious disorder is typically to assume the sick role, with all the attendant care, solicitous concern, and relief from responsibilities of normal life that this entails, even at the price of substantial cost in money, health, or freedom—that is, the motive is viewed as "senseless" in terms of any practical gain. In many cases, there also appears to be great satisfaction, perhaps partly unconscious, derived from manipulating the medical system and "fooling the experts." In this syndrome, patients may physically induce symptoms by deliberately infecting, poisoning, cutting, bruising, or otherwise injuring themselves.

COMMUNICATION

A good psychological/psychiatric IME report will display the following qualities, applicable in each instance to one's testimony as well.

BREVITY

"If I had more time, I would have written you a shorter letter," wrote Mark Twain. How many of us have suffered through reading bloated, rambling, redundant, and disorganized reports that take 30 to 40 pages to say what could have been said in 5 to 10? *Think* about your conclusions before you put them on paper. Without compromising quality, take the time to organize your findings so that they flow from the page into your reader's mind.

COMPREHENSIVENESS

This may sound like a contradiction to the above, but this pertains to content. Make sure you have covered all of the points that contribute to your conclusions. That is, do a thorough IME evaluation, including review of records, examining the claimant, and administering the specialized tests necessary to form an opinion, to a reasonable degree of psychological/psychiatric certainty, about the case.

TRANSPARENCY

Then, take your data and show the reader exactly how you arrived at your conclusions. Connect the dots and delineate how your conclusions and opinions flow seamlessly from the information obtained in your evaluation. Ambiguity is quicksand: if you can't support a conclusion with a test finding or clinical observation, don't blindly speculate. Some readers may disagree with your conclusions—in fact, if your conclusions differ from that of the plaintiff's expert, you can count on your findings being challenged. But you'll be less susceptible to criticism if your findings, and the bases for them, are clear.

CLARITY

The reader should not have to expend heroic effort to make sense of your report, so write in plain language. This does not mean dumbing down your conclusions, but simply invoking Einstein's dictum that "everything should be made as simple as possible—but no simpler." Remember, many people may be reading your report: physicians, lawyers, psychologists, case managers, and the like, so don't alienate your audience by confusing them. Feel free to use technical terminology and professional jargon where appropriate, as long as you explain what it means. In fact, the judicious use of "doctorese" can actually help: readers who are made to feel like they're being included in an exclusive club of secret knowledge are more likely to be sympathetic to your interpretation of the facts.

"The first step to rendering a diagnosis is to think of it" (Thibault, 1992), and the best diagnostic instrument is the expert's brain. In both the clinical and forensic settings, there is no substitute for the practitioner's knowledge, experience, and careful practice. Carefully evaluate the claimant, develop a credible case formulation, communicate your findings effectively, and you will serve the cause of justice by discouraging false injury claims and allowing the truly deserving to get what they need to pursue their lives.

REFERENCES

American Psychiatric Association. (2000). *Diagnostic and statistical manual of mental disorders* (4th ed., Text Revision). Washington, DC: Author.

Barton, W. A. (1990). *Recovering for psychological injuries* (2nd ed.). Washington, DC: ATLA Press.

Binder, L. M. (1992). Deception and malingering. In A. Puente & R. McCaffrey (Eds.), *Handbook of neuropsychological assessment: A biopsychosocial approach* (pp. 94–121). New York, NY: Plenum Press.

Dattilio, F. M., & Freeman, A. (Eds.) (2007). *Cognitive behavioral strategies in crisis intervention* (3rd ed.). New York, NY: Guilford Press.

Dattilio, F. M., & Sadoff, R. L. (2007). *Mental health experts: Roles and qualifications for court* (2nd ed.). Mechanicsburg, PA: Pennsylvania Bar Institute.

Dattilio, F. M., Sadoff, R. L., & Gutheil, T. G. (2003). Board certification in forensic psychology and psychiatry: Separating the chaff from the wheat. *Journal of Psychiatry and the Law, 31,* 5–19.

Dattilio, F. M., Tresco, K. E., & Siegel, A. (2007). An empirical survey of psychological testing and the use of the term "psychological": Turf battles or clinical necessity. *Professional Psychology: Research and Practice, 38,* 682–689.

Goldstein, R. L. (1988). Consequences of surveillance of the forensic psychiatric examination: An overview. *American Journal of Psychiatry,* 1243–1247.

Gutheil, T. G., & Dattilio, F. M. (2008). *Practical approaches to forensic mental health testimony.* Philadelphia, PA: Lippincott, Williams & Wilkins.

Heilbronner, R. L., Sweet, J. J., Morgan, J. E., Larrabee, G. J., & Millis, S. R. (2009). American Academy of Clinical Neuropsychology Consensus Conference statement on the neuropsychological assessment of effort, response bias, and malingering. *Clinical Neuropsychologist, 23,* 1093–1129.

Lipman, F. D. (1962). Malingering in personal injury cases. *Temple Law Quarterly, 35,* 141–162.

Miller, L. (1990). Litigating the head trauma case: Issues and answers for attorneys and their clients. *Cognitive Rehabilitation, 8*(3), 8–12.

Miller, L. (1992). Back to the future: Legal, vocational, and quality-of-life issues in the long-term adjustment of the brain-injured patient. *Journal of Cognitive Rehabilitation, 10*(5), 14–20.

Miller, L. (1993a). Psychotherapeutic approaches to chronic pain. *Psychotherapy, 30,* 115–124.

Miller, L. (1993b). Toxic torts: Clinical, neuropsychological, and forensic aspects of chemical and electrical injuries. *Journal of Cognitive Rehabilitation, 11*(1), 6–20.

Miller, L. (1993c). *Psychotherapy of the brain-injured patient: Reclaiming the shattered self.* New York, NY: Norton.

Miller, L. (1995). Toxic trauma and chemical sensitivity: Clinical syndromes and psychotherapeutic strategies. *Psychotherapy, 32,* 648–656.

Miller, L. (1996a). Malingering in mild head injury and the postconcussion syndrome: Clinical, neuropsychological, and forensic considerations. *Journal of Cognitive Rehabilitation, 14*(4), 6–17.

Miller, L. (1996b). Making the best use of your neuropsychology expert: What every neurolawyer should know. *Neurolaw Letter, 6,* 93–99.

Miller, L. (1997a). Neuropsychology of the toxic tort: Making the case for chemical injury. *Neurolaw Letter, 6,* 123–126.

Miller, L. (1997b). Traumatic brain injury, substance abuse, and personality: Facing the challenges to neuropsychological testimony. *Neurolaw Letter, 6,* 137–141.

Miller, L. (1997c). The neuropsychology expert witness: An attorney's guide to productive case collaboration. *Journal of Cognitive Rehabilitation, 15*(5), 12–17.

Miller, L. (1998a). Motor vehicle accidents: Clinical, neuropsychological, and forensic aspects. *Journal of Cognitive Rehabilitation, 16*(4), 10–23.

Miller, L. (1998b). Malingering in brain injury and toxic tort cases. In E. Pierson (Ed.), *1998 Wiley expert witness update: New developments in personal injury litigation* (pp. 225–289). New York, NY: John Wiley & Sons.

Miller, L. (1998c). *Shocks to the system: Psychotherapy of traumatic disability syndromes.* New York, NY: Norton.

Miller, L. (1999a). "Mental stress claims" and personal injury: Clinical, neuropsychological, and forensic issues. *Neurolaw Letter, 8,* 39–45.

Miller, L. (1999b). Psychological syndromes in personal injury litigation. In E. Pierson (Ed.), *1999 Wiley expert witness update: New developments in personal injury litigation* (pp. 263–308). Rockville, MD: Aspen.

Miller, L. (2001a). Not just malingering: Syndrome diagnosis in traumatic brain injury litigation. *Neurorehabilitation, 16,* 109–122.

Miller, L. (2001b). Crime victim trauma and psychological injury: Clinical and forensic guidelines. In E. Pierson (Ed.), *2001 Wiley expert witness update: New developments in personal injury litigation* (pp. 171–205). New York, NY: Aspen.

Miller, L. (2001c). Workplace violence and psychological trauma: Clinical disability, legal liability, and corporate policy. Part I. *Neurolaw Letter, 11,* 1–5.

Miller, L. (2001d). Workplace violence and psychological trauma: Clinical disability, legal liability, and corporate policy. Part II. *Neurolaw Letter, 11,* 7–13.

Miller, L. (2002). What is the true spectrum of functional disorders in rehabilitation? In N. D. Zasler & M. F. Martelli (Eds.), *Functional Disorders* (pp. 1–20). Philadelphia, PA: Hanley & Belfus.

Miller, L. (2007a). School violence: Effective response protocols for maximum safety and minimum liability. *International Journal of Emergency Mental Health, 9,* 105–110.

Miller, L. (2007b). Workplace violence: Practical policies and strategies for prevention, response, and recovery. *International Journal of Emergency Mental Health, 9,* 259–279.

Miller, L. (2007c). Traumatic stress disorders. In F. M. Dattilio & A. Freeman (Eds.), *Cognitive-behavioral strategies in crisis intervention* (3rd ed., pp. 494–527). New York, NY: Guilford Press.

Miller, L. (2008a). *Counseling crime victims: Practical strategies for mental health professionals.* New York, NY: Springer.

Miller, L. (2008b). *From difficult to disturbed: Understanding and managing dysfunctional employees.* New York, NY: AMACOM.

Mogil, M. (1989, May). Maximizing your courtroom testimony. *FBI Law Enforcement Bulletin,* pp. 7–9.

National Academy of Neuropsychology. (2000). Presence of third party observers during neuropsychological testing: Official statement of the National Academy of Neuropsychology. *Archives of Clinical Neuropsychology, 15,* 379–380.

Nies, K. J. & Sweet, J. J. (1994). Neuropsychological assessment and malingering: A critical review of past and present strategies. *Archives of Clinical Neuropsychology, 9,* 501–552.

O'Donnell, M. L., Creamer, M., Bryant, R.A., Schnyder, U. & Shalev, A. (2003). Posttraumatic disorders following injury: A empirical and methodological review. *Clinical Psychology Review, 23,* 587–603.

Parker, R. S. (1994). Malingering and exaggerated claims after head injury. In C. M. Simkins (Ed.), *Analysis, understanding, and presentation of cases involving traumatic brain injury.* Washington DC: National Head Injury Foundation.

Posey, A. J., & Wrightsman, L. S. (2005). *Trial consulting.* New York, NY: Oxford University Press.

Rachlin, S., & Schwartz, H. I. (1988). The presence of counsel at forensic psychiatric examinations. *Journal of Forensic Sciences, 33,* 1008–1014.

Rosen, G. M., & Taylor, S. (2007). Pseudo-PTSD. *Journal of Anxiety Disorders, 21,* 201–210.

Simon, R. I. (1995). Toward the development of guidelines in the forensic psychiatry examination of posttraumatic stress disorder claimants. In R. I. Simon (Ed.), *Posttraumatic stress disorder in litigation: Guidelines for forensic assessment* (pp. 31–84). Washington, DC: American Psychiatric Press.

Simon, R. I. (1996). Three's a crowd: The presence of third parties during the forensic psychiatric examination. *Journal of Psychiatry and Law,* 3–25.

Stone, A. A. (1984). The ethical boundaries of forensic psychiatry: A view from the ivory tower. *Bulletin of the American Academy of Psychiatry and the Law, 12,* 209–219.

Taylor, J. S. (1997). *Neurolaw: Brain and spinal cord.* Washington DC: ATLA Press.

Thibault, G. E. (1992). Clinical problem solving: Failure to resolve a diagnostic inconsistency. *New England Journal of Medicine, 327*, 26–39.

Travin, S., & Potter, B. (1984). Malingering and malingering-like behavior: Some clinical and conceptual issues. *Psychiatric Quarterly, 56*, 189–197.

Trimble, M. R. (1981). *Post-traumatic neurosis: From railway spine to whiplash.* New York, NY: Wiley.

Varney, N. R. (1990). Litigation concerning mild head injury. *Cognitive Rehabilitation, 8*(3), 30–33.

Vinson, D. E., & Davis, D. S. (1993). *Jury persuasion: Psychological strategies and trial techniques.* Little Falls, NJ: Glasser Legalworks.

CHAPTER 14

Employment Discrimination and Harassment

LIZA H. GOLD and WILLIAM J. STEJSKAL

INTRODUCTION

Before 1964, individuals who experienced harassment or discrimination had relatively little legal recourse. When the Civil Rights Act of 1964 was passed, federal and ensuing parallel state legislation created a variety of avenues, in addition to those provided by tort litigation, through which individuals who believe they have been unfairly treated in the workplace due to race, religion, gender, age, disability, or other inherent personal qualities, can seek legal redress. Passions and beliefs surrounding employment and basic concepts of fairness have generated one of the most dynamic areas of legal activity in American law over the past decades.

Employment law continues to evolve, fueled in part by more recent changes that have allowed for jury trials and large damage awards in harassment and discrimination cases. Just 5 days after taking office in January 2009, President Obama signed the Lilly Ledbetter Fair Pay Act into law, relaxing the statute of limitations under various civil rights laws and giving more people more time to file charges for pay discrimination and other civil rights employment violations. Similarly, in 2008, Congress enacted an amendment to the Americans with Disabilities Act (ADA), in large part in response to several recent Supreme Court decisions. These Court decisions narrowed the protection of the ADA and resulted in pressure to reverse the effect of these Supreme Court decisions through statutory amendment (Petrila, 2009).

As more laws and statutes making harassment and discrimination in the workplace illegal have been enacted over past years, employment litigation has increased (see www.eeoc.gov), as has the legal system's request for psychiatric assessment of emotional or psychological injuries related to such experiences. Psychiatric and psychological testimony may form the crux of legal arguments regarding causation and damages in harassment and discrimination litigation (Gold, 2004). Mental and emotional injuries constitute the bulk of exposure in much federal and civil litigation related to employment claims (Lindemann & Kadue, 1992; McDonald & Kulick, 2001). Virtually every federal employment discrimination lawsuit contains an allegation that the plaintiff suffered mental and emotional distress at the hands of the defendant employer (McDonald & Kulick, 2001). Psychiatrists and psychologists can best assist the finder of fact by careful review of mental status, timeline, and evaluation of causation damages, and other legally relevant psychiatric issues.

PREPARATION

ADDRESS SOURCES OF BIAS

Mental health experts conducting evaluations for claims of mental disorders and emotional distress in harassment and discrimination claims should monitor their own assumptions that may accompany these evaluations. Most individuals experience employment-related problems and conflicts as stressful, especially if they result in adverse financial or social consequences, whether or not they include real or perceived harassment and discrimination. In workplace evaluations, examiners should be careful to distinguish psychiatric illnesses from nonpathological and appropriate emotional reactions to workplace stress and distress.

Clinicians have a bias toward identifying distress as pathology (Gold, 2004; Gold & Shuman, 2009). Adverse employment events and the stress and distress that accompany them may precipitate or exacerbate illness in individuals with preexisting diagnoses or vulnerability to psychiatric disorders. Nevertheless, in and of themselves, intense and distressing feelings and complaints associated with them, such as anxiety, insomnia, tearfulness, or irritability, do not amount to diagnosable psychiatric disorders. "Though it may be stressful, unhappiness is not a psychiatric condition; neither is injustice. One may be miserably and justifiably unhappy about a work experience and not be psychiatrically injured" (Savodnik 1991, p. 188).

Harassment and discrimination experiences are not uncommon (see, e.g., Krieger et al., 2006; McMahon & Hurley, 2008) and occur on a continuum, from mild to profound and severe (Gold, 2004). The majority of such experiences can be conceptualized as equivalent to other types of noxious work stress and environments (Fitzgerald, Swan, & Magley, 1997). Exceptions to this general observation occur when the harassment involves violent and/or humiliating assaults or reactivation of previous traumatic experiences (Lenhart, 1996). Nevertheless, even relatively mild forms of harassment and discrimination can have psychological consequences, which, in certain individuals, can result in new onset psychiatric disorders or exacerbations of preexisting disorders (Bergman & Drasgow, 2003; Buchanan & Fitzgerald, 2008; Glomb, Munson, Hulin, Bergman, & Drasgow, 1999; Schneider, Swan, & Fitzgerald, 1997). All of these effects, regardless of preexisting conditions, may be compensable if liability is found.

Avoid Opining on Issues of Liability and Illegal Conduct

Mental health experts should be careful not to be drawn into questions involving liability or the legal definition of harassment and discrimination. The universe of adverse workplace experiences behaviors that may be personally perceived, experienced, or considered harassing or discriminatory is broad; the world of harassing and discriminatory behaviors in the workplace that has been deemed illegal is far narrower. The finder of fact, whether judge or jury, will determine whether illegal as opposed to legal but adverse or undesirable behavior for which an employer is liable has occurred. Since the issue of liability is purely legal, mental health experts cannot offer such opinions without crossing into the purview of the finder of fact and without going beyond the boundaries of their expertise. In addition, offering such opinions will compromise the credibility of mental health opinions that are within their expertise and which may assist the trier of fact in coming to legal determinations.

THE LEGAL CONTEXT OF HARASSMENT AND DISCRIMINATION CLAIMS

Mental health experts are not expected or required to be legal experts. Nevertheless, psychiatrists and psychologists who provide evaluations in harassment and discrimination litigation should begin by familiarizing themselves with the legal and psychiatric issues relevant to the various types of litigation associated with these claims. This will allow experts to focus on those aspects of the case that will be most helpful to those responsible for legal or administrative decisions in making the required determinations. Detailed review of the legal aspects of all types of these claims is beyond the scope of this discussion. However, experts should determine what legal standards and definitions are relevant, and whether considerations of such issues are properly legal or medical opinions.

For example, many employment and discrimination cases are brought under Title VII of the Civil Rights Act of 1964. This act does not provide any particular definition of harassment or discrimination. It also does not require that a psychological injury is necessary to establish a claim of actionable harassment (see *Harris v. Forklift Systems, Inc.*, 1993). In contrast, tort claims for personal injury related to harassment and discrimination often include a claim of intentional infliction of emotional distress. Severe injury must be present to establish the validity of this claim. In both Title VII litigation and tort litigation, causation must be established. In yet another arena in which discrimination and harassment complaints may arise, that of workers' compensation, causation may not be an issue, but the injury must demonstrably affect work functions and earning capacity in order to be compensable (see Gold, 2004; Gold & Shuman, 2009; Gold et al., 2009).

Some statutory antidiscrimination laws do provide relevant definitions with which clinicians should be familiar. For example, the Americans with Disabilities Act (1990) was designed to protect the civil rights of disabled individuals, including their employment rights. The ADA requires an employer to make "reasonable accommodations" for a disabled but qualified individual to enable that individual to perform essential job functions, unless the accommodation would impose an "undue hardship" on the employer. The terms *disability, reasonable accommodations, qualified individual, essential job functions,* and *undue hardship* are either defined statutorily or have been defined through case law. Whether a person has a statutorily defined disability or what accommodations are reasonable, are questions that form the basis of much ADA-related litigation. Expert opinions in these cases will require familiarity with these definitions.

THE REFERRAL

The initial conversation with the referring attorney provides the evaluator an opportunity to address several important preliminary matters. Foremost among these is the need to determine the goodness-of-fit between the needs/issues of the case, and the expertise of the evaluator. General clinical expertise is necessary but not sufficient to perform competent forensic mental health evaluations, whether in discrimination and harassment cases, or in other types of criminal or civil cases.

Knowledge of legal and professional standards, and of forensic evaluation methods and relevant scientific literature that apply to one area of forensic practice, does not necessarily equip the mental health professional to practice competently in a forensic domain outside their previous experience (Melton et al., 2007). Evaluators should undertake only those forensic mental health evaluations for which they have sufficient specialized competence to perform (American Academy of Psychiatry and the Law, 2005). The relevant legal issues, standards, definitions, and required mental health opinions in the particular harassment or discrimination case should be briefly discussed or noted when an attorney first contacts an expert to explore the expert's potential involvement in a harassment or discrimination case.

Because the amount of time needed to conduct an evaluation will vary considerably from case to case, and because evaluators should only accept referrals where there is a reasonable likelihood that they will have sufficient time to conduct an adequate multimodal evaluation, the evaluator should clarify with the referring attorney the procedural timeline of the case, including any deadlines for discovery, as well as the extent of documentary materials available to review and the availability of the subject (and any collateral sources) for examination/interview and the like. The complexity (and, therefore, the time demand) of evaluations is often difficult to appreciate until the evaluation is actually undertaken. Evaluators should ne-gotiate as much time as possible to conduct their evaluation, given the procedural constraints of the case. Referrals should be declined where there are procedural deadlines or other time parameters that could result in a precipitous, assailable evaluation.

FEE ARRANGEMENTS

Arrangements for payment of the evaluator's fees should be clarified in the initial discussion with the referring attorney. To avoid the influence of bias, evaluators do not work on a contingent fee basis (American Academy of Psychiatry and the Law, 2005; American Psychological Association [APA], 2002; Committee on Ethical Guidelines for Forensic Psychologists, 1991). For similar reasons, arrangements that involve payment of the evaluator's fee at the conclusion of their involvement of the case (regardless of outcome) should also be avoided, since this arrangement could threaten an evaluator's objectivity due to concern that their final invoice might not be paid if their opinions are not favorable to the referring attorney's position/theory in the case or if the outcome of the case results in no monetary damage awards.

An alternative arrangement that tends to mitigate bias due to this type of perverse financial incentive is one wherein the referring attorney agrees to provide funds at the outset of the evaluator's involvement in the case as a retainer for the evaluator's services (American Academy of Psychiatry and the Law, 2005). This initial payment reflects a specified number of hours of service at the evaluator's usual fee. The time spent by the evaluator in activities that pertain to the evaluation are then tallied against this retainer. As the time spent on the case grows, and as the initial retainer nears exhaustion, there should be provisions in the agreement for replen-ishing the retainer periodically with additional funds or timely payment of outstanding invoices. Any such agreements between an evaluator and the referring attorney should be explicitly deline-ated in a written agreement or contract, and should include trans-parent accounting of the evaluator's fees and professional activities (APA, 2002).

Mental health experts should be aware that in employment and discrimination cases, defendants can and often do include various city, state, or federal government agencies. Government agencies do not work on a retainer basis with experts, and instead typically request that the expert work on a private contractor basis. This contract is usually negotiated with the government agency's attorneys but managed by a financial department unrelated to the attorneys.

OBJECTIVITY IN EXPERT OPINIONS

In the initial discussion with the referring attorney, the evaluator should recognize that the attorney is operating as a partisan advocate for his or her client and, as such, will typically engage the evaluator in a manner that is calculated to lay the groundwork for a favorable analysis and opinion in the case. This stance can range from rational and matter-of-fact statements by the attorney regarding the manner in which he or she hopes the evaluation will support the theory of the case, to the selective distortion, constraining, or withholding of data that the attorney fears would run counter to their case. Whether the attorney represents the plaintiff or the defendant, the evaluators should clarify their commitment to conduct an objective evaluation consistent with prevailing standards of practice respecting assessment procedures, use of collateral sources, and so on. Evaluators should only accept those referrals where there is a reasonable likelihood that they will have recourse to the information and procedures necessary to conduct a valid and objective evaluation.

ISSUES FOR EVALUATION

Despite the wide scope of legal, administrative, or regulatory issues involved in workplace claims of harassment and discrimination, mental health evaluations in these cases typically involve a limited number of medicolegal issues:

- Whether the plaintiff has a psychiatric diagnosis, and if so, its duration and symptoms
- The etiology or causation of the disorder and, specifically, its relationship to the events in question
- Whether the disorder has resulted in a work-related or other type of impairment, dysfunction, or loss (i.e., damages)

- The plaintiff's prognosis, particularly in regard to issues of recovery, treatment, and functioning (Brodsky, 1987; Greenberg, Otto, & Long, 2003; Metzner, Struthers, & Fogel, 1994)

DIAGNOSIS

Examiners have to determine whether the plaintiff experienced emotional distress from the conduct in question and whether that emotional distress rises to a level where it meets *Diagnostic and Statistical Manual of Mental Disorders*, 4th edition, Text Revision (DSM-IV-TR; APA, 2000) criteria for a psychiatric diagnosis. Most types of employment litigation, even claims of intentional infliction of emotional distress, do not require the plaintiff to establish emotional injury or a DSM-IV diagnosis for alleged discriminatory or harassing behavior to be actionable. Nevertheless, claims of emotional harm, injury, or disability, when unaccompanied by physical injury, have historically been viewed with suspicion by the legal system (Shuman, 2002).

It is difficult, if not impossible, to establish severe distress and emotional injury if the plaintiff does not meet the criteria for a formal DSM-IV diagnosis. A DSM-IV diagnosis supports arguments that a severe injury entitling a claimant to damages actually occurred. Even in a Title VII claim, where psychological injury and, therefore a DSM-IV diagnosis, is not required for a plaintiff to prevail, the Equal Employment Opportunity Commission will compute compensatory damages on the basis of a consideration of the severity and duration of harm (Strubbe, Lindemann, & Kadue, 1999). A formal DSM-IV diagnosis strengthens such damage claims.

Arguments regarding the relevance and importance of DSM-IV diagnoses in litigation highlight the difficulties in utilizing psychiatric diagnoses designed for clinical purposes in nonclinical arenas, such as the legal system. The DSM-IV's diagnostic categories were never intended for use in nonmedical contexts. The imperfect fit between diagnostic emphasis in research and treatment and diagnostic emphasis in legal and administrative systems legitimately raises the question of the relevance of psychiatric diagnoses in litigation generally (Gold, 2002a; Gold & Shuman, 2009; Greenberg, Shuman, & Meyer, 2004).

However, the use of an established diagnosis can serve as a point of reference that enhances the value and reliability of psychiatric and psychological testimony (Gold, 2002a; Gold & Shuman, 2009; Halleck, Hoge, Miller, Sadoff, & Halleck, 1992; Shuman, 1989). Diagnostic categories also create a common language that can facilitate communication, and therefore legal or administrative decision making, when used appropriately. In addition, when a diagnosis is established, the subject of the evaluation can be assessed in relation to others of the same diagnostic category, which in turn can allow experts to draw reasonable connections, restrain ungrounded speculation, or refute unreasonable claims between symptoms associated with a diagnosis and arguments regarding causation, impairment, and damages or disability. The application of a diagnostic category also allows reasonable discussion of the course of a particular individual's illness and the likelihood of symptoms creating past, present, or future functional impairments.

Nevertheless, the fact that a plaintiff experienced or is experiencing emotional distress does not mean that he or she has a psychiatric illness. Examiners should be careful to distinguish psychiatric illnesses from nonpathological and expectable emotional reactions. As noted earlier, clinicians have a bias toward identifying distress as pathology (Gold & Shuman, 2009). If examiners determine that psychological symptoms rise to the level of a mental disorder, diagnoses should be made according to DSM criteria. Psychiatrists and psychologists should be certain to use standard methods of evaluation and differential diagnosis. They should also be prepared to support diagnostic conclusions with specific information gathered from both the clinical interview and record review. Idiosyncratic diagnoses based solely on "clinical experience" will not withstand cross-examination or examination for scientific reliability.

In addition, the evaluation of emotional distress should consider the role of litigation in the plaintiff's clinical presentation (Gold & Simon, 2001). Involvement in the litigation process is an extremely stressful experience. Individuals who file legal claims often are not prepared for the financial and emotional effort involved in proving their cases and the emotional toll these efforts can take. Litigation is widely acknowledged to exacerbate psychological symptoms regardless of diagnosis (Strasburger, 1999). Discrimination and harassment claims that include claims of psychological injury almost guarantee that any and all social, behavioral, family, and legal aspects of an individual's life will be examined in painful and public ways.

However, emotional distress and associated impairment due to the stress of litigation is not compensable, and should be identified separately from any underlying psychiatric disorder.

CAUSATION

A claim for harassment and litigation may be successful, depending on the type of litigation, absent demonstration of causation of psychological damage and attendant disability. However, large damage awards typically are dependent on the demonstration of a causal nexus between the events in question and the psychiatric or psychological injury. In tort law, whether conduct is intentional or negligent and leads to direct or indirect infliction of emotional distress, emotional harm damages will not be awarded unless the conduct "proximately" causes injury. The law in these cases seeks to determine whether one particular event precipitated, hastened, or aggravated the individual's current condition. (As noted, whether that conduct constituted illegal discrimination or harassment for which the defendant is liable is a legal, not medical opinion).

Evaluators should understand that the legal concept of causation and the medical concept of causation are not congruent. The legal concept of proximate cause is an elusive one, even within the law. The legal requirement for establishing proximate cause generally is not scientific certainty but, rather, "probability," "50.1%," "more likely than not," or "reasonable medical certainty" (Danner & Sagall, 1977). The traditional legal method of determining whether one event is the proximate cause of another is to ask whether one could "reasonably foresee" that the former would lead to the latter (Shuman, 2002; Simon, 1992). Practically speaking, proximate cause has come to mean the "recent" cause, that is, "the straw that broke the camel's back" (Simon, p. 550).

In contrast, the concept that many factors contribute to a negative psychological outcome or the development of a psychiatric or medical illness is axiomatic in all behavioral and medical sciences. Mental health experts examine and weigh multiple causative elements in the development of a theory of the etiology of any disorder. Psychiatric and psychological determinations of causation typically conclude that although certain factors may be more significant, a mental disorder has been precipitated by the interaction of a number of factors.

These may include preexisting vulnerability, substance use, family history, and other causes that often have nothing to do with the workplace.

Despite the conflicts inherent in the legal and psychiatric principles of causation, psychiatrists and psychologists recognize that external events can precipitate psychological injury or emotional harm that falls within both legal and psychiatric parameters of causation. Posttraumatic stress disorder (PTSD) and adjustment disorders by definition develop in response to an external event. Other anxiety disorders and mood disorders may also be precipitated or caused by external events. For example, a considerable literature has demonstrated that stressful life events also have a substantial causal relationship with the onset of episodes of major depression, for individuals both with and without identifiable genetic risk factors (Kendler, Karkowski, & Prescott, 1999; Shalev et al., 1998).

Nevertheless, examiners should not assume that any stressful, distressful, or even traumatic workplace event is causally related to any psychiatric diagnosis. The key to the evaluation of causation in any type of employment litigation lies in a thorough assessment of the workplace events, the circumstances surrounding these events, and the individual's life history. The spectrum of harassing and discriminatory behaviors may include many that result in psychologically damaging experiences. However, individuals may bring preexisting problems into the workplace or experience other sources of stress that may result in psychiatric problems.

As noted earlier, even relatively mild experiences of harassment and discrimination can provoke profound emotional reactions that can precipitate psychiatric illness or exacerbate preexisting illness. Claims of emotional injury caused by harassment and discrimination when accompanied by physical injury may be quite straightforward. Physical or sexual assault is readily acknowledged to cause or precipitate psychiatric or psychological harm under certain circumstances.

Although more difficult to demonstrate legally, psychological harm absent physical injury is a real, possible, and at times compensable outcome of discrimination and harassment experiences. Typically, diagnoses commonly associated with such events include depression, panic disorder, generalized anxiety disorder, and substance abuse or dependence, or, in the event of physical or sexual

trauma, PTSD. In individuals without preexisting Axis I or II disorders, psychological responses to harassment and discrimination
generally are proportional to the severity, intensity, duration, magnitude, frequency, and consequences (such as job loss) of their
experiences.

Nevertheless, examiners should not be too quick to assume a
causal nexus between harassment and discrimination, however
upsetting or distressing to the plaintiff, and a psychiatric disorder.
Assessments of causation in such cases should always include:

- Consideration of exposure to another stressor, either in the past
  or concurrent with present events, as the cause of a new
  disorder
- The extent to which the events in question caused a new
  disorder or exacerbated a preexisting disorder
- Whether a disorder would have occurred at all but for the
  events in question
- The presence and course of a preexisting disorder, with and
  without exposure to the events in question
- Whether the dynamics of the individual or the workplace are
  contributing to either the perception of causation or the attribution of preexisting problems to conflict in the workplace

Psychiatric theory does not propose or conclude that the inevitable
outcome of any event is the development of a mental disorder. Even
for adults exposed to a traumatic stressor as defined by DSM-IV,
epidemiological studies indicate that only 15% to 24% of adults
develop PTSD (Breslau, 2001; Kessler, Sonnega, Bromet, Hughes, &
Nelson, 1995; Yehuda & Wong, 2001; Perrin et al., 2007). When
evaluations are made retrospectively, as is often the case in litigation,
estimates of pathology are inflated (Melton et al., 2007) and diagnosis
of psychiatric illness is common (Long, Rouse, Nelsen, & Butcher,
2004; Rosen, 1995).

The evaluation of causation in harassment and discrimination
litigation can become particularly complex when individuals equate
adverse employment experiences, and the distress associated with
them, with traumatic experiences. Psychiatric illness can result from
chronic work-related stress (Gold & Shuman, 2009). This stress may
be the result of illegal activities. Attorneys will argue that unfair

treatment in the workplace is so stressful and psychologically harmful that it has caused psychiatric injury. Claims of psychiatric illness or injury resulting from nontraumatic stressors are common (Gold, 2002b).

Nevertheless, the overwhelming majority of workplace harassment and discrimination experiences, and workplace experiences such as job loss or conflict with coworkers or supervisors, although distressing, do not constitute traumatic stressors. Such experiences are not typically equivalent to traumatic stressors, and claims of PTSD causally related to such experiences, which often accompany the legal claims, are often unsupportable.

As noted, other psychiatric illnesses, such as mood disorders, adjustment disorders or non-PTSD anxiety disorders may be causally related to adverse workplace experiences. But conclusions that the presence of these disorders is causally related to the workplace events also require careful evaluation. Job loss, unfair or discriminatory treatment, and employment-related conflict, whether real or perceived, are stressful. Clinicians who assess individuals involved in employment-related conflict often mistake the stress and distress that follows exposure to any adverse event for psychiatric illness (Long, 1994; Rosen, 1995). However, failure to consider the contribution of earlier or concurrent unrelated traumatic events or stressors to the evaluee's illness, regardless of the alleged precipitant, may result in the false attribution of current symptoms to the employment events being litigated.

Alternative sources of an individual's psychological problems may include past or present exposure to traumatic experiences other than the events involved in the litigation. Other concurrent problems that can result in new-onset disorders include substance abuse disorders, medical conditions, and psychosocial stressors such as marital problems. Areas of inquiry should include family and personal relationships, financial problems, illness, death or loss of significant others, other job-related stress, and any other possible sources of tension or stress.

The possibility of diagnosed or undiagnosed preexisting disorders should also be considered. Disorders such as depression, panic attacks, and generalized anxiety are common. Panic disorder occurs in 1% to 2% of individuals over their lifetime. The lifetime risk of major depressive disorder varies from 10% to 25% for women and from 5% to 12% for men (APA, 2000). Many preexisting illnesses may be exacerbated by adverse events. If the individual has not been previously diagnosed or treated, or if an adequate history is not obtained, such exacerbations may appear to be new-onset disorders.

Evidence of preexisting disorders will not prevent individuals from prevailing in their claims. Tortfeasors must take their victims as they find them. The law recognizes that relatively little trauma may cause injury to someone who is vulnerable to harm. Such a plaintiff is often referred to as having a "glass jaw" or "eggshell skull." An individual with a history of prior illness or trauma may have a more profound reaction to stressful events or conflict than would another individual without such a history. However, the presence of another major life stressor or trauma, or a disorder predating the employment events in question, will make proof of a causal connection between the employment events and the mental injury more difficult.

In some cases, individuals with little or no insight into preexisting problems may genuinely but erroneously consider the workplace harassment or discrimination to be the cause of their psychological problems. Such false attributions may lead examiners to incorrectly assess causation by overlooking the central etiological significance of the individual's prior, long-standing emotional difficulties. This type of situation tends to arise in the context of adverse employment events or interpersonal conflict in the workplace, as often occurs when employees have substance abuse problems or personality disorders. Paranoid, antisocial, borderline, histrionic, and narcissistic disorders are those most frequently encountered in employment litigation (Lipian, 2001; Price, 1994).

Evaluation of the possibility that the individual has a personality disorder is essential. Personality disorders are commonly associated with behavioral problems and interpersonal conflicts which may result in adverse employment experiences. Since individuals with these disorders often do not take responsibility for their behaviors, they often interpret adverse experiences in the workplace as a form of discrimination or harassment. In addition, personality disorders are commonly associated with Axis I mood and anxiety disorders. Work-related stress or adverse events, such as lack of promotion, reprimand for poor performance, or job termination, personality disorders and their cognitive distortions, emotional reactivity, can precipitate or exacerbate associated Axis I disorders and the preexisting personality disorder. In these cases, the personality disorder rather than the workplace may actually be the cause of both the conflict and the Axis I disorders.

In making a diagnosis of a preexisting personality disorder, experts should exercise caution to distinguish the personality traits that define these disorders from characteristics that emerge in response to specific situational stressors. Clinicians are generally warned against the error of making a diagnosis of a personality disorder in the context of a specific external event or stressor (APA, 2000). This is particularly true in the context of harassment and discrimination litigation, where individuals may present as fragile, unstable, or histrionic as a result of their experiences and the stresses and difficulties of litigation. The accurate diagnosis of a personality disorder requires an evaluation of the individual's long-term patterns of functioning across a life span from early adulthood. Evidence of repetitive patterns and symptoms that would be indicative of a chronic, rather than an acute, condition should be identified in multiple spheres of functioning.

Finally, the identification of a history of alternative trauma exposure, preexisting psychiatric history, or a personality disorder should not be used to discount the potentially damaging effects of harassment and discrimination in the workplace. Individuals with preexisting Axis I or II disorders may have a more pronounced and reactive response to these experiences, in contrast to those without preexisting disorders whose responses, as noted above, should be relatively proportional to the circumstances and experiences. Evaluators then have to explain how and why this individual was perhaps more vulnerable or demonstrated a more exaggerated response than would be expected given the circumstances of the case.

DAMAGES

In tort law, an individual's level of impairment is the aspect of any psychiatric disorder most closely associated with assessment of damages (McDonald & Kulick, 2001). All levels of functioning and experience, from interpersonal relationships and work functioning to pain and suffering may be compensable, and thus require evaluation. No specific degree of impairment, dysfunction, or disability is required to be present, although damage awards tend to be directly proportional to the severity of injury as demonstrated by degree of functional impairment, particularly in cases of psychological injury.

Diagnosis is only one factor, and often not the most significant factor, in assessing the severity and possible duration of impairment or disability associated with psychological symptoms (American Medical Association [AMA], 2008; Gold & Shuman, 2009; Gold et al., 2009; Simon, 2002). Just as examiners should avoid the error of assuming a causal connection between a claim of discrimination and harassment and a psychological outcome, they should avoid assuming that any diagnosis is automatically associated with any specific degree of impairment or dysfunction. Even the severity of psychiatric symptoms and illness do not necessarily equate with functional impairment. The condition of the claimant before and after the occurrence of the incident or illness in question is more relevant to the assessment of impairment and loss of function than is any diagnosis alone.

Diagnostic categories should therefore be considered as a means of organizing thinking and using evidence-based data to understand the possible types of impairments associated with specific diagnoses. As clinicians are well aware, not everyone with a specific disorder will have all the possible impairments associated with that disorder. In addition, the loss of function may be greater or less than the diagnostic label or associated impairment might imply, and the individual's performance may fall short of or exceed that usually associated with the impairment (Gold & Shuman, 2009). For example, although depression is widely acknowledged to be a major source of disability (Murray & Lopez, 1996), not all individuals with depression experience symptoms that cause functional impairment.

Examiners should begin by analyzing the pattern associated with the development of impairment and compromised function (Gold & Shuman, 2009). Psychiatric disability rarely develops overnight. Careful examination of the individual's personal, work, and medical history should allow examiners to determine baseline function, whether it has been deteriorating steadily over time regardless of job demand; whether job demand has played a significant factor in developing disability; and whether other events, perhaps unrelated to the workplace, such as medical illness or family problems, have precipitated loss of function.

Psychiatrists and psychologists should use this type of analysis to compare the individual's functioning before and after the events in question and the development of the claimed emotional injury. Only this type of comparative evaluation will allow examiners to arrive at a reasonable determination of severity of impairment and disability. In discrimination and harassment claims, indeed in all claims where causation is relevant, plaintiffs tend to assert that all functional difficulties began after the employment events in question. Regardless of current functional status, such assertions should not be initially accepted as factual. An assessment of the pattern of development of impairment can help clarify such claims.

The evaluation of impairment should include an assessment of the severity of symptoms and the effect of these symptoms in all spheres of the claimant's functioning. As in causation, mental health experts should find a reasonable and proportional relationship between the active symptoms and claims of impaired function, unless the individual had a preexisting vulnerability to a more severe reaction to a lesser injury. Examiners should carefully review the history of the mental disorder, the history of the individual's ability to function over time, and his/her response to treatment or rehabilitation. The influence of other work-related factors, such as poor remuneration, interpersonal workplace conflict, or frustration with career, and non-work-related factors, such as social, family, or medical problems, should also be explored.

Other medical and psychiatric problems, in addition to the primary psychiatric disorder in question, can result in impairment. Examiners should consider whether individuals have impairments resulting from their psychiatric illness or another concurrent illness, such as substance abuse or depression. In addition, individuals involved in employment litigation or making disability claims often are not working. Secondary damaging effects typically arise when the beneficial personal, social, and financial aspects of work become unavailable. Often, financial and marital difficulties ensue. Examiners should distinguish impairment related to psychiatric illness from the consequences of unemployment (Gold & Shuman, 2009). Although both may be compensable, depending on the circumstances, the prognosis for each may be different. Effects that result directly from unemployment may be more easily reversed if the plaintiff begins working again.

Even with all this information, determining the specific nature of an individual's impairments and functional limitations due to psychiatric illness is a complex process. Psychiatric symptoms, even at a mild or moderate level, can create impairment, including work disability, particularly if the psychiatric illness results from employment-related events such as discrimination or harassment. Nevertheless, not every psychiatric symptom will cause work-related impairment in every individual, and not every individual who has a psychiatric symptom, or even a psychiatric disorder, will necessarily experience work impairment or disability.

Psychiatrists and psychologists should not rely on interviews and mental status examinations alone to determine level of disability. Opinions based solely on an evaluee's reports or on the evaluator's personal experience are not an adequate basis for conclusions. Familiarity with research literature helps evaluators avoid relying only on an evaluee's reports, stereotypic beliefs, or their own limited clinical experience. In addition, extensive review of relevant documentation and collateral third-party information is an essential part of the evaluation of impairment.

Assessments of all impairments should be as specific and detailed as possible. Psychological testing can be an important adjunct in this process. It may provide additional useful data, particularly regarding cognitive impairments, such as attention, comprehension, or memory and ruling out any factitious disorders or malingering (Gold & Shuman, 2009, Gold et al., 2009). Assessment of functional impairment should also include use of one or more of the widely available scales designed for this purpose if requested.

PROGNOSIS

Prognosis and the length of time that the plaintiff is likely to continue to experience impairment is also a significant part of the assessment of damages. The prognosis of the individual's illness is closely related to the degree and duration of an impairment or disability. Determination of the future degree of dysfunction should be based on the assessment of current impairment and comparative assessment of functioning before and after the events in question.

The assessment of prognosis should be informed by a thorough clinical evaluation as well as the epidemiological data regarding the natural course of the disorder. Again, the pattern of disability development may be informative, as it may indicate a deteriorating course over many years, or an individual who has a history of regaining function in between episodes of acute illness (Gold & Shuman, 2009).

In formulating opinions regarding prognosis, examiners should evaluate the extent to which treatment will restore the person's capacity to work (AMA, 2008). The effects of treatment can be a major factor in the course of the disorder and, therefore, in the determination of prognosis. The assessment of permanent impairment or disability should not be considered definitive until the claimant has received a sufficient trial of appropriate treatment. An individual who is quite symptomatic and impaired but has not obtained treatment may be someone whose condition will improve with appropriate treatment and, thus, have a good prognosis.

Prognostic assessment, even with adequate treatment, may be difficult. Psychiatric disorders, even with the best treatment, demonstrate many variations in the course of recovery, ranging from complete remission to the development of a chronic and debilitating illness. In addition, examiners should also consider the presence or severity of factors that significantly worsen prognosis. Comorbid psychiatric disorders, such as substance abuse or personality disorders, complicate recovery or remission. The individual's life history, the availability of personal and social support, and the status of other related medical or psychosocial problems may also play a role in prognostic assessment.

The relationship between prognosis, functional impairment, and long-term dysfunction also requires assessment of issues such as secondary gain, malingering, and lifestyle. It may be difficult to untangle the effects of characterological depression, poor motivation, personality conflicts, the secondary gain of unemployment, and lack of opportunity. Perhaps the most significant factor in recovery from impairment is motivation. Regardless of occupation, even minimal impairment may lead to permanent disability when the claimant is not motivated to obtain appropriate treatment or to recover previous level of functioning. Lack of motivation may be hard to distinguish from mental impairment, such as depression or avoidance, and requires careful assessment.

DATA COLLECTION AND INTERPRETATION

Collateral sources, whether as documents/records or third parties available for interview, have the potential to provide the forensic evaluator with essential information concerning the claims of the plaintiff (Heilbrun, Warren, & Picarello, 2003). The objectivity, accuracy, and validity of forensic mental health evaluations, including evaluations in employment discrimination and harassment cases, are enhanced when evaluation procedures are multimodal (Greenberg et al., 2003; Heilbrun, Rogers, & Otto, 2002), and include information from the subject/plaintiff, from psychological testing, and from collateral sources/records.

Information contained in records pertaining to the plaintiff's past employment, medical care, or mental health treatment is not susceptible to being distorted by the plaintiff's response style. Such records can be illuminating regarding preinjury baseline functioning, and may include observations that pertain to claimed psychological injuries or functional impairments. Information obtained from interviews with individuals familiar with the plaintiff (e.g., health care providers, coworkers, family members) can assist the evaluator by providing observational data about the plaintiff in multiple domains of functioning.

It is incumbent on the evaluator to assess the relevance and reliability of the information obtained from collateral sources. For example, medical records may be silent with respect to the claimed tortious event(s), but might depict a succession of physical complaints or syndromal exacerbations that track the timeline of events claimed by the plaintiff. Alternately, coworkers and family members could have allegiances, sympathies, or stakes (tangible and intangible) that might cause them to provide distorted or one-sided information to the evaluator. The evaluator must determine what weight they will assign to the information they obtain from third parties, as they attempt to triangulate, using multiple sources, an accurate formulation of the plaintiff's past and current psychological status.

Legal Records

Prior to interviewing the plaintiff, evaluators should review all available legal documents pertaining to the litigation. This will acquaint the evaluator with the allegations, claims, circumstances, and factual disputes that comprise the substance of the case. This review should include the plaintiff's initial complaint, the defendant's response, responses to interrogatories, deposition transcripts, and the like. While many of these documents are highly partisan in their purpose and tone, they will familiarize the evaluator with the main issues in the litigation.

THE CLINICAL INTERVIEW

In clinical practice, as opposed to forensic practice, the patient is typically relied upon and credited as the most therapeutically relevant source of information about both their objective and subjective experience; in the epistemology of psychotherapy, for example, standards of objective accuracy are often subordinated to the purpose of forming an empathic, uncritical appreciation of the patient's subjective experience for the purpose of promoting the well-being of the patient (Gabbard, 2005). In forensic practice, the evaluator's role and purpose are different; he/she must critically evaluate the objective accuracy of the data before him/her, including information from the subject/plaintiff, in order to confirm or disconfirm competing hypotheses regarding the claims of the plaintiff (Melton et al., 2007).

The clinical interview with the plaintiff should begin with full disclosure of the purpose and limits of the interview. At the outset of the initial interview, evaluators should clarify their role in the case, as well as the nature, scope, and purpose of the evaluation process. The applicable limits of confidentiality and privilege should be explained, along with the foreseeable uses of the evaluator's report and testimony. The nontherapeutic nature of the evaluation should be clarified (American Academy of Psychiatry and the Law, 2005; APA, 2002).

The direct evaluation of the plaintiff provides examiners with an opportunity to elicit information from the subject/plaintiff regarding the plaintiff's level of psychological functioning prior to the alleged discrimination or harassment, current functioning, and the nature and extent of the distress experienced as a result of the alleged actions of the defendant. In harassment and discrimination cases, the evaluators should spend considerable time discussing the plaintiff's work history: prior level of success or failure in the workplace, prior problems if any, jobs held, for how long, why the plaintiff left previous jobs, terminations, periods of probation or implementation of performance improvement plans, promotions, demotions, transfers, complaints, grievances, disability claims, and prior employment litigation.

The interview with the plaintiff should include an exploration of both current psychological functioning, as well as a review of developmental, social, occupational, medical, and mental health history. This retrospective exploration is essential; to evaluate both the plaintiff's claim that they have experienced impairment in a prior level of functioning, as well as claims that the alleged discrimination or harassment is the cause of any such impairment, evaluators must gather data that will enable them to consider the competing hypotheses raised by the plaintiff's claims.

Throughout the interview, the evaluator should be alert to distortions and exaggerations in the self-reported symptomatic picture, as well as in the plaintiff's attribution of causation for any such symptoms. In evaluating the disclosures and behaviors of plaintiffs during the interview, the evaluator should be mindful of the inferred motivation of the plaintiff to prevail in a cause of action. It is imperative that the evaluator recognizes that this motivation may affect the response styles of the plaintiff. Richard Rogers (2008) observed, "In personal injury cases, claimants may use two response styles in the same evaluation. They may minimize psychological problems (i.e., defensiveness) prior to the [tortious event] but grossly exaggerate their symptoms (i.e., malingering) following it" (p. 3). This view finds support in studies that observe that plaintiffs, including plaintiffs in employment litigation, disproportionately present positive depictions of their prior functioning compared to non-litigating controls (Lees-Haley et al., 1997), while accentuating negative aspects of their current functioning (Lees-Haley, 1997; Long et al., 2004).

PSYCHOLOGICAL TESTING

No psychological test score or profile of scores can ever be dispositive on any psycholegal issue (Greenberg et al., 2003; Heilbrun, 1992). Instead, psychological testing provides the evaluator with incremental data that can serve the "purpose of efficiently and objectively generating hypotheses" (Greenberg et al., 2003) regarding the plaintiff's current psychological state. Heilbrun suggested a number of standards regarding the selection of psychological instruments for use in forensic evaluations, asserting among other things that forensic evaluators should use instruments with adequate documented reliability, and whose relevance with respect to the legal issue, or to a psychological construct underlying the legal issue, has been demonstrated in research published in peer-reviewed journals.

General psychopathology and personality inventories such as the Minnesota Multiphasic Personality Inventory, Second Edition (MMPI-2; Butcher, Dahlstrom, Graham, Tellegen, & Kaemmer, 1989), the Millon Clinical Multiaxial Inventory-III (MCMI-III; Millon, Davis, & Millon, 1997), and the Personal Assessment Inventory (PAI; Morey, 1991), can provide information regarding aspects of plaintiffs' current psychological status that may be relevant to their claims of psychological injury (Archer, 2006). Because these instruments include validity scales, they can provide additional information regarding the plaintiff's response style.

Some specialized clinical assessment instruments, such as the Trauma Symptom Inventory (TSI; Briere, 1995), may also provide information relevant to plaintiffs' claims, and include validity scales that address response style. However, the research foundations of instruments such as the TSI are less robust with respect to the performance of their validity scales in nonclinical samples, when compared to instruments like the MMPI-2 (Franklin & Thompson, 2005; Pope, Butcher, & Seelen, 2006). Recent suggestions that the Rorschach Inkblot Method, a projective technique, may have some utility in employment discrimination and harassment evaluations are intriguing (Smith, Gacono, Evans, Kaser-Boyd, & Gacono, 2008), but the inability to detect the influence of response styles may continue to limit the viability of projective methods in forensic evaluation (Sewell & Rogers, 2008).

The degree to which a plaintiff's response style may be distorting their reports of psychological symptoms and distress can be assessed with instruments such as the Miller-Forensic Assessment of Symptoms Test (M-FAST; Miller, 2001), Structured Inventory of Malingered Symptomatology (SIMS; Widows & Smith, 2005) and the Structured Interview of Reported Symptoms (recently published as the SIRS-2; Rogers, Sewell, & Gilliard, 2010). Recent research has suggested that the SIRS, which has long been recognized for its value in detecting malingered psychosis in criminal pretrial and correctional populations (Melton et al., 2007), can also be effective in detecting feigned or exaggerated symptomatology in plaintiffs claiming trauma-related distress (Rogers, Payne, Berry, & Granacher, 2009).

Although psychological and neuropsychological testing can be useful in the evaluation of psychiatric impairment or diagnoses, they should not be used as the sole basis for such determinations. Nevertheless, psychological and neuropsychological tests can be valuable sources of information when conducted in conjunction with the direct examination of plaintiff, review of records, and integration of information from collateral sources.

RECORD REVIEW

Collateral sources of information often are essential in evaluating claims of employment discrimination and harassment. Some objective evidence of a psychiatric disorder and actual impairment is key evidence in coming to an opinion that a plaintiff does or does not have a psychiatric diagnosis, the causation of that diagnosis, and associated levels of impairment, if any. Some claims may encompass unique circumstances in which no collateral information is necessary. Generally, however, without access to such information, subsequent revelation of inconsistent or contradictory facts can seriously undermine conclusions and impeach the expert's credibility.

Collateral information in discrimination and harassment cases consists of formal written records obtained in the course of usual professional and business operations and third-party information obtained through personal interviews, witness statements, and depositions. The amount of either type of collateral information available depends on the circumstances of the claim. The legal discovery process should result in the provision of all past and recent treatment records, witness statements, depositions, and other background materials.

Written records may include a job description, psychiatric, substance use, and medical and pharmacy records. The value of these records in forensic assessments is obvious. In harassment and discrimination cases, past and current employment records may also be invaluable. Good evaluations and the absence of performance problems can reduce concern about workplace factors such as poor performance influencing a claim of discrimination. In contrast, employment records that contain documentation of personnel issues that precede a claim of discrimination might raise concerns that the claim represents an attempt to address workplace conflict or performance issues rather than work impairment based on psychiatric symptoms. Records may include disciplinary or personnel actions that have threatened the claimant's job stability and perhaps led to legal claims of discrimination.

Other records may also add evidence that support or refute claims of psychiatric injury and causation. Although difficult to obtain, academic records can shed light on an individual's intellectual abilities, earlier achievements or failures, limitations in functioning, or need for accommodations. They can also indicate whether an individual has a history of behavioral problems, an important historical aspect of certain disorders, including personality disorders.

Other professional evaluations, whether psychiatric or nonpsychiatric, can assist in determining the consistency of an individual's reports and allow comparison of diagnostic formulations. Evaluations that include psychological and neuropsychological testing can be helpful to establish validity of self-reports, clinical symptom patterns, and personality features of the individual. Finally, a variety of other personal records may be helpful, depending on the circumstances. Previous legal claims, disability claims, police and criminal records, military records, and financial records, including tax returns, can provide information relevant to an individual's previous psychiatric status and level of functioning. An individual's diaries or journals may also be useful, if contemporaneous and not kept for self-serving purposes to validate a legal claim.

THIRD-PARTY INFORMATION

Information from third parties can be useful in corroborating evaluees' accounts of their history, symptoms, and functioning. The reliability of all sources of collateral information should be taken into account, and the inherent bias of all informants as well as the consistency of reported information should be scrutinized. For example, family and friends often have firsthand knowledge of an evaluee's symptoms, evolution of disorder, and functional abilities. However, family members may be as invested in the success of the legal claim as plaintiffs themselves and may distort or exaggerate reports of the individual's mental symptoms in support of the claim. Written statements, depositions, or affidavits provided by third parties may be informative. However, mental health experts should be aware that they might be incomplete or biased, depending on the source. Multiple witness statements that seem to corroborate each other may be more reliable and credible.

COMMUNICATION

DISCUSS FINDINGS WITH THE ATTORNEY

After evaluation of the plaintiff and review of the collateral information, evaluators should be able to formulate their opinions. Opinions may be extensive and detailed or limited to the unsatisfactory conclusion that the evaluator lacks enough information to come to an opinion within a reasonable degree of certainty. Regardless, before committing anything to writing, the evaluator should call the retaining attorney and discuss how to proceed.

Discussion with the retaining attorney should include a candid review of findings and opinions. If additional information is needed, evaluators should request that it be provided, and opinions should not be finalized until this information is reviewed. However, assuming that evaluators have all the available information, it is up to the attorney to decide if he or she wants a written report. If the evaluator's opinions are unfavorable to the attorney's case, he/she may not want a report, and the expert's association with the case may come to an end.

If the retaining attorney feels that the expert's opinions will be of assistance, he/she may instruct the expert to not submit a report or to submit only a brief report, depending on the legal strategy being employed. In these cases, the evaluator's findings and opinions are likely to be disclosed through abbreviated expert disclosure statements and oral testimony. In most harassment and discrimination cases, however, the attorney will ask the mental health expert to produce a written report that more fully describes findings and opinions.

THE REPORT

There is no one set format for writing a report in harassment and discrimination cases. A variety of formats have been suggested for various types of forensic reports (Gold et al., 2009; Greenfield & Gottschalk, 2009; Melton et al., 2007; Silva, Leong, & Weinstock, 2003). Regardless of format, reports should provide enough information to support the opinions for which the expert is being consulted. In addition, evaluators should bear in mind that, typically, the intended audience of the report has not had medical or psychiatric training. Reports should therefore convey information and opinions in nontechnical language that can easily be understood.

Some attorneys will request a full evaluation report without limitations on the scope or depth of the assessment. If no questions have been provided, psychiatrists and psychologists should include all findings and opinions relevant to medicolegal issues in the case in addition to providing any data supporting their conclusions unless otherwise specified. These may include (but are not limited to):

- Degree of emotional distress and psychiatric diagnosis if any
- Causation of diagnosis
- Associated degree of impairment(s)
- Prognosis, including the expected course of the evaluee's disorder(s), likelihood of chronicity, and expected duration of the impairment and treatment recommendations

Attorneys may ask evaluators to answer a specific set of written questions. If specific questions are asked, psychiatrists and psychologists should limit themselves to providing opinions that are responsive to just these questions unless they feel that some relevant or significant aspect of the case is being overlooked.

As noted above, whether the conduct or behavior complained of actually constitutes illegal harassment or discrimination for which the defendant is liable is a legal opinion, not a medical one. Indeed, these are often the ultimate issues in front of the court. Experts, even if asked to do so, should not opine on whether harassment or discrimination actually occurred or whether the defendant is liable for the behavior or conduct in question.

REFERENCES

American Academy of Psychiatry and the Law. (2005). *Ethical guidelines for the practice of forensic psychiatry.* Bloomfield, CT: Author.

American Medical Association. (2008). *Guides to the evaluation of permanent impairment* (6th ed.). Chicago, IL: Author.

American Psychiatric Association. (2000). *Diagnostic and statistical manual of mental disorders* (4th ed., Text Revision). Washington, DC: Author.

American Psychological Association. (2002). Ethical principles of psychologists and code of conduct. *American Psychologist, 57,* 1060–1073.

Archer, R. P. (2006). *Forensic uses of clinical assessment instruments.* Mahwah, NJ: Erlbaum.

Bergman, M. E., & Drasgow F. (2003). Race as a moderator in a model of sexual harassment: An empirical test. *Journal of Occupational Health Psychology, 8,* 131–145.

Breslau, N. (2001). The epidemiology of posttraumatic stress disorder: What is the extent of the problem? *Journal of Clinical Psychiatry, 62* (Suppl.), 16–22.

Briere, J. (1995). *Trauma symptom inventory professional manual.* Odessa, FL: Psychological Assessment Resources.

Brodsky, C. M. (1987). Factors influencing work-related disability. In A. T. Meyerson & T. Fine (Eds.), *Psychiatric disability: Clinical, legal, and administrative dimensions* (pp. 49–65). Washington, DC: American Psychiatric Press.

Buchanan, N. T., Fitzgerald, L. F. (2008). Effects of racial and sexual harassment on work and the psychological well-being of African American women. *Journal of Occupational Health Psychology, 13,* 137–151.

Butcher, J. N., Dahlstrom, W. G., Graham, J. R., Tellegen, A., & Kaemmer, B. (1989). *Minnesota Multiphasic Personality Inventory-2 (MMPI-2): Manual for administration and scoring.* Minneapolis, MN: University of Minnesota Press.

Committee on Ethical Guidelines for Forensic Psychologists. (1991). Specialty guidelines for forensic psychologists. *Law and Human Behavior, 15,* 655–665.

Danner, D., & Sagall, E. L. (1977). Medicolegal causation: a source of professional misunderstanding. *American Journal of Law and Medicine, 3,* 303–308.

Fitzgerald, L. F., Swan, S., & Magley, V. J. (1997). But was it really sexual harassment? Legal, behavioral and psychological definitions of the workplace victimization of women. In W. O'Donohue (Ed.), *Sexual harassment: Theory, research, and treatment* (pp. 5–28). Boston, MA: Allyn and Bacon.

Foote, W. E., & Goodman-Delahunty, J. (2005). *Evaluating sexual harassment: Psychological, social, and legal considerations in forensic examinations.* Washington, DC: American Psychological Association.

Franklin, C. L., & Thompson, K. E. (2005). Response style and post-traumatic stress disorder (PTSD): A review. *Journal of Trauma and Dissociation, 6,* 105–123.

Gabbard, G. O. (2005). *Psychodynamic psychiatry in clinical practice* (4th ed.). Arlington, VA: American Psychiatric Publishing.

Glomb, T. M., Munson, L. J., Hulin, C. L.Bergman, M. W., & Drasgow, F. (1999). Structural equation models of sexual harassment: Longitudinal explorations and cross-sectional generalization. *Journal of Applied Psychology, 84,* 14–28.

Gold, L. H. (2002a). Psychiatric diagnoses and retrospective assessment of mental states. In R. I. Simon & D. W. Shuman (Eds.), *Retrospective assessment of mental states in litigation: Predicting the Past* (pp. 335–368). Washington, DC: American Psychiatric Publishing.

Gold, L. H. (2002b). Posttraumatic stress disorder in employment litigation. In R. I. Simon (Ed.), *Posttraumatic stress disorder in litigation* (2nd ed., pp. 163–186). Washington, DC: American Psychiatric Publishing.

Gold, L. H. (2004) *Sexual harassment: Psychiatric assessment in employment litigation.* Washington, DC: American Psychiatric Press.

Gold L. H, Anfang, S. A., Drukteinis, A. M., Metzner, J. L., Price, M., Wall, B.W., Zonana, H. V. (2009). AAPL practice guideline for the forensic evaluation of psychiatric disability. *Journal of the American Academy of Psychiatry and the Law, 36,* S3–S50.

Gold L. H., & Shuman, D. W. (2009). *Evaluating mental disability in the workplace: Model, process, and analysis.* New York, NY: Springer.

Gold, L. H, & Simon, R. I. (2001). Posttraumatic stress disorder in employment cases. In J. J. McDonald & F. B. Kulick (Eds.), *Mental and emotional injuries in employment litigation* (2nd ed., pp. 502–573). Washington, DC: Bureau of National Affairs.

Greenberg, S. A., Otto, R. K., & Long, A. C. (2003). The utility of psychological testing in assessing emotional damages in personal injury litigation. *Assessment, 10,* 411–419.

Greenberg, S. A., Shuman, D. W., & Meyer, R. G. (2004). Unmasking forensic diagnosis. *International Journal of Law and Psychiatry, 27,* 1–15.

Greenfield, D. P., & Gottschalk, J. A. (2009). *Writing forensic reports: A guide for mental health professionals.* New York, NY: Springer.

Halleck, S. L., Hoge, S. K., Miller, R. D., Sadoff, R. L., & Halleck, N. H. (1992). The use of psychiatric diagnoses in the legal process: Task force report of the American Psychiatric Association. *Bulletin of the American Academy of Psychiatry and the Law, 20,* 481–499.

Harris v. Forklift Systems, Inc., 510 U.S. 17 (1993).

Heilbrun, K. (1992). The role of psychological testing in forensic assessment. *Law and Human Behavior, 16,* 257–272.

Heilbrun, K., Rogers, R., & Otto, R. (2002). Forensic assessment: Current status and future directions. In J. R. P. Ogloff, (Ed.), *Taking psychology and law into the twenty-first century* (pp. 120–146). New York, NY: Kluwer.

Heilbrun, K., Warren, J., & Picarello, K. (2003). Third party information in forensic assessment. In A. M. Goldstein (Ed.), *Handbook of psychology: Forensic psychology*, Vol. 11 (pp. 69–86). Hoboken, NJ: John Wiley & Sons.

Kendler, K. S., Karkowski, L. M., Prescott, C. (1999). Causal relationship between stressful life events and the onset of major depression. *American Journal of Psychiatry, 156,* 837–841.

Kreiger, N., Waterman, P. D., Hartman, C., Bates, L. M., Stoddard, A. M., Quinn, M. M. . . . Barbeau, E. (2006). Social hazards on the job: Workplace abuse, sexual harassment and racial discrimination: A study of Black, Latino, and White low-income women and men workers in the United States. *International Journal of Health Services, 36,* 51–85.

Lees-Haley, P. R. (1997). MMPI-2 base rates for 492 personal injury plaintiffs: Implications and challenges for forensic assessment. *Journal of Clinical Psychology, 53,* 745–755.

Lees-Haley, P. R., Williams, C. W., Zasler, N. D., Marguilies, S., English, L. T., & Stevens, K. B. (1997). Response bias in plaintiffs' histories. *Brain Injury, 11,* 791–799.

Lenhart, S. A. (1996). Physical and mental health aspects of sexual harassment. In D. K. Shrier (Ed.), *Sexual harassment in the workplace and academia: Psychiatric Issues* (pp. 21–38). Washington, DC: American Psychiatric Press.

Lindemann, B., & Kadue, D. D. (1992). *Sexual harassment in employment law.* Washington, DC: Bureau of National Affairs.

Lipian, M. S. (2001). Personality disorders in employment litigation. In J. J. McDonald & F. Kulick (Eds.), *Mental and emotional injuries in employment litigation* (2nd ed., pp. 212–261). Washington, DC: Bureau of National Affairs.

Long, B. L. (1994). Psychiatric diagnoses in sexual harassment cases. *Bulletin of the American Academy of Psychiatry and the Law, 22,* 195–203.

Long, B., Rouse, S. V., Nelsen, R. O., & Butcher, J. N. (2004). The MMPI-2 in sexual harassment and discrimination litigants. *Journal of Clinical Psychology, 60,* 643–657.

McMahon, B. T., Hurley, J. E. (2008). Discrimination in hiring under the Americans with Disabilities Act: An overview of the national EEOC ADA research. *Journal of Occupational Rehabilitation, 18,* 103–105.

Melton, G. B., Petrila, J., Poythress, N. G., Slobogin, C., Lyons, P. M., Jr., & Otto, R. K. (2007). *Psychological evaluations for the courts: A handbook for mental health professionals and lawyers* (3rd ed.). New York, NY: Guilford Press.

Metzner, J. L., Struthers, D. R., & Fogel, J. D. (1994). Psychiatric disability determinations and personal injury litigation (pp. 232–241). In R. Rosner

(Ed.), *Principles and practice of forensic psychiatry*. New York, NY: Chapman & Hall.

McDonald, J. J., & Kulick, F. B. (2001). *Mental and emotional injuries in employment litigation* (2nd ed). Washington, DC: Bureau of National Affairs.

Miller, H. A. (2001). *Miller-Forensic Assessment of Symptoms Test (M-FAST): Professional manual*. Odessa, FL: Psychological Assessment Resources.

Millon, T., Davis, R. D., & Millon, C. (1997). *Manual for the Millon Clinical Multiaxial Inventory-III (MCMI-III)* (2nd ed.). Minneapolis, MN: National Computer Systems.

Morey, L. C. (1991). *The Personality Assessment Inventory*. Lutz, FL: Psychological Assessment Resources.

Murray C. J. L., & Lopez, A. D. (Eds.). (1996). *The global burden of disease: A comprehensive assessment of mortality and disability from disease, injuries and risk factors in 1990 and projected to 2020*. Cambridge, MA: Harvard University Press.

Perrin, M. A., DiGrande, L., Wheeler, K., Thorpe, L., Farfel, M., & Brackbill, R. (2007). Differences in PTSD prevalence and associated risk factors among World Trade Center disaster rescue and recovery workers. *American Journal of Psychiatry, 164*, 1385–1394.

Petrila, J. (2009). Congress restores the Americans with Disabilities Act to its original intent. *Psychiatric Services, 60*, 878–879.

Pope, K. S., Butcher, J. N., & Seelen, J. (2006). *The MMPI, MMPI-2, & MMPI-A in court: A practical guide for expert witnesses and attorneys* (3rd ed.). Washington, DC: American Psychological Association.

Price, D. R. (1994). Personality disorders and traits. In J. J. McDonald & F. B. Kulick (Eds.), *Mental and emotional injuries in employment litigation* (pp. 93–140). Washington, DC: Bureau of National Affairs.

Rogers, R. (Ed.). (2008). *Clinical assessment of malingering and deception* (3rd ed.). New York, NY: Guilford Press.

Rogers, R., Payne, J. W., Berry, D. T. R., & Granacher, R. P., Jr. (2009). Use of the SIRS in compensation cases: An examination of its validity and generalizability. *Law and Human Behavior, 33*, 213–224.

Rogers, R., Sewell, K. W., & Gilliard, N. D. (2010). *Structured Interview of Reported Symptoms, 2nd Edition: Professional manual*. Lutz, FL: Psychological Assessment Resources.

Rosen, G. M. (1995). The Aleutian Enterprise sinking and posttraumatic stress disorder: Misdiagnosis in clinical and forensic settings. *Professional Psychology: Research and Practice, 26*, 82–87.

Savodnik, I. (1991). The concept of stress in psychiatry. *Western State University Law Review, 19*, 175–189.

Schneider, K. T., Swan, S., & Fitzgerald, L. F. (1997). Job-related and psychological effects of sexual harassment in the workplace: Empirical evidence from two organizations. *Journal of Applied Psychology, 82,* 401–415.

Sewell, K. W., & Rogers, R. (2008). Dissimulation on projective measures. In R. Rogers (Ed.), *Clinical assessment of malingering and deception* (3rd ed., pp. 207–217). New York, NY: Guilford Press.

Shalev, A. Y., Freedman, M. A., Peri, T., Brandes, D., Sahar, T., Orr, S. P., & Pitman, R. K. (1998). Prospective study of posttraumatic stress disorder and depression following trauma. *American Journal of Psychiatry, 155,* 630–637.

Shuman, D. W. (1989). The *Diagnostic and Statistical Manual of Mental Disorders* in the courts. *Bulletin of the American Academy of Psychiatry and the Law, 17,* 25–32.

Shuman, D. W. (2002). Persistent reexperiences in the law and psychiatry: Current and future trends for the role of PTSD in litigation. In R. I. Simon (Ed.), *Posttraumatic stress disorder in litigation: Guidelines for forensic assessment* (2nd ed., pp. 1–18). Washington, DC: American Psychiatric Publishing.

Silva, J. A., Leong, G. B., & Weinstock, R. (2003). Forensic psychiatric report writing. In R. Rosner (Ed.), *Principles and practice of forensic psychiatry* (2nd ed., pp. 31–36). New York, NY: Oxford University Press.

Simon, R. I. (1992). *Clinical psychiatry and the law* (2nd ed.). Washington, DC: American Psychiatric Press.

Smith, B. L., Gacono, C. B., Evans, F. B., Kaser-Boyd, N., & Gacono, L. A. (2008). Rorschach assessment in tort and employment litigation. In C. B. Gacono & F. B. Evans (Eds.), *The handbook of forensic Rorschach assessment* (pp. 279–299). New York, NY: Routledge/Taylor & Francis.

Strasburger, L. H. (1999). The litigant-patient: Mental health consequences of civil litigation. *Journal of the American Academy of Psychiatry and the Law, 27,* 203–212.

Strubbe, M. R., Lindemann, B., & Kadue, D. D. (1999). *Sexual harassment in employment law* (1999 cumulative supplement). Washington, DC: Bureau of National Affairs.

Widows, M. R., & Smith, G. P. (2005). *Structured Inventory of Malingered Symptomatology: Professional manual.* Lutz, FL: Psychological Assessment Resources.

CHAPTER 15

Structural and Clinical Assessment of Risk of Violence

KENNETH TARDIFF and DAWN M. HUGHES

INTRODUCTION

In this chapter, we present the psychological and psychiatric factors in the assessment of the risk of physical violence. We discuss the core principles supported by empirical data that have been shown to be related to violent behavior that should encompass a forensic violence risk evaluation. We review the *structured method* as well as *clinical method* of measuring risk of violence. The structured method uses actuarial data and structured tests and rating instruments. The clinical method uses clinical data obtained from the interview of the patient and collateral sources about current and past violence.

Use of the structured method is readily evident in a myriad of settings, in both legal and civil matters, such as sentencing of violent offenders, mitigating or aggravating factors at capital sentencing, eligibility for parole, supervision during probation, release from psychiatric commitment, and civil inpatient commitment.

Use of the clinical method of assessing risk of violence by patients is expected of all clinicians who have a relationship with a patient for evaluation or treatment. The responsibility to assess the risk of violence exists when clinicians evaluate a patient in the emergency department and decide whether to discharge or admit; see a patient in an office setting for the first time and between outpatient visits; admit a patient to a hospital, order a level of observation; and provide other immediate treatment as the patient enters the hospital. It exists during in-hospital diagnosis and treatment, including monitoring level of observation for the patient and deciding whether seclusion or restraint should be used. It exists in the decision to discharge the patient and in the planning and implementation of care after discharge.

Overall, this chapter will describe the assessment of violence risk in forensic populations, both in the short and long term, by psychiatrists and psychologists, and by utilizing the clinical and structured method. What is consistent in both approaches is the sound reliance on the empirical factors that have been found to be present in cases of violent acting out and reoffending. Gone are the days of a "gut reaction" in the assessment of risk, and replaced are solid clinical analyses of the individual's psychological functioning, history, and current factors that may mitigate or aggravate risk. Thus, for anyone undertaking a forensic violence risk assessment, a solid and mastering read of the emerging literature in the field is imperative.

PREPARATION

A well-trained psychiatrist, psychologist, or other mental health professional should be able to assess an individual's short-term violence potential with assessment techniques analogous to those used in the short-term prediction of suicide potential. The time frame for both is several days to a week. Beyond that time, many factors may intervene after the initial decision is made about risk, as in the case of the stabilized schizophrenic patient who stops his or her medication or the abstinent spouse abuser who resumes drinking. As in the assessment of suicide risk, the evaluator focuses on the clinical aspects of the evaluation—namely, psychopathology—but also must take into consideration demographic, historical, and environmental factors that may be related to an increased risk of violence or suicide (Tardiff, Leone, & Marzuk, 2000).

The evaluation of violence potential is analogous to that of suicide potential. Even if the patient does not express thoughts of violence, the clinician should routinely ask the subtle question, "Have you ever lost your temper?" in much the same way as one would check for suicide potential with the question, "Have you ever felt that life was not worth living?" If the answer is "yes" in either case, the evaluator should proceed with the evaluation in terms of how, when, and so on, with reference to violence as well as suicide potential.

When making a decision about violence potential, the clinician also should interview family members, police, and other persons with information about the patient and about violent incidents to ensure that the patient is not minimizing his or her dangerousness. It is also important to contact or attempt to contact the patient's current and past therapists and review old charts for previous episodes of violence, police and arrest reports, and other available records such as judicial proceedings.

DATA COLLECTION

THE STRUCTURED ASSESSMENT OF VIOLENCE RISK

The debate regarding statistical versus clinical methods of violence prediction has been ongoing for at least the past 50 years (Dawes, Faust, & Meehl, 1989; Grisso & Appelbaum, 1992; Grove & Meehl, 1996; Melton et al., 2007). However, over the past two decades, as the courts have pressed for greater methodological rigor regarding expert's opinions, so has the field of violence risk prediction simultaneously evolved into a more sophisticated science, generating sound empirical correlates of violence (Monahan et al., 2001). In addition, the research and development of instruments and assessment tools to aid in the prediction of violence risk emerged (Quincy, Harris, Rice, & Cormier, 1998; Webster, Douglas, Eaves, & Hart, 1997).

Some have argued rather compellingly that structured methods of risk assessments occur along a continuum, with clinical (totally nonstructured assessments) at one end and purely actuarial and statistical methods occupying the other with a combination (structured professional judgment) absorbing the middle ground (Douglas, Ogloff, & Hart, 2003; Monahan, 2008). Furthermore, it would be incorrect to assert that structured assessments of violence risk are devoid of clinical judgment. In fact, clinical observations, psychosocial information gathering, and clinical data synthesis are often essential components that are incorporated and considered within the structured assessment tool itself.

Actuarial risk assessment measures are structured risk assessment tests utilized to estimate the relative probability that an individual will engage in future violence. They represent an explicit and formal format for arriving at violence risk. They are considered statistical, structured, and actuarial because they are derived from a combination of empirically supported risk factors based on known groups of violent offenders and patients, and, as such, they have been found to improve the accuracy of violence risk predictions (Rice & Harris, 1995; Grove & Meehl, 1996). In addition, structured risk assessment tools allow the forensic evaluator to communicate to the trier of fact specifically what factors were relied upon, and the empirical data supporting them, in making risk determinations to the court.

Another empirically based model of violence risk assessment represents a blending of clinical judgment, interview, and analysis with a formal assessment tool, often referred to as Structured Professional Judgment (Douglas & Kropp, 2002; Hart, 1998; Monahan, 2008). This method also adheres to guidelines for assessment, such as analyzing clinical data and information to uncover factors that have been identified in the literature as relating to violence risk (which are discussed further in this chapter) and utilizing an assessment tool, such as the Historical/Clinical/Risk Management-20 (HCR-20) violence assessment scheme. In fact, a cornerstone of forensic evaluations is the reliance on multiple sources of data, and the consistency among data points, to render a confident opinion. The structured professional judgment method acknowledges that violence risk prediction is not an exact science, that there may always be outliers and idiosyncratic case variables, and that certain circumstances dictate the need for professional discretion. Thus, the inherent combination of utilizing sound clinical data *and* an assessment tool provides a comprehensive approach to decision making thereby providing the evaluator with ample data to rely upon in making final conclusions as to the individual's low, moderate, or high violence risk.

Several factors should be taken into consideration when choosing the most appropriate risk assessment measure for the task at hand (Heilbrun, 1992). First and foremost, *what are you trying to measure*? Are you interested in estimating short- or long-term violence risk, the risk of reoffending, risk of community violence or prison violence, risk on parole, risk of sexual violence recidivism, or the risk of future domestic violence? Is the individual you are evaluating male or female, young or old, or an ethnic minority? Particular attention must be paid to utilize a measure that corresponds to the standardization sample in the corresponding group that one is assessing as well as knowledge of base rates of violence in that indexed group (Cunningham & Reidy, 1999). Given the high stakes of conclusive statements regarding violence risk and the potential deprivation of an individual's most basic rights, it is imperative that the forensic evaluator has received training and supervision in assessment methodology and encompasses an adequate command of the violence risk literature. Finally, the importance of communicating to legal decision makers the methods that were relied upon in arriving at a determination of relative risk, as well as potential limitations and margins of error, cannot be overstated.

In this section, we have listed risk assessment tools that have been extensively researched and validated in several populations and are met with wide use in the forensic evaluations of violent offenders. As stated previously, risk assessment measures are not without limitations and may not generalize to every sample. We have also included two domestic violence risk assessment tools for the identification of both reoffending and lethality risk in cases of intimate partner violence. Whereas the risk assessment literature is replete with samples of male violent community offenders, domestic violence offending and reoffending represent the majority of violent crimes toward women and are underrepresented in the discussion of violence risk. Empirical studies have identified prior domestic violence as the most common risk factor for intimate partner homicide, whether the woman or the male partner is killed (Browne, Williams, & Dutton, 1998; Moracco, Runyan, & Butts, 1998; Saunders & Browne, 2000), impressing on evaluators the need for a structured method to assess for this type of violent offending. In addition, in cases of intimate partner homicide, the victim or perpetrator or both have usually had prior contact with the criminal justice system, victim assistance agency, and/or health care facility (Sharps et al., 2001) demonstrating that opportunities do exist for the assessment of lethality risk.

HCR-20: Assessing Risk for Violence—Revised   The HCR-20 violence assessment scheme (Webster et al., 1997; Webster, Eaves, Douglas, & Wintrup, 1995) is an extensively researched 20-item broad-based checklist to assess for future violence in criminal and psychiatric populations. The HCR-20 was developed through a comprehensive analysis of the violence and dangerousness literature and subsequent factors that have been found related to future violence. It synthesizes these data into an instrument that incorporates clinical experience and is relatively straightforward to administer and score.

The value of the HCR-20 is that is incorporates risk markers from past, present, and future considerations of violence. There are 10 historical items, which were chosen based on the empirical link between past and future violence behavior across numerous research studies examining violence risk. The Historical Scale is calculated through a copious review of past documentation and collateral sources, and consists of risk indicators such as age at first offense, early maladjustment, extent of previous violence, history of major mental illness or personality disorder, psychopathology, interpersonal relationship and vocational instability, substance abuse problems, and prior supervision failure. The Clinical Scale assesses for the dynamic and changeable correlates of violence such as lack of insight, negative attitudes, and active symptoms of major mental illness, impulsivity, and unresponsiveness to treatment. Finally, the focal point of the Risk Management Scale is how the individual may adjust to future circumstances and relies on factors that may serve to mitigate or exacerbate violence, such as release and treatment plan, lack of social support, noncompliance, external stress, and other destabilizing factors.

After a careful analysis and scoring of the HCR-20, a judgment is made as to an individual's risk regarding the likelihood of future violence in the categories of low, moderate, or high risk. There are no fixed, arbitrary cutoff scores for the determination of violence risk, but rather structured professional judgments are rendered through an examination of the three factors on the HCR-20.

Hare Psychopathy Checklist—Revised   The Hare Psychopathy Checklist Revised (PCL-R; Hare, 1991, 2003) is a 20-item rating scale that is designed to assess for psychopathy in forensic populations. The PCL-R has been regarded as the most widely researched and best validated instrument for detecting criminal psychopathy and has been translated into multiple languages. It is a highly reliable instrument with associations to criminal behavior and recidivism. Because psychopathy has been found to be one of the factors most strongly associated with violence, the PCL-R is an essential tool in the assessment of violence risk and is often incorporated in other risk assessment measures as well.

Ratings on the PCL-R are derived from a semistructured interview and a review of collateral documentation and information to arrive at a total psychopathy score. Two central factors are generated that reflect the salient features of psychopathy: the affective–interpersonal factor (the callous, selfish, remorseless use of others) and the socially deviant factor (chronically unstable, irresponsible, impulsive, and antisocial lifestyle). Through extensive research and factor analyses, these two main factors were further parsed resulting in four validated and empirically supported subfactors: interpersonal, affective, impulsive lifestyle, and antisocial behavior. The PCL-R is a lengthy instrument designed to be administered and interpreted by individuals who are familiar with the field of psychopathy, forensic psychology, and the theory and research supported in the development of the PCL-R.

There is also an abbreviated version of the Hare Psychotherapy Checklist Revised—the PCL: Screening Version (PCL-SV)—which is a 12-item scale that can be administered in less than 90 minutes. The PCL-SV is based on subset of PCL-R items and is highly correlated with the PCL-R. However, the PCL-SV is not intended to replace the PCL-R, but rather to provide an expeditious manner to assess for the interpersonal, affective, and social deviance factors in both forensic and nonforensic populations and to screen for the possible presence of psychopathy. Cutoff scores alert the evaluator to follow up with the complete PCL-R to establish a more detailed and reliable assessment of psychopathy. The PCL-SV was developed for use in the MacArthur Violence Risk Assessment Study.

Violence Risk Appraisal Guide The Violence Risk Appraisal Guide (VRAG; Quincy et al., 1998) is a 12-item actuarial scale that is constructed to assess for general violence over the period of 7 to 10 years. Predictor variables were coded from institutional files of approximately 600 men from a maximum security forensic psychiatric facility in Canada. The VRAG utilizes quite an extensive review of the psychosocial history of the offender, such as family background, childhood conduct, antisocial and criminal behavior, psychological difficulties, and details of the index criminal offense. Multiple sources of information are reviewed, such as court and police records, psychiatric records, school records, and third parties such as family and friends. The Hare PCL-R score is additionally utilized in determining calculations of violence risk.

Unlike the HCR-20, which allows for structured professional judgment in the decision of violence risk, the VRAG does not, as the VRAG is purely an actuarial instrument. The VRAG authors assert that clinical expertise is important in the compilation of the relevant psychosocial data and substance that go into the computation of the total VRAG score. However, they specifically caution against combining clinical judgment with the VRAG actuarial score as that may lead to lower accuracy than actuarial scores alone.

Danger Assessment Scale   The Danger Assessment Scale (DA; Campbell, 2004) is a 20-item weighted instrument designed to assess the likelihood of lethality or near lethality occurring in a case of intimate partner violence. The DA is administered to the battered victim in a dichotomous yes/no format to assess for lethality risk factors. Weighted scoring of the DA is effective in assisting in safety planning as well as criminal justice options, such as more restrictive bail settings or lack of probation for the offender.

An 11-city case-control study was utilized to identify risk factors for intimate partner femicide and informed the assessment and revision of the DA (Campbell et al., 2003; Campbell et al., 2008). High recidivism and reassault in cases of intimate partner violence underscored the need for law enforcement, courts, victim assistance programs, and hospital emergency departments to have valid and systematic means of evaluating domestic violence cases and identifying those most likely to escalate to lethality. Risk factors include access to guns, threats to kill, increase in frequency and severity of violence, choking, forced sexual contact, threats to children, controlling and stalking behaviors, extreme jealousy, and a battered victim's belief that her partner could kill her. The combination of a high DA score with the woman's perception of danger represents a strong predictor of lethal situations.

Spousal Assault Risk Assessment Guide   The Spousal Assault Risk Assessment Guide (SARA; Kropp, Hart, Webster, & Eaves, 2000) was designed to assess risk of reoffending in cases intimate partner violence in the criminal justice system. The SARA is described as an instrumental means of coding professional judgment rather than a psychological test or actuarial instrument and requires both a psychological assessment of the perpetrator and clinical judgment. The SARA strongly encourages utilizing multiple sources of information to arrive at scoring determinations, such as both victim and perpetrator interviews, criminal justice records, and additional standardized instruments, especially the Hare Psychopathy Checklist (Hare, 1991).

THE CLINICAL METHOD OF ASSESSMENT OF RISK

The focus of this section is to describe methods to evaluate the risk of violence in the short term (within days or a week), because an increased risk of violence should result, as soon as possible, in preventive clinical actions such as change in medication, monitoring, and admitting to or discharge from a hospital. Unlike clinical methods of assessing the risk of violence, actuarial methods of assessing the risk of violence use structured instruments with items that are selected to measure areas thought to be related to the overall risk of violence in an individual. Usually, these items are scored and used to predict the long-term risk of violence after discharge from prison or forensic psychiatric treatment facilities. The actuarial method has been applied to psychiatric patients in the long-term prediction of violence; however, this does not assist the clinician in the treatment of a potentially violent patient, because the clinician managing such a patient is primarily interested in the risk of violence in the next few days to a week. A number of researchers have reviewed many instruments that assess the risk of violence by using actuarial methods. They found that greater integration of clinical, dynamic data more relevant to general adult psychiatry is needed in the assessment of the short-term risk of violence (Harris, Rice, & Camilleri, 2004; Kroner, Mills, & Reddon, 2005; Kumar & Simpson, 2005; Mills, 2005).

DATA INTERPRETATION

The model presented in this section describes at least 10 factors that must be evaluated in determining whether a patient poses a short-term risk of violence. These factors are not scored to produce a global numerical indication of risk, such as 6 out of 10 indicating risk but

4 out of 10 not indicating risk of short-term violence. Rather, information obtained in each area should be synthesized and weighed by the evaluator to form a clinical decision about short-term risk of violence. The clinician must keep in mind that some factors may be more important than others for the individual patient, such as a history of violence with alcohol use or accompanying noncompliance with medication or other aspects of treatment. Even after making a decision about the patient's risk of violence, the clinician must keep in mind that unexpected events can still occur that may provoke violence, such as resumption of alcohol or drug use or a patient's spouse asking for a divorce.

This model represents a consensus among experts that has not been empirically tested but has been used as a standard by clinicians both in testifying as expert witnesses in a number of malpractice suits and in daily practice.

APPEARANCE OF THE PATIENT

The appearance of the patient may prompt further scrutiny of the potential for violence. This applies both to the loud, agitated, angry-appearing patient who is impatient and refuses to comply with the usual intake procedures in the emergency department or clinic and to the quiet, guarded patient to whom one must carefully listen to detect subtle violent ideation. Dysarthria, unsteady gait, dilated pupils, tremors, and other signs of acute drug or alcohol intoxication dictate caution and serious consideration of the potential for violence, even though threats of violence may not have been expressed.

VIOLENCE IDEATION AND DEGREE OF PLANNING AND FORMULATION

The clinician should begin by assessing whether the patient has thoughts of violence toward other persons. As in the evaluation of suicide ideation, evaluation of violent ideation includes assessment of how well planned the ideation or threat is—that is, the degree of formulation. Relatively speaking, vague threats of killing someone, such as "I'm going to get even with her" or "She'll be sorry to see me," may not be as serious as the patient's saying, "I'm going to kill my wife with a gun because she had an affair," but do warrant further inquiry.

INTENT

If a patient has thoughts of harming someone, it is important to explore whether he/she really intends to do something or is just having thoughts of violence. This disclosure may arise during an outpatient treatment session, as an offhand comment on the inpatient unit, or during any other contact with the patient. The patient's mere thought of violence may not be sufficient for the clinician to take actions such as warning someone, changing medication, or hospitalizing the patient. For some patients, these thoughts of violence may seem intrusive, alien, and disturbing, and they will say that they do not intend to do anything to carry them out.

AVAILABLE MEANS

The availability of a means of inflicting injury or death is important in the assessment of violence potential. If the patient is thinking about getting a gun or already has one, the clinician should obviously take a threat of violence more seriously. The clinician always should ask a potentially violent patient if he or she has or has ready access to a gun. Vigorous efforts should be made to have the patient dispose of the gun or to have it taken from the patient by family members or others. Removal of the gun must be verified by a callback by staff. When guns are removed, the potential for homicide is reduced; however, that does not necessarily preclude the patient's attacking the victim in other, less lethal ways.

Available means also applies to the physical availability of the potential victim. How easily accessible is he or she to the patient? Does the potential victim live in a secluded place or in a city building without a doorman? Geography is another aspect of availability. A schizophrenic patient who threatens his/her father may be more of an immediate threat if actually living with the father as opposed to living in a different city or state at a distance from him.

PAST HISTORY OF VIOLENCE OR IMPULSIVE BEHAVIORS

A past history of violence or other impulsive behaviors is often related to future violence. Clinicians should ask about injuries to other persons, destruction of property, suicide attempts, reckless driving, reckless spending, criminal offenses, sexual acting out, and other impulsive behaviors. Past violence increases the risk of future violence by a patient. Episodes of past violence should be "dissected" in a detailed, concrete manner by the clinician. This includes obtaining details as to the time and place of past violence; who was present; who said what to whom; what the patient saw; what the patient remembers; what family members, friends, or staff members remember about the violent episode; why the patient was violent (e.g., because of psychosis); and what could have been done to avoid the violence. Often, there is a pattern of escalation of violence, whether it involves the dynamics of a couple in a domestic violence situation or the increasing agitation of a schizophrenic inpatient for whom interactions with other patients have become too intense.

The past history of violence should be treated as any other medical symptom. This includes noting the date of onset, frequency, place, and severity of violence. Severity is measured by degree of injury to the victim, from pushing to punching, causing injuries such as bruises, and onward to more serious injuries such as broken bones, lacerations, internal injuries, or even death. Severity, target, and frequency of violence can be measured by a written instrument such as the Overt Aggression Scale (Yudofsky, Silver, & Jackson, 1986). Information that should be obtained and recorded about past history of violence includes prior psychological testing, imaging, laboratory testing, and other evaluations, as well as past treatment, hospitalizations, and response to treatments.

PSYCHOSIS

Psychosis is not a diagnosis, but it is a symptom that can be found in a number of disorders, including schizophrenia, delusional disorder, neurological and medical disorders, substance abuse disorders, and mood disorders, especially with mania. When psychosis is present, regardless of the disorder, it increases the risk of violence (Anderson & Silver, 1999).

Schizophrenic patients can be delusional and can have ideas of persecution. Patients may present with aggressive and violent behavior. This may be due to decompensation due to inadequate medication or noncompliance with treatment. This leads to psychotic symptoms such as delusions and hallucinations. Such patients may believe that people are trying to harm them; that the police, the

FBI, or other organizations are spying on them; that some unknown mechanism is controlling their minds; or that the therapist is harming them (e.g., through medication). Patients with paranoid delusions in schizophrenia may react to these persecutory delusions by retaliating against the presumed source of the persecution. Patients with other types of schizophrenia may attempt to kill other persons because of some form of psychotic identification with the victim. Hallucinations associated with schizophrenia have been known to result in violent behavior and homicide (Andreasen et al., 1995; Dixon et al., 1991; Modestin & Ammann, 1996).

Other aspects of schizophrenia, apart from psychotic processes, can also result in violence. Sudden, unpredictable changes in affect may be associated with anger, aggression, and violent behavior. Some schizophrenic patients are violent because of generalized disorganization of thought and a lack of impulse control. Other schizophrenic patients may develop akathisia that is accompanied by purposeless excited psychomotor activity so that they may inadvertently come into physical contact with other patients, which may lead to fights. Schizophrenic patients also may use violence to attain what they want, to express anger, or to deliberately hurt others.

The psychotic paranoid patient, regardless of diagnosis, poses a problem because his/her delusions may not be obvious or the patient may attempt to hide them. Therefore, the evaluator must listen for subtle clues and should follow up regarding the assessment of violence toward others but must be careful not to confront the patient with insistent questioning about the presence of paranoid delusions (Taylor & Felthous, 2006). Auditory hallucinations can be associated with violent behavior. It is unclear whether command auditory hallucinations to harm other persons are associated with a greater risk of violent behavior or whether hallucinations in themselves are responsible for frustration, fear, disorganization, and violence.

Schizophrenic patients can be violent for reasons other than psychosis. Violence by these patients may be the result of comorbid alcohol or substance abuse due to the symptoms of intoxication or from a superimposed insult to the brain as a result of heavy alcohol or drug use with a lower threshold for violence. Comorbid medical and neurological disorders mentioned later in this chapter such as AIDS, dementia, hypoxia, and other metabolic processes may be associated with violence among schizophrenics. Mentally retarded schizophrenics may resort to violence out of frustration in response to either demands from family or staff members or an inability to verbalize their needs and conflicts. Antisocial or borderline personality disorders with schizophrenia increase the potential for violence. Finally, schizophrenics can be manipulative and use violence to control others or to express anger that is not part of the schizophrenic disorder per se.

Patients with delusional disorder can be violent, especially the paranoid and jealous types. The paranoid type involves harboring grudges against those whom the patient believes have wronged them. Patients with delusional disorder of the jealous type are known to retaliate violently against their spouses or loved ones.

A manic patient may become violent as a result of delusional thinking in which the patient believes he or she is being persecuted because of some special attribute. Manic patients usually put all their impulses, including violent ones, into action. A typical situation in which manic patients erupt with violence is when they feel contained and not free to do what they want to do, as in being told that they will be hospitalized against their will or being confronted by a nurse that insists that they take medication that they do not want or think that they do not need (McElroy et al., 1992).

ALCOHOL AND DRUG USE

Alcohol and drug use can exacerbate the psychopathology in other psychiatric disorders and can cause violence in persons with no other psychiatric disorder. It is important to recognize that alcohol and many drugs can produce violence through intoxication as well as withdrawal. Heavy use of alcohol and drugs can cause changes in the brain that may lead to chronic impairment and psychiatric symptoms related to violent behavior (Tardiff et al., 2005; Volavka & Tardiff, 1999). The ingestion of alcohol can be associated with aggression and violence as a result of disinhibition, particularly in the initial phase of intoxication. (Bushman, 1997; Langevin et al., 1987; McCormick & Smith, 1995). The release of inhibitions involves behaviors that would be unacceptable in the sober state, in this case, violence that erupts despite personal and societal restraints. Alcohol also produces impairment in tasks associated with the frontal lobes such as assessment, planning, organization of behavior, and ability to abstract. In an argument or other stressful situation, communication skills may not be sufficient to allow the intoxicated person to deal with the situation in a verbal rather than a physical manner; thus, violence occurs. Cognitive impairment of the brain caused by alcohol may exaggerate provocation through misinterpretation of real events as in perceiving a benign statement as an insult in a bar or in a marital discussion. The intoxicated person may not appreciate the consequences of violence because of cognitive impairment.

Cocaine, especially when absorbed through the nasal route, initially produces a feeling of well-being and euphoria. With continued use, particularly when the cocaine is taken intravenously or smoked in the form of crack, the euphoria turns to grandiosity, psychomotor agitation, suspiciousness, and, frequently, violence. Suspiciousness first becomes paranoid ideation and then paranoid delusional thinking. Thus, violence results from delusional thinking as well as from the stimulation, irritation, confusion, and psychomotor agitation effects of cocaine. Symptoms of intoxication typically disappear within 2 days after the last dose; however, the delusional thinking may last for a week or longer after the last dose (Denison, Paredes, & Booth, 1997; Linaker, 1994).

Violence may occur during intoxication with a number of hallucinogens, but less commonly than it occurs in phencyclidine (PCP) intoxication. Within 1 hour of oral use (5 minutes if the drug is smoked or taken intravenously), PCP can produce belligerence, ataxia, dysarthria, muscle rigidity, impulsivity, unpredictability, grossly impaired judgment, and violence. There also may be delusional thinking or delirium that can last longer than that produced by cocaine (Convit, Nemes, & Volavka, 1988).

With intense or prolonged amphetamine use, a feeling of well-being and confidence turns to confusion, rambling, incoherence, paranoid ideation, and delusional thinking, which are accompanied by agitation, fighting, and other forms of aggression (Miczek & Tidey, 1989).

Inhalants are substances containing hydrocarbons, such as gasoline, glue, paint, and paint thinners, which are used by young children and early adolescents to produce intoxication. Inhalant intoxication may be characterized by belligerence and violence as well as impaired judgment.

Anabolic steroids are used by young men to enhance muscle growth and performance in athletics. Reports and systematic studies have found that after several months of self-administering these drugs, these men become irritable, combative, and violent. Their irritability and violent outbursts disappeared within several months after discontinuation of steroids (Choi, Parrott, & Cowan, 1989; Pope & Katz, 1994).

PERSONALITY DISORDERS

Some personality disorders, particularly the antisocial and borderline types, increase the risk of violence (Bernstein, Useda, & Siever, 1993; Gunderson, Ronningstam, & Smith, 1991; Hare, Hart, & Harper, 1991; Herpertz et al., 1997; Kemperman, Russ, & Shearin, 1997).

Patients with antisocial personality are violent in order to seek revenge and/or to bolster their dominating presence. Frequently, the victims are strangers or superficial acquaintances. Characteristically, these patients show no remorse after the attacks and instead regret not inflicting more injuries on their victims whom they believe deserved the violence. Although these patients may appear glib and attractive, the clinician should expect violence if their self-esteem or inflated self-image is threatened.

The person with borderline personality can be violent in several contexts. Violence can be a manifestation of affective instability or manipulation and as such can be unpredictable. Individuals with borderline personality disorder have a pervasive pattern of instability in interpersonal relations, self-image, emotional states, and marked impulsivity. They are sensitive to real or imagined rejection. They form intense relationships with some people and expect these people to protect and rescue them. The failure of others to live up to these unrealistic expectations provokes rage, verbal and/or physical violence, suicidal behavior, or other self-injurious behaviors. Impulsivity is severe in borderline personality, and this also results in violence, suicide attempts, and other self-destructive behaviors.

Persons with narcissistic personality can be violent occasionally when angry because they are not given something they think that they deserve.

Persons with paranoid personality frequently threaten violence because they feel persecuted and/or discriminated against because of their race, gender, or other personal attribute. These feelings of persecution often lead to arguments with people in their lives. These patients often have thoughts or plans of violence but do not usually act on their violent thoughts; however, if violence occurs, it can be catastrophic, as in cases of mass murder.

Although intermittent explosive disorder is not a personality disorder, it seems appropriate to discuss it here. It is characterized by discrete episodes of loss of control resulting in serious violence toward persons or destruction of property. The violent episode is not the result of the physiological effect of a substance or medical disorder. The degree of the violent episode is grossly out of proportion to any provocation or environmental stressor. These patients may describe a sense of tension before the violence and a sense of relief afterward. Unlike the antisocial and borderline personality disorders, these patients feel remorseful after their violence. Between the violent episodes, these patients may appear to be stable and a model employee or spouse.

Posttraumatic Stress Disorder

To meet criteria for posttraumatic stress disorder (PTSD), the traumatically exposed person must have symptoms of reexperiencing the event, avoidance of reminders of the event or numbing of responsiveness, and symptoms of increased arousal or hypervigilance. Associated features may also include dissociation, affect regulation, and marked difficulties in interpersonal relationships. Whereas PTSD is twice as common in females, males with PTSD are more likely to act out aggressively. Patients with PTSD often direct aggression toward intimate partners, although persons or situations resembling the trauma may provoke and be the victims of violence. Higher rates of depression and alcohol and substance abuse have been found to co-occur in PTSD patients who attack intimate partners (Grieger, Benedek, & Ursano, 2008). Although more uncommon, because PTSD can result in a stress-response system that continues to operate as if a threat were actively present, individuals who are not characteristically aggressive but who suffer from PTSD may act out violently in response to a real or imagined threat of danger. One should take a detailed history of traumatic events and victimization experiences and current traumatic symptomatology as well as conduct a thorough assessment of, comorbid psychiatric conditions, such as depression, alcohol and drug use, and details of past violent behavior.

MENTAL RETARDATION

Aggressive behavior by the mentally retarded is a common problem (Citrome & Volavka, 1999). In a number of studies in the United States, Canada, and Europe of mentally retarded patients identified in residential facilities as problem cases, roughly a third were aggressive. Moderately retarded patients presented more severe violent behavior than the severely mentally retarded. Aggressive behavior was more frequent in the moderately retarded probably due to the reduced mobility of some the profoundly retarded. Most of the violent behaviors were directed at staff or other patients.

NEUROLOGICAL AND MEDICAL DISEASES AND VIOLENCE

There are a number of organic causes of violence involving focal or diffuse brain damage and medical disorders. Some are uncommon and some are fairly common. Violence due to organic causes generally is more likely than other types of violence to be triggered by modest or trivial stimuli, usually does not involve premeditation or planning, does not serve long-term aims or goals, and does not have a gradual buildup. Aggression is punctuated by long periods of calm and after outbursts patients are often upset or embarrassed (Anderson & Silver, 1999).

DEMENTIA

Behavioral disturbances are common in persons with dementia. Aggression is one of the main factors that lead to patients being placed in a nursing home. Aggression is most likely to emerge when a patient is asked to do something they resent or do not want to do. The target of violence in institutions often is the staff. Alzheimer's patients with delusions or hallucinations are more likely to be violent than those who do not have delusions or hallucinations.

TRAUMATIC BRAIN INJURY

Aggression commonly occurs after traumatic brain injury, usually during the acute stages of recovery from brain injury, and can endanger the safety of patients and caregivers. Patients experience agitation and confusion that can last from days to months. Subsequently, patients may develop low frustration tolerance and explosive behavior can be triggered by minimal provocation or occur without warning. These explosive episodes range in severity from irritability to violent outbursts that result in damage to property or attacks on others. In severe cases, the violent patients cannot remain in the community and are referred to psychiatric or other type of facilities.

Epilepsy

Most aggression associated with epilepsy occurs in general tonic-clonic seizures in the ictal phase (during the seizure) and often involves attempts to assist or restrain the patient. In the postictal phase (immediately after a seizure), the patient is confused and some aggression can occur. The occurrence of aggression in the interictal period (between seizures) is controversial.

AIDS Encephalitis

AIDS causes numerous behavior deficits, including dementia. Agitated behavior is common in severe cases and psychosis can develop with AIDS-related mania. Violence can be dangerous as patients may attempt to bite others or threaten them with a weapon such as a knife.

Electrolyte Imbalance and Hypoxia

Electrolyte imbalance can precipitate delirium and confused states. These patients may become agitated and aggressive. Sodium and calcium imbalances are most likely to be involved in these states. Cerebral hypoxia and hypoxemia, usually resulting from cardiac or pulmonary disorders, can cause delirium with confusion and aggression.

Endocrine Disorders

Hyperthyroid states can produce agitation and psychosis. Hypothyroid conditions produce depression, apathy, and lethargy. Long-standing hypothyroidism can produce myxedema psychosis, which causes extreme agitation and aggression. Hyperparathyroidism can cause psychosis and lead to violent behavior. Cushing's Syndrome due to adrenal tumors has high levels of cortisol, which can cause metabolic encephalopathy and psychosis with associated violence.

NONCOMPLIANCE WITH TREATMENT

A history of noncompliance with treatment should alert the clinician that the patient is at an increased risk of violent behavior. Noncompliance may be indicated by a history of irregular attendance at scheduled appointments or laboratory and other clinical workups, or by the patient's refusing to take certain medications for a psychiatric or medical disorder or deliberately missing doses of medication. Measuring the patient's blood levels of medication may assist the clinician in monitoring the patient's compliance with the medication regimen. Contact with the patient's family—with the consent of the patient—also may assist in determining whether the patient is taking medication as prescribed. Depot medication, administered by injection every two to four weeks, eliminating the need for daily oral dosing, particularly antipsychotic medications for schizophrenia and other psychotic disorders, also can be used to ensure compliance by these patients.

DEMOGRAPHIC CHARACTERISTICS

Demographic characteristics of patients should be considered in the assessment of violence potential. Young persons and men have been found to be at increased risk of violence, as are persons from environments of poverty, familial disruption, or decreased social control in which violence is considered an acceptable means of attaining a goal in the absence of other legitimate means or adequate education. The environment from which the patient comes is thus an important consideration in the determination of violence potential.

COMMUNICATION

Upon completion of a thorough forensic psychiatric or psychological evaluation, communication of the findings and opinions is warranted in some form. A written report may or may not be requested, depending upon jurisdiction requirements. Similarly, testimony at depositions, hearings, or trial may or may not occur. Regardless of the means of communication, written or oral, it is imperative that the evaluator remain mindful of the referral question that was asked as well as the limits of one's expertise. The evaluator should strive toward clarity and nonjargon interpretation of the information that has been gathered, with particular attention to separating facts of the case from his/her own professional opinion regarding violence risk. Explaining the statistical properties of a risk assessment tool and elaborating on the empirical studies that identified violence risk markers—such as the MacArthur Violence Risk Assessment Study— are important in laying the foundation for one's opinion. Adequate preparation is paramount in order to convey sound and reasoned opinions regarding violence risk that can be readily understood and digested by a lay professional.

Particular attention in violence risk assessment must be paid to communicating the different risks for violent offending that have been empirically supported in the literature with the specific factors present in the matter at hand, and why or why not they are considered significant in a present case. In addition, there are times an individual may have few statistical risk factors for future violence, but behave in a manner that signifies greater risk, such as a direct expressed threat of harm to another or the presence of active hallucinations, misperceptions of the intent of others, and paranoia with the intent to act on those misperceptions. Communicating this professional judgment of risk is warranted as well.

If one is utilizing a structured psychological measure or actuarial tool as part of an overall professional judgment of risk, the limitations of that measure must be reported. Moreover, reporting base rates for violence in a particular index population is crucial to establishing accuracy of statistical probabilities of risk for a given individual. Statements regarding risk should be stated in overall probabilities detailing the clinical, empirical, and case-specific descriptors that inform that assessment.

Obviously, the ultimate goal in violence risk assessment is not merely prediction, but the protection of individuals from the violent acts of another. Thus, in addition to an overall assessment of violence probability, risk management strategies—factors that may help to suppress or deter behaviors that signify risk—should be offered. Rather than historical or past correlates of violence, risk management focuses on dynamic and changeable circumstances in a particular individual's life whereby an intervention may have a positive altering effect. Examples include treatment for active substance abuse, inpatient or outpatient psychotherapy, and/or psychopharmacological interventions to reduce psychotic symptomatology.

REFERENCES

Anderson, K. E., & Silver, J. M. (1999). Neurological and medical diseases and violence. In K. Tardiff. (Ed.), *Medical management of the violent patient: Clinical assessment and therapy* (pp. 87–124). New York, NY: Marcel Dekker.

Andreasen, N. C., Arndt, S., Alliger, R., Miller, R., & Flaum, M. (1995). Symptoms of schizophrenia: Methods, meanings, and mechanisms. *Archives of General Psychiatry, 52,* 341–351.

Bernstein, D. P., Useda, D., & Siever, L. J. (1993). Paranoid personality disorder: A review of its current status. *Journal of Personality Disorders, 7,* 53–62.

Browne, A., Williams, K. R., & Dutton, D. C. (1998). Homicide between intimate partners. In M. D. Smith & M. Zahn (Eds.), *Homicide: a sourcebook of social research* (pp. 149–164). Thousand Oaks, CA: Sage.

Bushman, B. J. (1997). Effects of alcohol on human aggression: Validity of proposed explanation. *Recent Developments in Alcohol, 13,* 227–304.

Campbell, J. C. (2004). Helping women understand their risk in situations of intimate partner violence. *Journal of Interpersonal Violence, 19,* 1464–1477.

Campbell, J. C., Webster, D., & Glass, N. (2008). The Danger Assessment: Validation of lethality risk assessment instrument for intimate partner femicide. *Journal of Interpersonal Violence, 24,* 653–674.

Campbell, J. C., Webster, D., Koziol-McLain, J., Block, C. R., Campbell, D. W., Curry, M. A., et al. (2003). Risk factors for femicide in abusive relationships: Results from a multisite case control study. *American Journal of Public Health, 93,* 1089–1097.

Choi, P. Y., Parrott, A. C., & Cowan, D. (1989). High dose anabolic steroids in strength athletes: Effects upon hostility and aggression. *Journal of Psychopharmacology, 3,* 102–113.

Citrome, L., & Volavka, J. (1999). Violent patients in the emergency setting. *Psychiatric Clinics of North America, 22,* 789–801.

Convit, A., Nemes, Z. C., & Volavka, J. (1988). History of phencyclidine use and repeated assaults in newly admitted young schizophrenic men. *American Journal of Psychiatry, 154,* 1176–1183.

Cunningham, M., & Reidy, T. (1999). Don't confuse me with the facts: Common errors in violence risk assessment at capital sentencing. *Criminal Justice and Behavior, 26,* 20–43.

Dawes, R. M., Faust, D., & Meehl, P. E. (1989). Clinical versus actuarial judgment. *Science, 243,* 1668–1674.

Denison, M. E., Paredes, A., & Booth, J. B. (1997). Alcohol and cocaine interactions and aggressive behaviors. *Recent Developments in Alcoholism, 13,* 283–291.

Dixon, L., Haas, G., Weiden, P. H., Sweeney, J., & Frances, A. J. (1991). Drug abuse in schizophrenic patients: Clinical correlates and reasons for use. *American Journal of Psychiatry, 148,* 224–230.

Douglas, K. S., & Kropp, P. R. (2002). A prevention based paradigm for violence risk assessment: Clinical and research applications. *Criminal Justice and Behavior, 29,* 617–658.

Douglas, K. S., Ogloff, J. R., & Hart, S. D. (2003). Evaluation of a model of risk assessment among forensic psychiatric inpatients. *Psychiatric Services, 54,* 1372–1379.

Grieger, T. A., Benedek, D. M., & Ursano, R. J. (2008). Posttraumatic stress disorder, aggression, and violence. In R. I. Simon & K. Tardiff (Eds.), *Aggression and mental health* (pp. 123–140). Washington, DC: American Psychiatric Publishing.

Grisso, T., & Appelbaum, P. S. (1992). Is it unethical to offer predictions of violence? *Law and Human Behavior, 16,* 621–633.

Grove, W. M., & Meehl, P. E. (1996). Comparative efficiency of informal (subjective, impressionistic) and formal (mechanical, algorithmic) prediction procedures: The clinical-statistical controversy. *Psychology, Public Policy, and Law, 2,* 293–323.

Gunderson, J. G., Ronningstam, E., & Smith, L. E. (1991) Narcissistic personality disorder: A review of data on DSM-III-R descriptions. *Journal of Personality Disorders, 5,* 167–177.

Hare, R. D. (1991). *The Hare Psychopathy Checklist—Revised (PCL-R).* Toronto, ON: Multi-Health Systems.

Hare, R. D. (2003). *Manual for the Revised Psychopathy Checklist* (2nd ed.). Toronto, ON: Multi-Health Systems.

Hare, R. D., Hart, S., & Harper, T. J. (1991). Psychopathy and the DSM-IV criteria for antisocial personality disorder. *Journal of Abnormal Psychology, 100,* 391–398.

Harris, G. T., Rice, M. E., & Camilleri, J. A. (2004). Applying a forensic actuarial assessment (the Violence Risk Appraisal Guide) to nonforensic patients. *Journal Interpersonal Violence, 19,* 1063–1074.

Hart, S.D. (1998). The role of psychopathy in assessing for risk of violence: Conceptual and methodological issues. *Legal and Criminological Psychology, 3,* 123–140.

Heilbrun, K. (1992). The role of psychological testing in forensic assessment. *Law and Human Behavior, 16,* 257–272.

Herpertz, S., Gretzer, E. M., Steinmeyer, V., Muehlbauer, V., & Schuerkrens, A. (1997). Affective instability and impulsivity in personality disorder. *Journal of Affective Disorders, 44,* 31–37.

Kemperman, I., Russ, M. J., & Shearin, E. (1997). Self-injurious behavior and mood regulation in borderline patients. *Journal of Personality Disorders, 11,* 146–157.

Kroner, D. G., Mills, J. F., & Reddon, J. R. (2005). A coffee can, factor analysis and prediction of antisocial behavior: the structure of criminal risk. *International Journal of Law and Psychiatry, 28,* 360–374.

Kropp P. R., Hart, S. D., Webster, C. D., & Eaves, D. (2000). The Spousal Assault Risk Assessment (SARA) Guide: Reliability and validity in adult male offenders. *Law and Human Behavior, 24,* 101–118.

Kumar, S., & Simpson, A. I. (2005). Application of risk assessment for violence methods to general adult psychiatry: A selective review of the literature. *Australian New Zealand Journal of Psychiatry, 39,* 328–335.

Langevin, R., Ben-Aron, M., Wortzman, G., Dickey, R., & Handy, L. (1987). Brain damage, diagnosis, and substance abuse among violent offenders. *Behavioral Sciences and the Law, 5,* 77–86.

Linaker, O. M. (1994). Assaultiveness among institutionalized adults with mental retardation. *British Journal of Psychiatry, 164,* 62–78.

McCormick, R. A., & Smith, M. (1995). Aggression and hostility in the substance abuser: The relationship to abuse patterns, coping style, and relapse trigger. *Addictive Behaviors, 20,* 555–564.

McElroy, S. L., Keck, P. E., Pope, H. G., Hudson, J. I., Feadda, G. L., & Swann, A. C. (1992). Clinical and research implications of the diagnosis of dysphoric or mixed mania or hypomania. *American Journal of Psychiatry, 149,* 1633–1644.

Melton, G. B., Petrila, J., Poythress, N. G., Slobogin, C., Lyons, P., & Otto, R. K. (2007). *Psychological evaluations for the courts: A handbook for mental health professionals and lawyers* (3rd ed.). New York, NY: Guilford Press.

Miczek, K. A., & Tidey, J. W. (1989). Amphetamines: aggressive and social behavior. *National Institute of Drug Abuse Research Monographs, 94,* 68–79.

Mills, J. F. (2005). Advances in the assessment and prediction of interpersonal violence. *Journal of Interpersonal Violence, 20,* 236–241.

Modestin, T., & Ammann, R. (1996). Mental disorders and criminality: male schizophrenia. *Schizophrenia Bulletin, 22,* 69–82.

Monahan, J. (2008). Structured risk assessment of violence. In Tardiff, K. (Ed.), *Textbook of violence assessment and management.* Washington, DC: American Psychiatric Publishing.

Monahan J., Steadman, H. J., Silver, E., et al. (2001). *Rethinking risk assessment: The MacArthur Study of Mental Disorder and Violence.* New York, NY: Oxford University Press.

Moracco, K. E., Runyan, C. W., & Butts, J. (1998). Femicide in North Carolina. *Homicide Studies, 2*, 422–446.

Pope, H. G., & Katz, D. L. (1994). Psychiatric and medical effects of anabolic-androgenic steroid use: A controlled study of 160 athletes. *Archives of General Psychiatry, 51*, 375–386.

Quincy, V. L., Harris, G. T., Rice, M. E., & Cormier, C. A. (1998). *Violent offenders: Appraising and managing risk.* Washington, DC: American Psychological Association.

Rice, M. E., & Harris, G. T. (1995). Violent recidivism: Assessing predictive validity. *Journal of Consulting and Clinical Psychology, 63*, 737–748.

Saunders, D. G., & Browne, A. (2000). Intimate partner homicide. In R. T. Ammerman & M. Hersen (Eds.), *Case studies in family violence.* New York, NY: Kluwer Academic/Plenum Press.

Sharps, P. W., Koziol-McLain, J., Campbell, J. C., McFarlane, J., Sachs, C. J., & Xu, X. (2001). Health care providers' missed opportunities for preventing femicide. *Preventive Medicine, 33*, 373–380.

Tardiff, K., Leone, A. C., & Marzuk, P. M. (2000). Suicide risk measures. In A. J. Rush (Ed.), *Handbook of Psychiatric Measures* (pp. 61–270). Washington, DC: American Psychiatric Press.

Tardiff, K., Wallace, Z., Tracy, M., Piper, T., Vlahov, D., & Galea, S. (2005). Drug and alcohol use as determinants of New York City homicide trends from 1990–1998. *Journal of Forensic Sciences, 50*, 1–5.

Taylor, P. J., & Felthous, A. R. (2006). Introduction to this issue: International perspectives on delusional disorders and the law. *Behavioral Sciences and the Law, 24*, 235–240.

Volavka, J., & Tardiff, K. (1999). Substance abuse and violence. In K. Tardiff (Ed.), *Medical management of the violent patient: Clinical assessment of therapy* (pp. 153–177). New York, NY: Marcel Dekker.

Webster, C. D., Douglas, K. S., Eaves, D., & Hart, S. D. (1997). *HCR-20: Assessing the Risk for Violence (Version 2).* Vancouver, BC: Mental Health, Law, and Policy Institute, Simon Fraser University.

Webster, C. D., Eaves, D., Douglas, K. S., & Wintrup, A. (1995). *The HCR-20 scheme: The assessment of dangerousness and risk.* Vancouver, BC: Mental Health Law and Policy Institute, and Forensic Psychiatric Services Commission of British Columbia.

Yudofsky, S. C., Silver, J. M., & Jackson, W. (1986). The Overt Aggression Scale for the objective rating of verbal and physical aggression. *American Journal of Psychiatry, 143*, 35–39.

CHAPTER 16

Child Abuse and Neglect

GILLIAN BLAIR and ANNIE G. STEINBERG

INTRODUCTION

This chapter will offer the reader an approach to the forensic assessment of the child and adolescent when abuse, neglect, and/or exposure to violence has been alleged or confirmed. The importance of the role of the examiner cannot be underestimated in ensuring a child's safety and well-being. Critical decisions made in court often permanently affect the life of the child, his/her family, and the community at large. It is, therefore, incumbent upon the examiner either to possess the requisite knowledge of child development and experience upon interviewing a child or adolescent prior to accepting the role of evaluator, or to engage in partnership with a professional who has the necessary expertise to work directly with children and adolescents who have become the victims of abuse.

FEDERAL AND STATE LEGAL DEFINITIONS

The Child Abuse Prevention and Treatment Act (CAPTA) is the federal legislation that provides minimum standards that states must incorporate in their statutory definitions of child abuse and neglect (42 U.S.C.A. § 5106g(2)). The CAPTA definition of *child abuse and neglect* refers to "any recent act or failure to act on the part of a parent or caretaker, which results in death, serious physical or emotional harm, sexual abuse, or exploitation, or an act or failure to act which presents an imminent risk of serious harm." The

CAPTA definition of *sexual abuse* includes "the employment, use, persuasion, inducement, enticement, or coercion of any child to engage in, or assist any other person to engage in, any sexually explicit conduct or simulation of such conduct for the purpose of producing a visual depiction of such conduct"; or "the rape, and in cases of caretaker or interfamilial relationships, statutory rape, molestation, prostitution, or other forms of sexual exploitation of children, or incest with children" (42 U.S.C.A. § 5106g(4)).

An abused or neglected child is one whose parent or custodian inflicts, permits, or threatens physical or mental injury, excluding purely accidental events. Because legal definitions vary from state to state as per specific language, the forensic examiner should be familiar with the specific statutes (www.childwelfare.gov). While the federal definition of *maltreatment* is "the physical and mental injury, sexual abuse, negligent treatment, or maltreatment of a child under the age of 18 by a person who is responsible for the child's welfare under circumstances which indicate that the child's health or welfare is harmed or threatened," state definitions specify threshold criteria of particular relevance to the legal process and should be known to the forensic examiner. For example, in Pennsylvania (23 Pa. C.S.A. §6303), the standard is whether the abuse caused *serious* physical injury, mental injury, sexual abuse or exploitation, whether it created an *imminent risk* of serious physical injury to or sexual abuse or sexual exploitation, whether the neglect constituted *prolonged or repeated* lack of supervision. In, New Jersey, the standard is whether it caused or created a *substantial risk* of death or serious or protracted disfigurement, or if the neglect involved a *willfully* abandoned child (N.J. Ann. Stat. § 9:6-8.21).

Abuse may involve physical injury, sexual acts, emotional assaults, or any combination of these. *Neglect* can refer to the failure to provide sufficient food, safe shelter, necessary medical care, access to education, and/or emotional support. Abuse issues tend to carry more weight in court, partly because neglect is more difficult to define and less readily recognized and considered less critical to the life of the child (Cantwell, 1997). While it is widely acknowledged that neglect is the most prevalent form of maltreatment and its sequelae profound and long lasting, it remains elusive conceptually, bereft of a coherent theoretical framework. It also remains the subject of relatively little research and intervention, perhaps given its inextricable relationship to poverty, race, disability, and other socio-economic and class-based factors. While there are broad social implications to the alleviation of the stresses of poverty-related neglect, the roots of abuse and neglect are also extremely case specific.

More than 500,000 children, almost 1% of the population of children under the age of 18 years old, are in foster care on any given day (Child Welfare Information Gateway, 2009). The average age of children entering the foster care system is younger than a decade ago, with younger children now remaining in the system longest. Children in foster care are disproportionately African American or minority children. Errors made as a result of incomplete information or hasty evaluation in this domain can have a lifelong impact on the child. In each decision, there exists the possibility of error—the state can fail to act or intervene, leaving a child at risk; or the state can be overly intrusive, infringing on parental rights, harming a child, and wasting scarce resources. Once child protective services has been involved, there is still no guarantee of safety for the child; as many as half of the children killed by parents or caretakers are killed after they have come to the attention of the child welfare system.

Evaluations involving child abuse and neglect are particularly challenging because serious consequences can result if inaccurate information is reported. As an example, children may be subjected to continued maltreatment and may even die, parental rights may be terminated, families may be ruined, and the stigma of being accused of child abuse may lead to a suicide (Sattler, 1998). Unfortunately, even under the best of conditions, there may remain uncertainty about the facts, and it may not be possible to definitively state the degree to which a child is at risk. The forensic evaluator who recognizes the enormity of his/her task in such cases can better help to ensure the safety of the child by providing an assessment of the highest caliber that addresses the multifactorial risks (e.g., mental health, psychosocial, poverty, substance abuse, medical, etc.) and offers recommendations for relevant interventions that will ensure the safety of the child and family.

THE FORENSIC EVALUATIVE CONTEXT

Child abuse and neglect is an area encountered by forensic psychologists and psychiatrists in several distinct contexts. While this chapter largely addresses the civil context, some child abuse investigations result in criminal charges. The forensic evaluator in criminal proceedings, regarding acts of abuse against a child, follows the rules and standard of evidence with the burden of proof beyond a reasonable doubt, distinct from the preponderance of evidence that is required in civil proceedings that involve child abuse and neglect.

Forensic evaluators may be called on to conduct an initial assessment of the abuse or neglect of a child in the following circumstances:

- When either an allegation by the child, parent, or other party regarding harm to a child occurred in the context of an emerging family conflict or custody dispute.
- Symptoms of concern are exhibited by the child and the child welfare system, as representative of the state, has become involved in assessing the degree of injury or harm to the child that has resulted from a caretaker's act or omission. Sometimes the forensic evaluator is called upon to help distinguish between an abusive and accidental injury if the history and examination do not distinguish between the two.
- Civil litigation following an alleged or documented incident of abuse, to assist the attorney with respect to the credibility or preparation of a child witness.
- Civil litigation following an alleged or documented incident of abuse, with regard to the assessment of damages incurred by the child for the purposes of determining necessary interventions and/or monetary compensation.
- Criminal child abuse proceedings that focus not on the welfare of the child, but the accountability of the offender.
- Decision making regarding reunification following foster care placement for abuse and neglect, to advise in assessing parental capacity and the potential for harm to the child, or to help in deciding what will be in the best interest of the child who has been abused or neglected.

DEVELOPMENTAL FRAMEWORK

Because children are not miniature adults, it is critical to have a developmental understanding of children and adolescents, as this directly impacts on the assessment of abuse and neglect. The needs for protection and safety are different for infants and very young children than for adolescents, and the risks in many ways are greatest for the youngest. The youngest children cannot express what they have seen and experienced in language that can be understood by the court. The impact of an erroneous finding leaves the youngest child most vulnerable to a lethal outcome, making the role of the evaluator particularly important for this age group.

Understanding the needs of children at distinct stages of development and the associated parental tasks is critical in the assessment of child abuse and neglect (Barnum, 2002). In the domain of safety, the infant requires food, shelter, warmth, safety from physical harm, and routine medical care; toddlers need all of this as well as poisoning and accident prevention, and the school-age child autonomous safety and life skills. Children also need communication and understanding, cognitive support, discipline, and supervision, as well as emotional support, each appearing distinct at different phases of the developmental life. Examination of the developmental needs of children for advocacy, protection, and socialization in the context of the specific capacities of parents and caregivers has direct implications for all forensic evaluations involving abuse or neglect, even in civil cases, informing damages in addressing factors associated with the child's resilience and outcome prediction.

In addition to language and cognitive issues, school age children often feel pressured to give the interviewer what is (perceived as) desired, and the wording of the questions needs to be focused but not leading. Understanding how to generate a comfortable environment in which the child can relax, even play, is often critical in completing a meaningful evaluation, especially for this age group. With adolescents, evaluators must still assess vocabulary, and capacity to process language and abstractions in order to structure appropriate questions (Rosado, 2000). Interviewing the teenager who may understand the implications of full disclosure and who may have been groomed to respond in a certain way, who may wish to protect the integrity of the family, or may wish to challenge parental authority with a provocative, embellished narrative requires an empathic knowing of the dilemma of adolescence.

Behavioral observations of the child with a parent are essential in understanding the child, the nature of the abuse and its implications for the child's developmental trajectory. While gathering information from other sources is important, direct clinical assessment of the child and caregiver yields tremendous information about the child (as well as parent). Children can be very anxious in the presence of their parent, or move immediately to a caregiver role themselves when the parent has limitations such as a chronic depression. Observing how the parent reads and responds to the child's communication efforts, the level of comfort, mutual understanding, and shared pleasure are several of the many factors that shape the assessment.

Evaluations when there have been allegations of abuse or neglect often camouflage the early pursuit of child custody by one parent. Given that child custody evaluations incorporate extensive assessment strategies, emphasizing the critical identification of the "psychological parent," parental competence, and often, the subtle nuances of the best interests of the child, it is important to clarify the purpose of the evaluation as provided by the retaining party or the court. While the child-relevant information accumulated in child custody often involves scores of hours of observation, data gathering, and assessment, child abuse or neglect hearings are often afforded only minutes in the courtroom and a systematic evaluation of the child's developmental needs may not be heard. Regardless of the nature of the case, the forensic evaluator must present findings synthetically and in a way that is most relevant to the specific question before the court.

Children grow physically, emotionally, and cognitively by progressing through stages, but there is considerable variation in the way each individual child develops. Further, many factors affect the developmental trajectory, including trauma, illness, and the child's individual personality features in evolution. Knowledge of normative child development and its variations helps evaluators avoid the mistake of assuming that common behaviors reflect abuse experiences (Friedrich, Grambsch, Broughton, Kuiper, & Beilke, 1991; Poole & Wolfe, 2009).

The child's response to the interview itself is valuable information; does the child welcome the opportunity to talk openly and play, or does he/she appear timid, frightened, regressed, shut down? Responses to individual questions are also crucial. Is the child open until specific topics arise, when does the child begin to fidget, glance anxiously at the door, whisper, or ask to go to the bathroom? While children who have serious emotional disturbances or significant cognitive delays may not be able to provide a coherent and reality-based narrative, regardless of the age of the child, most children and adolescents can offer an enormous amount of information if the evaluation is developmentally matched with their status and current caregiver situation is taken into consideration. The capacity to distinguish real events from fantasy is another essential aspect of the evaluation, see below for a discussion of this topic.

THE VERY YOUNG CHILD

The outcome of many child abuse cases is determined by an evaluation of the child's credibility, and when the child's statement stands alone as evidence, it is easier for the defense attorney to attack the child's allegation on memory and suggestibility grounds (Vieth, 1998). The forensic evaluator must create an environment that assesses the child's communication and narrative, seek corroborative evidence, if any, and transmit a credible narrative for the court.

Contrary to beliefs about the accuracy of the report of a very young child, research has demonstrated that when children are first asked to tell about a recently experienced event by a nonbiased interviewer, their narratives are accurate, and the absence of suggestive techniques allows even very young preschoolers to provide highly accurate reports, although they may be sparse in details (Bruck, Ceci, & Hembrooke, 1998). The forensic evaluator rarely is the first to interview a child, but a cognitively intact child of almost any age can provide a relevant, honest, and rich account of what transpired, when time is available to allow for free play and the limited language level of the very young child is accommodated. For example, a 3-year-old who sustained immersion burns from scalding bath water at 2 years of age, held a doll down in a plastic tub and scolded the doll, "If you not being good, you going to the hot water."

When her stepfather returned to the waiting room, she opened the examination room door and whispered to him, "No more hot water, okay?"

If the abuse occurred before the child had extensive language, the child may also use gesture or act out what happened, for example, when a 4-year-old communicated how she had sustained life-threatening abdominal injuries by punching herself fiercely in the stomach with a mean expression on her face, nodding wide-eyed, and silently staring at the alleged perpetrator or pointing to his picture when asked if she remembered who had done this to her. The forensic evaluator must synthesize the primitive verbal accounts, gestures, play, and other behaviors of the child along with the physical findings and history to construct a relevant narrative and respond to the questions posed by the court.

REAL AND FANTASY, TRUTH AND LIES

Within a developmental framework, the capacity to distinguish real events from fantasy is an essential aspect of the evaluation of a child or adolescent. While there are many factors that may influence children's reports and significant potential for the misinterpretation of children's statements, the data do not support categorically discrediting the testimony of children, nor do they justify skepticism about reports made by children (Brown & Lamb, 2009; Ceci & Bruck, 1995; Klemfuss & Ceci, 2009). The complex arena of evaluating the accuracy of children's statements requires a foundation in child development and knowledge of the scientific field that has emerged, along with what Ceci and Bruck describe as "both common and uncommon sense." Accuracy is optimal in the first report of a child, presuming appropriate and nonleading questions; inaccuracy can be related to perception, poor recall, cognitive limitations, and other factors.

The forensic evaluator must address the child's understanding of truth and lies and what it means to the child to "tell the truth" (Poole & Lamb, 1998). Careful review of all transcripts, videotapes, and interview recall can help understand the potential effects of repeated interviews and depositions; suggestive questioning; and the role of interviewer bias, duration, and trajectory of the litigation, and other factors.

Analyzing the child's interview is an important component of the assessment of the credibility of the report. Detailed interviewing will help determine the consistency of the child's reports over time, as well as across informants. Child and adolescent specific details, such as the kind of pajamas worn, the cartoon viewed on television when the event in question occurred, and so on can often assist in corroborating the history. The child's report of what transpired may or may not be consistent over time, and many factors account for the recanting and revisions to the original narrative. How the child's account of abuse is conveyed also offers much information; if there are many child-relevant idiosyncratic details and language used to describe the abuse, the narrative is more likely to have been articulated first by the child and not embedded, suggested, or coerced by an adult.

DEVELOPMENTAL FACTORS THAT IMPACT MEMORY

Children need to perceive and understand their experiences before they can accurately store and retrieve them in an organized fashion (Dwyer, 2009). Very young toddlers do not have the language, cognitive ability or contextual framework to recount their experiences in a coherent way. From 3 to 6 years of age, children are able to encode, store, and retrieve their memories in an organized fashion if prompted with appropriate but not leading questions. Once school age, children can begin to use strategies for keeping information in memory, and by 7 to 8 years of age, children are beginning to learn how to rehearse memories and keep them in focus. As children get older, their knowledge base grows, and the memory is recalled based on how it fits with other experiences, as well as its distinctiveness from what was known by the child.

When children are young, many cannot distinguish reality from fantasy reliably, as their knowledge base is not large enough to cognitively understand what happened conceptually, nor do they have a relevant context in which their memories can be placed. Despite these developmental factors that impact memory, and the related potential for misleading or false evidence, even preschoolers are capable of recalling much that is forensically relevant.

SUGGESTIBILITY

Although young children may be vulnerable to leading questions and suggestibility, even very young children can provide accurate accounts (Blandon-Gitlin & Pezdek, 2009). The reliability of child recall is enhanced through the use of open-ended questions that encourage free narrative from memory; focused questions demanding yes/no or other short answers may limit memory retrieval (Lamb, Orbach, Hershkowitz, Esplin, & Horowitz, 2007). However, experimental studies showed that children who omitted information in response to open-ended questions were able to provide further details with focused questioning (Hutcheson, Baxter, Telfer, & Warden, 1995). The child's capacity to provide a reliable history can be considerably enhanced with the appropriate elicitation of information by trained forensic investigators using high quality interviewing techniques (Brown & Lamb, 2009).

Suggestibility increases with repeated interviews and questions, high stress situations, and intimidating interviewers; the process of suggestive interviewing techniques and impact of interviewer bias has been well described in the literature (Bruck, Ceci & Hembrooke, 1998; Bruck & Ceci, 2002; Goodman et al., 1999; Malloy & Quas, 2009). While open-ended, nonjudgmental questions can facilitate recall of details, more often, repeated interviews lead to inadvertent suggestions and forced choices, embedded information, and altered responses due to the child's desire to please the interviewer. In civil cases, the forensic evaluator often sees the child following multiple meetings and depositions; it is important to examine the consistency of the history and level of detail present in available transcripts. In some cities, allegations of child abuse and neglect are now addressed in child advocacy centers, where efforts are made to conduct a single forensic interview conducted by a trained individual and observed behind one-way mirrors and/or videotaped to minimize the negative impact of serial interviews on the accuracy of the child's responses. Transcripts and videos of this interview should be carefully reviewed by the forensic evaluator whenever available.

The child's capacity to qualify as competent to testify relates to his/her reliability and accuracy in recounting the narrative. This has become even more critical since the Supreme Court of the United States increased the significance of oath-taking competency requirements for child witnesses in criminal cases by expanding defendant's rights against the admissibility of hearsay from individuals who fail to testify at trial (*Crawford v. Washington*, 2004; *Davis v. Washington*, 2006; Lyon, Carrick, & Quas, 2009). When children are not competent to testify, their statements to the police and forensic interviewers are also not accessible (Raeder, 2007).

Evaluations of a child or adolescent include the assessment of the social, emotional, cognitive, linguistic, educational, medical, and developmental functioning of the child (and often the family as well), and a developmentally appropriate exploration of the child's perspective of the current situation and family relationships. While the forensic evaluator is not an investigator, it is often necessary to offer an opinion regarding how to understand the data, including its inconsistencies. The ethical forensic evaluator will examine the degree to which he/she has the requisite skills, experience, and knowledge base to undertake and competently conduct the evaluation utilizing established professional practice guidelines before agreeing to do so. This chapter will provide a guide for the forensic evaluation of the child or adolescent when child abuse or neglect has been alleged or confirmed.

PREPARATION

REFERRAL QUESTION AND SOURCES

Clearly articulated referral questions inform the evaluation and help to establish specific parameters for all parties. Understanding what the evaluation is expected to add to the legal decision-making process guides the form, structure, and scope of the evaluation. For example, videotaping often provides rich powerful data that cannot be obtained in other ways, particularly with young, nonverbal children, but many agencies, attorneys, and families are skeptical, and permission is often denied. Clear communication and a partnership with those requesting information may help the examiners to craft an evaluation that best answers the referral question, and provides the richest data for the case.

INFORMED CONSENT

In the absence of a court order, a crucial first step is the identification of those required to give informed consent, and if this is overridden by court order, understanding any limits to the scope of the evaluation. Absent a court order, written consent from all participants precedes record review, scheduling, and so on. It should be recognized that in evaluations of abuse and neglect, participation may not be voluntary, which can profoundly affect the relationship and dynamic between examiner and examinee (Melton, Petrila, Poythress, & Slobogin, 2007).

In giving consent, parties need to understand the purpose of the evaluation; what is expected of them; sources of collateral information; how information may be used, and identification of the recipients of the final report. In understanding the purpose and scope of the evaluation, evaluees need to appreciate the limits to confidentiality inherent in a forensic examination (Bernet, 2002). In structuring the evaluation, it is helpful to have a plan of who will be interviewed and in what order, whether psychological testing will be required and of whom, who will be observed with whom, and whether observations in home and/or school are required in addition to the office setting. It is also helpful to indicate to the retaining attorney the estimated time needed to complete the evaluation and prepare a report.

A comprehensive assessment of allegations of abuse or neglect requires data from numerous sources. This includes data from interviews, observations, and psychological testing, considered in the context of a carefully gathered history and corroborative data (Simon & Gold, 2007). An authorization by parents or the court to release collateral data from medical, psychiatric, educational, legal, and child protective agency sources, as well as to conduct interviews with those acquainted with the child (family members, child protection caseworkers, treating sources, teachers), may be facilitated by parents who understand the importance of these adjunct interviews. When a referral for a medical exam is warranted, it should be initiated at the beginning of the evaluation so that relevant findings can be incorporated in the report. Failure to gather information from multiple sources in complex evaluations is likely to lead to inadequate or inaccurate findings.

Obtaining consent to video or audiotape interviews is often challenging; there may be reluctance on the part of parents regarding privacy concerns, such as who might review the tapes, how they will be stored, and when and whether they will be destroyed. However, opposition to a potentially unassailable record of the evaluation is more often raised by attorneys seeking to avoid charges or preserve legal options, or by child protection agencies that may fear retribution over decision-making capacity and/or adherence to their own established protocol.

It is helpful to explain to parents and older children how the information generated in the evaluation will be communicated to others, for example, written report to the retaining party, verbal consultation, deposition, or court testimony. Parents should be informed that the report will not be made directly available to them.

PARTICIPANTS

Participants to the evaluation often extend beyond parents and child to include extended family members, foster parents, or other caregivers. Understanding the relationships between the parties helps the examiner decide how best to schedule interviews and psychological testing if warranted. This foundational work improves later efficiency.

RECORD COLLECTION

Careful review of all pertinent records is essential to a thorough evaluation. Unfortunately, not all referral sources automatically provide these records, and the examiner is tasked with obtaining relevant records for review prior to beginning the evaluation. Because parents may present a history at variance with official records, familiarity with the record allows the examiner to structure the interview, to know where and when to probe and challenge perceptions. In forensic assessment, the incentive for intentional distortion is recognized, but without a conscious desire to distort, informants may provide inaccurate or biased information. The use of multiple sources of information reduces the impact of bias (Heilbrun, Grisso, & Goldstein, 2009). Failure to obtain pertinent records at the outset may prolong the evaluation process, require additional interviews, lead to erroneous conclusions, even invalidate the findings.

In allegations of abuse or neglect, it is helpful to ask parents or caregivers to write a narrative about the child prior to meeting with either parent or child. Parental perceptions of a child can be both informative and illustrative of the parent–child relationship. The inclusion of photographs, artwork, or family videos helps the examiner to understand the child and family in the context of the specific referral questions. In addition to collateral sources provided by the referring agency, parents should be asked to provide the names of additional individuals most familiar with their child and the family.

OFFICE ENVIRONMENT

The conditions under which interviews occur include the consideration of a one way mirror and management of the attorney who may request to be present in civil cases. The room used for interviews and parent–child observations should be sufficiently large to accommodate families and child friendly with a play area and an array of developmentally and age-appropriate toys so that children will feel comfortable but not overstimulated (Haller, 2002). In addition to a selection of art materials, children evaluated for abuse or neglect often gravitate to toys representing home life, such as kitchen and cooking materials, toy baths, dolls, and so on. Having a supply of drinks and snacks, even diapers, on hand for young children is often helpful in avoiding interruptions to the evaluation session.

DATA COLLECTION

An evaluation begins with a review of the records, with particular attention paid to prior allegations of abuse or neglect, and any earlier evaluations of participants. Understanding the history and the family dynamic allows for a stepwise approach to data collection.

It is generally helpful to first meet at least once with the parents together to gain insight into their own relationship as well as their perspective about their child. Recognizing that the examiner is familiar with the parents may also allay the child's anxiety regarding the evaluation. Ideally, parent–child observations are scheduled after the individual interviews with parents and child to avoid perceptions of alliances that may arise in the joint session.

PARENT INTERVIEW

It is important to gather information regarding family of origin; abuse and neglect history for each parent; prior child protection agency involvement with the family; and medical, developmental, psychiatric, substance abuse, educational, employment, marital, and legal history. Parents should be asked to describe their relationship with the child, and their understanding of why the evaluation was requested. It can be instructive to observe whether the parent remains child-focused during the interview or is more interested in following a different agenda. Behavior checklists are a useful way to gather data regarding a parent's perception of the child's behavior, and should be reviewed with the parents after completion. When parent interviews reveal previously unknown information (e.g., a psychiatric history in a parent), an authorization for release of records should be requested and additional interviews conducted after these records are reviewed. Other adults, such as foster parents or extended family members, should be interviewed to elicit more information about the child, his/her experiences, needs, and quality of their attachment and relationships; the focus of these interviews is to gather information rather than to elicit opinions regarding the validity of abuse and neglect allegations.

CHILD INTERVIEW

Children should be interviewed alone, although with a very young or particularly anxious child, it may be helpful to have a parent/caregiver present initially. If a sibling is part of the evaluation, seeing the children together first may allay anxiety. Explain the purpose of the evaluation to the child in an age- and developmentally appropriate fashion. Examiners need to build rapport with the child; this can be achieved by chatting with the child about something important to them such as a recent birthday, a family pet, school, and so on. It is helpful to give the child permission to disagree with the examiner, and this can be practiced with praise given when the child appropriately disagrees. Exploring the difference between the truth and a lie enables the examiner to understand if and how the child understands these abstract concepts. During the forensic evaluation, as distinct from a forensic interview at a child advocacy center where art materials but no toys are provided, children should feel free to interact with play materials available to them.

In recent years, a number of protocol-driven interviews have been developed to ensure that nonsuggestive questions are used, improve interview techniques and the quality of data, and provide structured techniques that operationalize guidelines and bridge the gap between theory and practice; Yuille's Step-Wise Interview technique establishes rapport with the child, then assesses the child's verbal skills before introducing the concerning event (Lamb, Orbach, Hershkowitz, Esplin, & Horowitz, 2007; Brown & Lamb, 2009). Open-ended and nonsuggestive questions are initially used to encourage a narrative from the child and specific questions are only used to seek clarification. Forensic evaluators should be familiar with their utility as well as how to select and adapt the relevant instruments depending on the function of the interview, its process, and how to adapt the interview when rapport is diminishing, the child's anxiety is rising, or cognitive–linguistic deficits become evident as the interview progresses.

PARENT–CHILD OBSERVATION

Prior to the observation, the parent is informed that the examiner will not take an active role initially, and that the parent is expected to structure the interaction with the child and to address the child's behavior as they would out of the office. Observation of parent and child is pivotal in assessing the quality of the attachment and the strength of the relationship. The sensitivity of the parent's response to the child is associated with the secure attachment of the child, and assessment of this relationship can be achieved with structured interaction, play assessment, and parent perception interviews (Larrieu & Bellow, 2004). Attachment, as a perpetually developing relationship, is adaptive to various situations, and young children develop a range of strategies to help them cope with a parent who may be abusive or neglectful; a healthy attachment relationship can ensure that a child recovers from sustained abuse. Anxious attachment resulting from maltreating relationships has long-term developmental consequences and in most forensic evaluations involving abuse or neglect, attachment is a critical issue that merits careful assessment.

Observations can occur in the office setting or in the home, though less feasible. The office setting affords the opportunity to observe how a parent sets limits in an unfamiliar setting; how attuned the parent is to the child; the child's need for proximity and reassurance from the parent, and the parent's capacity to soothe and comfort the child. Careful observation will reveal a parent's comfort level in following the lead of the child, whether the parent needs to control or "showcase" the child; or involve the examiner in the interaction. In addition to observing parent–child interactions during free-play, the examiner may impose structured conditions, such as asking the parent to teach the child a challenging task or asking the child the clean up at the end of the session. In-home observations can involve typical parent–child interactions during meals, around the completion of homework, and so on (Budd, 2001).

PSYCHOLOGICAL TESTING

Psychological testing of parents can be a useful source of information, providing objective support for working hypotheses and counterbalance bias (Bernet, 2002; Gould, 2006; Quinnell & Bow, 2001). Heilbrun noted that "agreement across multiple sources of information, such as self-report, collateral records, psychological testing . . . and collateral interviews, makes it more likely that the information is accurate" (Heilbrun, Warren & Picarello, 2003; Kraemer, Kazdin, Offord, Kessler, Jensen, & Kupfer, 1997; Heilbrun et al., 2009). Psychological testing of children, although not diagnostic of abuse (American Academy of Child and Adolescent Psychiatry, 1990; American Academy of Child and Adolescent Psychiatry Work Group on Quality Issues, 1997), has a place in evaluations involving abuse and neglect. Psychological testing of parents can be invaluable, particularly in uncovering unacknowledged or undiagnosed psychopathology, personality disorders, cognitive issues, coping deficits, and so on. Objective and projective personality testing can be helpful and informative as part of the evaluation. Data generated from these instruments can be confirmatory or suggest alternative explanations for observed behavior. The involuntary nature of forensic evaluations raises concerns of intentional distortion (in interview and in certain psychological tests) that may threaten the validity of self-report measures. Utilizing multiple sources of information is one way to reduce self-report distortion if present (Melton et al., 2007).

It is important to select psychometrically sound psychological tests (Murrie, Martindale & Epstein, 2009). Melton et al. (2007, p. 48) identified 12 factors to be considered in determining the appropriateness of a specific psychological test. The need for, and scope of, any psychological testing is determined on a case-by-case basis; based on the referral questions posed, or guided by history or record review. For example, intelligence testing of either parent or child is typically only considered when questions are raised regarding the cognitive capacity of a parent, or when a child's special needs might be critical to answering a referral question. Psychological testing is most helpful if it precedes any interviews, as test data may suggest areas of inquiry that might otherwise be overlooked. In addition, examiner bias is minimized when psychological testing occurs prior to interviews or observations of parent–child interactions.

The Minnesota Multiphasic Personality Inventory, 2nd Edition (MMPI-2) is typically chosen as a reliable objective test of personality. The publication in 2008 of the Restructured Form (MMPI-2-RF) is a welcome addition to personality assessment of parents or other adults being evaluated in the context of abuse, neglect, or custody questions (Ben-Porath & Tellegen, 2008). In addition to its shorter length, the Restructured Form offers a number of salient reference groups for profile comparisons often helpful in abuse and neglect proceedings, for example, normative, psychiatric inpatient, outpatient, forensic pretrial and inmate, and custody. The Millon Clinical Multiaxial Inventory-III (MCMI-III) is an alternative and widely used objective test. Considerably shorter than either version of the MMPI-2, the MCMI-III has utility with those unable to tolerate the time demanded by the MMPI-2-RF.

Although not favored by many, projective techniques such as the Rorschach and the Thematic Apperception Test (TAT), can serve as a rich source of data reflecting unconscious thought processes that can inform the interview process or confirm objective data and clinical presentation in interview (Quinnell & Bow, 2001). They allow clinicians to formulate a hypothesis about the clinical picture. When tests of cognitive functioning are warranted, the Wechsler Adult Intelligence Scale—Fourth Edition (WAIS-IV) is the test of intellectual functioning commonly chosen by psychologists conducting evaluations of parents.

DATA INTERPRETATION

At the end of data collection, the evaluator may become overwhelmed by the need to synthesize an enormous amount of information. When all results are consistent and confirm the findings of the other parts of the evaluation, when psychological testing results are consonant with the clinical interview and the history, and the interpretation of each component results in minimal confusion for the forensic evaluator, articulating the opinion and responding to the posed questions is facile. However, in many cases, findings diverge in ways unexpected, presenting ambiguity and lingering uncertainty. This section will offer a systematic approach to reaching a sound and evidence-based opinion, even when some reported information does not "fit." In this domain, much like other complex areas of forensic psychiatry and psychology, outlier information can also be reported and placed into an appropriate context. The forensic evaluation of child abuse has also been described as responding to the four "Wh" questions, each to a different degree depending on the nature of the case: "What happened? What harm did it cause? What help can the parent provide? What hope is there for the future?" (Barnum, 2002). While the questions of each case may be limited, it was noted that it is always helpful to attend to each of these four questions to some degree.

PHYSICAL EVIDENCE

The assessment of the physical evidence of abuse or neglect is assisted by a combination of a review of the medical records and direct contact with the providers who initially evaluated the child whenever possible, as this often reveals critical information not captured in a cautiously scribed medical note documenting the specifics of the injury in an objective manner. For example, "full-thickness burns of the back, buttocks, and legs with sparing of the posterior knees and inguinal folds" may be better explained by flexion of the child and forced immersion than the reported accidental fall into the bathtub.

In cases of child neglect, charting the declining growth pattern and developmental arrest of the child is a first step toward confirmation of the suspected neglect. Weight gain after restoration of nutritional support confirms its earlier absence. However, in cases of emotional neglect, offering nutrition does not address the fundamental issue, that the child's psychological and social needs have not been met, and oftentimes, no weight gain occurs with the availability of food alone; such cases require a nurturing relationship that may take more time to develop. Overall, the rapid achievement of previously arrested developmental milestones confirms the restoration of the emotional, social, and cognitive stimulation needed for healthy development and may be evidence of its previous absence as well.

MENTAL STATUS EXAMINATION

The mental status of the child provides critical information as well. Cognitive, behavioral, and emotional limitations such as the unwillingness to discuss the events may interfere with obtaining adequate information from the interview process. The child's use of language in the construction of the narrative, inclusion of sensory details, and idiosyncratic child vocabulary all contribute to the credibility of the history. The evolution of the child's disclosure in the interview, display of knowledge about what transpired, and the degree to which this does or does not exceed the normal capacity for a child of that age and experience provides more information for the evaluator. Consistency of the narrative over time and the congruence of affect with the content of the narrative can also provide additional clues to the child's credibility. It is important to consider that the child may not manifest expected affective responses due to psychological coping mechanisms such as dissociative defenses; details may be blocked by repression; and because earlier childhood experiences also establish expectations, abusive experiences may be experienced as normative and not particularly traumatic in the context of the lives of some children or adolescents.

The forensic evaluator must determine how compatible the original disclosure or narrative is with parental report, adjunct historians, physical evidence, and the remainder of the information in evidence. The presence of motivation to shape, suggest, coach, or frankly coerce the child must also be considered when assessing the credibility of the child's narrative. Themes emerging in free play, reenactments of the trauma, exaggerated sexual features, and the nature of the artistic productions of a child are often very helpful; art and play can rarely be coached. These media also are well suited for the articulation of experiences that are difficult to express in words due to language, cognitive, or affective limitations. Fantastic imagery, while not closely related to reality, does not rule out the possibility that the child has truly experienced abuse and is utilizing creative imagery to make sense of or distract from the confusing and overwhelming past.

Assessing physical abuse in the context of a forensic evaluation is often facilitated by the review of physical evidence—metabolic laboratory findings, burns, bruises, scars, dislocations, and radiographic evidence of fractures old and new, often incompatible with the history provided. The child may also exhibit signs and symptoms characteristic of past experiences of inflicted physical pain—wincing, easy startling, wariness, hypervigilance near adults, emotional withdrawal, preoccupation with aggressive fantasy figures, dissociation, and heightened aggression in play and in relatedness. A preference to remain in the interview and reluctance to leave with parents may also suggest fear of parents.

Assessing neglect is complex and involves not only the parents' acts and omissions in caring for the child and gaining access to health care, education, nutrition, and housing, but also emotional support, engagement, intimacy, and stimulation. It is important to factor in the vulnerability and attachment experiences of the child, and his or her developmental disabilities or other special needs. In the assessment of neglect, information about the child at home is vital; the state of the home, refrigerator, personal space of the child, sleeping arrangements, other parties in the home, both reported and non-reported, interpersonal dynamics, and other factors can be ascertained best with a home visit. It is important not to confuse poverty with neglect; many families have little, but the children are well loved and cared for. In abuse and neglect evaluations, home visits are a routine component of the evaluation, and in cases involving the child welfare system, investigators and ongoing caseworkers who have conducted home visits should be interviewed. In the office, children who have experienced emotional neglect may act out and assume pseudomature roles; may request or even beg for snacks, toys, and other small objects; and inappropriately seek affection from and physical proximity with the evaluator.

Sexual Abuse Evaluations

A developmental perspective to the assessment of child sexual abuse is necessary to determine if the child shows age-inappropriate sexual knowledge or if he/she is inexplicably familiar with sexual matters far beyond his/her developmental stage. Sexualized play and precocious or overly sexualized or seductive behavior during the interview reiterates this atypical and inappropriate familiarity. Often, a child's statement relates progression from games and play to sexual activity, and sometimes the description of abuse relates elements of pressure or coercion. The child's behavioral and/or affective response to a dressed versus undressed doll, or typically "private" parts of the doll's anatomy can also indicate exposure to sexually explicit material, either through experiences of abuse or media inappropriately seen by the young viewer.

The use of anatomically correct dolls remains somewhat controversial, but it is clear that the dolls should never be used as a "test" for abuse; evaluators should possess training and knowledge specific to the forensic assessment of child sexual abuse if they are to be used (Quinn, 2002). Manual examination of a doll's genitals, including digital penetration of orifices, is common behavior in young, presumably nonabused children, but explicit positioning, mouthing, and sucking the doll's penis suggest detailed knowledge of sexual acts and a higher probability of sexual abuse (Everson & Boat, 1994). While some evaluators have cited the efficacy and detailed the appropriate use of anatomically correct dolls, others do not utilize these dolls, as they can potentially engender excitement, overstimulation, and curiosity in all children.

Children need to be interviewed several times, rather than relying on the history provided during a single visit. When the child returns for a second visit, there is a notable increase in comfort with the interview situation and the use of the materials (e.g., dollhouse) in the office. Several interviews with the child also afford the forensic evaluator the opportunity to assess the consistency of the story line, emergent themes over time, the nature of relatedness with the evaluator, and the degree to which the child has been coached to present a particular history by nature of the explicit repetition of narrative.

There is a large middle range or what has been described as the "gray area" in the spectrum of child sexual abuse allegations in which molestation cannot easily be proven or disproven (Schetky & Green, 1988). It is not always easy or possible to differentiate the exaggerated, sexual responsiveness within a family from the early onset of an incestuous relationship, between hugging, touching, and kissing in a family and inappropriate fondling. Schetky and Green note that in true cases of child sexual abuse, the child is initially reticent to disclose and discuss the abuse; will rarely confront one parent, even if the other is present; is usually fearful in the presence of the offender; and usually demonstrates signs and symptoms of child sexual abuse. In contrast, cases that are not substantiated and ultimately found to be false are characterized by children who discuss the abuse promptly with the parent, confront the alleged offender easily and often while seeking the parent's approval, appear comfortable in the presence of the alleged offender, and do not exhibit objective signs and symptoms of abuse despite the report of the parent, who often has prominent paranoid and hysterical personality features.

Although review of research findings on the symptomatology of sexually abused children does not support the existence of a single syndrome that is applicable to all or most sexually abused children, there is a spectrum of symptoms among sexually abused children that ranges from those symptoms that are more discriminating for sexual abuse, including alterations in sexualized behavior, to those that are less discriminating, including a variety of stress reactions such as increased anxieties, sleep disturbances, bed wetting, depression, and others. Indeed, many sexually abused children display no symptoms (Corwin, 1995).

COMMUNICATION

The evaluative data and findings must be responsive to the specific referral questions. Prior to initiating the evaluation, the forensic evaluator must ensure that the attorney or agency has articulated the questions to be addressed as well as to whom the report should be distributed. Having this framework supports the communication of findings and recommendations succinctly and ensures that the report respond effectively to the areas of most concern to the requesting party, though there may be additional and unrelated areas of discussion based on the information gathered during the evaluation process.

While the existence of physical indicators of abuse (bruises, malnutrition, burns and scars, semen, sexually transmitted diseases, vaginal or rectal tears or enlargements, etc.) may seem like easily comprehensible, irrefutable data, the forensic evaluator should review carefully the medical evidence and note its presence and relevance as they are most often not intuitively understood by the lay person or the judge. For example, one judge cast aside a finding of semen in the vaginal introitus of a 5-year-old girl with an intact hymen, noting that only several live sperm were found, believing that if sexual abuse had truly occurred, there would have been millions of sperm. The explanation that no sperm should be found inside of a 5-year-old child shifted his decision-making process and the child was maintained in foster care pending further evaluation of her stepfather, mother, and the safety of her home.

The forensic evaluator's role in an abuse case often involves explaining what has actually transpired in clear and simple terms as the nature of child abuse is unfathomable to most individuals. In a case of severe injury without a clearly identifiable perpetrator, it was the elaborate explanation about the week that had passed as the child slipped into a coma that clarified for the judge that regardless of the abuse, medical neglect had resulted in the near lethal injury to the child and warranted her permanent removal from her home, given the aggravated circumstances and the delay to seek treatment that resulted in the condition in which she had arrived to medical attention.

Often, the referring attorney requests verbal feedback prior to the completion of the report and this is most often provided via telephone consultation. The forensic evaluator is thus afforded the opportunity to make recommendations to the attorney regarding the manner in which to best proceed with the least negative impact for the child, the child's suitability for court testimony, need for and recommendations of specific therapy modalities or other interventions, and current concerns regarding the safety of the child.

At the conclusion of the evaluative process, verbal feedback may also be given to parties involved in the litigation prior to the finalization of the report and in close consultation with the retaining attorney; several contexts in which this may be particularly informative or beneficial are noteworthy.

Feedback to parents in an abuse or neglect case may be further diagnostic of their insight, capacity to process unwanted information, management of negative affect, and ability to accept responsibility for their actions. Feedback occasionally results in additional critical information that shapes the findings in the final report as well. An example of this can be seen in a case of a child who had experienced life-threatening injuries of unknown etiology. When told that the child had explicitly stated who had injured her, her parents looked down, but did not ask who their daughter had identified. When another family member in the room noted that the identification of the perpetrator would probably lead to incarceration, her parents remained silent and shifted uncomfortably.

Feedback to parents also informs the examiner of the parents' preparation for and willingness to change and capacity to work effectively with mental health and social service professionals in the future. Feedback in the evaluative process, while not intentionally therapeutic, may be beneficial in helping parents understand how their narrative is perceived and how the data or objective material does not match their perception of reality, and may prepare them to better understand and accept the legal consequences of the abuse and neglect that has impacted their family.

In a civil case, feedback to parents can be helpful as litigation can become inextricably woven with the life narrative and experiences of the child (and parents). Litigation can span a substantial portion of childhood, when personality structure is still evolving and habituated behaviors, such as school avoidance, are developing. Feedback can also help parents understand the need for developmental or psychological/psychiatric evaluation and treatment, the impact of courtroom testimony on their child, and may result in their acceptance of a less than hoped for legal settlement as it may be in the developmental interest of their child. This type of feedback should only be undertaken in careful consultation with the retaining attorney or agency.

Feedback to the child in the context of a case involving child abuse and/or neglect can be offered in a developmentally matched and appropriate fashion, and can affirm the child's narrative and experiences, help the child to feel heard, understood, and valued. The forensic evaluation can be difficult, even traumatic for a child, but feedback can offer a sense of meaning and place the evaluative process in a context, and ideally, provide some closure to a challenging period in the child's life.

Written reports are addressed and released to the requesting party, whether it be the court (and addressed to the judge), attorney, or child protective agency. Parents requesting copies of the report are referred to their attorney or the child's attorney to obtain a copy; the report often has information that is difficult for them to process alone and in the absence of an understanding of the legal context.

In general, it is helpful to present the expert opinion on the first page of the report so that all parties will have easy access to them; many judges receive extensive documentation prior to a hearing or trial and facilitating visual access to the findings of the evaluation improves the likelihood that the summary will be considered by the court. Identification of the sources of information relied upon by the forensic examiner, as well as a detailed history by each relevant source, review of the relevant records, and a detailed description of the examination (with minimal jargon) should be included. Cases involving ambiguity and uncertainty with respect to risk, identification of perpetrators, parental capacity, and the like merit particularly careful wording in order to protect the forensic examiner from repercussions incurred by angry parties.

Reports can be written individually but in a multidisciplinary evaluation, a single report may be issued and cosigned; the report should identify the expert who will be available for testimony if required. This decision should be made in consultation with the retaining attorney, and may be based on the specifics of the case (e.g., medically fragile child) or the pragmatics of the anticipated date of testimony and availability of the individual examiners.

The perceptions, values, and cultural beliefs of the forensic evaluator need to be examined closely to avoid bias, as issues involving child abuse and neglect evoke strong emotions. Understanding agendas in child abuse and neglect–related evaluations is helpful in developing realistic expectations of the interpersonal outcome of feedback; in some cases, all parties will be unhappy with the evaluator's findings and recommendations; the forensic examiner should utilize colleagues for peer supervision and support with these challenging cases.

REFERENCES

American Academy of Child and Adolescent Psychiatry. (1990). *Guidelines for the clinical evaluation for child and adolescent sexual abuse.* Retrieved from http://www.aacap.org/cs/root/policy_statements/guidelines_ for_the_ clinical_evalution_for_Child_and_Adolescent_Sexual_Abuse

American Academy of Child and Adolescent Psychiatry Work Group on Quality Issues. (1997). Practice parameters for the forensic evaluation of children and adolescents who may have been physically or sexually abused. *Journal of the American Academy of Child and Adolescent Psychiatry*, *36*, 423–442.

Barnum, R. (2002). Parenting assessment in cases of neglect and abuse. In D. H. Schetky & E. P. Benedek (Eds.), *Principles and practice of child and adolescent forensic psychiatry* (pp. 81–96). Washington, DC: American Psychiatric Publishing.

Ben-Porath, Y.S. & Tellegen, A. (2008). *The Minnesota Multiphasic Personality Inventory-2 Restructured Form: Manual for administration, scoring, and interpretation*. Minneapolis, MN: University of Minnesota Press.

Bernet, W. (2002). Child custody evaluations. *Child and Adolescent Psychiatric Clinics of North America*, *11*, 781–804.

Blandon-Gitlin, I., & Pezdek, K. (2009). Children's memory in forensic contexts: Suggestibility, false memory, and individual differences. In B. L. Bottoms, C. J. Najdowski, & G. S. Goodman (Eds.), *Children as victims, witnesses and offenders: Psychological science and the law* (pp. 57–80). New York, NY: Guilford Press.

Brown, D., & Lamb, M. E. (2009). Forensic interviews with children: A two-way street. In K. Kuehnle & M. Connell (Eds.), *The evaluation of child sexual abuse allegations: A comprehensive guide to assessment and testimony* (pp. 299–325). Hoboken, NJ: John Wiley & Sons.

Bruck, M., & Ceci, S. J. (2002). Reliability and suggestibility of children's statements. In D. H. Schetky & E. P. Benedek (Eds.), *Principles and practice of child and adolescent forensic psychiatry* (pp. 137–147). Washington, DC: American Psychiatric Publishing.

Bruck, M., Ceci, S. J., & Hembrooke, H. (1998). Reliability and credibility of young children's reports: From research to policy and practice. *American Psychologist*, *53*(2), 136–151.

Budd, K. S. (2001). Assessing parenting competence in child protection cases: A clinical practice model. *Clinical Child and Family Psychology Review*, *49*(1), 1–18.

Cantwell, H. B. (1997). The neglect of child neglect. In M. E. Helfer, R. S. Kempe, & R. D. Krugman (Eds.), *The battered child* (pp. 247–373). Chicago, IL: University of Chicago Press.

Ceci, S. J., & Bruck, M. (1995) *Jeopardy in the Courtroom: A Scientific Analysis of Children's Testimony*. Washington, DC: American Psychological Press.

Child Welfare Information Gateway. (2009). Retrieved from http://www.childwelfare.gov/pubs/factsheets/foster.cfm

Corwin, D. L. (1995). Child sexual abuse assessment and professional ethics: Commentary on controversies, limits, and when to just say no. *Journal of Child Sexual Abuse*, *4*, 115–122.

Crawford v. Washington, 541 U.S. 36 (2004).

Davis v. Washington, 547 U.S. 813 (2006).

Dwyer, R. G. (2009, October). The child as witness: Evaluating allegations of sexual abuse. Paper presented at the Annual Meeting of the American Academy of Psychiatry and the Law, Baltimore, MD.

Everson, M. D., & Boat, B. W. (1994). Putting the anatomical doll controversy in perspective. *Child Abuse and Neglect, 18,* 113–129.

Friedrich, W. N., Grambsch, P., Broughton, D., Kuiper, J., & Beilke, R. L. (1991). Normative sexual behavior in children. *Pediatrics, 88,* 456–464.

Goodman, G. S., Redlich, A. D., Qin, J., Ghetti, S., Tyda, K. S., Scaaf, J. M., & Hahn, A. (1999). Evaluating eyewitness testimony in adults and children. In Hess, A.K., Weiner, I.B. (Eds.), *The Handbook of Forensic Psychology* (pp. 218–272). New York, NY: John Wiley & Sons.

Gould, J.W. (2006). *Conducting scientifically crafted child custody evaluation* (2nd ed.). Sarasota, FL: Professional Resource Press.

Haller, L. H. (2002). The forensic evaluation and court testimony. *Child and Adolescent Clinics of North America, 11,* 689–704.

Heilbrun, K., Grisso, T., & Goldstein, A.M. (2009). *Foundations of forensic mental health assessment.* New York, NY: Oxford University Press.

Heibrun, K., Warren, J., & Picarello, K. (2003). Third party information in forensic assessment. In Goldstein, A. M. (Ed.), *Forensic psychology: Vol. 11 of Handbook of psychology* (pp. 69–86). Hoboken, NJ: John Wiley & Sons.

Hutcheson, G. D., Baxter, J. S., Telfer, K., & Warden, D. (1995). Child witness statement quality: Question type and errors of omission. *Law and Human Behavior, 19,* 631–648.

Klemfuss, J. Z., & Ceci, S. (2009). Normative memory development and the child witness. In K. Kuehnle & M. Connell (Eds.), *The evaluation of child sexual abuse allegations: A comprehensive guide to assessment and testimony* (pp. 153–180). Hoboken, NJ: John Wiley & Sons.

Kraemer, H., Kazdin, A., Offord, D., Kessler, R., Jensen, P., & Kupfer, D. (1997). Coming to terms with the terms of risk. *Archives of General Psychiatry, 54,* 337–343.

Lamb, M. E, Orbach, Y., Hershkowitz, I., Esplin, P. W., & Horowitz, D. (2007). A structured forensic interview protocol improves the quality and informativeness of investigative interviews with children: A review of research using the NICHD Investigative Interview Protocol. *Child Abuse and Neglect, 31,* 1201–1231.

Larrieu, J. A., & Bellow, S. M. (2004). Relationship assessment for young traumatized children. In J. D. Osofsky, (Ed.), *Young children and trauma: Intervention and treatment.* New York, NY: Guilford Press.

Lyon, T. D., Carrick, N., & Quas, J. A. (2009). Young children's competency to take the oath: Effects of task, maltreatment, and age. *Law and Human Behavior, 34,* 141–149.

Malloy, L. C., & Quas, J. A. (2009). Children's suggestibility: Areas of consensus and controversy. In K. Kuehnle & M. Connell (Eds.), *The evaluation of child sexual abuse allegations: A comprehensive guide to assessment and testimony* (pp. 267–297). Hoboken, NJ: John Wiley & Sons.

Melton, G., Petrila, J., Poythress, N., & Slobogin, C. (2007). *Psychological evaluations for the courts: A handbook for mental health professionals and lawyers* (3rd ed.). New York, NY: Guilford Press.

Murrie, D., Martindale, D. A., & Epstein, M. (2009). Unsupported assessment techniques in child sexual abuse evaluations. In K. Kuehnle & M. Connell (Eds.), *The evaluation of child sexual abuse allegations: A comprehensive guide to assessment and testimony* (pp. 397–420). Hoboken, NJ: John Wiley & Sons.

Poole, D. A., & Lamb, M. E. (1998). *Investigative interviews of children: A guide for helping professionals.* Washington, DC: American Psychological Association.

Poole, D. A., & Wolfe, M.A. (2009). Child development: Normative sexual behaviors that may be confused with symptoms of sexual abuse. In K. Kuehnle & M. Connell (Eds.), *The evaluation of child sexual abuse allegations: A comprehensive guide to assessment and testimony* (pp. 101–128). Hoboken, NJ: John Wiley & Sons.

Quinn, K. M. (2002). Interviewing children for suspected sexual abuse. In D. H. Schetky & E. P. Benedek (Eds.), *Principles and practice of child and adolescent forensic psychiatry* (pp. 149–159). Washington, DC: American Psychiatric Publishing.

Quinnell, F. A., & Bow, J. N. (2001). Psychological tests used in child custody evaluations. *Behavioral Sciences and the Law, 19*, 491–501.

Raeder, M. S. (2007). Comments on child abuse litigation in a "testimonial" world: The intersection of competency, hearsay, and confrontation. *Indiana Law Journal, 82*, 1009–1027.

Rosado, L. M. (2000). *Understanding adolescents: A juvenile court training curriculum.* Washington, DC: American Bar Association.

Sattler, J. M. (1998). *Clinical and forensic interviewing of children and families: Guidelines for the mental health, pediatric and child maltreatment fields.* San Diego, CA: Author.

Schetky, D. H., & Green, A.H. (1988). *Child sexual abuse: A handbook for health care and legal professionals.* New York, NY: Brunner Mazel.

Simon, R., & Gold, L. (Eds.). (2007) *Textbook of forensic psychiatry* (5th ed.) Washington, DC: American Psychiatric Publishing.

Vieth, V. I. (1998). When a child testifies: Getting the jury to believe the victim. *ABA Child Law Practice, 17*, 22.

CHAPTER 17

Abuse and Neglect of Adults

CARLA RODGERS and MARK SIEGERT

INTRODUCTION

The two primary areas of adult abuse that come to the attention of forensic psychiatrists and psychologists are elder abuse and domestic violence. The problem of abuse in the United States is all too common. It is estimated that as many as 2 million older adults are mistreated each year in the United States (National Research Council, 2003; Swagerty, Takahashi, & Evans, 1999). Another estimate is that between 4% and 10% of the elderly in this country, defined as being over the age of 65, will experience some form of abuse (Levensky & Fruzzetti, 2003). In one study of a large, community-based population involving primary care patients, 1 out of 20 women had experienced domestic violence in the previous year; 1 out of 5 had experienced violence in their adult life, and 1 out of 3 had experienced violence at some point in their lives (McCauley et al., 1995). Risk factors for elder abuse include the elderly individual having dementia, noncompliance with activities of daily living or medical treatment, and lack of rapport between caregiver and patient (Coyne, Reichman, & Berbig, 1993; Swagerty et al., 1999).

Both elder abuse and domestic violence include psychological/ emotional abuse, which is a broad category that includes broadly three types of abuse: verbal abuse, physical abuse, and financial exploitation (Levensky & Fruzzetti, 2003). By verbal abuse we do not mean the occasional arguments that individuals living in close proximity will inevitably engage in, but the systematic use of threats and/or ongoing use of demeaning words and phrases with the object of controlling and/or intimidating the victim. Examples include the individual who constantly berates his/her spouse, saying that the spouse is stupid, ugly, or that no one else would have them, or the elderly person whose caretaker may ridicule him/her for physical problems such as urinary incontinence, needing assistance to walk, or name calling, such as stupid or senile (particularly when examples of memory loss appear).

The term *physical abuse* speaks for itself. There is never a situation where one adult should feel justified in hitting, pinching, kicking, shoving, or in any other way physically assaulting another adult. This is the type of abuse that gets the most media coverage because it is so obviously damaging. Certain individuals, however, such as the demented elderly individual, may at times require some physical restraint, such as a Posey vest, to make sure they do not fall out of bed or a chair. This type of nonviolent physical restraint is for the purpose of making sure the elderly person does not injure him/herself, not for the purpose of expressing the caretaker's anger or frustration, or for the aforementioned desire of one individual to inappropriately control another.

The third type of abuse is financial exploitation. An example is the recent real-life criminal conviction of Anthony Marshall, the son of Brook Astor, the 105-year-old doyenne of the wealthy Astor family. Ms. Astor, who died in 2007, had cash and assets valued at approximately $200 million. Her son, Mr. Marshall, was convicted of defrauding her and literally stealing art objects while his mother was suffering from advanced Alzheimer's disease. It was also alleged that Mrs. Astor was suffering from physical neglect, including a lack of bathing and feeding, which is yet another form of elder abuse (Berger, 2007).

Because these victims are intimidated by their abusers, and when elderly they may also be cognitively impaired, forensic mental health evaluations can be difficult, and it is important that the evaluator remain sensitive to the almost captive situations that abused adults may find themselves in. A discussion of how to structure and formulate the interview(s), as well as how to formulate important questions, appears in detail in the following sections.

PREPARATION

Preparation for an evaluation of adult abuse requires clarity of the task at hand, as there are some very distinct challenges that come with these evaluations. First, as previously noted, there are two often quite different types of evaluation that are categorized together as adult abuse: domestic abuse and elder abuse. Throughout this chapter, the authors will address both types of abuse largely as if they were entirely distinct phenomena. However, the overlap is often great, particularly when there is no age-related cognitive decline and no distinctive issues of loss of capacity to care for oneself. Therefore, the reader is advised to be alert for the overlap between the two types of abuse, even though, for heuristic purposes, they will often be treated as separate in this section.

A forensic psychiatrist or psychologist cannot do a competent evaluation without a prior understanding of the *characteristics* of the alleged abuse situation (e.g., domestic violence or elder abuse), the *type* of alleged abuse (e.g., verbal abuse, physical abuse, financial exploitation), the person(s) alleged to be the victim, and the person(s) alleged to be the perpetrator of the abuse. In addition, the forensic psychiatrist or psychologist must know the *scope* of the alleged abuse, as well as the *setting* of the alleged abuse (Melton, Petrila, Poythress, & Slobogin, 2007). Therefore, the first task of the evaluator is to obtain as clear a description of the concern or problems as possible; that is, the clinician needs to get a clear *referral question,* preferably with all available background documentation. Without clarity, the evaluator cannot reasonably prepare for the evaluation. The clinician needs to know if this is part of an existing litigation with interested parties and/or criminal charges, as these may well bias the information given or withheld. The evaluator must be aware that this evaluation may serve the interests of a specific party, and that data could, of course, be skewed by the person making the referral. Therefore, the clearer the referral question, the clearer the specific concerns (including the alleged type, scope, and setting of the abuse), and the clearer the situation and persons involved are presented from the start, the more likely an accurate evaluation will follow.

In abuse cases, important areas for obtaining information include obtaining knowledge of possible outcomes. Negative effects following evaluations of both domestic violence and elder abuse can and do occur. In domestic violence situations with minor children involved, the outcome of these evaluations can include living situations, visitation, and custody. Such an agenda can be a hidden agenda of one of the parties (Melton et al., 2007). In the case of elder abuse, the elder person may be separated from those who provide his/her social and familial ties, as well as access to his/her community, friends, and relatives. These types of situations, at times, turn a well-intentioned evaluator into the agent of change, leading to an elder person who is significantly less happy than they were in the abusive situation. Some resolutions, particularly those involving moving a person into a long-term care facility, or moving a person out of the community where the elder has relatives and friends, can be permanent and depressing. With knowledge of the various possible outcomes, the forensic psychiatrist or psychologist may be able to carefully word reports such that they cause as little negative outcome as possible. For this reason, it becomes ethically necessary to understand the various possible outcomes of the evaluation and to be sure that one's words in the report do not make it unduly easy for one party to misuse the report for an untoward gain.

Abuse evaluations require the examiner to determine in advance how to plan and structure the evaluation. This requires knowledge not only of the alleged abuse, but also knowledge of the victim, and all relevant parties to the claim. At this point, evaluations of domestic violence for persons who are not elderly and for elder abuse can take different paths. For domestic violence claims of someone who is not elderly, one is usually able to conduct an evaluation without significant time given to evaluating the cognitive status and competence of the person alleged to be the victim (Sprehe, 2003). For elder abuse, the cognitive status and competence of the victim usually must be assessed more carefully, which can at times be relatively simple, but at others, it can be quite complex. In the elderly, it can be important to consider the time of day of the evaluation, as "sundowning" can significantly affect those over 60 years of age who may be less clear and more symptomatic by the afternoon and evening. If a late afternoon or evening evaluation is unavoidable, and if the elderly person shows cognitive deficits, it may be good practice to schedule even a brief follow-up appointment early in the day to confirm that the functioning found in the elderly patient is an accurate or best portrayal of the information and cognitive status of that individual.

In cases where cognitive decline is suspected, if the evaluator is not a psychologist trained in cognitive assessment or neuropsychology, a referral to a respected psychologist with such training is a good and sometimes a necessary practice, as significant cognitive declines are often able to be hidden when cognitive or neuropsychological testing is not administered.

COLLATERAL INFORMATION

For evaluations of both domestic violence and elder abuse, collateral information can be extremely helpful, and in some situations, necessary, if one is to get an accurate forensic understanding. This is so because in these types of cases, the victim might not be entirely forthcoming—volitionally out of fear, shame, or other conscious motives, for defensive and/or unconscious reasons (where the person being evaluated is unable to accept aspects of the situation that are unpleasant and therefore denied or repressed), or especially in cases of elder abuse, when the person being evaluated may not know or accept genuine and at times severe cognitive deficits. Using collateral sources can pose specific problems: there are often competing interests and/or cognitive or psychiatric problems in the collateral source which can lead to inaccurate information being presented to the examiner. In contrast, information from third parties can, in some cases, shed important light on many aspects relevant to these evaluations, including reporting observed signs of abuse, bringing up questions of the veracity of the person(s) making the claim, highlighting the various interested parties, and bringing up other forensically relevant information. Collateral sources may be family members, medical personnel, social service workers, police officers, correctional workers, various documented histories, and prior forensic reports.

Ethical standards are well established for both psychiatrists and psychologists by their respective professional organizations (American Academy of Psychiatry and the Law, 2005; Committee on Ethical Guidelines for Forensic Psychologists, 1991; an updated version of this document is presently under review). Areas requiring extreme care include finding out whether the person being examined is competent to consent to the evaluation. The nature and purpose of the evaluation, who retained the expert, and the limits of confidentiality must be discussed with the person being examined for competency. In the case of individuals who are not competent, or where there is a question of the capacity to understand and knowingly agree to continue, it is important to do one's best to obtain informed consent in various manners, which can include a court order, the client's guardian, and the client's attorney. In cases where these auxiliary sources do not exist, it is important to document that thought was given to obtaining consent and the barriers that were encountered as the examiner attempted to obtain consent.

Another important area is the examiner's competence to conduct forensic evaluations in the specific area being examined (Siegert & Weiss, 2007). Experience is necessary to conduct an ethical evaluation, but definitions of appropriate or necessary experience vary. With the elderly, and those of questionable ability to meaningfully understand and agree to participate, psychologists and psychiatrists must possess a level of knowledge and understanding of both the appropriate legal requirements in the jurisdiction, as well as knowledge of the appropriate population, such as geriatrics, cognitive decline, and dementia. Psychological and neuropsychological testing may be important to get accurate and factual data, as it may be the only way to get a relatively full, objective assessment of the person's cognitive or psychiatric status. Confidentiality must be understood and respected, with the examiner disclosing information only to those legally entitled.

DATA COLLECTION

At this point, when the preparation is complete, all of the records described above should have been reviewed. It is worth noting that unless specifically requested, it is, unfortunately, common that references to various types of psychological testing are excluded from medical records when they are sent. Consequently, asking the evaluee and/or their caregivers if testing has been administered can be important. The forensic psychiatrist or psychologist has by now determined which, if any, collateral sources will be interviewed, and it is time to begin the interview(s).

INTERVIEWING THE EVALUEE

A good forensic psychiatric or psychological interview is essential to conducting a good psychiatric or psychological evaluation. In addition to the clinical evaluation, one conducts an investigation of areas of forensic import. Forensic evaluations of abuse must include a psychosocial history, and in the case of adult abuse, they must include a history of childhood physical and emotional abuse(s), as well as any history of childhood exploitation, as these are risk factors for becoming involved in similar situations in adulthood. Of course, a careful history of prior adult involvement in abusive relationships is essential. It is also essential to interview suspected victims of abuse alone, particularly not in the presence of the suspected perpetrator, for the obvious reason that various kinds of fear and intimidation are quite possible (Lachs & Pillemer, 1995).

MENTAL STATUS EXAMINATION

The mental status examination is very important. It is also important to note that the mental status examination, no matter how thoroughly administered, routinely misses certain types of cognitive deficits. Cognitive, neuropsychological, and at times, personality-based psychological testing can be the only way to uncover forms of subtle or concealed cognitive deficits.

MENTAL STATUS EXAMINATION IN THE ELDERLY

If the person is elderly, detailed identifying information should be asked, including questions to see if the individual retains basic information. For example, one might ask the birthplace, the person's current address including the zip code, and the telephone number including the area code. If the person is using computers, an email address, and frequented websites may be helpful in determining the evaluee's awareness and retention of basic information. Orientation questions should include asking the current location (perhaps including the street address where the evaluation is occurring). Asking for the current year, month, date, and day of the week are all potentially helpful. One might ask how the person came to the evaluation. Does the elderly person believe that the location of the evaluation is a private residence, office, hospital, and so on? Asking about self-care, who provides it, and what is included may be important. Does the person possess a valid driver's license and, at present, operate a motor vehicle? Does the evaluee vote? Because questions about voting are often answered in the affirmative, asking when the person last voted can be illuminating.

Questions about education are helpful, not only for memory, but also to help gauge expectations for the person. A recitation of the names of schools from grammar school up, as well as asking the rough grades a person obtained, can guide rough expectations. One can ask where the various schools are located, rough dates of attendance, graduation, and degrees. It should be noted that in some states, a high school diploma is awarded to *all special education students* merely for attending their programs, and a high school diploma cannot, by itself, be taken as an indication that the person being evaluated had a relatively normal cognitive development.

Asking about finances can be particularly important, as elder abuse is frequently associated with resentment about financial dependency. Financial exploitation is clearly one type of abuse. Does the evaluee know his/her current income? Does he/she know the basis for the income? Does he/she know the name of his/her bank or other financial institutions? Does he/she know if the income is directly deposited or mailed? Does the evaluee know the current expenses, or the typical cost of a few ordinary items? Does he/she write checks? If so, does he/she sign in the correct place, and so on? These are only a few possible questions, but they highlight a direction that may prove very illuminating, as some elderly persons superficially and socially appear quite intact until asked specific questions.

Because some people's cognitive declines are not obvious, when evaluating victims of elder abuse, it is important to consider cognitive or neuropsychological testing, as it can be the only way to have a clear picture of cognitive functioning. In milder cases, cognitive testing may seem unnecessary. In our experience, it is often in what appeared to be milder cases or what looked like age-related cognitive decline, that cognitive testing may find that there are deficits that are more significant and debilitating than was thought prior to testing.

Personality-based psychological testing can also be extremely helpful, especially when one wants to know the presence and level of various symptoms, as well as the possible presence of some troubling or hidden symptoms. For example, paranoia, personality disorder, and/or underlying psychotic thinking may be present but hidden. The American Psychological Association (1998) reminds the forensic examiner that "neuropsychological evaluation and cognitive testing remain the most effective differential diagnostic methods in discriminating pathophysiological dementia from age-related cognitive decline, cognitive difficulties that are depression-related, and other related disorders" (p. 1298). Psychological tests are not always reliable and valid and do not always have appropriate normative data for comparison. It is the responsibility of a competent and ethical psychologist to be sure that any testing administered meets these standards. Furthermore, careful consideration of whether the tests administered would meet the requirements of a *Daubert* challenge is important for a forensic evaluation.

MEDICAL HISTORY TAKING

For all forensic mental health evaluees, the medical history is important, since medical illness can adversely affect mental status. A specific area of interest in the elderly is the cardiopulmonary system. There is already some age-related decline in cardiopulmonary function in the vast majority of elderly individuals. If the elderly evaluee is or has been a smoker, or has had a history of unhealthy nutrition leading to elevated cholesterol and low-density lipoproteins, or does not and possibly did not have a history of exercise, the evaluee is at increased risk for cardiopulmonary compromise. One should ask about a history of high blood pressure (hypertension), heart attack (myocardial infarction), stroke (cerebrovascular accident), emphysema, and asthma. Any one of these can result in cognitive compromise and/or mood dysfunction. Additionally, since the evaluator has reviewed the medical records, obtaining a medical history from the evaluee is a good way to determine the accuracy of one's self-perception.

The compromised elderly individual may be at higher risk for abuse. The evaluator should also check to see if the elderly person knows which medications he or she is taking, and how these medications are supposed to be taken. Individuals who are confused about their medications may overdose or underdose themselves, again resulting in mental status changes. In the intact but physically compromised elderly who do not dispense their own medication, this history can help the evaluator determine if the evaluee is actually receiving his/her medication or is a victim of neglect.

For the victims of domestic violence who are generally younger and female, a history of physical trauma is important. There may be evidence of old healed injuries, and these require inquiry. The location of such injuries is important. Victims of domestic violence are 13 times more likely to sustain injuries to the breast, chest, or abdomen, while injuries of accident victims are more likely to involve the periphery of the body (Rodgers & Gruener, 1997).

In all evaluations, a history of medication use; medication allergies; and substance, alcohol, and tobacco use should be reviewed. Evidence of inconsistency with the medical records may be useful to explore.

ADDITIONAL MENTAL STATUS CONSIDERATIONS
FOR ADULTS INCLUDING THE ELDERLY

Many of the preceding considerations are central to any thorough mental status examination, not just the elderly. For everyone evaluated, a careful and detailed drug and alcohol history is essential, as will be described in the "Communication" section. A history of legal difficulties, including both criminal and civil involvements, may prove relevant. The social network, including people in one's daily life, can prove quite revealing, as abuse victims of all ages can become quite isolated, hiding the abuse from the sight of many people (Brandl, Steigel, Dyer, Heilser, & Otto, 2006; Lachs & Pillemer, 1995).

PSYCHOLOGICAL TESTING

For the purposes of evaluating adult abuse, there are two primary categories of psychological testing that can be very helpful—at times, crucial—in a well-done forensic examination. The two categories of psychological testing are personality testing and cognitive or neuropsychological testing.

Personality testing offers a view into the behavioral and emotional characteristics of the victim. Certain types of behavior patterns, particularly some of the personality disorders, may suggest volatility, fear of abandonment, and increased risk of overly engaging in overheated interactions. If personality tests are used, the psychologist is well advised to use only those tests that will pass a *Daubert* challenge, as the court has determined minimum scientific standards which apply to psychological testing, and it is the current authors' opinion that most psychological tests on the market would not successfully pass this challenge. Tests with validity scales are particularly encouraged, as they offer the possibility of looking at the veracity of the claim, the likelihood of symptom exaggeration or malingering, and often offer a stronger base to defend a report if a *Daubert* challenge is undertaken.

Cognitive or neuropsychological testing can be very important, if not essential, in cases where there is suspected dementia, or when knowing the degree of dementia or other cognitive decline is important. Brief screening instruments, such as the Mini-Mental Status Examination, frequently miss important cognitive deficits, and therefore are not adequate in cases where dementia is not clear-cut. In cases where behaviors exist that are consistent with dementia and pseudo-dementia, or cases in which the impact of some level of dementia is important to making decisions (such as financial capacity, undue influence, or even placement decisions), it is often only possible to get a clear reading of the cognitive functioning if one administers these tests. Cognitive or neuropsychological testing often can give a very clear, detailed picture not only of cognitive status or deficit, but also of the way a decline functions or impacts a person's thinking and reactions. Therefore, in cases where dementia or other cognitive disorders is suspected but not clear-cut, cognitive or neuropsychological testing is strongly encouraged. In cases of obvious and fairly severe dementia, cognitive testing may be desired to document the degree of deficit, or to establish a baseline for future comparisons.

INTERVIEWING COLLATERAL SOURCES

Interviewing collateral sources requires a different emphasis; as the purpose of the interview is to obtain information about someone else, one cannot typically ask the level of personal questions being asked of the evaluee, even if one thinks it might be prudent. One's goal should be obtaining the perspective and recollection of the various sources on all of the relevant information described above. Additionally, one should carefully ask about the collateral's relationship with the person who's central to the evaluation. Asking relevant collaterals, including police, neighbors, family members, and so on, what they've witnessed or heard, and about any noted changes in the personality and habits of the victim, is essential. One must remain thoughtful of the relationship of the collateral to the alleged victim, and be aware of any potential gain for the collateral by presenting the material in a manner that is less than entirely open, direct, and honest. If the collateral is the person suspected of abuse, one hopes for, but doesn't expect honest and direct answers. Skillful interviewing should attempt to make the suspected perpetrator as comfortable as possible in reporting what occurred, which hopefully will yield more information than if one is taking an adversarial position.

DATA INTERPRETATION

At this point in the process, the evaluator has reviewed all of the documentation discussed previously, collateral information, the results of the face-to-face evaluation with the subject and any collateral sources, and any psychological testing that's been administered. Based on the totality of these resources, the evaluator is now in a position to form a forensic opinion. Among the issues the evaluator may be asked to address is whether the evaluee has in fact been a victim of abuse and/or neglect, whether the evaluee is experiencing a mental disorder as a result of this abuse, whether there is a preexisting mental condition, and the interplay of any abuse and mental disorder(s).

GENERAL CONSIDERATIONS

One of the primary tasks in evaluations regarding abuse is looking for consistent and inconsistent data sources. For example, there may be a police report in which the victim of abuse called 911 for help, told the operator that he/she was being physically abused by his/her partner, but later in the emergency room the same victim might say that the injuries were the result of an accident, not abuse. Depending on the skill of the interviewer and the rapport established in the face-to-face evaluation, the interviewer may or may not ask about such an inconsistency. Regardless of whether questions are directly asked, the forensic expert will have to do his/her best to interpret any discrepancies, and try to form an opinion as to whether the abuse actually occurred.

If there is no finding of abuse, the issues in the legal matter may be moot, although there may be a significant psychopathological problem in the evaluee that the evaluator should not ignore. If the forensic psychiatrist or psychologist diagnoses an emergent problem, he/she must make recommendations for immediate treatment and make sure the evaluee is safe until he/she can get to treatment. An example would be an evaluee who reveals the presence of active suicidal ideation with a plan. The forensic referral source must be contacted and, at the least, be informed of the treatment recommendations made to the evaluee.

According to the ethical guidelines of the American Academy of Psychiatry and the Law (2005), forensic psychiatric evaluators should strive for honesty and objectivity, and "should not distort their opinion in the service of the retaining party" (p. 3). Psychologists have the same obligation (Committee on Ethical Guidelines for Forensic Psychologists, 1991). In order to support the goal of all forensic reports, which is to report honestly and objectively, one must watch for a potential tendency to let one's desire to help the victim of abuse, especially if there are physical consequences of this abuse, overpower one's objectivity. It never hurts to be reminded that it is unethical for the forensic mental health evaluator to attempt to influence the outcome of an abuse case by skewing his/her report beyond what the data objectively offer (American Academy of Psychiatry and the Law; Committee on Ethical Guidelines for Forensic Psychologists). One's obligation is to provide a clear and objective opinion, supported by the evidence. This report can then be used by the court, government agencies, or whatever other legal entity is involved in determining the outcome.

MEDICAL STATUS

Although important in every forensic mental health evaluee, the medical status of an elderly person is especially significant because of the effect that it has on the elderly person's mental status. Elderly persons have more physical and cognitive comorbidity than their younger counterparts, so their medical status can have a profound effect on their mental status (Devanand & Pelton, 2009). In addition to making observations about the person's physical presentation, such as whether he or she is underweight or has poor hygiene, the evaluator must review the physician's notes and any diagnostic studies, including magnetic resonance imaging (MRI) and blood work. Elevated hemoglobin, blood urea nitrogen, and sodium levels in the blood work can indicate that the person is dehydrated, and therefore may not be functioning at an optimal cognitive level.

A history of cerebrovascular accident (CVA) may tell the evaluator that the elderly individual is permanently cognitively impaired. Hyponatremia, excessive urine osmolality and sodium, and decreased serum osmolality indicates that that the evaluee is suffering from the syndrome of inappropriate antidiuretic hormone secretion (SIADH; Ferry & Pascual-Y-Baralt, 2009). This is also called *water intoxication*. Among other causes, this syndrome, which can result in significant cognitive compromise, can be a side effect of antidepressant medications, and should be looked for, especially in the elderly, when the records indicate a sudden change in mental status with the onset of starting an antidepressant. Other medical problems that can have an effect on either mood, cognition, or both are anemia, vitamin B_{12} deficiency, hypothyroidism, and various infections. All of these should be looked for in any forensic mental health evaluation, but especially in the elderly.

A common cause of mental impairment can be the combination of medications the elderly evaluee is taking. As an example, this author participated in the evaluation of an individual who appeared demented and had a rapid heart rate. A review of medications showed that the evaluee was on thioridazine and meperidine, both of which are highly anticholinergic, having a deleterious effect on both the brain and the heart. Discontinuation of both medications resulted in the normalization of heart rate and marked improvement in mental status.

If the evaluator does not have a sufficient medical background to interpret these medical records, he/she should get assistance from a physician in interpreting these records; the medical status of the evaluee should not be ignored.

ALCOHOL AND SUBSTANCE ABUSE DATA INTERPRETATION

What is the significance of a substance abuse history for the victim of elder abuse or domestic violence? First of all, the abused individual may be putting himself in jeopardy by using poor judgment when intoxicated or high. Second, the abuser may be responding out of frustration with the victim's substance/alcohol use, or the abuser may actually be using along with the victim, and the disinhibition experienced by both parties can result in abuse. Finally, the abuser may be encouraging alcohol or substance abuse in the victim, and may be providing these substances, sometimes in order to control the victim.

In the face-to-face evaluation, and possibly in collateral evaluations, the evaluator will have obtained specific information about alcohol and substance use. In order to determine whether this use constitutes abuse, the evaluator will additionally have to look at records to see if the alcohol or substance use has affected the individual's functioning in social and occupational roles (American Psychiatric Association [APA], 2000). For example, if the individual being examined reports the use of alcohol at a significantly excessive level, or the daily use of crack cocaine is reported, the determination of substance abuse is easier. However, evaluees are often highly inaccurate in reporting their alcohol and/or drug intake, frequently minimizing or denying excessive usage (Wettstein, 2004). It is when the evaluee reports two to three beers or glasses of wine per day, or smoking marijuana on the weekends only, that the issue of substance and/or alcohol misuse becomes less clear.

Alcohol or substance use assessment is frequently a part of mental health records, and such an assessment should have been conducted routinely on psychiatric patients; therefore, the evaluator should carefully look for this material when reviewing collateral data, particularly from outpatient and inpatient mental health records. Another source for this information can be personnel records, particularly if the evaluee has a history of tardiness or absence from work, or if there is an actual notation that the individual is intoxicated or high on the job. Police and/or jail records may also indicate problems with substance.

The duration of a substance or alcohol problem should be considered because cognitive impairment can result from long-term alcohol and substance use. Viewing blood work findings can be helpful, even without a documented alcohol abuse history, since alcohol affects liver function, which may be reflected in the liver function tests, such as albumin level, and in liver enzymes. Spikes in gamma glutamyl transferase (GGT) can indicate a recent alcohol binge. An increase in carbohydrate-deficient transferring (CDT) is another useful marker for heavy alcohol consumption (Heitala, Koivisto, Anttila, & Niemela, 2006). These lab results are not pathognomonic for excessive alcohol intake, but can indicate that further inquiry must be made (or can support abuse in a known history).

For the individual known to use cocaine, a cardiac history can help the evaluator interpret the extent of the evaluee's use. A minority of individuals who are susceptible to the effects of cocaine on the heart, which causes vasoconstriction of the coronary arteries, can experience chest pain, a myocardial infarction, or sudden death on a first or second use of this substance. Many chronic users, however, will manifest cardiac changes, which can result in the electrocardiogram (ECG) indicating ischemic damage (Schuckit, 2009). Again, such a finding has to be made in conjunction with a cocaine use history, since there are many causes of ischemic change on the ECG. However, such ECG changes or history of a myocardial infarction in a young person suggest a high level of suspicion in the evaluator, and should result in additional investigation, especially if the evaluee has not been forthcoming, has no cardiac risk factors, and no family history of heart disease. General laboratory findings will probably be normal if substances other than alcohol or cocaine are abused, so a meticulous review of the records and very specific questioning during the evaluation is required.

It is common for evaluees in the active phase of their abuse to come to an examination with alcohol or substances on board. If the evaluator suspects this, he/she should gently confront the evaluee about whether any substances or alcohol were used prior to the examination. Less frequently, an evaluee will ask for a bathroom break and will ingest substances/alcohol during that break. If the evaluator notices a marked change in behavior after the break, questioning about alcohol or substance abuse during the break is indicated. Obviously, if corroborated, such use can be interpreted as the evaluee's being significantly dependent on their substance of choice.

COMMUNICATION

CONTACTING THE REFERRAL SOURCE

Before setting down one's findings on paper, it is incumbent upon the evaluator to contact the referring attorney, agency, or whoever asked for the evaluation to be performed (Wettstein, 2004). The purpose of this contact, usually a telephone call, is to let the referral source know what your findings are. If they are unfavorable to the referral source, the call allows the referral source options, including deciding that no report should be written or asking you to proceed with the written report regardless of the negative findings. The call to the referral source also provides the opportunity to review any inconsistencies between the interview and collateral data with your referral source, and to ask for additional collateral data if they exist. Additionally, your referral source can tell you what the time frame is for the report submission, since expert discovery deadlines may be subject to change.

REPORT ORGANIZATION

It is helpful to referral sources, most of whom are not trained in mental health care, to use bullet points and/or subject headings in your report (Wettstein, 2004). Topics such as mental status examination and medical history should be separate, and using headings makes them easier to read and easier to locate for future reference when looking at the report.

CONFIDENTIALITY

It is important to note in the report that the interviewer has told the evaluee that the data from the evaluation will not be held in confidence, as is usually expected in a psychiatrist or psychologist's office, because the interviewer will be writing a report and may be asked questions under oath. It is further important to document that the evaluee has been informed that the psychiatrist/psychologist is not forming a traditional doctor–patient (or client) treatment relationship, and if treatment is required, the examiner would not be the provider rendering this treatment. The interviewer should document receiving a clear verbal or written consent from the evaluee, stating that he/she is willing to be evaluated under these circumstances. If the evaluee is not competent, or if there are significant concerns as to competency, it is important to document any attempts to obtain consent, including from a guardian (if one exists), or an attorney (if one exists). If it is not possible to get consent from a source that has the authority to consent, then one should document the evaluator's concerns about the evaluee's capacity to consent, and that the evaluator has considered and determined that there are no known available sources to give consent. For the demented elderly evaluee, the interviewer may have had to repeat these concepts more than once, and in simplified language. The evaluator might have asked the evaluee to repeat what was said regarding the limits of confidentiality, and then discuss what it means. If these occurred, they should be documented in the report.

CHIEF PSYCHOLOGICAL/EMOTIONAL COMPLAINTS

The individual being evaluated may or may not have a chief psychological/emotional complaint as a result of the abuse. Because of intimidation or fear of further abuse, denial, or other concerns such as placement of oneself or one's children, the evaluee may deny any psychological problems and may also deny the actual abuse. As stated in an earlier section, it is critical that during the evaluation of the victim, the alleged perpetrator is not present (Lachs & Pillemer, 1995). Who was present during the evaluation should be explicitly stated in the report. Even if the perpetrator of the abuse is not in the interview room, the evaluee can still feel intimidated and be frightened of additional abuse just for being interviewed if the perpetrator is still at large, residing with, or having regular contact with the victim. If the individual denies any psychological problems as a result of abuse, the evaluator should record behavioral observations in the mental status examination section of the report, and opine on the significance of the behaviors in the opinion section.

The evaluee may respond to the interviewer by talking about anxiety and/or depression, which is common in abused individuals (McCauley et al., 1995). A brief description of the evaluee's symptoms, preferably in his or her own words, is useful to characterize psychological damage. If the evaluee is not forthcoming, the interviewer may choose to omit this section.

HISTORY OF PRESENT ILLNESS

Demographic information may be included in this section or in a separate section of the report. In addition to age, gender, and marital status, it is important to describe the living arrangements of the evaluee because this information will help determine if the individual was at risk of abuse, and/or is at current risk. Living situations include shelters, assisted living facilities, nursing homes, and so forth. Writing a description of the person's daily activities, during the week and on the weekend, can help the reader of the report understand when the individual is in contact with the alleged abuser, and what impact that contact has on the victim's ability to function. Daily activities are one useful measure of the extent of psychological impairment in abuse cases. Noting the evaluee's description of how he/she came to have bruises, cuts, burns, or other indicia of physical violence can also be useful (Jayawardena & Liao, 2006). One should communicate in the report if accidents such as falling down stairs and hitting oneself with a door are blamed, and the individual seems to have repeated accidents. It is especially important to note this if the physical damage sustained by the victim is not consistent with the reported accidents. For financial abuse, one needs to address the relevant claims and relevant source material describing the abuse.

If the evaluee has acknowledged psychological problems, a temporal description of those symptoms in terms of when the victim is in contact with the alleged abuser may be helpful, especially if the victim is denying any abuse. Even if the alleged abuser is incarcerated or for some other reason is no longer in contact with the victim, he/she may be embarrassed to acknowledge once having been a victim of abuse. The daily activities review can help reveal in the report the level of impairment while the abuse was active, including any long-term sequelae. If the victim is forthcoming about the abuse and its effect on him/her, specific exploration of the nature of the abuse and the victim's response should be included in this section.

MEDICAL HISTORY

While this history should be obtained in all forensic evaluations, it is especially important to describe in reports about the elderly. Many infirmities, such as an inability to walk without assistance as a result of a CVA, may predispose an individual to abuse. Possible causes include the evaluee's not moving fast enough or well enough to satisfy the alleged abuser, or the alleged abuser's being annoyed or tired of being the victim's caretaker. A careful review of medications prescribed and medications actually taken is critical, since an elderly person can become sedated or confused by multiple medications and therefore may be at higher risk of abuse.

For domestic violence victims, a history of repeated injuries, such as broken ribs or other bones, may support the contention that the individual has been abused. Additionally, a history of multiple miscarriages in a woman of childbearing age should be noted, since pregnant women can be at risk of domestic violence by their significant others during the pregnancy (Jasinski, 2004).

MENTAL HEALTH TREATMENT HISTORY

Through self-report and/or collateral data, a history of mental health treatment at any point in a victim's life should appear in any forensic report regarding psychological status. Current mental health care, including medications, should also be listed, and can be included under this section. The fact that domestic violence and elder abuse can affect the mental health of the victim is clear. However, individuals with certain mental disorders, such as dementia, depression, or personality disorders, may be more likely to become victims of abuse, including violence (Hiday, Swartz, Swanson, Borum, & Wagner, 1999).

SOCIAL AND FAMILY HISTORY

Since an important risk factor for present abuse is a history of previous abuse, including childhood abuse, it is important to have any such history in the report (Parish & Stromberg, 2009). This section of the report can include information regarding whether the victim him/herself experienced abuse in the past, or whether there is a pattern of abuse in the environment, either in the victim's immediate family or in his/her peer group. Also of interest is the family history of mental illness, since this may predispose the victim to psychological problems, which can predispose the victim to abuse.

Either in this section, or in a different section, a detailed alcohol and substance use history of the victim should be obtained, since alcohol and substance use often accompanies abuse (Mossman, 2004). Equally important is to note the history of alcohol and substance use in the abuser, if such history can be obtained. Legal and military history can be important if either the victim or the abuser has a history of arrests, including difficulties with authority that might result in an outcome like a dishonorable discharge from the service. A history of civil litigation may also be helpful, especially if financial abuse or exploitation is suspected. Clearly, even if the evaluee is denying current abuse, a history of any past abuse, such as rape, should be noted in the report.

MENTAL STATUS EXAMINATION

In this section, or separately, the evaluator can record the behavior of the evaluee. Is the individual acting in a fearful manner? Behaviors indicating fear can be hugging oneself protectively, curling up in the chair, visibly shrinking away from the evaluator, a halting or soft voice, and poor eye contact. If the evaluator has asked the victim about his/her behavior in the evaluation, it is useful to the reader of the report to know the victim's explanation and any notable manners or affect while describing this. Questions about how the victim feels when the alleged abuser is present can be included in this section of the report. A brief cognitive screen like the Folstein Mini-Mental Status Examination can be administered, and definitely should be considered in the elderly (Folstein, Folstein, & McHugh, 1975; Folstein, Folstein, White, & Messer, 2009). The results should be in the report. Areas like concentration may be impaired in an abuse victim of any age. If the victim is a mild to moderately demented elderly person, the ability to attend to questions, in addition to the Folstein score, should be noted in the mental status section of the report. Obviously, the usual mental status examination questions regarding mood, hallucinations, delusions, and suicidality must be addressed in the forensic mental health report.

PHYSICAL OBSERVATIONS

Unlike the usual forensic psychiatric/psychological report—which does not typically contain a physical examination—a report about the abuse of an elderly victim, or a victim of domestic violence, may include a section on the evaluator's observations of any physical manifestations of abuse, such as bruises, fractures, burns, or lacerations. Equally important may be the signs of neglect, such as cachexia, poor skin turgor from dehydration, poor dentition, and poor hygiene. In addition to noting these physical findings, the report can include the victim's explanation of physical findings, which may be critically important. The victim may be able to give a credible explanation of injuries, but any inconsistencies must be noted. This is also true of the victim's hygiene and nutritional status.

PSYCHOLOGICAL TESTING

All psychological tests that were administered should be listed and all relevant findings described. It is important that the most recent versions of psychological testing be used in keeping with the guidelines for forensic psychologists. Psychological testing may be directed at clarifying cognitive deficits or personality styles and symptoms. Both of these can be important in the overall understanding leading to the opinion, and the contribution of the test to the opinion should be clearly laid out. It is important that the reader is presented this material in clear, easy-to-understand language, free from the jargon that often accompanies psychological test reports. Keeping in mind that the reader is likely an attorney or judge with little or no exposure to psychological testing, tailoring the clarity of language to the needs of the reader will make test results useful and lend weight to their findings.

OPINION SECTION

This may be the only section that the person requesting the report actually reads in detail. This section can include a restatement of the purpose of the evaluation, a discussion of the findings, the diagnostic impression, and recommendations for treatment and/or safety of the evaluee, if recommendations are requested by the retaining party. This section of the report may lean heavily on collateral data, especially if the evaluee is demented and cannot give a full coherent history, or if the evaluee is too intimidated by the abuser to be fully forthcoming. If collateral sources are used, the report should be sure to address considerations of any possible bias or gain by the collateral source. Police and hospital emergency room reports can be especially helpful in establishing cases of physical abuse. Calls to 911, or transcripts of such calls, can be helpful in establishing the abuse, and can be quoted verbatim in this as well as other sections of the report. Additionally, a discussion of the findings should include any nonverbal behavioral cues, especially of fearfulness, particularly if the evaluee has denied abuse but exhibits inconsistent nonverbal behaviors. A similar discussion should be undertaken if there are physical findings of abuse and/or neglect.

For the individual whose finances are suspected of being misappropriated by a spouse or caretaker, collateral data such as police reports and a forensic accountant's report may be helpful. Even a review of the victim's checkbook, with his/her consent, may be useful, particularly if the evaluator has an opportunity to ask the evaluee about various expenditures to determine if the evaluee understands current activity with his/her assets. This information should also be included in the interpretation of findings.

With verbal abuse, a summary of the data as they appear in other parts of the report is useful, especially if there is a pattern of verbal abuse, such as when the victim needs ambulatory assistance or assistance at meal times. Again, collateral data may be very useful to cite in this section, especially firsthand accounts of observers who have witnessed the verbal abuse.

As previously discussed, one problem the evaluator may struggle with in writing reports on victims of domestic violence or elder abuse is remaining truly objective. Striving for objectivity is an ethical goal in all forensic evaluation and report writing (Wettstein, 2004). Objectivity may be difficult in these cases when victims seem particularly vulnerable, eliciting the evaluator's desire to help. However, it is important to keep in mind that not only will the report be more useful if an objective writing style is maintained; it will be more credible and lend more weight to its opinions.

REFERENCES

American Academy of Psychiatry and the Law. (2005). *Ethics guidelines for the practice of forensic psychiatry.* Bloomfield, CT: Author.

American Psychiatric Association. (2000). *Diagnostic and statistical manual of mental disorders* (4th ed., Text Revision). Washington, DC: Author.

American Psychological Association. (1998). Guidelines for the evaluation of dementia and age-related cognitive decline. *American Psychologist, 53,* 1298–1303.

Berger M. (2007, August 14). Brooke Astor, 105, aristocrat of the people dies. *New York Times,* p. A1.

Brandl, B., Steigel, L. A., Dyer, C. B., Heilser, C. J., & Otto, J.M. (2006). *Elder abuse detection & intervention: A collaborative approach.* New York, NY: Springer.

Committee on Ethical Guidelines for Forensic Psychologists. (1991). Specialty guidelines for forensic psychologists. *Law and Human Behavior, 15,* 655–665.

Coyne, A. C., Reichman, W. E., & Berbig, L. J. (1993). The relationship between dementia and elder abuse. *American Journal of Psychiatry, 150*, 643–646.

Devanand, D. P., & Pelton G. H. (2009). Psychiatric assessment of the older patient. In B. J. Sadock, V. A. Sadock, & P. Ruiz (Eds.), *Kaplan and Sadock's comprehensive textbook of psychiatry* (9th ed., pp. 3952–3958). Philadelphia, PA: Williams & Wilkins.

Ferry, R. J., & Pascual-Y-Baralt, J. F. (2009). Syndrome of inappropriate anti-diuretic hormone. Retrieved October 22, 2009, from http://emedicine.medscape.com/article/924829-overview

Folstein, M. F., Folstein, S. E., & McHugh, P. R. (1975). "Mini-mental state": A practical method for grading the cognitive state of patients for the clinician. *Journal of Psychiatric Research, 12*, 189–198.

Folstein, M. F., Folstein, S. E., White, T., & Messer, M. A. (2009). *Mini-Mental State Examination, 2nd Edition: User's manual.* Lutz, FL: Psychological Assessment Resources.

Heitala, J., Koivisto, H., Anttila, P., & Niemela, O. (2006). Comparison of the combined marker GGT-CDT and the conventional laboratory markers of alcohol abuse in heavy drinkers, moderate drinkers and abstainers. *Alcohol Abuse, 41*, 528–534.

Hiday, V. A., Swartz, M. S., Swanson J. W., Borum, R., & Wagner, H. R. (1999). Criminal victimization of persons with severe mental illness. *Psychiatric Services, 50*, 62–68.

Jasinki, J. (2004). Pregnancy and domestic violence: a review of the literature. *Trauma, Violence, and Abuse, 5*, 47–64.

Jayawardena, K. M., & Liao, S. (2006). Elder abuse at end of life. *Journal of Palliative Medicine, 9*, 127–136.

Lachs, M. S., & Pillemer, K. (2004). Elder abuse. *Lancet, 364*, 1263–1272.

Lachs, M. S., & Pillemer, K. (1995). Current concepts: Abuse and neglect of elderly persons. *New England Journal of Medicine, 332*, 437–443.

Lachs, M. S., & Pillemer, K. (1995). Current concepts: Elder abuse. *New England Journal of Medicine, 332*, 437–443.

Levensky, E. R., & Fruzzetti, A. E. (2003). Partner violence: assessment, prediction, and intervention. In W. O'Donohue & E. R. Levensky (Eds.), *Handbook of Forensic Psychology* (pp. 715–735). San Diego, CA: Elsevier.

McCauley, J., Kern, D. E., Koldner, K., Dill, L., Schroeder, A. F., DeChant, H. K., . . . Derogatis, L. R. (1995). The "battering syndrome": Prevalence and clinical characteristics of domestic violence in primary care internal medicine practices. *Annals of Internal Medicine, 123*, 737–746.

Melton, G. B., Petrila, P., Poythress, N. G., & Slobogin, C. (2007). *Psychological evaluations for the courts: A handbook for mental health professionals and lawyers* (3rd ed.). New York, NY: Guilford Press.

Mossman, D. (2004). Understanding prediction instruments. In R. I. Simon & L. H. Gold (Eds.), *Textbook of forensic psychiatry* (pp. 501–523). Washington, DC: American Psychiatric Publishing.

National Research Council. (2003). *Elder mistreatment: Abuse, neglect, and exploitation in an aging America*. Washington, DC: Author.

Parish B., & Stromberg S. (2009). Physical and sexual abuse of adults. In B. J. Sadock, V. A. Sadock, & P. Ruiz (Eds.), *Kaplan and Sadock's comprehensive textbook of psychiatry* (9th ed., pp. 2579–2583). Philadelphia, PA: Williams & Wilkins.

Rodgers, C., & Gruener, D. (1997). Sequelae of sexual assault. *Primary Care Update Ob/Gyns, 4*, 143–146.

Schuckit, M. A. (2009). Alcohol-related disorders. In B. J. Sadock, V. A. Sadock, & P. Ruiz (Eds). *Kaplan and Sadock's comprehensive textbook of psychiatry* (9th ed., pp. 1268–1288). Philadelphia, PA: Williams & Wilkins.

Siegert, M., & Weiss, K. (2007). Who is an expert? Competency evaluations in mental retardation and borderline intelligence. *Journal of the American Academy of Psychiatry and the Law, 35*, 346–349.

Sprehe, D. J. (2003). Geriatric psychiatry and the law. In R. Rosner (Ed.), *Principles and practice of forensic psychiatry* (pp. 651–659). New York, NY: Arnold.

Swagerty, D. L., Takahashi, P. Y., Evans, J. M. (1999). Elder mistreatment. *American Family Physician, 9*, 2804–2812.

Wettstein, R. M. (2004). *The forensic examination and report*. In R. I. Simon & L. H. Gold (Eds.), *Textbook of forensic psychiatry* (pp. 139–165). Washington, DC: American Psychiatric Publishing.

CHAPTER 18

Education and Habilitation

MARK J. HAUSER, ROBERT F. PUTNAM, and GREGORY I. YOUNG

INTRODUCTION

Understanding the mental health professional's role in education and habilitation requires a basic working knowledge of applicable laws, including the United States Constitution and various statutes and regulations.

United States Constitution

10th Amendment   Education is not a fundamental right guaranteed by the Constitution. This amendment states that "powers not delegated to the United States by the Constitution, nor prohibited by it to the States, are reserved to the States, respectively, or to the people." Therefore, education becomes the duty of state governments, which provide public education as an entitlement. Individual states are responsible for educating school-aged residents, financing education through taxes, and enforcing school attendance.

14th Amendment   The key notions in this regard are "equal protection" and "due process." This Amendment states that "no state shall make or enforce any law which shall abridge the privileges or immunities of citizens of the United States . . . without due process of law." Concerning "equal protection," if a state elects to provide education to some, it must provide equal education to all. Affirmed by the Supreme Court of the United States in *Brown v. Board of*

Education (1954), this right was extended to students with disabilities by lower federal courts in such landmark cases as *Pennsylvania Association for Retarded Children v. Commonwealth of Pennsylvania* (1972) and *Mills v. Board of Education of the District of Columbia* (1972).

The "due process" clause establishes that education is a property right that cannot be taken away without notice and an opportunity to be heard—both of which schools must provide prior to suspension or expulsion. Moreover, due process also protects students from unwanted stigmatization: Schools must provide prior notice and guarantee the right to a hearing should a student wish to protest being labeled "mentally retarded" or "emotionally disturbed."

ANTIDISCRIMINATION LEGISLATION

Although the federal government does not directly control education, it does have the capacity to pass legislation that significantly affects virtually every aspect of school operations. Federal antidiscrimination legislation prevents states and school authorities from treating students differentially on the basis of race, color, national origin, sex, or handicapping condition. This legislation also protects students from harassment and hate crimes that interfere with a student's participation or ability to benefit from a district's programs or activities. Schools must comply with this legislation if they receive any federal funding for any purpose:

- Title VI of the Civil Rights Act of 1964 prohibits discrimination based on race, color, or national origin.
- Section 1983 of the Civil Rights Act of 1871 states that any person whose constitutional rights or rights under federal law have been violated by a government official may sue for damages in federal court and the official may be held liable for damages.
- Title IX of the Education Amendments of 1972 prohibits discrimination based on sex.
- Title II of the Americans with Disabilities Act of 1990 guarantees equal opportunities for individuals with disabilities in employment, public accommodation, transportation, state and local government services, and telecommunication. Subtitle A is particularly important to schools, as it addresses disability-based

discrimination in the programs, services, or other activities of local as well as state governments.

- Section 504 of the Rehabilitation Act of 1973 prohibits discrimination against an otherwise qualified individual based solely on a handicapping condition in any program or activity that receives federal funding.

EDUCATIONAL LEGISLATION

Federal educational legislation affects schools by requiring schools to comply with various policies and practices in order to receive federal funding:

- *Family Educational Rights and Privacy Act.* The Family Educational Rights and Privacy Act of 1974 (FERPA) is an amendment to the Elementary and Secondary Education Act of 1965. Schools will receive funds only if they adhere to pupil record-keeping procedures outlined in this law. The law protects confidentiality and parent access to school records about their children. Parents have access to all official school records of their children, the right to challenge the accuracy of those records, and the right to have a hearing regarding their accuracy. Moreover, student records are available only to those in the school setting with legitimate educational interest, and parental consent must be obtained before records are shared with outside agencies.
- *Protection of Pupil Rights Amendment.* The Protection of Pupil Rights Amendment of 1978 represents an additional embellishment of the Elementary and Secondary Education Act of 1965. If a survey, analysis, or evaluation is funded by the U.S. Department of Education, schools are required to obtain written parental consent before a student can be required to submit to a survey, analysis, or evaluation that reveals certain types of personal information. Schools must also develop policies ensuring that parents have the opportunity to review surveys prior to their distribution, so that parents can elect to opt out of such surveys on behalf of their children.
- *No Child Left Behind Act.* The No Child Left Behind Act of 2001 (NCLB) furthered the Elementary and Secondary Education

Act of 1965 to include stricter regulations about how federal monies could be used and provided assistance to schools with students with low socioeconomic status. The purpose of the NCLB is to close achievement gaps with a combination of accountability, flexibility, and choice. The NCLB requires state-wide reading and mathematics tests each year for students in grades 3 through 8. Each state was charged with achieving academic proficiency for all students within 12 years, and districts were to document progress towards that goal each year. The NCLB enabled public school choice for pupils, and required heightened qualifications for classroom teaching.

• *Individuals With Disabilities Education Improvement Act.* The Individuals with Disabilities Education Improvement Act of 2004 (IDEIA) is probably the most important piece of federal legislation to know and understand for those conducting forensic assessments in the schools. Previously known as the Education for the Handicapped Act (EHA) before it was transformed into the Individuals with Disabilities Education Act (IDEA), the IDEIA outlines policies and practices for the education of children with disabilities. Part B of the IDEIA provides funds to states that provide a free and appropriate education (FAPE) to all children with disabilities. Under the IDEIA, FAPE is defined as an educational program that is individualized to a specific child, designed to meet that child's unique needs, provides access to the general curriculum, meets the grade-level standards established by the state, and from which the child receives educational benefit. In order to receive these funds, states must demonstrate that students with disabilities receive special education and related services in accordance with an individualized education program.

DEVELOPMENT OF THE INDIVIDUALIZED EDUCATION PROGRAM

An individualized education program (IEP) is developed for each child with a disability. It is a written statement developed by the IEP team. The team includes the parents; regular education teachers; special education teachers; representative of the school; the child, when appropriate; and other professionals with knowledge that is relevant to the given child. When developing the IEP, the team must consider the child's strengths, parental concerns, data provided by the initial evaluation or the most recent evaluation, and information about the child's academic, developmental, and functional needs.

The IDEIA outlines the required information to be included in the IEP, including the child's current functional performance and academic achievement, and how any disabilities may affect the child's participation and progress in the general curriculum. The IEP must have clear and measurable academic or functional annual goals as well as benchmarks or objectives to meet that goal. Specific plans describing how goals will be measured and how often evaluations of the goals will be made must also be included (e.g., quarterly progress notes).

Importantly, the IEP must include any special education services, accommodations, and modifications that will be provided to the child in both regular educational and special educational settings. *Accommodations* are the actual teaching supports and services that the student may require to successfully demonstrate learning. Examples of accommodations are additional time, preferred seating, a taped book, or a scribe. Accommodations in the IEP are often specified for the administration of statewide, standardized tests.

Modifications, as listed in the IEP, are the changes made to curriculum expectations in order to meet the needs of the student. Modifications are made when the expectations are beyond the student's level of ability. An example of a modification is inclusion of the student in the same activity but with individualized expectations and materials. IDEIA also mandates that all services be evidence based and empirically supported. If the child's services are provided in a separate classroom, the IEP must identify the reason for the student being removed from the regular education classroom. Included in this plan are detailed information identifying the dates that services will start and the frequency, duration, and locations of all services.

Due Process Procedures

The IDEIA includes a number of due process procedures, designed to ensure that a student is receiving a free and appropriate education. Once an IEP is proposed to the student's parents or guardian, the parents have the right to accept the IEP, reject the IEP completely, or partially reject the IEP. The school district or parents can request a mediation meeting in which both the school district and the parents present their sides to a state department of education mediator to attempt to mediate the dispute.

If this is not successful, a resolution meeting can be scheduled with a state department of education representative in which both sides present their rationale. The purpose of the meeting is for the parent of the child to discuss the due process complaint, and the facts that form the basis of the due process complaint, so that the local education agent (LEA) has the opportunity to resolve the dispute that is the basis for the due process complaint.

If disputes cannot be resolved at this level, a due process hearing is held in which both sides—the parents and the school district—present their case before an appointed state education hearing officer. Each side usually has an attorney, and witnesses (e.g., evaluators, school district staff) are sworn in and present evidence for both sides through direct testimony. Parents may represent themselves or hire an advocate to represent them. Each side is afforded cross-examination of each witness. The hearing officer has 60 days to issue a published decision on the matter.

PREPARATION

Under the IDEIA, a student can be referred by a parent, guardian, teacher, or administrator for an evaluation to determine whether that student has a disability. After the referral is made, the parents of the child must provide consent before the evaluation can be conducted—even if the referral was made by the parents themselves.

Informed consent should include an explanation of the reasons for assessment, details about the types of tests that will be used and the evaluation procedures involved, who will be able to access the results, and the specific use to which the results will be put. Information must be presented in the consenting adult's native language, with easily understood vocabulary and syntax, and while schools may take action without parental consent with clear and documented evidence that parents have repeatedly failed to respond, due process procedures are preferable when feasible (Knauss, 2001). Consent is not required if the parents cannot be located, the rights of the parents have been terminated, or there is another individual who has been appointed by a court to represent that child.

Assessments intended to screen students as part of their regular education curriculum in an attempt to make instructional decisions do not require parental consent (Alexander, 2006). Although health professionals can review student records, participate in teacher consultation, and conduct student screenings without parental consent, parents should be notified if ongoing involvement is anticipated (Burns, Jacob, & Wagner, 2008).

If parents disagree with the school district's evaluation, the IDEIA allows them to obtain independent educational evaluation of their child at public expense once the school district's evaluation has been completed. In this context, an "independent" evaluation is one that is conducted by a qualified examiner who is not employed by the school district, while "public expense" means that the school district pays for the evaluation outright or otherwise ensures that the evaluation is provided at no cost to the parent.

DATA COLLECTION

An evaluation conducted by or contracted by the school district must be completed within 45 days of obtaining consent. The goal of evaluation is to gather relevant functional, developmental, and academic information in order to determine if the child has a disability, as well as to provide information relative to the strengths and weaknesses of the student and to provide recommendations to the student's IEP team.

It is imperative to link the assessment to intervention. The school district may contract for an assessment conducted by an outside evaluator, or an assessment may be obtained by the student's parent or guardian from any professional. These assessments, upon presentation to the school district, must be reviewed by the student's IEP team within 10 days of their presentation to the school district.

According to the IDEIA, the evaluation process must be multifaceted, with multiple assessment methods that reach a comprehensive conclusion on the basis of observation, review of background information, and collation of information from other professionals. Test results must provide accurate information about the student's developmental, functional, and academic abilities. Assessments should use information collected from teachers, parents, and—depending on a given child's age—students themselves.

Further IDEIA requirements include technically sound and scientifically valid assessments, with careful consideration of the potential effects of race, culture, gender, age, linguistic preference, and known disability in order to avoid biased results. Moreover, the assessor must be trained and knowledgeable about the measures to be employed. Assessments must be performed in the student's native language by a linguistically competent test administrator.

If an outside evaluation—not conducted by school district staff—is being conducted, it is important to determine what the referring questions are from the perspectives of both the family and the school. The following areas should be addressed uniformly:

- What are the major concerns (problem identification) of the parents/school staff that are referring the child/student?
- What is the student's current status in the specific areas of concern (academic, social, communication, social, or behavioral functioning)?
- What are the current services provided to the student on his or her IEP?
- Is the student making meaningful effective progress in these areas?
- Is this progress commensurate with the student's intellectual functioning?

Accommodations are designed to enable the student to access grade level content and stay on the same track as peers. Modifications basically alter the expectations, lowering content standards. For example, a concern that parents may have is that their child with a disability has not made effective progress in his/her school program. It is important to determine in what specific area the parent or school district has identified concerns—that is, academic or prosocial—and to select the optimal assessment instruments for appraising current functioning in that area and informing relevant recommendations.

The ultimate goal of the evaluation is to inform the student's IEP with appropriate recommendations. School districts are required to review evaluations within 10 working days of their receipt. Failure to seek information directly from the school district staff—for example, reviewing the current IEP and previous school assessments, conducting interviews with school staff, having the staff complete rating scales, or observing students in their classrooms—may serve to erode the school's confidence in the validity of the evaluator's opinions. Receiving information solely from the parents—or gathering information only from assessments conducted in the office—may further limit the utility of findings and their impact on the student's IEP.

DATA INTERPRETATION

SPECIFIC LEARNING DISABILITIES

Numerous disabilities may be considered when determining a student's eligibility for special education services, including autism, visual impairment/blindness, hearing impairment/deafness, emotional disturbance, mental retardation, multiple disabilities, orthopedic impairment, other health impairments, specific learning disability, speech and language impairment, and traumatic brain injury.

One major change attending the reauthorization of the IDEIA was a shift that allowed students to become eligible for special education as a result of failing to respond to the regular education curriculum. This change allowed what is typically referred to as response to intervention (RTI) to have legal bearing in schools. Approximately half of the students who receive special education services qualify on the basis of specific learning disabilities (LDs; President's Commission on Excellence in Special Education, 2002).

Traditional school assessments for LDs have used what is historically called the discrepancy model, which compares students' academic achievement (as tested by a standardized test) with the students' intelligence quotient (IQ). If the discrepancy between the two scores was viewed as significant, then the student would qualify for special education. In recent years, this practice has taken a significant amount of criticism. Discrepancies are often not significant until students reach third grade or beyond. Thus, the traditional model has been deemed the "wait to fail" model (Vaughn & Fuchs, 2003). This notion is specifically intended to point out that students often do not receive the instructional supports that they may need to achieve until they have already fallen significantly behind in their scholastic careers.

Current research shows that many LDs can be prevented with early application of effective instruction. Unfortunately, there is an over-identification of children with special needs because of ineffective instruction. Many students' difficulties can be prevented if the instructional quality were to be enhanced early on in the student's academic career (Vellutino, Scanlon, Small, & Fanuele, 2006).

RTI allows students to be assessed more frequently and with greater sensitivity to change. Through the use of curriculum-based assessments (CBAs) and curriculum-based measurements (CBMs; Deno, 1985), which are both essential components of assessment of RTI, students' direct academic functioning can be assessed and compared to their peers or to national norms. This can allow teachers to monitor students' growth and support them before a significant deficit develops.

GENERAL CONSIDERATIONS

An evaluation for educational purposes helps inform the parents and school district staff of the student's current status, his/her progress, and types of supports and interventions that will help the student in school, at home, and in the community. The areas of assessment should provide data that will assist the evaluator in determining the specific skill strengths and weaknesses, and how the student approaches and uses specific stimuli and materials. It is most helpful to gather interview information from the parents and significant educational staff, and complete an observation of the student in his or her school (where feasible), as well as conduct a direct assessment of the student using norm-referenced testing instruments. Using assessment instruments that have been used in previous assessments is helpful in determining the rate of progress a student is making. The use of the same serial assessment instruments, where possible, reduces the confounding of the results by eliminating the variable of different assessment instruments, which may measure similar skills in slightly different ways.

COGNITIVE

The cognitive assessment allows the examiner to assess the student's overall cognitive functioning such as intellectual functioning and strengths and weaknesses in this area. Usually, data will be gathered on the overall IQ of the student as well as specific subareas such as short- and long-term memory. Additional information will be provided on the general information, cognitive reasoning, processing speed, and other areas that will impact on the student's ability to learn information and the rate of growth expected. A variety of tests may be broken up into several different components to assess cognitive areas such as reasoning and understanding language. There are a number of assessments that are used to measure cognitive functioning, including the following:

- Wechsler Intelligence Scale for Children—4th Edition (WISC-IV)
- Wechsler Preschool Primary Scale of Intelligence—3rd Edition (WPPSI-III)
- Wechsler Adult Intelligence Scale—4th Edition (WAIS-IV)
- Stanford-Binet, Fifth Version (SB-V)
- Kaufman Assessment Battery for Children—2nd Version (K-ABC-II)
- Woodcock-Johnson Test of Cognitive Abilities—3rd Edition (WJ-III-COG)
- Differential Ability Scales—2nd Edition (DAS-II)

ACADEMIC ACHIEVEMENT

Norm-referenced academic assessments provide information on the current performance of the student in reading, mathematics, written expression, and spelling. This information will provide a current status of the student's performance in these areas as well as the student's strengths and weaknesses. Specific information concerning the specific student's skill deficits in each area will help the student's IEP team determine skills deficits and thus direct the instruction to remediate these deficiencies.

For example, a determination of whether a student has a fluency deficit or comprehension deficit would be helpful in determining the type of intervention to recommend. In addition, a current status assessment would determine if the student is making effective progress in this area. There are a number of assessments that are used to measure academic functioning, including:

- Woodcock-Johnson III NU Tests of Achievement (WJ-III NU)
- Wechsler Individual Achievement Test—Third Edition (WIAT-III)
- Wide Range Achievement Test—Fourth Edition (WRAT-IV)

Problem Behavior

According to the IDEIA, functional behavior assessment is the recognized methodology in this regard. The goal of a functional behavior assessment is operational definition of specific problem behaviors, to determine and understand the specific contextual variables that increase the probability of the behavior as well as the functions or motivations of the behavior. These data are helpful in determining the most effective and efficient interventions, teaching socially appropriate replacement behaviors that effectively and efficiently gain the function of the problem behavior, and supporting systems to reinforce the desired behavior and replacement behaviors. A functional behavior assessment usually consists of an interview with the student as well as with significant persons in the student's environment, in addition to direct observation of the student in that environment. The data assist in the development of a hypothesis regarding the context and functions of the student's behavior.

Communication

Many students with disabilities have concomitant disorders of communication. These include students with autism, developmental disabilities, and/or behavior disorders. Data should be collected to determine the current type and status of communication disorder, and these should be interpreted in light of appropriate diagnostic criteria.

Social Skills

Students with autism, emotional/behavior disorders, and/or developmental disabilities often have social skills deficits. A norm-referenced social skills assessment provides data on the type and extent of relevant social strengths and weaknesses—involving peer relations, assertiveness, and compliance. Where a previous assessment has been conducted in this area, follow-up investigation assists the evaluator in determining the rate of progress being achieved (Luiselli, McCarty, Coniglio, Zorilla-Ramirez, & Putnam, 2005). Global and norm referenced scales for this purpose include the following:

- Behavior Assessment System for Children—2nd Edition (BASC-2)
- Achenbach System of Empirically Based Assessment (ASEBA)

- Social Skills Intervention System (SSIS)
- Social Responsiveness Scale (SRS)

ADAPTIVE BEHAVIOR

Adaptive behavior deficits are often observed for students with autism and developmental disabilities. Since the goals of educational programming include teaching each student to be as independent as possible, skill acquisition data assume particular importance. These assessments should provide data on the extent of the adaptive behavior skill deficits, with specific attention to such areas as personal hygiene skills, toileting, and dressing. Comparison to data from previously administered assessments—if available—will provide the evaluator with an opportunity to determine the rate of progress being achieved. Examples of these assessments include the following:

- Scales of Independent Behavior—Revised (SIB-R)
- Vineland Adaptive Behavior Scales (VABS)

COMMUNICATION

REPORTS

The goal of these evaluations is not simply to provide numerical values regarding the child's functioning—rather, it is to identify conditions that will enable a child to learn most effectively (Tilly, 2002). Assessment as part of the problem solving process is directly linked to intervention, in contrast to more traditional assessment activities in which the goal is typically to make a diagnostic decision.

When communicating the results of the evaluation, it is important to bear in mind how such results will be used. Assessment data inform the evaluator about the current status of the students in the areas assessed, students' strengths and weaknesses, supports to assist students in skill acquisition, and—where possible—students' current rate of learning. These results should be presented in a fashion that school personnel and parents alike can both use and understand.

The most important part of these reports is the "recommendations" section. Incorporating information gathered from the school staff through review of school records, including progress reports and evaluations, previous and current IEPs, interviews with relevant educational staff, completion of rating scales by school staff, and—where possible—observations of the current school program will increase the validity and persuasiveness of evaluation results. The IDEIA requires school districts to use evidence-based interventions, so the evaluator should be prepared to highlight the "evidence" on which the recipients of his or her report are compelled to rely.

The evaluator should try to determine and communicate whether the student has made meaningful progress in areas of specific concern (i.e., academic, social skills, problem behavior, or adaptive behavior). The goal of the IEP team, after all, is to ensure that the student is making meaningful progress. Comprehensive and coherent reports will assist the team in determining whether to maintain, change, or abandon the current IEP.

In light of the foregoing considerations, the reports should contain readily identifiable reference to the following:

- Types of accommodations (e.g., use of computer, visual supports, timed or untimed assessments)
- Evidence-based interventions (e.g., specific reading interventions, applied behavior analysis)
- Timing and duration of interventions (e.g., 1 hour per day, twice per week)
- Location of interventions (e.g., general classroom, small group setting)
- Training levels and competencies (e.g., board-certified behavior analyst, master's level speech and language therapist with clinical certification, training in autism)
- Monitoring requirements (e.g., type, frequency)

TESTIMONY

An evaluator may be called to testify at a due process hearing, as a witness for the parents, as a witness for the school district, or as the court's appointee (i.e., as a guardian ad litem). This may be because either side feels that the IEP is not designed appropriately to confer meaningful benefit to the student or the IEP is not being implemented as designed. The evaluator may be subpoenaed by either side or both.

In the due process hearing, direct testimony will be given by the evaluator and then he or she most likely will be cross-examined. The evaluator, depending on experience and credentials, may be qualified as an expert witness by the hearing officer. The evaluator will be asked to specify the extent of his/her knowledge of the student and then to discuss how the evaluation was conducted, the results of the evaluation, and the recommendations made by the evaluator. The evaluator will usually be asked if his/her recommendations were incorporated in the IEP and if the IEP as implemented would result in meaningful benefit to the student. The evaluation, if conducted as outlined above and communicated appropriately, will usually provide this information.

REFERENCES

Alexander, A. M. (2006, March 28). Latest legal issues impacting general education interventions. Workshop presented at the National Association of School Psychologists meeting, Anaheim, CA.

Americans with Disabilities Act of 1990, 42 U.S.C. § 12101 et seq.

Brown v. Board of Education, 347 U.S. 483 (1954).

Burns, M. K., Jacob, S., & Wagner, A. R. (2008). Ethical and legal issues associated with using response-to-intervention to assess learning disabilities. *Journal of School Psychology, 46,* 263–279.

Civil Rights Act of 1871, 42 U.S.C. § 1983 et seq.

Civil Rights Act of 1964, 42 U.S.C. § 2000d et seq.

Deno, S. L. (1985). Curriculum-based measurement: The emerging alternative. *Exceptional Children, 52,* 219–232.

Education Amendments of 1972, 20 U.S.C. § 1681 et seq.

Elementary and Secondary Education Act of 1965, 20 U.S.C. § 7801 et seq.

Family Educational Rights and Privacy Act of 1974, 20 U.S.C. § 1232 et seq.

Individuals with Disabilities Education Improvement Act of 2004, 20 U.S.C. § 1400 et seq.

Knauss, L. K. (2001). Ethical issues in psychological assessment in school settings. *Journal of Personality Assessment, 77,* 231–244.

Luiselli, J. K., McCarty, J. C., Coniglio, J., Zorilla-Ramirez, C., & Putnam, R. F. (2005). Social skills assessment and intervention: Review and recommendations for school practitioners. *Journal of Applied School Psychology, 21,* 21–38.

Mills v. Board of Education of the District of Columbia, 348 F. Supp. 866 (D.D.C. 1972).

No Child Left Behind Act of 2001, 20 U.S.C. § 6301 et. seq.

Pennsylvania Association for Retarded Children (P.A.R.C.) v. Commonwealth of Pennsylvania, 343 F. Supp. 279 (E.D. Pa. 1972).

President's Commission on Excellence in Special Education. (2002). *A new era: Revitalizing special education for children and their families.* Jessup, MD: U.S. Dept. of Education.

Protection of Pupil Rights Amendment of 1978, 20 U.S.C. § 1232h.

Rehabilitation Act of 1973, 29 U.S.C. §794 et seq.

Tilly, D. W. (2002). Best practices in school psychology as a problem-solving enterprise. In A. Thomas & J. Grimes (Eds.), *Best practices in school psychology-IV* (pp. 21–36). Bethesda, MD: National Association of School Psychologists.

Vaughn, S., & Fuchs, L. S. (2003). Redefining learning disabilities as inadequate response to instruction: The promise and potential problems. *Learning Disabilities Research and Practice, 18,* 137–146.

Vellutino, F. R., Scanlon, D. M., Small, S., & Fanuele, D. P. (2006). Response to intervention as a vehicle for distinguishing between children with and without reading disabilities: Evidence for the role of kindergarten and first-grade interventions. *Journal of Learning Disabilities, 39,* 157–169.

CHAPTER 19

Child Custody and Parental Fitness

GERALD COOKE and DONNA M. NORRIS

INTRODUCTION

From the early Roman period extending through English and American history, children were viewed as "chattel" to be used, abused, and/or disposed of by their fathers (Derdeyn, 1976; Mason, 1994). The desires of women as mothers or wives were only secondarily considered to the wishes of their husbands, who, as heads of household, governed their homes as if they were kings. This was regardless of the poverty or wealth of the father's financial circumstances. If the child had wealth, however, this was seriously considered in any custody decisions. In *De Manneville v. De Manneville*, a classic legal case from the early 19th century, the English Court reaffirmed the rights of the father to custody of the child unless the child was propertied and his/her life was at risk (Wright, 1999). In the new colonies, early American law was modeled after English law. The father's role was sacrosanct and unchallenged as primary custodian of all children. Into the 20th century, the "Tender Years Doctrine," advocating for mothers as the primary nurturers initially of infants and later expanded to include all children, became the standard utilized by the courts in custody matters (Sadoff & Billick, 1981).

With the growing and mixed feelings regarding women's suffrage, some argued that divorced women should have closer scrutiny before gaining custody of minor children, who needed moral upbringing (Massachusetts Association Opposed to the Extension of Suffrage to Women, 1912). In that period in American history, divorced women were not readily accepted into "polite" society. Declaring that the courts should be heard in these matters, Judge Cardozo determined that for children a dual role existed for the courts: to stand as *parens patriae* and to determine their best interests (*Finlay v. Finlay*, 1925). Thereafter, the "Best Interests Standard," primarily considering the rights and needs of children, not parents, became and remains the determinant doctrine on custody matters in this country. When investigating custody matters, the evaluator must be familiar with the specific state statutes and any professional and/or court guidelines that govern the process. The importance of considering physical and psychological factors in any assessment was carefully explored by *Beyond the Best Interests of the Child* (Goldstein, Freud, & Solnit, 1973). This expanded the presence of mental health professionals in the family courts to assist the judiciary in their decisions regarding children.

In 2004, there were approximately 2.2 million (7.5/1,000) marriages in the United States, with a divorce rate of 3.6/1,000 (Centers for Disease Control and Prevention, 2005). Many of these families include children whose lives are greatly impacted by their parents' decisions to separate and divorce (Wallerstein & Johnson, 1990). It is notable that the majority of decisions regarding custody are by agreement between the parents and do not become entangled in prolonged conflicts often portrayed in the media. However, divorce and custody conflicts within the court system are a different matter and may become quite contentious, expensive, and, in a few instances, even dangerous for the parties, the attorneys involved, and the evaluators (Hanley, 2003; King, Douthat, & Piloto, 2003; Koontz, 2004; Morse, 2008). Although the aforementioned situations portray frightening scenarios, it is important to understand that experts involved in performing these assessments may be harassed by parties being evaluated. Such incidents may result in claims of fraud, charges of malpractice, and complaints of unethical and unprofessional conduct, and culminate in investigations by professional licensure boards (Lion & Herschler, 1998; Miller, 1985; Norris & Gutheil, 2003).

PREPARATION

In planning the assessment process, evaluators must review the particular guidelines and ethical considerations as defined by their discipline governing his/or her clinical practice to assure that the professional standards are met. Some jurisdictions may have certain mandated guidelines and a format that must be followed in evaluating and presenting the written assessment to the court. The clinical evaluator must perform an in-depth assessment for the court, which generally covers many hours of clinical work. Therefore, there are certain parameters that need to be clear before starting the evaluative process to assure that integrity of the work will not be compromised.

When possible, any preliminary discussion regarding the evaluator's availability to work with this matter should be done in the presence of both attorneys or at least on the telephone. If this is not possible, limit discussion to general availability, approximate time needed to accomplish the work, and the fee schedule. It is helpful to review with the attorneys the anticipated scope of the work generally planned in these evaluations; however, any discussion of the potential case material must be avoided. In line with most professional guidelines, do not agree to interview only one party without the opportunity to see both parents (if possible), all caretakers, and any others who may provide important information regarding the well-being and care of the children. Parental fitness may be considered as multifactorial sets of skills including the abilities to understand and carry through appropriate caretaking and nurturing of the children's physical and emotional development.

As outlined by Barnum (2003), a series of parental tasks should be evaluated for all appropriate stages of child development: infancy, toddlerhood, school age, and adolescence. The assessment should identify for the court the parental strengths encompassing their abilities to support the children's cognitive gains, appropriate progress, provide supervision, and permit independence as age appropriate. Also included in the evaluation is an assessment of parental deficits, which will provide the court with an accurate and comprehensive understanding of the scope of limitations that may compromise the child's safety and future growth and development. In addition, clarify with the attorneys that the evaluative findings will be submitted in the final report with the specific order of the court and are not subject to prior approval and/or modification. If there are errors, these should be corrected and submitted in writing in an addendum.

The professional evaluator must address clearly who is financially responsible for the cost of the assessment. Is it the court, the parties, or the state department of children's and family services? If the work is to be paid in some proportion by the parties, review the court's order regarding payment, and address with the attorneys the need for prior retainer before commencing the work. It is a troubling matter to pursue payment with the parties once the assessment is completed. One party may not want to pay for the work, as he/she may feel the evaluation was unfavorable to his/her interests. And, finally, before starting a new assessment, ascertain that the evaluator has appropriate personal rest and the time to complete a thorough report that will be attentive to the necessary details of the evaluation.

DETERMINING THE PROPER FOCUS AND SCOPE

The professional relationship between the evaluator and the examinees is one of respect and cordiality, but it is not a psychotherapy relationship. Maintain a professional demeanor and avoid solicitous comments or responses, which may lead the parent to believe that they are favored or disfavored in some manner. The lack of confidentiality for the assessment process and any information revealed or discovered must be clearly stated to the parties and documented by the evaluator in the record. Evaluators undertaking custody evaluations must understand that they are working for the court and must focus their assessment on addressing the court's questions. When there is ambiguity regarding the scope of the assessment, the court is readily available to clarify these concerns. If the evaluator does otherwise, he/she risks losing credibility with the court, attorneys, and the parties and may place the entire evaluative process in jeopardy. Child forensic authorities (Benedek & Schetky, 1985; Herman, 2003; Norris & Ferguson, 2003; Schetky & Haller, 1983) discuss special concerns, that is, sexual violence, new reproductive techniques, transcultural conflicts as they impact custody decisions, and the need for a clear and unbiased assessment regarding the potential impact of these factors on the child's well-being. The professional who is a novice in this work must be aware that the roles of psychotherapist and evaluator are distinct in boundaries and responsibilities and must not be confused (Strasberger, Gutheil, & Brodsky, 1997).

TIMING

The plan for the initiation and completion of the assessment is often impacted by the parties' schedules, which may already have established separate visitations with the children built around the school day (for older children) or other plans. Therefore, the assessment appointments should, if possible, accommodate these vacation plans during the academic year and during the summer period. When feasible, it is important to establish interviews with the parents—to separately, and/or when the level of conflict allows, together—soon after the court's initial order.

Some parents may be so overwhelmed by their emotions of anger, agitation, and/or fearfulness in the case of domestic violence that they are not able to sit in the same room with the other party, and should be offered the opportunity to be seen alone. It is generally helpful to encourage parents to start the interview with their main concerns about what prompted the current court and evaluative process. Why are you in court? This may serve to reduce their anxiety about this assessment and permit them some sense of control by telling their own story in this new setting with the evaluator. When the question of custody is raised, much is on the line, and many parents may find it difficult to feel comfortable and to participate freely in the process. The evaluator should keep in mind that the court will need to have the completed evaluation about the parties and children prior to rendering decisions regarding custody of the children. Therefore, it is important to provide the completed report as soon as feasible. Generally, the court may ask that this is completed within 3 to 4 months. Due to the complexity of these matters, it may be necessary to ask the court for an extension of the evaluation time. The court is appreciative of an interim report discussing the information still outstanding and the reasons for the delay.

Ethical Issues

It is the ethical responsibility of the evaluator to attempt to maintain an honest and balanced perspective regarding the findings in the evaluations before the court and to know the statutes and guidelines that govern the work. Some states may have guidelines for the evaluations, which are reference points to consider but are not mandates. If there are reasons to deviate from a planned action in the assessment, document the reasons and be prepared to discuss their rationale.

While the court may order this assessment, it is still important to review with the parties the nature of the professional contact, the plan to obtain information, and the written agreement, which provides the necessary permissions to contact others who may have important knowledge about the child. It is also critical to clarify the parties' understanding of this process once it has been reviewed. If there is any concern that a party is confused or that information has been misinterpreted in any manner, this will need to be addressed by the court and the attorneys prior to continuing the assessment.

During the process of the evaluation, important information may surface of abuse, neglect, or violent behavior, which places the children or others in the household at risk. As a mandated reporter, the evaluator must follow through with this responsibility, regardless of the ongoing current court assessment.

Evaluator conflicts of interest may compromise the assessment and result in a loss of professional work, compensation, and professional esteem. As soon as any conflicts of interest are recognized, discuss these with the attorneys. When conflicts are determined to be of significance, it will be necessary to inform the court and recuse yourself from participating in the assessment.

CONFIDENTIALITY

The parents must be alerted in the initial interview regarding the lack of confidentiality for any information that is discovered during the process of these interviews. Nothing is "off the record," and any information discovered and determined pertinent may be reported to the court. In some states in which the custody of children is being addressed, the judge may determine that there is no confidentiality for mental health records, including the parents. One of the major difficulties that some parents may have with this interview process is that they may forget that this assessment is part of an ongoing legal process. Since the examiner is focused on parental concerns regarding the children, and inquiring about these in a thoughtful manner without judgment, parents may misconstrue the nature of the relationship as more in line with therapy. Therefore, it is appropriate to periodically remind parents of the limits of any confidentiality.

DATA COLLECTION

There are several general guidelines to data collection in child custody evaluations. These are well summarized by Martindale (2007). Before beginning the evaluation process, the evaluator needs to obtain a copy of the court order. There are several reasons for this. First, in some states, a court-ordered evaluation provides immunity from legal action, which is not the case in the absence of a court order (*Hughes v. Long et al.*, 2001). Thus, even if the parties have agreed to the evaluation, the evaluator should ask that this be put into a formal court order. Second, the court order defines the scope of the evaluation. All evaluations will, of course, include the parents (or persons in parental roles) and the children. However, some evaluations need to include significant others, grandparents, or others, depending on the issues that have been raised in litigation. Third, the court may want the evaluator to address certain special issues such as a parent's drug or alcohol use, mental health history, physical or sexual abuse, or the possibility of parental alienation. Such special issues will drive further data gathering.

Custody evaluators must use multiple data-gathering methods (Martindale, 2007). These include, but are not limited to, interview, psychological tests, forms and assessment techniques filled out by each parent regarding each child, legal petitions, responses to petitions, orders, various other records, contact with third-party collaterals, observation of each parent's interaction with the children, and interview. Each of these areas will be discussed in detail below. The ultimate purpose of the custody evaluation is to offer an opinion regarding what custody arrangement is in the best interest of the children. While the legal statutes governing child custody evaluations vary from state to state, many states further define the factors relevant to that determination. In Pennsylvania's statute (Pa. C.S.A. Section 5328), for example, the primary factor is which party is more likely to encourage contact with another party. It then goes on to list 14 other factors that, by implication, must be assessed by the custody evaluator where relevant. These are:

1. The parental duties performed by each party on behalf of the child
2. Need for stability and continuity in the child's education, family life, and community life
3. Availability to extended family
4. Child's sibling relationships
5. Present and past abuse

6. Well-reasoned preference of the child based on child's maturity and judgment
7. Attempts of a parent to turn a child against the other parent
8. Which party is more likely to maintain a loving, stable, consistent, and nurturing relationship with the child
9. Which party is more likely to attend to the daily physical, emotional, developmental, educational, and special needs of the child
10. Proximity of the residences of the parents
11. Each party's availability to care for the child or make appropriate child care arrangements
12. The level of conflict between the parents and the willingness and ability of the parents to cooperate with one another
13. The history of drug or alcohol abuse of a party or a member of a party's household
14. The mental and physical condition of a party or a member of a party's household

The data collection process must address such issues where relevant.

INTERVIEWING THE PARENTS

Prior to moving into a history specific to custody, the evaluator takes a personal history. This includes education; family and childhood; occupation; social relationships; substance use; and treatment for mental, emotional, and medical problems. Even though the evaluator is not focusing on custodial issues, a lot of relevant information may emerge. For example, taking the occupational history, which includes work hours and travel, is often an indirect way of exploring the parent's availability to the children. In current times, it is not unusual that both parents are employed. Therefore, the fact that one parent is working away from the home is not necessarily a factor against him or her eventually obtaining custody of the children.

There is, of course, some degree of variability in terms of the areas explored on interview, and the detail in which each area is explored. The following is not meant to be all-inclusive. First, it is necessary to get important date parameters, for example, dates of marriage, in-home separation, physical separation, divorce final, and so on. It is helpful to review the character of the courtship. This is often a tip-off when there is a history of misuse and abuse in the marital relationship.

The next step is to explore the problems in the marriage/relationship. How detailed this is depends on the time since separation. This may be quite important if the separation is recent. However, if the separation is remote in time, such as 7 to 8 years, many other factors have since intervened that will be more important. The same is true when it comes to exploring child care during the marriage. Clearly, there will be much more material to review if the separation occurred when the child was 12 years old as opposed to when the child was 6 months old. Typically, it is while discussing child care that information is gathered on who attended to which of the children's needs, involvement in school, medical care, activities, and parenting along such dimensions as rewards and punishments, and so on.

The interview then proceeds to what happened at the time of separation and thereafter. A chronological account is developed with changes in custody arrangements, important incidents, and the like. In this process, information about parenting practices is likely to be reiterated, as well as information from the list contained in the statute. The interview concludes with what each parent wants as a custodial arrangement, and why each believes this is in the best interest of the children. Since this is the crucial issue, it may include a summary of factors already discussed.

INTERVIEWING THE CHILDREN

The approach to interviewing children varies in part based on their age. Also, evaluators differ regarding a formal office interview of the children. Some evaluators do not interview children under the age of 5 or 6, unless there is a child sexual abuse allegation. This is because children under 5 are so influenced by recent events that they cannot provide an overall perspective. However, even if a formal interview is not conducted, it is important to see the children regardless of their age, even with very young infants.

Some evaluators see the children with each parent in the office and then make a home visit. Others will only perform a home visit if the children are young. Each setting may provide important information about the child interacting in the presence of the parents with a stranger, and an observation of the parent's ability to help the child manage the new situation. For example, in trying to determine each parent's involvement in child care, the evaluator could not expect to get reliable information from a 4-year-old regarding which parent bathes him/her. Most likely, the answer will be based on who bathed the child the day before.

Even with older children, the interviewer must be careful not to lead or inadvertently influence the children's responses. Also, before beginning to explore content, the evaluator needs to establish rapport with the children. However, this has already been partially accomplished through the two home visits, which will be discussed later in this chapter. This author generates a list of questions of areas to explore based on the information obtained in the parent interviews. This will almost always include issues related to child care and other activities with the children, participation in and style of helping with homework, discipline, rules, expression of affection, critical incidents the child may have observed, and many other areas.

The questions should be phrased in as nonleading a manner as possible and balanced so that the evaluator is asking about both parents. For example, if the mother has alleged that when father does homework with the children, he yells at the children and gets the children upset, the evaluator should not ask if Dad yells at the children when they do homework together. Instead, the evaluator should ask who does homework with the children, how Mom does it and how Dad does it. If the children have special needs, a critical issue is which parent is most attentive to those needs, but again, this should be approached in the same nonleading and balanced manner.

Evaluators may disagree on whether the children should be put in the position of being directly asked their preference for a custodial arrangement. Typically, older children feel strongly about this and will state a preference, even if not asked. Younger children may be more ambivalent or hesitant. Some evaluators first determine that the children know what the current arrangement is (younger children may not be able to keep track of this), and then ask how it is working out and whether he/she would like to change it in any way. Others tell the children that the evaluator is not going to ask them for their view, with the aim of making the children feel comfortable that they will not be put on the spot with this question. Some children will blurt out an uninvited statement of preference. In this case, an undertaking about why this has occurred is in order. At times, the children have been prepped by the parent to come in with an answer, even without a question. More important than the preference is that the reasons be explored from the perspective of the legal guideline that gives more weight to a "consistent and well reasoned preference."

The evaluator has to be sensitive to reasons for a preference that may actually be detrimental to the children. For example, a younger child may wish to be with the parent that allows unrestricted time on video games, rather than with the parent who places a reasonable limit. Similarly, an older child may express a preference to be with the parent who does not check up on where the child is going and with whom, or who doesn't set limits on when the child needs to be home, how late at night he/she can talk on the cell phone, and so forth.

PARENTING FORMS AND PSYCHOLOGICAL TESTS

Some custody evaluators ask each parent to fill out some sort of "parent questionnaire." Others elicit this information on interview regarding the health, pregnancy, and development of the child. The form of interview typically asks the parent to provide information on the child's developmental landmarks, educational history, and current status, and medical history and current status. In addition, there are typically questions pertaining to parenting practices, including how the parent expresses affection to the child, what the parent disciplines for and how the parent disciplines, rules and chores in the house, the child's food preferences, the child's greatest needs and how the parent attempts to meet those needs, the child's favorite activities and interests, the child's organized activities and the parent's participation in these, the child's greatest abilities and strengths, and the child's dislikes.

It is also important to have each parent describe what they view as their own strengths and weaknesses as a parent and those of the other parent. Some evaluators include a form on which the parent indicates what percentage of child care functions each parent and/or another caretaker such as a nanny or grandparent performed. This includes such things as dressing, cooking meals, helping with homework, taking to doctor/dentist appointments, and the like. While it is true that a parent may not report accurately on these forms, their responses can be compared with one another, with the child's report and with information from third-party contacts. This will be discussed further in the section on data interpretation.

There are standardized forms on which parents can rate children in terms of both problem behaviors and adaptive skills (e.g., the Behavior Assessment System for Children—2nd Edition [BASC-II], Reynolds & Kamphaus, 2004). These are helpful in obtaining each parent's view of each child. Again, a comparison of each parent's perception can provide important information relevant to custodial recommendations, and this also will be discussed further in the data interpretation section.

Not all custody evaluators administer psychological tests, and their necessity in a custody evaluation is a subject of disagreement (Emery, Otto, & Donahue, 2005). In addition, in some states, the evaluator must petition the court to obtain psychological testing and provide a rationale. Additional cost may be a factor here as well. Those who feel they are unnecessary point out, correctly, that they provide no direct information about parenting. However, those evaluators who do use them point out that psychological functioning as assessed, in part, by testing can have a bearing on parental ability. Also, where one parent makes allegations that the other has personality characteristics that impact on custodial issues, the testing, along with other sources of information, can be useful in either confirming or disconfirming the presence of these personality characteristics.

There are hundreds of psychological tests for use with adults. Psychologists tend to have favorite batteries, and this author will focus on one such assemblage. Ackerman and Ackerman (1997) surveyed psychologists and determined that the most commonly used tests are the following (the percentages refer to the percentage of evaluators surveyed who indicated they used that test): Minnesota Multiphasic Personality Inventory (MMPI/MMPI-2; 91.5%); Rorschach Inkblot Technique (47.8%); Wechsler Adult Intelligence Scale—Fourth Edition (WAIS-R; 42.8%); Millon Clinical Multiaxial Inventory II/III (34.3%); Thematic Apperception Test (29.4%); Sentence Completion (22.4%). All other tests ranged in percentage of use from 11.4% to 2.5%.

A well-balanced battery may include, for example, the MMPI-2 and the Rotter Incomplete Sentences Blank (Rotter, 1950), along with the BASC-2, Parents Questionnaire, Personal History Questionnaire, and Custody History Questionnaire. Despite the frequent use of the

Rorschach (utilizing the Exner system) in the past, it appears to be declining in frequency of use, based on the popularization of an accumulation of research data demonstrating that this measure overpathologizes the test taker and lacks substantial validity (Wood, Nezworski, Lilienfeld, & Garb, 2003).

As noted above, these instruments were not developed specifically to assess factors related to child custody. Numerous attempts have been made in recent years to develop such specific instruments (e.g., ASPECT, Ackerman & Schoendorf, 1992; Custody Quotient, Gordon & Peek, 1989). However, numerous reviewers (e.g., Grisso, 2003) have concluded that these instruments, despite their face validity, lack methodological soundness and empirical validity, and thus they are rarely used by custody evaluators.

The use of specialized instruments is in part driven by issues raised in the specific custody case. For example, if there is an allegation of substance abuse, there are scales on general personality tests, such as the MMPI-2, as well as other instruments such as the Michigan Alcohol Screening Test (MAST; Selzer, 1971). While the frequent use of intelligence testing for adults is both surprising and usually of little relevance, such testing would be important if there were an allegation of limited intellectual ability (e.g., reasoning, judgment) impacting on parenting. The evaluator will take a substance abuse history and look for evidence that this is an ongoing problem, and may ask for a specialty evaluation and/or drug/alcohol screens and/or suggest to the court a need for ongoing follow-up.

Because testing and parenting forms may take many hours (typically, 4 to 6 hours) to complete, parents frequently ask if they can take the tests and forms home with them. This issue has been discussed by other writers in the field (e.g., Sparta & Stahl, 2006), and the present authors agree with their position that this is not an acceptable. In fact, we have found that, in this day of Blackberrys and similar devices, that even in the office it is necessary to check on the parents frequently to assure they are not checking with others to get information they otherwise do not have. For example, a father might call his new wife to get the name of the child's teacher because she has been more involved in school than he has. Obviously, determining that the father does not know the name of the teacher is critical information that could be lost if the forms went home or if the father could simply call to get the information.

Psychological testing of children is also controversial. Some evaluators do this routinely, but in some jurisdictions the evaluator must obtain permission from the court and provide a rationale, and again there may be a cost factor. It is somewhat surprising how often intelligence testing is performed (58.2%), while other frequently used materials are the Children's Apperception Test (36.8%), the Rorschach (27.4%), and projective drawings such as the Kinetic Family Drawing (18.4%) (Ackerman & Ackerman, 1997). We have found that a modified Children's Incomplete Sentences Blank—with additional sentence stems regarding each parent—will generate relevant information about the child's perception of and feelings about each parent. Since most children in custody evaluations are below the age where objective personality testing can be administered, evaluators must rely on projective techniques, which have even weaker reliability and validity.

The present authors would recommend that findings from psychological tests, for both the parents and the children, be interpreted cautiously and conscientiously. Tests should be used to generate hypotheses, which can then be confirmed or disconfirmed by direct observation, history, and/or third party collaterals. The evaluator may be asked why the testing was or was not indicated.

HOME VISITS

The American Psychological Association's *Guidelines for Child Custody Evaluations in Family Law Proceedings* (2009) favor a comprehensive series of examinations that may include observations of interactions between the parents and the children. While some evaluators do this in the office, others make the observations in a home visit to each of the parents when the children are with that parent. The home visit provides the opportunity for several important observations that the observation of the interaction in the office does not. It also allows the evaluator to meet twice with the children prior to the office visit, on the children's own territory, which fosters development of rapport. However, there may be circumstances under which visiting the home is not appropriate or when one should be accompanied by an officer of the court.

One part of the observation is of the physical characteristics of the home. An evaluator can quickly discern if this is or is not a child-oriented environment. For example, are the children's rooms decorated to their tastes and interests? Are there photographs of the family, including the other parent? Is the child's artwork displayed? Are there activity schedules, chore charts, and the like on the refrigerator or elsewhere? Are there appropriate toys, games, books, videos, and so on? Are the child's needs for privacy met? How neat and clean is the house? We have seen homes where one would not know a child lived there—and, in fact, on occasion we have seen homes where one would not know a parent lived there.

Critics of home visits argue that the parent can prepare by cleaning up and/or decorating the house, and can engage in positive behaviors with the child that is not their typical way of interacting. However, it is certainly appropriate for a parent to clean up, organize, and so on. If, despite this, the house is messy, dirty, and disorganized, it carries even more weight. Also, even though parents may try to put their best foot forward, they usually revert to habit fairly quickly. Also, the evaluator can usually tell from the children's behavior whether the parent's behavior is typical or atypical. Sometimes this is subtle in terms of a confused look by the child. Other times, it is blatant, such as when the psychologist coauthor was leaving a home visit at the same time the father was leaving in the car with the child. The child turned toward the father and said, "Why are we using the seat belt today, Daddy?"

The home visit also allows for observation of the parent and child in a naturalistic setting. While not all home visits result in situations that allow all of the following to be observed, the evaluator should try to assess the following aspects of the parental interaction: support of the relationship with the other parent; verbal and physical expression of affection; patience; tolerance of upset; a balance of helpfulness/ support with promoting age-appropriate independence; teaching; repetition and reinforcement; communicating and playing at the children's level; communication of understanding of the children's feelings; effective/appropriate limits and discipline; modeling and reinforcing manners; and effective utilization of distraction.

Often, the verbal interaction will demonstrate the parent's level of knowledge about friends, schoolwork, activities, schedules, and the like. The evaluator also assesses the interaction of the children with the parent, including but not limited to initiation and response to physical interaction, response to limits and discipline, presence or

absence of manipulativeness, encouragement of appropriate independence, and manners. If there is more than one child, the evaluator
also assesses the quality of the children's interaction with each other
and the parent's ability to balance attention, promote fairness, and so
forth. Assessing the physical setting, the behavior and the verbal-
izations of parent and child often also provides information about
hygiene, safety, and nutrition.

COLLATERAL CONTACTS

In providing history, parents often either intentionally or uninten-
tionally skew positive factors in their own favor and skew negative
factors in portraying the other parent. Some of this "he says—she
says" kind of material can never be sorted out and verified. But some
can through observation, test findings, input from the children, and,
often most importantly, from objective third-party collaterals. The
evaluator has both parents sign release-of-information forms.
School-year custodial arrangements often are strongly influenced
by each parent's involvement in school academics and activities.

School records may provide some insight into this, but even more
important is contact with school staff. This is sometimes problematic.
Some schools, particularly private schools, are advised by their
attorneys not to speak with a custody evaluator. If the evaluator
deems the information to be crucial in a particular case, this resistance can be overcome by a court order. If the evaluator is able to
speak to the guidance counselor, teachers, and others, important
information can be obtained regarding each parent's involvement
with school. The evaluator then compares this with what each parent
stated about his or her own and the other parent's involvement.

Similarly, pediatric records will sometimes show who brought the
child, who signed for inoculations, and so on. Speaking to the pediatrician can also provide information on the parents' interaction with
the children, follow-through on medical recommendations, and the
like. Past babysitter and day care providers may also be able to provide
important information on involvement in child care and the parent–
child bond. The problem with present babysitters is that if their income
depends on a parent, they are not likely to be a reliable source.

If either or both parents have been in psychiatric/psychological
treatment, drug/alcohol treatment, and/or marital therapy, it may be

necessary to contact various treatment providers. Most relevant is whether any past or present mental condition impinged on or continues to impinge on parenting. In cases where there are allegations of child sexual abuse, the evaluator needs to obtain all prior medical and psychological evaluations pertaining to that issue, as well as reports from children and youth services or similar investigative agencies. If a child has special needs (e.g., autism spectrum), the evaluator also needs to speak with the specialists who have evaluated or treated the child.

Some evaluators do not preclude the parents from providing "character references" from friends, relatives, and so on. However, these generally are not found to be objective sources, so that the information obtained is often not useful. The psychologist coauthor typically will not speak to the children's grandparents unless a parent is living with them after the separation, and/or they have been very involved in child care, again because of the likelihood that they will not be objective. However, if a person has been a friend of both parents, then he or she does speak to them. The psychiatrist coauthor maintains an open policy about talking with family members. While they may present a biased view, the grandparents also may offer important insights about the children, observing parenting behaviors, and/or family incidents that may or may not be verified later by outside sources, but still may be important considerations regarding additional investigation pathways.

Neighbors who knew both as a couple can also be helpful. However, the evaluator must be careful to determine if friends or neighbors have "taken sides" since the separation and weigh the information accordingly. The same rule applies to evaluating the input from the parents of the children's friends. If relocation is an issue, then the evaluator must obtain information about the new neighborhood, schools, and so on. The parents can be asked to provide this information, but there are also websites that provide data on school systems.

SIGNIFICANT OTHERS

In some custody evaluations, the assessment must go beyond the parents and the children. If either or both parents have a significant other who is involved with the children or have remarried, then these individuals must also be part of the evaluation. If neither parent feels the significant other of the parent is a major issue in the custody evaluation, then this can easily be accomplished by having the significant other present for the home visit to observe their interaction with the children, and to conduct a brief separate interview with the significant other. However, in some cases, one or both parents believe that the significant other is a major issue. This may require more in-depth interview and testing of the significant other. If there are allegations that grandparents are a major issue, particularly in terms of alienating the children from the other parent, they may have to be evaluated as well.

DATA INTERPRETATION

As is obvious from the preceding section, by the time the data-gathering process has been completed, there is often a mountain of data from multiple sources. Organizing and interpreting the data is often a difficult task. There are many approaches to this.

It may be helpful to label certain "salient points." This is defined in part by the issues raised by each of the parents, but also may be generated by information from the children or third-party collaterals. In a typical case, there may be approximately 8 to 12 salient points. Some of these are factors that need to be addressed independent of whatever recommendation is made for the custody arrangement. For example, if one or both parents is using the children to convey messages to the other parent, this may result in a recommendation that they stop doing so.

Salient points will vary from case to case, but often include the following:

- Who was the primary caretaker during the marriage?
- What effect has this or other factors had on the children's past and current bond with each parent?
- Who is more knowledgeable about the children's needs, feelings, behavior, and the like, and is better able to respond to those needs?
- Which parent is more likely to encourage the children's relationship with the other parent?
- Which parent is more accessible to the children both physically and emotionally?

- Which parent provides more stability to the children in terms of the parent's emotional makeup, and in terms of continuity of household, school, church, friends, extended family, and so on?
- What is the child's preference, and is it a consistent and well-reasoned preference? Some statutes and/or some judges do not require or want the evaluator to directly question the children about their preference. Others leave it to the professional judgment of the evaluator.

For each salient point, the sources of data (which would have already been presented in the text of the report) can be summarized. For example, part of meeting the children's needs is involvement in their schooling. In summarizing this point, multiple sources of data can be used. Frequently on the questionnaires and on interview, parents will exaggerate their involvement and minimize that of the other parent. Data interpretation requires interpreting other information to determine which position is supported. Thus, school records and contacts may show that one parent was frequently at teacher conferences and back-to-school nights and signed permission slips, while the other parent rarely did. Interview of school/league athletic coaches may reveal that one parent was a coach and transported to and attended practices and games.

However, this is not just about time spent with the children, but the quality of the interaction; in one situation where the mother was the one at the conferences, she talked only about herself and her needs. The children may provide information that one parent was the one who primarily communicated with teachers, supervised homework, picked up from school when sick, and so forth. Parents of friends may indicate that at school plays, concerts, and the like, it is one parent who has been present and the other has been absent. Each of the other salient points is handled in a similar manner. In addition, a comparison of the parent questionnaires and BASCs, when compared with the evaluator's impressions of the child, along with information from schools, therapists, and so on, will often indicate which parent has a more accurate understanding of the child. A comparison of personality test findings with allegations by one parent about the other (e.g., an anger control problem) may help to confirm or disconfirm that allegation.

Often, by the time all the salient points have been developed by the evaluator, the recommendation follows logically from the accrued data. However, there are always individual factors that have to be considered. In the preceding example, let us say that the most involved parent was the mother. However, they had agreed that she would be the stay-at-home parent and he would work to supply a lifestyle she wanted (e.g., private school, country clubs). Thus, the father worked long hours, but was involved when he could be, and the children reported very positive interactions with him. Since the separation, the father has now taken a much more active role. He attends to business when the children are with the mother, working extra hours at those times so he can be with the children on his custodial time when they get home from school and on his weekends. Thus, though the children have always been more with their mother, they now have a closer and more involved relationship with their father, prize this, and have a consistent and well-reasoned preference for equal time with both parents.

As in the example, each salient point must be looked at closely and balanced against others in reaching a recommendation for a custody arrangement. Three possible types of physical custody recommendations usually result from this analysis: primary custody for the mother with partial custody for the father; primary custody for the father with partial custody for the mother; or equally shared custody. The evaluator must clearly connect the salient points to the recommendation. Legal, as opposed to physical, custody has to do with decision making in major areas such as education, medical care, and religion. In most cases, legal custody is shared no matter what the physical custody arrangement. However, if one parent has demonstrated a lack of cooperation or involvement in one of those areas, particularly if this is based on cognitive or emotional problems, then the recommendation may be that the other parent have legal custody.

There are two areas in particular in which data interpretation requires additional analysis. One of these is when one parent alleges sexual abuse of the child by the other parent. In such cases, interviews of the children should be recorded, preferably by videotape. The evaluator needs to be cognizant of the research on interviewing children in child sexual abuse cases (e.g., Ceci & Bruck, 1995), and to be sensitive to the possibility that a parent has either fabricated the allegation or overreacted to something innocuous said or done by the child. Of course, it is always possible that sexual abuse has occurred, and this requires integration of the psychological evaluation of the alleged perpetrator and the parent bringing the allegation, the records of the pediatrician and children and youth services, and the interviews of the children.

The other area is in relocation cases. These cases involve one of the parents' desire to move to a different geographical area. This is the parent who already has primary custody or who is petitioning for primary custody for purposes of the relocation. For example, several cases in Pennsylvania have defined the criteria that the court, and hence the evaluator, must explore:

- The potential advantages of the move and the likelihood that it will improve the quality of life for the custodial parent and the children, and is not a "whim."
- Integrity of motive—not to frustrate the rights of the non-custodial parent. Included here is also the willingness of the custodial parent to cooperate with alternative visitation arrangements.
- Availability of realistic, substantive visitation that will foster the relationship of the child and the noncustodial parent (*Gruber v. Gruber*, 1990).

In Massachusetts, by way of contrasting example, there is a somewhat different emphasis. The well-being of the custodial parent should be considered in determining the best interest of the child in case of removal from the jurisdiction. Preferences of young children (ages 9 to 13) not to move to California with the custodial parent should be treated with caution by the judge making the decision (*Hale v. Hale*, 1981).

If the evaluator is unable to visit the scene of the proposed relocation, information should be obtained regarding the new location, utilizing pictures of the house (if possible), information on the school and neighborhood, accessibility to family and friends, and so on. Depending on the court order, the evaluator will integrate these data to make a custody recommendation that includes whether the custodial parent should be permitted by the court to relocate, or will just present the data for the court to make the ultimate determination.

COMMUNICATION

REPORT WRITING

The report first presents the identifying information and the authority (e.g. Court Order) under which the evaluation has taken place. Some judges want the report to go only to the attorneys, and do not want to see it until it is formally entered into evidence. Others want to receive the report at the same time as the attorneys, and the relevant instruction is usually included in the court order for the evaluation. The report then lists who was seen, when they were seen, and what procedures were utilized (e.g. interview, testing, home visits). There is a section on records reviewed and interviews of third-party collaterals and the relevant information obtained from these.

When the report moves into the interview, different evaluators approach it somewhat differently. However, the report needs to include from each of the parents his or her account of the history of the marriage and the problems/issues in the marriage, history of child care, and the events that have transpired since the separation. A section is devoted to the results of testing and one to the observations at the home visits. Another section describes the interview and testing of the children. The summary then reviews each salient point and the data that support the evaluator's opinion on each of the points. The evaluator then lays out the recommendation for legal and physical custody. Any recommendation for therapy, co-parenting counseling, mediation, and so on, should also be included. The report should indicate that the opinions are held to a reasonable degree of psychiatric/psychological/scientific certainty, and are based on what the evaluator believes is in the best interest of the children.

TESTIMONY

Many texts, chapters, and articles have been written regarding how a mental health expert should approach testimony (e.g., Hess, 2006), and it is beyond the scope of this chapter to describe that in detail. Thus, only factors specific to testimony in child custody cases will be presented here.

The parties in custody litigation often settle after the report is issued, and therefore testimony is not needed. If it does proceed to court, custody cases present a different situation than criminal and other civil cases. In most other cases, the attorney and the expert should meet to prepare the testimony and discuss anticipated cross-examination. However, in custody cases, whether this is allowed varies by jurisdiction and judge. This is because technically the expert's client is usually not either parent. In some cases, the children will have their own attorney to look out for their interests.

The expert is the court's witness, but the critical focus is ultimately on the children and their best interests. Thus, unless the court order specifically allows the expert to prepare with the attorney whose adult client is "favored" by the report, the expert should refuse. In some cases, the court will stipulate that the expert can meet with the attorney who will call the expert, but only if the attorney for the other parent is present. In other instances, the attorney whose client is not favored will ask the court for a deposition of the expert. Generally, both attorneys will be present for this presentation.

Once the custody evaluator is on the witness stand, the role should not be that of an advocate, but rather a neutral educator of the court. Some judges want a full recitation of what is in the report. However, if the judge has read the report, the court usually requests that the evaluator briefly highlight the findings and recommendations, and then has the other attorney proceed with cross-examination. In addition to being thoroughly familiar with the case file, the evaluator needs to keep up to date on research dealing with the factors related to children's adjustment following divorce, the effects of relocation, and so on.

REFERENCES

Ackerman, M.J., & Ackerman, M. C. (1997). Custody evaluation practices: A survey of experienced professionals (revisited). *Professional Psychology: Research and Practice, 28,* 137–145.

Ackerman, M., & Schoendorf, K. (1992). *ASPECT: Ackerman-Schoendorf Scales for Parent Evaluation of Custody—manual.* Los Angeles, CA: Western Psychological Services.

American Academy of Child and Adolescent Psychiatry. (1997). *American Academy of Child and Adolescent Psychiatry practice parameters for child custody evaluation.* Washington, DC: Author.

American Psychological Association. (2009). *Guidelines for child custody evaluations in family law proceedings*. Washington, DC: Author.

Barnum, R. (2003). Parenting assessment in cases of neglect and abuse. In D. H. Schetky and E. P. Benedek (Ed.), *Principles and practices of child and adolescent forensic psychiatry* (pp. 81–95). Washington, DC: American Psychiatric Publishing.

Benedek, E., & Schetky, D. (1985). Custody and visitation: Problems and perspectives. *Psychiatric Clinics of North America, 8*, 857–873.

Ceci, S., & Bruck, M. (1995). *Jeopardy in the courtroom: A scientific analysis of children's testimony*. Washington, DC: American Psychological Association.

Centers for Disease Control and Prevention. (2005). *Divorces*. Retrieved May 30, 2010, from www.cdc.gov/nchs/fastats/divorce.htm

Derdeyn, A. (1976). Child custody in historical perspective. *American Journal of Psychiatry, 133*, 1369–1375.

Emery, R. E., Otto, R. K., and Donahue, W. T. (2005). A critical assessment of child custody evaluations. *Psychological Service in the Public Interest, 6*, 1–29.

Finlay v. Finlay, 148 N.E. 624 (NY 1925).

Goldstein, J. A., Freud, A., & Solnit, A. M. (1979). *Beyond the best interests of the child*. New York, NY: Free Press.

Gordon, R., & Peek, L. A. (1989). *The Custody Quotient: Research manual*. Dallas, TX: Wilmington Institute.

Grisso, T. (2003). *Evaluating competencies: Forensic assessments and instruments* (2nd ed.). New York, NY: Kluwer Academic/Plenum Press.

Gruber v. Gruber, 583 A.2d. 434 (Pa. Super. 1990).

Hale v. Hale, 429 N.E.2d 340 (Mass. App. 1981).

Hanley, R. (2003, March 5). Accountant accused of hiring hit men to kill his divorce lawyer. *New York Times*, B5.

Herman, S. P. (2003). Child custody evaluations. In D. H. Schetky and E. P. Benedek (Eds.), *Principles and practices of child and adolescent forensic psychiatry* (pp. 69–79). Washington, DC: American Psychiatric Publishing.

Hess, A. K. (2006). Serving as an expert witness. In A. K. Hess & I. B. Weiner (Eds.), *Handbook of forensic psychology* (3rd ed., pp. 652–697). Hoboken, NJ: John Wiley & Sons.

Hughes v. Long et al., 242 F.3d 121 (3rd Circ. 2001).

King, R. P., Douthat, B., & Piloto, C. (2003, November 11). Palm beach divorce turns deadly. *Palm Beach Post*, p. 1A.

Koontz, R. A. (2004, September 16). In the midst of divorce case, wife charged with trying to have husband killed. *Plain Dealer*, p. B5.

Lion, J. R., & Herschler, J. (1998). The stalking of clinicians by their patients. In J. R. Meloy, Jr. (Ed.), *The psychology of stalking: clinical and forensic perspectives* (pp. 163–173). New York, NY: Academic Press.

Martindale, D. A. (2007). Introduction to the Association of Family and Conciliation Courts' Model Standards of Practice for Child Custody Evaluation. *Family Court Review, 45,* 58–60.

Mason, M. A. (1994). *From father's rights to children's rights: The history of child custody in the United States.* New York, NY: Columbia University Press.

Massachusetts Association Opposed to the Extension of Suffrage to Women. (1912). The equal custody of children by parents. Retrieved May 30, 2010, from www.masshist.org/findingaids/doc.cfm?fa= fa0121

Miller, R. D. (1985). Harassment of forensic psychiatrists outside of court. *Bulletin of the American Academy of Psychiatry and the Law, 13,* 337–343.

Morse, D. (2008, November 8). Man fights divorce efforts: MD man accused of killing children. *Washington Post,* p. B2.

Norris, D., & Ferguson, Y. (2003). Transracial and transcultural adoption in the United States. In D. H. Schetky & E. P. Benedek (Eds.), *Principles and practices of child and adolescent forensic psychiatry* (pp. 117–126). Washington, DC: American Psychiatric Publishing.

Norris, D., & Gutheil, T. G. (2003). Harassment and intimidation of forensic psychiatrists: An update. *International Journal of Law and Psychiatry, 26,* 437–445.

Reynolds, C. R., & Kamphaus, R. W. (2004). *Behavior Assessment System for Children, Second Edition (BASC-2).* Circle Pines, MN: AGS Publishing.

Rotter, J. (1950). *Incomplete Sentences Blank.* San Antonio, TX: Psychological Corporation.

Sadoff, R. L., & Billick, S. (1981). The legal rights and difficulties of children and divorce. In I. R. Stuart & L. E. Abt (Eds.), *Children of separation and divorce: Management and treatment* (pp. 4–16). New York, NY: Van Nostrand Reinhold.

Schetky, D., & Haller, L. (1983). Parental kidnapping. *Journal of the American Academy of Child Psychiatry, 22,* 279–285.

Selzer, M. L. (1971). The Michigan Alcohol Screening Test: The quest for a new diagnostic instrument. *American Journal of Psychiatry, 127,* 1653–1658.

Sparta, S. N., & Stahl, P. M. (2006). Psychological evaluation for child custody. In S. N. Sparta & G. P. Koocher (Eds.), *Forensic mental health assessment of children and adolescents* (pp. 203–229). New York, NY: Oxford University Press.

Strasberger, L. H., Gutheil, T. G., & Brodsky, A. (1997). On wearing two hats: Role conflict in serving as both psychotherapist and expert witness. *American Journal of Psychiatry, 154,* 448–458.

Wallerstein, J., & Johnson J. (1990). Children of divorce: recent findings regarding long-term effects and recent studies of joint and sole custody. *Pediatrics in Review, 11,* 197–204.

Wood, J. M., Nezworski, T. M., Lilienfeld, S. O., & Garb, H. N. (2003). *What's wrong with the Rorschach.* San Francisco, CA: Jossey-Bass.

Wright, D. C. (1999). *De Manneville v. De Manneville*: Rethinking the birth of custody law under patriarchy. *Law and History Review, 17,* 247–306.

CHAPTER 20

Americans With Disabilities Act Evaluations

LISA DRAGO PIECHOWSKI and URROOJ REHMAN

INTRODUCTION

The Americans with Disabilities Act (ADA, 1990) and the Americans with Disabilities Act Amendments Act (ADAAA, 2008) are federal laws designed to protect the rights of individuals with disabilities who wish to have access to or participate in certain aspects of American society, including the competitive labor market. Persons who meet the definition of disability under ADA are entitled to protection from discrimination by employers, either for having a disability, having a history of a disability, or being perceived as disabled. ADA evaluations differ from other work-related disability evaluations (e.g., disability benefit eligibility), in that the ADA examinee is seeking continued access to the workplace through the protections accorded under ADA rather than compensation due to an inability to work. In cases of psychiatric disability, forensic psychiatrists and psychologists may be called upon to assist the employer or the court in determining if an individual is disabled according to ADA definitions, and if so, whether the individual is "qualified," that is, able to perform his/her occupational duties with or without accommodations. The evaluator may also be asked to describe the "reasonable accommodations" that would allow the individual to perform the "essential functions" of his/her occupation.

There are several different circumstances under which a forensic evaluation may be sought from a psychologist or psychiatrist. This can occur when an employee identifies him/herself as having a disability and requests accommodations from the employer. For example, after a hospital informs its nurses that they will be required to work rotating shifts, an employee identifies himself as having bipolar disorder and requests the accommodation of being assigned to the day shift only. In other circumstances, an employer would like to accommodate the employee, but is unsure as to what accommodations would be most appropriate and practical. Sometimes, an employer requests an evaluation when the employer seeks to understand the cause of an employee's behavior, especially when this behavior is atypical of the employee, becomes distracting or concerning to other employees, or raises questions of workplace safety. The employer needs to understand if the employee's behavior is due to a disability rather than being a reflection of a lack of motivation, poor interpersonal skills, or willful disregard of rules or expectations. Personality traits (as opposed to personality disorders) and discomfort with general work stress do not constitute disabilities under ADA. Employee behavior that may trigger such an evaluation includes missing time from work, getting into arguments with coworkers or supervisors, making bizarre statements, or acting in a manner that is perceived to be threatening. Finally, an evaluation may be sought when the employee seeks to return to work following a long absence related to mental health issues. This is similar to a "fitness for duty" evaluation (see Chapter 13 in this volume). In this case, the employer may be seeking to know if the employee is now capable of returning to work and if so, whether specific accommodations would be required.

ADA evaluations occur within a complex legal context. Despite having features in common with other disability evaluations, ADA evaluations are unique in that they require strict attention to the particular contours of ADA law. Evaluators must be familiar with the ADA definition of disability and understand concepts such as impairment in major life activities, essential job functions, reasonable accommodations, and direct threat. Stakes in ADA evaluations are high, as the outcome may result in the loss of important civil rights for the examinee. Careful attention must be given to ethical considerations, including objectivity, confidentiality, role conflict, and the duty to warn or protect the examinee or others from imminent harm. The evaluation should be designed to address specific referral questions which typically include determining if there is a diagnosable mental illness as defined by ADA; if there are substantial limitations in major life activities as a result; if the examinee is able to perform the essential functions of job with or without accommodations; describing reasonable accommodations; and/or determining if the examinee presents a direct threat to self or others. These findings should then be communicated to the referral source in the form of a coherent, well-reasoned written report.

PREPARATION

UNDERSTANDING THE LEGAL BACKGROUND

The ADA was enacted in 1990 as an outgrowth of the civil rights movement. The ADA is comprised of five titles: Title I relates to employment discrimination, Title II to public services and transportation, Title III to public accommodations, Title IV to telecommunications, and Title V for miscellaneous provisions. This chapter focuses primarily on issues related to Title I.

The ADA defines *disability* as a physical or mental impairment that substantially limits one or more of the major life activities, a record of such impairment, or being regarded as having such an impairment (42 U.S.C. §12102(2)). Thus, the presence of a *Diagnostic and Statistical Manual of Mental Disorders,* 4th edition, Text Revision (DSM IV-TR) diagnosis by itself does not qualify someone as disabled. The ADA requires that the mental illness must substantially limit one or more major life activities that the average person does every day with little effort such as sleeping, breathing, learning, eating, and so forth. Under ADA, a "qualified individual with a disability" means an individual with a disability who, with or without reasonable accommodation, can perform the essential functions of the employment position that such individual holds or desires. "Essential job functions" are determined by a number of factors including the employer's judgment, a written job description prepared prior to advertising or interviewing applicants for the job, the actual work experience of employees on the job, and collective bargaining agreements. The term *reasonable accommodations* refers to a modification or adjustment to a job, the work environment, or work procedures in order to enable a qualified individual with a disability to enjoy an equal employment opportunity. Examples of reasonable accommodations include making existing facilities readily accessible to and usable by individuals with disabilities, job restructuring, part-time or modified work schedules, reassignment to a vacant position, acquisition or modification of equipment or devices, appropriate adjustment or modifications of examinations, training materials or policies, the provision of qualified readers or interpreters, and other similar accommodations. Employers are not required to provide accommodations that would cause an undue hardship to the employer by involving significant difficulty or expense.

Certain diagnoses or conditions are excluded from coverage under ADA. For example, an employee or applicant who is currently engaging in the illegal use of drugs cannot claim a right to protection under ADA based on substance abuse or dependency. The DSM-IV-TR V-Codes, which include relational stressors and stressful life events, are not considered mental disabilities for the purposes of ADA. In addition, certain conditions related to impulse control or sexual behavior, such as compulsive gambling, kleptomania, pyromania, transvestitism, transsexualism, pedophilia, exhibitionism, voyeurism, and gender identity disorders not resulting from physical impairment, are denied the status of disability in the ADA (42 U.S.C. §§12211(b)(1)–(3)).

Title I does not apply if the individual poses a "direct threat" to self or others in the workplace, if such threat cannot be eliminated through reasonable accommodations. An employer need not hire or retain a person who poses a direct threat. For example, an employer may fire an employee with paranoid personality disorder who threatens to physically injure his/her boss and divulges this plan to a coworker. In contrast, the ADA does not allow an employer who believes that all individuals with mental illnesses are dangerous to refuse to hire an individual with no prior history of violence, simply because that person has a mental illness. In determining if a direct threat is present, factors such as the duration of the risk, severity of potential harm, likelihood of potential harm, and imminence of potential harm should be considered. A history of suicide attempts, a perception of danger by others, or even verbal or written threats alone are not sufficient to establish the presence of direct threat absent a display of recent violent behaviors or a plan to commit violence (Wylonis, 1999).

The ADA was intended to be broad and inclusive, but over time, court rulings led to a narrower interpretation of *disability*. The ADAAA sought to correct this trend. The ADAAA was designed to broaden the scope of coverage and overturned several Supreme Court of the United States decisions that made it difficult to establish the existence of a disability (§2 (a)–(b)). The definition of *disability* was to be construed more broadly, and the term *substantially limits* was to be interpreted as a less demanding standard (§4(1)–(2)). Furthermore, the ADAAA prohibits consideration of mitigating measures such as medication, assistive technology, accommodations, or modifications when determining whether an impairment substantially limits a major life activity. Impairments that are episodic in nature or in remission must be assessed in their active state. The term *major life activities* was defined more specifically (§4(3)). The meaning of *regarded as having an impairment* was clarified such that an individual meets this requirement if the individual establishes that he or she has been subjected to an action prohibited under ADA because of an actual or perceived physical or mental impairment regardless of whether the impairment actually limits, or is perceived to limit, a major life activity (§4(a)(3)(A)).

As noted earlier, the ADA has shaped various Supreme Court decisions since its enactment in 1990. The 1999 decision in *Cleveland v. Policy Management Systems Corporation* highlighted the unique definition of *disability* under ADA as distinct from definitions under other federal programs (specifically Social Security Disability). In *Cleveland*, the plaintiff suffered a stroke and applied for Social Security disability benefits (SSDI). She was denied these benefits when she was able to return to work, but was subsequently awarded SSDI after being terminated from her job. She filed a claim against her employer for failing to provide reasonable accommodations. The employer argued that her statement on her SSDI application (that she was unable to work) prevented her from making a claim that she was a qualified individual with a disability under ADA. The Court disagreed, ruling that an individual who had applied for and/or received Social Security disability benefits would not be automatically precluded from pursuing an employment-related ADA claim. The claimant, however, must be able to explain why these seemingly inconsistent claims (being unable to work and being able to work with accommodations) would be justified.

The "direct threat" provision of ADA was addressed in *Chevron U.S.A., Inc. v. Echazabal* (2002). Specifically, this case spoke to the issue of whether an employer can decline to hire an individual with a disability in a job that would pose a risk to the employee's own health and safety. Chevron had refused to hire Echazabal after his doctor opined that Echazabal's liver condition would be exacerbated by exposure to workplace substances. Echazabal asserted that the ADA should not allow an employer to discriminate against an employee for concerns about his own health and safety. The Court, however, agreed with Chevron's position, noting that an employer that knowingly hired an individual in a position that placed him at risk would be acting in conflict with Occupational Safety and Health Administration (OSHA) mandates to protect employees from harm. The Court found that a determination of *direct threat* should be based on current medical knowledge and an individualized assessment of the employee's or applicant's ability to safely perform the essential functions of the job.

The issue of what constitutes a *substantial limitation* was the basis of the ruling in *Toyota Motor Manufacturing, Kentucky, Inc. v. Williams* (2002). Toyota argued that Williams did not meet the definition of a qualified individual with a disability under ADA since she had failed to demonstrate that her impairment prevented or restricted her from performing tasks that were of central importance to most people's daily lives and had permanent or long-term impact. This ruling set a demanding standard for meeting the definition of disability under ADA, and was expressly addressed in the ADAAA which noted that the *Toyota* court "interpreted the term 'substantially limits' to require a greater degree of limitation than was intended by Congress" (§2(a)(5)(7), (b)(4)–(5)).

Perhaps the most significant Supreme Court decision to date involving ADA issues is *Sutton v. United Air Lines, Inc.* (1999). *Sutton* and two similar cases (*Albertson's, Inc. v. Kirkinburg*, 1999; *Murphy v. United Parcel Service, Inc.*, 1999) dealt with the issue of *mitigating measures*. *Sutton* involved two individuals with nearsightedness who were rejected for jobs as commercial pilots by United for not meeting the airline's uncorrected vision standard. The Court ruled that the plaintiffs were not "disabled" under ADA because they were not "substantially limited" due to the fact that their nearsightedness could be corrected with eyeglasses or contact lenses. The Court found that in determining substantial limitation, corrective measures must be taken into account. Similar reasoning was employed in *Albertson's*, which involved a truck driver with monocular vision, and *Murphy*, which concerned a commercial vehicle driver with high blood pressure. In effect, these rulings allowed employers to terminate or refuse to hire an individual because of a physical or mental condition and subsequently argue that the individual was not "disabled" under ADA because the condition was not serious enough to substantially limit the individual's functioning. Like *Toyota*, *Sutton* was specifically addressed in the ADAAA, which noted that "the purposes of this act are . . . to reject the requirement enunciated by the Supreme Court in [*Sutton*] and its companion cases that whether an impairment substantially limits a major life activity is to be determined with reference to the ameliorative effects of mitigating measures" (§2(b)(2)).

THE REFERRAL

The ADA evaluation process is usually initiated by an employer who is seeking clarification about the employee's status or need for accommodations, from an employee seeking accommodations from an employer, or by the legal representative of either party. As with any forensic evaluation, the first step is for the evaluator to clarify the reason for the referral, the specific questions to be addressed in the evaluation, and the context in which the evaluation will be utilized. Most ADA evaluations occur outside of litigation and many ADA disputes are resolved without further legal action. Although this relieves the evaluator from the need to testify in court, it places a heavier burden on the evaluator, whose work may not be subject to outside review or questioning, to ensure that the evaluation is objective and comprehensive, and that the conclusions are carefully reasoned.

ETHICAL CONSIDERATIONS

Before accepting a referral for an ADA evaluation, there are a number of things the evaluator should consider. ADA evaluations, like most forensic evaluations, require affirmative consideration of ethical issues. These issues, which include objectivity, confidentiality, role conflict, and handling potential threats, should be considered before agreeing to accept the referral and should be revisited frequently during the course of the evaluation.

Objectivity is required of the evaluator regardless of which party is retaining and/or paying for the evaluator's services. Although this may seem straightforward, the evaluator should consider if his or her relationship to or feelings about any party has the potential to compromise objectivity. This is particularly relevant when the evaluator is frequently retained by a specific employer or attorney. The evaluator should be careful to consider how a desire to please or see eye to eye with the referral source might affect his/her ability to perform a fair and impartial evaluation. Threats to objectivity might also arise when the evaluator has strong feelings, for or against, about the inclusion of individuals with disabilities in the workplace. The evaluator must take care not to inject personal opinions or political views into the evaluation process.

Confidentiality is problematic in all forensic evaluations. Although typical doctor–patient expectations of confidentiality are not part of most forensic evaluations, this fact must be made clear to all parties prior to beginning the evaluation. The examinee must indicate his or her understanding and acceptance of this condition. The examinee must be informed as to how the information obtained in the evaluation will be shared and who will and will not have access to these data. Despite the fact that the evaluator will be creating a report that will be shared with the employer, attorneys, or other parties, the evaluator should be careful not to include unnecessary private data that has no direct bearing on the referral questions.

Role conflict arises when the evaluator occupies two distinct roles in relation to either the referral source or the examinee. Not all role conflicts can be (or must be) avoided. The evaluator, however, must be alert to the potential pitfalls that threaten the validity or objectivity of the evaluation. Role conflicts include, for example, situations in which the evaluator is an employee of the entity requesting the evaluation and when the evaluator is currently, or has previously, treated the examinee.

Much has been written about the differences between the roles of independent evaluator and treatment provider (for example, Greenberg & Shuman, 1997; Greenberg & Shuman, 2007; Strasburger, Gutheil, & Brodsky, 1997). Maintaining a therapeutic relationship with a patient can be extremely difficult while acting as an independent evaluator. Likewise, treatment providers are trained to focus on the patient's subjective experience and to treat the patient's condition rather than to focus on the objective and legal contours of the patient's life. Thus, treatment providers may have difficulty functioning as impartial judges of disability for individuals who may be long-standing patients. The treatment provider may feel obliged to advocate for the patient's disability, even when such a stance is not fully warranted by the patient's condition.

Another type of role conflict arises when the evaluator is an employee of the employer requesting the evaluation. This occurs, for example, when the evaluator works in an occupational medicine department established by the employer. Occupational medicine departments typically offer treatment as well as evaluation to employees. It is important to clearly inform the employee about the nature of the evaluator's relationship to the employer, and that in the current circumstance, evaluation, and not treatment, is being provided. It is essential that the evaluator not offer diagnosis or treatment advice to the employee in the course of the evaluation, as this would further blur the distinction between these roles.

Issues of danger to self or others often arise in ADA evaluations. As discussed earlier in this chapter, employers are not required to retain or accommodate an employee who presents a direct threat to others in the workplace. In these situations, the evaluator must balance a number of competing concerns and duties. Most states have laws regarding the "duty to warn" or "duty to protect" when others are directly threatened. These duties are not obviated by the fact that the psychiatrist or psychologist is performing a forensic evaluation. Thus, the evaluator must be prepared to think through and respond to potentially dangerous situations in a manner that protects the rights and well-being of all those concerned and is consistent with the demands of state laws.

PRELIMINARY REVIEW

Once the evaluator has decided to accept a referral for an ADA evaluation, the evaluator should review the information provided by the referral source in order to determine if sufficient material has been provided. The evaluator typically needs to review employment records, the job description, a description of any problematic behavior noted at work, and the employee's medical records. The latter may need to be obtained directly from the employee, as the employer is unlikely to have access to such records. If the employee has made a request for specific accommodations, the evaluator should understand what this entails and the employer's concerns or questions about implementing the requested accommodations. The evaluator should review the referral questions to make sure that he or she understands the specific questions being asked, as well as to determine if the type of evaluation needed is within the scope of the evaluator's training, experience, and knowledge. This will allow the evaluator to plan the actual evaluation process and determine the methods that will be employed. Finally the evaluator should clarify the nature of the feedback being requested by the referral source—that is, whether there will be oral feedback, a written report, or both. The evaluator should be aware of any time constraints or deadlines involved in the evaluation and should make certain that the time frame is realistic.

Informed Consent

Before beginning the actual evaluation, the evaluator must attend to obtaining informed consent from the examinee. The examinee should be clearly informed of the nature and purpose of the evaluation, the expected use of the data obtained, the role of the evaluator relative to the examinee and to the referral source, whether the evaluator will be providing feedback directly to the examinee, and the fact that the evaluation is not being compelled by the evaluator. The evaluator should be certain that the examinee understands this information completely and consents freely to the evaluation before proceeding. It is a wise practice to document this through a signed written consent form.

DATA COLLECTION

Data collection in an ADA evaluation should be directly linked to the purpose of the evaluation and the specific referral questions. In general, ADA evaluations require obtaining data to address one or more of the following issues:

- Is there a diagnosable mental illness as defined by ADA?
- Are there substantial limitations in major life activities as a result?

- Can the examinee perform the essential functions of the job in question with or without accommodations?
- What reasonable accommodations are needed?
- Does the examinee present a direct threat?

As with any forensic evaluation, the use of multiple data sources is recommended. The data sources typically utilized in an ADA evaluation include information obtained from written records and documents, from interviewing collateral sources, from the examinee in the clinical interview, and psychometric test data.

Records and Collateral Data

Written records can be very helpful in establishing the examinee's condition and functioning over time. These records include those related to the examinee's condition, such as medical records; records related to the examinee's baseline functioning, such as school records or previous employment records; and records related to the examinee's current functional capacity, such as recent employment evaluations. The evaluator should also review a detailed written job description in order to determine the core duties of the examinee's job. If the examinee has been involved in any disciplinary action at work, the evaluator should review the relevant written documentation, as well as any documentation generated by the examinee, such as grievances, complaints, or requests for accommodations.

Beyond written records, the evaluator should consider directly interviewing collateral sources such as treatment providers, supervisors, coworkers, and/or family members. Interviews have certain advantages over written documentation in that this more dynamic format allows the evaluator to address specific questions or areas of concern that may be absent in written records. Collateral interviews can occur either before or after meeting with the examinee. The examinee's consent should be obtained prior to contacting potential collateral sources.

Clinical Interview

The clinical interview is the core of an ADA evaluation. The evaluator should be sure to allot sufficient time for this interview. This will allow the evaluator to obtain the examinee's history and information about the examinee's current situation and concerns, and to directly observe the examinee's behavior, presentation, and responses. A complete mental status examination should be documented. The examinee should be asked about the onset of his or her condition, treatments and treatment outcomes, periods of exacerbation and remission, and current symptoms. It is essential to elicit information about how the manifestations of the examinee's condition affect his or her functioning in all areas of life, including social, educational, personal, and occupational. If applicable, the examinee should be asked about the nature of the accommodations being sought and how these accommodations relate to the manifestations of the examinee's condition and the performance of essential job duties. If the evaluation was prompted by a particular incident in the workplace, the employee should be asked about this event.

PSYCHOMETRIC ASSESSMENT

Psychological and/or neuropsychological testing may be useful in an ADA evaluation, but it is important to differentiate between examinees who are job applicants and examinees who are employees. The use of preemployment examinations to potentially screen out applicants with disabilities is prohibited by ADA, including psychological tests that are used to support a diagnostic determination. Thus, psychological testing must be used very cautiously with job applicants. However, when examining individuals who are already employed, psychological testing may provide useful information related to establishing a diagnosis, understanding current symptoms, or determining the examinee's functional capacity relative to the job requirements. Testing may be especially relevant when the examinee is reporting a disability related to cognitive functioning, such as attention deficit/hyperactivity disorder (ADHD), or when the evaluator is attempting to distinguish personality traits from true psychopathology.

DATA INTERPRETATION

The evaluator must now interpret the evaluation data in order to respond to the referral questions. As noted previously, referral questions typically relate to the presence of a diagnosable condition, the effects of this condition on the examinee's functioning, the examinee's ability to perform essential job functions, the need for and nature of accommodations, and/or whether the employee presents a risk of harm.

DIAGNOSIS

The definition of *disability* under ADA is specific and is not synonymous with definitions related to other federal programs (such as SSDI). *Disability* under ADA is defined as "a physical or mental impairment that substantially limits one or more of the major life activities of such individual; a record of such an impairment; or being regarded as having such an impairment" (42 USC §12102(2)). Thus, the starting point in determining if an examinee meets the ADA definition of disability is to establish the examinee's specific diagnosis(es). The DSM (current edition) should be the basis for reaching diagnostic conclusions. The examinee's presentation should be compared to the diagnostic criteria listed in the DSM. Diagnostic opinions should be supported by a description of the examinee's symptoms as they relate to these criteria. As noted previously, not all DSM diagnoses are recognized as disabilities under the ADA. Exclusions include many impulse control disorders (e.g., kleptomania), sexual disorders (e.g., pedophilia), and all V-Codes. Personality traits (as opposed to personality disorders) do not meet the ADA definition of disability. Although substance abuse/dependence can form the basis for ADA protection, current on-the-job use of alcohol or drugs is not protected, assuming the employer forbids this and applies the same rules to all employees. In addition, a remote history of alcohol or drug abuse, absent recent use, is not considered a disability under ADA.

FUNCTIONAL IMPAIRMENT

The ADA definition of disability includes a functional component. The diagnosed condition must substantially limit one or more major life activities. What constitutes a *major life activity* was first described in the ADA and subsequently expanded upon in the ADAAA. Examples of major life activities include caring for oneself, performing manual tasks, walking, seeing, hearing, speaking, breathing, learning, working, sitting, standing, lifting, and mental and emotional processes such as thinking, concentrating, and interacting with others. A substantial limitation is one that restricts an individual's ability to perform a major life activity as compared to the ability of the average person in the general population to perform the same activity. The ADAAA includes language noting that mitigating measures, including assistive devices, auxiliary aids, accommodations, and medical therapies and supplies have no bearing in determining whether a disability qualifies under the law. The ADA also requires that conditions that are episodic or in remission, such as epilepsy or post-traumatic stress disorder, be assessed in their active state. With this in mind, the evaluator must determine if the examinee's condition substantially limits the performance of one or more life activities. The evaluator's opinion should be supported by clear examples of how the examinee's functioning is limited by his/her condition. For example, in the case of depression, "feeling sad" would not describe a functional impairment, but "diminished concentration resulting in an inability to comprehend written instructions" would meet this criterion. If possible, multiple examples should be given of the examinee's functional limitations, including those not related to the work setting.

CAUSATION

The causal connection between the examinee's diagnosed condition and the difficulties being experienced in the workplace must be explored. Sometimes an employee with a disability may be experiencing problems at work that are unrelated to the condition. For example, an employee with documented depression may start coming in to work late. It must be determined if this tardiness is due to impairment from the depression or to some other issue. Changes in work behavior can be related to personal problems, lack of interest in one's job, personality conflicts with coworkers, and financial issues, among others. Accommodations are warranted only if the employee's difficulties are directly related to the disabling condition.

WORK CAPACITY

Employers are not required to accommodate an employee who cannot perform the essential job functions. Essential functions are the core duties of a job in contrast to peripheral duties. For example, an essential job duty of an elementary school teacher is to instruct students individually and in groups, using various teaching methods such as lectures, discussions, and demonstrations. A peripheral job duty would be creating attractive bulletin boards in the classroom.

Therefore, the evaluator needs to have a clear understanding of the essential duties of the examinee's job and the education and training requirements. This information should be obtained from a careful review of the job description and from discussion with the employer. In addition to being able to perform the essential job duties, the employee must have the requisite education and training to perform the job in question. The employer is not required to accommodate an employee who does not meet these basic job requirements. For example, someone applying for a job as an elementary school teacher wouldn't be considered qualified if he or she lacked the relevant teacher certification. Likewise, a position requiring the visual inspection of parts in a factory could not be performed by someone who is blind. With the data obtained through the evaluation process, the evaluator should compare the examinee's work capacity to the requirements of the job in question.

ACCOMMODATIONS

If the examinee meets all three criteria discussed above (diagnosed condition, substantial limitations in major life activities, ability to perform essential job functions), he or she would be considered a qualified person with a disability. An employer is required to provide "reasonable accommodations" to enable an employee with a disability to maintain his or her job unless to do so would be an "undue hardship." Although it is not the evaluator's role to determine whether or not an accommodation is "reasonable," evaluators are often asked to suggest accommodations that would allow the employee to continue working. The evaluator should have some sense of the types of accommodations that are most likely to be considered reasonable. To suggest accommodations that are unrealistic or impractical would do little to assist either the employer or the employee. For example, if an employee with an anxiety disorder becomes agitated when working in an open area, it might be a reasonable accommodation to relocate the employee's work station to a quieter area. However, promoting the employee to a manager's job so that she could have a private office is not likely to be considered a reasonable accommodation. The evaluator should consider types of accommodations such as allowing the employee to take more frequent breaks, giving the employee written instead of verbal directions, allowing time off or flexible scheduling to attend psychiatric appointments, moving the employee's work station, or transferring the employee to another position of the same level, if available. Gold and Shuman (2009) described a number of accommodations that are not considered "reasonable." These include creating a new position, eliminating essential job functions, reducing performance standards, eliminating performance evaluations, providing a "stress-free" work environment, altering a position to reduce stress, excusing an employee from uniformly applied disciplinary policies, reassigning or transferring another employee or supervisor, promoting the employee, arranging a transfer if no vacant positions are available, providing erratic or indefinite leave, and providing treatment for or monitoring of the employee's condition. These lists are far from exhaustive. Recommendations for accommodations should be individualized and based on the employee's specific limitations, nature of the job, and options realistically available to the employer.

THREAT ASSESSMENT

An employee who poses a direct threat to the health and safety of self or others in the workplace is not considered a qualified person under ADA. Sometimes the evaluator will be asked to determine if the examinee does pose such a threat. In doing so, the evaluator should consider nature and severity of the potential harm, the duration of the risk, the likelihood that harm will occur, and the imminence of the potential harm. It is important to differentiate between real and perceived threats, such as when coworkers or supervisors misinterpret manifestations of mental illness as threatening when they are not.

Assessing potential threat is inherently difficult. In essence, the evaluator is being asked to predict the likelihood that some behavior will occur in the future. In terms of the potential for self-harm, the evaluator should assess not only suicidal ideation and history, but also the potential for other types of self-injurious behavior. In addition to intentional self-harm, the evaluator should consider whether other aspects of the employee's condition are likely to put him or her in danger. For example, an employee who needs to take sedating psychotropic medications during the work day might need to avoid operating heavy machinery or driving a vehicle. When danger to others is the focus of concern, the evaluator may want to employ instruments designed to assist in collecting information relevant to the assessment of threat in the workplace. For example, the Workplace Assessment of Violence Risk (WAVR-21) is a 21-item checklist that identifies static and dynamic risk factors associated with workplace targeted or intended violence (White & Meloy, 2007).

It is important to keep in mind that *direct threat*, as defined in ADA, refers to "a significant risk of substantial harm to the health or safety of the individual or others that cannot be eliminated or reduced by reasonable accommodation" (42 U.S.C. §12113(b)). A finding of direct threat must be based on objective, factual evidence, rather than on subjective perceptions, irrational fears, or stereotypes about people with disabilities. It is important to carefully document the evidence that supports the evaluator's opinion. In doing so, the evaluator should describe the nature and severity of the potential harm, the duration of the risk, the likelihood that harm will occur, and the imminence of the potential harm. Specific examples or behavioral descriptions are very useful. If the threat is such that it could be reduced or eliminated by specific accommodations or interventions, this should be noted and the relevant accommodations described.

Finally, if the evaluator determines that a direct threat does exist, he or she must take immediate action, as necessary, to ensure the safety of the examinee or others. This could include, among other things, notifying the employer or law enforcement authorities or arranging for emergency psychiatric care for the examinee. If valid safety concerns exist, the evaluator should never delay the release of this information until the written report is completed.

COMMUNICATION

A written report is usually expected at the conclusion of the evaluation. The report should be clear, succinct, and without reliance on professional jargon. All sources of information should be cited. The evaluator should include information about the history of the examinee's condition, past and current treatments, the impact of the condition on major life activities, current functioning, the need for accommodations, and suggestions for accommodations (if requested).

In communicating the evaluation findings to the referral source, it is essential to frame the findings in language consistent with ADA definitions and rules. Failure to do so can lead to misperceptions or misrepresentations of the evaluator's opinions. At the same time, the evaluator should remember that he or she is not being asked to render a legal determination of disability, but is providing an expert psychological or psychiatric opinion to the employer or to the court regarding the issues in question.

Organizing the report into sections facilitates comprehension and clarity. The report should begin with identifying information and describe the source, context, and specific purpose for the referral. There should be a statement documenting that informed consent was obtained from the examinee. The report should then list all sources of information utilized in the evaluation, including written records, collateral sources, and (if applicable) psychological and neuropsychological testing procedures.

The evaluator should next present the data obtained in the course of the evaluation. In doing so, the evaluator should avoid interjecting opinions or conclusions at this point in the report, as this often confuses the reader. The evaluator should provide a detailed description of the clinical interview and behavioral observations of the examinee. Information obtained from records and collaterals should be summarized and clearly attributed to its source. This is particularly important, as information obtained from different sources may be inconsistent or contradictory. Psychological test data should be presented so that they are comprehensible to a lay reader. It is best to avoid relying on statistical concepts to explain test findings. A better approach is to use descriptive language, such as "average" or "poor."

The report should then address the interpretation of data. This section is shaped by the specific questions the evaluator was asked to address. If this includes establishing the presence of a disabling condition, a full DSM-IV-TR diagnosis should be provided. Specific functional limitations resulting from the diagnosed condition should be described in detail. As noted by Gold and Shuman (2009), it is important to include specific examples regarding impairments, functional capacity, and limitations. Discussion of impairments should not be limited to the workplace, but should include limitations experienced in all aspects of the examinee's life. The report should indicate that determination of whether an impairment substantially limited the examinee's performance of major life activities was made without consideration of mitigating measures such as medication, assistive technology, accommodations, or modifications.

The examinee's capacity to perform the essential functions of his/her job should be discussed. The evaluator should make reference to the job description and list what he/she considers to be the essential job functions. The examinee's ability to perform each function should be described. The evaluator should discuss whether these functions could be performed with and without accommodations.

If assessment of threat was requested as part of the evaluation, the evaluator must include discussion of this in the report regardless of whether the evaluator believes such a threat exists. The nature, duration, and severity of the threat should be described. If applicable, specific recommendations to reduce this risk should be outlined. If the evaluator determines that no valid threat exists, this should be explicitly stated. The evaluator may also wish to describe alternative interpretations of the employee's behavior that was mistakenly perceived to be threatening.

The evaluator may be asked to suggest reasonable accommodations that would allow the examinee to perform his or her job. These suggestions are most useful if they are described in sufficient detail, are practical, and are not unnecessarily costly. It is helpful, when possible, to suggest several different accommodations to address the issues. This gives the employer some alternatives should one of the suggestions prove to be unworkable.

REFERENCES

ADA Amendments Act of 2008 (ADAAA), P.L. 110–325 (2008).

Albertson's, Inc. v. Kirkinburg, 527 U.S. 555 (1999).

Americans with Disabilities Act of 1990 (ADA), 42 U.S.C. §§12101 et seq. (1990).

Chevron U.S.A., Inc. v. Echazabal, 536 U.S. 73 (2002).

Cleveland v. Policy Management Systems Corporation, 526 U.S. 795 (1999).

Gold, L., & Shuman, D. (2009). *Evaluating mental health disability in the workplace*. New York, NY: Springer.

Greenberg, S., & Shuman, D. (1997) Irreconcilable conflict between therapeutic and forensic roles. *Professional Psychology: Research & Practice, 28,* 50–57.

Greenberg, S., & Shuman, D. (2007). When worlds collide: Therapeutic and forensic roles. *Professional Psychology: Research & Practice, 38,* 129–132.

Murphy v. United Parcel Service, Inc., 527 U.S. 516 (1999).

Strasburger, L., Gutheil, T. G., & Brodsky, A. (1997). On wearing two hats: Role conflict in serving both as therapist and expert witness. *American Journal of Psychiatry, 154,* 448–456.

Sutton v. United Air Lines, Inc., 527 U.S. 471 (1999).

Toyota Motor Manufacturing, Kentucky, Inc. v. Williams, 534 U.S. 184 (2002).

White, S., & Meloy, R. (2007). *The Workplace Assessment of Violence Risk (WAVR-21).* San Diego, CA: Specialized Training Services.

Wylonis, L. (1999) Psychiatric disability, employment and the Americans with Disabilities Act. *Psychiatric Clinics of North America, 22,* 147–158.

CHAPTER 21

Civil Commitment

DAVID F. MRAD and CLARENCE WATSON

INTRODUCTION

Within the United States, individual jurisdictions have long held the power to commit their mentally ill citizens to institutions under two broad authorities, *parens patriae* and police power. The power of the state to commit individuals who are incapable of caring for themselves evolved from a similar authority held by English kings to act as "general guardian to all infants, idiots, and lunatics" (Harvard Law Review Association, 1974, p. 1207). In the United States, that authority as applied to the mentally ill was upheld by the Massachusetts Supreme Judicial Court in the 1845 decision *In re Oakes* (Harvard Law Review Association). That decision established the groundwork for future courts to involuntarily commit the mentally ill for treatment and protection from harm (Perlin, 1989).

The "police power" of the state is its "inherent power to protect the public," and is used to protect society's interest rather than the interest of the committed patient (Harvard Law Review Association, 1974). In the 1905 Supreme Court of the United States decision, *Jacobson v. Commonwealth of Massachusetts*, the constitutional authority of the state to exercise its police power was established when the Court upheld a state law requiring citizens to be vaccinated for smallpox. Technically, it is this power, which authorizes states to prevent individuals from engaging in activities harmful to themselves and others, that permits states to commit individuals who are actively suicidal but not otherwise incapable of caring for themselves.

Application of these powers was rarely overseen or restricted by the courts until the 1970s. During that decade, critical decisions, such as *Jackson v. Indiana* (1972), *Lessard v. Schmidt* (1972), *O'Connor v. Donaldson* (1975), and *Addington v. Texas* (1979) reshaped the landscape of civil commitment (Mrad & Nabors, 2006). States could no longer commit individuals simply because they were mentally ill and in need of treatment, and the commitment process required much more judicial oversight with many more constitutional protections.

PREPARATION

The process of determining whether to utilize civil commitment laws is complex due to variation in case specific factors, limitations in clinicians' ability to predict future violent or suicidal behaviors, and the impact on establishing a therapeutic alliance with the patient. Fundamentally, these determinations require knowledge of civil commitment criteria in a given jurisdiction, which vary from state to state. Regardless of the jurisdiction, the essential requirements of civil commitment laws include the presence of mental illness and a degree of risk of harm to the patient or to others due to the patient's mental illness (Bagby, Thompson, Dickens, & Nohara, 1991). The ever-present tightrope between the patient's need for psychiatric treatment and the patient's guaranteed civil liberty rights must be carefully traversed by the clinician. Within this context, clinicians must be prepared to evaluate the patient's current symptoms and collect relevant historical information when a patient may be unable or unwilling to cooperate fully with the examination.

THE REFERRAL

Most often an evaluation for civil commitment comes about during a crisis situation where a patient is believed to be at risk of harming him/herself or others. In such situations, the patient may be brought to the emergency department by ambulance, police, family, or friends after expressing the intent to engage in or actually engaging in self-injurious or violent behaviors. Similarly, a patient may be referred by their outpatient treating clinician with concerns about the need for involuntary psychiatric treatment. These situations typically rely on emergency civil commitment laws, which may be initiated by clinicians without an initial court determination. Such emergency commitment without a court hearing allows immediate and necessary treatment interventions to be implemented in urgent situations.

A patient may also require evaluation for civil commitment during an inpatient psychiatric hospitalization. This may occur in at least three distinct ways. First, a patient who was previously committed on an emergency basis may need to have the civil commitment extended beyond the provisional period allowed by the emergency commitment. An evaluation of the patient's ongoing need for involuntary treatment beyond the initial emergency period will be required to continue the civil commitment. As a safeguard, statutes require a judicial review process to weigh the need for continued involuntary commitment versus patients' right to exercise their civil liberties. Second, a patient who was initially hospitalized voluntarily may at some point refuse further treatment and request immediate discharge against medical advice. Under these circumstances, the continuation of treatment against the patient's wishes will require an evaluation for civil commitment. Finally, in some states where an inpatient has been adequately stabilized but has a history of treatment noncompliance and frequent hospitalizations, an evaluation for outpatient civil commitment may be initiated prior to discharge into the community (Appelbaum, 2005).

In addition to the standard civil commitment laws that apply to the general public, some states have specialized civil commitment laws that provide involuntary treatment for violent sex offenders who pose an ongoing risk of danger at the completion of their criminal sentences (*Kansas v. Hendricks*, 1997). Under these specialized statutes, incarcerated sex offenders are referred for evaluation prior to their release into the community to determine if various criteria for commitment are present, including the number of previous sexual offenses, the severity of those offenses, a congenital or acquired mental abnormality, and dangerousness.

DETERMINING THE PROPER FOCUS AND SCOPE OF THE EVALUATION

The focus and scope of the evaluation is dependent on the relevant statutory provisions for civil commitment in each state jurisdiction. As these provisions vary, it is critical that clinicians be intimately familiar with the civil commitment laws of the jurisdictions in which they practice. For example, while statutes usually require that mental illness places a patient in substantial or imminent risk of danger to harm himself or others, some jurisdictions vary on whether an overt dangerous act is required or if "grave disability" or "inability to care for oneself" is required (Schwartz, Mack, & Zeman, 2003). Knowledge of the relevant statutory scheme for civil commitment will allow the clinician to delineate the pertinent details of a patient's clinical presentation and psychiatric history during these assessments.

Additionally, a number of jurisdictions require that involuntary treatment be provided via *the least restrictive alternative*, which is dependent on the patient's clinical presentation (*Lake v. Cameron*, 1966). Accordingly, the clinician's evaluation must consider potential alternatives to involuntary inpatient hospitalization, such as day treatment programs, group home placement, or other outpatient settings as appropriate. Such an analysis requires the clinician to examine factors such as the stability of available social supports, the success or failure of treatment in similar settings historically, and the severity of the patient's current psychiatric symptoms.

TIMING OF THE EVALUATION

The timing of the evaluation is often dictated by the emergence of severe psychiatric symptoms that carry a high risk of dangerousness; therefore, the clinician often assesses the patient on an emergency basis. Depending on the patient's symptoms, for example, acute agitation and self-injurious or violent behaviors, the clinician must take measures to optimize safety for the patient and staff prior to initiating the examination. Such measures may include minimizing environmental stimuli or administering emergency medications to decrease agitation. Such interventions may also improve the patient's ability to participate meaningfully in the clinical interview. Similarly, demands by a voluntary patient for immediate hospital discharge against medical advice will compel the clinician to consider civil commitment prior to discharge. An evaluation for outpatient civil commitment, on the other hand, may take place at any point during the initial hospitalization as part of the discharge planning process.

COLLATERAL INFORMATION

It is critical for the clinician to obtain relevant collateral information regarding the patient's recent symptoms and behaviors, social stressors, and psychiatric history in order to assess adequately the need for civil commitment. In situations where the patient is uncooperative with the examination, family, friends, and outpatient providers must be contacted for such information. Regardless of the patient's level of cooperation, the clinician should not rely solely on the patient's account of recent events leading to the evaluation, as there may be motivation to minimize significant historical details to avoid treatment. As these evaluations usually occur in the context of an emergency, collateral information should be sought even in the absence of the patient's consent.

It should be noted that in situations where an individual is suicidal, there exists an inherent conflict in the clinician–patient relationship; the clinician is viewed as an obstacle to the patient's desired outcome. Consequently, the patient's family, friends, and outpatient treating clinician may provide the most accurate information to aid the clinician in the assessment. In addition, police officers and paramedics who accompany the patient to the emergency department may possess critical information regarding the patient's recent behaviors or statements that may also guide the clinical determination of the need for civil commitment.

ETHICAL ISSUES

Given the inherently intrusive nature of involuntary treatment on individuals' civil liberty rights, clinicians have an ethical obligation to base their decisions on clinical factors that directly relate to the relevant statutory criteria for civil commitment. Accordingly, clinicians must exercise due diligence in obtaining all relevant clinical data prior to a determination for the need to civilly commit an individual. This further requires the clinician to remain aware of legislative changes to the commitment laws in their jurisdiction.

As with other areas in the doctor–patient relationship, the clinician is under an ethical obligation to avoid unnecessary breaches of confidentiality in the absence of the patient's consent (American Psychiatric Association, 2009). However, testimony and communications to mental health courts as required by law for the purposes of civil commitment are permitted without patient consent. Throughout the evaluation process, some patients may experience negative emotions, as they perceive that their liberties have been stripped away. Treating clinicians must remain cognizant of these concerns and make efforts to preserve patient dignity and foster the therapeutic alliance as appropriate.

THE EXAMINER'S COMPETENCY

Depending on the jurisdiction—and often at the sole discretion of the presiding judge—the type of clinician who is legally qualified to examine a patient for the purpose of emergency civil commitment may be a licensed physician, clinical psychologist, or psychiatric nurse (Schwartz et al., 2003). Continued civil commitment beyond the emergency period allowed by the relevant statute often requires an examination by a licensed physician, such as a psychiatrist. Accordingly, depending on the clinician's background, they will be subject to the ethical requirements of their specific profession. Regardless of the specific credentials required by each jurisdiction, clinicians must have knowledge of the various risk factors for suicide, violence, and inability to care for oneself in the setting of mental illness. Clinicians must also have a working knowledge of the relevant civil commitment laws in their jurisdiction to consider properly those risk factors prior to initiating civil commitment procedures. This is particularly important in order to avoid the haphazard disregard of patient's civil rights in the absence of a careful risk assessment.

CONFIDENTIALITY

The clinician's obligation to protect the patient's confidentiality persists at all stages of the civil commitment process. While the emergent nature of evaluations for civil commitment may require the clinician to contact the patient's family members and friends for collateral information, care must still be taken to minimize unnecessary disclosures of the patient's confidential information. However, professional ethical standards allow the clinician to determine whether disclosures are necessary in light of emergency situations that the civil commitment process usually involves (Appelbaum & Gutheil, 2007). Further, communication of protected information to persons authorized by statute in order to facilitate the civil commitment process is permitted.

DATA COLLECTION

Determining What Information Is Needed

As with all forensic evaluations, the information necessary to address the referral issue goes beyond a simple clinical interview and must encompass several key areas, many of which cannot be assessed by interview alone. The exact nature of the information needed is dependent on the jurisdiction. For instance, some state statutes require a recent overt act to prove that there is a risk of dangerousness, while others do not (Melton, Petrila, Poythress, & Slobogin, 2007). This is one of the many reasons that examiners must be familiar with the statutes and rules of the jurisdictions in which they work, in order to properly address the relevant commitment criteria. Werth (2001) reviewed the commitment criteria of all the states and focused specifically on the self-harm criteria. All of the states required a diagnosed mental illness and a documentation of danger to self or others for commitment. At least minimal definitions of the necessary type of mental illness were provided by 44 jurisdictions. Thirty-four of these had explicit descriptions of dangerousness to self. Most of the jurisdictions required that the dangerousness to self be a direct result of the mental illness, and some also required that the patient be incapable of making reasonable treatment decisions.

Mental Disorder

This is perhaps the area in which psychiatrists and psychologists usually feel most comfortable and confident. It is a mainstay of traditional clinical training. For that same reason, most are likely to feel little need for guidance in collecting data to make this determination. Nevertheless, there are a few important points to consider. Does the state specify or define the types of disorders that qualify for commitment or alternatively are some disorders specifically excluded or addressed by some alternate procedure? Parry (1994) summarized the standards for extended commitment in all 50 states and the District of Columbia and found that the types of disorders typically had to be "severe" or "gross." He found that many jurisdictions specifically excluded some disorders, most frequently "mental retardation, epilepsy, developmental disabilities, drug addiction, and alcoholism" (p. 323).

The reliability of a diagnosis is also more important in civil commitment assessments than in traditional clinical practice. It is important that the examiner consider the criteria established in *Diagnostic and Statistical Manual of Mental Disorders*, 4th edition, Text Revision (DSM-IV-TR; American Psychiatric Association, 2000). In standard clinical practice, clinicians may reach diagnostic impressions quickly based on a few key symptoms and vast experience. When offering a diagnosis that will be used as a qualifying mental disorder for the patient's loss of liberty, it is incumbent on the examiner to be able to address the accepted criteria, either to demonstrate their presence or to explain why a patient may still have the disorder in their absence.

Typically, in the context of civil commitment evaluations, examiners might expect a defensive presentation on the part of the patient but are less likely to expect or consider exaggeration or feigning of symptoms. Although such a presentation is much less likely, it does sometimes occur, most commonly when the patient is without resources and seeking a place to provide for their basic necessities or a record to support disability claims. For that reason, examiners should not disregard typical indicia of malingering (e.g., atypical presentations or inconsistencies in presentation or history).

DANGER TO SELF

As with diagnosing mental disorders, assessing risk of suicide is a common experience in most clinical practice. It is often a key component in a civil commitment assessment. Reviewing the factors related to increased risk of suicide is beyond the scope of this chapter and can be found in many other places in the literature (American Psychiatric Association, 2003; Mrad & Nabors, 2006). We will summarize some of the key factors that should be considered in assessing suicide risk. Those factors might be categorized as:

- *Mental disorders.* Although the presence of a qualifying mental disorder has already been mentioned as a requirement for commitment, the nature and severity of the mental disorder is also a consideration in the determination of suicide risk. Evaluators should be considering the following diagnostic issues. Does the patient suffer from a major mood disorder or schizophrenia? The presence of depressive disorders is widely recognized as being associated with a higher risk of suicide. More specifically, and perhaps more importantly, a high degree of hopelessness more than depression alone has been shown to be a good predictor of suicide attempts. Additionally, the evaluator should consider whether a depressed patient also has symptoms of anxiety or agitation, since the presence of anxiety has been shown to increase the risk of suicide in depressed patients. Schizophrenia, particularly paranoid type or schizophrenia accompanied by depressive symptoms also presents a greater risk of suicide. Does the patient have a substance abuse/dependence problem? The presence of substance abuse, especially the abuse of alcohol and sedative drugs has also been associated with an increased risk. Additionally, the evaluator should consider whether the patient has an underlying personality disorder, since borderline, antisocial, avoidant, and dependent personality disorders have been associated with higher suicide risk.

- *Demographic characteristics.* Clinicians are commonly aware of the typical demographic characteristics that are associated with increased risk for completed suicide but, of course, must not rely too heavily on these group differences when making individual risk assessments. These factors can augment but not replace a thorough individualized suicide risk assessment. Although women have a higher rate of suicide attempts, men (who generally use more lethal means) are at greater risk of completing suicide. Caucasians consistently have a higher suicide rate than most other racial groups. As a group, the elderly are at greater risk of suicide than younger adults, but there seems to be an interaction among demographic factors in that African American males are at greater risk in young adulthood than old age.

- *Previous attempts and current ideation.* The evaluator should ask about current suicidal ideation and past suicide attempts, recognizing that more reliable information about the latter might be obtained from collateral sources. Past suicide attempts and other self-harm behavior have been shown to be an especially good predictor of suicide, but the patient may be embarrassed or resistant to acknowledging this behavior. When patients acknowledge past attempts, a number of questions arise.

How recent were the past attempts? What was the lethality of the attempts? What, if any, factors precipitated the attempts? Did the patient demonstrate ambivalence by seeking assistance, or were they discovered as the result of some unexpected event (e.g., spouse arriving home early)?

Some patients will acknowledge the act but mischaracterize it as unintentional, such as an accidental overdose of some drug of abuse or a vehicular accident. In these instances, family or friends may be able to provide context to better assess the actual intent.

The evaluator must also consider current suicidal ideation, about which the same collateral sources are of much less utility. The evaluator should consider several issues in exploring suicidal ideation. How frequent are the suicidal thoughts? Does the patient quickly dismiss them or dwell on them? Are the thoughts about suicide specific and detailed? Has the patient considered a method? Have they contemplated a specific time or place? Have they rehearsed or initiated some portion of the plan?

- *Social support.* In general, patients living alone and those having no family or friends are at greater risk for suicide. Additionally, supportive family and friends can provide important collateral information and potential assistance in alternatives to commitment. The presence of family members, however, is not always a protective factor. Family conflicts are often precipitating events for suicide attempts. Evaluators should inquire about the quality of the relationships. Are there ongoing conflicts? Have there been physical altercations? Do conflicts lead to alcohol abuse?
- *Other risk factors.* Although a number of idiosyncratic factors might also need consideration in each specific case, there are some additional factors that should be routinely considered. Does the patient have a history of poor impulse control or is he/she currently suffering from a disorder that promotes impulsivity? Particularly if the patient is facing a number of situational stressors, his/her problem-solving skills or deficits should be evaluated. Because religious devoutness, regardless of denomination, has been linked to lower suicide rates, the evaluator should explore the patient's religious beliefs. Does he/she identify with a specific religion? What are the religion's tenets concerning afterlife and suicide? Does he/she regularly

attend church services; how firmly does he/she adhere to religious beliefs? Finally, examiners should routinely consider the availability of firearms. Even if a patient is not reporting a specific suicide plan involving firearms, the presence of a firearm increases the potential for lethal attempts.

Evaluators may find two resources particularly helpful in conducting assessment of suicide risk. The first is the *Practice Guideline for the Assessment and Treatment of Patients With Suicidal Behaviors* (American Psychiatric Association, 2003), available on the American Psychiatric Association website. This guide can serve as an excellent information gathering structure to assist the clinician in considering the relevant risk factors. Another useful resource is the book *How to Identify Suicidal People* (White, 1999).

GRAVE DISABILITY

As Melton et al. (2007) point out, all states provide for commitment of individuals who present a risk to themselves not from suicide but from grave disability—an inability to meet their basic needs. How *grave disability* is defined varies from state to state and once again emphasizes the importance of specific knowledge of the rules in one's jurisdiction. Typically, the examiner will be inquiring or observing to determine whether patients are capable of engaging in basic activities of daily living. Can they feed, clothe, and clean themselves? Can they provide for their shelter and properly attend to basic medical needs? In regard to the latter, the examiner may have to assess the patient's capacity for making medical treatment decisions. The examiner may be able to obtain information from collateral sources about the patient's actual behavior in caring for his or her needs. To assess the patient's decision-making capacity regarding treatment, the examiner might consider using the MacArthur Competence Assessment Tool—Treatment (MacCAT-T), a semistructured interview designed to assist in assessing a patient's ability to make rational treatment decisions (Grisso & Appelbaum, 1998).

DANGER TO OTHERS

In the past two decades, perhaps no area of forensic practice has received more attention, both in terms of research and practice recommendations, than the assessment of risk to others. While the work is far from over, the substantial progress generated in this area might be best demonstrated by the contrast between two landmark works by John Monahan and others (Monahan, 1981; Monahan et al., 2001). As with suicide risk, the literature in this area is far beyond the scope of this chapter. Excellent reviews can be found in Melton et al. (2007) and Conroy and Murrie (2007). The latter text also provides a useful model for conceptualizing and conducting risk assessments. That model emphasizes several considerations about the referral question that are critical in civil commitment risk assessments. For instance, the examiner should be considering the time period covered by the prediction, the type of violence and the causal connection with a qualifying mental condition. The examiner would want to know how imminent a risk of violence must be to qualify for commitment in their state. He or she needs to know if a specific type of violence risk, such as "bodily injury," is required, and also must know what sort of causal relationship to a specific type of mental disorder is required. For instance, in a very specific subset of civil commitments, sexual predator commitments, a qualified risk might arise from a "personality disorder or abnormal mental condition" (*Kansas v. Hendricks*, 1997). In traditional civil commitments, a jurisdiction might require a causal relationship between violence risk and some specified condition, such as a "severe mental disease or defect."

Once an examiner knows the specifics of the civil commitment referral question, he/she faces the task of determining what information is necessary to render a professionally responsible opinion. One of the controversies generated by the advance in research and development of risk assessment instruments is whether assessments of violence risk are best done by clinical judgment or actuarial methods. Few practitioners will rely on actuarial methods alone, but instead use actuarial instruments as a source of data like other assessment methods, such as psychological tests, interviews, and behavioral observations to inform their clinical judgment.

We will not review those actuarial instruments in this chapter. Most of the existing actuarial instruments were developed to predict violence in offender populations or they were designed to predict specific types of violence, such as sexual predation or domestic violence. One notable exception is a product of the MacArthur Study mentioned above (Monahan et al., 2001). The Classification of

Violence Risk (COVR), which is now commercially available, was derived from the MacArthur findings and is based on a psychiatric population outside of the criminal justice system (Monahan et al., 2005). If this or a different actuarial method is used, then the examiner will need to exercise clinical judgment in determining whether there are factors that modify the risk potential estimate. In the absence of an actuarial instrument, examiners will typically consider several issues in developing a clinical estimate of risk:

- *Base rates.* If it is available, and commonly it is not, examiners should consider the base rate for violence in the group to which the patient belongs in order anchor one's opinion. Conroy and Murrie (2007) list several studies that provide some base rate data, but local base rate data, if available, is always preferable.
- *Personal characteristics.* Unlike suicide risk, risk for violence to others generally declines with age. Historically, males have been considered at greater risk for violence than females, but that difference did not hold up in the MacArthur Study (Monahan et al., 2001). There was a difference in violence pattern with women more likely to commit violence against a family member and in the home.

   The examiner should also obtain a detailed account of past violence. Has the patient been arrested, convicted, or hospitalized for past violent acts? Has he/she used a weapon against someone in the past? Has he/she caused serious injury? How frequent and recent has past violence been? This question is especially important in jurisdictions requiring a recent violent act for commitment. These are also questions for which collateral information from police and hospital records or family members should be obtained if at all possible.
- *Clinical factors.* There are a number of clinical factors that need to be explored in relation to violence potential. Does the patient demonstrate evidence of psychopathy? Although they used a noncorrectional population, the MacArthur study found scores on the Psychopathy Checklist—Screening Version (PCL-SV) (Hart, Cox, & Hare, 1995) to be one of the best predictors of violence (Monahan et al., 2001).

   Based on the MacArthur findings, examiners should also assess whether the patient has a pervasive suspiciousness of others; although, actual delusions do not appear predictive of violence. Hallucinations, as well, do not generally increase the risk of violence, but hallucinations commanding violence are associated with higher risk. Thus, with psychotic patients, it is important for examiners to explore the exact nature of hallucinations and even with nonpsychotic patients to assess for high levels of suspiciousness.

The presence of substance abuse problems has generally been considered a risk factor for violence. That relationship was clearly supported in the MacArthur study findings (Monahan et al., 2001). Some states allow for special commitments of substance abusers, but even with general commitments based on mental disease or defect, the presence of substance abuse needs to be explored, since the risk potential increases dramatically for mentally ill patients who also abuse substances. The MacArthur report did not distinguish the effects of different types of substances. Meloy (2000), however, emphasized that alcohol and psychostimulant drugs are especially associated with violence. Therefore, it is important to explore the specific pattern of substance abuse.

- *Situational factors.* Mental health professionals, used to assessing characteristics of the individual patient, sometimes overlook the important situational factors that contribute to violence risk. This long-standing oversight was pointed out almost three decades ago by Monahan (1981). The examiner should explore the patient's current living situation. Does he/she have a stable place to live? Does he/she have a steady source of income? Is he/she involved in a turbulent relationship? Has he/she experienced any recent losses? Are there specific potential victims toward whom he/she feels anger or by whom he/she feels threatened? Does he/she have weapons readily available? In his/her neighborhood, does he/she feel a need to carry a weapon for protection?

DATA INTERPRETATION

GENERAL CONSIDERATIONS

In order to determine the need to utilize civil commitment provisions in a particular case, clinicians must weigh available clinical data to guide their assessment for the risk of dangerousness as defined in their jurisdiction. Such a determination requires more than collecting a checklist of risk factors; it must include clinical reasoning regarding how these factors taken together impact the clinical picture. Generally, clinicians first make a determination whether a patient is currently suffering from a diagnosable mental disorder. Clinicians then determine whether the patient's mental disorder along with his/her identified risk and protective factors meet the dangerousness threshold. It should be noted that while some commitment statutes explicitly require a causal connection between the identified mental illness and dangerousness, other statutes require only that an individual meet both criteria (Schopp, 2006).

While studies have demonstrated clinicians' inability to predict future suicidal or violent behaviors with accuracy, the objective of data interpretation is not for predictive purposes, but to identify and minimize the high potential for dangerousness in the setting of mental illness (Lidz, Mulvey, & Gardner, 1993; Simon & Hales, 2006). Accordingly, all relevant information from a patient's self-report of symptoms, past psychiatric history, and family and other collateral reports must be weighed together to assess that risk. Additionally, while structured assessment instrument tools may assist in identifying these risks, clinicians should not rely on these instruments alone, as they do not possess the specificity or sensitivity necessary for that purpose (Appelbaum & Gutheil, 2007). The clinician's interpretation of all available data, including structured instruments, must guide clinical judgment in these matters.

MENTAL ILLNESS

As noted previously, the presence of a mental illness is required by civil commitment statutes. Assessing whether that mental illness places a person or others in imminent risk of harm requires the clinician to consider the quality and severity of the individual's psychiatric symptoms. As part of this assessment, the clinician must consider the likely consequences of the patient being left untreated. Clinicians must also consider the best course of treatment for a particular mental illness, as involuntary hospitalization may not always represent the best therapeutic alternative. For example, the decision to civilly commit a patient for involuntary hospitalization may be influenced by the potential for regression or dependency reinforcement in a particular patient within the hospital setting (Melton et al., 2007). Accordingly, a clinician not only must identify a particular diagnosis, but must also determine the appropriate course of treatment in light of the likely response to treatment. Regardless of these concerns, it is paramount that clinicians utilize all legal safeguards available to minimize the risk of danger as it relates to mental illness.

RISK OF DANGER TO SELF

When assessing whether an individual presents a danger to him/herself, the clinician must weigh known risk factors against the individual's specific protective factors. This requires a critical examination of the clinical data collected and how that information collectively affects the overall risk of danger to self. Accordingly, clinicians must consider risk factors such as current psychiatric symptoms, including depressed mood, hopelessness, anxiety, and suicidal ideation; historical data, including personal and family history of suicide attempts; current psychosocial stressors; and access to weapons. It is important not only to consider the mere presence of risk factors, but also to consider the severity of those risk factors (American Psychiatric Association, 2003). The individual's protective factors can then be considered in the context of the severity of the risk factors.

For example, when weighing the significance of previous suicide attempts, the clinician must consider the risk versus rescue potential of the suicide attempts. The risk potential is measured by the potential lethality of method used, while the rescue potential is measured by the likelihood of being discovered and rescued following the attempt (Weisman & Worden, 1972). Such information, along with the presence of similar psychosocial stressors and the loss of previous protective factors, will guide the clinician's assessment for dangerousness to self. Other risk factors must also be analyzed in this manner to estimate the overall risk and to determine if an individual meets the civil commitment criteria for dangerousness in a particular jurisdiction.

The quality of a patient's suicidal thoughts should also be explored by the clinician. Factors to be identified by the clinician include the frequency and intensity of the suicidal thoughts; the development of a suicide plan; the lethality of the suicide plan; rehearsals of the suicide plan; and final arrangements made by the patient (e.g., giving away possessions) (Melton et al., 2007). These factors may indicate to the clinician how imminent the threat of harm is to the patient. Finally, clinicians must bear in mind that an individual's characterization potential for self-harm may be strongly influenced by a desire to mislead the clinician in order to remove obstacles to achieving an ultimate goal. Accordingly, an individual's self-report must also be scrutinized when weighing the protective factors and risk factors for dangerousness to self.

RISK OF DANGER TO OTHERS

As with the risk of danger to self, the data informing the risk of danger to others must be interpreted collectively in order to evaluate adequately the appropriateness of civil commitment. Generally, the data interpretation must be aimed at identifying the imminent risk of violence that would necessitate involuntary treatment. Authors have identified 10 risk factors that must be considered together for adequate assessment of short-term risk of violence. Those factors include appearance or affect; violent ideation and degree of planning; violent intent; access to victim and weapons; history of violence; substance use; psychosis; personality disorders; noncompliance with treatment; and demographics associated with violence (Tardiff, 2008).

When weighing these risk factors together, clinicians must bear in mind that the single best predictor of future violence is a history of violent behaviors (Klassen & O'Connor, 1988). Accordingly, clinicians must give significant weight to this risk factor when present. Further, clinicians must consider patient accounts of past violent behavior along with collateral reports, as patients may minimize this critical factor to avoid treatment. A careful review of psychosocial stressors involved in prior violent episodes and the likely recurrence of similar stressors will instruct the clinician regarding the acute risk of violence. In addition to weighing these factors together, the nature of each risk factor must be scrutinized individually. For example, the mere presence of a psychotic disorder alone may not necessarily increase the risk of violence. However, psychotic illness with auditory hallucinations commanding violent behavior is known to increase the risk of violence (Monahan et al., 2001).

INABILITY TO CARE FOR ONESELF

Of the legal criteria for the use of civil commitment, the inability to care for oneself is likely the most ambiguous. This criterion allows the clinician some flexibility to commit patients in situations when no overt threat of harm to self or others is made by the patient. Instead, consideration is given as to whether an individual is unable to provide for his or her own basic needs in the community within the context of that person's mental illness. Accordingly, information regarding the impact of mental illness on an individual's level of functioning and the availability of social supports to assist the individual should be weighed together to determine the degree of impairment.

Often, individuals who qualify for civil commitment due to inability to care for self are unable or unwilling to provide reliable description of their level of functioning. As a result, clinicians must review the available data for indicators that mental illness, such as psychosis or dementia, represents a passive risk of harm to the patient (Appelbaum & Gutheil, 2007). Information provided by collateral sources, such as family members, is essential for reliable assessment of functioning in the community setting. Taking these factors together, clinicians determine the individual's relative risk of danger with special consideration to factors such as serious medical illness, limited access to food or shelter, and environmental hazards, which an individual may be independently unable to manage due to mental illness.

COMMUNICATION

In some circumstances, when a hearing must be held after only a few days of emergency hospitalization, at most a brief report of the significant findings and the evaluator's recommendation regarding continued commitment may be all that is required or desired. Testimony at the commitment hearing, in those cases, may be the principal method of communicating the evaluator's opinion and the reasoning behind it. When there is a longer period of evaluation, usually followed by the possibility of a more extended commitment, the court would be better served by a more thorough report preceding the testimony.

Before addressing report content specifically, there are a number of controversial issues among forensic clinicians, particularly regarding communicating information about risk of violence toward others. Should evaluators offer an "ultimate issue" opinion? If they do, should that opinion be expressed as a dichotomy or as a risk level? If risk is presented as a level, should it be expressed in categories, probabilities, or frequencies? These issues have been debated among forensic clinicians and researchers without resulting in a clear consensus or standard of care. Regarding perhaps the most controversial topic, the "ultimate issue," courts will frequently expect, and when possible, require an opinion from the evaluator. Furthermore, in some settings, such as evaluations by hospital staff to determine whether to seek long-term commitment, the courts may not become involved unless the evaluator offers an opinion that the patient is dangerous and meets the requirements for commitment.

REPORT ORGANIZATION

The organization and content of reports varies widely among evaluators. Realizing that some of differences are a matter of personal style and preference, we believe that there are some elements that make a report more understandable to its consumers and ultimately more useful to the court and subsequent treating clinicians.

- *Referral issue.* Defining the referral issue may seem obvious, but the benefits are not. Reports often become part of a record and may be viewed years later out of context. Assessing the relevance and meaning of a report at that point is aided by knowledge of the exact purpose of the evaluation. More immediately, defining the referral question in terms of the exact commitment criterion in the jurisdiction demonstrates to the consumer (usually the court) that the examiner understood and will address the specific issues that the court must decide.
- *Sources of data.* An exhaustive listing of all evaluation procedures, including all documents reviewed and collateral contacts made, allows all parties a fair opportunity to assess the thoroughness of the evaluation and to prepare properly any challenges. Often, it serves the additional purpose of preventing

unnecessary challenges, because the party that might disagree with the opinion can, nevertheless, recognize the solid foundation on which it rests.

- *Present illness.* Giving a detailed account of the circumstances and course of the present episode provides the court with a description of the patient's current functioning and assessment of whether the condition is worsening. It also will indicate which options may have been exhausted in treating the disorder in a less restrictive environment.
- *Psychiatric history.* A thorough account of psychiatric history is often necessary to support a diagnosis. Additionally, when a court has to decide whether to involuntarily confine a patient in a hospital, knowing his/her past treatment response can be quite valuable. The history of past treatment also informs the court about a patient's compliance in an out-of-hospital setting.
- *History of violence.* Ultimately, a court's decision about commitment will turn more on their potential for violence to self or others than on their diagnosis and mental status. It is critical to document past violent acts and to relate them to the patient's mental state at the time. Some patients, for instance, may have a history of substance abuse related or instrumental violence that is essentially unrelated to their mental disorder. It is especially important for the examiner to document recent violence and to highlight any pattern of violence escalation.
- *Diagnostic impression.* As mentioned earlier, clinicians often develop a working diagnosis that may be changed or specified as they learn more about the patient. For the purpose of civil commitment, a definitive diagnosis may be less important than a specification of severity, since many statutes require a severe or gross disorder to justify commitment. If a patient's exact diagnosis is unclear, but the differential diagnoses being considered would all meet the criteria for commitment in the jurisdiction, it is important to make this explicit. The exact diagnosis, while relevant for treatment and prognosis, may not be critical to the commitment decision.
- *Opinion and recommendations.* In most instances, the court will expect the examiner's opinion on whether the patient meets the criteria for commitment. It is also appropriate for the examiner to point out any data that are inconsistent with their opinion or

any deficits in the data (such as missing medical records or difficulty interviewing the patient) that might lessen the reliability of the opinion.

- *Prognosis.* In determining whether to commit a patient, the court will benefit from any information the examiner can offer regarding the likelihood of improvement with and without treatment. When possible, it is also useful to point out how the patient might fare in a less restrictive treatment alternative.

TESTIMONIAL ISSUES

For clinicians with little or no experience testifying, the prospect of courtroom testimony, even in the less contentious setting of a civil commitment, can be anxiety provoking. New expert witnesses sometimes benefit from awareness of two important principles: (1) it is not about them; and (2) they must tell the truth. Although these principles seem apparent, inexperienced witnesses sometimes personalize an opposing attorney's attempts to discredit their testimony. They also sometimes experience the process as a test of wits with the attorney, where a clever, plausible response might be offered to "score a point" in spite of the fact that it is actually not true.

- *Foundation of opinion.* Just as in a report, it is important when testifying to demonstrate that the examiner was, in fact, aware of and addressed the criteria that the court must consider. It is also useful to specify all the sources of data that went into the evaluation to emphasize the sound foundation upon which the examiner's opinion rests.
- *Making the data relevant.* It is particularly helpful to the court if the testifying expert organizes testimony in a manner that tracks the criteria on which the court must make its decision. In civil commitment determinations the court must determine whether the patient has a threshold mental condition, such as a "severe" or "gross" mental disease or defect, and then must determine if the disorder results in a particular functional condition, such as danger to self or others or grave disability. If the expert addresses each of these elements and identifies the particular data points that demonstrate their presence or absence, they will have provided the court with testimony that will be directly useful and relevant.

REFERENCES

Addington v. Texas, 441 U.S. 418 (1979).

American Psychiatric Association (2000). *Diagnostic and statistical manual of mental disorders* (4th ed., Text Revision). Washington, DC: American Psychiatric Association.

American Psychiatric Association (2003). *Practice guideline for the assessment and treatment of patients with suicidal behaviors*. Retrieved August 7, 2009, from www.psychiatryonline.com/pracGuide/pracGuideTopic_14.aspx

American Psychiatric Association. (2009). *The principles of medical ethics with annotations especially applicable to psychiatry*. Washington, DC: Author.

Appelbaum, P. S. (2005). Assessing Kendra's law: Five years of outpatient commitment in New York. *Psychiatric Services, 56*, 791–792.

Appelbaum, P. S., & Gutheil, T. G. (2007). *Clinical handbook of psychiatry & the law* (4th ed.). Philadelphia, PA: Lippincott Williams & Williams.

Bagby, R., Thompson, J. S., Dickens, S. E., & Nohara, M. (1991). Decision making in psychiatric civil commitment: An experimental analysis. *American Journal of Psychiatry, 148*, 28–33.

Conroy, M. A., & Murrie, D. C. (2007). *Forensic assessment of violence risk: A guide for risk assessment and risk management*. Hoboken, NJ: John Wiley & Sons.

Grisso, T., & Appelbaum, P. S. (1998). *MacArthur competence assessment tool for treatment (MacCAT- T)*. Sarasota, FL: Professional Resource Press.

Hart, S., Cox, D., & Hare, R. (1995). *The Hare Psychopathy Checklist: Screening Version*. Toronto, ON: Multi-Health Systems.

Harvard Law Review Association (1974). Developments in the law: Civil commitment of the mentally ill. *Harvard Law Review, 87*, 1190–1406.

Jackson v. Indiana, 406 U.S. 715 (1972).

Jacobson v. Commonwealth of Massachusetts, 197 U.S. 11 (1905).

Kansas v. Hendricks, 521 U.S. 346 (1997).

Klassen, D., & O'Connor, W. A. (1988). A prospective study of predictors of violence in adult male mental health admissions. *Law and Human Behavior, 12*(3), 143–158.

Lake v. Cameron, 364 F. 2d 657 (D.C. Cir. 1966).

Lessard v. Schmidt, 349 F. Supp. 1078 (1972).

Lidz, C. W., Mulvey, E. P., & Gardner, W. (1993). The accuracy of prediction of violence to others. *Journal of the American Medical Association, 269*, 1007–1011.

Meloy, J. R. (2000). *Violence risk and threat assessment: A practical guide for mental health and criminal justice professionals*. San Diego, CA: Specialized Training Services.

Melton, G. B., Petrila, P., Poythress, N. G., & Slobogin, C. (2007). *Psychological evaluations for the courts: A handbook for mental health professionals and lawyers* (3rd ed.). New York, NY: Guilford Press.

Monahan, J. (1981). *Predicting violent behavior: An assessment of clinical techniques.* Beverly Hills, CA: Sage.

Monahan, J., Steadman, H., Silver, E., Appelbaum, P., Robbins, P., Mulvey, E., . . . Banks, S. (2001). *Rethinking risk assessment: The MacArthur study of mental disorder and violence.* New York: Oxford University Press.

Monahan, J., Steadman, H. J., Appelbaum, P. S., Grisso, T., Mulvey, E. P., Roth, L., . . . Silver, E. (2005). *The classification of violence risk.* Lutz, FL: Psychological Assessment Resources.

Mrad, D. F., & Nabors, E. (2006). The role of the psychologist in civil commitment. In A. M. Goldstein (Ed.), *Forensic psychology: Emerging topics and expanding roles* (pp. 232–259). Hoboken, NJ: John Wiley & Sons.

O'Connor v. Donaldson, 422 U.S. 563 (1975).

Parry, J. (1994). Involuntary civil commitment in the 90s: A constitutional perspective. *Mental and Physical Disability Law Reporter, 18*, 320–336.

Perlin, M. (1989). *Mental disability law: Civil and criminal (Volume 1).* Charlottesville, VA: Michie.

Schopp, R. F. (2006). Two-edged swords, dangerousness, and expert testimony in capital sentencing. *Law and Psychology Review, 30*, 57–101.

Schwartz, H. I., Mack, D. M., & Zeman, P. M. (2003). Hospitalization: Voluntary and involuntary. In R. Rosner (Ed.), *Principles and practice of forensic psychiatry* (2nd ed.) (pp. 107–115). New York, NY: Arnold.

Simon, R. I., & Hales, R. E. (Eds.) (2006). *The American psychiatric publishing textbook of suicide assessment and management.* Arlington, VA: American Psychiatric Publishing.

Tardiff, K. (2008). Clinical risk assessment of violence. In R. I. Simon, & K. Tardiff (Eds.), *Textbook of violence assessment and management* (pp. 3–16). Arlington, VA: American Psychiatric Publishing.

Weisman, A. D., & Worden, J. W. (1972). Risk rescue rating in suicide assessment. *Archives of general psychiatry, 26*, 553–560.

Werth, J. (2001). U.S. involuntary mental health commitment statutes: Requirements for persons perceived to be a potential harm to self. *Suicide & Life-Threatening Behavior, 31*, 348–357.

White, T. W. (1999). *How to identify suicidal people: A systematic approach to risk assessment.* Philadelphia, PA: Charles Press.

CHAPTER 22

Competency to Consent to Treatment

NICOLE FOUBISTER and MARY CONNELL

INTRODUCTION

In 1914, Justice Benjamin Cardozo wrote, "Every human being of adult years and sound mind has a right to determine what shall be done with his own body" (*Schloendorff v. Society of New York Hospital*, 1914, p. 93).

Forensic assessment of competence to consent to treatment is a focused examination that is conducted for a specific psycholegal reason. It goes beyond the assessment all health care providers conduct during the "informed consent" process when the practitioner needs to establish that the individual understands and consents to treatment procedures. By contrast, the evaluation of competence must focus on the process of reasoning leading up to the treatment decision making rather than on the decision itself (Buchanan & Brock, 2001). Assessment of the individual's capacity to consent to treatment combines traditional clinical assessment of cognitive functioning with assessment of psychiatric symptoms in a structured interview and, if indicated, formal psychological assessment.

Traditionally paternalistic with physician-driven decision making, the practice of medicine has become increasingly patient focused, with respect for a patient's rights to autonomy. The age-old view of "doctor knows best" has been replaced with regard for a patient's right to self-determination. At the heart of an adult's right to make legally and medically significant decisions lies the concept of competence; however, a discussion of competence cannot be undertaken without first examining the doctrine of informed consent, a relatively new development in tort law.

Determination of competence in civil law means the individual is able to provide informed consent. *Informed consent* is a term that was first introduced in the California case of *Salgo v. Leland Stanford Junior University Board of Trustees* (1957). Ultimately, competent patients have a right to make informed treatment decisions for themselves. Melton, Petrila, Poythress, and Slobogin (1997) observed that "the informed consent doctrine serves to humanize the clinician–patient relationship and to restore the balance in authority between the clinician and the patient, on whose body or mind the proposed treatment would intrude" (p. 177).

Informed consent requires three essential elements: requisite information, which includes the disclosure of risks, benefits, and alternatives, including no treatment; decision-making capacity on the part of the patient; and consent that is voluntary and free of coercion or undue influence. Thus, the doctrine of informed consent requires competency, disclosure, and voluntariness.

The topic of competency is fraught with controversy, which emanates largely from the absence of uniform and clear legal standards for incompetency, coupled with the absence of a consensus in the professional community on appropriate procedures for competency determination (Applebaum, Lidz, & Meisel, 1987). Courts now recognize and respect the right of a competent adult patient to consent to or refuse medical procedures and treatment and informed consent is a legal and ethical precondition for medical treatment except in emergency situations.

Requests for assessment of competence are most commonly made when patients are refusing a recommended treatment. Courts have expanded the liability of health care professionals who fail to obtain informed consent and under tort law a provider may be held liable for battery or negligence for treating patients who have not given valid consent. Therefore, an assessment of competence should be requested whenever there is a suspicion of impaired decision making regardless of whether a patient is accepting or refusing treatment recommendations.

PREPARATION

"Given the requirement of competence for valid informed consent, the assessment of the patient's capacity to make decisions is an intrinsic aspect of every physician patient interaction" (Applebaum, 2007, p. 1837). Competency to consent to treatment involves a determination that the individual can make a *voluntary* and *knowing* decision to receive the treatment being proposed. *Voluntary* means that the individual feels free to decline or accept the treatment and is under no duress to accept it. *Knowing* refers to understanding the nature of the disorder requiring treatment and the risks, benefits, and alternatives of the proposed treatment.

Competency may be assumed unless there is some indication of a limitation in the decision-making capacity or constraints on the individual's freedom to consent voluntarily. The assessment of competence to consent to treatment involves both clinical observation and, potentially, formal testing, to determine whether the individual has the capacity for knowing and voluntary consent for the proffered treatment (Beauchamp & Childress, 2001).

Competence, which is defined as the quality or condition of being legally qualified to perform an act and/or make decisions, is a legal concept that represents a specific judgment made by the courts. Competence and capacity are also considered medicolegal or psycholegal concepts, frequently utilized interchangeably in the medical literature. Forensic examiners often render an opinion regarding decisional capacity or the mental soundness of treatment decisions.

Adults are presumed competent unless it is shown that a mental disease or defect impairs their understanding of the nature or consequences of the act in question. While there is a presumption of competence in adults, minors are considered to lack the competency to consent (see Chapter 11). In most jurisdictions, individuals whose judgment has been deemed to require appointment of guardians generally are considered to lack competence for all legal purposes.

THE REFERRAL

Referrals for competency to consent to treatment are often sought when a patient of uncertain competence is refusing a prescribed treatment. These requests commonly include the mentally ill, brain damaged, elderly, and children. Referrals for assessments may also be requested in patients undergoing high-risk procedures and this type of referral is often sought to protect the physician from potential future liability.

DETERMINING THE PROPER FOCUS AND SCOPE OF THE EVALUATION

Regardless of how a referral is made, it is essential that the evaluating clinician have a very clear and comprehensive understanding of the referral question and why the referral is being sought. In addition, the risks, benefits, and alternatives to treatment, including no treatment, should be clear to the evaluator, as this will be an essential element of the evaluation.

TIMING

Timing of the evaluation and preparation of the report, if requested, will depend largely on the acuity of the medical condition. Examiners must clarify precisely when the results are needed to insure the examination can be completed within the required time frame. An additional consideration is the number and structure of interviews that may be required. Fluctuations in mental status that may affect performance may occur secondary to multiple factors, including, for example, the time of day, such as sundowning seen in delirium; setting; medications; and changes in clinical condition. For this reason, several interviews may be necessary for an accurate assessment.

COLLATERAL INFORMATION

Opinions offered in evaluations conducted for courts are based on multiple data sources selected to address the referral question in the most relevant and reliable way possible (Grisso, 2003; Heilbrun, 2001). This includes not only the data collected directly from the examinee through interview and, where appropriate, testing, but also review of documents from, and potentially interviews with, third-party sources (Heilbrun, Warren, & Picarello, 2003). These collateral sources of information increase the examiner's certainty as opinions are formulated; divergent data generates new hypotheses to be explored, while convergent data increases reliability of findings. Efforts should be made to obtain collateral information from sources such as family members or nursing staff who know about the examinee's functioning across a broad range of settings. Such information will assist the examiner to form accurate and defensible opinions.

ETHICAL ISSUES

As noted in the *Ethics Guidelines for the Practice of Forensic Psychiatry* (*AAPL Guidelines*; American Academy of Psychiatry and the Law, 2005), "a forensic evaluation requires notice to the evaluee and to collateral sources of reasonably anticipated limitations on confidentiality" (p. 1). Despite the fact that a clinician is called upon to perform an assessment of a person's capacity to consent to treatment, this does not abrogate the clinician's responsibility to provide full disclosure of the purposes of the evaluation and with whom the information obtained during the course of the evaluation will be shared.

Examiners must also maintain objectivity and guard against the incursion of personal biases and prejudices. Value judgments, an inevitable part of capacity and competence determinations (Koppleman, 1990), must be carefully distinguished from empirical data that can be stated with reasonable medical certainty (Rosner, 2003). An awareness of countertransference, or how the examiner's own history and reactions influence the assessment of another person, is essential in all clinical evaluations. A treating clinician should generally avoid agreeing to perform an evaluation for legal purposes or to offer expert opinion to courts as suggested in both the *AAPL Guidelines* and the *Specialty Guidelines for Forensic Psychologists* (Committee on Ethical Guidelines for Forensic Psychologists, 1991).

The examination should be scheduled to occur in a quiet area free of distractions which affords some privacy to the examinee. If the examination is to be audio- or video-recorded, preparations should be made including advance notice to the parties so that any necessary consent can be obtained.

DATA COLLECTION

Forensic assessment of competence to consent to treatment requires both a general assessment of the individual's psychological functioning and specific assessment of the capacities relevant to treatment decisions. In competency assessments, the examiner maintains a forensically neutral role, refrains from providing information or teaching the examinee about the examinee's diagnosed condition, and serves instead as an examiner of the necessary capacities. The examiner does not champion any particular treatment choice and is not expected even to formulate an opinion about the most appropriate treatment course. Assessment is on capacities, not on how they are exercised in a specific instance.

For the general assessment, the following elements are included:

- General background data, including demographic information, level of education achieved, work history, interpersonal relationships, leisure pursuits.
- Medical and mental health history both for the examinee and for family members.
- Legal history, including criminal adjudications, civil litigation, and any challenges to or court actions regarding guardianship.
- Screening for cognitive impairment that might limit understanding of treatment options—the Mini Mental State Examination (MMSE) or a brief measure of intellectual functioning may reveal impairment in verbal understanding or reasoning that could influence the examinee's ability to grasp complex constructs. Initial screening may be followed by more comprehensive assessment if there are indications of limited cognitive capacity. Impaired memory or concentration, limited verbal expressive ability, and other such deficits, if present, may bear on capacity to understand and appreciate treatment options.
- Screening for symptoms of psychopathology—thorough document review and clinical interview, the examinee is evaluated for symptoms of severe psychopathology that might interfere with competence to make treatment decisions. The presence of a disorder does not, in itself, imply lack of competence. If a disorder is present, it is necessary to determine whether the symptoms affect decision-making capacity.

Standardized instruments are available for assessing competence to consent to treatment, and vary in terms of their psychometric strength. Reviewing the decisional capacity assessment instruments focusing on consent in treatment, Dunn et al. (2006) identified 15 instruments. All 15 instruments assessed understanding, but only 9 assessed all four constructs generally identified as the prongs of treatment competence—understanding, appreciation, reasoning, and expression of a choice (Grisso & Appelbaum, 1995). Those 9 instruments are briefly described next.

1. *Competency Interview Schedule (CIS)*. The CIS utilizes the structured interview format (Bean, Nishisato, Rector, & Glancy, 1994). It was standardized on inpatients with major depression being considered for electroconvulsive treatment. The instrument has good interrater reliability, reasonable test–retest reliability, good internal consistency, and ratings are found to agree well with expert judgments (Bean et al., 1994). Administration time was not reported.

2. *Assessment of Consent Capacity for Treatment (ACCT)*. The ACCT was standardized on adults with mild to moderate mental retardation and adults without mental retardation. Administration involves the presentation of three vignettes regarding recommended treatments and takes about 45 minutes (Cea & Fisher, 2003). Interrater reliability and internal consistency are excellent (Bean et al., 1994). Criterion validity was reported by Dunn et al. (2006) to be good in that control subjects were rated higher than those with mild retardation, and the latter were found to perform better than those with moderate mental retardation, on understanding, acceptance, and reasoning questions.

3. *Hopemont Capacity Assessment Interview (HCAI)*. The HCAI is a semistructured interview in which the examiner presents hypothetical vignettes involving eye infection and CPR (Edelstein, 1999). Administration takes 30 to 60 minutes. Dunn et al. (2006) found that item inspection raised doubt that the construct of reasoning was being adequately assessed. Interrater reliability and internal consistency were reported by Dunn et al. to be good but test–retest reliability was reportedly poor. Validity was moderately good for understanding as evinced by correlation with the MMSE but appreciation and reasoning did not perform well (Dunn et al., 2006).

4. *Understanding of Treatment Disclosures, Perception of Disorder, Thinking Rationally About Treatment, Expressing a Choice*. These

are the original MacArthur instruments (Appelbaum & Grisso, 1995; Grisso, Appelbaum, Mulvey, & Fletcher, 1995), and they relied on treatment vignettes presented through semistructured interview (Grisso & Appelbaum, 1995). Administration took from 60 to 90 minutes. Standardized variously on patients with schizophrenia, major depression, bipolar disorder, medical illness, residents of long-term care facilities and control subjects, the instruments were found to have generally high interrater agreement on most items and varying test–retest reliability and measures of validity (Dunn et al., 2006).

5. *MacArthur Competence Assessment Tool—Treatment (MacCAT-T).* The MacCAT-T assesses four constructs of decisional capacity: understanding reasoning, appreciation, and expressing a choice (Grisso & Appelbaum, 1998). A semistructured interview guides the clinician through the assessment of capacity to make the actual treatment decision with which the examinee is faced. The examiner using the MacCAT-T must understand in considerable detail the patient's treatment options that are under consideration. This instrument was standardized on patients with schizophrenia, major depressive disorder, dementia/cognitive impairment, control subjects, and medical patients. Psychometric properties demonstrated respectable reliability and variable indices of validity, with correlation with previous MacArthur instruments and the MMSE and with performance in understanding and reasoning, but not appreciation, being worse among patients with dementia than those without. Administration time may vary and generally ranges from 15 to 20 minutes (Dunn et al., 2006).

6. *Structured Interview for Competency and Incompetency Assessment Testing and Ranking Inventory (SICIATR).* The SICIATR (Tomoda et al., 1997), a structured interview, was standardized on psychiatric and medical inpatients. Reliability and validity, examined in limited research, were respectable with medical patients demonstrating higher competency levels than psychiatric inpatients, sensitivity being 0.83 and specificity being 0.67 (Kitamura et al., 1998). The administration time is 20 minutes.

7. *Competency to Consent to Treatment Instrument (CCTI).* The CCTI, also known as the "Standardized Consent Capacity Instrument," relies on the presentation of hypothetical vignettes in

a structured interview format. The CCTI was standardized on patients with Alzheimer's disease, Parkinson's disease, any dementia, and control subjects (Marson, Ingram, Cody, & Harrell, 1995). Psychometric properties are good and administration takes 20 to 25 minutes (Dunn et al., 2006).

8. *Vignette method described by Schmand et al. (1999).* Schmand, Gouwenberg, Smit, and Jonker (1999) described the presentation of a vignette in a structured interview. The technique was standardized on a sample of older subjects with and without dementia. Research revealed poor agreement with psychiatric judgments. The procedure was reported to have moderate correlation with the *MMSE*. There was no information available regarding interrater reliability and administration time was not reported. (Dunn, 2006).

9. *Vignette method described by Vellinga et al. (2004).* Vellinga, Smit, Van Leeuwen, van Tilburg, and Jonker (2004) described another assessment method that relies on presentation of a vignette or the actual treatment decision in a structured interview. The examiner gathers relevant information for a competency determination. Research found poor agreement with physician and family member judgments. No information was available regarding interrater reliability or administration time (Dunn, 2006).

Dunn et al. (2006) found that the *MacArthur Competence Assessment Tool—Treatment* had the most empirical support of the instruments described above. They observed, however, that other instruments might be equally or better suited to certain situations. Each of these instruments or techniques offers some standardization of the assessment process. Psychometric advantages, however, may be somewhat offset by inferential gaps that occur with the use of these instruments and at this stage of development of the field of assessment of treatment competence, many examiners continue to rely primarily on interview and collateral contacts.

DATA INTERPRETATION

The integration and interpretation of data should focus on the individual's capacity or incapacity to make treatment decisions rather than on an ultimate declaration of competence. When the data are not consistent or clear and the determination cannot be made, then both the data in support of a finding of competency and the data that argue against such finding should be clearly set forth to assist the fact finder. The ultimate competence judgment may rest on balanced consideration of the degree of severity of consequences and the individual's capacities, a decision that invokes moral or values considerations and may best be made by the court (Grisso, 2003).

The data can be conceptualized along a continuum of capacities, from clear absence to unquestionable presence of all of the relevant capacities. The capacities are:

- *Understanding*—the examinee's cognitive capacity to understand treatment options.
- *Acceptance*—the examinee's capacity to accept reasonable treatment recommendations.
- *Decision making*—the examinee's treatment decision making capacity.
- *Communicating*—the examinee's capacity to communicate treatment decisions.
- *Autonomy*—the examinee's freedom to make decisions without coercion.

Clearly, there are likely to be divergent data on each point and the task of integration is to find the greatest convergence of the data, identifying points in support and those that refute the conclusion. When an opinion cannot be derived from the data and it is not reasonable to believe more information would clarify the issue, the discord must simply be described so that the fact finder has the data necessary to make a competence determination.

COMMUNICATION

REPORT ORGANIZATION

Examiners should strive to produce clear and concise reports that furnish the data necessary to assist with the legal question or dispute at hand. Prior to beginning the evaluation, the examiner should have a clear understanding with the referring source about whether a formal report is being requested. If it is determined that a report is needed to be generated, the examiner should construct a plan for organizing the data. A competence assessment report should indicate what areas of functioning were evaluated, what factors were considered relevant, and why. Keep your audience in mind, as a report intended for legal purposes is not akin to a report written for clinical purposes. In a forensic report, the data must be linked to the relevant psycholegal issues at hand. To this end, minimize technical jargon while maintaining the quality and accuracy of the report. The report should clearly describe how competence for one purpose should not be confused or generalized for competence for other purposes. Although the terms *capacity* and *competence* are both utilized in the medicolegal literature, there remains disagreement among experts on the use of these terms. Many support using the term *capacity* in an assessment to avoid confusion with *competence*, which is a legal determination. For the purposes of this chapter, we recommend utilizing the term *capacity* as well as offering a final opinion on the ultimate issue, which has also been the source of debate.

DEMOGRAPHIC INFORMATION

Identification data permits the reader to quickly obtain a generalized overview of the age, gender, and education of the person being evaluated to conceptualize the findings. The level of education attained by the examinee should be included because it may be relevant to considerations of current cognitive functioning and offer some possible information about baseline cognitive capacity. The date of each interview and of the report should also be included.

LEGAL BACKGROUND AND SOURCE OF REFERRAL

Reports identify the referral source, reasons for the request, and purpose of the evaluation. An outline of the specific legal question the examiner is being asked to address should be included as well as the legal standard under which the evaluation will be considered.

SOURCES OF INFORMATION

The examiner should list all persons examined and interviewed as well as the location, dates, and duration of the contacts. It is also helpful to document who accompanied the examinee to interviews.

All documents that were reviewed should be listed and organized chronologically or grouped by type. Relevant documents may include medical and mental health records, psychological testing, educational records, and criminal records. Other documents that illuminate the examinee's functioning, specifically in decisional capacities, may also be included. Documents may be summarized within the report as well, to provide the reader with what the examiner considered salient and to further the development of the nexus between findings and conclusions. Documents that were requested but not available for review should also be listed with an explanation for why they were not available for review.

CONFIDENTIALITY AND NOTIFICATION OF PURPOSE

The report should include a description of the notification of purpose discussion that was held with the examinee and with any substitute decision maker who accompanied the examinee or otherwise spoke for the examinee. This may include specifically a discussion of the limits of confidentiality, to whom the report is released, and how the examinee can access or amend the report (Health Insurance Portability and Accountability Act of 1996 [HIPAA], 1996). The examinee's understanding of this discussion should also be probed and documented.

PSYCHOSOCIAL HISTORY

This section should include information that is relevant to the psycholegal question and the information may be garnered from interviews with the examinee as well as from other sources. The developmental history, family history, and education are reviewed. Educational history should include any learning disabilities, mental retardation, special education, and behavioral disruptions such as suspensions and expulsions. Work history is reviewed including relevant information such as promotions, terminations, write-ups, or disciplinary actions and reasons for moving from position to positions. Military history might include promotions, awards, cross-training, and disciplinary actions such as courts martial, nonjudicial punishment ("Article 15s"), or a less than honorable discharge. Also relevant may be the examinee's sexual and marital history, drug and alcohol history, and any criminal adjudication. The source of each piece of information should be clearly designated.

MEDICAL HISTORY

This section should include the examinee's past and current medical conditions. Particularly important may be any history of seizures, head injuries (indicating loss of consciousness and outcome), medications that may affect cognition such as those prescribed for dementia or for major mental disorders. Current medications and their possible effects on cognition, behavior, and emotions should be noted. Information may be obtained from the examinee as well as from current and old records.

LEGAL HISTORY

Of potential relevance may be juvenile and adult arrests as well as civil actions such as lawsuits, worker's compensation claims, or other legal actions. Review of the actual court documents may, however, be beyond the scope of the examination and reliance on the reports of others about the nature and outcome of legal proceedings may also be risky. For this reason, it may be preferable to make reference to "reported" legal actions and to provide the reader with only that which is clearly relevant and is undisputed.

MENTAL HEALTH HISTORY

Assessments should include a comprehensive review of mental health treatment. Relevant data may include current and past mental health diagnoses, psychiatric hospitalizations or outpatient treatment, and medications. Treatment and medication compliance should also be reviewed. Additionally, the review should include any history of suicide attempts, self injurious behaviors, or other indications of difficulty functioning independently.

BEHAVIORAL OBSERVATIONS

In describing the examinee's presentation for and behavior during the examination, it is important to include a description of the circumstances of the evaluation, parties present, and whether the examinee was recently medicated. This section should contain a complete mental status examination including descriptions of appearance, speech, affect, perception, apperception, thought process and content, attention, memory, orientation, judgment, insight, and cognition. It is recommended that examiners concretely describe behaviors. For example, rather then stating, "patient demonstrated bizarre behaviors," note "patient reported that there was an impending bomb attack and crawled under his bed where he stated he was seeking shelter."

Summary of Special Studies

Clinically relevant data such as physical examination, laboratory tests, imaging studies, electroencephalograms (EEGs), and neurological examination should be included with a jargon-free description. This may include the examinee's medical illnesses that may cause a change in mental status and impair capacity, including hepatic encephalopathy; encephalitis; metabolic derangements, such as, for example, changes in sodium levels; thyroid function tests; severe anemia; abnormalities of blood urea nitrogen (BUN) and creatinine; hyperglycemia; and hypoglycemia. The presence of evidence of delirium might call for review of laboratory findings that could illuminate which of the wide range of potential etiologies might be at play. For example, postoperative or medicated patients or those with infections may evince changes in white blood cell count, urinalysis, and blood cultures.

Summary of Psychological Testing

Psychological testing, both that accomplished recently and in the past, should be summarized. Psychiatric examiners should consider including the full report of the examining psychologist since a summary might exclude data important to the reader.

Impression

In a competency assessment, the data should be organized so as to make clear the nexus between data and conclusions. This portion of the report should summarize all significant material including information supporting the examiner's opinion and data that appeared contrary. Inconsistencies or contradictions in data should be noted with explanations provided when possible. An explanation should then be provided regarding how the data were valued or weighed. This section may contain general findings regarding the examinee's cognitive, behavioral, and emotional functioning; diagnoses made by treating mental health professionals and recommended treatments, including psychotropic medications; and even potentially prognostications. The examiner, however, focuses specifically on the issues significant to competency determination. Psychiatric diagnoses, if offered, should be provided using the most recent *Diagnostic and Statistical Manual of Mental Disorders* (DSM) terminology. Opinions regarding competence to consent to treatment should be deferred until the Findings and Recommendations section.

FINDINGS AND RECOMMENDATIONS

Here, the examiner provides the final opinion, expressed clearly and definitively. The opinion may be stated with a "reasonable degree of medical or psychological certainty." If the examiner is unable to form a final opinion, this should be stated. The opinion should follow logically from the content of the report and should include the examiner's reasoning. Statement of a psychiatric diagnosis does not provide sufficient evidence for the resolution of the legal question or provide a complete rationale or basis for an opinion. Examiners should include specific examples from the data in support of and in contradiction to their opinions and relate any psychiatric diagnosis to the opinion. Psychodynamic themes should be avoided, as they are irrelevant in determining capacity. Finally, any weaknesses in the examination process, such as time constraints, missing data, examinee's lack of cooperation, effects of the examinee's medical condition or medications, should be acknowledged and their potential effects on the findings described.

The report must contain sufficient data to support the final opinion and the reader should not need to review additional documents in order to understand how a conclusion was reached. The utility of the report is enhanced by openness and clarity in presenting the data and its nexus to the opinion. The findings should be expressed in the context of the legal criteria or psycholegal question, how each legal element was evaluated, what factors were considered relevant, and why. Finally, the examiner should make clear that competence for one purpose should not be confused with competence for another or with general competence.

REFERENCES

American Academy of Psychiatry and the Law. (2005). *Ethics guidelines for the practice of forensic psychiatry*. Bloomfield, CT: Author.

Appelbaum, P. S. (2007). Assessment of patients' competence to consent to treatment. *New England Journal of Medicine, 357*, 1834–1840.

Appelbaum, P. S., Lidz, C., & Meisel, A. (1987). *Informed consent: Legal theory and clinical practice*. New York, NY: Oxford University Press.

Appelbaum, P. S. & Grisso, T. (1995). The MacArthur Treatment Competence Study, I: Mental illness and competence to consent to treatment. *Law and Human Behavior, 19*, 105–126.

Bean, G., Nishisato, S., Rector, N. A., & Glancy, G. (1994). The psychometric properties of the Competency Interview Schedule. *Canadian Journal of Psychiatry, 39*, 368–376.

Beauchamp, T. L., & Childress, J. F. (2001). *Principles of biomedical ethics* (5th ed). New York, NY: Oxford University Press.

Buchanan, A. E., & Brock, D. W. (2001). Determinations of competence. In T. A. Mappes & D. DeGrazia (Eds.), *Biomedical ethics* (5th ed., 109–114). New York, NY: McGraw-Hill.

Cea, C. D., & Fisher, C. B. (2003). Health care decision-making by adults with mental retardation. *Mental Retardation, 41*, 78–87.

Committee on Ethical Guidelines for Forensic Psychologists. (1991). Specialty guidelines for forensic psychologists. *Law and Human Behavior, 15*, 655–665.

Dunn, L. B., Nowrangi, M. A., Barton, M. B., Palmer, W., Jeste, D. V., & Saks, E. R. (2006). Assessing decisional capacity for clinical research or treatment: A review of instruments. *American Journal of Psychiatry, 163*, 1323–1334.

Edelstein, B. (1999). *Hopemont capacity assessment interview manual and scoring guide*. Morgantown, WV: West Virginia University.

Grisso, T. (2003). *Evaluating competencies: Forensic assessments and instruments*. New York, NY: Kluwer Academic/Plenum Press.

Grisso, T., & Appelbaum, P. S. (1995). The MacArthur Treatment Competence Study, III: Abilities of patients to consent to psychiatric and medical treatments. *Law and Human Behavior, 19*, 149–174.

Grisso, T., & Appelbaum, P. S. (1998). *Assessing competence to consent to treatment: A guide for physicians and other health professionals*. New York, NY: Oxford University Press.

Grisso, T., Appelbaum, P. S., Mulvey, E. P., & Fletcher, K. (1995). The MacArthur Treatment Competence Study, II: Measures of abilities related to competence to consent to treatment. *Law and Human Behavior*, *19*, 127–148.

Health Insurance Portability and Accountability Act of 1996 (HIPAA), Pub. L. No. 104-191, 110 stat. 1936.

Heilbrun, K. (2001). *Principles of forensic mental health assessment*. New York, NY: Kluwer Academic/Plenum Press.

Heilbrun, K., Warren, J., & Picarello, K. (2003). Third party information in forensic assessment. In A. M. Goldstein (Ed.), *Handbook of forensic psychology* (pp. 69–86). Hoboken, NJ: John Wiley & Sons.

Kitamura, F., Tomoda, A., Tsukada, K., Tanaka, M., Kawakami, I., Mishima, S., & Kitamura, T. (1998). Method for assessment of competency to consent in the mentally ill: Rationale, development, and comparison with the medically ill. *International Journal of Law and Psychiatry*, *21*, 223–244.

Koppleman, L. M. (1990). On the evaluative nature of competency and capacity judgments. *International Journal of Law and Psychiatry*, *131*, 209–329.

Marson, D. C., Ingram, K. K., Cody, H. A., & Harrell, L. E. (1995). Assessing the competency of patients with Alzheimer's disease under different legal standards. *Archives of Neurology*, *52*, 949–954.

Melton, G. B., Petrila, P., Poythress, N. G., & Slobogin, C. (2007). *Psychological evaluations for the courts: A handbook for mental health professionals and lawyers* (3rd ed.). New York, NY: Guilford Press.

Rosner, R. (2003). *Principles and Practices of Forensic Psychiatry* (2nd ed). New York, NY: Oxford University Press.

Salgo v. Leland Stanford Junior University Board of Trustees, 154 Cal. App.2d. 560, 317 P.2d. 170 (1957).

Schloendorff v. Society of New York Hospital, 211 N.Y. 125, 105 N.E. 92 (1914).

Schmand, B., Gouwenberg, B., Smit, J. H., & Jonker, C. (1999). Assessment of mental competency in community-dwelling elderly. *Alzheimer Disease and Associated Disorders*, *13*, 80–87.

Tomoda, A., Yasumiya, R., Sumiyama, T., Tsukada, K., Hayakawa, T., Matsubara, K., . . . Kitamura, T. (1997). Validity and reliability of Structured Interview for Competency and Incompetency Assessment Testing and Ranking Inventory. *Journal of Clinical Psychology*, *53*, 443–450.

Vellinga, A., Smit, J. H., Van Leeuwen, E., van Tilburg, W., & Jonker, C. (2004). Competence to consent to treatment of geriatric patients: Judgments of physicians, family members, and the vignette method. *International Journal of Geriatric Psychiatry*, *19*, 645–654.

CHAPTER 23

Guardianship

ERIC Y. DROGIN and THOMAS G. GUTHEIL

INTRODUCTION

Guardianship is "the most inclusive method of substitute decision-making for persons who have been adjudicated incompetent" (Parry & Drogin, 2007, p. 138), whereby "a finding of deficient capacities results in someone other than the patient having to make the decision in question" (Appelbaum & Gutheil, 2007, p. 186). Guardianship constitutes "a legal mechanism by which the state delegates authority over an individual's person or estate to another party," and "is probably the most ancient aspect of mental health law" (Melton, Petrila, Poythress, & Slobogin, 2007, p. 370). As described by Adkins and Ciccone (2010):

> Legal approaches to guardianship can be traced to Egyptian and Greek legal writings. Many of our current approaches to guardianship are derived from Roman law. After the fall of the Roman Empire, English rules on guardianship evolved through the Visigothic Code . . . to the commentary of Lord Coke in the early 17th century. American guardianship law has its roots in colonial law. In colonial times, the expectation was that the immediate family would care for the incompetent individual. The colony had an ability to act to protect the interest of the incompetent if necessary. (p. 274)

Jurisdiction-specific guardianship laws have been in place in every one of the United States for almost three decades (Drogin &

Barrett, 2003). They occasionally provide a labeling distinction between *guardianship* and *conservatorship*—with the former focusing on the individual's self-care and the latter focusing on financial and property issues—but have increasingly tended to address all related functional abilities under the broad heading of "guardianship" (Parry & Drogin, 2007).

Guardianship evaluations are often conducted utilizing a multi-disciplinary "team" approach that draws on the distinct and over-lapping skills of physicians, psychologists, social workers, and other health care professionals (Drogin & Barrett, 2010). It is also worth noting that while guardianship evaluators are autonomous experts offering independent forensic opinions on a case-by-case basis, the "team" notion is optimally extended to include both doctors and lawyers when it comes to fostering "a collaborative approach to the issues of competence, treatment refusal, and vicarious decision-making, resulting in improvements in the quality of care" (Gutheil, Bursztajn, Kaplan, & Brodsky, 1987, p. 446).

Ensnaring respondents of every age, diagnosis, and socio-economic status, guardianship evaluations are particularly fasci-nating because of the way in which they draw together so many diverse competencies within the same legal context. Can the exam-inee drive, vote, marry, live alone, contract for medical care, devise property, or otherwise handle financial matters? To what extent, with how much assistance, and with whom as a source of that assistance? This chapter provides a practically focused overview of resources and approaches for engaging in this rewarding as well as challenging mode of forensic service.

PREPARATION

The experienced expert has long ago been disabused of the notion that one can simply sweep into the hospital ward or examining room, ask some questions, give some tests, and walk away with a supportable forensic conclusion. Nowhere in forensic psychiatry or psychology is this more readily apparent than with guardianship evaluations, which in their broad sweep ultimately involve the assessment of a life to the present date, the gauging of the future of that life, and the determination of who will be running that life. Laying the groundwork for such evaluations requires careful, stepwise planning that may play weeks or even months before the initial face-to-face examination is conducted.

SOURCES OF INFORMATION

Guardianship decisions are optimally informed by collateral interviews and detailed documentation of a medical, nursing, educational, occupational, military, correctional, legal, and personal nature (Drogin & Barrett, 2010). When pursuing such information, the evaluator must nonetheless bear in mind that the guardianship examination is a present state assessment of current functional capacity that is enriched—but never supplanted—by historical data. Following are considerations for obtaining and incorporating preparatory material from each of the aforementioned domains.

Medical   The examinee's alleged disability may be the result of any number of medically related causes. Is there a chronic physical or psychological condition—or some interrelated presentation in which, for example, depression is potentiated by chronic pain? What is the examinee's current medication status? Should the guardianship evaluator be on the lookout for the sedating effects of a particular currently prescribed medication, or for effects of some less than desirable combination of medications (Mallet, Spinewine, & Huang, 2007)? What is the examinee's history of utilization of medical services, and how is this likely to affect his or her rehabilitation prospects, understanding of future medical care options, or willingness to participate in a series of forensic mental health evaluations?

Nursing   Guardianship examinees of all ages are frequently encountered in nursing care facilities, due to conditions associated either with (1) advanced age or (2) traumatic brain injury or other incidents requiring long-term rehabilitative treatment. Is the examinee prone to "sundowning" effects (Staedt & Stoppe, 2005), or has he/she become generally disaffected as a result of prolonged residential placement? The examinee's residence in such facilities is often predicated upon prior determinations of temporary or long-term disability that may be readily available from the medical chart. Those providing day-to-day assistance in these settings are often fruitful sources of information about functional capacities of direct relevance to guardianship determinations. To what extent does the examinee anticipate or direct routine aspects of daily care? Is the examinee even aware that he/she is currently residing in a nursing facility?

Educational   In order to gauge a guardianship examinee's current cognitive status and future cognitive recovery potential, it is necessary to gain an understanding of his or her baseline level of educational attainment. Related to this notion is the examinee's prior exposure to various measures typically administered to assess this construct. When psychological testing identifies what appears to be a limited degree of vocabulary improvement in a specified period of time, just what was the examinee's educationally determined level of oral fluency in the first place? A lack of educational exposure to mathematical calculations can have a substantial influence on an examinee's capacity for managing financial matters. Comparative educational deficiencies can also be reflected in responses to basic mental status examination questions (Glymour, Kawachi, Jencks, & Berkman, 2008).

Occupational   Considerations here are similar to those attaching to notions of educational attainment, with additional psychosocial elements. Occupational history is associated not only with intellectual capacity and with exposure to relevant issues, but also with task approach (Strickler, Whitley, Becker, & Drake, 2009). Is the examinee likely to attempt to "take charge" of the examination, or is he or she going to be a passive participant only? One advantage of a reasonably comprehensive work record is the subsequent opportunity to inquire about these details during clinical and forensic interviewing. For many examinees, their work lives spanned decades and may encompass some of the most gratifying, disappointing, or otherwise significant events in their adult lives. Employment records may also provide useful access to supervisors, supervisees, and other coworkers.

Military   Military service is often recalled in terms of singularly defining moments and lasting friendships, amounting to rich fodder for the identification of collateral sources and for subsequent interviewing. Records from years of service—active or reserve—address issues of discipline, cognitive status, and skills attainment as well as medical history (Jones, Fear, Greenberg, Hull, & Wessely, 2009). These records can often be quite difficult to obtain quickly, so planning and filing one's request in advance will be important. In cases where posttraumatic stress disorder is or was once a factor, military documentation may be useful in confirming the nature of combat experiences even if the examinee's file does not reflect any history of related psychiatric treatment.

Correctional The guardianship examinee's arrest, jail, or prison records may yield useful information on a plethora of issues, including substance abuse, stress tolerance, suicidal ideation, antisocial personality, and general intellectual functioning (Fisher, Roy-Bujnowski, Grudzinskas, Clayfield, Banks, & Wolff, 2006). Will the examinee recall the dates and locations of various spans of incarceration? What sorts of treatment or training programs were undertaken?

How does his/her history of faring under circumstances of confinement comport with current or recent records of hospitalization or nursing home care? Such information will be relevant not only to the assessment of current cognitive and personality functioning but also prognosis and recommendations for future placement.

Legal Records associated with civil actions such as personal injury lawsuits may include results—or at very least clues for the retrieval—of prior medical evaluations to establish or disprove such injuries. In addition, the guardianship examinee may have been examined with regard to child custody proceedings where custodial status was an issue (Gould & Martindale, 2007). Records associated with criminal proceedings will contain several of the same useful elements as identified above for correctional records. Is prior counsel available to shed some light on the contents of legal records, and to comment on his/her experience with the litigant? To what extent can the guardianship examinee recall key aspects of what were likely to have been a highly significant series of events?

Personal Collateral contacts with friends and relatives are a well-established method for supplementing forensic mental health evaluations (Ewing, 2006)—both in the provision of direct information concerning the guardianship examinee and in establishing connections to the various sources of documentation described above. Interviewees can describe how the examinee fared over the course of his or her lifetime and what programmatic and other resources were tapped in his or her support. Central to the guardianship evaluator's considerations of substituted judgment issues (Drogin & Barrett, 2003) will be the information that interviewees can supply regarding the examinee's hopes, dreams, aspirations, and personal preferences. Interviewees may also surface as candidates for the role of the guardian should a sufficient degree of impairment be established for a finding of full or partial disability.

Practical Considerations

The guardianship examination may be conducted in a variety of different locations, at times dictated by professional schedules or caretaker availability, and under any number of circumstances—for example, criminal incarceration, nursing home placement, and the family home. Drogin and Barrett (2010) have identified several practical considerations in preparing for data collection (pp. 51–60) that are condensed and updated as follows:

- *Specific legal question.* In every case, competence is decision specific. What, exactly, has the guardianship evaluator been asked to do? Guardianship statutes, regulations, and case law provide highly detailed direction and are often unique from jurisdiction to jurisdiction (Ford, 2009). Knowing and tracking the exact legal question is critical; otherwise, it will be extraordinarily difficult to "reverse engineer" the results of one's examinations when it comes time to draft a report and the realization dawns that critical issues were not addressed during interview and testing.
- *The role of counsel.* To what extent should counsel be involved or even present? On the one hand, the availability of the examinee's lawyer may facilitate the examination by alleviating concerns and placing the examiner's presence in the proper context, although, on the other hand, there may be concerns about contamination of obtained results in the form of "third-party observer" effects (Horwitz & McCaffrey, 2008).

- *Authorization.* Merely showing up on the scene, claiming to be "the doctor" and starting to ask questions will often aid the guardianship evaluator's cause very little, even when armed with a court order (Drogin & Barrett, 2010). It is best to contact host facilities ahead of time, and perhaps to convey a copy of the court's order in advance, prior to the scheduled examination. Setting the scene for testing and interview in advance can mean avoiding considerable wasted time at the later introduction stage.
- *Scheduling.* Was the guardianship examinee able to make and keep an appointment with the evaluator? Although not much should be made of a single missed appointment—this could happen to anyone, irrespective of cognitive status (Daniels & Jung, 2009)—repeated failures to show (and perhaps an inability to recall the reasons for these failures) may have clinical significance.
- *Location.* What are the respective evaluative merits and practical advantages—or disadvantages—of meeting in the evaluator's office, the attorney's office, the hospital, the nursing home, the jail, or the courthouse? It is well understood that setting can influence the results of evaluations and treatment alike (Mario et al., 2009).

DATA COLLECTION

MENTAL STATUS

Mental status domains for elderly—and other—guardianship examinees will include several specific components (Read & Weinstock, 2010, p. 510), as augmented below:

1. Alertness and attention
   a. Level of arousal
   b. Orientation (to person, place, and time)
2. Cognitive functions
   a. Memory
       i. Immediate recall (of three random items)
       ii. Short-term recall (after 5 to 10 minutes)
       iii. Long-term recall (at the end of the interview; this is also conveyed by accurate reporting of history)

   b. Language
      i. Fluency (including absence of word-finding difficulty)
      ii. Comprehension (of verbal narrative or of written material from a book or magazine)
      iii. Repetition
      iv. Reading and writing for comprehension
   c. Visual
      i. Figure copying
      ii. Ability to recognize faces and emotional expressions (as depicted in drawings or photographs)
   d. Numerical skill
      i. Arithmetic
      ii. Valuation (of currency and other comparative amounts)
   e. Reasoning
      i. Level of abstraction (from interview material, proverbs, and similarities)
      ii. Logical conclusions
   f. Executive functions
      i. Working memory (for example, recalling the purpose of the current interview)
      ii. Ability to focus
      iii. Distractibility
      iv. Ability to shift set (i.e., to adopt a change of interview subject matter)
3. Perception and thought
4. Affect and mood, response and modulation

These critical mental status categories for a fully realized guardianship evaluation—modified in their internal foci and emphases for the particular case at hand—will establish the subsequent course of standardized psychological testing as well as clinical and forensic interviewing.

Psychological Testing

Typical measures of cognitive functioning and personality are detailed elsewhere in this book as they pertain to most forensic psychological examinations. Drogin and Barrett (2010) have identified—among others—the following assessment measures that are particularly relevant for the assessment of strengths and weaknesses that make up the various components of a guardianship evaluation (pp. 92–96):

- Adult Functional Adaptive Behavioral Scale (Spirrison & Sewell, 1996)
- Community Competence Scale (Searight & Goldberg, 1991)
- Competency Interview Schedule (Douglas & Koch, 2001)
- Decision-Making Instrument for Guardianship (Moye, 2003)
- Direct Assessment of Functional Status (Mariani, 2004)
- Functional Independence Measure (Timbeck & Spaulding, 2004)

What these and similar measures have in common is their overtly forensic focus on the guardianship examinee's functional abilities, as opposed to feeding into what in some instances can properly be characterized as the *irrelevance of diagnosis* (Read & Weinstock, 2010, p. 512). *Specific competence* (Appelbaum & Gutheil, 2007, p. 185) is the watchword in these cases. The examinee's ability—or lack thereof—to perform a series of often statutorily defined and meticulously itemized functions constitutes a performance that may or may not result in an ultimate forensic finding of "disability" (Parry & Drogin, 2001, p. 91). Guardianship evaluators should strive to avoid the pitfall of focusing upon "diagnosis rather than functional capacity" (Gutheil, 2007, p. 516).

CLINICAL AND FORENSIC INTERVIEWING

Guardianship evaluators will engage in the usual structured and structural interviews they might perform in any clinical examination—forensic assessment is not a context for "leapfrogging" over the usual obligation to understand the person with whom one is confronted—before moving forward to a consideration of the specific—and diverse—disability components encountered from jurisdiction to jurisdiction (Bolton & Pinals, 2006; Hurme, 2007). In other words, as in any court-related endeavor, the guardianship evaluator should "conduct a standard psychiatric examination, including a mental status, and obtain additional relevant information" (Gold et al., 2008, p. S15).

Drogin & Barrett (2003, p. 309) have provided the following sample domains—blended, of course, with clinical considerations indicated above—for addressing one statutorily defined construct for guardianship:

- Identifying Information
- Orientation
- Education
- Finances
- Self-Care
- Social Contact and Leisure Pursuits
- Testamentary Capacity
- Medical Care
- Driving an Automobile
- Voting
- Behavioral Response
- Review

Experienced forensic clinicians will note the inclusion of "Driving an Automobile" among these domains. Some states specifically call for consideration of this particular competency within the overall construct of guardianship. It is a good example of how the courts will sometimes expect guardianship evaluators to opine on issues for which they have minimal practical training. As a general rule, our forensic colleagues would do well by "leaving driving assessment to motor vehicle agencies" (Appelbaum & Gutheil, 2007, p. 154).

DATA INTERPRETATION

ETHICAL ISSUES: CLINICAL

The American Psychiatric Association provides *The Principles of Medical Ethics with Annotations Especially Applicable to Psychiatry* ("Principles of Medical Ethics"; 2009) while the American Psychological Association provides the *Ethical Principles of Psychologists and Code of Conduct* ("Ethics Code"; 2002). These sources of guidance apply to forensic as well as mainstream clinical practice, but our focus in this section is primarily on the latter. Following are a few representative examples of how each document addresses issues frequently encountered in guardianship cases.

Contractual Arrangements Issues of agency are likely to color the interpretation of guardianship evaluation data—not to the extent, for example, of influencing a choice of diagnosis, but rather in framing the forensic question in contemplation of whom the expert considers to be his/her "client." According to the Principles of Medical Ethics (2009), contractual arrangements "should be explicitly established" (p. 5). The psychologists' Ethics Code (2002) states that when psychologists are involved in providing services "at the request of a third party," they "attempt to clarify at the outset of the service the nature of the relationship with all individuals or organizations involved," including "the role of the psychologist" and also "an identification of who is the client" (p. 1065).

Lifetime Learning The Principles of Medical Ethics (2009) indicate that "psychiatrists are responsible for their own continuing education and should be mindful of the fact that theirs must be a lifetime of learning" (p. 8). For guardianship evaluators, the most important topics to track may involve culture and aging, but will also include all aspects of relevant psychiatric knowledge, skill, training, education, and experience. Similar requirements are reflected in the psychologists' Ethics Code (2002), with its direction that "psychologists undertake ongoing efforts to develop and maintain their competence," including a requirement that in these evaluative settings they should be "reasonably familiar with the judicial or administrative rules governing their roles" (p. 1064).

Personal Examination According to the Principles of Medical Ethics (2009), "the psychiatrist may permit his or her certification to be used for the involuntary treatment of any person only following his or her personal examination of that person" (p. 9). As guardianship proceedings are likely to result in similar deprivations of liberty and medical choice, we would encourage evaluators to recognize in their data interpretations the primary importance of a clinician's direct observations. The psychologists' Ethics Code (2002) does not make a similarly overt declaration for any particular form of assessment, indicating instead that there are circumstances under which a personally conducted examination is not "practical" (p. 1071). Nonetheless, every effort should be made to conduct a personal examination in guardianship evaluations.

ETHICAL ISSUES: FORENSIC

The American Academy of Psychiatry and the Law provides *Ethics Guidelines for the Practice of Forensic Psychiatry* ("AAPL Guidelines"; 2005) while the Committee on Ethical Guidelines for Forensic Psychologists (a joint undertaking of the American Psychology–Law Society and the American Academy of Forensic Psychology) provides the *Specialty Guidelines for Forensic Psychologists* ("AP-LS Guidelines"; 1991). Following are a few representative examples of how each document addresses common issues in guardianship cases.

Confidentiality   This is a particularly knotty issue in the context of guardianship evaluations, given that a central aspect of this form of forensic service involves collateral consultation with a range of friends, relatives, custodians, and service providers. According to the AAPL Guidelines (2005), "psychiatrists should maintain confidentiality to the extent possible, given the legal context" (p. 1). The extent to which limitations have been placed on disclosure to collateral contacts should be taken into account when interpreting the data derived from those sources. The AP-LS Guidelines (1991) place a similar premium upon confidentiality issues by calling for a sensitivity to these issues and for forensic psychologists to "conduct their professional activities in a manner that respects those known rights and privileges" (p. 660).

Informed Consent   Guardianship evaluations proceed not from a presumption of incompetency, but nonetheless from an understanding that incompetency is quite likely to be present. The AAPL Guidelines (2005) state that "if the evaluee is not competent to give consent, the evaluator should follow the appropriate laws of the jurisdiction" (p. 2)—a situation complicated, of course, by the fact that it is conducting the examination that enables the evaluator to establish the presence or absence of competency. The degree to which the examinee does or does not understand the disclosure of data will bear considerably upon the fashion in which such data are interpreted. In addition to asserting that informed consent should be obtained unless an evaluation is "court ordered," the AP-LS Guidelines (1991) encourage evaluators to provide "reasonable notice" to the examinee's attorney before proceeding when the examinee "may not have the capacity to provide informed consent" (p. 659).

Belief in a Treatment Relationship   According to the AAPL Guidelines (2005), "psychiatrists have a continuing obligation to be sensitive to the fact that although a warning has been given, the evaluee may develop the belief that there is a treatment relationship" (p. 2). This is all the more likely in that a very substantial portion of guardianship evaluations are (1) conducted in hospital or nursing home settings where "doctors" of all sorts constantly come and go; and (2) performed upon persons with dementia. The AP-LS Guidelines (1991) address notifying the examinee about the "purpose" and "nature" of forensic services more generally (p. 659), without addressing any "continuing obligation" where a misperceived treatment relationship is concerned. Data interpretation will clearly be affected by the possibility that the examinee believes disclosures are being made to secure treatment instead of to address a potential deprivation of liberty. The more skilled and empathic the examiner may be, the more likely the examinee is to slip into an inappropriate treatment mind-set; the examiner should be alert to this slippage and repeat forensic warnings as needed.

INTERPRETIVE DIVERSITY: CULTURE AND AGING

Diversity issues are as critical in interpreting the results of guardianship evaluations as they are in any other form of forensic endeavor. The two primary diversity issues encountered in this context are culture and aging:

1. *Culture.* Perspectives on disability, aging, medication, family roles, and other issues central to guardianship determination play out with astonishing diversity in various cultures in the United States and abroad. The American Psychological Association (2003) has promulgated *Guidelines on Multicultural Education, Training, Research, Practice, and Organizational Change for Psychologists* that identify racial and ethnic diversity statistics and describe how psychologists—and others—can "recognize the importance of multicultural sensitivity/responsiveness to, understanding of, and understanding about racially and ethnically different

individuals" (p. 385), with particular attention to how evaluators can "ascertain whether the constructs assessed by their instruments have the same meaning across cultures, as well as the same function across cultures" (p. 389).

2. *Aging.* The American Psychological Association's *Guidelines for Psychological Practice with Older Adults* (2004) have identified a number of considerations valuable to the interpretation of data obtained from evaluations conducted with older persons. These include such clinical dimensions as:

   - Social and psychological dynamics of the aging process
   - Biological and health-related aspects of aging
   - Cognitive changes in older adults
   - Problems in daily living for older adults
   - The expression of psychopathology in older adults
   - The interpretation of measures initially created for use with younger populations
   - The interpretation of measures created for older adults
   - The evaluator's own attitudes and beliefs regarding the aging process

These are critical interpretive considerations for conducting guardianship evaluations, particularly when one considers that "it is by now axiomatic that the population of most North American and European countries is aging" (Petrila, 2007, p. 337), with the result that the primary focus of guardianship research as well as practice is now oriented toward persons aged 65 years and older (Drogin, 2007). Further developing one's understanding of "gerontology, neuropsychology, rehabilitation psychology, neuropathology, psychopharmacology, and psychopathology in older adults" will assist the evaluator "to evaluate age-related cognitive decline and dementia" (American Psychological Association, 1998, p. 1300). A helpful reference in this regard is the American Psychiatric Association's current *Practice Guideline for the Treatment of Patients with Alzheimer's Disease and Other Dementias* (2007).

THE (POTENTIAL) GUARDIAN

The court's charge to the guardianship evaluator may include an invitation—or an order—to comment or opine on the characteristics of the ideal guardian for the examinee in question. This is a reasonable task in light of the voluminous information that evaluators will have amassed and their assessment of the examinee's unique needs. It is distinct from what evaluators may also be asked to do: to opine on the suitability of a specific, contemplated guardian, which is a function—so often fraught with the confrontation of deep-seated and complex family dynamics (Isenberg & Gutheil, 1981)—that in our opinion is best left to the investigative resources and judgment of the court itself.

Appelbaum & Gutheil (2007) have compiled a list of the "characteristics of the ideal guardian" (pp. 205–206), which are excerpted and condensed as follows:

- *Availability.* Decisions in the clinical sphere often must be made rapidly, on short notice, and at unpredictable times. Ideally, the guardian must be both geographically and temporally available. One implication of this criterion is that if a guardian ever wishes to take a vacation, some sort of coverage must be arranged, in advance of need, by another party empowered in the same manner, because there is no guarantee that the ward's clinical status will remain stable in the interim. The same is true, of course, for the ward's financial and social status.
- *Competence.* Disturbed wards not infrequently come from disturbed families in which no available family member possesses sufficient capacity to grasp the complexities of major decisions. Attainment of sufficient background knowledge, even in a stable family member, might require formal training in the issues of concern to the ward's life. This might include attainment of an educated layperson's knowledge of rudimentary psychopharmacology and advantages and disadvantages of various residential and treatment options.
- *Empathic intuition.* This refers to the often desirable quality in a guardian of being able to make a difficult determination according to what the ward would want were he or she sane, competent, and possessed of sound judgment. At issue is the guardian's ability to make truly vicarious decisions. A guardian's assumptions about a ward's desires will, of course, reflect to some extent the guardian's own values or the guardian's

preconceptions regarding people in situations similar to that being experienced by the ward.

- *Freedom from conflict of interest.* The guardian should be free from contamination of purpose by any conflicting interest. Such interests might include psychological, psychosocial, or socioeconomic concerns that would or might interfere with objective substituted judgment. When family members serve as guardians, these matters wax complex. There may exist the empathy desired of guardians, but this may be balanced by an inevitably ambiguous psychological and practical involvement with the ward.
- *Willingness.* Guardianship can at times be a sinecure, but occasionally it can also be a burdensome, even overwhelmingly demanding role. It may require not only expenditure of time and energy, but tolerance of disruption of one's schedule and private life, tolerance of the emotional conflict deriving from the role, and tolerance of the ingratitude, vituperation, and even litigation of the ward. Not surprisingly, even adequate remuneration has often been insufficient to persuade potential guardians—including attorneys—to take the job.

COMMUNICATION

Appelbaum & Gutheil (2007) have provided a "Checklist for Testifying in Court" (pp. 308–309), selected components of which are excerpted and adapted here for their particular relevance to the guardianship evaluator's appearance on the witness stand:

- Recall that the role of the witness is to inform the court.
- Clear sufficient time in the schedule to permit unhurried participation.
- Present testimony clearly, audibly, and comprehensibly.
- Attempt to have impressive credentials spelled out and entered into the record.
- Avoid responding to discrediting cross-examination as a personal attack.
- Attend to specific questions and remain within their scope when answering.
- Remember the concept of "reasonable medical certainty."

- Describe the data first, and interpret meanings or conclusions later.
- Tell the truth to the extent you are best able.
- State when a question cannot be answered.
- Beware of qualifying phrases, metaphors, and analogies.
- Exercise concern regarding the examinee's presence in court.

The preceding reference to "reasonable medical certainty" reflects an issue that has bedeviled medical and research scholars for decades: What, exactly, does this term mean? For example:

> Reasonable medical certainty. What is that? I am afraid to report that after having attempted to study the subject for many, many hours, I have discovered that the status of reasonable medical certainty is quite uncertain. In fact, I can make the statement that I am certain that reasonable medical certainty is an uncertain legal concept. (Rappeport, 1985, p. 5)

> Reasonable medical certainty, in my opinion, should express the psychiatrist's highest level of confidence in the validity and reliability of his opinion. . . . It cannot be directly translated into the legal scale of levels of proof. It is the obligation of the trier of fact, rather than the expert witness, to make that translation in its decision. . . . (Diamond, 1985, p. 123)

> The problem, of course, is that few jurisdictions have defined the term. If the jurisdiction in which the expert is testifying has done so, the expert should learn it and be prepared to use it if questioned. If there is no accepted legal definition, experts should adopt one of their own. . . . Another option, is to ask the attorney who raised the question to define it. . . . (Miller, 2006, p. 286)

When possible, of course, "experts could avoid the term altogether and directly testify how confident they are in their opinion" (Gianelli, 2010, p. 40). The guardianship evaluator—by virtue of having to incorporate so many different sources of information, in the context of a multiply determined legal construct with a host of stepwise determinations—is at least as vulnerable as any other forensic practitioner to the issues raised in these discussions of "reasonable medical certainty." Care should be taken to address these issues in reports and in pretrial discussions as appropriate. Blanket pronouncements on competency, however eagerly sought by counsel and the courts, are particularly suspect where the controlling statute calls for determinations of partial versus limited guardianship and the separate assessment of a specified list of abilities and disabilities.

The exceptional degree of reliance on external documentation and other collateral sources—present, to be sure, in other forms of forensic work, but rarely to this extent—makes the guardianship evaluator a target for a common cross-examination gambit in which counsel asks "what assumptions you made on taking the case" (Gutheil & Dattilio, 2008, p. 70). To reply reflexively that there were "none" may seem to the judge and jury as defensive as it is inaccurate. Care should be taken in such cases to distinguish "assumptions"—initial working hypotheses the expert stands ready to see disproven—from the "conclusions" that attend a fully executed, unbiased evaluation. Implicit in all of this is a good faith approach that acknowledges competency as the default conclusion.

Another issue related to database sufficiency involves attempts by counsel to withhold forensically relevant information as a means for influencing the guardianship evaluator's opinion. Research by Gutheil and Simon (2002) resulted in nearly half of a sample of forensically experienced respondents reporting that they had been subjected to withholding, although in some cases it is clear that attorneys "honestly believe that the document is not relevant to the expert question being asked" (p. 59). The point at which the guardianship evaluator is composing his or her report and its "listing of everything you reviewed" (Gutheil, 2009, p. 97) presents a good opportunity for approaching counsel once more to make sure that all relevant documentation has been obtained.

REFERENCES

Adkins, J. A., & Ciccone, J. R. (2010). Expert witness testimony in conservatorship proceedings. *Journal of the American Academy of Psychiatry and the Law, 38*, 273–275.

American Academy of Psychiatry and the Law. (2005). *Ethics guidelines for the practice of forensic psychiatry.* Bloomfield, CT: Author.

American Psychiatric Association. (2007). *Practice guidelines for the treatment of patients with Alzheimer's Disease and other dementias* (2nd ed.) Washington, DC: Author.

American Psychiatric Association. (2009). *The principles of medical ethics with annotations especially applicable to psychiatry.* Arlington, VA: Author.

American Psychological Association. (1998). Guidelines for the evaluation of dementia and age-related cognitive decline. *American Psychologist, 53,* 1298–1303.

American Psychological Association. (2002). Ethical principles of psychologists and code of conduct. *American Psychologist, 57,* 1060–1073.

American Psychological Association. (2003). Guidelines on multicultural education, training, research, practice, and organizational change for psychologists. *American Psychologist, 58,* 377–402.

American Psychological Association. (2004). Guidelines for psychological practice with older adults. *American Psychologist, 59,* 236–260.

Appelbaum, P. S., & Gutheil, T. G. (2007). *Clinical handbook of psychiatry and the law* (4th ed.). Philadelphia, PA: Lippincott Williams & Wilkins.

Bolton, M. A., & Pinals, D. A. (2006). Interstate transfer of guardianships. *Journal of the American Academy of Psychiatry and the Law, 34,* 416–418.

Committee on Ethical Guidelines for Forensic Psychologists (1991). Specialty guidelines for forensic psychologists. *Law and Human Behavior, 15,* 655–665.

Daniels, M. K., & Jung, S. (2009). Missed initial appointments at an outpatient forensic psychiatric clinic. *Journal of Forensic Psychiatry and Psychology, 20,* 964–973.

Diamond, B. L. (1985). Reasonable medical certainty, diagnostic thresholds, and definitions of mental illness in the legal context. *Bulletin of the American Academy of Psychiatry and the Law, 13,* 121–128.

Douglas, K. S., & Koch, W. J. (2001). Civil commitment and civil competence: Psychological issues. In J. R. Ogloff & R. A. Schuller (Eds.), *Introduction to psychology and law: Canadian perspectives* (pp. 353–374). Toronto, ON: University of Toronto Press.

Drogin, E. Y. (2007). Guardianship for older adults: A jurisprudent science perspective. *Journal of Psychiatry and Law, 35,* 553–654.

Drogin, E. Y., & Barrett, C. L. (2003). Substituted judgment: Roles for the forensic psychologist. In I. B. Weiner (Series Ed.) & A. M. Goldstein (Vol. Ed.), *Comprehensive handbook of psychology: Vol. 11. Forensic psychology* (pp. 301–312). Hoboken, NJ: John Wiley & Sons.

Drogin, E. Y., & Barrett, C. L. (2010). *Evaluation for guardianship.* New York, NY: Oxford University Press.

Ewing, C. P. (2006). Collateral interviews reconsidered. *Monitor on Psychology*, *37*(7), 83.

Fisher, W. H., Roy-Bujnowski, K. M., Grudzinskas, A. J., Clayfield, J. C., Banks, S. M., & Wolff, N. (2006). Patterns and prevalence of arrest in a statewide cohort of mental health care consumers. *Psychiatric Services*, *57*, 1623–1628.

Ford, D. D. (2009). Fundamental issues to understand before accepting a guardianship litigation engagement. *The Advocate*, *48*(3), 77–80.

Gianelli, P. C. (2010, Spring). "Reasonable scientific certainty": A phrase in search of a meaning. *Criminal Justice*, 40–41.

Glymour, M. M., Kawachi, I., Jencks, C. S., & Berkman, L. F. (2008). Does childhood schooling affect old age memory or mental status? *Journal of Epidemiology and Community Mental Health*, *62*, 532–537.

Gold, L. H., Anfang, S. A., Drukteinis, A. M., Metzner, J. L., Price, M., Wall, B. M., . . . Zonana, H. V. (2008). AAPL practice guideline for the forensic evaluation of psychiatric disability. *Journal of the American Academy of Psychiatry and the Law*, *36*, S3–S50.

Gould, J. W., & Martindale, D. A. (2007). *The art and science of child custody evaluations*. New York, NY: Guilford Press.

Gutheil, T. G. (2007). Common pitfalls in the evaluation of testamentary capacity. *Journal of the American Academy of Psychiatry and the Law*, *35*, 514–517.

Gutheil, T. G. (2009). *The psychiatrist as expert witness* (2nd ed.). Arlington, VA: American Psychiatric Publishing.

Gutheil, T. G., Bursztajn, H., Kaplan, A. N., & Brodsky, A. (1987). Participation in competency assessment and treatment decisions: The role of a psychiatrist-attorney team. *Mental and Physical Disability Law Reporter*, *11*, 446–449.

Gutheil, T. G., & Dattilio, F. M. (2008). *Practical approaches to forensic mental health testimony*. Philadelphia, PA: Lippincott Williams & Wilkins.

Gutheil, T. G., & Simon, R. I. (2002). *Mastering forensic psychiatric practice: Advanced strategies for the expert witness*. Washington, DC: American Psychiatric Publishing.

Horwitz, J. E., & McCaffrey, R. J. (2008). Effects of a third party observer and anxiety on tests of executive function. *Archives of Clinical Neuropsychology*, *23*, 409–417.

Hurme, S. B. (2007). Crossing state lines: Issues and solutions in interstate guardianship. *Stetson Law Review*, *37*, 87–142.

Isenberg, E. F., & Gutheil, T. G. (1981). Family process in legal guardianship for the psychiatric patient: A clinical study. *Bulletin of the American Academy of Psychiatry and the Law*, *9*, 40–41.

Jones, N., Fear, N. T., Greenberg, N., Hull, L., & Wessely, S. (2009). Occupational outcomes in soldiers hospitalized with mental health problems. *Occupational Medicine, 59*, 459–465.

Mallet, L., Spinewine, A., & Huang, A. (2007). The challenge of managing drug interactions in elderly people. *The Lancet, 370*, 185–191.

Mariani, C. (2004). Monitoring of functional deficits in neurology: Dementias. *Neurological Sciences, 25*, S33.

Mario, B., Massimiliano, M., Chiara, M., Alessandro, S., Antonella, C., & Gianfranco, F. (2009). White-coat effect among older patients with suspected cognitive impairment: Prevalence and clinical implications. *International Journal of Geriatric Psychiatry, 24*, 509–517.

Melton, G. B., Petrila, P., Poythress, N. G., & Slobogin, C. (2007). *Psychological evaluations for the courts: A handbook for mental health professionals and lawyers* (3rd ed.). New York, NY: Guilford Press.

Miller, R. D. (2006). Reasonable medical certainty: A rose by any other name. *Journal of Psychiatry and the Law, 34*, 273–289.

Moye, J. (2003). Guardianship and conservatorship. In T. Grisso (Ed.), *Evaluating competencies* (2nd ed., pp. 309–310). New York, NY: Plenum Press.

Parry, J. W., & Drogin, E. Y. (2001). *Civil law handbook on psychiatric and psychological evidence and testimony.* Washington, DC: American Bar Association.

Parry, J. W., & Drogin, E. Y. (2007). *Mental disability law, evidence and testimony: A comprehensive reference manual for lawyers, judges and mental disability professionals.* Washington, DC: American Bar Association.

Petrila, J. (2007). Introduction to this issue: Elder issues. *Behavioral Sciences and the Law, 25*, 337.

Rappeport, J. R. (1985). Reasonable medical certainty. *Bulletin of the American Academy of Psychiatry and the Law, 13*, 5–15.

Read, S. L., & Weinstock, R. (2010). Forensic geriatric psychiatry. In R. I. Simon & L. H. Gold (Eds.), *Textbook of forensic psychiatry* (2nd ed., pp. 505–528). Arlington, VA: American Psychiatric Publishing.

Searight, H. R., & Goldberg, M. A. (1991). The Community Competence Scale as a measure of functional daily living skills. *Journal of Mental Health Administration, 18*, 128–134.

Spirrison, C. L., & Sewell, S. M. (1996). The Adult Functional Adaptive Behavior Scale (AFABS) and psychiatric inpatients: Indices of reliability and validity. *Assessment, 3*, 387–391.

Staedt, J., & Stoppe, G. (2005). Treatment of rest-activity disorders in dementia and special focus on sundowning. *International Journal of Geriatric Psychiatry, 20*, 507–511.

Strickler, D. C., Whitley, R., Becker, D. R., & Drake, R. E. (2009). First person accounts of long-term employment activity among people with dual diagnosis. *Psychiatric Rehabilitation Journal*, 32, 261–268.

Timbeck, R. J., & Spaulding, S. J. (2004). Ability of the Functional Independence Measure (FIM) to predict rehabilitation outcomes after stroke: A review of the literature. *Physical and Occupational Therapy in Geriatrics*, 22, 63–76.

CHAPTER 24

Psychiatric and Psychological Malpractice

ERIC Y. DROGIN and DONALD J. MEYER

INTRODUCTION

The specter of malpractice litigation is so pervasive that younger doctors may be surprised to learn just how recently it assumed its current proportions. Practitioners still active today can recall when the American Psychological Association decided to investigate whether lawsuits were enough of a risk for its members to seek coverage at all—especially when group policies might cost as much as "$100 for three years, or $33 figured annually" (APA Committee on Malpractice Insurance, 1952, p. 677). Over the course of the past 10 years, the cost of psychological malpractice policies in some states has steadily approached $3,000 per year (Wagner, 2002), while the average psychiatric malpractice policy currently costs over $6,000 per year (Daly, 2010).

Increasing premiums reflect a growing number of lawsuits, which in turn reflect a greater demand for psychiatric and psychological forensic experts, although "spiraling consultation fees for experts in every professional discipline have compelled lawyers to take affirmative steps to contain costs" (Drogin & Barrett, 2007, p. 468). None of the clinical subspecialties has escaped the proliferation of malpractice claims. The risk that forensic practitioners may be sued "though not great, has nonetheless increased beyond the level of insignificance that once existed" (Greenberg, Shuman, Feldman,

Middleton, & Ewing, 2007, p. 446). This is primarily because of the steady erosion of expert immunity in state court decisions nationwide, due to "concern that the safeguards cited by courts to ensure honest expert witness testimony—that is, potential prosecution for perjury and cross-examination—are not effective" (Binder, 2002, p. 1820). Forensic practitioners shielded from malpractice suits may still face the wrath of litigants in the form of complaints to a state medical or psychological board (Belar & Deardorff, 2009) or to the ethics committees of professional societies.

To understand the elements of a malpractice suit, one must understand certain legal concepts: negligence, the standard of care, and legal causation (Meyer, Simon, & Shuman, 2010). Negligence in common English usage means carelessness or recklessness. However, as a legal term of art, negligent conduct is conduct falling below the standard of care. Standard of care is also a legal term of art. While jurisdictional definitions may vary slightly, in general the standard of care is defined as the conduct of an average, prudent individual in similar circumstances.

The standard of care applies to all conduct, not just the actions of professionals. Persons doing repairs to their homes' walkways use yellow tape and detours to conform with the requisite standard of care due a passerby. A professional cleaner alerts the public that the floor is wet to conform with the requisite standard of care. Absent those prudent actions, it could be alleged that an individual's conduct was negligent. The applicable standard of care due by the defendant is decided at trial by the *trier of fact*. In a bench trial, the judge serves as the trier of fact. In a jury trial, the jury assumes that role.

Not all harms are legally compensable. Compensation may be sought for harms that were caused by ordinary or intentional negligent conduct.

The harm must be directly caused by the negligent conduct. Legal causation is known as "proximate cause" and is conceptually different from the scientific causation with which clinicians are more familiar. Scientific cause typically includes multiple factors that draw on research from a wide range of scientific disciplines. While scientific causes are discovered, legal causation is decided in a court of law by the trier of fact (Baranoski, 2009). Proximate cause or legal causation rests on the concepts of the *but for* test and *foreseeability*:

(1) but for the negligent conduct, the harm would not have occurred; and (2) the harm was also a foreseeable consequence of the negligent conduct.

In a malpractice suit, the plaintiff (patient) alleges injury by the defendant (clinician). Mental health treatment is not without underlying risks and not all harms stemming from treatment are legally compensable. Those harms which were directly (proximately) caused by clinical acts that fell below what an average, reasonable prudent clinician would do in similar circumstances are legally defined as below the requisite standard of care, proximately caused and therefore negligent and compensable (Meyer et al., 2010, p. 208).

The standard of care or clinician duty to the patient is shaped not only by the words average and prudent but also by the words *in similar circumstances*. Although vast knowledge is accumulated by psychiatrists and psychologists during the course of several years of training and practice, the requisite standard of care in a malpractice suit is shaped by the specific facts and circumstances at trial such as patient diagnosis, acuity of condition, accuracy of history, treatment adherence, and interprofessional and institutional resources.

Malpractice cases also proceed with geographical sensitivity to just whose standard of care is employed as a benchmark. Some legal jurisdictions use the locality rule for their definition of the standard of care. These jurisdictions ask the trier of fact to decide what would be the conduct of an ordinary, prudent individual from that specific geographic area. More commonly, jurisdictions rely on a national standard, acknowledging that knowledge and standards freely move across state boundaries. Under this majority approach, the defendant's actions are measured against the standard of conduct nationwide (Parry & Drogin, 2007, pp. 350–351).

When determination of the standard of care involves knowledge that is outside the experience of trier of fact (judge or jury), the law provides for expert testimony. Though typically retained by either the plaintiff or defense attorney, the service of expert testimony is to educate the trier of fact: experts advocate for an objectively based opinion and, in contrast to the attorneys, are not advocates for a side.

Federal Rule of Evidence (FRE) 702 states that "if scientific, technical, or other specialized knowledge will assist the trier of fact to understand the evidence or determine a fact in issue, a witness qualified as an expert by knowledge, skill, experience, training or education, may testify thereto in the form of an opinion or otherwise." Experts offering testimony should be familiar with the legal regulation of admissibility. While some jurisdictions have retained the rule of "general acceptance" described in *Frye v. United States* (1923), most jurisdictions rely on the FRE, consistent with the opinions of the Supreme Court of the United States in three pivotal cases: *Daubert v. Merrell Dow Pharmaceuticals, Inc.* (1993), *General Electric Co. v. Joiner* (1997), and *Kumho Tire Co. v. Carmichael* (1999).

In *Daubert*, the Supreme Court overturned the *Frye* rule, asserting that admissibility was to be determined by the trial judge based upon the testimony's relevance to the case at trial and its reliability (trustworthiness). Reliability should be assessed on the basis of whether the scientific field's principles and methodologies (1) have been or can be tested; (2) have been peer reviewed; (3) have a known error rate; and (4) have gained general acceptance—the last of these components reflecting the ongoing influence of *Frye*.

Mental health experts might reasonably have wondered how those standards of reliability would apply to their testimony, which involved case-specific extrapolation and did not fit the model of bench science. In *Kumho* (1999) the Supreme Court opined:

> A federal judge may properly consider one or more of some specific factors—whether the theory or the technique (1) can be and has been tested; (2) has been subjected to peer review or publication; (3) has (a) a high known or potential rate of error, and (b) standards controlling the technique's operation; and (4) enjoys general acceptance within a relevant scientific community—where such factors are reasonable measures of the testimony's reliability. The trial judge may ask questions of this sort not only where an expert relies on the application of scientific principles, but also where an expert relies on skill- or experience-based observation. (p. 642).

In *Joiner* (1997), the Supreme Court reified that expert testimony must be relevant and reliable and based on established knowledge within the field and not on just the opinion of an expert. The Court specified that "experts commonly extrapolate from existing data. But nothing in either *Daubert* or the Federal Rules of Evidence requires a district court to admit opinion evidence which is connected to existing data only by the *ipse dixit* [he, himself, said it] of the expert" (p. 515).

Mental health experts have a wide range of resources on which to rely to found their case specific opinions within the framework of existing science: the research literature, textbooks, review articles, treatment guidelines, diagnostic instruments, and special studies. While an expert opinion may be well founded, experts should be mindful there is no iron-clad algorithm which of itself can delineate a case-specific standard of care.

In addition to the legal requirements for a court's credentialing a practitioner as an expert and the expert's opinion as admissible, increasingly "health care disciplines . . . have independently established general ethical guidelines for their respective members" (Melton, Petrila, Poythress, & Slobogin, 2007, p. 87). In *Austin v. American Association of Neurological Surgeons* (2001), a federal appeals court gave strong support to a professional society's role in the regulation of the conduct of health care providers offering expert testimony. Professional societies have stressed that an expert have actual, current expertise with the issues at trial and that the expert function objectively, independently, and within the bounds of accepted scientific knowledge.

The standard of care is not to be confused with the "standard of proof," which defines the degree of certainty with which an allegation must be proven. Malpractice must be proven by a preponderance of the evidence, that is, more likely than not. Clear and convincing, the middle standard of proof usually applies to matters of citizenship or parental rights. Beyond a reasonable doubt is reserved for criminal trials. Clinicians may be painfully surprised that with their reputations, savings, and even livelihoods at stake, verdicts in their cases will be based upon the least stringent of the available standards of proof.

The responsibility for establishing this standard—the "burden of proof"—is that of the "plaintiff," the person bringing the lawsuit against the doctor. The burden of proof consists of two interrelated components: the "burden of persuasion" and the "burden of production" (Clermont & Yeazell, 2010). The former addresses the plaintiff's obligation to convince the court that the doctor committed malpractice, while the latter addresses the plaintiff's obligation to deliver the sort of evidence that would support that conclusion.

An alternative to the traditional malpractice system—and its daunting costs and infuriating delays—uses malpractice "tribunals" that screen cases for proper substantiation. In addition, "many states now utilize a variety of methods, such as proactive legislation which may cap the amounts of plaintiff awards, govern mediation, and determine the form of the physician's apology as integral parts of action plans to address liability reform" (Norris, 2007, p. 287).

PREPARATION

STEPPING FORWARD AS AN "EXPERT"

Clinicians who proffer themselves as experts can anticipate a series of issues that may be raised regarding their qualifications to serve.

Appropriate Discipline and Specialization Due to expediency, inexperience, or a combination thereof, counsel may view different mental health experts as fungible—that is, he/she may not perceive any relevant differences between psychiatrists and psychologists, or between clinical psychologists and school psychologists. Disciplines and specializations may overlap considerably, but the critical issues here are those of *authenticity* and *credibility*. It may be that every mental health professional is aware of the need to monitor patients for the ongoing efficacy and safety of certain prescribed medications; however, does a psychologist truly possess the knowledge, skill, training, education, and expertise to speak articulately to this issue on cross-examination? Along similar lines, although he or she may be an informed consumer of psychological test results, is a psychiatrist sufficiently well informed to address issues in the selection, administration, scoring, and interpretation of such measures?

Conflicts of Interest Any real or perceived conflict of interest can be a serious challenge to an expert's credibility. Experts should have no prior or independent knowledge of a case. They should have nothing personally, professionally, or economically to gain or lose from the outcome of the litigation. Experts who have a personal or professional ax to grind about a certain professional issue may best direct that motivation to avenues of social policy rather than testifying in court. Experts are educators of the trier of fact, not legal advocates.

Experts sometimes wrongly believe they can simply rise above conflicts simply because they are experts: they have become unduly confident in their ability to be objective where others might not. Experts in general would be better served to ask themselves if others might perceive a conflict of interest: in a court of law, what others perceive will be the litmus test for the expert's credibility.

Some of these conflicts are more subtle than others. What should be done when both the defendant and the expert are recognized members of a small professional community in the same largely rural jurisdiction? What if both doctors continue to compete for the same sources of grant funding, attended the same undergraduate program, or served on the same large panel at a national scientific convention? In addition to individual soul-searching and collegial or institutional ethics consultation, the potential must be fully disclosing to counsel of such potential conflicts, and the best practice is to ensure that attorneys for both sides have signed off on attenuated connections that are ultimately deemed acceptable.

Level of Actual and Recognized Expertise   Experts must have real and current knowledge, training and experience regarding the issues at trial to which they will testify. As illustrated by the federal case of *Blanchard v. Eli Lilly* (2002), doctors whose expertise is based solely on reading and long-past experience will face vigorous cross-examination if not exclusion. Experts are cautioned to eschew the narcissistic inducements of the adversarial process and remain squarely within their actual expertise. More than one expert has been forced to quickly construct a tree that would support the limb out onto which the expert wrongly crawled (Gutheil, 2009).

It is not necessary, however, to be the nation's predominant expert in the defendant's general area of practice—as much as one's lofty professional status may thrill counsel and feed into his or her notion of a "battle of the experts." Nor is it necessary to possess a high research profile concerning every discernible aspect of the treatment or assessment situation that gave rise to the present lawsuit. For example, the patient in question may have been physically challenged, African-American, female, and artistically gifted. There would be few if any experts in any discipline who would be prohibitively qualified in each of these areas, although it would be difficult to overstate the importance of possessing sufficient "cultural competence" regarding relevant aspects of the treatment dyad in question (Brown, 2009; Rogers-Sirin & Sirin, 2009). An expert's overall length of service may be raised on cross-examination, but is unlikely to result in an outright ban on admissibility (Drogin, in press).

Prior Commitment to Relevant Perspectives   The potential expert may have published, lectured, or testified on a topic that either supports or undercuts the defendant's own theory of what should have occurred in treatment. Such preserved statements are unlikely to constitute a conflict of interest—unless, for example, they reference the defendant himself or herself—but understandably they are of considerable interest to counsel. For a plaintiff's expert, prior statements consistent with the defendant's perspective are not necessarily fatal to the expert's participation, particularly where they can be distinguished in some fashion, or when they go to issues that are not central to the case at hand. The same can be said of prior statements by a defense expert that *do* run afoul of the defendant's point of view. What may be particularly problematic are incidents in which the potential expert appears to have endorsed diametrically opposing perspectives in the course of earlier trials or depositions.

Experts will do well to remember that whatever they say under oath will be memorialized for the duration of their career. Prior testimony will be brought back by opposing counsel if it undermines or contradicts the expert's present opinion.

Prior or Pending Negative Experiences   There are few persons—including expert witnesses—who can presume to have walked through life unscathed by any problematic incidents. Doctors may be subject to pending lawsuits or board complaints themselves, or they may have been the focus of civil litigation or licensure action at some time in the past. Even if the outcome of such situations was mostly or entirely positive, retaining counsel will need to be informed of this and to draw his or own conclusions. The same can be said of other negative brushes with officialdom, however supposedly minor these may have been, and even if they can safely be characterized as the product of some "youthful indiscretion" some decades before. Prior failure to obtain licensure or board certification—even if such distinctions were eventually achieved—may constitute fodder for cross-examination (Drogin, 2007). It may also be that the potential expert's testimony was looked upon with disregard in a prior appellate opinion.

REVIEWING CATEGORIES OF MALPRACTICE

Appelbaum & Gutheil (2007) identify several "common forms of psychiatric malpractice" (pp. 118–125) that in most cases are directly applicable to the circumstances of psychologists as well. Mastery of the issues reflected in these various categories—as updated and annotated in this section—contributes to a "toolkit" of competencies for the plaintiff's or defendant's expert witness.

Misdiagnosis of Psychiatric Disorders   In and of itself, misdiagnosis would serve as relatively ineffectual basis for a malpractice suit (Parry & Drogin, 2001). In order for "harm" to ensue from the putative "breach of duty" to provide an accurate diagnosis, some form of injury would need to have been caused by the doctor's error. Typical negative results of such mislabeling would include negligent use of somatic treatments, negligent failure to prevent patients from harming themselves, negligent failure to prevent patients from harming others, all as described below. In addition, it may be that the patient was damaged by the stigma associated with an inappropriate diagnosis—for example, a loss of employment occasioned by an alleged disorder for which no "reasonable accommodation" (Pollet, 1995) was available in the workplace.

Negligent Use of Somatic Treatments   The two main subcategories here are (1) negligent administration and monitoring of psychotropic medications (Wettstein, 1992); and (2) negligent application of physical interventions such as electroconvulsive therapy (ECT; Smith, 1996) or transcranial magnetic stimulation. This category of malpractice is, of course, typically ascribed to the psychiatrist defendant; psychologists would do well to consider what expanding one's scope of practice on the basis of increasingly available "prescriptive authority" (Greenberg, 2010) would mean both for malpractice insurance fees and for the increased liability a fee hike would reflect. This would also prove an exception to the general notion of same-discipline expertise, as psychiatrists could serve handily as experts on the medication-related practices of psychologists.

Negligent Use of Psychotherapy   Given the wide variety of distinct, integrative, and eclectic psychotherapies from which doctors have always been able to draw (Goldfried & Norcross, 1995)—"currently, there are more than 450 schools of psychotherapy" (Simon, 2005, p. 9)—it may be less one's choice of treatment modality that incurs malpractice liability than the specific fashion in which one has chosen to apply it. It is far easier for plaintiff's counsel to establish that the defendant's psychotherapy notes fail to comport with published treatises on how to conduct a given form of treatment than it is to wade through decades of academic crossfire on which approach is the most effective in a particular situation. Indeed, failure to maintain adequate notes no matter what brand of psychotherapy was employed is a particularly damning and all too commonly observed phenomenon in these cases. Subsumed under this category are also cases involving the alleged mishandling or implantation of "recovered memories" (Appelbaum & Gutheil, 2007).

Negligent Failure to Prevent Patients From Harming Themselves   These cases arise on both inpatient and outpatient bases. The former will involve a complex blend of clinical and administrative issues that invariably call for an in-depth review of the institutional "chain of command" and of the evidence reflected in staffing books, training protocols, telephone logs, and the like. The latter adds the additional aspect of premature discharge or botched transfer (IACFP Practice Standards Committee, 2010), reaching beyond the walls of the clinic or hospital to invite commentary on the living situation and support systems into which the patient was discharged (Simon & Shuman, 2008). Due to the diversity of disciplines involved and the dramatic nature of the damages in question, these cases are likely to involve a phalanx of experts with varying professional backgrounds.

Negligent Failure to Prevent Patients From Harming Others   The dynamics here are essentially those present in the context of "negligent failure to prevent patients from harming themselves," but with an additional twist: the need to determine just what role it is that the alleged victim may have played in the causation of that person's injury. Plaintiffs and defendants alike—aided by the insights of their respective experts—will examine closely the extent to which the patient may have been stigmatized, taunted, ignored, or otherwise inappropriately engaged by others during the institutional or postdischarge period in question. Such evidence as caregiver instructions and the participation of friends and family in follow-up planning can play a significant role in identifying accurate and equitable proportions of blame in these cases.

Sexual Activity Between Patients and Therapists and Other Boundary Violations   Lamb and Catanzaro (1998) determined that a sample of 553 psychologists reported involvement in the following nonsexual boundary issues: providing psychological services to a relative, friend, or lover of a current client; initiating nonsexual touching with a client; attending a client's special event (e.g., a wedding); remaining at a party after accidentally encountering and interacting with a client and interacting with a client at that party; and attending a small social gathering with knowledge that a client would be present. Clearly, some of these activities are associated with lesser potential harm than others. Sexual activity with clients and their immediate family is universally proscribed.

Negligence in Supervision   Liability from the supervision of mental health professionals typically is determined by the licensure, institutional setting, if any, and the choice, if any, of the clinician being supervised (Meyer, 2006). When the supervisor has the authority to control the clinician, for example the owner or director of a clinic employing mental health professionals, the supervisor may have exposure to vicarious liability by the legal doctrine of *respondeat superior*—"let the master answer" (Roszkowski & Roszkowski, 2005). In training settings in which the trainee clinician has dependent licensure by the state board, the independently licensed senior professionals in charge of the trainee will similarly have exposure to vicarious or indirect liability. *Cohen v. State of New York* (1976) illustrates a court's view of how lack of supervision of a junior trainee was the proximate cause of a patient's suicide. Supervision may be legally required as in the case of psychiatrists who supervise psychiatric nurse practitioners. Supervision which is voluntarily sought by a treating clinician who is independently licensed confers substantially less liability on the supervisor whose duty in this case is to the supervisee and not to the patient (*Schrader v. Kohout*, 1999).

Common to all allegations of negligent supervision is the question of what the supervisor knew, could have known, and should have known. When the supervision occurred within an institutional setting, the institution's policies for credentialing and quality assurance will be reviewed for clinical adequacy and adherence. Supervisory conduct and institutional policies and procedures that reflect reasonable prudence offer substantial protection against harm that was otherwise not foreseeable.

Negligent Split or Collaborative Treatment Split or coordinated mental health care involves ongoing therapies provided by two or more clinicians to a patient (Meyer, 2002; Mossman & Weston, 2010). Classically, split treatment was a dyad of a nonphysician psychotherapist providing verbal therapies teamed with a psychiatrist who prescribed psychotropic medications. In recent years, psychiatry and psychology have proffered a series of verbal individual and group therapies that target a specific diagnosis or even a specific set of symptoms. Patients with treatment-resistant affective disorders and personality disorders are commonly being treated with complex somatic regimens, individual psychotherapies, individual or group cognitive–behavioral therapy or dialectical behavior therapy, and individual or group skills–based training, to name just a few. The result is that the patients with the most intractable illness who also carry the highest risk for poor therapeutic outcomes are being treated by an expanded team of mental health subspecialists.

Neither mental illness nor its treatment is parsed along the lines of professional training or discipline. Adjudication of malpractice in cases of coordinated care will decide the requisite standard of care of the individual practitioners: which duties belong to one practitioner alone and which are shared. Subspecialty practitioners may wrongly believe that their duties do not extend beyond subspecialty expertise. There is no interdisciplinary barrier for the observation and assessment of and response to patient adherence, patient risk, or a patient emergency.

Clinicians are advised to work only with others whom they regard as competent, licensed, and appropriately insured. Clinicians also have to reconcile themselves to providing time for requisite interprofessional collaboration, time for which they will not be reimbursed.

Abandonment   In these cases, the precipitating action in question will be the doctor's allegedly inappropriate termination of an ongoing treatment relationship, perhaps complicated by a botched attempt to refer to another provider. To what extent was the patient "ready" to leave therapy, or to cease to take prescribed medications? What was the apparent impetus for cessation of treatment—for example, did this involve personal or professional frustration on the part of the doctor, or payment difficulties on the part of the patient? Those analyzing psychotherapy notes will typically look to see if the termination was broached at a particular point in treatment, processed with the patient appropriately, and then effectuated with sensitivity to resiliency, resources, and follow-up where indicated.

Breach of Confidentiality   This may have occurred in the form of an unguarded public statement, an incompletely redacted conveyance of treatment-related documents to an insurance company or collateral therapist, or even the insufficient protection of data stored in computers or office file cabinets. In addition to sources of ethical guidance tailored to specific needs of psychiatrists and psychologists (as described later in this chapter), the American Psychological Association has promulgated "Record Keeping Guidelines" (2007) observing that "the nature and extent of the record will vary depending upon the purpose, setting, and context" of the services provided (p. 993). Breaches of confidentiality may also involve the discussion of clinical issues via intercepted electronic mail, or failure to sound-proof treatment rooms.

Preliminary Communication With Counsel

In preparation for conducting the malpractice-related evaluation, the expert will of course be communicating with counsel on various occasions. It is useful to gain an understanding of counsel's own current theory of the case—where he or she feels the proceedings are currently, and where they are likely to go. If counsel responds with the notion that "I don't want to bias you," the expert can convey in response that this is not an issue of tailoring one's opinion to counsel's expectations, but rather an attempt to determine what issues are anticipated to be relevant to the case at hand, so that important data do not go unrequested and so that important theories do not go unexplored.

In turn, the expert should accept the obligation not to jeopardize counsel's case by communicating in a forensically untoward fashion. Comments that might make perfect sense when consulting with fellow mental health professionals may serve to open up gratuitously problematic avenues of cross examination in the months and years to come. Experts are best advised to speak on the telephone, write letters, and send electronic mail messages as if each such statement will eventually be reviewed by the jury. Premature conveyance of incomplete or speculative opinions is unhelpful, as are the unconsidered characterization of certain forms of evidence as "necessary" or of certain books or articles as the "best" or "authoritative" sources of guidance.

Consultation with counsel is necessary. Unstructured communications with the defendant doctor are strictly off limits for the plaintiff's expert, and may be a source of considerable concern for the defendant's expert. Some lawyers actually deputize their clients to identify, recruit, and even retain the expert on their own. This is typically due to some combination on counsel's part of laziness, overwork, or conviction that the defendant would be more likely to know "who the best experts are." Conversations with the defendant during the preparation phase may be discoverable by the plaintiff. Any such interaction should be cleared through and discussed with counsel in advance.

DATA COLLECTION

EXISTING RECORDS

In order to determine whether the defendant doctor has erred to the extent that malpractice may have occurred, the expert will naturally want to obtain all of the relevant information in counsel's possession, and to specify additional items as well. Such items are likely to include some combination of the following as obtained directly from the treatment record:

- Intake documentation
- Records of prior treatment and assessment
- Psychotherapy notes
- Prescription records
- Consultations with other professionals
- Collateral contacts
- Psychological testing reports and data
- Records of kept and cancelled appointments
- Telephone or electronic mail contacts with the patient
- Correspondence with insurers

Such information should not be too difficult for counsel to obtain. Under normal circumstances, strict confidentiality and privilege rules would exist; however, here, the patient has typically waived such rights when electing to bring a lawsuit against the doctor. The expert should of course bear in mind that he or she is not in a position simply to distribute such information further—for example, to other expert witnesses involved in the case—except at the express direction of counsel or the court.

When counsel asks the expert "how much of this material you want," a reasonable response would be "everything you are in a position to provide." This avoids the specter of the expert having requested information that was subsequently denied by counsel, while at the same time it allows counsel to hold back information properly designated as subject to the "attorney–client privilege," such as communications with the defendant concerning trial strategy. Naturally, the expert will not want to encourage counsel by this device to withhold information merely because it may be damaging to counsel's theory of the case, and there is certainly nothing wrong with making appropriately collegial reference to this notion—particularly in cases where counsel and the expert may be encountering one another for the first time. Such issues are better addressed "at the inception of a professional relationship, rather than at its premature and stressful termination" (Drogin & Barrett, 2007, p. 473). Gutheil, Bursztajn, Hilliard, and Brodsky (2004) have noted that in the case of late withdrawal from a legal matter, "the expert risks leaving the retaining attorney and the client in the lurch, and bad feelings, at the very least, are one of the likely outcomes" (p. 390). Many experts will include in their fee agreement a statement that the expert will rely on counsel to furnish all relevant documentation as discovery permits to clarify expectations from the beginning.

In addition to materials culled from the clinical case file itself, the expert may also request documentation of the defendant doctor's professional history and copies of the legal processes of the case which have taken place thus far. Such relevant information may include the following:

- Academic transcripts
- *Curricula vitae*
- Legal or criminal records
- Prior professional discipline (state board, hospital, professional society)
- Initial and amended complaints
- Responses to interrogatories
- Transcripts of depositions
- Motions and orders in the case at hand
- Pertinent statutes, regulations, and case law

ONLINE DOCUMENTATION

There is a growing recognition of the difficulties faced by psychiatrists and psychologists in preventing untoward disclosures via social networking sites such as Facebook and MySpace (Lehavot, Barnett, & Powers, 2010; Taylor, McMinn, Bufford, & Chang, 2010). What remains essentially untested in the forensic context is the extent to which it is appropriate for evaluators to seek out information from these sites pertaining to litigants. It may be more prudent at this juncture for counsel to be asked whether such information exists and whether it can or should be obtained—by counsel, possibly pursuant to a court order—in the instant case. Online documentation in the form of mainstream press accounts is presumably far less likely to run afoul of the sensibilities of the judge or jury, while blogging statements frequently accompanying such articles are of questionable value under any circumstances. When experts determine that it is appropriate to pursue online documentation, they should consider these issues carefully and make sure to keep track of when and where such information was obtained.

COLLATERAL CONTACTS

Data obtained from third-party sources "enhances the face validity of the examination and the competence of the expert in the eyes of the legal decision maker" (Otto, Slobogin, & Greenberg, 2007, p. 191). As with online documentation, the expert will want to proceed on the basis of consultation with counsel, with a well-articulated rationale for why such data are being sought, and with the ability to trace the source and location of any information obtained. Plaintiff's experts will strive to avoid the inference that they were engaging in a "fishing expedition" or even a "witch hunt" when contacting those personally or professionally affiliated with the defendant doctor; similarly, defense experts will want to be able to establish that seeking collateral contacts amounted to more than assembling "testimonials" in a fashion more properly the task of counsel—and in a way that, ironically, might serve to enable the submission of more of the other side's detrimental information to the extent that this is seen as the introduction of "character evidence" (Sanchirico, 2001).

FORENSIC EXAMINATION

Some malpractice cases include a clinical forensic examination of the defendant doctor as well as the plaintiff. It may be that a chronic disability or some other relevant condition was a contributing factor to the incidents precipitating the lawsuit, and defense counsel may want to establish this as a mitigating or other explanatory factor. Perhaps this has already been asserted, and now plaintiff's counsel wishes to commission his or her own examination in rebuttal.

Under these circumstances, one of the most complicated aspects of data collection will be the sophistication of the examinee. Psychiatrists and psychologists vary in their experience and understanding of various interview methods, test of cognitive ability, and personality assessment measures. Of particular importance may be their prior exposure to the nature, utilization, and interpretation of malingering tests and other "measures of effort"—instruments that are often susceptible to the effects of coaching whether the examinee is a mental health professional or not (Brennan et al., 2009).

The expert should (1) make an *a priori* determination of the defendant doctor's own evaluative sophistication, and (2) review the extant professional literature for any studies describing how mental health professionals tend to present on the assessment measure in question (e.g., Garfinkel, Bagby, Waring, & Dorian, 1997). The dynamics and assessment variables of these examinations overlap considerably with those addressed in the American Psychiatric Association's *Guidelines for Psychiatric "Fitness for Duty" Evaluations of Physicians* (2004).

DATA INTERPRETATION

ETHICAL ISSUES: CLINICAL

The American Psychiatric Association provides *The Principles of Medical Ethics with Annotations Especially Applicable to Psychiatry* ("Principles of Medical Ethics"; American Psychiatric Association, 2009), while the American Psychological Association provides the *Ethical Principles of Psychologists and Code of Conduct* ("Principles of Psychologists"; 2002). These sources of guidance apply to forensic as well as mainstream clinical practice, but our focus in this section is primarily on the latter. Following are a few representative examples of how each document addresses issues frequently encountered in malpractice cases.

Discrimination According to the Principles of Medical Ethics (2009), "a psychiatrist should not be a party to any type of policy that excludes, segregates, or demeans the dignity of any patient because of ethnic origin, race, sex, creed, age, socioeconomic status, or sexual orientation" (p. 3). The Principles of Psychologists (2002) target discrimination with regard to "age, gender, gender identity, race, ethnicity, culture, national origin, religion, sexual orientation, disability, economic status, or any basis proscribed by law" (p. 1064)—a similar if slightly more expansive list.

Sexual Activity The Principles of Medical Ethics (2009) state unequivocally that "sexual activity with a current or former patient is unethical" (p. 4). While the Principles of Psychologists (2002) similarly direct that "psychologists do not engage in sexual intimacies with current therapy clients/patients," a complex calculus is provided with regard to those treated formerly, such that "psychologists do not engage in sexual intimacies with former clients/patients for at least two years after cessation or termination of therapy," with a list of numerous circumstances to be considered "even after a two-year interval," including such issues as "the circumstances of termination" and "the client's/patient's current mental status" (p. 1073).

Boundaries of Competence According to the Principles of Medical Ethics (2009), "a psychiatrist who regularly practices outside of his or her area of professional competence should be considered ethical" (p. 5). The applied definition of the word *regularly* must be defined by the individual ethics tribunal adjudicating an actual ethics complaint. The Principles of Psychologists (2002) appear to adopt a somewhat stricter stance in stating that "psychologists provide services, teach, and conduct research with populations and in areas only within the boundaries of their competence, based on their education, training, supervised experience, consultation, study, or professional experience" (p. 1063), although there is also a provision for venturing—in "emergencies"—into activities for which they may not possess the "necessary training," with the understanding that such activities will be "discontinued as soon as the emergency has ended" (p. 1064).

Confidentiality The Principles of Medical Ethics (2009) establish that "a psychiatrist may release confidential information only with the authorization of the patient or under proper legal compulsion" (p. 6). A similar approach is reflected in the direction provided by the Principles of Psychologists (2002), which indicate that "psychologists may disclose confidential information with the appropriate consent of the organizational client, the individual client/ patient, or another legally authorized person on behalf of the client/patient unless prohibited by law" (p. 1066). Both sources of guidance recognize that various emergent situations may override this obligation.

Delegation According to the Principles of Medical Ethics (2009), "the physician should not delegate to the psychologist or, in fact, to any nonmedical person any matter requiring the exercise of professional medical judgment" (p. 8). The Principles of Psychologists (2002) institute a parallel requirement to the effect that "psychologists do not promote the use of psychological assessment techniques by unqualified persons, except when such use is conducted for training purposes with appropriate supervision" (p. 1072).

Ethical Issues: Forensic   The American Academy of Psychiatry and the Law provides *Ethics Guidelines for the Practice of Forensic Psychiatry* ("AAPL Guidelines"; 2005) while the Committee on Ethical Guidelines for Forensic Psychologists (a joint undertaking of the American Psychology-Law Society and the American Academy of Forensic Psychology) provides the *Specialty Guidelines for Forensic Psychologists* ("AP-LS Guidelines"; 1991). Following are a few representative examples of how each document addresses common issues in malpractice cases:

- *Informed Consent.* The AAPL Guidelines (2005) state that "the informed consent of the person undergoing the forensic evaluation should be obtained when necessary and feasible," and that "if the evaluee is not competent to give consent, the evaluator should follow the appropriate laws of the jurisdiction" (p. 2).

  The AP-LS Guidelines (1991) similarly direct that "unless court ordered, forensic psychologists obtain the informed consent of the client or party, or their legal representative, before proceeding with such evaluations and procedures," with the slightly different requirement—in terms of specific measures to be undertaken—that "in situations where the client or party may not have the capacity to provide informed consent or the evaluation is pursuant to court order, the forensic psychologist provides reasonable notice to the client's legal representative of the nature of the anticipated forensic service before proceeding. If the client's legal representative objects to the evaluation, the forensic psychologist notifies the court issuing the order and responds as directed" (p. 659).
- *Treatment and evaluation.* According to the AAPL Guidelines (2005), "psychiatrists who take on a forensic role for patients they are treating may adversely affect the therapeutic relationship with them . . . treating psychiatrists should therefore generally avoid acting as an expert witness for their patients or performing evaluations of their patients for legal purposes . . . when requirements of geography or related constraints dictate

the conduct of a forensic evaluation by the treating psychiatrist, the dual role may also be unavoidable; otherwise, referral to another evaluator is preferable" (pp. 3–4).

Addressing this topic, the AP-LS Guidelines (1991) indicate that "when it is necessary to provide both evaluation and treatment services to a party in a legal proceeding (as may be the case in small forensic hospital settings or small communities), the forensic psychologist takes reasonable steps to minimize the potential negative effects of these circumstances on the rights of the party, confidentiality, and the process of treatment and evaluation" (p. 659).

- *Evaluation without examination.* The AAPL Guidelines (2009) state that "for certain evaluations (such as record reviews for malpractice cases), a personal examination is not required. In all other forensic evaluations, if, after appropriate effort, it is not feasible to conduct a personal examination, an opinion may nonetheless be rendered on the basis of other information. Under these circumstances, it is the responsibility of psychiatrists to make earnest efforts to ensure that their statements, opinions, and any reports or testimony based on those opinions, clearly state that there was no personal examination and note any resulting limitations to their opinions" (p. 3).

The approach of the AP-LS Guidelines (1991) is quite similar, directing that "forensic psychologists avoid giving written or oral evidence about the psychological characteristics of particular individuals when they have not had an opportunity to conduct an examination of the individual adequate to the scope of the statements, opinions, or conclusions to be issued. Forensic psychologists make every reasonable effort to conduct such examinations. When it is not possible or feasible to do so, they make clear the impact of such limitations on the reliability and validity of their professional products, evidence, or testimony" (p. 663).

SPECIAL INTERPRETIVE CONSIDERATIONS

Experts reviewing events which preceded a suicide do so reminding themselves of the tendency towards hindsight bias leading to the conclusion that the patient's suicide was foreseeable. The law of malpractice requires ordinary not extraordinary treatment. The standard of care at the time of review may have matured from the standard of care at the time of the suicide. Experts need to apply the standard of care at the time of the events in question.

Experts need to separate incompetence from the bell shaped curve effect: nearly identical treatment experiences can and do produce widely varied outcomes, though gathering toward the mean. A tragic end may have been preceded by appropriate care that was no different than the care received by other, more fortunate patients on the curve (Blinder, 2004, p. 319).

There is no technology currently that allows for accurate prediction of violence or suicide and consequently no standard of care of prediction to which clinicians can be held. Clinicians are held to the standard of care of their assessment of risk. While good documentation is very effective in the defense of a clinician, no harm was ever proximately caused only by poor documentation. There must be more.

Reasonable people can come to differing conclusions about a complex set of facts. Simon (2002) notes that "an examination of the parameters of what constitutes acceptable suicide risk assessment finds marked disagreement among respected clinicians, academics, and researchers who testify as experts in suicide cases" (p. 340). Finally, Berman, Jobes, and Silverman (2006) maintain that "the determination of clear and imminent danger is a clinical judgment. There simply is no actuarial approach to this assessment" (p. 279).

"The standard of care should be distinguished from the quality of care" (Simon, 2006). As observed by Knoll and Gerbasi (2006), "even the most well-intended expert may be thwarted by subjectivity and cognitive illusions" (p. 215). "Forensic countertransference" is every bit a real phenomenon as is its clinical counterpart (Gutheil & Simon, 2002, p. 566). Treatment failure—even when seemingly inexplicable in a given case—should not reflexively be equated with psychiatric or psychological negligence.

COMMUNICATION

Accusatory histrionics have a tendency to gratify victims and their families but may do little to sway judges and jurors, whose role it is to view the available evidence from as objective and dispassionate a perspective as possible. For plaintiff's counsel, rather than encouraging his/her expert to mount an *ad hominem* attack, "a way must be found to convey both the spirit and the technique of the competent mental health professional and to encourage the fact finder to mourn that individual's absence from the field at that crucial juncture when injury occurred or when the opportunity to diagnose or heal effectively was irreparably lost" (Drogin & Barrett, 2007, p. 482). For similar reasons, when defense counsel has encouraged his or her expert to heap scorn upon the plaintiff's expert rather than to identify what may have been positive in the work performed by the defendant doctor, this strategy may backfire as well.

This is not to suggest in any way that all malpractice-related testimony must eschew criticism at all costs. A plaintiff's expert must be prepared to opine and defend that no prudent clinician would have done as the defendant did and that the defendant's misconduct caused the plaintiff's harm. When prior clinical or current forensic errors are apparent, it is entirely appropriate to point this out with appropriate professionalism. In fact, one commonly observed phenomenon is the understandable reluctance of experts to point out one another's flaws in some cases:

> An expert on the stand for a deposition or trial may be asked for an opinion about the opposing expert or colleague. Inescapably, this places a potential strain on the collegial relationship. Separate retaliatory ethics complaints and even suits for slander may be the result. . . . The expert is torn between the wish and burden to testify truthfully under oath and concern with "fouling one's own nest." (Gutheil & Dattilio, 2008, p. 140)

Irrespective of the demeanor of the witnesses for either side, the fact that reports and ensuing testimony in a malpractice case are themselves a referendum on the quality of professional work means that there is especial pressure on experts to ensure that forensic error is minimized. If not, excruciating courtroom scenes may be the result. For the testifying expert whose report is being scrutinized by opposing counsel:

> One looming "mistake" is problematic enough in the face [of] cross-examination. Should there be more than one error discovered by the

forensic psychological consultant, an effective strategy for the attorney is . . . to ask whether there might, in fact, be any *other* problems with the protocol in question. "Not that you know of, Doctor? I'm sure the court will be glad to provide you with a few minutes to check and make *absolutely sure*." After an appropriate interval, counsel then trots out the next error for discussion. . . . (Drogin, 2007, pp. 252–253)

Of course, no matter how much time is expended on the forensic report, "in a malpractice context the cross-examining attorney may attempt to mislead the jury by counterposing the amount of time the treating doctor has spent with the patient against the necessarily shorter time the expert has spent doing an evaluation of that same patient," a strategy that can be met by the expert taking pains to assert that "he or she holds the more objective opinion, because he or she does not have the bias of the wanting to advocate for the client as the treating expert may have" (Gutheil & Dattilio, 2008, pp. 68–69).

REFERENCES

American Academy of Psychiatry and the Law. (2005). *Ethics guidelines for the practice of forensic psychiatry*. Bloomfield, CT: Author.

American Psychiatric Association. (2004). *Guidelines for psychiatric "fitness for duty" evaluations of physicians*. Arlington, VA: Author.

American Psychiatric Association. (2009). *The principles of medical ethics with annotations especially applicable to psychiatry*. Arlington, VA: Author.

American Psychological Association. (2002). Ethical principles of psychologists and code of conduct. *American Psychologist, 57*, 1060–1073.

American Psychological Association. (2007). Record keeping guidelines. *American Psychologist, 62*, 993–1004.

APA Committee on Malpractice Insurance. (1952). The case for and against malpractice insurance for psychologists. *American Psychologist, 7*, 677–683.

Appelbaum, P. S., & Gutheil, T. G. (2007). *Clinical handbook of psychiatry and the law* (4th ed.). Philadelphia, PA: Lippincott Williams & Wilkins.

Austin v. American Association of Neurological Surgeons, 253 F.3d 967 (7th Cir. 2001).

Baranoski, M. (2009, March). *Beyond prediction: Paradigms for appraisal and management of psychiatric risk in clinical practice*. Psychiatry grand rounds presentation, Beth Israel Deaconess Medical Center, Boston, MA.

Belar, C. D., & Deardorff, W. W. (2009). *Clinical health psychology in medical settings: A practitioner's guidebook* (2nd ed.). Washington, DC: American Psychological Association.

Berman, A. L., Jobes, D. A., & Silverman, M. M. (2006). *Adolescent suicide: Assessment and intervention* (2nd ed.). Washington, DC: American Psychological Association.

Binder, R. L. (2002). Liability for the psychiatrist expert witness. *American Journal of Psychiatry, 159,* 1819–1825.

Blanchard v. Eli Lilly, 207 F. Supp. 2d 308 (2002).

Blinder, M. (2004). Suicide, psychiatric malpractice, and the bell curve. *Journal of the American Academy of Psychiatry and the Law, 32,* 319–323.

Brennan, A. M., Meyer, S., David, E., Pella, R., Hill, B. D., & Gouvier, W. M. (2009). The vulnerability to coaching across measures of effort. *Clinical Neuropsychologist, 23,* 314–328.

Brown, L. S. (2009). Cultural competence: A new way of thinking about integration in therapy. *Journal of Psychotherapy Integration, 19,* 340–353.

Clermont, K. M., & Yeazell, S. C. (2010). Inventing tests, destabilizing systems. *Iowa Law Review, 95,* 821–859.

Cohen v. State of New York, 382 N.Y.S.2d 128 (1976).

Committee on Ethical Guidelines for Forensic Psychologists. (1991). Specialty guidelines for forensic psychologists. *Law and Human Behavior, 15,* 655–665.

Daly, R. (2010). Was vital component omitted from healthcare reform? *Psychiatric News, 45,* 5.

Daubert v. Merrell Dow Pharmaceuticals, Inc., 509 U.S. 579 (1993).

Drogin, E. Y. (in press). Expert qualifications and credibility. In D. Faust (Ed.), *Ziskin's coping with psychiatric and psychological testimony* (6th ed.). New York, NY: Oxford University Press.

Drogin, E. Y. (2007). The forensic psychologist as consultant: Examples from a jurisprudent science perspective. *Journal of Psychiatry and Law, 35,* 245–260.

Drogin, E. Y., & Barrett, C. L. (2007). Off the witness stand: The forensic psychologist as consultant. In A.M. Goldstein (Ed.), *Forensic psychology: Emerging topics and expanding roles* (pp. 465–488). Hoboken, NJ: John Wiley & Sons.

Frye v. United States, 293 F. 1013 (D.C. Cir. 1923).

Garfinkel, P. E., Bagby, R. M., Waring, E. M., & Dorian, B. (1997). Boundary violations and personality traits among psychiatrists. *Canadian Journal of Psychiatry, 42,* 758–763.

General Electric Co. v. Joiner, 522 U.S. 136 (1997).

Goldfried, M. R., & Norcross, J. C. (1995). Integrative and eclectic therapies in historical perspective. In B. M. Bongar & L. E. Beutler (Eds.),

Comprehensive textbook of psychotherapy: Theory and practice (pp. 254–273). New York, NY: Oxford University Press.

Greenberg, R. P. (2010). Prescriptive authority in the face of research revelations. *American Psychologist, 65,* 136–137.

Greenberg, S. A., Shuman, D. W., Feldman, S. R., Middleton, C., & Ewing, C. P. (2007). Lessons for forensic practice drawn from the law of malpractice. In A.M. Goldstein (Ed.), *Forensic psychology: Emerging topics and expanding roles* (pp. 446–461). Hoboken, NJ: John Wiley & Sons.

Gutheil, T. G. (2009). *The psychiatrist as expert witness* (2nd ed.). Washington, DC: American Psychiatric Publishing.

Gutheil, T. G., Bursztajn, H., Hilliard, J. T., & Brodsky, A. (2004). "Just say no": Experts' late withdrawal from cases to preserve independence and objectivity. *Journal of the American Academy of Psychiatry and the Law, 32,* 390–394.

Gutheil, T. G., & Dattilio, F. M. (2008). *Practical approaches to forensic mental health testimony.* Philadelphia, PA: Lippincott Williams & Wilkins.

Gutheil, T. G., & Simon, R. I. (2002). *Mastering forensic psychiatric practice: Advanced strategies for the expert witness.* Washington, DC: American Psychiatric Publishing.

IACFP Practice Standards Committee. (2010). Standards for psychology services in jails, prisons, correctional facilities, and agencies. *Criminal Justice and Behavior, 37,* 749–808.

Knoll, J. K., & Gerbasi, J. (2006). Psychiatric malpractice case analysis: Striving for objectivity. *Journal of the American Academy of Psychiatry and the Law, 34,* 215–223.

Kumho Tire Co. v. Carmichael, 526 U.S. 137 (1999).

Lamb, D. H., & Catanzaro, S. J. (1998). Sexual and nonsexual boundary violations involving psychologists, clients, supervisees, and students: Implications for professional practice. *Professional Psychology: Research and Practice, 29,* 498–503.

Lehavot, K. L., Barnett, J. E., & Powers, D. (2010). Psychotherapy, professional relationships, and ethical considerations in the MySpace generation. *Professional Psychology, Research, and Practice, 41,* 160–166.

Melton, G. B., Petrila, P., Poythress, N. G., & Slobogin, C. (2007). *Psychological evaluations for the courts: A handbook for mental health professionals and lawyers* (3rd ed.). New York, NY: Guilford Press.

Meyer, D. J. (2002). Split treatment and coordinated care with multiple mental health clinicians: Clinical and risk management issues. *Primary Psychiatry, 9,* 56–60.

Meyer, D. J. (2006). Psychiatric malpractice and administrative inquiries of alleged physician misconduct. *Psychiatric Clinics of North America, 29,* 615–628.

Meyer, D. J., Simon, R. I., & Shuman, D. W. (2010). Professional liability in psychiatric practice and requisite standard of care. In R. I. Simon & L. H. Gold (Eds.), *Textbook of forensic psychiatry* (2nd ed., pp. 207–226). Arlington, VA: American Psychiatric Publishing.

Mossman, D., & Weston, C. G. (2010). Splitting treatment: How to limit liability risk when you share a patient's care. *Current Psychiatry, 9*, 43.

Norris, D. M. (2007). A medical malpractice tribunal experience. *Journal of the American Academy of Psychiatry and the Law, 35*, 286–289.

Otto, R. K., Slobogin, C., & Greenberg, S. A. (2007). Legal and ethical issues in accessing and utilizing third-party information. In A. M. Goldstein (Ed.), *Forensic psychology: Emerging topics and expanding roles* (pp. 190–205). Hoboken, NJ: John Wiley & Sons.

Parry, J. W., & Drogin, E. Y. (2001). *Civil law handbook on psychiatric and psychological evidence and testimony.* Washington, DC: American Bar Association.

Parry, J. W., & Drogin, E. Y. (2007). *Mental disability law, evidence and testimony: A comprehensive reference manual for lawyers, judges and mental disability professionals.* Washington, DC: American Bar Association.

Pollet, S. L. (1995). Mental illness in the workplace: The tension between productivity and reasonable accommodation. *Journal of Psychiatry and Law, 23*, 155–184.

Rogers-Sirin, L., & Sirin, S. R. (2009). Cultural competence as an ethical requirement: Introducing a new educational model. *Journal of Diversity in Higher Education, 2*, 19–29.

Roszkowski, M. E., & Roszkowski, C. L. (2005). Making sense of respondeat superior: An integrated approach for both negligent and intentional conduct. *Southern California Review of Law and Women's Studies, 14*, 235–285.

Sanchirico, C. W. (2001). Character evidence and the object of trial. *Columbia Law Review, 101*, 1227–1307.

Schrader v. Kohout, 522 S.E.2d 19 (Ga. App. 1999).

Simon, R. I. (2002). Suicide risk assessment: What is the standard of care? *Journal of the American Academy of Psychiatry and the Law, 30*, 340–344.

Simon, R. I. (2005). Standard-of-care testimony: Best practices or reasonable care? *Journal of the American Academy of Psychiatry and the Law, 33*, 8–11.

Simon, R. I. (2006). Medical errors, sentinel events, and malpractice. *Journal of the American Academy of Psychiatry and the Law, 34*, 99–100.

Simon, R. I., & Shuman, D. W. (2008). Psychiatry and the law. In R. E. Hales, S. C. Yudofsky, & G. O. Gabbard (Eds.), *The American Psychiatric Publishing textbook of psychiatry* (5th ed., pp. 1555–1599). Arlington, VA: American Psychiatric Publishing.

Smith, S. R. (1996). Malpractice liability of mental health professionals and institutions. In D. W. Shuman & B. D. Sales (Eds.), *Law, mental health, and mental disorder* (pp. 76–98). Belmont, CA: Thomson Brooks/Cole.

Taylor, L., McMinn, M. R., Bufford, R. K., & Chang, K. B. (2010). Psychologists' attitudes and ethical concerns regarding the use of social networking websites. *Professional Psychology, Research and Practice, 41*, 153–159.

Wagner, M. K. (2002). The high cost of prescription privileges. *Journal of Clinical Psychology, 58*, 677–680.

Wettstein, R. M. (1992). Legal aspects of prescribing. In M. S. Keshavan & J. S. Kennedy (Eds.), *Drug-induced dysfunction in psychiatry* (pp. 9–19). Washington, DC: Hemisphere Publishing.

CHAPTER 25

Fitness for Duty

LISA DRAGO PIECHOWSKI and ALBERT M. DRUKTEINIS

INTRODUCTION

A fitness for duty (FFD) evaluation is initiated by an employer to assess an employee's capacity to perform his or her job duties in a safe and competent manner in the context of a possible mental impairment. The FFD evaluation is usually triggered when an employee's behavior is identified as being disruptive, bizarre, or threatening; or impedes work performance. Similar to other "disability" evaluations, FFD evaluations compare the employee's functional capacity to the demands of the occupational setting (Gold et al., 2008). However, unlike other disability evaluations, whereby the employee makes his or her mental state an issue by claiming impairment, in an FFD evaluation, the employer raises the issue of the employee's work capacity. Fundamentally, the context of the FFD evaluation creates a tension between the needs of the employer to maintain a safe and productive workplace and the privacy rights of the employee. This situation presents unique challenges and requires knowledge of and attention to the procedural and substantive nuances inherent to the process.

CIRCUMSTANCES LEADING TO AN FFD

A number of circumstances may raise concerns that could warrant an FFD evaluation. These include:

- *Impairment in employee performance.* With employee performance, the most common circumstance is when the employer suspects or has evidence of impaired performance by an employee. The employer may have observed uncharacteristic performance problems, sometimes accompanied by behavioral changes that are sufficiently dramatic to require attention. The employee's behavior may be immediately problematic or could suggest the possibility of future disturbance.

- *Disruption to and/or threat in the workplace.* This is the second most common circumstance. It may present in the form of harassment, aggression, inappropriate behaviors, and/or overt or covert threats to harm colleagues, customers, or the employer. The Occupational Safety and Health Act (OSHA) requires employers to take reasonable steps to maintain a safe workplace for all employees (U.S. Department of Labor, 1996). In addition, employers risk incurring vicarious liability when an employee inflicts harm on other employees or the public under the legal theory of *respondeat superior.*

- *Return-to-work evaluation.* The Family and Medical Leave Act (FMLA) provides certain employees with up to 12 weeks of unpaid, job-protected leave per year when (among other things) the employee is unable to work because of a serious health condition (29 U.S.C., 1993). Some employees are able to receive disability benefits while absent from work. FMLA certification is typically provided by the employee's treating physician, and challenges by the employer are limited. However, following a prolonged leave of absence, especially when due to a mental disorder, the employer may request a FFD evaluation to determine if the employee has sufficiently recovered and is able to perform his or her job competently and safely. This is particularly likely if significant performance problems or troubling behaviors preceded the leave of absence.

- *Evaluation of employees in specialized jobs requiring mental stability or greater stress tolerance.* FFD evaluations are also frequently sought to assess applicants for and employees already working in jobs or professions for which a history of mental or personality disorders may be unacceptable to the employer. Police officers, firefighters, secret service agents, and others in public service fall into this category. Physicians, dentists, psychiatrists, psychologists, and other professionals also may be required to submit to an FFD evaluation if they have demonstrated impairment that has been brought to the attention of their respective professional licensing board.

- *Claim Under the Americans with Disabilities Act (ADA).* (42 U.S.C., 1990). This circumstance can involve applicants or employees who assert they have an impairment that should be reasonably accommodated—in which case they are raising the issue of mental impairment. The employer may seek a FFD evaluation to corroborate the impairment and/or to determine whether the employee can still perform the essential functions of the job (see Chapter 20 on ADA claims for a more detailed discussion).

LEGAL AND ETHICAL CONSIDERATIONS

Typically in FFD evaluations, it is the employer, and not the employee, who is raising the issue of the employee's mental condition. This circumstance creates unique legal and ethical concerns for the evaluator (Anfang & Wall, 2006). One such concern stems from the employee's right to privacy. Although laws concerning employee privacy vary from state to state, federal law, including the ADA and the Health Insurance Portability and Accountability Act (HIPAA) protect the employee's rights regarding disclosure of medical and health information to the employer (Health Insurance Portability and Accountability Act, 1996). On the other hand, the FFD evaluation requires a thorough exploration of the employee's personal, psychiatric, and medical history. Thus, the evaluator must balance the need to obtain sufficient information with the employee's right to keep certain information private.

For the evaluator, it is risky to undertake a FFD evaluation without obtaining a complete history. Missing or inaccurate historical information may compromise the reliability of the evaluator's diagnostic impression and lead to mistaken conclusions about the degree of the employee's mental impairment. This is particularly true when the potential for workplace violence is at issue. Nevertheless, when the FFD evaluation yields detailed personal information about the employee, much of which may not be directly related to the employee's job duties, the evaluator must safeguard this information and should share only the minimum data necessary to address the employer's concerns.

The evaluator should be aware of the degree to which the employee's participation in the FFD evaluation is being compelled by the employer. Employees in some occupations (e.g., police officers) can be mandated to attend a FFD evaluation. In other circumstances, the employer may imply that the employee is required to attend, even if this is not the case. Regardless, the evaluator is never in a position to compel the employee's participation and the evaluator should take care not to mislead the employee in this regard. It is essential that the evaluator obtain informed consent from the employee before beginning the evaluation.

Occasionally, employers may seek a FFD evaluation on spurious grounds as a way of dealing with problematic workplace issues. One of the most common examples of this is when the intent of the employer is to attribute a performance or administrative problem to the employee's mental condition, in order to avoid addressing what is really an organizational issue. Employee performance problems can be the result of nonclinical personal/employee issues and/or supervisor or organizational disputes. An FFD evaluation should be sought only when the employer has reasonable cause to believe that the employee's problematic functioning is related to a mental health condition. A vague or undocumented suspicion about a mental condition may not be sufficient to initiate an FFD evaluation. Moreover, an unwarranted FFD evaluation diverts attention from the real issues affecting employee performance and inappropriately intrudes into the employee's private life.

The agency relationship between the evaluator and the employer is another area of potential conflict. In most cases, FFD evaluations are performed by psychiatrists or psychologists retained by the employer, even though their position is that of an independent examiner. This is a routine concern for evaluators who work in an occupational medicine department established by the employer, where the dual roles of evaluator and treatment provider inevitably blur agency boundaries. Although most FFD evaluators are contracted consultants and not employees, role confusion is nonetheless possible. It is important to inform the employee clearly about the nature of the evaluator's relationship to the employer. The evaluator should exercise caution not to offer diagnosis or treatment advice directly to the employee and should advise the employee that theirs is not a treatment relationship. Regardless of the fact that the employer has requested and is paying for the evaluation, it is incumbent upon the evaluator to perform an objective evaluation of the employee and not allow his/her relationship, financial or otherwise, with the employer to influence his/her opinion.

Evaluators should be aware that employers seeking FFD evaluations may have unrealistic expectations about what the evaluator can deliver. Evaluators should have sufficient experience in conducting such assessments, coupled with a clear understanding of their professional limitations as well as those of the evaluation, to ensure that no misunderstandings emerge between the employer and the evaluator. Outlining the inherent limitations of the evaluation is especially important when attempting to assess the potential for violent behavior. The employer may believe it is possible to determine this with greater certainty than is actually feasible. It is, therefore, incumbent upon the evaluator to advise his/her referral source, from the beginning and unambiguously, what to expect from the FFD evaluation, especially with regard to the limited potential to predict future behavior.

Finally, it should be kept in mind that FFD evaluations, like all clinical and forensic functions, must meet the ethical guidelines of the American Psychiatric Association, the American Psychological Association, and/or the American Academy of Psychiatry and the Law (American Psychiatric Association, 2006; American Psychological Association, 2002; American Academy of Psychiatry and the Law, 2005). If these guidelines and conditions cannot be met, the FFD evaluation should not take place.

PREPARATION

DEALING WITH REFERRAL SOURCES

Referrals for FFD evaluations may come from a number of sources, but in one way or another they are usually linked to the employer. Sources may include an employee assistance program (EAP), the human resources (HR) department, an occupational medicine department, employer administration, or a third-party vendor. One of the roles of an EAP or occupational medicine department is to diagnose and treat the employee, but it is still an extension of the workplace. The EAP and the occupational medicine department inevitably will become drawn into the specific concerns and needs of the employer, despite their best attempts to insulate themselves from them.

Establishing clear boundaries for the FFD evaluation, along with specifying both the scope and the limits of the evaluation, often result in the denial of initial requests for evaluations. As stated previously, a major obstacle is the unrealistic expectations of the employer, most notably when an administrative or personnel issue is presented in the guise of a suspected mental disorder. Another hurdle is timing. It may be urgent for the referral source to reach a quick resolution of a problem, even though relevant information is lacking and will take more time than anticipated to retrieve. Or the FFD evaluator may recognize that a psychiatric emergency exists that requires immediate intervention. In such a circumstance, it is critical that the evaluator communicate this to the employer, to preclude any misconception about the evaluator's function. In short, the substantive issues for an FFD evaluation must take a backseat to the emergent clinical needs of the employee.

Also at issue, in some cases, is lack of awareness on the part of the employer regarding the type and depth of the historical information (medical and personnel records and other important data) that must be produced and reviewed before the evaluator can offer any opinions. Vague or unsubstantiated allegations against the employee, undocumented hearsay, witnesses unwilling to come forward, and other essential data lacking corroboration all can impede the FFD evaluation and compromise the veracity of any opinion. As with the preevaluation discussion with the employee, the evaluator should raise and address these issues during first contact with the referral source, to ensure there is no misunderstanding.

The FFD evaluator often must decide whether an FFD evaluation is necessary and appropriate under the circumstances presented (Anfang & Wall, 2006). Therefore, in the initial contact with the referral source, one important objective of the FFD evaluator is to identify, as clearly as possible, the specific workplace behaviors of concern to the employer and determine why they are not being handled via routine administrative procedures. Where there is ambiguity, or in the absence of more detailed information from the referral source, the evaluator should seek to fill in those blanks before scheduling the evaluation. The evaluator should also outline the scope of the evaluation to the employer, including specifying the types of consent forms and authorizations that will be required of the employee, so that all of this paperwork can be addressed at the workplace in advance of the evaluation.

When there is immediate concern for the safety of the employee, coworkers, or the workplace generally, administrative leave with pay is often advisable, so that everyone has sufficient time to gather data before the evaluation takes place, and in an environment free of discord. In the event that the employee's behavior presents an imminent danger, police involvement may be necessary.

Finally, the evaluator should discuss candidly with the referral source the length of the evaluation, the type of diagnostic tools that may be needed (e.g., psychological testing), and the timing of both preliminary and final reports. Attending to such details is required of the evaluator if he or she is to assess properly the reasonableness of the FFD request; but to the employer who is eager to address and remedy an imminent problem, it may seem little more than a burdensome and time-consuming prelude. Anything less than this level of due diligence would, however, be misleading and could result not only in unrealistic expectations but, in a worst-case scenario, liability for both the employer and evaluator.

COMMUNICATING WITH THE EMPLOYEE

Prior to beginning the evaluation, it is imperative to provide complete and accurate information to the employee regarding the nature of the evaluation and the possible outcomes or consequences. Many FFD evaluations are "forced," or at least leveraged using threat of termination. The FFD evaluator must establish his or her own parameters for the evaluation and obtain the employee's informed consent before beginning the evaluation.

The employee should be told about the scope of the evaluation and the potential consequences or outcomes (including loss of employment) that might be taken by the employer as a result of it. The employee should be informed that this is not a superficial discussion of the immediate precipitants that led to the evaluation, but by necessity involves a full psychiatric or psychological inquiry into the employee's personal life, as well as related employment issues. The employee must also understand that the evaluation is much more than a simple statement regarding his or her fitness—either fit or unfit for duty. Rather, the evaluator is required to establish the basis for all his or her opinions, and that this may include highly personal and sensitive information, which the employee might think irrelevant.

In addition to revealing this information to the evaluator, the employee must be informed about how this information might be used and the extent to which it may be disclosed to others. The evaluator must make every effort not to unnecessarily release private information to the employer, such as sensitive or embarrassing personal history that is, in fact, not pertinent to the evaluation. Nevertheless, the employee must understand that he or she will be expected to give blanket consent, and that it will be up to the professional discretion of the evaluator as to what information to release and distribute.

The employee must be made aware of the need to authorize the release of medical and mental health records, his/her personnel file, and any other relevant job information to the evaluator. In many cases, ancillary interviews with supervisors, coworkers, and family members may be deemed necessary. The employee must also be willing to allow the release of the evaluation results to the referral source within the workplace—although either the employer or employee has the right to restrict who actually receives the results. For example, an agreement may be reached that only the HR representative or the occupational medicine department will receive it, not the employee's supervisor.

It is important to acknowledge the *de facto* agency relationship that the FFD evaluator will have with the employer. Thus, the FFD evaluator must emphasize that his or her role is as a nonclinical, independent assessor who is, at the same time, an agent of the employer. One effective way to facilitate this discussion is to provide to the employee, in advance of the evaluation, authorization forms outlining precisely what information will be released to the employer/employer's representative, so that there is no question about what will or will not be divulged.

DATA COLLECTION

Broadly speaking, there are four sources of data available to the FFD evaluator. These are (1) information obtained from written records and documents; (2) information obtained from interviewing collateral sources; (3) information obtained from the employee in the clinical interview; and (4) psychometric test data.

The evaluator typically reviews written records prior to meeting with the employee. The evaluator should begin by inspecting the records that have been provided to ensure that the necessary documentation is present. Certain material should be considered essential. This includes a detailed job description and a written account of the incident that led to the referral (ideally by someone who witnessed the event). Other useful material includes disciplinary records, performance reviews, the job application and/or employee's resume, and other information contained in the employee's personnel file. The evaluator should also request the name and contact information for the employee's manager or supervisor. It is important to obtain medical and psychiatric treatment records to review, but these are usually not available prior to meeting with the employee. Such records are rarely in the possession of the employer and authorization to obtain these records must be requested from the employee. If law enforcement has been involved in the case, there may be access to criminal records or other legal documentation such as restraining orders.

COLLATERAL INTERVIEWS

In addition to reviewing written records, it may be important for the evaluator to interview individuals who have direct knowledge of the employee and the behavior in question. Appropriate collateral sources may include the employee's supervisor and/or coworkers, EAP personnel, the employee's medical and mental health treatment providers, and individuals, such as family members, who are familiar with the employee's functioning outside of the work environment. The evaluator must obtain authorization from the employee before contacting EAP personnel and treatment providers; and should obtain consent from the employee before contacting coworkers, family members, or other individuals who may not know that an FFD is taking place. Also, the evaluator should obtain consent from the employer before contacting anyone at the workplace.

CLINICAL INTERVIEW

The core of the evaluation is the clinical interview. This allows the evaluator to obtain information from the employee's point of view and to observe the employee so as to directly assess his or her functioning first hand. A full mental status examination should be performed. It is particularly important to be alert for signs of disordered thinking, confusion, poor impulse control, agitation, mood instability, limited insight, or poor judgment. Any indication of possible substance abuse issues should be noted.

The evaluator must be prepared to cover a wide range of topics in the interview. A thorough history—that is, personal, social, educational, vocational, medical, psychiatric, military, legal, and substance abuse history—must be obtained. The evaluator should inquire about how the employee has dealt with disappointments and frustrations in the past. Relationships with family and romantic partners should be explored, with special attention paid to how conflicts were resolved. Inquiries regarding any history of violent behavior or of threatening violence, the extent of the employee's current alcohol and drug use, any recent losses (e.g., divorce, bankruptcy), history of head injury or other health issues, use of medications, and nature of the employee's living situation and social support system should be addressed.

The employee should be queried in detail about the specific incident that led to the evaluation. Does the employee's account differ substantially from that of the employer? If the employee acknowledges the behavior described by the employer, does the employee agree that the behavior was problematic? Does the employee express remorse for the behavior? The employee's relationship with others in the workplace should be explored. How does the employee get along with his/her supervisors and coworkers? Are there particular individuals with whom the employee has difficulty dealing, or does he/she have problems with almost everyone?

Psychometric testing can generate additional information that is useful to the FFD evaluator. Testing is usually directed toward assessing psychopathology, cognitive functioning, and/or the presence of factors associated with an increased risk of violent or disruptive behavior. There is no "standard protocol" of psychological tests in FFD evaluations. Test selection should be based on the specific circumstances of the evaluation, the characteristics of the employee being evaluated, and the referral questions the evaluator is being asked to address. The following discussion provides examples of instruments that may be employed to address the questions of a FFD evaluation. This list is not exhaustive, as there are many other instruments that are useful and appropriate for these purposes.

The Minnesota Multiphasic Personality Inventory, 2nd Edition (MMPI-2; Butcher, Dahlstrom, Graham, Tellegen, & Kaemmer, 1989) is the most commonly used instrument to assess psychopathology. It consists of 567 true or false questions and requires a fifth-grade reading level. It takes approximately 60 to 90 minutes to complete. There is substantial research on the MMPI-2 and its use in forensic evaluations. A number of validity scales are imbedded in the MMPI-2 to assist the evaluator in determining if the examinee is attempting to overplay or minimize psychopathology. The MMPI-2 is frequently used in FFD evaluations to address questions of psychopathology. In addition to the MMPI-2, the Millon Clinical Multiaxial Inventory (MCMI; Millon, 1994) may be used when the evaluator suspects that personality characteristics may underlie the behavioral issues in the workplace. This instrument consists of 175 true or false items and can be completed in 25 to 30 minutes. An eighth-grade reading level is required.

When the employee's cognitive functioning is at issue, testing can help determine the presence and extent of deficits in attention, memory, concentration, or executive functions that would interfere with the performance of the employee's occupational duties. The Wechsler Adult Intelligence Scale (WAIS) can be used to assess overall intellectual functioning as well as well as many specific components of cognitive functioning (Wechsler, 2008). The Wechsler Memory Scale (WMS) provides an in depth assessment of memory functioning (Wechsler, 2009). Its scores correspond to those of the WAIS thus facilitating comparisons between expected and actual memory functioning. Both the WAIS and the WMS are individually administered and require approximately 90 minutes each. If a briefer assessment of intellectual functioning is appropriate, an instrument such as the Wechsler Abbreviated Scale of Intelligence (WASI), which can be administered in 30 minutes, may be used (Wechsler, 1999). Scores on the WASI can provide an estimate of WAIS IQ scores, but do not provide detailed information about specific cognitive functions. Also, the total IQ score may vary from that obtained on the WAIS-IV, due to the fact that the number of calculated scales has been reduced to four.

The Repeatable Battery of Neuropsychological Status (RBANS) provides an overview of functioning in several key cognitive areas (Randolph, 1998). It can be individually administered in approximately 30 minutes. It should be noted that the RBANS is not a substitute for a full neuropsychological battery, but it may assist the evaluator in identifying potential problem areas that can then be explored through additional assessment.

FFD evaluators are often asked to assess the degree of risk the employee presents in terms of the potential for future threatening, dangerous, or seriously disruptive behavior. It must be remembered that no psychological test exists that can provide a definitive answer to this question. Many risk assessment instruments designed for and normed on other populations (e.g., convicted felons, sex offenders) may be inappropriate for use with employees. In addition, most risk assessment instruments presume there has been at least one documented incident of violent behavior. FFD evaluations are frequently conducted on individuals without such a history.

Several instruments have been specifically designed to assist the evaluator in collecting information relevant to the assessment of threat in the workplace and are more appropriate for use in a FFD evaluation. These instruments are not "psychological tests" and do not generate a quantitative score, but provide a structure for collecting data. One example, the Workplace Assessment of Violence Risk (WAVR-21), a 21-item checklist, identifies static and dynamic risk factors associated with workplace targeted or intended violence (White & Meloy, 2007). Other similar tools include the Workplace Violence Risk Assessment Checklist, and the Employee Risk Assessment (ERA-20; Hall, 2001; Bloom, Webster, & Eisen, 2002).

DATA INTERPRETATION

The FFD evaluator must approach data interpretation with caution, as the stakes in FFD evaluations are high. The employee stands to lose his or her job or may be deprived of basic privacy rights. In addition, the safety of others in the workplace may depend on an accurate interpretation of the FFD evaluation findings. In an ideal situation, all the evaluation data will be consistent and the evaluator will feel confident in reaching conclusions and expressing his/her opinion. In reality, this almost never happens. The evaluator must contend with conflicting data from various sources and must be prepared to weigh and analyze the data in order to resolve these discrepancies.

Data interpretation should begin by reexamining the referral questions. Typically, the FFD evaluator is asked to address questions such as:

- Is there evidence of a psychiatric condition?
- Is the employee's behavior related to this condition?
- If present, how do symptoms of this condition affect the employee's ability to perform his/her job duties safely and effectively?
- What accommodations, interventions, or adjustments might allow the employee to perform his/her job duties safely and effectively?
- Is the employee now fit to return to work, or if not, under what conditions, if any, might the employee be fit to return to work in the future?

Each question should be examined in light of the data collected in the evaluation. Because data from different sources may yield different information, the evaluator must consider the relative reliability and validity of the data from each source.

Written records, especially those created prior to the onset of the problematic behavior in question, can provide useful information regarding the employee's baseline functioning, allowing comparisons with the employee's present functioning. Written records, however, are based on the information available to the author at the time the record was created and care must be taken not to reach inaccurate or incomplete inferences as a result. For example, records from a primary care physician might not include information about work-related issues or marital problems. This does not necessarily mean those problems were not occurring at the time, as it is possible they were just not mentioned to the physician or the physician chose not to document this information in the records. The objectivity of the author of the records must also be taken into consideration. Treating providers, especially psychotherapists, are trained to focus on the patient's subjective view of his or her life. This point of view is likely reflected in their records. Personality issues between a supervisor and an employee may affect the way information is reported in the employee's personnel file. Similar influences may affect information obtained from collateral interviews. One way to overcome this potential bias is to consider information from a variety of sources, looking for convergence of data from sources independent of one another.

Information obtained directly from the employee may be influenced by the fact that the employee fears job loss, prosecution, or other unwanted consequences. Lack of insight related to mental illness can also affect the accuracy of the employee's self-report. To address this, self-report information can be compared to the evaluator's direct observation of the employee during the interview. In addition, the internal consistency of the information provided by the employee can be scrutinized by looking for patterns of behavior rather than focusing on single events.

Psychological test data should be evaluated in light of the psychometric properties of the instruments utilized, especially information regarding reliability and validity. The evaluator should consider the population on which the test was normed and the questions the test was designed to address. Care should be taken to not over- or under-interpret test data. As mentioned earlier, there is no psychological test that can provide a definitive answer to the question of whether an employee is fit to return to work.

When interpreting FFD evaluation data, particular attention should be given to certain issues that can be related to especially problematic behavior in the workplace. These include substance abuse, thought disorder, anger control problems, chronic interpersonal difficulties, and a history of violent or threatening behavior. When several of these factors are simultaneously present, the potential for problematic behavior is likely to be higher. Overall, factors that may lead to distorted perceptions of events or interactions (e.g., thought disorder, personality disorder, intoxication) combined with factors that may diminish behavioral control (e.g., intoxication, anger control problems, history of violent behavior) are cause for concern. When such factors are present, the evaluator should consider the availability of current or potential mitigating factors such as the use of psychotropic medication, psychotherapeutic treatment, or abstinence from substance use.

Some evaluations may yield data that does not support the presence of a psychiatric condition in the employee. Such circumstances include intentional behavior (e.g., the employee does not complete work because he/she finds it boring), a one-time reaction to a stressful situation (e.g., employee yells at a coworker for losing an important document), or unusual, but not pathological, personal characteristics or beliefs (e.g., employee does not believe women should be in positions of authority). In other evaluations, there may be evidence of a psychiatric condition, but the problematic behavior is unrelated to this condition. For example, the evaluation may reveal that the employee meets the diagnostic criteria for an eating disorder, but the symptoms of this disorder cannot explain why the employee threatened a coworker. In interpreting the evaluation data, it is important to clarify if and how the problematic behavior is linked to a psychiatric condition.

COMMUNICATION

Verbal Communication

Communication of the evaluator's findings, verbally and in writing, is the final step in the FFD evaluation process. Although a written report is almost always called for, giving the employer immediate verbal feedback is often very helpful. This is particularly important when issues relating to workplace safety are involved. The evaluator must be cognizant of his or her obligations under "duty to warn" laws. If, in the course of the evaluation, material emerges that gives the evaluator reason to believe that the employee presents an imminent threat, the evaluator should take appropriate steps as required by law in the jurisdiction where the evaluation is taking place. In no circumstances should the evaluator delay in providing information to the employer when safety issues are at stake.

Verbal feedback also affords the evaluator the opportunity to ensure that the employer clearly understands the evaluator's findings. This helps avoid situations in which the employer takes action based on a misinterpretation of the written report. A conversation between the evaluator and the employer allows the employer to ask questions about any findings that may be confusing and gives the evaluator the chance to clarify his or her opinions.

The Written Report

Whether verbal or written, all communication to the employer must be clear, succinct, and germane to the referral questions.

The evaluator should strenuously avoid providing information, especially information of a private nature, if such material is not essential to answering the employer's referral questions. FFD reports should not be confused with clinical psychiatric or psychological evaluation reports. The FFD evaluator must remember that the purpose of the FFD evaluation is to provide the employer with information about the employee's capacity to perform his/her work functions efficiently and safely. Communicating unnecessary information to the employer, even though an authorization has been given, can still be a needless intrusion on the employee's privacy and could subject the employer to becoming the unwitting possessor of extraneous protected health information. The FFD evaluator should consider whether the disclosure of such information is essential.

In determining the appropriate level of information disclosure, the FFD evaluator should consider where his or her report is to be directed. Diagnostic information, for example, may be more appropriately disclosed in a report going to the occupational medicine department than one directed to human resources. In the latter case, when the report is destined for the employee's personnel file, the employer may prefer that such information not be included, or be kept separate, as having this information creates an additional obligation on the part of the employer to safeguard and restrict access to it. In addition, specific diagnostic information may not be useful in a report that will be read by nonclinical personnel. When in doubt, it is better to err on the side of not disclosing private health information to the employer. If necessary, the evaluator can always provide additional detail; however, it is not possible to take back information once it has been disclosed.

The evaluator should keep in mind that readers of the report are quite likely to be lay people who are unfamiliar with psychiatric terminology. It is important that the evaluator explain his or her findings in plain English, avoiding the use of jargon or references to esoteric concepts. It is helpful to remember that the employer is more interested in maintaining a safe and productive workplace than in being schooled in the intricacies of psychopathology.

Many evaluators find it useful to organize the written report into sections. The first section should include the employee's identifying information, indicate the source of the referral, and include a brief statement describing the reason for the evaluation. The date or dates in which the employee was seen and the sources of data (e.g., written records, clinical interview, psychological testing) should be outlined. This should be followed by a section describing the circumstances or events that led to the employee being referred for evaluation.

Following this, the evaluator may include a section describing the information obtained during the course of the evaluation both from the employee and from other sources. Again, the evaluator is cautioned to use extreme care in choosing the data to include. Any personal history of a highly sensitive nature that has no relevance to the opinions provided by the evaluator should not be included. Conversely, the evaluator should never withhold important information that is necessary to satisfactorily address the referral questions simply because it is of a personal nature.

It is also important to address as directly as possible the workplace issue that led to the FFD referral. Often, the facts regarding this situation may be in dispute and the available information may be ambiguous. This can create a situation in which the evaluator's final opinion is contingent on a factual resolution of the dispute. A caveat is in order here: FFD evaluators never take on a fact-finding role, as this will inevitably lead to presumptive and erroneous opinions. This can be difficult to avoid, because the referral source may incorrectly assume that the evaluator's expertise in mental health enables him or her to resolve such factual disputes—another unrealistic expectation. The approach to take here is to relay options for consideration based on how the facts resolve, as opposed to assuming facts and, thereby, potentially sabotaging one's own opinion when a different version of the facts is later accepted.

Whether the evaluator chooses to include the formal diagnosis in the report to the employer depends on a variety of circumstances. The evaluator should ask him/herself whether communicating the specific diagnosis is truly necessary to address the referral questions of the evaluation. When the decision is made to include diagnostic information, it should be consistent with criteria and format of the *Diagnostic and Statistical Manual of Mental Disorders* (American Psychiatric Association, 2000). The clinical formulation cannot exist in isolation, however, and must be related to the specific work situation and job duties of the employee. Aspects of the employee's job such as the degree of contact with the public, the need to work collaboratively with other employees, access to weapons or dangerous materials, or the use of heavy machinery are examples of relevant factors that should be considered when interpreting clinical information. Organizational dynamics should factor into the formulation as well. These include, for example, the degree of flexibility, tolerance, time pressure, and conformity that are present in the work environment.

The evaluator's ultimate opinion regarding the employee's fitness for duty should be clearly delineated in a separate section at the end of the report. It should be noted that this is the only section of the report that many employers will actually read. Thus, it is particularly important that this section be brief and clear.

COMMUNICATING INFORMATION ABOUT RISK OF VIOLENCE

When workplace disruption or violence is a concern, great care should be taken to communicate this information accurately. Although it is feasible to assess threat, predicting future behavior with a high degree of certainty is not possible. Employers sometimes have unrealistic expectations or assumptions regarding the violence prediction. The evaluator should make clear the limitations inherent in making predictions to avoid misunderstandings and misinterpretations. Generally, opinions regarding violence risk should be expressed in terms of situational variables. In other words, given this set of circumstances, the employee presents a low, moderate, or high risk. This risk would increase given certain (specified) factors and would decrease given certain (specified) factors. All statements regarding violence risk should be based on empirically sound data, noting that the opinions are dependent on personal and/or employment circumstances.

MAKING RECOMMENDATIONS

Where a mental condition suggests or points to impairment of an employee's ability to function at work, the final opinion the evaluator communicates does not have to be a simple fit or unfit for duty. Rather, the evaluator has a range of options, including:

- Leave of absence to restore fitness for duty
- Temporary or permanent modification of the job description, based on the assessed mental condition

- Recommendations for further investigation of organizational factors
- Consideration of short- or long-term disability for the employee
- Reasonable accommodation for impairment
- More extensive inquiry into an employee's concern over supervisory practices

In the event that an employee is determined to be fit for duty, in spite of or in the absence of a mental condition, an FFD evaluator may want to recommend a formal work agreement between the employee and employer that outlines in detail the types of behavior that will be tolerated and those that will not; how such behavior may be monitored or reported; the consequences misbehavior shall invoke; and the type of mental health treatment the employee shall take part in, should it be deemed necessary. With regard to the latter issue, it is important to note that the employer cannot enforce treatment, beyond identifying problem behaviors that have once again manifested, and suggesting mental health treatment that may or may not prevent their occurrence. If and when an FFD evaluator is asked to reevaluate an employee, it should be, accordingly, based on problem behaviors, not on whether the employee has conformed to treatment recommendations. In most cases, therefore, what prompts administrative action is not that the employee has failed to comply to treatment, but that the treatment might have prevented the unacceptable behavior.

If appropriate, the evaluator may offer the employer suggestions for more effectively managing the employee. Such suggestions might include moving the employee's work station to a quieter location, setting firm limits regarding behavioral expectations, encouraging the employee to engage in additional training or work with a mentor, for example. The evaluator should consider alerting the employer to possible "red flags"—that is behavioral cues on the part of the employee that could signal the early onset of problematic behavior. When making suggestions, however, it should be remembered that employers sometimes use FFD evaluations to resolve thorny personnel or organizational issues. Therefore, the FFD evaluator must be vigilant not to extend his or her opinions into administrative matters that go beyond the scope of the FFD evaluation. In the end, an evaluator's recommendations should be based on the employee's mental condition and how it affects the employee and the workplace, within the framework of the workplace environment.

REFERENCES

American Academy of Psychiatry and the Law. (2005). *Ethics guidelines for the practice of forensic psychiatry*. Bloomfield, CT: Author.

American Psychiatric Association. (2000). *Diagnostic and Statistical Manual of Mental Disorders* (4th ed., Text Revision). Washington, DC: Author.

American Psychiatric Association. (2006). *The principles of medical ethics with annotations especially applicable to psychiatry*. Arlington, VA: American Psychiatric Press.

American Psychological Association. (2002). Ethical principles of psychologists and code of conduct. *American Psychologist, 57*, 1060–1073.

Americans with Disabilities Act, 42 U.S.C., Sec. 12101 (1990).

Anfang, S. A., & Wall, B.W. (2006). Psychiatric fitness-for-duty evaluations. *Psychiatric Clinics of North America, 29*, 675–693.

Bloom, H., Webster, C. D., & Eisen, R. (2002). *The Employee Risk Assessment Guide, Version 1*. Toronto, ON: workplace.calm Inc.

Butcher, J. N., Dahlstrom, W. G., Graham, J. R., Tellegen, A., & Kaemmer, B. (1989). *Manual for the administration and scoring of the MMPI-2*. Minneapolis, MN: University of Minnesota Press.

Family and Medical Leave Act, 29 U.S.C., Sec. 2611 (11) (1993).

Gold, L. H., Anfang, S. A., Drukteinis, A. M., Metzner, J. L., Price, M., Wall, B. W., . . . Zonana, H. V. (2008). AAPL practice guideline for the forensic evaluation of psychiatric disability. *Journal of the American Academy of Psychiatry and the Law, 36*, S3–S50.

Hall, H. V. (2001). Violence prediction and risk analysis: Empirical advances and guidelines. *Journal of Threat Assessment, 1*(3), 1–39.

Health Insurance Portability and Accountability Act, 5 U.S.C.A. Sec. 601 (1996).

Millon, T. (1994). *Manual for the Millon Clinical Multiaxial Inventory (MCMI-III)*. Minneapolis, MN: National Computer Systems.

Randolph, C. (1998). *Repeatable battery for the assessment of neuropsychological status (RBANS)*. San Antonio, TX: Psychological Corporation.

U.S. Department of Labor (1996). Occupational Safety and Health Administration, Guidelines for preventing workplace violence for healthcare and social service workers. *OSHA*, 3148.

Wechsler, D. (1999). *Wechsler Abbreviated Scale of Intelligence*. San Antonio, TX: Psychological Corporation.

Wechsler, D. (2008). *Wechsler Adult Intelligence Scale* (4th ed.). San Antonio, TX: Pearson.

Wechsler, D. (2009). *Wechsler Memory Scale* (4th ed.). San Antonio, TX: Pearson.

White, S., & Meloy, R. (2007). *The Workplace Assessment of Violence Risk (WAVR-21)*. San Diego, CA: Specialized Training Services.

CHAPTER 26

Psychological Autopsy

FRANK M. DATTILIO and ROBERT L. SADOFF

INTRODUCTION

Medical autopsies, otherwise known as post-mortem examinations, are medical procedures that consist of a thorough examination of a corpse to determine the cause and manner of death and to evaluate any disease or injury that may be present. History tells us that the ancient Egyptians were one of the first civilizations to practice the removal and examination of internal organs and remains (Starr, 1991). However, the traditional autopsy's intellectual founder, Giovanni Morgagni, was an Italian physician who lived from 1682 to 1771. He is the celebrated father of the modern pathological autopsy (Annon, 1995). Since Morgagni's introduction of this procedure, the medical autopsy has been performed daily throughout the world with the primary intention of determining the cause of death. The results of medical autopsies are usually accepted as scientific evidence and are used to clarify matters in forensic cases in which the cause of death is uncertain.

In the same fashion, the "psychological autopsy" (PA) is often used to assist medical examiners in death classifications, particularly when there is some doubt as to whether or not a decedent committed suicide. In cases of suicide, PAs are mostly used to gather information about the circumstances of an individual's life, as well as their death, in order to attempt to understand the possible reasons for suicide (Hawton et al., 1998; Scott, Swartz, & Warburton, 2006; Simon, 1998).

PAs are usually conducted by behavioral scientists, forensic psychologists, or psychiatrists with specialized training and experience in the area. They may also be conducted by multidisciplinary teams as well, with law enforcement investigators, medical personnel, chaplains, and mental health workers working in mutually dependent roles (Annon, 1995; Litman, 1989; Otto, Poythress, Starr, & Darkes, 1993; Poythress, Otto, Darkes, & Starr, 1993).

While it may appear to many that just about any mental health professional can conduct PAs, there is a truly specific need for training and expertise in the areas of clinical psychodiagnostics and assessment. A solid knowledge of clinical psychology and/or psychiatry is necessary, along with a firm understanding of psychopathology when determining one's mental state at the time of death. This is particularly so if the death involves auto-erotic-type disorders that may be intertwined with anxiety, depression, and even psychotic disorders. The training received by clinical/forensic psychologists and psychiatrists is ideal for this work because of the issues involved. The reader is referred to Dattilio and Sadoff (2007) for a detailed explanation of the specific training of mental health professionals for a better understanding of which professionals may possess the appropriate training to conduct PAs.

We strongly recommend that professionals conducting PAs are duly licensed in their respective jurisdictions and also maintain the appropriate board certification. It is also essential that they have experienced some involvement in working on one or two PAs prior to testifying in court.

The goal of PAs is primarily to assist a medical examiner or coroner in determining the manner of unexplained death. When such cases find their way into the court, they may be used to settle criminal cases, the state's questions, workers' compensation claims, malpractice suits, or even cases involving insurance claims (Simon & Shuman, 2002).

PAs have also been used in cases involving autoerotic deaths (Sauvageau, 2008). These involve accidental deaths occurring during individual (usually solitary) sexual activity in which a device, apparatus, or prop was employed to enhance the sexual stimulation of a decedent, which resulted in an unintentional death (Byard &

Branwell, 1991). Accidental death can also be due to drugs or unintentional gunshot wounds.

The PA is a tool that has been more fluidly used since 1958 (Biffl, 1996; Litman, Curphey, Shneidman, Farberow, & Tabachnick, 1963; Shneidman & Farberow, 1961). It was first developed by Edwin Shneidman, who was one of the directors of the Los Angeles Suicide Prevention Center, conducing PAs in collaboration with the Los Angeles County Medical Examiner's Office under the direction of Theodore Curphey (Snider, Hane, & Berman, 2006). Since that time, more than 20 major PA projects have been conducted in North America, Europe, Australia, New Zealand, Israel, Taiwan, and India since their introduction in the 1950s (Isometsae, 2001). The trend appears to be increasing as the incidences of more unexplained deaths escalate (Dattilio, 2006).

The psychological autopsies are clearly difficult and complicated procedures that beget uncertainty. The ongoing criticism of such autopsies is very likely to continue in the future as it has in the past (Selkin & Loya, 1979; Stengel, 1973) due to the questionable use of precise scientific technology as opposed to medical autopsies. One should be reminded that nothing is perfect and that the psychological autopsy is sometimes the only assessment that we have in light of the fact that the decedent is no longer available for questioning and direct examination. Archaeologists and anthropologists use similar techniques all the time in examining historical facts from individuals and civilizations that lived thousands of years ago. However, with psychological autopsies and forensic settings, due to the scrutiny and demands of rules of evidence or standards, such as *Frye* & *Daubert*, any expert opinion offered through psychological autopsies is likely to continue to be challenged on its validity and reliability. As a result, conclusions must always be stated in terms of relative probabilities and the limitations of techniques, particularly when testifying in such cases. In order to make a good case for its effective use, it will also be important for experts to have a listing of citations in which psychological autopsies have been accepted in other courts of law in various jurisdictions.

The PA is actually a set of post-mortem investigative procedures that help ascertain and evaluate the role that physical and psychological factors play in the death of an individual (Weisman &

Kastenbaum, 1968). They have since been applied to many retrospective and equivocal death situations and involve mortality reviews and root cause analysis with regard to decedents with the aim of identifying cause of death. Equivocal deaths are usually undetermined deaths where the manner and cause may be known, but the circumstances surrounding an individual's passing were unclear.

PAs have also been used in some cases to determine the degree of mental illness that existed prior to the death (Gustafsson & Jacobsson, 2000). Because the subject is deceased in all cases of equivocal death, the entire truth may never be known. Accordingly, equivocal death autopsies must rely on a means of indirect assessment. It must be emphasized that even though psychological autopsies are an investigative technique, there are psychological elements in any behavioral analysis that must be maintained.

There are a slew of research articles in the professional literature pertaining to the use of PA and equivocal death investigations. Many of these articles outline the pros and cons to the use of such autopsies due to the fact that the procedure has come under scrutiny in the past (Snider et al., 2006). For one, PAs have a number of weaknesses. They suffer from the unavailability of the decedent for direct observation or questioning. Obviously, this makes the type of evaluation extremely arduous and more complicated than most evaluations that are typical of mental health professionals because specific details or elaboration are unobtainable (Sadoff & Dattilio, 2008; Ogloff & Otto, 1993). What is more, investigations may be complicated by the number of individuals who have something to gain based on the results, such as the decedent's survivors, third party beneficiaries, insurance companies, and other individuals involved with the case. Probably the most critical has been the lack of standardized protocol and methods for conducting PAs, which can sometimes have a profound effect on the results obtained (Ritchie & Gelles, 2002).

More recently, some have called for the standardization of PAs in attempts to address the *Daubert* challenge (Snider et al., 2006). This would reduce the variable skills training and sensitivity of interviewers and improve the overall question of the procedure's reliability (Werlang & Botega, 2003). As a result, the validity and reliability

issue of PAs has been a major concern among critics of the procedure. This no doubt poses significant problems for PAs, particularly
when they are introduced into the forensic forum as admissible
evidence. This has recently raised the issue under the *Daubert* standard derived from the Supreme Court decision, *Daubert v. Merrell
Dow Pharmaceuticals, Inc.* (1993). According to *Daubert*, the foundation
of "scientific knowledge" must be grounded in methods and procedures of science and possess scientific validity and reliability. Some
have suggested that, depending on how PAs are conducted, they may
still meet the requirements of that standard (Ault, Hazelwood, &
Reboussin, 1994).

On the positive end, there is much to be said for the use of PAs,
aside from the fact that they are much needed. This procedure
complements the skill of the medical examiners in determining the
cause of death of an individual and may increase the amount of
data for decision making. The information developed through the
PA also serves to piece together reasons why an individual may
have gravitated toward accidental or even purposeful death. PAs
and their constituent elements have struggled to achieve consensual validation or operational standardization, particularly with
aspects of content, validity, and reliability. This is due, in part, to
the fact that the process of reviewing the psychological aspects of a
victim's life is fraught with numerous obstacles, such as availability of records, inconsistency in recollections, family members' or
friends' refusal to speak about the deceased, and the possible biases
of the examiner. Furthermore, the purpose of a given PA may
itself be an issue, depending upon the manner in which it is used
(LaFon, 1999).

PREPARATION

One of the first steps that forensic psychologists and psychiatrists
need to take is to educate retaining counsel on exactly what is
entailed in embarking on a psychological autopsy. This involves
making clear the potential pitfalls and limitations of the autopsy
and how such a report may be rebuffed by opposing counsel. It is
also important to synthesize with retaining counsel the specific
questions to be answered with the autopsy report and what

essentials need to be presented to the judge or jury. Young (1992) and Ebert (1987) provide an excellent example of what forensic psychologists and psychiatrists will encounter in the process of conducting a psychological autopsy. These details are reviewed later in this chapter.

DATA COLLECTION

THE NEED FOR STANDARDIZED PSYCHOLOGICAL AUTOPSY PROTOCOLS

Unfortunately, in the past, one of the areas of concern has been the fact that suicide psychological autopsies (SPAs) or equivocal death psychological autopsies (EDPAs) have not been adequately addressed with regard to standardized protocol. Many experts in the field have called for the need for standardization, particularly in meeting the Daubert challenge (Snider et al., 2006). A standardized protocol would serve as a template in essential aspects of inquiries during interviews and reviewing of materials in order to achieve the objective. Such protocols would be applied to interviews, particularly those involving close friends and family members, in order to deal with biases that may occur in addressing the recollections of the decedent.

Interviews have been a particular area of concern regarding their vulnerability to bias, as outlined in the literature (Beskow, Runeson, & Asgard, 1990; Maris, Berman, & Silverman, 2000). Some results have shown that close friends and family members are somewhat protective of the decedent and more likely to project biased opinions, particularly if they are concerned that their statements might become publicly known, as in the case of publicized matters (Young, 1992; Selkin & Loya, 1979). It is also the issue that many of these interviews should be achieved within a few weeks of the decedent's death, and certainly no later than 6 months due to memory factors, as well as other reasons. This may be a problem, particularly if the case extends 6 months to a year subsequent to the death.

TEMPLATE PROTOCOL FOR PSYCHOLOGICAL AUTOPSIES

Young (1992) provides a skeletal outline of procedures for conducting psychological autopsies. In his article, Young adapted guidelines from Shneidman (1981), which are outlined in an expanded template below, but greatly enhanced by the first author of this chapter. Clinicians might find this guideline helpful as a protocol when conducting both SPAs and EDPAs.

- *Identifying information.* This includes such components as the decedent's name, age, address, marital status, occupation, and religion. Such demographic information is important initially for several reasons. For one, it is important to be able to identify all of the ongoing data due to documentation that is reviewed. Also, in some vein, minor details such as the decedent's address, marital circumstances, work-related atmospheres, and even religious affiliation may have some bearing on the cause of death.
- *Details of death.* All of the details surrounding the death are extremely important, including photographs and even, at times, making visits, if possible, to the site where the decedent expired. Police reports will often provide information as to with whom the decedent interacted prior to his or her death, with the circumstances surrounding the death, time, atmosphere, and length of time between the actual time of death and when the body was discovered.
- *Decedent's history.* Contact with these individuals and pursuit of this information is vital for a number of reasons. Each is outlined below:
  - *Siblings.* Oftentimes, illnesses with siblings are similar, particularly with issues involving mental illness. Therefore, speaking with siblings and understanding their courses of illness, whether or not they experienced any depression or mental illness, often helps in understanding the psychological dynamics of the decedent.
  - *Marriage.* The history of marital relationships, long-term live-in relationships, or any promiscuity and sexual activity, is all-important in trying to conceptualize the decedent's lifestyle. If the decedent was involved in marital and/or family counseling, these records would be essential to obtain in order to search for clues about the state of mind.
  - *Medical illnesses and treatments.* These data can be extremely helpful, particularly if there was a medical illness that was life threatening or recent significant losses occurred.

- ○ *Suicide attempts.* Any history of suicidal attempts, gestures, or even documentation about thought content or "off-the-cuff statements" must be included.
  - ○ *Death history of decedent's family.* The number of deaths in the decedent's family should be noted, particularly regarding who they were, how they died, when they died, what the circumstances were, and the impact that the deaths had on the decedent during his/her lifetime. Family members are often able to provide this information, particularly whether the decedent took family members' deaths hard, whether there were any subsequent periods of depression, and whether this coincided in close proximity to his/her death.
  - ○ *Decedent's pattern of reactions to stress.* It is essential to attempt to understand stress patterns and reactions, which can be discerned from not only records, but also by talking with close friends, family members, spouses, or children.
- *Recent tensions or anticipated trouble.* This is another vital area, particularly if the individual was laboring under any financial stress or any type of impending stressor that may have involved legal problems or potential incarceration, shame, or embarrassment. This could also involve the anticipation of the end of intimate relationships, infidelities, or even the lack of intimate relationships.
- *Role of alcohol and other drugs in overall lifestyle in death of decedent.* Any long history of illicit drug or alcohol use, abuse, dependence, or failed treatments, is vital.
- *Decedent's interpersonal relationships.* When Aaron T. Beck and associates were studying suicidality, one of the tasks they conducted was to interview many of the close friends of individuals who had successfully committed suicide in order to understand their psychodynamics and their effect on relationships with the decedent (Beck, Resnik, & Lettieri, 1974). This is another area to consider in attempting to understand whether there were any complications involving interpersonal relationships and dynamics that may have contributed to an untimely death.
- *Fantasies, dreams, thoughts, premonitions, or fears of the decedent relating to death, accident, or suicide.* Any of the information that

can be determined through family members or friends close to the decedent would also be extremely useful.

- *Changes in the decedent's habits, hobbies, eating patterns, sexual behavior, and other life routines before death.* Often, individuals who commit suicide engage in radical changes in routine behaviors. The forensic expert would need to detect any changes in any of these areas.

- *Information related to the "lighter side" of the decedent.* This would include such components as "upswing," successes, and plans. In a particular case, where mania or bipolar illness may be suspected, understanding highs and lows in the individual's life, mood swings or any types of erratic behaviors, or moods should be considered. Attempts to determine whether or not unrealistic expectations may have led to disappointment and subsequent depression would be an important link to the potential for suicide.

- *Assessment of intentional acts.* The role of the decedent in his/her own demise is extremely important when attempting to discern a cause of death. Three types of death are often outlined: intentional death in which the decedent plays a direct conscious role in his/her demise; unintentional death in which the decedent plays no role in his/her demise; subintentional death in which the decedent plays some covert, unconscious role in his/her demise. Shneidman (1981) reported that for a 2-year period, 26% of all natural, accidental, and homicidal deaths in Marin County, California, were deemed to be subintentional. A good example of subintentional death might be an accidental overdose of cocaine in which the individual had been struggling with depression and stress, but not necessarily making any clear and direct overtures toward suicide. In essence, the carelessness of using cocaine may have been a part of the addiction, along with a reckless disregard for potential death. Hence, one dies at his/her own hand without the specific or conscious intent of committing suicide.

- *Rating of lethality.* Often, suicidal cases have components that access perturbation and lethality. Perturbation refers to how agitated and disturbed one becomes at a particular moment.

Lethality reflects the propensity to do something impulsive while having access to a method of death.

- *Reaction of informants to decedent's death.* Interviewing informants and family members who receive word of a loved one's death is very important, particularly with regard to their reaction and whether or not they anticipated it or feared it.

Additional Factors

In addition to the above, Ebert (1987) offers a guideline of 26 factors to consider when conducting autopsies. These factors include the following:

1. Illicit drug or alcohol history
2. Suicide notes
3. Writings, diaries, notes, etc., by the deceased
4. Books owned or read by the deceased
5. Interpersonal relationships with friends, acquaintances, parents, siblings, coworkers, supervisors, relatives, physicians, mental health professionals, and teachers
6. Marital relationships and history of long-term relationships
7. Mood
8. Psychosocial stressors
9. Presuicidal behavior
10. Language (i.e., analyze tapes, recollections, or conversations and writings for morbid content)
11. Prescription medications, interaction effects of legal and/or illegal compounds
12. Medical history
13. Mental status exam of the decedent's condition prior to death—assess orientation, memory, attention, concentration, mood and affect, hallucinations or delusions, cognition, intelligence, language, and judgment
14. Psychological history
15. Laboratory studies
16. Coroner's report
17. Motive assessment

18. Reconstruction of events occurring on the day prior to the decedent's death
19. Assess feelings regarding death, as well as preoccupations and fantasies
20. Military history
21. Death history of family
22. Family history
23. Employment history
24. Educational history
25. Familiarity with methods of death
26. Police reports

While it may not be essential to collect data on every single one of the 26 factors listed above, this list can serve as a guideline of factors to aid clinical forensic psychologists or psychiatrists in conducting psychological autopsies.

DATA INTERPRETATION

LaFon (1999) has suggested that there are actually two types of psychological autopsies: the suicide psychological autopsy and the equivocal death psychological autopsy.

Suicide Psychological Autopsy (SPA)

The PA has been used by mental health professionals to assist medical examiners in death classifications. Various sources of information are used in this type of autopsy for the examination, including interview data from family, friends, coworkers, and acquaintances, as well as physical autopsy, toxicology reports, and an examination of the death scene characteristics. Clinical opinions center on the manner of death, whether it be an accident, natural causes, homicide, suicide, or undetermined origin.

With the SPA, the aim is to understand the psychosocial factors that have contributed to the suicide. Data are collected and maintained in a database for the purpose of future prevention efforts. In a sense, the term *PA* may actually be a misnomer when applied to suicide in which the manner of death has already been determined. However, at times, there may be question as to whether or not one truly intended to die, or may have been attempting to achieve another purpose (Sauvageau, 2008). A classical example is with autoerotic deaths in which individuals who engage in different types of autoerotic activities, such as hanging or certain types of bondage activities for sexual excitation may experience unintentional death. A recent example occurred with the 72-year-old actor, David Carradine, who was found hanging in the closet of his Bangkok hotel suite in June of 2009. Carradine's official cause of death was determined to be due to asphyxiation. However, the position in which the actor's body was bound raised some question initially as to whether the death was truly a suicide. A public autopsy was conducted, followed by a private one hired by the actor's family. The pathologist, Michael Baden, had initially questioned whether the death was a suicide; however, it was eventually determined that the cause of death was indeed asphyxiation, which, in this case, is an inability to breathe due to self-infliction. Whether this was deliberate or accidental remains unclear. In cases such as this, experts conducting SPAs would specifically look at issues surrounding any history of depression, social and psychological pressures, or circumstances that might implicate the potential for the involvement of suicidal intent. The issue in this case pertained to the ligatures or "ties that bind," with marks on Carradine's body raising questions as to whether it was an intended suicide (Dobuzinskis, 2009).

Other cases of suicide with no visible precursor may call for an SPA as a means of helping family and friends come to grips as to why an individual would take his/her life without any indication that anything was wrong or seriously disturbing the decedent.

EQUIVOCAL DEATH PSYCHOLOGICAL AUTOPSY (EDPA).

In contrast to the SPA, the EDPA is a separate and distinct procedure in that the primary purpose is to assist in the actual determination and the manner of death classification, that is, why a particular individual died and whether it was indeed suicide, homicide, accidental death by natural causes, or an undetermined reason. Consequently, appropriate action may follow suit, particularly where there are cases of questionable criminal charges involved. A good example of this is presented in a case example by Dattilio (2006).

In cases of EDPA, data are not necessarily collected and stored in large databases, but are used in the medical examiner's forensic investigation, for a criminal defense, or even by a prosecutor on a case-by-case basis. LaFon (2008) argues that even though SPAs and EDPAs are similar, there is a distinct difference in their purpose and that individuals in the professional literature have a tendency to lump the two together under the rubric of "PA" without any specifier.

EDPAs are concerned with any information that might reveal cognition, emotion, behaviors, relationships, medical history, social pressures, and coping mechanisms, as an integral aspect of what occurred (Ebert, 1991; Gelles, 1995). The gathering of vital information is the reason that the use of SPAs or EDPAs has been pivotal in investigating cases of suicidal or accidental death (Annon, 1995; Shneidman & Farberow, 1961; Lacks, Westeveer, Dibble, & Clemente, 2008). However, there are times when the actual manner of death is not clear. It is estimated that between 5% and 20% of all deaths are equivocal (Schneidman, 1981).

One of the circumstances in which this question becomes crucial is in charges of criminal homicide, such as murder or manslaughter, and when the death actually occurred as a result of suicide. In cases of criminal homicide, the issues may be multifaceted. One example may be whether the act was premeditated or accidental. In addition, an EDPA may also be conducted on the victim of a homicide in order to determine whether or not the victim may have had propensities towards violence and possibly assaulted someone who, in self-defense, committed an unpremeditated murder.

In his article, Dattilio (2006) outlines a very interesting case that involves an accidental suicide in which the defendant was charged with criminal homicide in the death of his former girl-friend. The defendant was eventually vindicated based on evidence presented at trial, which outlined the fact that the victim had a history of depression, substance abuse, acute stress at the time of death, emotional instability, a previous diagnosis of cancer, a history of suicide attempts, a criminal history, and was facing incarceration. All of these circumstances contributed to a determination of reasonable doubt by the jury, which also considered the angle of the gunshot wound and powder burns on the hands of the decedent. The jury concluded that the victim did indeed commit suicide.

In addition to criminal cases, EDPAs are also important in insurance cases as well. In one early case, the California Supreme Court declared in *Searle v. Allstate Life Insurance Company* (1985) that mental capacity was very relevant to determining the presence of suicidal intent, and specified that "if the insured did not understand the physical nature and consequences of the act, whether he was sane or insane, then he did not intentionally kill himself" (p. 439). In light of this and similar cases, Botello, Weinberger, and Gross (2003) emphasize the importance of collecting information that will "provide a picture of the decedent's lifestyle and his or her behavior and mental state near the time of death" (p. 92).

INTERPRETATION: CASE EXAMPLES

In addition to the use of psychological autopsies to detect the manner of death in suicide cases or equivocal death cases where homicide may be involved, forensic experts have also utilized psychological autopsies in determining the degree of pain and suffering prior to death. In one case of an airline crash, Sadoff (unpublished transcript) relied on the medical autopsy material of Cyril Wecht, a noted forensic pathologist, to determine the length of time estimated that each decedent lived and was conscious prior to death following the crash. Dr. Wecht estimated that from his study of the autopsy material, each individual had been conscious for approximately two minutes prior to death following the fiery crash. Based on the forensic autopsy reports conducted by Dr. Wecht and interviews of a number of survivors of the crash, Dr. Sadoff was able to determine various states of anxiety, fear, and depression at various points prior to death. He divided the time from the announcement by the captain that the plane would not make it safely to Chicago and that he was trying to land at a closer airport. Individuals began praying, holding hands, calling loved ones, and realizing, at various times, that they would not survive. It was only through the determination of others on board that estimates could be made as to what feelings were experienced by the victims of the crash. This is not a typical psychological autopsy, but does incorporate the techniques utilized in PAs in order to arrive at an opinion to be used within a reasonable degree of medical certainty in a court of law.

Another example of a psychological autopsy involves the drowning death of a young man who was on a canoe trip with friends when a storm developed and capsized the boat. It was only through interviews with survivors that Dr. Sadoff was able to ascertain the fear and emotional distress experienced by the victim prior to his death. One survivor recalled the victim yelling and screaming that he could not swim, that he was not going to make it and to tell his mother and father that he loved them. Another survivor was thrown overboard with the victim, but was able to swim to safety and was not able to save the decedent. Attempts were made to hold on to the victim, but he was not able to maintain his hold, slipped away, and drowned. The survivor was able to discuss the comments made and his observations of the body movements (i.e., the thrashing around and panic) expressed by the victim.

COMMUNICATION

Communication of the results of a psychological autopsy is extremely important, particularly to a presiding judge and/or jury. First and foremost, it is important to educate the court on exactly what is entailed with a psychological autopsy, why such is conducted, and how it has been used in the past. Establishing credibility is essential, not only with regard to the credentials of the forensic examiner conducting the autopsy, but also the value (not the mere weight) of such a procedure. This often sets a good foundation for a process that will undoubtedly be attacked on cross-examination. One issue that is important is the degree of professional certainty that an examiner is able to make, particularly because he or she did not have direct contact with the decedent. However, carefully documenting the evidence base that exists with interviews with families and reviewing records is important for ensuring that the process is credible to both judge and jury. Such highlights, as the use of "convergent validity" when records reviewed by multiple sources come to the same conclusion, need to be highlighted and bolstered for purposes of credibility. Also, it is important to convey the fact that psychological autopsies are used in many countries throughout the world.

WRITTEN REPORT

Once all of the relevant data and information have been collected, psychological autopsies require the production of a written report with sections that convey the reason for the evaluation, a complete listing of sources of information and interviews, a summary of facts, an accounting of pertinent and significant factors, medical treatment, psychiatric history, and conclusions. The report should be constructed with headings that lead the narrative forward to the ultimate conclusion.

Reports should be written in a clear, concise, and jargon free manner. Verbose wording may impede the reader's understanding. Reports that are jumbled or disorganized will also detract from the veracity of the findings. The enhanced outline provided earlier as a "Template Protocol for Psychological Autopsy" may prove particularly useful in developing an inclusive yet accessible report format. Readers may also want to refer to Dattilio (2006) as an additional guideline in this regard.

REFERENCES

Annon, J. S. (1995). The psychological autopsy. *American Journal of Forensic Psychology, 13*(2), 39–48.

Ault, R. L., Hazelwood, R., & Reboussin, R. (1994). Epistemological status of equivocal death analysis. *American Psychologist, 49*, 72–73.

Beck, A. T., Resnik, H. L., & Lettieri, D. (Eds.). (1974). *The prediction of suicide*. Bowie, MD: Charles Press.

Beskow, J., Runeson, B., & Asgard, U. (1990). Psychological autopsies: Methods and ethics. *Suicide and Life-Threatening Behavior, 20*, 307–323.

Biffl, E. (1996). Psychological autopsies: Do they belong in the courtroom? *American Journal of Criminal Law, 24*, 123–146.

Botello, T. E., Weinberger, L. E., & Gross, B. H. (2003). Psychological autopsy. In R. Rosner (Ed.), *Principles and practice of forensic psychiatry (2nd ed.)* (pp. 90–94). London, UK: Arnold Press.

Byard, R. W., & Branwell, N. H. (1991). Autoerotic death definition. *American Journal of Forensic Medicine and Pathology, 12*, 74–76.

Dattilio, F. M. (2006). Equivocal death psychological autopsies in cases of criminal homicide. *American Journal of Forensic Psychology, 24*(1), 5–22.

Dattilio, F. M., & Sadoff, R. L. (2007). *Mental health experts: Roles and qualifications for court* (2nd ed.). Mechanicsburg: Pennsylvania Bar Institute.

Daubert v. Merrell Dow Pharmaceuticals, Inc., 509 U.S. 579 (1993).

Dobuzinskis, A. (2009). David Carradine died of asphyxiation: Pathologist. Retrieved August 23, 2009, from Reuters web site: http://www.reuters.com/article/entertainmentNews/idUSTRE5610CD20090702

Ebert, B. W. (1987). Guide to conducting a psychological autopsy. *Professional Psychology: Research and Practice, 18*, 52–56.

Ebert, B. W. (1991). Guide to conducting a psychological autopsy. In K. N. Anchor (Ed.), *Handbook of medical psychotherapy* (pp. 249–256). Lewiston, NY: Hogrefe & Huber.

Gelles, M. G. (1995). Psychological autopsy: An investigative aid. In M. I. Kurke & E. M. Scrivner (Eds.), *Police psychology into the 21st century* (pp. 337–355). Hillsdale, NJ: Erlbaum.

Gustafsson, L., & Jacobsson, L. (2000). On mental disorder and somatic disease and suicide: The psychological autopsy study of one hundred suicides in North Sweden. *Nordic Journal of Psychiatry, 54*, 383–395.

Hawton, K., Appleby, L., Platt, S., Foster, T., Cooper, J., Malmberg, A., et al. (1998). The psychological autopsy approach to studying suicide: A review of methodological issues. *Journal of Affective Disorders, 50*, 269–276.

Isometsae, E. T. (2001). Psychological autopsy studies: A review. *European Psychiatry, 16*, 379–385.

Lacks, R. D., Westeveer, A. E., Dibble, A., & Clemente, J. (2008). Equivocal death investigation: Case study analysis. *Victims and Offenders, 3*, 150–164.

LaFon, D. S. (1999). Psychological autopsies for equivocal deaths. *International Journal of Emergency Mental Health, 1*, 183–188.

LaFon, D. S. (2008). The psychological autopsy. In B. E. Turbey (Ed.), *Criminal profiling: An introduction to behavioral evidence analysis* (3rd ed) (pp. 419–429). San Diego, CA: Elsevier Academic Press.

Litman, R. E. (1989). Five hundred psychological autopsies. *Journal of Forensic Sciences, 34*, 638–646.

Litman, R. E., Curphey, T., Shneidman, E. S., Farberow, N. L., & Tabachnick, N. (1963). Investigations of equivocal suicides. *Journal of the American Medical Association, 184*, 924–929.

Maris, R. W., Berman, A. L., & Silverman, M. M. (2000). *Comprehensive textbook of suicidology*. New York, NY: Guilford Press.

Ogloff, J., & Otto, R. (1993). Psychological autopsy: Clinical and legal perspectives. *St. Louis Law Review, 37*, 607–646.

Otto, R. K., Poythress, N., Starr, L., & Darkes, J. (1993). An empirical study of the reports of APA's peer review panel in the congressional review of the USS *Iowa* incident. *Journal of Personality Assessment, 61*, 425–442.

Poythress, N., Otto, R. K., Darkes, J., & Starr, L. (1993). APA's expert panel in the congressional review of the USS *Iowa* incident. *American Psychologist, 48*, 8–15.

Ritchie, E., & Gelles, N. G. (2002). Psychological autopsy: The current department of defense effort to standardize training and quality assurance. *Journal of Forensic Science, 47*, 1370–1372.

Sadoff, R. L., & Dattilio, F. M. (2008). *Crime and mental illness: A guide to courtroom practice.* Mechanicsburg, PA: Pennsylvania Bar Institute.

Sauvageau, A. (2008). Autoerotic deaths: A seven-year retrospective epidemiological study. *Open Forensic Science Journal, 1*, 1–3.

Scott, C. L., Swartz, E., & Warburton, K. (2006). Psychological autopsy: Solving the mysteries of death. *Psychiatric Clinics of North America, 29*, 805–822.

Searle v. Allstate Life Insurance Company, 38 Cal.3d 425 (1985).

Selkin, J., & Loya, F. (1979). Issues in the psychological autopsy of a controversial public figure. *Professional Psychology, 10*, 87–93.

Shneidman, E. S. (1981). The psychological autopsy. *Suicide and Life-Threatening Behavior, 11*, 325–340.

Shneidman, E. S., & Farberow, N. L. (1961). Sample investigation of equivocal suicide deaths. In N. L. Farberow & N. E. Shneidman (Eds.), *The cry for help* (pp. 118–128). New York: McGraw-Hill.

Simon, R. I. (1998). Murder masquerading as suicide: Post-mortem assessment of suicide risk factors at the time of death. *Journal of Forensic Sciences, 43*, 1119–1123.

Simon, R. I., & Shuman, D. W. (2002). Remembering the future: Policy implications for the forensic assessment of past mental states. In R. I. Simon & D. W. Shuman (Eds.), *Retrospective assessment of mental states in litigation: Predicting the past* (pp. 445–451). Arlington, VA: American Psychiatric Publishing.

Snider, J. E., Hane, S., & Berman, A. L. (2006). Standardizing the psychological autopsy: Addressing the Daubert standard. *Suicide and Life-Threatening Behavior, 36*, 511–518.

Starr, C. G. (1991). *A history of the ancient world.* New York, NY: Oxford University Press.

Stengel, E. (1973). The psychology of suicide. *Life-Threatening Behavior, 3*, 166–168.

Weisman, A. D., & Kastenbaum, R. (1968). *The psychological autopsy: A study of the terminal phase of life (Community Mental Health Journal Monograph Series, 4)*. New York, NY: McGraw-Hill.

Werlang, S. G., & Botega, N. J. (2003). The semi-structured interview for psychological autopsy: An inter-rater reliability study. *Suicide and Life-Threatening Behavior, 33*, 323–330.

Young, T. J. (1992). Procedures and problems in conducting a psychological autopsy. *International Journal of Offender Therapy and Comparative Criminology, 36*, 43–52.

PART 3

FORENSIC PRACTICE CONSIDERATIONS

CHAPTER 27

Developing and Operating a Forensic Practice

STANLEY L. BRODSKY and WILLIAM H. REID

INTRODUCTION

Many mental health professionals are interested in forensic work. Most of them do not realize that forensic practice is really a subspecialty, with some elements that require special knowledge and experience. Having said that, there is nothing magical or exotic about forensic practice; it is no more stressful or complex than any other subspecialty. But it is different.

Clinicians often consider forensic work in order to make money, ease third-party-payer hassles, lessen paperwork, avoid some of the administrative rules of modern clinical practice, or decrease malpractice risk. They should think carefully before deciding that forensic practice is the answer to their dreams. The objectives can usually be met with less trouble by finding other ways to simplify one's professional life.

In this chapter, we refer to *forensic practice* as work that involves assessment and consultation to the legal process, often leading to a role of "expert" or "expert witness." We will not describe the many other kinds of forensic work, such as treatment in forensic settings, correctional psychology or psychiatry, or academic pursuits. We will address work that involves consultation or participation in litigated (or potentially litigated) matters, by private practitioners and consultant clinicians employed by agencies, institutions, and universities. When there are significant differences in practice style, case opportunities, or work responsibilities among these forensic practice worlds, we will point them out.

THE "RETAINING ENTITY" AND OTHER PLAYERS

We will often refer to a *retaining entity*. The term is a bit unwieldy, but describes any attorney, court, agency, or other entity that hires (retains) a mental health professional, either individually or through his/her employer (e.g., clinic, university). Private practitioners are usually retained by lawyers. Professionals whose work is part of their agency or academic employment may work on behalf of an agency or facility (such as a secure hospital), or on behalf of a client (e.g., a lawyer or insurance company) who has contracted with their employer (Gutheil, 2009b).

In any case, it is important to understand that the lawyer with whom one is working is not "your" lawyer, and should not be referred to as such. He or she is merely someone who has retained an expert to help with his client's problem.

Similarly, we will often refer to an attorney who represents the side opposite the retaining entity as the *opposing lawyer*. It should be understood that this "opposing" attorney opposes the retaining attorney and his/her case, not the expert.

People interviewed or examined by forensic practitioners are often clients of a retaining or opposing attorney or someone else (such as an insurance company); they are rarely the forensic examiner's "patient," and should not be referred to as such. What one calls the person assessed indicates how one understands the process. He or she may be the *litigant*, the *plaintiff*, the *defendant*, or the *evaluee*, but never one's patient or client.

A PATH LESS TAKEN

For psychiatrists and clinical psychologists, the path to a clinical service career is often a well-marked, well-traveled road. The clinical elements of training segue directly into positions offering clinical assessment and treatment services. The training is directly related to the tasks at hand.

Developing a practice in forensic mental health is a different matter. Most training sites do not offer extensive forensic training or forensic practice opportunities. This chapter addresses the procedures and knowledge that psychologists and psychiatrists should acquire in order to start a forensic practice. One may begin either fresh from residency or postdoctoral training, or later in a clinical career.

Either choice involves at least four principles:

1. Forensic work is based in solid clinical training, knowledge, and experience. A forensic clinician's primary usefulness lies in his or her clinical expertise. Familiarity with forensic principles allows one to use and convey that expertise in a way that is useful to legal or administrative situations.
2. Forensic work is not for those who are looking for an "easier" practice. The demands are extensive, the work is often public, and thin-skinned professionals often find themselves sorely tested.
3. Forensic work in the United States calls for adaptation to a context in which adversarial challenges and procedures are the norm. Unlike the typical collaborative and collegial milieu of clinical work, forensic tasks often involve attorneys who dispute findings and opposing experts who come to different conclusions.
4. The demand for objectivity, neutrality, and comprehensiveness is more persistent and pervasive than in customary clinical work. In clinical work, the therapeutic alliance is assumed; action often may reasonably be taken based on incomplete information, and advocating for the best interests of patients/clients is routine. In forensic practice, such advocacy is inappropriate; detached impartiality with regard to the evaluee or case is required. One may, and often should, advocate vigorously and articulately for one's *opinions*, which may favor a litigant, but the difference between this and advocating for a litigant *per se* is very important.

THE NEW PRACTITIONER

The most straightforward route to early-career forensic practice is simply to take a forensic fellowship or postdoctoral year as part of one's training. Senior trainees and recent graduates should consider such formal training, in which one receives complete, efficient, up-to-date, practical tutoring from good teachers, and makes important practice and career contacts in the process. In addition, we do not recommend that new graduates move immediately into exclusively forensic practice, particularly without a fellowship.

For those who wish to begin traditional practice and also develop forensic aspects without full-time subspecialty training, the process is similar to that for established clinicians. The main difference is that new practitioners may not have a financial "cushion" of established patients and income as they wait for their forensic practice to grow. Forensic practices, particularly those without agency employment or contracts, often grow more slowly than traditional clinical ones (another good reason to maintain traditional practice while doing forensic work).

EVOLVING A FORENSIC PRACTICE FROM A TRADITIONAL "CLINICAL" ONE

Many established psychiatrists and psychologists want to shift part or all of their practices to forensic work. One common reason is the labyrinthine paperwork that surrounds third-party payments. Others are drawn by the vision of better, but sometimes illusory, compensation. Still others are attracted by the challenge and puzzle-solving aspects of forensic work, some imagining they will add a bit of "drama" to their daily work.

Unlike those who come from a forensic training program, many general clinicians who shift their career emphasis have not been exposed to important discussions about, and supervision in, the fundamental roles and potential ethical conflicts they will encounter. In one of the most cited articles about the distinctions between clinical and forensic work, Greenberg and Shuman (1997) identified a number of basic differences between clinical and forensic work, saying that in forensic endeavors:

- The attorney is the client (in private consultations).
- The assessing clinician is neutral rather than supportive.
- Competencies and evaluation techniques are often targeted to legal claims/issues.
- The diagnostic tasks, although clinically based, are often related to the legal issues at hand.
- Litigant statements are not taken at face value, but are scrutinized carefully, often via collateral sources.

- Forensic evaluations are usually more structured than routine clinical ones.
- The relationship with the evaluee or other litigant is not therapeutic, but evaluative and commonly within an adversarial context.
- Critical judgment is expected.

BIAS

Letting go of one's commitment to the welfare of the evaluee or other litigant is an important shift in thinking for clinicians. That patient-care interest is replaced by a more detached relationship of impartial assessment or participation, with primary obligations to objective evaluation of records, individuals, and case situations. The court's requirement for honesty and objectivity is a very high priority, which must not be subrogated by either the evaluee's "interest" (e.g., if he/she were to be viewed as a patient) or the contractual relationship with the retaining entity.

It may be helpful to remember that the objectivity of one's findings is important to the retaining attorney as well as the court. Practical and ethical lawyers want to hear the truth about their cases, not just supportive fluff. They know that their experts' opinions are likely to be vigorously challenged and must be easily defensible. Most lawyers are grateful to know when experts' findings do not support their cases, so that they can make accurate decisions.

Even with the best intentions and clarity of purpose, objectivity can be compromised in several ways, most of which can be addressed with a little common sense. One compromise process has been called the "allegiance effect": Murrie, Boccaccini, Johnson, and Janke (2008), studying forensic evaluators, observed strong but unconscious allegiances and partiality in assessors. Many forensic clinicians view themselves as free of significant bias (Commons, Miller, & Gutheil, 2004); many others realize that some level of bias, of one kind or another, is likely to be present in virtually every forensic and non-forensic matter (Gutheil, 2009b; Gutheil & Simon, 2004).

What can a responsible expert do to minimize bias and prevent it from significantly affecting the work and the case? Four concepts seem important: *recognition* of potential bias, the *relevance* of a particular bias to the case at hand, the *extent and effect* of the bias on the case, and the exerting of professional *controls* over that potential effect. Forensic clinicians are not expected to understand absolutely everything about their unconscious objectivity, but can draw on various self-checks, consultants, and colleagues to review their procedures, findings, and inferences (Murrie et al., 2009).

Liability in Forensic Practice

A disclaimer is in order: This isn't legal advice; it's just our opinion.

Liability generally arises from a duty that one person or entity has to another. Forensic professionals have duties to the lawyers who retain them, and perhaps to other people involved in the forensic matters. For example, they must be reasonably diligent, avoid misre-presentation, provide adequate work quality, act in good faith, and not improperly abandon a retaining entity. They have a strong duty of truthfulness to the court. Negligent breach of a duty may cause damage to someone, for which the negligent person (the expert, potentially) may be found liable. Other considerations, civil and criminal, that may apply in some situations include contempt of court, perjury, and spoliation of evidence. Experts should be insured. In our experience, most forensic work incurs fewer malpractice allegations than general clinical work, but one should be sure his or her insurance policy covers the expected activities. Some mal-practice policies cover forensic work without an additional rider; others don't.

PRINCIPLES OF FORENSIC WORK

Courts and lawyers seek experts with clinical expertise and with some understanding of the legal process at hand. They do not need quasi-attorneys or clinicians who act like lawyers. The basic task is to understand your clinical discipline and how it applies to the forensic arenas in which one is involved. Still, one must know how legal procedures and rules apply to forensic work, and when retaining attorneys may have acted improperly.

An attorney who retained one of the authors for a forensic evaluation instructed his client not to speak to evaluators retained by the other side. It was important that the expert inform the attorney that in the case at hand, it was improper to instruct his defendant to be silent.

Forensic professionals in litigated matters, particularly those in private practice, are usually retained by a lawyer, not by the judge or court. The common belief that expert witnesses are often "friends of the court" misunderstands both the U.S. judicial system and the definition of that phrase.

- *Understand the case.* Forensic practitioners must understand the point of the legal exercise in which they are involved. That means understanding, and being comfortable with, both cases themselves and the common roles forensic professionals have in them.
- *Credibility.* Forensic matters necessarily highlight the credibility of those who offer opinions to courts; one's background information and past testimony are easily accessible to lawyers and courts. The expert must have, and maintain, a very good reputation in both clinical and forensic work. One should not be a "hired gun" (that's the lawyer's job). The impression that one is a "bought" witness is one of the most damning indictments of forensic credibility. Scrupulous efforts at openness and objectivity work to reduce that impression.
- *Treater vs. expert.* A clinician who is treating a litigant or other party with an interest in a case, or who has done so in the past or anticipates doing so in the future, should not present himself as an impartial evaluator or be an expert witness (i.e., offer opinions) in a case involving that person. This strong proscription has important bearing on both the case and the treatment. The many likely conflicts are described well elsewhere (e.g., American Psychology-Law Society, 2008; Reid, 2008; Strasburger, Gutheil, & Brodsky, 1997).
- *"Expert" witness versus "fact" witness.* Expert witnesses offer conclusions and opinions to a court. Their expertise, backgrounds, and the foundations of their opinions are subject to considerable scrutiny by the court and opposing counsel. Fact witnesses, however, describe, under oath, what they actually have heard or seen firsthand, without drawing conclusions or offering opinions. Treating clinicians are commonly called to testify as fact witnesses (Gutheil, 2009b).

Kinds of Cases

The kinds of legal matters in which one engages often select themselves, based on one's background and interests (e.g., a psychologist who specializes in assessment, or a psychiatrist experienced in psychopharmacology), and what one chooses to accept. Individuals may wish to consider different kinds of forensic referrals, but should be aware of the limitations of their expertise. For example, clinicians who are not specially trained and experienced in child and family work should not accept child custody cases.

- *Negligence.* Negligence matters include, but aren't limited to, civil lawsuits that involve alleged malpractice (in which the *standard of care* and *damage* to patients are usual issues), personal injury (especially emotional damages), workplace discrimination and harassment.
- *Criminal matters.* These usually involve assessments for competency to stand trial, criminal responsibility ("insanity"), mitigation of charges or sentences, release from custody, eligibility for the death penalty, or juvenile matters such as waiver to adult court.
- *Competency and capacity matters.* These cover a very broad range, such as the ability to make a will (testamentary capacity), to manage one's affairs (e.g., financial, health care), to make a contract, to consent to some action, to refuse consent, to "proceed" (usually to trial), and to parent. Competency varies with the task expected, and may include the ability to resist the harmful influence of others.
- *Guardianship, conservatorship, and incompetent parenting.* These imply a broad lack of capacity or a special need for protection in matters of caring for oneself, child custody, parenting, children's best interests, and potential harm associated with parental visitation.
- *Disability, impairment of fitness, and workers' compensation matters.* These usually allege an inability to do something, such as work at a job or practice a profession. Uncomplicated disability assessment is sometimes an exception to the "treater *versus* evaluator" proscription mentioned elsewhere; treating clinicians commonly offer opinions about disability.

- *Civil commitment.* These involve involuntary hospitalization or outpatient care, forensic issues commonly seen in general clinical practice. Opinions about mental illness causing danger to self, danger to others, or grave disability are often offered by treating clinicians (usually psychiatrists). Many special commitment proceedings, such as those coming after criminal court adjudication, those associated with marked danger to others (e.g., transfer to a facility for particularly violent patients), and those associated with alleged sexually violent predators, should be performed by nontreating evaluators.
- *Second opinions.* Although not often thought of as a forensic process, second opinions and consultations to treating clinicians or treatment teams about patients' dangerousness, readiness for discharge, eligibility for civil commitment, or even diagnosis or treatment are common in both clinical and forensic practice. Sometimes the consultation has a specifically legal purpose; more often, it is done for clinical or risk management reasons.

FORENSIC PRACTICE ETHICS

Ethics principles and ethical practices are addressed throughout this chapter. We will touch upon a few before moving to the practical sections.

Most ordinary clinical duties are not created in the kinds of work we describe herein, primarily because no doctor–patient relationship exists. Many ethics principles do apply, however, including some that do not arise in routine clinical work (Gutheil, 2009a).

One reason to belong to respected professional organizations is the expectation that one will adhere to their ethics guidelines. Since much ethics enforcement is done by organizations such as the American Psychiatric Association or American Psychological Association, being a member provides the public with at least a modicum of reassurance that one accepts their guidelines and has not been censured by them.

One must avoid misrepresenting experience and credentials to attorneys and other parties. Some new forensic professionals are tempted to overstate their backgrounds to appear more desirable for a case referral or more credible to a court. Lack of forensic experience is not always viewed as a weakness; for some jurors and attorneys it implies that one is a clinician, and not tainted by the legal system.

There is a risk of being used by attorneys, law enforcement, or agencies. Although most experts work hard to remain objective and adhere to the truth as they advocate for their opinions, it is common for retaining attorneys to attempt to "woodshed" experts (i.e., to try to manipulate them into using words that support the lawyer's case). It is also common for lawyers to encourage experts to use their influence to reach some nonprofessional goal, such as to punish a criminal, oppose the death penalty, rescue a child from a bad parent, or compensate a deserving plaintiff. Remember that the forensic role should be solely professional. Once accepting work on a case, one should indulge his or her social or political views elsewhere, in some more appropriate forum.

Forensic consultants acting in forensic roles often discover reportable, illegal, or unethical behavior by others during the course of their work. One may or may not be generally obligated to report *clinicians* who are reasonably believed to be impaired or to have behaved improperly (e.g., exploited a patient). Discuss legal and ethical obligations with the retaining lawyer or entity, but remember that the retaining lawyer is not "your" attorney; his or her allegiance is to his client, not to the expert. Remember, too, that *any obligation one may have to the attorney's client are quite different from the attorney's obligation. Experts are probably not entitled to the same protections that the lawyer may enjoy with regard to not reporting.* It is a good idea to document one's concerns in the notes, along with the reasons for whatever action is taken or not taken. When in doubt, contact an experienced attorney of your own, or query the agency to which such reports are usually made.

An expert acting in a forensic role may or may not be generally obligated to report suspected patient abuse, neglect, or exploitation discovered in the course of reviewing individual or organizational behavior. (Legally reportable conditions are often not limited to known or proved ones, but may include reasonable or good faith suspicion as well.) In many instances, discussion with the retaining attorney or entity, along with an expectation that reportable behavior will be communicated if required, will resolve the issue.

One of the authors was frequently involved in cases alleging sexual behavior between clinicians and patients. Knowing that his state law required reporting of even suspected sexual activity, he contacted the State medical licensing board to ask about reporting duties in forensic matters. A written opinion was provided that he did not have to report clinicians directly when working in an expert witness role, but should recommend that attorneys be certain that plaintiffs understand the importance of reporting and provide appropriate contact information. (*This opinion may or may not apply to readers of this chapter.*)

RELATIONSHIP WITH THE RETAINING ENTITY (E.G., ATTORNEY)

In most forensic practice matters, one's only professional relationship should be with the retaining entity. When potential litigants contact professionals directly to inquire about forensic consultation, the rule of thumb is not to discuss their problems, express opinions, or make agreements. One should politely say that he or she does not work directly for litigants, and that talking with the potential litigant directly may interfere with any possible eventual involvement. One should not recommend a specific lawyer or comment about the case; the professional role at this point should be unequivocal lack of involvement.

PRO SE LITIGANTS

When litigants represent themselves (act *"pro se"*), the line between retaining entity and litigant relationship becomes quite blurred. We recommend that experts, particularly inexperienced ones, avoid acting on behalf of *pro se* litigants, or at the least work in part through a judge or attorney who has been appointed to oversee the process (oversight lawyers are often appointed, particularly in criminal cases). In our experience, many problematic relationships, including occasional harassment and lawsuits, can arise from working with *pro se* litigants, many of whom do not understand the law and/or the expectations of working with a forensic expert.

One of the authors was called by a man whose wife had left him and moved in with their current family therapist. He was looking for an expert to testify that this was unethical. The man was told that the potential expert would be happy to speak with his attorney about the case, but could not discuss working with him directly. The man said that he was acting *pro se*. The potential expert politely declined and terminated the conversation.

Initial Contact The typical first contact with attorneys is through a telephone inquiry (or by email), but we recommend that the first exchange of significant information be by telephone or in person. The conversation usually begins with a brief description of the case and the issues involved, as well as questions about the forensic clinician's eligibility and willingness to work on the case. The lawyer has probably already learned something about the potential expert, but still seeks information about that person's relevant knowledge, forensic experience, professional credibility, and ability to work well in the case. The lawyer also wants a professional who is reliable and easy to work with. Attorneys do not want to be surprised by experts who are contentious (not the same as firmly defending one's opinions and ethics), tardy, or not conscientious about deadlines and responsibilities.

Attorneys often ask about potential experts' general views of the facts presented in an initial call, and are interested in how one thinks about, or would address, the issues at hand; however, they rarely (and should not) ask for an opinion during an initial contact. A discussion of how the expert might proceed and how he or she generally approaches such cases is reasonable. It is inappropriate, and arguably unethical, for an expert to offer a specific opinion based solely on a lawyer's recitation of his/her side of the case.

This is a time for the forensic professional to be prudently cautious about the nature of the task, particularly if he or she has no experience with the lawyer. Occasionally, attorneys imply that they want an early commitment to their side of the case, before data are gathered, or they imply that allegiance to the attorney is more important than truth and objectivity. One should decline such relationships.

Sometimes initial contact comes from someone other than the attorney, such as a legal assistant, paralegal, or an investigator acting on a lawyer's behalf. It is reasonable to carry on the above discussion with such a person. If the lawyer has delegated the task of calling prospective experts to the litigant, however, one should politely decline to discuss the matter and recommend that his/her lawyer call instead. Speaking at length with a litigant or potential litigant can interfere significantly with one's usefulness and objectivity in a case.

Don't believe everything the lawyer says about the case. If you are taking notes, indicate that those notes are the attorney's version of the facts. ("Facts," in legal parlance, are not necessarily "true." They are often merely one litigant's or lawyer's interpretation of the information, often colored to support his/her side of the case.)

Notes taken during the initial conversation (and subsequent ones) are very likely to be "discoverable" (i.e., can be demanded by the other side) if you are retained. Never be flippant or cavalier, and do not make premature comments. There may some ambiguity about whether attorney-communicated information, say about case strategy, is discoverable or protected by attorney work-product rules. (Note that experts themselves generally have no "work product" protections; that's a lawyer privilege. Note also that at this writing, *federal* case discovery rules are expected to change to limit discovery of some expert materials, attorney conversations, and report drafts.)

One often finds that the lawyer's inquiry raises issues outside potential experts' expertise. When that is the case, or when one doesn't wish to participate for some other reason, consider helping the attorney find another expert or other useful information. Being cordial helps build a practice and reputation.

The Working Relationship   The most common working relationship is that of contracting to provide a service to a retaining entity. The forensic professional should not consider himself or herself a part of the lawyer's "team" in the sense of assuming one side's advocacy position. A lot of forensic work is consultative, but the work often goes beyond being a consultant (e.g., when one is asked to express opinions on behalf of a litigant). The lawyer or other retaining entity pays for time spent rendering services, such as record review, consultation, assessment, or expressing opinions— the forensic expert should view those services with case needs in mind, but the services themselves should be nonpartisan unless it is clear that a more strategic role is appropriate and does not conflict with other participation in the same matter.

For example, it is sometimes appropriate and ethical for a psychologist or psychiatrist to help a lawyer with litigation strategy, such as by analyzing parts of the opposing side's arguments, but such activities may, and often do, create a conflict with the objectivity required for offering opinions to a court. Such experts often should not testify about their opinions and/or should expect vigorous challenges to their objectivity.

One should not begin work on a forensic matter until he or she has the following in hand:

- An accurate case description
- A clear understanding of the expert's expected role
- A clear and binding fee agreement
- All available, relevant records (not just summaries or chronologies prepared by attorneys)
- The freedom to review the records completely
- A general schedule of the case, including deadlines
- The retaining entity's understanding of one's work style and ethics, how one reviews materials, and future communication with the attorney
- An understanding that the attorney will represent one's opinions, if any, accurately, and only after they have actually been rendered. (Unfortunately, a few lawyers occasionally express experts' opinions in documents before they have actually been rendered, sometimes even before the expert has been retained. Do not tolerate this improper behavior!) (Gutheil, Simon & Hilliard, 2001)

Who gathers the records and other information? The lawyer or other retaining entity. This is not the expert's task. Attorneys are skilled at getting releases and obtaining school, hospital, prison, youth, military, and occupational records. Ask the lawyer for assurance that all the available and relevant records have been sent for review. Some records may not be available when one accepts the referral, but they should be received in time to consider them when forming opinions for reports or testimony. If important records are not received, try to ascertain whether they were purposely withheld by the retaining entity. When records are simply not available, that fact should be noted along with a disclaimer about the potential effect on the validity and reliability of your opinions.

BEGINNING WORK

RECORD REVIEW

There is no mystery here; just do a thorough review. We suggest you take notes, while remaining aware that your notes are discoverable.

Sometimes one can form limited opinions without reviewing all records. Those opinions should contain disclaimers and *caveats* as professionally and ethically appropriate. One may offer preliminary impressions to the retaining entity after limited review, but be cautious about the phrasing of those impressions to others; they should not be defined as "opinions."

After the records have been reviewed, the next step often is to discuss with the lawyer your preliminary thoughts, any need for further records, and what comes next in the process, such as an in-person examination or report. When retained by one side in litigation, one usually should not write a report without talking with the lawyer. Some other matters (e.g., straightforward assessments for judges, agencies, or insurance companies) often involve report-writing without additional contact.

One should sometimes give the attorney feedback after a limited, preliminary review, particularly if the findings appear to be heading in an unexpected direction. Lawyers hate surprises.

Many cases, especially civil ones, are settled or resolved at this point, since the lawyers now have more information with which to assess their positions. Settlement or other resolution is usually a good thing, saving resources for all concerned.

NOTE TAKING AND COMMUNICATIONS

Everything the expert creates is likely to be "discoverable" by the other side. This is particularly true in civil cases. Except in extraordinary circumstances, nothing you create is "work product"; that phrase refers to lawyers' work, not experts', even if one happens to be a lawyer himself.

Do not be snide or cavalier in notes, letters, or emails. Don't send drafts or carry on a case-related conversation by email unless the attorney requests it. That doesn't mean one should refrain from sending emails or taking notes; just be aware that others are likely to see them sooner or later.

Talk with the attorney after your review, and be cautious about writing reports without being instructed to do so. Like written notes, one's oral conversations are likely to be discoverable to the extent one remembers them. If asked at deposition, for example, what was discussed, one must make an effort to recall to the extent feasible.

Do not destroy notes, records, emails, phone messages, or report drafts unless you are certain that doing so is proper. In particular, once a subpoena for records is received, which is routine when the other side is about to depose an expert, safeguard all records that exist at that point.

Be objective when discussing the case with the lawyer. Cover the pros and cons of the findings in terms the attorney can understand. He/she wants to know what the expert is thinking, wants clear and concise information, and wants to see that the expert can articulately and without ambivalence convey his/her findings to the court. If one's findings seem ambiguous or his/her views are ambivalent, now is the time to talk about them and try to find clarity. Use this early discussion, going back and forth over the details, to become as concise as the findings allow before writing a report or testifying.

What if one's findings don't seem to support the retaining entity's case? Most of the time, that's not really bad news. Lawyers benefit from experts' negative findings almost as much as they do from findings that support their cases. They need to know both strengths and weaknesses in order to evaluate case merits accurately, abandon frivolous pursuits, promote reasonable settlements, and help their clients accept the truth about their situations. In addition, if one finds that there are few merits in the proposed psychiatric or psychological issues, clarifying that fact may protect the attorney from later criticism for not pursuing the case. Be able to see the big picture and prioritize the findings accordingly, but don't shade opinions toward what the lawyer seems to want.

EVALUATIONS AND INDEPENDENT MEDICAL EXAMINATIONS

More specific information about assessments is provided elsewhere in this book. We'll present a few basic guidelines:

- *Standardize the evaluation procedures.* If a lawyer presses for an immediate examination, slow down and go through the usual routine. Some criminal responsibility evaluations are exceptions; they should take place as soon as feasible after the alleged criminal act, *but after defense counsel is appointed and notified.* In such situations, it may be acceptable to talk with the retaining attorney or court by telephone, come to a verbal agreement, quickly gather available information, and proceed directly to the attorney's office or jail.
- *Communicate through the retaining attorney or entity.* Do not communicate directly with opposing counsel or the evaluee except to verify times or give directions.
- *Attend to the safety of all concerned.* Privacy must take a back seat to safety and security.
- *Consider recording most or all evaluations.* Video recording (but not surreptitious recording) is common for many kinds of assessments, and provides accurate documentation, increased credibility, decreased liability, and help when writing reports. At the same time, retaining parties almost always should be consulted before recording is initiated. They may have case-related reasons to oppose recording. Jails and prisons may prohibit recording equipment. Some experts question whether or not even unobtrusive recording interferes with evaluation outcome, but this criticism does not have good empirical support.
- One of the authors (WHR) does not allow an attorney for either side to be present during evaluations except under very unusual circumstances. He understands that the evaluee sometimes has a right to have his or her lawyer present, and opposing attorneys, particularly, may wish to be in the room; however, he is concerned about interference with the evaluative process. The other (SLB) shares those concerns but permits attorneys to be present provided the lawyer is out of the evaluee's sight and remains silent. In any case, if there is a court order or other legal demand allowing attorney presence, one may either accept it and include an appropriate description or caveat in reports and testimony, or decline the evaluation.
- *Do not perform direct services to evaluees except in emergencies.* If you treat, or anticipate treating, an evaluee or other interested

party, avoid becoming an expert witness in the same case. In that instance, you may become a "fact witness," and testify solely about what you saw or heard rather than about conclusions and opinions. Crises such as acutely suicidal or homicidal evaluees should be immediately reported to the attorney and, depending on circumstances, may require other protective or clinical action.

- *As already noted, do not **forensically** interview an arrestee before defense counsel is appointed.* When criminal responsibility is an issue, it is desirable to interview the defendant as soon as possible after the alleged crime. Nevertheless, if one is asked by an officer or prosecutor to see a person soon after he or she is arrested, ask if defense counsel has been appointed, document the answer, and decline if the arrestee has not yet had benefit of defense counsel. It is ethical to evaluate and treat an unrepresented arrestee or defendant for clinical purposes, but do not perform a forensic evaluation (and understand that treatment ethically precludes a later expert role in most cases). If the arrestee, now a patient rather than an evaluee, blurts something out about the alleged events, one may record it, as well as his or her impression of the person's state of mind (e.g., delirious, intoxicated, psychotic, or not) at the time. Do not pursue the topic with the person unless it is clinically necessary.

REPORTS AND AFFIDAVITS

Much of a forensic professional's usefulness and influence is through reports or affidavits. Most experts are far more likely to be asked to express findings and opinions in report form than in testimony. Reports and affidavits are usually sent to the retaining lawyer or other entity for forwarding to the appropriate decision maker (e.g., court, agency) or opposing lawyer. In some practices, they may be requested directly from a decision-making insurance company, agency, or court.

Reports and affidavits are lasting representations of one's opinions, abilities, expertise, and effectiveness. They formally convey opinions and/or other information to others; they organize and clarify one's findings; they are a tool for resolving cases; they establish how one's expertise might be used later in the litigation process;

and they help focus the expert's study before testimony. They are often the only product of the evaluating expert that lawyers and decision makers ever see. These are compelling reasons to *take your time and do them right.*

FORMAT AND STYLE

Forensic reports are different from clinical ones in format, content, and intent. *Forensic Mental Health Evaluations* by Heilbrun, Marczyk, and DeMatteo (2002) presents sample reports by experts in various areas of forensic practice; Reid's forensic practice development *Syllabus* (2010) contains a number of examples as well. Others are available from many sources, including forensic colleagues whose work one respects. When in doubt about the format of a particular report, and the use to which it will be put, ask the person who requested it.

Be aware of the legal requirements and format issues for particular reports. Cases have been dismissed because of improperly written reports. In some jurisdictions, for example, plaintiffs' reports in malpractice cases must carefully include duty, breach of that duty, damage, and causation for each item of negligence alleged. In many federal reports, experts must touch upon every topic about which they may later testify. Many jurisdictions and types of cases require certain inclusions, such as lists of cases in which one has testified or specific expert qualifications. When in doubt, ask.

Include relevant disclaimers and *caveats.* Experts who have not personally evaluated the people about whom they are opining, or who do not have all relevant records for review, should say so and briefly comment about whether or not those omissions are important to the opinion. If a report is preliminary, which is very common, the expert should label it as such. If examination conditions were inadequate, one should describe the problem and its possible effect on findings.

Short reports are usually better than long ones, but may actually take longer to write. We disagree with writers who recommend exhaustive treatises when they have not been specifically requested. Long reports may seem scholarly, but they often obfuscate important points and may provide extraneous information to which the other side is not entitled. Our general rule of thumb is not to include content unrelated to the essential evaluation issues unless asked to do so by the retaining entity.

Lawyers often offer to send the expert a report or affidavit template, and sometimes to draft the opinions themselves. Responsible experts do not let lawyers (or anyone else) write their reports or attribute opinions to them that they have not genuinely rendered. Attorneys may supply the format or provide guidance about the relevance of certain content, but all opinions and the words that support them should come directly from the expert.

Use relevant legal terms correctly but sparingly. Forensic experts are expected to have a basic understanding of the point of the case and of a few relevant legal terms, but they should not try to sound like lawyers. Misunderstanding and misusing terms such as *reasonable medical/professional certainty*, *rely*, *foreseeable*, *competent*, and others can severely damage a case. For example, *reasonable medical (or professional) certainty* almost always means, simply, "more likely than not" (there are exceptions in a handful of jurisdictions). Clinicians with little forensic experience often assume that the phrase refers to something far more certain.

PROOFREAD THE REPORT CAREFULLY

Double-check everything. Confirm dates, places, testing scores, citations, spelling, grammar, and so forth. Then check everything again. When we read forensic reports, we are often startled by obvious errors or contradictions that affect the writer's accuracy and clarity, and the impression he/she makes on eventual readers.

Use excellent grammar and spelling. One should write with the care employed for a term paper that absolutely must receive an "A." Grammar and spelling are important to meaning. In addition, the clients who are most important to you will notice mistakes such as incorrect plural pronouns (e.g., "they" for "he or she"), misplaced apostrophes (e.g., in plurals or incorrect possessives), and the like. Consider investing in a grammar guide such as Strunk & Whites' venerable *The Elements of Style*.

Don't let reports leave your office if they don't look very professional. Send originals on quality letterhead. Do not expend this much time and effort on something that looks and feels cheap in your client's hand.

"EMERGENCY" REPORTS

Lawyers and agencies often call at the last minute and ask for "just a quick report," with some very short deadline. Resist that temptation. First, "emergency" requests of any kind should raise a red flag. Doing things outside one's usual professional routine automatically increases the likelihood of problems in the report. The premise for the report may be faulty; there may not be adequate time to learn about the case; or the evaluation may be incomplete.

Second, doing things outside one's usual professional routine substantially increases the likelihood of future problems with the attorney or retaining entity, especially if expert and attorney have not exchanged written agreements and the expert has not obtained a retainer. Rush work has a very high rate of nonpayment.

Third, experts should resist allowing requesting lawyers to unreasonably shift deadline problems onto their own shoulders. The lawyer has almost always had months to accommodate the deadline. In some such cases, her or she has simply received a report he didn't like and is seeking a quick fix. In others, the lawyer has "dropped the ball" and hopes you will save the day. Be polite, but resist being manipulated into poor or incomplete work.

DISCOVERY

Nothing the expert does should be hidden from the discovery process (the procedure through which each side is entitled to see what may be used against it at trial). Do not destroy copies of anything sent to the attorney or retaining entity (including drafts, letters, or emails), nor destroy anything once records have been subpoenaed. Early versions of reports that are typed over as part of routine word processing are not, so far as we know, considered drafts that must be saved for discovery. Reports that are sent to the attorney or other requesting entity, however, whether electronically or in print, must be kept and may be discoverable.

TESTIMONY

One may be asked to testify in depositions, hearings, or trials. (Affidavits and some other communications are also a form of testimony, but we're speaking of live appearances.) Testimony itself is addressed elsewhere in this book, but here are a few practice principles.

SCHEDULE DEPOSITIONS AND TRIALS WITH CARE

Depositions can usually meet the expert's schedule. Trials are much less flexible; the lawyers must balance lots of people and factors. They will try to meet the needs of the expert, but one should be reasonable. Most lawyers prefer that expert depositions not take place in the expert's own office, though some practitioners feel more at ease there.

Don't assume that court dates are set in stone. Once one has agreed to a date, one must be available for it, but it may be possible to schedule some flexible activity at the same time. In civil cases particularly, most trial dates will be changed or the case resolved before trial. Indeed, most civil matters and many criminal ones never go to trial at all.

THE EXPERT'S CREDIBILITY *WILL* BE QUESTIONED

Past trial and deposition testimony, licensing, hospital privilege status, references on the Web, and publications are all easily available to lawyers and may be highlighted by the other side. One should let retaining lawyers know the strengths and weaknesses of his or her background before testifying (and preferably before being retained). Be scrupulously honest when testifying, explain answers well but briefly, and avoid cavalier comments.

Testimony is neither a collegial process nor a scientific one. It is usually respectful, but cross-examination is necessarily adversarial. Be able to tolerate public criticism, even animosity. Experts should not be adversaries themselves, but must endure questioning from lawyers who vigorously oppose the side for which they are testifying. Be polite. Avoid defensiveness. Stick to important points so long as they are defensible. And don't take it personally.

HAVE A PRETESTIMONY CONFERENCE WITH THE RETAINING ATTORNEY

Do not simply show up to testify. If the attorney doesn't think conference is needed, press for one anyway in order to be prepared, to go over questions that may be asked, and to encourage the retaining lawyer to ask about the findings you believe are most important.

TESTIMONY IS ALMOST ALWAYS PUBLIC INFORMATION

Questions about one's professional practice are to be expected, but one should not give out a social security number, home address, or family details. If a judge demands an answer to personal questions that should remain private (such as financial information not reasonably related to a case), politely ask for an exception (and be prepared to give a reason).

DEPOSITIONS

These are usually "discovery" depositions, opportunities for the other side to learn what will be said at trial. One may also testify in a "trial deposition" in lieu of coming to court, in which case the testimony may be heard in its entirety by the trier. Depositions are routine in civil cases but uncommon in criminal ones. The setting may seem informal, but remember that anything a deponent says under oath may be read back in court, has the same weight as trial testimony, and is likely to become part of a public record. A deposition is often a useful portent to the questions that will be asked at trial.

A *subpoena duces tecum* is a demand to produce records and files, or to bring them to a deposition. It comes from an attorney, not a judge. One may question, or even decline, onerous or overly personal demands, but should do so through the retaining lawyer. Do not try to keep case-related items from the other side, or remove them from the file, unless absolutely sure it is legal and ethical.

Schedule and bill for depositions through the retaining attorney or entity, even though the opposing attorney may be responsible for the deposition costs. In some cases, the opposing attorney may bring a check to the deposition, but this should be arranged by the retaining attorney, not the expert. Discuss payment with the retaining attorney beforehand (see next section); do not be placed in a position of having to bill the opposing lawyer.

Many depositions are videotaped; selected parts may be shown to the judge and/or jury at trial. If the deposition is being videotaped, that fact is usually known beforehand and the expert should dress and behave as if actually in court. Direct most answers to the camera, since the answer is intended for the judge or jury, not the questioner. If the deponent does not speak to the camera, the jury may feel more like eavesdroppers than the targets of one's answers.

FEES, BILLING, AND COLLECTIONS

FEES AND BILLING

Several financial concepts stand out as important to forensic practice success, including the following:

- *Implications of a low-volume practice.* Forensic practice is a low-volume, relatively high-dollar "business." In clinical practice, individual clients' fees vary from a few tens of dollars to a few thousand over a long time. This may sound like a lot to many people, but success usually depends on maintaining a substantial number and flow of patients. In forensic work, however, every case is likely to result in hundreds, usually thousands, of dollars in fees for service. That means that a gain of one or two cases is an important financial gain, and a loss of (or loss of opportunity for) one or two cases is an important loss. Maintaining good service and availability is thus very important to practice success, and to one's ability to decline inappropriate cases.
- *Bill scrupulously.* Forensic psychiatry and psychology are, at their foundation, clinically based pursuits, but maintaining a successful practice is a businesslike activity. Keeping track of time, much as lawyers do, is important to that success. Attorneys and other retaining entities understand the concept of charging for time, and are not put off by it.
- *Never charge a contingency fee.* Forensic consultants and experts may charge either by the hour (day) or by the task, but never in any way that depends on the outcome of the forensic matter. Simple contingency fees are easy to recognize and avoid (e.g., if "your side" wins one gets paid; if not, one doesn't get paid). A "letter of protection," seen particularly in some workers'

compensation matters, is almost as bad (and unacceptable, in our view). A letter of protection involves an attorney's sending his/her client to a clinician for evaluation and/or treatment with the promise that the clinician will be paid immediately from the proceeds of any successful litigation, but if the litigation fails, the lawyer backs away and the clinician must bill the injured party. (The clinician is often asked to testify on behalf of the injured party.) Another, more subtle but often unacceptable fee arrangement is the lawyer's asking the expert to delay his/her fee until after the case has been resolved. In all of these cases, the expert is placed in a position of having a financial incentive in the litigation.

- *Court orders for fees.* It is not uncommon for government agencies or large organizations (such as insurance companies) to contract for fees and pay them after some period of weeks or months. When considering whether to accept such a contract, one should be certain that the terms of the agreement include all of the characteristics necessary to actually be paid the full amount for one's time and expenses. Smaller governmental entities such as county courts or boards of commissioners, for example, may decrease payments after the work has been done, blaming budget problems or excessive charges. In our experience, carefully specifying one's hourly rate, billing regularly as charges are incurred, and being very clear about the conditions of the contract (such as whether travel time and waiting time are covered) are crucial to avoiding billing problems.

- *Clarity, in writing.* Be very clear about rates and fees, what is charged (e.g., travel time, waiting time, cancellations, allowances for meals and lodging), responsibility for payment, and schedule and method of payment. Except in insurance or governmental matters, the financial agreement should not be directly with a litigant, even though that person/entity may be the source of the lawyer's own compensation.

- *Require a retainer against billings or refundable deposit.* This should be done at the beginning of a case and when substantial time is anticipated for reports or testimony. Some entities (such as many government agencies) cannot pay retainers or deposits, but they should be a part of one's practice routine.

- *Realize your value.* One should not be unreasonable about his/ her experience, expertise, or fees, but should understand his/ her competence and value to the retaining entity. Don't believe lawyers who say that they can't afford to pay for *this* case, but have big plans for future ones. That's a red flag for both business and ethics.

Most fee problems (and other problems as well) are visible early in one's relationship with the lawyer or other retaining entity. Be very cautious if the attorney does not agree to a retainer, is late with payments, wants a quick review or assessment, or does not send all the materials needed to do a proper review or evaluation.

Some forensics professionals charge a flat rate for frequently repeated services such as competency or disability evaluations. One should be careful that the fixed rate doesn't create an ethics or credibility problem, such as a temptation to short-change services in order to make them more profitable. This caution applies particularly to professionals in private practice.

Do not work without a retainer except as noted. Everyone who has been in practice for very long has been "stiffed." Allowing a client's debt to mount unreasonably is a common source of delinquent accounts.

Do not testify with a large bill outstanding. There are substantial ethical, practical, and credibility problems associated with testifying while the lawyer withholds a major part of the payment. Remove the money issue by requiring that the outstanding bill be paid and/or a reasonable deposit received before deposition or trial. Then be scrupulously honest and prompt in returning any unused portion of the deposit.

We suggest six additional guidelines for billing in forensic practice:

1. Be fair.
2. Itemize statements.
3. Keep raw time and billing sheets available for inspection.
4. Do not "nickel and dime" clients.
5. Never cheat or pad billings.
6. Do not charge interest on overdue bills (charging interest is subject to legal procedures and rarely worth it).

COLLECTIONS

Expectations Start the collection process on the right foot: Expect an adequate retainer and prompt payment. Strongly consider not testifying, and perhaps refraining from releasing reports or opinions, when the outstanding bill is large. Consider requiring a reasonable deposit for estimated time spent in expensive activities (e.g., preparing complex reports or testimony, travel, complex examinations). Have a clear understanding with attorneys that payment must be current or reliably guaranteed before spending valuable time and perhaps canceling other activities.

Most lawyers and many agencies pay their bills promptly. Government agencies usually honor their contracts, but may take months to send payment. A few lawyers and some government entities (usually small local ones) make it hard to collect what one is owed. One potential source of collection problems is the plaintiff's attorney who has invested considerable resources into a civil case, perhaps in a faraway state, and loses. Once the case is resolved and the expert is no longer relevant, the lawyer has little motivation to pay the bill other than his or her own sense of fairness. Get an adequate deposit before committing to time or travel.

When bills are overdue, don't waste time with the firm's or agency's accounts payable clerks. They are not decision makers. Talk to the person who can write the check.

Serious Collection Problems When an expert knows he or she has the job and deserves to be paid, he should not allow himself to be bullied by a lawyer who threatens to sue or besmirch the expert's reputation, or implies that the work was poor. Whether or not one is eventually paid is unlikely to affect what such people say anyway, and other lawyers often know that the cheating attorney is not credible. Nevertheless, if a lawyer or other influential person is saying or writing bad and untrue things, consider pursuing the matter legally. It's slander or libel, and damage to one's reputation is damage to one's livelihood.

Know how to find a lawyer who sues other lawyers, for the rare times when things get nasty. Lawsuits for nonpayment are generally "contract" issues, fairly simple and usually successful, but not worth the expert's trouble for small amounts. The process begins with a letter from one's lawyer and is usually resolved once the debtor knows that the expert will not tolerate the unpaid bill. Do not threaten to sue if there is no real intention to do so. State bar associations have complaint processes, but they are rarely helpful in billing disputes.

MARKETING

Marketing is a broad process, not simply advertising. One's reputation, quality of work, and quality of service are the most effective marketing tools. Most successful forensic clinicians don't do much or any direct marketing. Lawyers usually find experts by talking with other lawyers. They sometimes search the Web, ask clinicians for suggestions, or look for authors of professional articles that are relevant to their cases. If one decides to market directly, he or she should remember that the target is potential forensic referral sources, not patients or colleagues. Those sources are almost always certain kinds of attorneys, such as defense, prosecution, and plaintiffs' lawyers who specialize in personal injury, malpractice, criminal matters, or family law (Gutheil, 2009b; Berger, 1997).

Experts who perform services for other professionals, such as psychological testing or nursing consultations, may find it useful to let relevant professionals in those fields know of their availability. Experts who practice in a particular geographic area may wish to notify similar forensic professionals in other locations, so that they can refer inquiries that they cannot accept. Professionals with practices similar to one's own, in the same location, are a much less likely source of referrals. Enjoy direct peers, and learn from them, but don't expect many referrals.

Be easy to work with. Once a lawyer or other client engages an expert, the quality of service is judged in part by the quality of the relationship. This doesn't mean be exceptionally friendly or bending to unethical expectations; it means understanding the client's needs, being available and attentive, knowing one's field(s) of expertise, and caring about the work.

Several often-suggested marketing activities are unlikely to be useful. Tasteful announcements to attorneys and agencies may help, but should not include a brochure, curriculum vitae, or case list. Teaching in continuing education programs, hospital risk management, judges' groups, or law schools is a good way to contribute and become locally known. Media interviews on newsworthy topics may be useful for some kinds of referrals, but avoid being a regular media feature. Service organization membership and other networking is common among those with local practices, but one should do it because he wants to, not for marketing. Some professionals send regular, brief email newsletters discussing current or interesting topics.

We do not recommend spending money, time, or energy on brochures, legal directories, Yellow Pages listings or other advertisements, flashy Internet pages, social networking sites, expert directories (online or print), paid referral membership services, or the many online solicitations that will come along. Don't believe people who send emails saying they can increase referrals through some "expert listing" or "expert finder" website. Professionals who do pay to belong to a referral service should be certain they are not paying for referrals themselves or doing anything else that may be construed as fee-splitting or kickbacks.

INTERNET MARKETING

Tasteful Internet pages can help in marketing. They should be individual, perhaps educational, not just a page on some large commercial or organization website. It takes time and experience to develop a successful Web presence. Don't expect fast results, and don't spend energy or money with website developers or marketers who have no idea what a forensic expert does or what the market is.

One should not expect miracles from marketing through the Internet. Our advice is to limit Internet marketing to one's own website. The quality of website content makes a big difference. Don't let a teenager design it. Use a reliable hosting service, not a local Internet service provider that may go out of business. Many professionals choose to get their own domain name rather than using a crowded sub-URL that no one can remember.

The website should be professional, not glitzy. Avoid hints of advertising or testimonial. Learn about search engine placement, but don't pay anyone for it; the emails one gets about website traffic are almost always scams, and from people who have no idea how to maximize a forensics website. Try to follow practice website traffic with simple monitoring software. Take a look at successful forensic practice websites such as www.reidpsychiatry.com (primarily educational, but also a significant source of referrals).

Access and Availability

Successful experts make it easy for lawyers or other retaining entities to find them. New attorney calls should be a high priority. Return missed calls immediately. If potential clients reach another expert before one calls back, or if reaching the potential expert is inconvenient, one will never know what was missed.

Consider a toll-free number for communication stability and caller encouragement. Long distance costs are far less expensive than they were a few years ago, but a toll-free number is a convenience that may cause potential clients in other geographic areas to put one's name at the top of their lists. And toll-free numbers don't change when one moves, even across the country.

Have the office phone answered by an intelligent, professional person, not an impersonal answering service or voicemail. Test office telephone and email procedures frequently to be sure they are responsive to callers. When potential clients make email inquiries, suggest a call to discuss the matter. Telephone calls also allow one to assess the situation and caller, and establish important preliminary "ground rules." One may then choose to exchange information electronically, but we don't recommend discussing case information by email.

OFFICE PROCEDURES

Office staff often have more contact with clients and their employees than do experts themselves. They are usually the first people that potential clients hear. They are the public face of the practice and the interface between the expert and his or her clients. Excellent staff give excellent results. Do background checks on new staff. Train them in basic security procedures. If someone else cleans the office, lock everything daily (cleaning people can be very curious). Be aware of, and deal with, the substantial security risks associated with email. Take steps to keep your files and practice secure.

The phone is your main interface with clients and potential clients. Written material is a close second. Avoid having clients experience voicemail, especially if it is not checked several times a day. Email is useful, but it doesn't replace telephone contact in most forensic matters.

Log everything that enters or leaves the office, including phone calls, letters, records received, deliveries, and visitors. Make file notes of telephone conversations, scheduling agreements, and billing changes. Experts usually must list what they have reviewed in their reports and depositions; it is much easier to refer to a log than to shuffle through stacks of paper.

Have procedures for keeping track of current and past cases, case types, past testimony, and referral sources, as well as a system for tracking current cases and deadlines. These allow one to be aware of priorities, analyze practices, monitor referral sources, and adhere to jurisdiction rules about documenting testimony.

Client and evaluee records must be secure, but also accessible. One will often have to locate records after months, even years of hiatus. Logging and tracking files for easy access is an important staff responsibility. Consider creating a very accessible main file that contains notes, reports, and other frequently addressed information. In addition, there should be a financial file with time sheets and billing records. Bulk records occupy a great deal of space in forensic practices; one needs lots of on-site storage space. Once cases are resolved (but not before), one may use (secure) off-site archive storage. Get the retaining entity's permission before destroying old files. We suggest keeping primary and financial files indefinitely.

Opposing lawyers occasionally ask for copies of past deposition and trial testimony. If one keeps depositions or other transcripts, they may have to be produced unless one can reasonably establish that doing so would create an onerous task (e.g., searching through piles of off-site storage, for which one may charge a reasonable fee). Use a good shredder for disposing of obsolete records; don't just send them to a landfill. If you use a recycler or shredding service, be sure the records are rendered unreadable.

Learn to budget. Compensation in private forensic practice usually comes in fairly large amounts, but infrequently. Slack periods and long payment delays are routine. One must be responsible for such things as income tax deposits, employee salaries and benefits, prompt client refunds, and practice insurance in addition to family expenses. It is very helpful to keep a separate account for retainers and deposits, as a reminder that the money cannot be spent until it has been earned, and to make it easy to send prompt refunds. More than one forensics client has told the authors that the promptness of their refunds—and the fact that an expert actually refunded money to them in the first place—was a factor in future referrals.

CONCLUSIONS

- *Practice well.* Appreciate the boundaries of your knowledge and competence. Be thorough and careful. Be certain that your work is seated in current and accepted procedures. Be serious about ethics. Have a consultant or colleague to whom you can turn when you feel puzzled or stymied.
- *Quality begets quality; quality begets success.* You will have no trouble competing with psychologists or psychiatrists who are poorly trained, lazy, sloppy, unethical, or just don't get the point of the forensic exercise.

REFERENCES

American Psychology-Law Society. (2008). Specialty Guidelines For Forensic Psychology, 4th draft. Retrieved June 15, 2010, from http://www.apls.org/aboutpsychlaw/92908sgfp.pdf

Berger, S. H. (1997). *Establishing a forensic psychiatric practice: A practical guide.* New York, NY: W. W. Norton & Co.

Commons, M. L., Miller, P. M., & Gutheil, T. G. (2004). Expert witness perceptions of bias in experts. *Journal of the American Academy of Psychiatry and the Law, 32,* 70–75.

Greenberg, S. A., Shuman, D. W. (1997). Irreconcilable conflict between therapeutic and forensic roles. *Professional Psychology: Research and Practice, 28,* 50–57.

Gutheil, T. G. (2009a). Ethics and forensic psychiatry. In S. Bloch & S. Green (Eds.), *Psychiatric ethics* (4th ed.) (pp. 435–452). New York, NY: Oxford University Press.

Gutheil, T. G. (2009b). *The psychiatrist as expert witness* (2nd ed). Washington, DC: American Psychiatric Press.

Gutheil, T. G., & Simon, R. I. (2004). Avoiding bias in expert testimony. *Psychiatric Annals, 34,* 258–270.

Gutheil, T. G., Simon, R. I., & Hilliard, J. T. (2001). The phantom expert: Uncontested use of the expert's name and/or testimony as a legal strategy. *Journal of the American Academy of Psychiatry and Law, 29,* 313–318.

Heilbrun, K., Marczyk, G., & DeMatteo, D. (2002). *Forensic mental health evaluations: A casebook.* New York, NY: Oxford University Press.

Murrie, D. C., Boccaccini, M. T., Johnson, J. T., & Janke, C. (2008). Does interrater (dis)agreement on Psychopathy Checklist scores in sexually violent predator trials suggest partisan allegiance in forensic evaluations? *Law and Human Behavior, 32,* 352–362.

Murrie D. C., Boccaccini, M. T., Turner, D. B., Meeks, M., Woods, C., & Tussey, C. (2009). Rate (dis)agreement on risk assessment measures in sexually violent predator proceedings: Evidence of adversarial allegiance in forensic evaluations? *Psychology, Public Policy, and Law, 15,* 19–53.

Reid, W. H. (2008). The treatment-forensic interface. *Journal of Psychiatric Practice, 14,* 122–125.

Reid, W. H. (2010). Syllabus: Developing a forensic practice: Principles, practice, ethics. Available from reidw@reidpsychiatry.com or www.psychandlaw.org

Strasburger, L. H., Gutheil, T. G., & Brodsky, A. (1997). On wearing two hats: Role conflict in serving as both psychotherapist and expert witness. *American Journal of Psychiatry, 154,* 448–456.

CHAPTER 28

Interstate Practice

ROBERT L. SADOFF and FRANK M. DATTILIO

INTRODUCTION

Most forensic psychiatrists and psychologists practice almost exclusively in the states in which they reside and are duly licensed. There is no national license for psychologists or physicians, and each state or province maintains its own licensing laws. Some mental health professionals may be licensed in multiple states or provinces because they work in contiguous jurisdictions (e.g., Pennsylvania, New Jersey, Delaware, and New York) and seek access to a correspondingly broad variety of opportunities.

Multistate licensure is particularly important for forensic psychiatrists because the American Medical Association (1998) has declared that testifying in court is tantamount to the practice of medicine. Therefore, theoretically (and in some cases practically), one needs a medical license in order even to testify in court. The same holds true for psychologists in certain states, but varies by jurisdiction (http://www.asppb.org) (see Figure 28.1). Forensic psychiatrists and psychologists may draw some measure of comfort from the fact that testimony in federal court is not bound by requirements of local state licensure—although, of course, the court will expect the expert to be properly licensed in his or her home jurisdiction.

Forensic examinations are occasionally conducted in an evaluator's home state, for a trial that is set to occur in a different state where that evaluator is not licensed. Most states will not proceed against those who testify on rare occasion without a requisite license—particularly

	Temporary License Granted	Psychologists in Other States Can Only:
Alabama	No	Testify as expert witness but no psychological practice or services allowed other than the testimony
Alaska	Yes—psychologist (1 year) or psychological associate (2 years) under supervision	None
Alberta	Yes—up to 1 year	None
Arizona	Yes—only if the board requires an additional examination	Serve in emergency relief capacity no more than 20 days per year; testify as expert witness no more than 20 days per year; consult on a limited basis no more than 20 days per year.
Arkansas	No	Serve in emergency relief capacity; consult on a limited basis (one-time case consultation)
British Columbia	Yes—for 15 consecutive days (twice in any calendar year)	None
California	No	Serve in emergency relief capacity (30 days in any calendar year); testify as expert witness (30 days in any calendar year); consult on a limited basis (30 days in any calendar year); other (30 days in any calendar year)
Delaware	No	Other
District of Columbia	No	Serve in emergency relief capacity; testify as expert witness; consult on a limited basis; other
Florida	No	Testify as an expert witness; consult on a limited basis; other
Georgia	Yes	Serve in emergency relief capacity
Hawaii	Yes—for a period not to exceed 90 days within a calendar year	Testify as expert witness; consult on a limited basis
Idaho	No	Testify as expert witness

Figure 28.1   Out-of-State Psychologists
Courtesy of Association of State Provincial Psychology Boards (www.asppb.org/handbookpublic/handbookreview.aspx).

Illinois	No	Serve in emergency relief capacity; testify as expert witness
Indiana	Yes	None
Iowa	No	Serve in emergency relief capacity; testify as expert witness; consult on a limited basis; other
Kansas	Yes—15 days during the calendar year	Testify as expert witness
Louisiana	No	Serve in emergency relief capacity (duration of practice defined by emergency declaration issued by the governor); testify as expert witness (not to exceed 30 consecutive calendar days); consult on a limited basis (not to exceed 30 consecutive calendar days); other
Manitoba	No	Serve in emergency relief capacity
Maryland	No	Testify as expert witness
Massachusetts	No	Consult on a limited basis (one day per month)
Michigan	No	None
Minnesota	No	Serve in emergency relief capacity; testify as expert witness; consult on a limited basis
Mississippi	Yes	Testify as expert witness (with board approval and not exceeding 10 days during a consecutive 12-month period); consult on a limited basis (not exceeding 10 days during a consecutive 12-month period)
Missouri	Yes—individuals who are applying for a license but need to begin to practice immediately	Other (provision allows for 15 days in a 9-month period so any of the activities below may be done during those 15 days, any time worked during a day would = 1 of the 15 days, do not have to report to the board at all) Serve in emergency relief capacity; testify as expert witness; consult on a limited basis

Figure 28.1   (Continued)

Montana	No	Testify as expert witness (report to board if services will exceed 10 days in a calendar year, may not exceed 60 days); Consult on a limited basis (report to board if services will exceed 10 days in a calendar year, may not exceed 60 days); other
Nebraska	Yes	Consult on a limited basis (30 days per year)
Nevada	Yes—good for 1 year and is not renewable	Testify as expert witness; consult on a limited basis
New Brunswick	Yes—each case reviewed on an individual basis	Serve in an emergency relief capacity; testify as expert witness
New Hampshire	No	None
New Jersey	No	Serve in emergency relief capacity (not to exceed 10 days in any 90-day period); testify as expert witness (not to exceed 10 days in any 90-day period); consult on a limited basis (not to exceed 10 days in any 90-day period); other (not to exceed 10 days in any 90-day period)
New Mexico	Yes—6 months	None
New York	Yes—must reside in this state for a period of not more than 6 months prior—valid for a period of not more than 12 months	None
North Carolina	Yes—not more than 30 days in any calendar year	Serve in emergency relief capacity (5 days in a calendar year); testify as expert witness; consult on a limited basis (5 days in a calendar year)
North Dakota	No	Other (up to 30 days per year)
Nova Scotia	No	Serve in emergency relief capacity
Ohio	No	Serve in emergency relief capacity (letter of permission); testify as expert witness (letter of

Figure 28.1   (Continued)

		permission); consult on a limited basis (letter of permission); other (letter of permission)
Oklahoma	No	Serve in emergency relief capacity; testify as expert witness (no more than 5 days is allowed); consult on a limited basis (no more than 5 days is allowed)
Ontario	Yes	None
Oregon	Yes—good for 180 days, no more than 6 months	Testify as expert witness, but cannot deliver direct psychological services to an individual while in Oregon
Pennsylvania	Yes	Serve in emergency relief capacity (if no more than 14 days, is exempt form notifying the board); testify as expert witness (if no more than 14 days, is exempt from notifying the board); consult on a limited basis (if no more than 14 days, is exempt from notifying the board)
Puerto Rico	No	Testify as expert witness (no other services allowed)
Rhode Island	Yes	Serve in emergency relief capacity; testify as expert witness; consult on a limited basis
Saskatchewan	No	Testify as expert witness (must register only if actually seeing and assessing the client)
South Carolina	No	Serve in emergency relief capacity (certification with American Red Cross); testify as expert witness (need temporary permit); consult on a limited basis (need temporary permit)
South Dakota	No	Serve in emergency relief capacity; testify as expert witness; consult on a limited basis

Figure 28.1   (Continued)

Tennessee	Yes	Serve in emergency relief capacity; testify as expert witness
Texas	Yes	None
Vermont	Yes—no more than 10 days or 80 hours in a 12-month period	None
Virginia	No	Testify as expert witness; consult on a limited basis (must work with a Virginia licensed psychologist)
Washington	Yes	None
West Virginia	Yes—no more than 10 calendar days per year	None
Wisconsin	No	Serve in emergency relief capacity; testify as expert witness; consult on a limited basis

Figure 28.1 (Continued)

as such circumstances are rarely brought to the attention of licensing boards. There are, however, instances in which an evaluator's nonlicensed presence is so frequent that the relevant authorities will pursue a criminal indictment. This is particularly likely to occur in cases in which the mental health professional testifies for the defense in criminal cases or for the plaintiff in medical malpractice cases.

In addition, physicians may institute civil litigation against a "hired gun" who frequently testifies against colleagues in a state in which he or she is not licensed. Some states have specifically limited the exposure of malpractice defendants to testimony by full-time plaintiffs' experts. Pennsylvania, for example, has the Medical Care Availability and Reduction of Error Act (MCARE, 2002), which prohibits physicians from testifying regarding the medical standard of care without active engagement in clinical practice or teaching (or retirement less than 5 years ago), practice in a specialty similar to that of the defendant, and board certification if the defendant also possesses such certification. Many forensic psychiatrists or psychologists no longer treat patients, and such rules would render them ineligible to testify against a colleague who is sued for malpractice by a former treatment patient.

Reasonable Fees for Interstate Practice

There are a number of nationally known forensic psychiatrists and psychologists who are called upon to testify in high profile media cases. These experts are primarily teachers of forensic psychiatry or psychology who have earned a national reputation through their publications, lectures, and successful prior testimony in similar cases. Most forensic psychiatrists limit their practice to the state or states in which they are duly licensed and in which they have offices. However, for those few who are called to nationally prominent cases, they may be required to spend many hours in preparation and at trial. As an example, the psychiatrists appointed by the prosecution in the John W. Hinckley, Jr., case, indicated that they had spent several hundred hours over the course of a year in preparing for the trial. Similarly, those forensic psychiatrists appointed by the defense in the John DuPont case in Pennsylvania, also had spent several hundred hours in preparation and many scores of hours during the trial proceedings.

Billing for Services Rendered

How does one charge for such cases when travel is a basic part of the preparation and of the trial? It is prudent to have an hourly fee for most cases in which one is involved. However, there may need to be a daily fee when several days are reserved for a particular case away from home. The daily fee should reflect the hourly fee times 8 or 10 hours per day. It is not appropriate to charge for time that one sleeps (e.g., a 24-hour day). If one is working 12 to 14 hours per day on a case, it is appropriate to charge for the hours one spends on the case. All expenses, of course, are paid by the attorneys hiring the expert witness.

Should the mental health expert travel first class and stay in first-class accommodations? That question became an ethical issue on a case when a senior forensic psychiatrist invited a young colleague, who had a specialty in communication issues and signing for the deaf, to travel across country on a high-profile case. The senior psychiatrist accepted the first-class accommodations and the fine dinners and hotels without question. However, the young colleague, who was not used to such treatment, questioned the ethical concerns she had about accepting such luxuries. She questioned whether that was seductive, whether it was appropriate, and whether she would be compromised in her opinion by accepting such accommodations and expenses.

Gutheil, Slater, Commons, and Goodheart (1998) have written on sharing of fees when one is involved in more than one case at a time away from home. For example, experts will have to determine how to allocate expenses when flying from one site to another for professional purposes. Such determinations become particularly important when an expert elects to review records from these and other cases while in transit.

Time Allocation

One of the problems of having an interstate practice is how one allocates time to cases within a busy schedule, especially when also engaged in forensic teaching and in treating patients. Concerning the latter, it is extremely difficult to perform and testify concerning forensic evaluations when providing treatment, due to the need to reschedule psychotherapy appointments when the expert is away from home—in some instances, for several days or even weeks at a time. The psychiatrist coauthor has had the experience of traveling to England, Canada, Israel, Germany, and Vietnam in order to conduct examinations and testify in cases involving military personnel stationed overseas. There may also be the unpredictably timed but inevitable last-minute call to court, as well as cases that run over into an additional day (or days) of expert testimony.

In conducting assessments away from home, one will often discover a need to spend more than the initially allotted period of time with an examinee, returning after several hours' worth of examination on one day to continue on a second day. Scheduling may be complicated still further by the need to accommodate the schedules of additional evaluators, who may be local experts conducting psychological testing and perhaps participating in the clinical and forensic examination as well.

With the steady ongoing growth of forensic psychiatry and psychology as a form of supplemental practice, with the increasing institution of forensic fellowship programs, and with the increased training of skilled forensic psychiatrists and psychologists in residency and internship programs throughout the country, the need to call on "national" experts has diminished. There are times, of course, when counsel will want to include such experts, particularly in a high-profile case with prominent media coverage. There are experts in psychiatry and psychology in various subspecialties that are called upon when a particular diagnosis arises in a criminal or civil case.

In some very high-profile cases where there are adequate funds, a number of forensic experts may be called to participate at different levels and perform different functions within the overall process. For example, in the John DuPont case in Pennsylvania, there were a number of experts hired by the defense, all of them having different functions in consulting with the defense attorneys. The same is true for the case of John W. Hinckley, Jr., where there were four mental health experts on each side, all hailing from different home jurisdictions.

One complicating aspect of conducting an interstate forensic practice is the risk undertaken by counsel on cross-examination concerning the motivation for obtaining geographically diverse expertise. The psychiatrist coauthor has been asked several times why the counsel needed to call a doctor from "Jenkintown, Pennsylvania" to—for example—the "Great Commonwealth of Virginia" when it was clear there were a number of experts in Virginia who could have been called. The negative implication in such situations is that one's cause of action is so weak that it had to be bolstered either by a particularly courtroom-savvy "national" expert—or by one who wouldn't have to show his or face locally after offering the testimony in question. In order to resolve such issues, it may be prudent for visiting experts to be paired with locally respected colleagues, sharing discernibly different duties but contributing to the same overall mental health theory of the case.

In summary, it is a rewarding but challenging experience to have an interstate practice. One should be very selective in the cases one accepts, and it is often prudent for counsel to accept your recommendation of a respected local colleague either to take on the case alone or to participate with you.

REFERENCES

American Medical Association. (1998). *AMA policy compendium*. Washington, DC: Author.

Association of State and Provincial Psychology Boards (www.asppb.org/ handbookpublic/handbookreview.aspx).

Gutheil, T. G., Slater, F. E., Commons, M. L., & Goodheart, E. A. (1998). Expert witness travel dilemmas: A pilot study of billing practices. *Journal of the American Academy of Psychiatry and the Law, 26*, 21–26.

Medical Care Availability and Reduction of Error Act, 40 P.S. § 1303. 512 (2002).

CHAPTER 29

Conceptualization and Assessment of Malingering

RICHARD ROGERS and ROBERT P. GRANACHER, JR.

INTRODUCTION

Given the highly consequential nature of forensic evaluations, it is entirely understandable why a minority of examinees deliberately distort their clinical presentations by adopting a response style, such as malingering or defensiveness. Therefore, psychological and psychiatric assessments should routinely consider response styles as an essential component of their appraisals. This chapter begins with a conceptual framework for malingering and then outlines a systematic approach to its assessment.

Malingering is characterized in the *Diagnostic and Statistical Manual of Mental Disorders*, 4th edition, Text Revision (DSM-IV-TR) as "the intentional production of false or grossly exaggerated physical or psychological symptoms, motivated by external incentives" (American Psychiatric Association, 2000, p. 739). Malingering requires more than feigned symptoms. It must be purposeful falsification in pursuit of an external goal, which must be carefully ascertained by the evaluator and never inferred from the circumstances. In addition, the magnitude of feigning is important; minor or isolated amplifications of symptoms are unlikely to meet the definitional standard of "grossly exaggerated."

Malingering is a V-Code classification used to describe problems that "may be the focus of clinical attention" (p. 731); it is *not* a diagnosis with formal inclusion and exclusion criteria. Unlike diagnostic criteria, DSM-IV simply lists four screening items that raise the suspicion of malingering: psycholegal contexts, antisocial personality disorder (APD), discrepancies with objective findings, and uncooperativeness. As noted by Rogers (2008), three items (forensic contexts, APD, and uncooperativeness) are ineffective—even as screens—because they rely on common rather than distinguishing characteristics. For instance, all forensic evaluations involve a psycholegal context; therefore, this item cannot possibly assist forensic practitioners in distinguishing between malingered and genuine presentations. Unfortunately, some poorly trained practitioners continue to blatantly ignore V-Code classification of malingering, as established by DSM-IV, and attempt to "diagnose" malingering based on these ineffective screen items. Left unchallenged, such egregious practices can produce catastrophic results in both criminal and civil matters with four out of five forensic examinees being wrongly classified as malingering (Rogers, 2008).

DOMAINS OF MALINGERING

Determinations of malingering entail a careful, multistep process that integrates individualized clinical findings with standardized data. The assessment of malingering is not a monolithic process but must be considered carefully within specific domains, such as feigned mental disorders, feigned cognitive impairment, and feigned medical complaints (Rogers & Bender, 2003). Each domain requires specific tasks for malingerers. With feigned mental disorders, malingerers must decide which symptoms to report, and create a plausible onset and course to their putative disorders. In stark contrast, feigned cognitive impairment necessitates "effortful failure"; when provided with standardized measures, malingerers must put forth believable effort and then make plausible errors. Unlike the other domains, feigned medical complaints are more complex (Granacher & Berry, 2008). As observed by Mittenberg, Aguila-Puentes, Patton, Canyock, and Heilbronner (2002), some malingerers report an array of common but distressing symptoms, whereas others specialize in one symptom (e.g., pain) or a complex syndrome (e.g., fibromyalgia or chronic fatigue). Although malingering can span multiple domains, research on prototypical malingerers (Rogers, Salekin, Sewell, Goldstein, & Leonard, 1998) suggests that most forensic (98.0%) and nonforensic (91.2%) malingerers focus primarily on a single domain. Importantly, each domain has specific detection strategies for the identification of malingering (see Data Collection).

Construct Drift Many referrals from forensic and correctional settings have engaged in manipulative acts and may be seeking unwarranted medications or privileges (Vitacco & Rogers, 2005). In numerous instances, these individuals may be "playing the system"; however, care must be taken to not to facilely equate these manipulations with malingering. As noted previously, the classification of malingering is a painstaking process that must be established in a multistep process using the appropriate detection strategies. Forensic practitioners should exercise care that construct drift does not occur with the use of vague terms such as "overreporting" or "inadequate effort" on psychological measures (Rogers, Sewell, & Gillard, 2010).

Confusion of Secondary Gain With Malingering The construct of secondary gain has disparate meanings in professional practice (Rogers & Reinhardt, 1998). For the two well-established conceptualizations, psychodynamic practice and behavioral medicine, secondary gain is unrelated to malingering because it lacks intentional falsification. From a psychodynamic perspective, secondary gain is an unconscious process to protect an individual from intrapsychic conflict. From a behavioral medicine perspective, the individual is unaware that their illness behavior is being reinforced by caretakers and health professionals. In both instances, examinees lack the intentional motivation for the maintenance of an impaired condition.

More recently, the construct of secondary gain has been introduced to forensic practice, but it lacks the theoretical basis and empirical investigations found with the psychodynamic and behavioral-medicine approaches. From a forensic perspective, secondary gain cannot be directly measured and should never be inferred. Although many claimants become financially dependent on their disability payments, it is impermissible to extrapolate that secondary gain is perpetuating the disability (Rogers & Payne, 2006).

Malingering Precludes Genuine Disorders Most forensic experts clearly realize that malingering and genuine disorders are not mutually exclusive. Nonetheless, we have observed many civil and forensic reports in which the clinical investigation appeared to stop once the classification of malingering was established. Once, malingering is established, forensic practitioners bear the onerous diagnostic task of evaluating genuine mental disorders. While complicated by the presence of malingering, each examinee still deserves a comprehensive assessment of Axis I and II disorders as they relate to the referral issue.

PREPARATION

Prior to the evaluation, forensic practitioners should have an opportunity for an unhurried review of the past clinical and clinical–forensic records. Depending on the nature of the consultation, other records may be germane to a consideration of response styles. For independent medical examinations, the insurance company may have detailed documentation of symptoms and impairment regarding the onset and course of the mental disorders. For insanity evaluations, witnesses' accounts of the defendant's behavior are often available. They may provide valuable insights about the defendant's behavior and utterances at the time of the offense. Thus, the prior review of records is tailored to the available records and the referral question.

An important consideration is whether the prior assessments include standardized (e.g., Minnesota Multiphasic Personality Inventory, 2nd Edition [MMPI-2]) or specialized (e.g., Structured Interview of Reported Symptoms-2 [SIRS-2]) assessments of malingering or other response styles. Although this chapter focuses on malingering, data indicating that the examinee has minimized his/ her psychopathology or responded inconsistently on psychological measures may have important, albeit indirect, implications for malingering. If data are available on malingering, forensic practitioners must then decide about replication (i.e., readministration of the same measures) and augmentation (i.e., administration of additional malingering measures). Given the critical importance of malingering to forensic consultations, both replication and augmentation will be warranted in most cases.

DATA COLLECTION

Assessments of malingering integrate idiographic (e.g., individualized findings) and nomothetic (e.g., test results) data. Given the

importance of these determinations, interview findings and observations should be buttressed by standardized data, whenever possible. By the same token, standardized data should not stand alone in
malingering determinations; only through extensive interviews and
collateral information can definite conclusions be achieved about
malingering and its motivational differences from factitious disorders and other feigning presentations.

One complication of malingering assessments is the enduring
folklore about malingering indicators. For example, many forensic
practitioners erroneously believe that inconsistencies are the hall-
mark of malingering. For example, Edens, Poythress, and Watkins-
Clay (2007) found that correctional psychiatrists relied on inconsistencies for most (89%) of their malingering determinations.
Inconsistencies, common in genuine patient populations (Jackson
& Rogers, 2005), are ineffective for the assessment of malingering
and must be ruled out before MMPI-2 interpretations of feigned
mental disorders can even be considered (Greene, 2008).

DETECTION STRATEGIES

How can forensic practitioners avoid folklore and other pitfalls in
their assessments of malingering? *Detection strategies* provide theoretically sound and empirically validated methods for the evaluation
of malingering. In most instances, these strategies are specific to a
particular domain. Rogers (2008) delineated the components of
detection strategies. As its foundation, the detection strategy must
have a conceptual basis related to malingering or other specific
response style. To ensure methodological rigor, it must have standardized methods of assessment so that systematic differences can
be evaluated via effect sizes. As the capstone, its accuracy of classification must be demonstrated based on relevant comparisons. On
this point, a measure of feigned posttraumatic stress disorder (PTSD)
must be able to distinguish between malingered and genuine
PTSD. It is not sufficient to provide only broad (malingered PTSD
and general outpatients) or irrelevant (malingered PTSD and unimpaired college students) comparisons.

Detection strategies are divided into two broad categories: *unlikely* and *amplified* detection strategies (Rogers, Jackson, Sewell, &
Salekin, 2005). Unlikely detection strategies involve highly unusual

clinical characteristics or symptoms that are almost never observed in genuine patients. In contrast, amplified detection strategies are observed in genuine patients but not to the degree or magnitude reported by feigners. In the interest of space, domains and general categories of detection strategies are illustrated in this chapter (see Rogers, 2008, for a more comprehensive coverage).

1. Feigned mental disorders (domain) and unlikely (general category) detection strategies:
   ○ *Rare symptoms.* This strategy uses clinical characteristics that are very uncommon among genuine patients with mental disorders. Feigners often do not discriminate between infrequent and common items.
   ○ *Symptom combinations.* This strategy uses item pairs for which each item (i.e., clinical characteristic) is relatively common but their combined presence would be very uncommon in genuine patients with mental disorders. Not cognizant of this low probability, feigners often report unusual item pairs.
2. Feigned mental disorders (domain) and amplified (general category) detection strategies:
   ○ *Indiscriminant symptom endorsement.* Even with extensive comorbidity, genuine patients with mental disorders do not report most possible clinical characteristics. In contrast, some feigners believe "the more, the better" and report an unrealistic number or proportion of clinical characteristics.
   ○ *Symptom severity.* Even with marked impairment, genuine patients with mental disorders are usually selective about the number of symptoms and clinical characteristics reported as "extreme" in intensity. In contrast, some feigners are indiscriminant in reporting extremely intense clinical characteristics.
3. Feigned cognitive impairment (domain) and unlikely (general category) detection strategies:
   ○ *Magnitude of error.* When patients with genuine cognitive impairment fail items, they tend to make predictable errors. In contrast, some feigners do not appear to consider which items should be failed and make very uncommon errors.
   ○ *Violation of learning principles.* All persons putting forth genuine effort should demonstrate predictable patterns of learning (e.g., recognition is easier than recall). Some feigners do

not consider these patterns of learning; their performance is incongruent with learning principles.

4. Feigned cognitive impairment (domain) and amplified (general category) detection strategies:
   ○ *Floor effect.* Even for patients with genuine cognitive impairment, some items are "too simple to miss." Some feigners do not consider the item difficulty in deciding which items to intentionally fail.
   ○ *Symptom validity testing.* When provided with two equally probable choices, patients with genuine cognitive impairment may fail many items but should rarely score significantly below chance (i.e., 50%). Some feigners decide indiscriminately to fail most items and score markedly below chance.

Granacher and Berry (2008) underscored the challenges for evaluating somatic malingering of medical disorders. Although the physiological basis of deficit (e.g., certain visual defects) can sometimes be ruled out, health care providers cannot equate nonorganic impairments to malingering. In addition to factitious disorders, consideration must also be given to somatoform disorders, which can also produce nonorganic physical symptoms. Within the medical domain, formal detection strategies have not been standardized and formally tested. However, valuable indicators have been identified that will be subsequently summarized.

SELECTED MEASURES: FEIGNED MENTAL DISORDERS

Practitioners must choose from a broad range of standardized measures for the assessment of feigned mental disorders. For the purposes of this chapter, we focus primarily on comprehensive measures (i.e., rather than screens) that include multiple detection strategies and have been extensively tested with both simulation designs and known-group comparisons. As a result of this process, two multiscale inventories were selected: MMPI-2 (Butcher, Dahlstrom, Graham, Tellegen, & Kaemmer, 1989) and the Personality Assessment Inventory (PAI; Morey, 2007). In addition to the multiscale inventories, one specialized measure was chosen specifically for the assessment of feigned mental disorders: the SIRS-2 (Rogers, Sewell, & Gillard, 2010).

MMPI-2 The MMPI-2 is a personality inventory that has multiple validity scales used to evaluate malingering and other response styles. The MMPI-2 is often used by practitioners, who do not have extensive training relevant to its forensic applications and appropriate use for the assessment of malingering. Therefore, this subsection begins with common pitfalls:

- Avoid automated interpretation of validity scales. Despite their convenience, computerized interpretations are often not current with the malingering literature and may not be explicit in disclosing the basis for their interpretations.
- Avoid interpretations of inconsistent profiles. As observed by Greene (2008), random or inconsistent profiles may erroneously produce extreme elevations on feigning indicators. Therefore, it is completely inappropriate to interpret these indicators as evidence of feigning when the profile is determined, chiefly through Variable Response Inconsistency (VRIN) and True Response Inconsistency (TRIN), to be inconsistent.
- Avoid using the MMPI-2 clinical scales as indirect evidence of malingering. Some practitioners use the clinical scales to question the genuineness of an examinee's clinical presentation. Because there is no "signature" or specific MMPI-2 code type for particular mental disorders, the clinical scales cannot be used as indirect evidence of feigning. The most common profile for genuine patients has no clinical scales elevated (i.e., "within-normal-limits" or WNL) profile (Greene, 2008); however, these patients still have symptoms and presenting complaints. Therefore, these discrepancies are common in genuine patients and cannot be used in the determination of malingering.
- Exercise caution with specific diagnoses. Rogers, Sewell, Martin, and Vitacco (2003) conducted an extensive meta-analysis with 65 MMPI-2 feigning studies that were supplemented by additional diagnostic research. They found that genuine patients with PTSD and schizophrenic disorders often *averaged* marked elevations (e.g., 80T or higher) and extreme elevations (e.g., 100T or higher) were not uncommon. Thus, genuine patients with specific disorders may not be distinguishable from malingerers.

MMPI-2 determinations of feigned mental disorders are typically limited to extreme elevations on feigning indicators. Practitioners have two basic choices: extensive preparation or expert consultation. For preparation, they should be well versed in the MMPI-2 malingering meta-analyses and other large scale studies (e.g., Rogers et al., 2003) and have received formal training in their forensic applications. For consultation, they should judiciously select forensic experts with research and other credentials for the assessment of malingering. Recent data suggest that Fp and Ds scales may be superior to others in making a feigning classification that minimizes false positives (i.e., wrongly classifying genuine patients as feigners).

As a final note, the MMPI-2-Revised Format (MMPI-2-RF; Ben-Porath & Tellegen, 2008) was recently published with substantially modified validity scales. With minimal data on their effectiveness for assessing feigned mental disorders (Tellegen & Ben-Porath, 2008), it is likely to be years before the body of research justifies their use with suspected malingering in forensic cases. Initial forensic studies (Sellbom, Toomey, Wygant, Kurcharski, & Duncan, 2010; Rogers, Gillard, Berry, & Granacher, 2010) produced promising yet disparate results.

PAI The PAI has superior psychometric properties to the MMPI-2, but lacks its extensive database on malingering. Notably, its low reading level (i.e., fourth grade) is a definite advantage for certain forensic populations with limited literacy. Like the MMPI-2, the PAI also had multiple indicators of feigning that utilize specific detection strategies.

A critical review (Sellbom & Bagby, 2008) and a recent meta-analysis (Hawes & Boccaccini, 2009) highlight some of the strengths and weaknesses of the PAI for the assessment of feigned mental disorders. Although not stressed in the PAI manual (Morey, 2007), inconsistent profiles can produce marked elevations on feigning indicators, such as Negative Impression (NIM) scale. Similar to the MMPI-2, feigning indicators should not be used with inconsistent PAI profiles. An additional concern involves the Rogers Discriminant Function or RDF. Although it appears to function very well in clinical simulation studies, its accuracy is only modest in forensic studies, especially those using known-group comparisons.

In a review of 25 investigations, Hawes and Boccaccini (2009) provide strong empirical evidence for the NIM scale and the Malingering (MAL) index. Their data indicate that NIM > 110T or MAL > 4 have very high specificities (0.98 or higher) suggesting that these cut scores produce very few false-positives. Because the sensitivities are generally modest (<0.40), practitioners will need to combine the PAI with other standardized measures in order to improve their accuracy for determinations of feigned mental disorders.

SIRS-2 Rogers, Sewell, and Gillard (2010) substantially revised the original SIRS (Rogers, Bagby, & Dickens, 1992) utilizing much of the cumulative data from the last 18 years. The SIRS-2 is a fully structured interview that standardizes all questions, follow-up inquiries, and clinical ratings. As a result of this standardization, its interrater reliability is impressive and averages 0.98 for the primary scales. As a result, the reliability of individual scores is excellent with very small standard errors of measurement (SEM) and 95% confidence levels.

The SIRS-2 uses a multistep model for the classification of feigned presentations and genuine disorders. The basic rule for the classification of feigning (i.e., ≥3 scales in the probable range or ≥1 scales in the definite range) is augmented by new classification scale (RS Total) and two new indexes (MT and SS). These additional rules allow for the more accurate classification of both feigners and genuine patients (Overall Correct Classification = 0.91) with a very small false-positive rate (2.5%).

The generalizability of the SIRS-2 is established across gender and ethnicity. Regarding the latter, a Spanish SIRS-2 was developed via independent translations by three bilingual psychologists, a separate back-translation, and further refinements. Two studies (see Rogers et al., 2010) examined its comparability with bilingual outpatients and its discriminant validity with monolingual outpatients.

OVERVIEW OF MEASURES FOR FEIGNED COGNITIVE IMPAIRMENT

Dozens of feigned cognitive measures are available, many with specialized goals. Rather than attempt a selected review, this section provides a useful overview which should assist practitioners in deciding on their needs for expert consultation. We strongly recommend that practitioners gain further background for cases potentially involving feigned cognitive impairment. Boone's (2009) *Assessment of Feigned Cognitive Impairment* should be a primary reference. In addition, Rogers (2008) includes valuable chapters on feigning as it relates to traumatic brain injuries, memory impairment, and neuropsychological deficits.

A primary consideration in selecting feigned cognitive measures is whether multiple detection strategies are effectively used. Many of the simple screens rely solely on the "floor effect" attempting to identify feigners via repeated failures on items that are "too simple to miss." Two related problems with this approach include: (1) most feigners do not need to appear that impaired to achieve their objectives, and (2) simple coaching (e.g., "get the easy items correct") can foil this strategy.

Two examples of measures using multiple detection strategies are the Validity Indicator Profile (VIP; Frederick, 1997) and the Word Memory Test (WMT; Green, 2003). The VIP assesses each examinee's rate of success over items of increasing difficulty; this unlikely detection strategy is termed *performance curve* because genuine patients demonstrate a predictable decrease, plotted on a graph as a curve, whereas many malingerers do not. It also includes amplified detection strategies, such as the previously described *symptom validity testing*. In contrast, WMT indicators utilize only amplified detection strategies, although it is possible to consider *violations of learning principles* (e.g., better recall than recognition).

Practitioners, typically in consultation with malingering experts, also need to consider how well the measures match with the purported deficits. Should a measure of feigned memory deficits (e.g., the WMT) be used to assess questionable intellectual functioning? While not always feasible, matching the measure to the deficit in question is highly desirable.

The selection of measures should also consider whether to use *specialized* versus *embedded* measures. To this point, we have focused on specialized measures that were developed specifically to evaluate feigned cognitive impairment. As discussed by Sweet, Condit, and Nelson (2008), embedded measures refer to indicators that were developed and validated within actual tests of ability. Although not necessarily the case, current embedded measures were developed retrospectively and limited to the existing test items. Unlike specialized measures, these embedded indicators are limited to the extent that they can rigorously test specific detection strategies. However, embedded measures have several advantages (Sweet et al., 2008) including (1) the indicators are hidden in the larger test therefore potentially more difficult to foil, and (2) the indicators can be applied retrospectively to past test administrations.

OVERVIEW OF PROCEDURES FOR FEIGNED MEDICAL COMPLAINTS

Feigned medical complaints, as previously noted, covers a complex array of symptoms, syndromes, and diagnoses. As a result, psychological measures play a limited role. One exception is the Health Problem Overstatement (HPO) scale of the Psychological Screening Inventory (PSI; Lanyon, 2003). Initial data on the HPO scale indicates that it is markedly elevated in those feigning medical complaints when compared to medical and psychiatric inpatients. The HPO is composed of three factor scales that have potential in screening for feigned medical complaints: negativity/physical complaints, fatigue, and general poor health (Walters, Berry, Lanyon, & Murphy, 2009).

Psychologists and psychiatrists are increasingly consulted by healthcare providers regarding response styles among medical patients (Granacher & Berry, 2008). There are three basic ways to malinger a medical examination: (1) presentation of false cognitive or neuropsychological signs and symptoms; (2) presentation of false psychiatric signs and symptoms; and (3) presentation of false somatic signs and symptoms. It is also possible to have a documented physical injury and yet produce feigned psychological symptoms (Berry & Granacher, 2009). The presentation of nonpsychological or physical symptoms to a medical provider is termed somatic malingering. For mental health referrals, somatic malingering is often presented as a disorder of neurological functioning even though other organ system presentations may occur (e.g., orthopedic). For a more detailed explanation of these potential presentations, the reader is referred to the texts by DeMyer (2004) and Gorman (1993).

The procedures necessary to detect cases of somatic malingering are primarily art forms of medicine and, as noted above, psychological measures play a limited role in detecting feigned somatic presentations with the exception of the MMPI-2, Fake Bad Scale. The common potential presentations of somatic malingering include: (1) oculomotor eye signs; (2) dysfunctions of voice, swallowing, and breathing; (3) vomiting; (4) disturbances of standing and gait; (5) tremors; (6) disorders of vision; (7) disorders of sensation; (8) pseudoepileptic seizures; (9) fevers; and (10) pain.

The procedures necessary to detect these presentations rely primarily on the physician-conducted physical examination with particular emphasis on the organ system that may be presented as a feigned somatic disorder. Primarily, the detection methods employed by physicians are based on identification of nonanatomical or nonphysiological presentations of apparent neurological and physical disorders. Physiological or pharmacological tests may be applied in some instances to confirm a diagnosis of somatic malingering. As Bogduk (2004) has warned physicians, malingering is not a diagnosis but is a behavioral pattern for which there are no established diagnostic criteria. He cautioned that particularly for patients who present with pain, malingering cannot be proved, but it can only be refuted if a genuine source of pain can be established. An example is a positive response to pharmacological diagnostic blocks by needle insertion demonstrating that the complaint of pain is genuine and, by implication, refutes the hypothesis that the patient is malingering pain. When positive, diagnostic blocks provide objective data on whether a patient is malingering pain. When negative, responses to diagnostic blocks do not exclude a genuine complaint of pain, because bona fide patients may have a source of pain that is not amenable to testing with diagnostic blocks.

The detection of feigned seizures is best determined by a neurologist with special training in epilepsy. The patient is placed into an electroencephalographic (EEG) laboratory with split-screen video recording. This method enables the neurologist to monitor the brain waves of the patient and graph them electronically while providing a video screen of patient behavior, which can be directly observed for correlation with the electrophysiologic activity of brain function. Observed epileptic seizures should correlate directly with observed electrical activity consistent with the seizure. When these correlations do not exist, the diagnosis of pseudoepilepsy or nonepileptic seizures can be made. Unfortunately, as a diagnostic procedure, approximately 40% of patients with nonepileptic seizures also have epilepsy (Bruni, 2000).

While psychological tests are generally ineffective in detecting somatic malingering, the Lees-Haley Fake Bad Scale (FBS; Lees-Haley, English, & Glenn, 1991) is worthy of consideration. Larrabee (1998) has demonstrated that FBS is the most effective scale to detect somatic malingering and other MMPI-2 validity scales (e.g., F, Fb, and Fp) are often ineffective in assessing feigned somatic complaints. Nelson, Sweet, and Demakis (2006) conducted a meta-analysis on 19 MMPI-2 studies from forensic practices that met rigorous inclusion criteria. With a pooled sample of 1,615 dissimulators and 2,049 genuine patients, the largest effect sizes were observed for the FBS (0.96) and O-S scale (0.88). Moreover, a rigorous examination of medical and neurological samples indicates that almost no genuine patients have marked elevations (i.e., FBS $\geq$ 30; Griffenstein, Fox, & Lees-Haley, 2007); therefore, such elevations are not likely to represent credible presentations. The present evidence, from multiple studies, indicates that the FBS appears to be the best validated MMPI-2 scale for detecting somatic malingering (Berry & Schipper, 2007).

The recently published MMPI-2-RF includes the Fs-r scale, specifically designed to assess somatic feigning. However, the initial data (Tellegen & Ben-Porath, 2008, p. 29) demonstrates very high correlations with the F constellation (i.e., F, Fb, and Fp) for both simulators of mental disorders ($M\ r = .93$) and simulators of somatic feigning ($M\ r = .86$). In light of these very high correlations, Fs-r cannot be expected to distinguish somatic malingering from other feigned presentations.

DATA INTERPRETATION AND CLASSIFICATION

This section focuses on feigned mental disorders because of the extensive research and the ability to focus on several selected measures: the MMPI-2, PAI, and SIRS-2. The basic principle is to have classifications of malingering be based on multiple methods that preferably combine interview-based approaches with paper-and-pencil approaches. Whenever feasible, standardized measures should be used as a method of verifying of malingering classifications. However, barriers due to language, reading level, or cognitive abilities may occasionally prevent this from occurring. The process of interpretation and classification is conceptualized as two steps: (1) determination of feigned mental disorders and (2) determination of malingering motivation.

Determination of Feigned Mental Disorders

The first step in determining feigned mental disorders is to rule out other explanations for the anomalous findings. As previously noted, multiscale inventories are vulnerable to random or inconsistent responding. Because the evaluator does not directly participate in the test administration after a brief introduction, he/she cannot observe whether the examinee is psychologically engaged in the task or responding carelessly to the items. Because feigning indicators on random profiles are extremely elevated in most cases, inconsistent responding must be ruled out before any determination of feigned mental disorders is even considered. For all measures of feigned mental disorders including the SIRS-2, an acquiescent response style (i.e., "yea-saying") must be ruled out prior to any standardized testing. This process is simply accomplished during the initial interview by observing whether the examinee responds affirmatively irrespective of the question and its content. It is easily distinguishable from other response styles by asking questions with contradictory content, such as "Do you enjoy playing sports?" and, after a brief interval, "Are sports something you dislike?"

The second step is determining the accuracy of the measurement. For standardized measures, practitioners should examine the standardized errors of measurement and the 95% confidence levels. When these numbers are very small, practitioners should have a high level of confidence in their results. For example, the MMPI-2 F scale has a 95% confidence of 7.1 raw points (22.1T points). Therefore, a raw F score of 10 from a male client has 95% likelihood of falling between 3 (equivalent to 45T) and 17 (equivalent to 89T). In contrast, the SIRS-2 uses only raw scores for its classification; the primary scales average only 1 point for 95% confidence levels. Thus, the 95% confidence level for most SIRS-2 scores of 10 would fall between 9 and 11. In practical terms, the SIRS-2 yields much more reliable individual scores than the MMPI-2. This finding regarding large SEMs on the MMPI-2 continues to hold for the recently published MMPI-2-RF.

The third step is the accuracy of classification which is typically expressed in terms of utility estimates. A major, if not foremost, concern is false-positives (i.e., misclassifying genuine patients as feigners). For example, the PAI NIM scale (cut score $\geq$ 92T) has a relatively low false-positive rate for the clinical standardization sample of 5.9%, which becomes higher in inpatients (Morey, 2007). In comparison, the SIRS-2 has a very low false-positive rate of 2.5%. The rate is achieved by use of multiple classification rules and by removing the group that is "too-close-to-classify" (i.e., the indeterminate group; Rogers, Sewell, Martin, & Vitacco, 2010).

As noted, the classification of feigned mental disorders should be a multimethod appraisal with its determination based on established detection strategies. Given the highly consequential nature of these determinations, marginal cases should be considered as "dissimulation" and not categorized as feigned mental disorders. As such, dissimulation should not be considered for the classification of malingering.

DETERMINATION OF MALINGERING MOTIVATION

Unlike the classification of mental disorders, the determination of malingering motivation deemphasizes the use of standardized measures. Instead, extensive clinical interviews are used to explore the examinee's possible motivations. Inquiries can evaluate the examinee's goals both directly and indirectly. For instance, the examinee can be asked directly, "What do you hope this evaluation will accomplish for you?" Some examinees are surprisingly candid in describing their goals. However, most endeavors are multidetermined. An unhurried examination of different motivations is needed. On occasion, collateral sources can provide insights into the examinee's goals and motivation.

As previously discussed, motivations cannot be simply inferred from the circumstances. For example, the first author evaluated the competency to stand trial of a male defendant facing capital charges with compelling evidence of his involvement (e.g., a videotape and a confession). A facile assumption would be that the defendant was feigning a psychotic disorder to delay trial proceedings. However, it was the examiner's opinion that the feigning was primarily motivated by a more immediate desire to avoid gang-based violence directed at the defendant. While the classification was malingering, an understanding of the motivation remains essential.

COMMUNICATION

Clarity and accuracy are the watchwords in communicating conclusions about malingering to the courts and other decision makers. Regarding clarity, it is essential that malingering and other clinical terms are clearly communicated. In many instances, it is equally important to clarify what the term *does not mean*. Please consider the following example:

> The claimant is inconsistent and unreliable in describing her Axis I symptoms; therefore, it was critically important to rely more on collateral sources than her own account. It is my conclusion that she was genuinely attempting to disclose her symptoms, but was hampered by the severity of her impairment. Her unreliability should not be confused with malingering. I found no credible evidence during interviews and testing that she was attempting to fabricate or grossly exaggerate her symptoms.

The accuracy of malingering determinations is sometimes obfuscated in forensic reports. Reports should correctly reflect the strength of the findings. When the feigning indicators have large 95% confidence levels, this limitation should be stated explicitly. Likewise, when these indicators have substantial false-positive rates, it is the ethical responsibility of practitioners to make this error rate known so that the results can be fully and fairly evaluated by factfinders. Given the importance of malingering determinations, *deception by omission* may have equally grave consequences as *deception by commission*. Therefore, forensic reports and testimony about malingering should reflect the whole truth, including any uncertainties in reaching this classification.

REFERENCES

American Psychiatric Association. (2000). *Diagnostic and statistical manual of mental disorders* (4th ed., Text Revision). Washington, DC: Author.

Ben-Porath, Y. S., & Tellegen, A. (2008). *Minesota Multiphasic Personality Inventory-2 Restructured Form (MMPI-2-RF)*. San Antonio, TX: Pearson Assessments.

Berry D. T. R., & Granacher, R. P. (2009). Feigning of psychiatric symptoms in the context of documented severe head injury and preserved motivation on neuropsychological testing. In J. E. Morgan & J. J. Sweet (Eds.), *Neuropsychology of malingering casebook* (pp. 170–179). New York, NY: Psychology Press.

Berry, D. T. R., & Schipper, L. J. (2007). Detection of feigned psychiatric symptoms during forensic neuropsychological examinations. In

G. J. Larrabee (Ed.), *Assessment of malingered neuropsychological deficits* (pp. 226–263). New York, NY: Oxford University Press.

Bogduk, N. (2004). Diagnostic blocks: A truth serum for malingering. *Clinical Journal of Pain, 20,* 409–414.

Boone, K. B. (2009). *Assessment of feigned cognitive impairment.* New York, NY: Guilford Press.

Bruni, J. (2000). Episodic impairment of consciousness. In W. C. Bradley, R. B. Daroff, G. M. Fenichel, & C. D. Marsden (Eds.), *Neurology and clinical practice* (3rd ed., pp. 9–18). Boston, MA: Butterworth Heinemann.

Butcher, J. N., Dahlstrom, W. G., Graham, J. R., Tellegen, A. M., & Kaemmer, B. (1989). *MMPI-2: Manual for administration and scoring.* Minneapolis, MN: University of Minnesota Press.

DeMyer, W. E. (2004). *Technique of the neurologic examination* (5th ed.). New York, NY: McGraw-Hill.

Edens, J. F., Poythress, N. G., & Watkins-Clay, M. M. (2007). Detection of malingering in psychiatric unit and general population prison inmates: A comparison of the PAI, SIMS, and SIRS. *Journal of Personality Assessment, 88*(1), 33–42.

Frederick, R. I. (1997). *The Validity Indicator Profile.* Minneapolis, MN: National Computer Systems.

Gorman, W. F. (1993). *Legal neurology and malingering: Cases and techniques.* St. Louis, MO: Green.

Granacher, R. P., Jr., & Berry, D. T. R. (2008). Feigned medical presentations. In R. Rogers (Ed.), *Clinical assessment of malingering and deception* (3rd ed.; pp. 145–156). New York, NY: Guilford Press.

Green, P. (2003). *Green's Word Memory Test for Microsoft Windows.* Edmonton, Alberta: Green's Publishing.

Greene, R. L. (2008). Malingering and defensiveness on the MMPI-2. In R. Rogers (Ed.), *Clinical assessment of malingering and deception* (3rd ed., pp. 159–181). New York, NY: Guilford Press.

Griffenstein, M. F., Fox, D., & Lees-Haley, P. R. (2007). The MMPI-2 Fake Bad Scale in detection of noncredible claims. In K. B. Boone (Ed.), *Assessment of feigned cognitive impairment* (pp. 210–235). New York, NY: Guilford Press.

Hawes, S., & Boccaccini, M. (2009). Detection of overreporting of psychopathology on the Personality Assessment Inventory: A meta-analytic review. *Psychological Assessment, 21*(1), 112–124.

Jackson, R. L., & Rogers, R. (2005). Malingering. In J. Payne, J. R. Byard, T. Corey, & C. Henderson (Eds.), *Encyclopedia of forensic and legal medicine* (pp. 417–424). Oxford, UK: Elsevier.

Lanyon, R. (2003). Assessing the misrepresentation of health problems. *Journal of Personality Assessment, 81*(1), 1–10.

Larrabee, G. J. (1998). Somatic malingering on the MMPI and MMPI-2 in litigating subjects. *Clinical Neuropsychologists, 12,* 179–188.

Lees-Haley, P. R., English, L. T., & Glenn, W. J. (1991). A fake bad scale on the MMPI-2 for personal-injury claimants. *Psychological Reports, 68,* 203–210.

Mittenberg, W., Aguila-Puentes, G., Patton, C., Canyock, E. M., & Heilbronner, R. L. (2002). Neuropsychological profiling of symptom exaggeration and malingering. *Journal of Forensic Neuropsychology, 3,* 227–240.

Morey, L. C. (2007). *An interpretive guide to the Personality Assessment Inventory* (2nd ed.). Odessa, FL: Psychological Assessment Resources.

Nelson, N. W., Sweet, J. J., & Demakis, G. J. (2006). Meta analysis of the MMPI-2 Faked Bad Scale: Utility and forensic practice. *Clinical Neuropsychology, 20,* 39–58.

Rogers, R. (2008). Detection strategies for malingering and defensiveness. In R. Rogers (Ed.), *Clinical assessment of malingering and deception* (3rd ed., pp. 14–35). New York, NY: Guilford Press.

Rogers, R., Bagby, R. M., & Dickens, S. E. (1992). *Structured Interview of Reported Symptoms (SIRS) and professional manual.* Odessa, FL: Psychological Assessment Resources.

Rogers, R., & Bender, S. D. (2003). Evaluation of malingering and deception. In A. M. Goldstein (Ed.), *Comprehensive handbook of psychology: Forensic psychology* (vol. 11, pp. 109–129). New York, NY: John Wiley & Sons.

Rogers, R., Gillard, N. D., Berry, D. T. R., & Granacher, R. P., Jr. (2010). *Effectiveness of the MMPI-2-RF validity scales for the detection of feigned mental disorders: A known-groups study.* Manuscript submitted for publication.

Rogers, R., Jackson, R. L., Sewell, K. W., & Salekin, K. L. (2005). Detection strategies for malingering: A confirmatory factor analysis of the SIRS. *Criminal Justice and Behavior, 32,* 511–525.

Rogers, R., & Payne, J. W. (2006). Damages and rewards: Assessment of malingered disorders in compensation cases. *Behavioral Sciences and the Law, 24,* 645–658.

Rogers, R., & Reinhardt, V. (1998). Conceptualization and assessment of secondary gain. In G. P. Koocher, J. C., Norcross, & S. S. Hill, III (Eds.), *Psychologist's desk reference* (pp. 57–62). New York, NY: Oxford University Press.

Rogers, R., Salekin, R., Sewell, K., Goldstein, A., & Leonard, K. (1998). A comparison of forensic and nonforensic malingerers: A prototypical analysis of explanatory models. *Law and Human Behavior, 22*(4), 353–367.

Rogers, R., Sewell, K. W., & Gillard, N. (2010). *Structured Interview of Reported Symptoms-2 (SIRS-2) and professional manual.* Odessa, FL: Psychological Assessment Resources.

Rogers, R., Sewell, K. W., Martin, M. A., & Vitacco, M. J. (2003). Detection of feigned mental disorders: A meta-analysis of the MMPI-2 and malingering. *Assessment*, *10*, 160–177.

Sellbom, M., & Bagby, R. M. (2008). Response styles on multiscale inventories. In R. Rogers (Ed.), *Clinical assessment of malingering and deception*. (3rd ed., pp. 182–206). New York, NY: Guilford Press.

Sellbom, M., Toomey, J., Wygant, D., Kucharski, L., & Duncan, S. (2010). Utility of the MMPI-2-RF (Restructured Form) validity scales in detecting malingering in a criminal forensic setting: A known-groups design. *Psychological Assessment*, *22*(1), 22–31.

Sweet, J. J., Condit, D. C., & Nelson, N. W. (2008). In R. Rogers (Ed.), *Clinical assessment of malingering and deception* (3rd ed., pp. 14–35). New York, NY: Guilford Press.

Tellegen, A., & Ben-Porath, Y. S. (2008). *Minnesota Multiphasic Personality Inventory-2 Restructured Form: Technical manual*. Minneapolis, MN: University of Minnesota Press.

Vitacco, M. J., & Rogers, R. (2005). Assessment of malingering in correctional settings. In C. L. Scott & J. B. Gerbasi (Eds.), *Handbook of correctional mental health* (pp. 133–153). Washington, DC: American Psychiatric Publishing.

Walters, G., Berry, D., Lanyon, R., & Murphy, M. (2009). Are exaggerated health complaints continuous or categorical? A taxometric analysis of the Health Problem Overstatement Scale. *Psychological Assessment*, *21*(2), 219–226.

CHAPTER 30

Transcultural Considerations

SEEMA GARG, FRANK M. DATTILIO, and PIETRO MIAZZO

INTRODUCTION

We undoubtedly live in an era of cultural awareness due to the fact that the past several decades have witnessed the greatest influx of immigrants to the United States since the turn of the 20th century. The United States of America is currently experiencing the greatest rise in immigration in 100 years. It is estimated that more than one million undocumented immigrants are arriving annually, the vast majority of whom hail from Asia and the Hispanic worlds (McGoldrick, Giordano, & Garcia-Preto, 2005). This influx has had a major impact on the characterization of diversity with a rapid emergence for multicultural awareness throughout the United States. Consequently, incorporating cultural acknowledgment into our clinical assessments and opinions is essential.

The role of culture in forensic psychological and psychiatric assessments has received increasing attention in recent years. In 2000, the American Psychiatric Association (APA) recognized the importance of cultural variables in the *Diagnostic and Statistical Manual of Mental Disorders*, 4th edition, Text Revision, and included "an outline for cultural formulation" in the appendix for diagnosticians to follow. By doing so, the APA pointed out that it is important to maintain a conscious focus on any sources of bias that may arise due to cultural differences. This aspect of the diagnostic and statistical manual will receive even greater emphasis with the release of *DSM-5*, which is scheduled for publication in May 2012. It is important for forensic evaluators to recognize how cultural norms and values can influence professional judgments, particularly so with forensic psychologists and psychiatrists.

CULTURAL IDENTITY

The extent to which cultural identity affects an individual's daily functioning depends on many factors, including educational attainment, professional contact outside of the home, how long one has lived in this country, and whether one has continued to reside in a similar community that reflects one's cultural heritage. An individual's cultural background can often define such characteristics as the role that a man or woman plays in life, the roles of children and elders, or of extended family members, and the obligations of each family member to the entire family unit's functioning. It also has significant bearing on their feelings about anyone outside of their culture, affecting the family in general, as well as boundaries and behavioral interaction with each other.

Cultures can also have strong roles in defining what is normal and what is deviant. Both the fields of psychology and psychiatry focus on behavior that is considered deviant from the "norm." However, there are times when a minority culture may accept something as being very normal as opposed to the "dominant" culture that considers it to be abnormal. The question at hand relates to which set of criteria should be used in judging whether something is "normal or abnormal." There is a long-standing proverb that reads, "When in Rome, do as the Romans do." This basic tenet suggests that anything else would be considered out of place. However, the question is, "Do we think and act as Romans do, even if we are not in Rome?" Surely, one's cultural heritage greatly influences how one thinks and behaves and how one integrates into a foreign society. Much of this depends on what age an individual enters into a new culture and how one becomes introduced or acculturated. Consequently, if one is already at an adult age by the time one becomes introduced to a new culture, some of one's customs and habits may already be well established and ingrained, making the assimilation to a new culture more difficult. This may clearly involve thought and belief styles, as well as behavioral protocols for dealing with others.

Acknowledging the role of culture in forensic assessments is essential in order to reduce biases. However, it is also important to keep in mind that focusing on culture can also "taint" the assessment by stereotyping a particular group of individuals without consideration of individual differences. The use of culture as a defense can contribute to stereotyping and stigmatization of entire groups or communities.

There are a number of benefits to understanding an individual's cultural background that can also help to explain the reasons behind someone's behavior and put it into context, so that it makes more sense. Within a forensic context, this can provide a level of understanding of the origin of the accused individual's behavior and the level of volition and the intent with which he/she thinks and acts. "Since culture shapes personal identity, emotional responses, and patterns of reasoning, it can be expected to influence motivation and intent in situations involving criminal actions" (Kirmayer, Rousseau, & Lashley, 2007).

A classic example is the Japanese female defendant who appeared before a judge in the United States and made every effort not to make eye contact with His Honor. In her particular culture, looking directly into the eyes of such an authority would be a clear sign of disrespect, whereas the judge, an American-born and -bred product of the East Coast of the United States, found it to be a sign of disrespect, although the judge did remark that he was impressed by the fact that the woman repeatedly bowed to him throughout the sentencing.

At the same time, one should also bear in mind that cultural interpretations of behavior can be misused in the forensic context. The risk of using cultural context in a forensic setting is that it can be taken as a justification for many different kinds of behaviors. That might be perfectly reasonable and necessary in a clinical setting; however, in a courtroom setting, the task is to judge intent for the purpose of applying the law. If cultural explanations are misused in a forensic context, the results may be very troubling to the community. As an example, a very light sentence was imposed on a severe sex offender when he committed an offense against an ethnic minority (Kirmayer, Rousseau, & Lashley, 2007).

CLINICAL FORENSIC INTERVIEWS AND MENTAL STATUS EXAMINATIONS

Conducting clinical interviews and mental status examinations in culturally sensitive cases can be precarious, especially if the examiner is not familiar with the specific nuances of the culture or background of the examinee. Such cultural variations may have a profound effect on eye contact, speech, posture, and so forth. Therefore, what may be a cultural means of cordiality could be misconstrued as manipulativeness or evasiveness. For example, with Hispanic cultures, it is not uncommon for the individuals to arrive late for a doctor's visit with the anticipation that they are giving the doctor more time to prepare and take care of other items. Sometimes this is viewed as a sign of courtesy in the Hispanic culture as opposed to being viewed as a sign of tardiness or disrespect in the American culture.

Other areas that need to be considered are form and content for mental status examinations, particularly with individuals who are from different cultures than the examiner, or are not fluent in the English language.

SEATING ARRANGEMENTS

Depending on whether or not an examiner is evaluating a male or female, seating arrangements may involve differences in proximity. For example, females from a Muslim background may not wish to sit close to a male examiner, because it is against their faith to sit too close to a male. Also, face-to-face eye contact may be too intimidating at times, depending on the circumstances; however, this may be unavoidable, particularly when psychologists are conducting psychological testing. Handshakes may also be intimidating to certain cultures and should be avoided.

It should also be kept in mind that females from some cultures insist on having their spouse or a male family member with them during the examination, despite the evaluator's request that they be seen alone. In addition, in some cultures, it is considered a sign of respect to address the male member(s) of the family when explaining the evaluation process, even if it is a female who is being evaluated. The men can be considered as the "gatekeepers of the family" when dealing with outsiders. Therefore, body posture, eye contact, and verbal engagement need to be taken into consideration, depending on the culture. The behavior or attitude of an individual may have more to do with cultural differences than with the psychological disposition of the individual.

Also, people from some cultures might find it more respectful to respond to examiners in monosyllabic responses with either "yes" or "no" as opposed to long elaborations. Even when asked to elaborate, they may be reticent to do so as a sign of respect. It should also be noted that in some cultures, individuals may come to an examination bearing a gift, such as a cake or bread. This can be a normal sign of respect in some cultures, and not necessarily an attempt at manipulation or to win over the examiner.

Use of Language Interpreters

In this chapter, the words *translator* and *interpreter* are used interchangeably. However, every effort should be made to seek "translation" and not "interpretation," which implies input from the translator's perspective, rather than verbatim translation.

Very often forensic examiners may find themselves in the presence of a language translator due to the fact that the examinee may not have a fluent command of the English language. First and foremost, examiners should make every effort to attempt to find a forensic psychologist or psychiatrist who speaks the language of the examinee. In some of the more common languages, such as Spanish, this may not be so difficult in that there are often a number of Spanish speaking psychiatrists/psychologists who can conduct forensic evaluations. However, in those languages in which psychiatrists or psychologists may be less readily available, a professional translator will be necessary.

Forensic psychologists and psychiatrists need to make every attempt to utilize professional forensic translators who are trained specifically in simultaneous or consecutive translation that is verbatim. This is important since they are specifically educated on how not to embellish or to make their own interpretation of what they think the individual is attempting to communicate. This is so often the case when amateur translators are used, such as family members or relatives, or even neighbors of the defendant. Professional translators, who can be utilized through forensic translation services of many different languages, know specifically how to translate effectively and are even certified as official translators.

It is also important to understand that when interpreters are used, the examinee will be relating more directly to the interpreter and, therefore, eye contact and body language may be directed to the individual conducting the translation. There may also be problems if the interpreter is of a different culture but speaks the particular language of the examinee, which needs to be taken into account. For example, in the case where the languages of Ukrainian and Russian are involved, many Ukrainians speak Russian and vice versa. However, some of the older Ukrainian adults may have difficulty with a Russian translator who speaks Ukrainian due to the history of tension between those two nations. This always needs to be taken into consideration and factored into the forensic examination, especially when psychological testing is being translated.

CULTURE AND GENERAL PSYCHOLOGICAL ASSESSMENTS

Psychological tests and assessments need to be validated for the population with which they are being used. Psychologists or other forensic examiners using psychological testing or appraisals must take precaution to use instruments that are cross culturally reliable and valid, otherwise, the testing can lead to a biased conclusion. Even though no test is truly "culturally fair," there are some cultural factors that can influence the accuracy of test results. These include the level of language fluency, the variability of verbal and visual concepts across cultures, the level of the examinee's acculturation, the testing setting, and the interpersonal process between the test administrator and the examinee.

Many neuropsychological tests have not been translated or normed on populations with different cultural backgrounds (Mahurin, Espino, & Holifield, 1992). One study found that there were significant performance differences between felons of various ethnic groups on a battery of 27 neuropsychological tests (Selby, Jeffrey, & Laver, 2001). This is a significant factor since such test data can be used in courts and correctional facilities to make decisions about sentencing, parole violation potential, and treatment planning. This also may have a profound effect on the outcome of such evaluations, particularly where individuals are required to use interpreters (deArmas, 1997).

This concept gives rise to debate over whether or not one should assume that standard psychological tests are transportable from one culture to another, and whether or not the use of translators impedes the evaluation process. Culture and language issues may be overlooked by many who attempt to provide multicultural evaluations to the court. A classic example of this occurs with bilingual psychologists who choose to spontaneously translate a psychometric instrument printed in English for someone from a different culture speaking a different language. This often occurs when a translated version of an instrument is not available or nonexistent. In this case, the examiner translating the material is sometimes under the false assumption that the testee will share the presumption about the values and content of the test items simply because it has been translated into their particular language. This is typical of many tests, but most pronounced for the psychologist who uses intelligence tests.

For example, the WAIS-III (Wechsler Adult Intelligence Scale-III) was recently replaced by the WAIS-IV (Wechsler Adult Intelligence Scale-IV). For years, however, the only Spanish translation of the Wechsler Intelligence Scale was the EIWA (Escala de Inteligencia Wechsler para Adultos) (Wechsler, 1968). This has recently been replaced by the Spanish translation of the WAIS-III (Escala de Inteligencia de Wechsler Para Adultos-III; (Publicaciones de Psicologia Aplicada, 1999).

When the initial form of the WAIS appeared, no updated translation followed; therefore, to compensate, many Spanish speaking psychologists simply administered the English version of the WAIS and translated the items for the examinee as they encountered them during the test. Unfortunately, dilemmas may arise when administering this instrument, seriously jeopardizing the validity of the overall assessment.

A case in point involves one of the items on the comprehension subtest (a measure of ability to think abstractly), which asks, "What does this saying mean—shallow brooks are noisy?" The literal Spanish translation for this saying is "Los Riachuelos poco profundos son ruidosos," which essentially is a verbatim translation of the phrase "shallow brooks are noisy." Unfortunately, this phrase falls short of the concrete meaning of the proverb, suggesting instead the abstract generalization "shallow people talk a lot" (Wechsler, 1981, p. 132). A more appropriate translation for this concept is the very common phrase among most Hispanic cultures, which is "Perro que ladra no muerde." This literally translates to "barking dogs don't bite," which is a proverb more reflective of the symbolic nature of the culturally accurate phrase "shallow brooks are noisy." This is a clear example of how the central intent of the question may deviate significantly and be completely misunderstood due to the assumption that verbatim translation may suffice to convey the true meaning of the proverb. What's more, the psychologist administering the test may be fooled into thinking that this translation is sufficient since other terms can be translated without this misunderstanding. This may seduce the translator into believing that all items are universal when, in fact, they are not. This is an excellent example of cross-cultural misunderstanding.

Another issue that deserves mention is the aspect of cultural variations in instruments, as well as interview techniques that multi-lingual experts encounter. Being culturally sensitive and well versed in a particular language is still not sufficient for total accuracy, particularly due to the existence of variations of certain cultures. A classic example is with the use of the Minnesota Multiphasic Personality Inventory (MMPI; versions I and II), which is now translated into Spanish (see Pope, Butcher, & Seelen, 2000). Surprisingly, this test, as well as others that have been translated into Spanish, fails to reflect the diversities among those subcategories of Spanish speaking cultures. For this reason, it is important to attempt to collect different versions of certain tests translated into Spanish in order to reflect this specific culture and dialect in the interest of facilitating an accurate assessment. The interpretation of certain phrases and expressions may vary depending on the culture and may even have a profound impact on the responses given by the individual being examined. This is true for a number of other languages as well, such as Arabic or Chinese.

Furthermore, there is the assumption that standardized psychological tests are intrinsically transportable from one culture to another. With appropriate linguistic translation, administration by a "native" tester and (less frequently) the provisions of familiar content, tests can be used with different cultures (Greenfield, 1997). However, there are certain cultural variabilities that cannot be ignored, even with the common spoken language.

In addition to linguistics, the aspect of knowing one's culture is important, particularly when speaking the language or using an interpreter. While it is sometimes not easy to find an individual of the same culture, one should strive for that goal, particularly since it may make a difference in understanding the specific nuances pertaining to the culture of the examinee. The next best alternative to an evaluator of the same culture is to utilize translators of the same culture.

There are, however, several problems inherent in this alternative. For one, it is often rare to find a professional translator utilizing or fluent in the specific language involved. Hence, nonprofessional translators may not translate as accurately due to lack of fluency and proficiency in both languages, as well as lacking the experience in translating in formal cases where technical language may be involved. Secondly, a mental health professional is likely to miss some of the subtle affectual qualities conveyed in a statement that is transported through a translator as opposed to being experienced directly. The pace of responding, the tone of voice, as well as critical pauses, can be clues in the detection of malingering. Use of a translator may have a profound effect on the results of the evaluation, particularly where issues of remorse may be involved. This is particularly true when forensic examiners utilize friends or relatives of the examinee as translators. Such persons may try to "help" by fortifying or even substituting the examinee's statements—with predictably misleading results.

Finally, certain sensitive issues may inhibit an individual being evaluated, for example, the use of a translator who is the opposite sex of the examinee. A third party is also one more reason that may serve to inhibit self-disclosure in an examinee, especially with evaluations that occur under emotionally intense situations. In many cultures, issues of feeling shame and saving face can play a critical role in everyday life. If the examiner inquires about something that causes the examinee to feel ashamed, one may not be able to get important information. Although the examiner may have more success in obtaining information by inquiring in an indirect manner, one may still have difficulty getting sufficient details for the purpose of the evaluation.

The issue of cultural sensitivity is important for those who speak the language as well as those using translators. Simply knowing the language or even maintaining a remote conceptualization of a particular culture may not aid in detecting the fine details that may be so crucial at times in making effective determinations in our assessments. Professionals evaluating individuals of different cultures have an obligation to remain sensitive to these issues in order to strive for accuracy in the assessment.

Another example of the importance of reducing bias in testing is the Competency Screening Test (CST), which has been criticized for being biased against defendants with a negative view of the legal system. Individuals who express cynicism about the criminal justice process could be incorrectly scored as incompetent, contributing to the test's undesirably high false-positive rate (Melton, Petrila, Poythress, & Slobogin, 2007).

Different cultures have different socially acceptable ways of allowing people to express their problems. In some cultures it is acceptable to do so by focusing on somatic complaints, but not to express emotions. A person may ostensibly say the problem is one thing, when the real issue is something entirely different, which they may not be permitted to say. Knowing what areas are considered taboo to discuss can help a forensic expert explore the real sources of the problem.

Many times, families handle their problems internally and avoid turning to those outside of the family. They may fear shame and humiliation if their personal struggles are openly discussed with an outsider who is passing judgment on them. They may need to feel the evaluator is actually their ally, before they will open up, requiring ongoing contact that is more therapeutic in nature. However, forensic evaluators often do not have the time or opportunity to create such a relationship, role conflicts aside.

CULTURE AND FORENSIC PSYCHOLOGICAL ASSESSMENTS

The forensic evaluator must consider how cultural awareness can be used to elicit and make sense of relevant information that might otherwise be ignored. One does not, of course, institute a "therapeutic alliance" as would be employed in encouraging a reticent psychotherapy patient to disclose; nor is one's display of cultural awareness a tactic to lull the examinee into a false sense of security. When guilelessly and forthrightly conveyed, the forensic evaluator's visible sensitivity to—and respect for—cultural nuances is an appropriate undertaking designed to obtain the fullest and most accurate accounting of the examinee's perspective.

Boundaries surrounding both the evaluator and the examinee in a forensic context are very different from those found in a general psychological assessment, in which the evaluator can be seen as an ally who is trying to understand and appreciate the problem with hope of providing some help. The goal is not so much to judge as it is to understand. In a forensic context, however, the individual being evaluated is being confronted by a stranger, who is asking highly personal questions and is not offering the protection of confidentiality. In fact, one's statements may be used against one in a legal forum. Thus, the forensic evaluator may often be seen as an unwelcome intruder. Different cultures treat outsiders in different ways. Knowing these differences can help reduce some of the barriers to gathering accurate information.

CIVIL CONTEXTS

When conducting a psychological assessment, it is important to consider the specific purpose of the assessment—whether it relates to the criminal process (such as competency to stand trial, an insanity evaluation, sentencing) or civil issues such as child custody and divorce, financial disputes, or competency to make a will (need to know who are the natural heirs, which can be defined by the particular culture).

Culture can affect an interviewee's responses. If the interviewee hails from a culture in which exaggeration of experiences is encouraged, then he/she may exaggerate some aspect of an incident in order to meet cultural expectations.

> Individuals' attitudes towards truth and deception are of significance in the psychiatric assessment of malingering. These attitudes in turn must be understood and evaluated from the perspective of the cultural norm that underlies them. This cultural aspect contributes to the difficulty in assessing examinees for malingering and deception. (Bunnting, Wessels, Lasich, & Pillay, 1996)

In addition, there is wide cultural diversity in nonverbal behaviors such as eye contact and emotional expressiveness. Any interpretation of an interviewee's behavior must take into account those cultural differences. An example of how cultural differences can result in misunderstandings in a psychological assessment:

> Puerto Rican women are taught to lower their eyes and avoid eye contact. American therapists are taught to read lack of eye contact as an indication of inability to relate to others. Jewish patients routinely

inquire about the therapist's credentials, which many groups would perceive as a challenge and affront but is for them a needed reassurance. (McGoldrick et al., 1982, p. 24)

Standards of wrongfulness can vary across societies and cultures. For example, culture can play a major role within the context of decisions about child abuse, child custody, adoption, and termination of parental rights. When a family hails from a minority background, there may be many differences in how a "normal" family typically functions compared to the mainstream culture. In order to conduct an adequate assessment of each parent's abilities, it will be important to be aware of the cultural norms involved. Examples of some of the questions that need to be considered in a custody evaluation are: (1) What are normal boundaries within a given culture? What is "normal" parenting? (This could affect child custody evaluations.) (2) Is cosleeping considered normal or not? And until what age? (3) What are acceptable methods of discipline? (4) What are the cultural boundaries around privacy? (5) What are the cultural boundaries between generations?

Consider an example of an Asian family being assessed for a child custody evaluation by a Westerner. There are likely to be a number of unspoken beliefs shared by the family, both about the examiner and about what is best for the child. Western culture is very focused on individual achievements, and the impact of the nuclear family. Asian cultures often focus on the best interests of the group over individual achievement, and place a high value on the contributions of extended family members. As such, it would be important to remain sensitive to those cultural differences when trying to decide what is in the best interest of these children.

In many Asian cultures, marriage is viewed as a union of two families, not just two people. As such, a divorcing couple may need to consider the roles of extended family members in deciding what is best for the children. They may also defer to their elders, even if they do not agree with them, because that is part of the culture of respect for elders.

There are many cultures that consider maintaining "family honor" to be of the utmost importance. Often in such cultures, all the actions of an individual reflect directly on the entire family's reputation. As an example, in some Indian families it is considered shameful to marry outside, or below, one's caste. Think of an heiress marrying a taxi driver. If one person does something that causes any member of the family to feel shame, or to "lose face," the culture may approve of the family taking certain measures to restore their reputation. The question then becomes, what are acceptable sorts of responses from family members? Is "honor killing" of one or both parties condoned in such situations? Would there be any differences in how such an action was treated, compared to murdering someone without the motivation of restoring family honor?

Consider another example of a traditional culture, where a woman's value is closely tied to her family's reputation, and vice versa. If premarital sex is considered taboo, but the parties have a consensual relationship, then do they deserve to be punished or ostracized? If so, who should be punished, and what should the punishment be? Would only the female be punished, or would the male also be punished? And what about their respective families—should they also be punished or ostracized in some way? What if a married woman is raped? In some cultures, this can be blamed on the woman as "having an affair," or "being seductive," and is considered adequate grounds for divorce.

Another area where cultural differences can become important in civil legal matters is the area of finances and property distribution. The forensic examiner will need to be aware of the rules involving financial transactions within the family. Is everyone expected to share whatever they have, so that there is no distinction between what belongs to an individual as opposed to the family? In that case, what happens if one member of the family contends that he is owed money by another family member, and decides to take the matter to court? Are there some culturally accepted standards in deciding how to determine adequate compensation for property disagreements? What about cultural differences in inheritance practices, i.e., the oldest son may receive all of the estate (primogeniture), but is also burdened with the responsibility for caring for the remaining parent, educating younger siblings, and marrying off their sisters (Obama, 2004)?

CRIMINAL CONTEXTS

Sensitivity to cultural issues is also important in a forensic criminal evaluation. "Forensic psychiatrists provide clinical care in correctional and forensic hospital settings where issues related to ethnicity are not only relevant but attenuated, because of the greater proportion of ethnic minorities in these settings" (Hicks, 2004, p. 21). "Ethnicity is an important independent predictor of admission to psychiatric medium or high security units. Black patients of Caribbean origin are up to 10 times more likely than white Americans to be admitted to medium-security units (McKenzie, 2004, p. 37). Other studies have found that Caucasian defendants are more likely than defendants of an ethnic minority to have a successful insanity plea. In contrast, African-American defendants were nearly twice as likely as Caucasians to be referred to a strict secure facility for evaluation (Pinals, Packer, Fisher, & Roy-Bujnowski, 2004).

When examinees hail from a different culture, they may have had experiences in their country of origin that shape their response to the legal system of the United States. If they experienced a repressive legal system in their country of origin, they may react to the United States legal system in the same way. According to Matthews and Tseng (2004), the examiner's questions "may be interpreted as hostile and interrogative," while "the examiner himself may be seen as sadistic and voyeuristic," with such suspicions engendered by "psychiatric abuses in the examinee's country of origin" (p. 108). Unless these responses are interpreted within the context of the examinee's culture, the examiner may mistakenly conclude that the examinee is unduly guarded, suspicious, paranoid, or even delusional.

Different cultures have different taboos on what can or cannot be discussed. As an example, a victim of a sexual assault may be unwilling to discuss the details of the assault, because that violates a cultural norm. This may, however, be misconstrued as the examinee being not forthcoming or manipulative. Some cultures may also prohibit a younger member of the family from criticizing an elder member. The intent of remaining silent may be to maintain respect for the elder family member, not necessarily to consciously deceive the forensic examiner.

"Bringing awareness of cultural concerns to the attention of judges and jurors can play an important role in improving the functioning of the justice system. It is worth asking whether some social or cultural circumstances are so familiar or taken for granted that they are not recognized or given weight as explanations for criminal actions" (Kirmayer et al., 2007, p. 100).

The forensic examiner needs to consider what is normal within the culture. Female genital mutilation offends Western sensibilities, whereas some areas of Africa require this of a woman in order for her to be marriageable (i.e., piercing). The idea behind such mutilation is that a woman who is capable of sexual pleasure is likely to stray if she is not sexually satisfied by her husband. She is seen as "unclean" unless she has this procedure, and is unlikely to be selected as a marriage partner. Knowing the cultural differences is important if charges are brought against those who performed the procedure.

A person's cultural background can affect the capacity to form a criminal intent, or ability to control behavior. "For example, the Japanese mother who tries to kill her child and herself may be following the cultural template of *otaku*—joint suicide—in which, because of cultural values, the lives of the mother and child are linked. The intent then is not murder as a separate act, but the completion of a suicide in which the child is included as an extension of the self" (Kirmayer et al., 2007, p. 100).

Cultural factors can explain motives, and result in mitigation of a sentence. In Oregon, and in other states, there is a defense of "extreme emotional disturbance," which can be used to reduce a charge of murder to manslaughter. Cultural factors can play an important role in determining whether this defense applies and can be used to establish a "diminished capacity" defense.

There are some syndromes that are recognized as being psychiatric disorders in a particular culture, but are not described in the regular classifications of psychiatric disorders. Some examples include episodic, sudden homicidal behavior (called *amok*) (from Malay *amoq*), criminal behavior which occurs during a dissociated or possessed state (called malignant *latah*) (Middle Eastern origin), or culturally associated murder/suicide behavior by a family (called *ikashinjiu* in Japan). A person who commits an act of culturally related violence may be seen as lacking responsibility for this behavior within that culture.

Cultural factors could also play an important role in determining the choice of good rehabilitation programs. If one is sent back to one's family or community after legal entanglement, it will be important to know what sort of environment one is returning to. Will the person be accepted by his family and reintegrated into the community? How does the family understand the illegal behavior, and what is their attitude towards the returning individual? It will be important to consider the reactions of family and community members to a psychiatric illness and deviant behavior. Will one have the necessary support and structure to make a successful rehabilitation?

TRANSFERENCE AND COUNTERTRANSFERENCE

Another issue to consider is the role of transference and counter-transference—when the evaluator and examinee are the same ethnic background, as opposed to differing backgrounds. What if they come from different ethnic or religious backgrounds that have typically not gotten along—such as Israelis versus Palestinians, or Hindus versus Muslims? How does this impact the interaction? Is there a sense of identification and safety if both are from the same background? Could this lead to sharing more information than they normally would? Would there be an implicit assumption that certain behaviors will be considered "understandable and forgivable," because the culture tends to dismiss them, even if the law takes them seriously? Would the examinee have an unrealistic expectation of favorable treatment from an evaluator who was of the same ethnic background? As an example, how is abuse defined and handled in different ethnic communities? Also, would being from the same culture suggest that certain things will be kept secret from the courts (because the examinee identifies with the evaluator and thinks of him as a friend), even though the *Miranda* rights have been delivered?

CONCLUSION

In summary, it is important to be sensitive to cultural factors that may influence interpretations of behavior, feelings, and intent in forensic evaluations. This chapter has provided a number of suggestions on how to reduce culturally based biases in forensic assessments. Whenever possible, it is important to use professional translators, instead of family members, to ensure exact, unembellished translations. Psychological tests and assessments should be validated for the population on which they are being used. This is important, because test data can be used to make decisions about sentencing, parole violation potential, and treatment planning. The forensic evaluator should be aware of the possibility of boundary violations, which can take place whether the evaluator is from the same culture as the examinee, or from a very different one. Awareness of cultural norms around appropriate expression of emotions will help the evaluator understand the examinee's verbal and nonverbal behaviors. In addition, awareness of cultural norms surrounding the roles of different family members can be an important part of child custody evaluations. Cultural norms around gender appropriate behavior can greatly influence every-day interactions.

Behavior that is considered criminal in the dominant culture may be considered justifiable in a minority subculture, thus contributing to a better understanding of criminal intent, as well as prospects for rehabilitation. While it is impossible to provide a firm road map on how to navigate any particular culture, hopefully this chapter has raised some issues that will make forensic evaluators more sensitive to cultural factors that could improve their assessments.

REFERENCES

Bunnting, B. G., Wessels, W. H., Lasich, A. J., & Pillay, B. (1996). The distinction of malingering and mental illness in black forensic cases. *Medicine and Law, 15,* 241–247.

deArmas, A. (1997). The use of interpretation in forensic psychological evaluations. *Forensic Examiner, 6*(11/12), 37.

Greenfield, P. M. (1997). You can't take it with you: Why ability assessments don't cross cultures. *American Psychologist, 52,* 1115–1124.

Hicks, J. W. (2004). Ethnicity, race, and forensic psychiatry: Are we color-blind? *Journal of American Academy of Psychiatry and the Law, 32,* 21–33.

Kirmayer, L. J., Rousseau, C., & Lashley, M. (2007). The place of culture in forensic psychiatry. *Journal of American Academy of Psychiatry and the Law, 35,* 98–102.

Mahurin, R. K., Espino, D. V., & Holifield, E. B. (1992). Mental status testing in elderly Hispanic populations: Special concerns. *Psychopharmacology Bulletin, 28,* 391–399.

Matthews, D., & Tseng, W. (2004). Culture and forensic psychiatry. In W. Tseng & J. Streltzer (Eds.), *Cultural competence in clinical psychiatry* (pp. 107–123). Arlington, VA: American Psychiatric Publishing.

McGoldrick, M., Giordano, J., & Garcia-Preto. (2005). *Ethnicity and family therapy* (3rd ed). New York, NY: Guilford Press.

McGoldrick, M., Giordano, J., Pearce, J. K. (1982). *Ethnicity and family therapy*. New York, NY: Guilford Press.

McKenzie, K. (2004). Commentary: Ethnicity, race, and forensic psychiatry—Is being unblinded enough? *Journal of American Academy of Psychiatry and the Law, 32,* 36–39.

Melton, G. B., Petrila, J., Poythress, N. G., & Slobogin, C. (2007). *Psychological evaluations for the courts: A handbook for mental health professionals and lawyers* (3rd ed.). New York, NY: Guilford Press.

Obama, B. (2004). *Dreams from my father: A story of race and inheritance*. New York, NY: Crown.

Pinals, D. A., Packer, I. K., Fisher, W., & Roy-Bujnowski, K. (2004). Relationship between race and ethnicity and forensic clinical triage dispositions. *Psychiatric Services, 55,* 873–878.

Pope, K. S., Butcher, J. N., & Seelen, J. (2000). *The MMPI-2 and MMPI-A in court*. Washington, DC: American Psychological Association.

Publicaciones de Psicologia Aplicada. (1999). *Manual de Aplicacion y Corrección*. San Antonio, TX: Psychological Corporation.

Selby, M. J., Jeffrey, A., Laver, G. (2001). The effects of cultural experience on neuropsychological performance in a forensic population. *American Journal of Forensic Psychology, 19*(4), 75–85.

Wechsler, D. (1968). *Escala de Inteligencia Wechsler para Adultos*. New York, NY: Psychological Corporation.

Wechsler, D. (1981). *Wechsler Adult Intelligence Scale—Revised*. New York, NY: Psychological Corporation.

APPENDIX A

Scientific Glossary

A

ABERRANT BEHAVIOR: Irregular behavior that deviates from what is considered normal. The use of the term implies that the behavior in question is performed in secret and mainly for reasons of self-interest, as for example in the case of certain unusual sexual practices.

ADAPTIVE BEHAVIOR: A type of behavior that is used to adjust to another type of behavior or situation. This is often characterized by a type of behavior that allows an individual to change an unconstructive or disruptive behavior to something more constructive.

ADDICTION-BASED IMPAIRMENT: Brain damage is a common and potentially severe consequence of long-term, heavy substance abuse that specifically involves the impairment of cognitive functioning—mental activities related to acquiring, storing, retrieving, and using information.

ADDICTION MEDICINE: A medical specialty that deals with the treatment of addiction. Incorporated within the specialty are the processes of detoxification, rehabilitation, harm reduction, abstinence-based treatment, individual and group therapies, oversight of halfway houses, treatment of withdrawal-related symptoms, acute intervention, relapse prevention, and long-term therapies designed to fortify recovery.

ADDICTIONS WITHOUT SUBSTANCE: Psychological dependency on such things as gambling, food, sex, pornography, computers, video games, Internet, work, exercise, idolizing, watching TV or certain types of non-pornographic videos, spiritual obsession, cutting, and shopping may be counted as "addictions" as well and cause guilt, shame, fear, hopelessness, failure, rejection, anxiety, or humiliation.

ADDICTIVE DISORDER: A disorder characterized by the chronic use of an agent, resulting in the development of tolerance, physical dependence, and finally drug-seeking behavior.

ADJUSTMENT DISORDER: An adjustment disorder is an emotional or behavioral reaction to an identifiable stressful event or change in an individual's life that is considered maladaptive or somehow not an expected healthy response to the event or change. The reaction must occur within three months of the identified stressful event or change happening. The identifiable stressful event or change in the life of a child or adolescent may be a family move, parental divorce or separation, the loss of a pet, birth of a sibling, etc.

AFFECTIVE: Dynamics influenced by or resulting from the emotions. This pertains to arousing feelings or emotions.

ALGORITHMS: A step-by-step list of directions that need to be followed to solve a problem. The instructions should be simple enough so that each step can be done without thinking about it.

ALZHEIMER'S DISEASE: Alzheimer's disease is the most common cause of dementia—the loss of intellectual and social abilities severe enough to interfere with daily functioning. In Alzheimer's disease, healthy brain tissue degenerates, causing a steady decline in memory and mental abilities.

AMNESIA: A condition in which memory is disturbed or lost. Memory in this context refers either to stored memories or to the process of committing something to memory. The causes of amnesia have traditionally been divided into "organic" and "functional." Organic causes include damage to the brain, through physical injury, neurological disease, or the use of certain (generally sedative) drugs. Functional causes are psychological factors, such as mental disorder, posttraumatic stress or, in psychoanalytic terms, defense mechanisms.

ANABOLIC STEROIDS: Anabolic steroids are man-made substances related to male sex hormones. Medical uses of anabolic steroids include some hormone problems in men, late puberty, and muscle loss from some diseases. Psychoses can be produced by these drugs.

ANTISOCIAL BEHAVIOR: Behavior that lacks consideration for others and that may cause damage to society, whether intentionally or through negligence.

ANTISOCIAL DISORDERS: Include a long-standing pattern (after the age of 15) of disregard for the rights of others. There is a failure to conform to society's norms and expectations that often results in numerous arrests or legal involvement as well as a history of deceitfulness where the individual attempts to deceive people or use trickery for personal profit. Impulsiveness is often present, including angry outbursts, failure to consider consequences of behaviors, irritability, and/or physical assaults.

ANTISOCIAL PERSONALITY DISORDER: A pervasive type of chronic mental illness in which ways of thinking, perceiving situations, and relating to others are dysfunctional. This disorder involves a pervasive pattern of disregard for, and violation of, the rights of others that begins in childhood or early adolescence and continues into adulthood.

APPRAISALS: Provide insightful, objective information that is invaluable in the decision-making process, highlight areas of strength and those areas requiring further development, provide information relating to the most appropriate way to manage an individual.

ASPERGER'S DISORDER: A developmental disorder that affects an individual's ability to socialize and communicate effectively with others. Individuals with Asperger's disorder typically exhibit social awkwardness and an all-absorbing interest in specific, narrow topics.

ATAXIA: Ataxia describes a lack of muscle coordination during voluntary movements, such as walking or picking up objects. A sign of an underlying condition, ataxia can affect one's bodily movements, speech, eye movements, and the ability to swallow. Persistent ataxia usually results from damage to the cerebellum—the part of the brain that controls muscle coordination. Many conditions may cause ataxia, including alcohol abuse, stroke, tumor, cerebral palsy and multiple sclerosis. It is also possible to inherit a defective gene that may cause one of many ataxia variants.

AUTISM: One of a group of serious developmental problems called autism spectrum disorders (ASD) that appear in early childhood, usually before age 3. A pervasive developmental disorder characterized by severe deficits in social interaction and communication, by an extremely limited range of activities and interests, and often by the presence of repetitive, stereotyped behaviors.

Autoerotic Deaths: Individuals who engage in different types of autoerotic activities, such as hanging or certain types of bondage activities for purposes of sexual excitation, may experience unintentional death.

Automatism: Spontaneous verbal or motor behavior; an act performed unconsciously.

Autonomic Nervous System: The part of the peripheral nervous system that acts as a control system functioning largely below the level of consciousness, and controls visceral functions (i.e., reflex, etc.). The ANS affects heart rate, digestion, respiration rate, salivation, perspiration, diameter of the pupils, micturition (urination), and sexual arousal. Whereas most of its actions are involuntary, some, such as breathing, work in tandem with the conscious mind.

Axis I Diagnosis: Axis I diagnoses include the following: disorders evident from infancy/childhood/adolescence (ADHD, eating disorders, Tourette's), organic mental disorders (dementia arising from Alzheimer's, basically anything that has a physical medical cause, i.e., a brain tumor), psychoactive substance use disorders (drug dependence), psychosis (e.g., schizophrenia) mood disorders (depression, bipolar disorder), anxiety/neuroses (panic disorder, phobias, OCD, PTSD,) somatoform disorders, dissociative disorders (multiple personality disorder, psychogenic fugue), sexual disorders (exhibitionism, fetishism, etc.), sleep disorders.

Axis II Diagnosis: Axis II refers to the following: personality disorders (paranoid, avoidant, obsessive–compulsive, passive–aggressive, histrionic, borderline). Also includes developmental delays (mental retardation, autism, language and speech disorders, etc.).

B

Baseline Function: Provides data about a participant's performance prior to instituting an intervention. It also allows for predicting a participant's future performance in the absence of an intervention, and it indicates the normal variability in the participant's performance.

BEHAVIORAL SELF-REGULATION: Refers to the self-directive process through which patients transform their mental abilities into task related skills. This is the method or procedure that patients use to manage and organize their thoughts and convert them into skills used for learning. It is the process of continuously monitoring progress toward a goal, checking outcomes, and redirecting unsuccessful efforts. In order for patients to be self-regulated they need to be aware of their own thought process, and be motivated to participate actively in their own learning process.

BEST INTERESTS STANDARD: Primarily considering the rights and needs of children in custody matters.

BIPOLAR DISORDER: A mood disorder characterized by the occurrence of manic or hypomanic episodes, often in conjunction with major depressive episodes. Formerly labeled *manic depression*, accurate diagnosis of this condition is particularly dependent upon a thorough clinical history, as the patient may present as elated on one occasion and despondent on another.

BODY DYSMORPHIC DISORDER: A disorder that involves a pre-occupation with imagined or exaggerated defects in appearance or function. Unconsciously, the motivation may involve deep-seated and long-standing feelings of self-loathing, which are now projected onto a more objectifiable physical or mental impairment following an index injury or no injury.

BORDERLINE PERSONALITY DISORDER: A personality disorder described as a prolonged disturbance of personality function in an individual (generally over the age of 18 years, although it is also found in adolescents), characterized by depth and variability of moods. The disorder typically involves unusual levels of instability in mood; black-and-white thinking, or splitting. The disorder often manifests itself in over idealization and devaluation episodes, as well as chaotic and unstable interpersonal relationships, self-image, identity, and behavior, as well as a disturbance in the individual's sense of self. In extreme cases, this disturbance in the sense of self can lead to periods of dissociation.

BRAIN DAMAGE: The destruction or degeneration of brain cells, often with an implication that the loss is significant in terms of functioning or conscious experience. It is a common term that is very broad in scope, covering a vast range of specific diagnoses.

BRAIN DYSFUNCTION: Brain dysfunction may be widespread (diffuse) or limited to a specific area (localized). Diffuse dysfunction is caused by disorders that affect large areas of the brain (i.e., infections, very high or low blood pressure, metabolic abnormalities, severe or blunt head injuries, etc.) and localized brain dysfunction is caused by disorders that affect a specific area of the brain (i.e., tumors, strokes, penetrating injuries, etc.). Diffuse damage tends to affect consciousness, making arousal difficult (causing stupor) or impossible to arouse (causing coma). Localized damage tends to affect specific functions. However, the severity of brain dysfunction depends on the extent of brain damage as well as the specific location.

C

CARBOHYDRATE-DEFICIENT TRANSFERRIN: A laboratory test used to help detect heavy ethanol consumption. Carbohydrate-deficient transferrin is elevated in the blood of heavy alcoholism, but raised levels can also be found in a number of medical conditions.

CARDIOPULMONARY SYSTEM: The cardiopulmonary system consists of your heart and lungs, which are located in the thoracic cavity of the body. The most important function of the cardiopulmonary system is with respect to the flow and regulation of blood between the heart and the lungs, a process that centers on the connection between the heart and the lungs made through the pulmonary artery.

CEREBRAL HYPOXIA: Cerebral hypoxia technically means a lack of oxygen supply to the outer part of the brain, an area called the cerebral hemisphere. However, the term is more typically used to refer to a lack of oxygen supply to the entire brain. This condition may result in death. See Autoerotic Deaths.

CEREBROVASCULAR ACCIDENT: A cerebrovascular accident (CVA) is another name for a stroke. It is damage to the brain caused by a disruption of the blood supply to a part of the brain. This disruption of blood supply can be caused by a blood clot or by a ruptured artery. A CVA can affect cognition, speech, memory, and other mental functions.

CHEMICAL DEPENDENCE: This refers to a primary illness or disease that is characterized by addiction to a mood-altering chemical. Chemical dependency includes both drug addiction and alcoholism (addiction to the drug alcohol). A chemically dependent person is unable to stop drinking or taking a particular mood-altering chemical despite serious health, economic, vocational, legal, spiritual, and social consequences. It is a disease reflected across all demographics such as age, sex, race, religion, and economic status. It is progressive and chronic and if left untreated can be fatal.

CHILD ADVOCACY CENTER: In 1995, a small group of concerned professionals and community leaders met to consider a better, more sensitive way to respond to children who had been battered or sexually abused. These individuals envisioned a place where hurting children would have a safe, easy place to talk about difficult, frightening experiences. As a result of this commitment and concern, child advocacy centers were created.

CHRONIC PAIN: While acute pain is a normal sensation triggered in the nervous system to alert you to possible injury and the need to take care of yourself, chronic pain is different. Chronic pain persists. Pain signals keep firing in the nervous system for weeks, months, even years. There may have been an initial mishap (e.g., sprained back, serious infection), or there may be an ongoing cause of pain (e.g., arthritis, cancer, ear infection), but some people suffer chronic pain in the absence of any past injury or evidence of body damage. Many chronic pain conditions affect older adults. Common chronic pain complaints include headache, low back pain, cancer pain, arthritis pain, neurogenic pain (pain resulting from damage to the peripheral nerves or to the central nervous system itself), psychogenic pain (pain not due to past disease or injury or any visible sign of damage inside or outside the nervous system).

CLINICAL NEUROPSYCHOLOGY: This is a subspecialty of clinical psychology that focuses on the diagnostic assessment and treatment of patients with brain injury or neurocognitive deficits.

COGNITIVE: Comes from the Latin term, to think or perceive. It relates to conscious intellectual activity (as thinking, reasoning, or remembering) pertaining to the mental processes of perception, memory, judgment, and reasoning, as contrasted with emotional and volitional processes.

Cognitive–Behavioral Psychotherapy: Cognitive–behavioral therapy is based on the idea that our *thoughts* cause our feelings and behaviors, not external things, like people, situations, and events. The benefit of this fact is that we can change the way we think to feel/act better even if the situation does not change. This approach aims to teach the person new skills on how to solve problems concerning dysfunctional emotions, behaviors, and cognitions through a goal-oriented, systematic procedure.

Cognitive Decline: A decline in memory and thought processes.

Cognitive Impairment: A condition, typically found in children, where the child has some type of problems with their ability to think and learn. This condition most readily presents itself when the child is at school and expresses difficulty with subjects such as reading or mathematics, involving far more problems than expected for a child with normal development at his or her chronological age.

Cognitive Status: Current level of functioning involving thought and perception at a given time.

Compulsive Gambling: An uncontrollable urge to gamble despite harmful negative consequences or a desire to stop.

Convergent Validity: When records reviewed by multiple sources come to the same conclusion.

Conversion Disorder: Here, the essential feature is the presence of sensory or motor deficits that appear to suggest a neurological or medical illness or injury. The unconscious motivation typically involves the attempted resolution of psychological conflicts, such as dependency wishes, by channeling them into physical impairment. Alternatively, there may be an actual symbolic "conversion" of a particular psychological conflict into a representative somatic expression. Exacerbations are typically precipitated by psychosocial stresses related to job or family—or the stress of the accident itself—with resultant financial and legal hassles.

D

Dangerousness: A nonmedical term used to denote risk; causing danger; perilous; risky; hazardous; unsafe; able or likely to cause physical injury:

DECISION-MAKING CAPACITY: The ability of an individual to make his/her own health care decisions. Questions of capacity sometimes extend to other contexts, such as capacity to stand trial in a court of law, and the ability to make decisions that relate to personal care and finances.

DELIRIUM: A serious disturbance in a person's mental abilities that results in a decreased awareness of one's environment and confused thinking. The onset of delirium is usually sudden, often within hours or a few days. Delirium can usually be traced to one or more contributing factors, such as a severe or chronic medical illness, medication, surgery, or drug or alcohol abuse.

DELUSION: False belief: a persistent false belief held in the face of strong contradictory evidence, especially as a symptom of a psychiatric condition; mistaken notion: a false or mistaken belief or idea about something inconsistent with cultural beliefs.

DELUSIONAL THINKING: Delusional thinking is characterized by the presence of recurrent, persistent non-bizarre delusions that are inconsistent with cultural beliefs. When this is ongoing or pervasive, it is referred to as a delusional disorder.

DEMENTIA: Dementia isn't a specific disease. Instead, it describes a group of symptoms affecting intellectual and social abilities severely enough to interfere with daily functioning. It is caused by conditions or changes in the brain. Different types of dementia exist, depending on the cause. Alzheimer's disease is the most common type of dementia. Memory loss generally occurs in dementia, but memory loss alone doesn't mean one has dementia. Dementia indicates problems with at least two brain functions, such as memory loss along with impaired judgment or language. It can cause confusion and the inability to remember people and names. It may accompany changes in personality and social behavior. However, some causes of dementia are treatable and even reversible.

DEVELOPMENTAL LIMITATIONS: These include a delay with typical developmental abilities (i.e., speech, ambulation, etc.).

DISORIENTATION: Loss of one's sense of direction, position, or relationship with one's surroundings. Mental confusion or impaired awareness, especially regarding place, time, or personal identity.

DISSOCIATION: A trance state representing a partial or complete disruption of the normal integration of a person's conscious or psychological functioning. Dissociation can be normal, as in day-dreaming, or a response to trauma or drugs and perhaps allowing the mind to distance itself from experiences that are too much for the psyche to process at that time. Although some dissociative disruptions involve amnesia, the vast majority of dissociative events do not. (See "Multiple Personality Disorder" and "Dissociative Identity Disorder" following).

DISSOCIATIVE EVENTS: Dissociation involves a disruption of episodic memory—we expect there to be a continuity of historical memories but suddenly there is a deficit that cannot be accounted for (i.e., people experience themselves simply spacing out for a period of time and wondering what just happened).

DISSOCIATIVE IDENTITY DISORDER (DID):   A severe form of dissociation, a mental process, which produces a lack of connection with a person's thoughts, memories, feelings, actions, or sense of identity. DID is believed to stem from a particular trauma or series of traumas during one's lifetime. The dissociative aspect is thought to be a coping mechanism—the person literally dissociates him/herself from a situation or experience that is too violent, traumatic, or painful to assimilate within the conscious self.

DYSARTHRIA: A condition that results in distorted speech. It results in difficulty with controlling or coordinating the muscles you use when you speak, or weakness of those muscles. Dysarthria is often characterized by slurred or slow speech that can be difficult to understand. Common causes of dysarthria include stroke, brain injury, brain tumor, conditions that cause facial paralysis or weakness, and degenerative disorders. Dysarthria may also be caused by certain medications, such as sedatives or narcotics.

DYSFUNCTION: A patient's mental or physical abnormality leading to clinical distress and typically symptomatic of a diagnosable disorder.

DYSTHYMIC DISORDER: This mood disorder reflects chronically depressed mood that is manifested for the bulk of the day during the majority of days in any minimum 2-year period.

E

ELECTROCONVULSIVE THERAPY (ECT):   A procedure in which electric currents are passed through the brain, deliberately triggering a brief seizure. Electroconvulsive therapy seems to cause changes in brain chemistry that can immediately reverse symptoms of certain mental illnesses. It often works when other treatments are unsuccessful. This procedure may be conducted bilaterally or unilaterally and usually causes retrograde amnesia as a side effect.

ELECTROENCEPHALOGRAPH (EEG): An instrument used for recording the electrical activity of the brain, usually by means of electrodes placed over the scalp. It is used to diagnose tumors of the brain or to study brain waves, etc.

EMPIRICAL STUDIES: This involves a manner of gaining knowledge by means of direct observation or experience. It is used to answer research questions, which must be precisely defined and explained using data. These data can then be tested with a suitable experimental design. Depending on the outcomes of the experiment, the theory on which the hypotheses and predictions were based will be either supported or rejected.

ENCEPHALITIS: Although the term *encephalitis* literally means "inflammation of the brain," it usually refers to brain inflammation resulting from a viral infection. Encephalitis may lead to dementia and other neurological and psychological conditions.

ENCEPHALOPATHY: A condition characterized by altered brain function and structure. It is caused by diffuse brain disease.

EPIDEMIOLOGICAL DATA: The data collected from public health research that helps inform evidence-based medicine for identifying risk factors for disease and determining optimal treatment approaches to clinical practice and for preventative medicine.

EQUIVOCAL DEATH PSYCHOLOGICAL AUTOPSY (EDPA): The EDPA is a separate and distinct procedure in which the primary purpose is to assist in the actual determination and the manner of death classification; that is, why a particular individual died and whether it was due to suicide, homicide, accidental death, death by natural causes, or due to an undetermined reason.

ETIOLOGICAL: Relating to the cause or origin of a disease.

EXAGGERATION: The patient has true symptoms or impairments caused by the injury, but represents them to be worse than they truly are. This is probably the most common form of malingering in clinical forensic practice.

EXHIBITIONISM: The pattern of behavior displaying naked parts of the body to other people. The display can be quick or prolonged to

one or more unsuspecting individuals, usually for the purpose of
shocking the victim.

EXTENSION: A patient has experienced symptoms or impairments
caused by the injury, and these have now recovered or improved,
but he/she may falsely represent them as continuing unabated, or
even as having worsened over time.

F

FABRICATION: The patient has no symptoms or impairments resulting from a specific injury or condition, but represents that he/
she has. Symptoms may be atypical, inconsistent, or bizarre, or
they may be perfect "textbook" replicas of genuine syndromes.
In common litigation practice, this wholesale invention of an
impairment syndrome is the rarest form of malingering.

FACTITIOUS DISORDER: This is diagnostically separated from the
somatoform disorders, and is defined as the deliberate production, manipulation, or feigning of physical or psychological signs
and symptoms. Because the intentionality of symptom production
is conscious and deliberate, it is not classified as a somatoform
disorder; however, unlike malingering, where a utilitarian motive
for the deception can usually be discerned (e.g., money), the
motive in factitious disorder is typically to assume the sick role,
with all the attendant care, solicitous concern, and relief from
responsibilities of normal life that this entails, even at the price
of substantial cost in money, health, or freedom.

FALSE-NEGATIVE RATE: The proportions of cases in which a diagnostic test indicates no disease for a diseased patient.

FALSE-POSITIVE RATE: The proportions of cases in which a diagnostic
test indicates a disease for a disease-free patient.

FAMILY EDUCATIONAL RIGHTS AND PRIVACY ACT: The Family Educational Rights and Privacy Act of 1974 (FERPA) is an amendment to
the Elementary and Secondary Education Act of 1965. Schools will
only receive funds if they adhere to pupil record-keeping procedures outlined in this law. The law protects confidentiality and
parent access to school records about their children. Parents have
access to all official school records of their children, the right
to challenge the accuracy of those records, and have the right to
have a hearing regarding their accuracy. Moreover, student

records are only available to those in the school setting with legitimate educational interest, and parent consent must be obtained before records are shared with outside agencies.

FIVE AXES: A five-level diagnostic system published by the American Psychiatric Association to classify illnesses and disorders. When considered together, these five levels give the treatment provider a complete diagnosis that includes factors influencing a psychiatric condition. This is important for effective treatment planning.

Axis I is reserved for clinical disorders and developmental and learning disorders.

Axis II is for personality disorders or mental retardation.

Axis III is for medical and/or physical conditions or disorders.

Axis IV indicates factors contributing to, or affecting, the current psychiatric disorder and treatment outcomes, usually called "stressors."

Axis V is reserved for the GAF (global assessment functioning).

FORENSIC COUNTERTRANSFERENCE: The surfacing of a forensic evaluator's own repressed feelings through identification with the emotions, experiences, or problems of a person undergoing evaluation, or feelings toward the attorneys in the case. Rendering a completely unbiased forensic opinion is full of challenges, because of conscious and unconscious responses to evaluees or attorneys. The forensic psychiatrist/psychologist may be affected by the nature of the alleged crime and/or by the potential effects of the evaluation on the outcome of the trial.

FORENSIC PSYCHIATRIST: Forensic psychiatrists may work with courts evaluating an individual's competency to stand trial, defenses based on mental diseases or defects (e.g., the "insanity" defense), and sentencing recommendations. There are two major areas of criminal evaluations in forensic psychiatry. These are competency to stand trial (CST) and mental state at the time of the offence (MSO). Forensic psychiatrists also conduct evaluations in civil and administrative proceedings that include civil competence, will contests, defenses, and emotional injuries among other issues.

FORENSIC PSYCHOLOGIST: Forensic psychologists work with courts in evaluating the defendant's sanity or insanity (which relates to criminal responsibility) at the time of the offense. Forensic psychologists provide sentencing recommendations, treatment recommendations, and any other information the judge requests, such as information regarding mitigating factors, assessment of future risk, and evaluation of witness credibility. Forensic psychologists also conduct evaluations in civil and administrative proceedings that include civil competence, will contests, defenses, and emotional injuries among other issues.

G

Gamblers Anonymous (GA): A 12-step program for problem gamblers. The only requirement for GA membership is a desire to stop gambling.

Gender Identity Disorders: This is a formal diagnosis used by psychologists and physicians to describe individuals who experience significant gender dysphoria (discontent with the biological sex that they were born with).

General Tonic–Clonic Seizures: Tonic–clonic seizures (formerly known as grand mal seizures) are a type of generalized seizure that affects the entire brain. Tonic–clonic seizures are the seizure type most commonly associated with epilepsy and seizures in general, though it is a misconception that they are the only type. Such seizures may be malingered.

H

Hallucinations: This involves sensing things while awake that appear to be real, when they have actually been created by the mind, for example: feeling bodily sensations (tactile hallucinations), such as a crawling feeling on the skin or the movement of internal organs; hearing sounds (auditory hallucinations), such as music, footsteps, windows or doors banging; hearing voices when no one has spoken (the most common type of hallucination) (these voices may be critical, complimentary, neutral, or may command someone to do something that may cause harm to themselves or to others); seeing patterns, lights, beings, or objects that aren't there (visual hallucinations); smelling a foul or pleasant odor (olfactory hallucinations); and taste distortions (gustatory hallucinations).

Hallucinatory Experiences: Hallucinatory experiences commonly are associated with psychiatric or medical illness. However, they can occur also in "normal" individuals, and more people experience hallucinations than come into contact with psychiatric services. Reports of cultural and ethnic variation in the experience of hallucinations also suggest that hallucinations are not necessarily pathological phenomena.

HIGHER FUNCTIONING AUTISM SPECTRUM: High-functioning autism is at one end of the autistic spectrum. Signs and symptoms are less severe than with other forms of autism. In fact, an individual with high-functioning autism usually has average or above average intelligence.

HISTRIONIC DISORDER: Histrionic personality disorder (HPD) is defined by the American Psychiatric Association as a personality disorder characterized by a pattern of excessive emotionality and attention seeking, including an excessive need for approval and inappropriate seductiveness, usually beginning in early adulthood. These individuals are lively, dramatic, enthusiastic, and flirtatious.

HYPERACTIVITY: Hyperactivity can be described as a physical state in which a person is abnormally and easily excitable or exuberant. Strong emotional reactions, impulsive behavior, and sometimes a short span of attention are also typical for a hyperactive person.

HYPERTHYROIDISM: Hyperthyroidism (overactive thyroid) is a condition in which the thyroid gland produces too much of the hormone thyroxine. Hyperthyroidism can significantly accelerate the body's metabolism, causing sudden weight loss, a rapid or irregular heartbeat, sweating, and nervousness or irritability. The hypermetabolic state may rarely simulate mania or hypomania.

HYPERVIGILANCE: Abnormally increased arousal, responsiveness to stimuli, and scanning of the environment for threats.

HYPOCHONDRIASIS: The conviction that one has a serious illness or injury, in the face of numerous medical pronouncements to the contrary. Unlike somatization disorder, hypochondriacs tend to focus on one or a few chosen symptoms and remain preoccupied with them, although the focus may shift over time from one symptom or disorder to another, e.g., from memory impairment to headaches to dizziness to limb weakness. Unlike conversion disorder, there may be no actual observed or experienced impairment per se: It is the *fear* of dire impairment that is the problem.

Often, the unconscious motivation involves a deflection of anxiety away from issues of broader psychosocial concern, such as career or relationships, with a focus on a more delimited, and hence "controllable" source of concern in the form of somatic symptoms and fear of further injury.

Hypothyroidism: Hypothyroidism (underactive thyroid) is a condition in which the thyroid gland doesn't produce enough of certain important hormones. This disorder may simulate depression by causing lethargy, lack of energy, and other symptoms.

I

Ictal Phase: A major motor seizure is known as a grand mal or a tonic–clonic seizure. These seizures occur in three phases. The first is the preictal or aura phase. It is followed by the ictal phase, which is the seizure itself. The final stage is the postictal phase.

Idiosyncratic: A characteristic, habit, mannerism, or the like, that is peculiar to an individual.

Imaging: The visual examination of an object, such as a body part, for the purpose of medical diagnosis, using any of a variety of usually computerized techniques, such as ultrasonography or spectroscopy.

IME: Abbreviation for the term *independent medical evaluation*. This involves an examination that is intended to be completely objective.

Impaired Memory: Inability to remember or recall bits of information or behavioral skills. Impaired memory may be attributed to pathophysiological or situational causes that are either temporary or permanent.

Individuals with Disabilities Education Improvement Act: The Individuals with Disabilities Education Improvement Act of 2004 (IDEIA) is probably the most important piece of federal legislation to know and understand for those conducting forensic assessments in the schools. Previously known as the Education for the Handicapped Act (EHA) before it was transformed into the Individuals with Disabilities Education Act (IDEA), the IDEIA provides funds to various states that provide free and appropriate education (FAPE) to all children with disabilities. Under the IDEIA, FAPE is defined as an educational program that is individualized to a specific child, designed to meet that child's unique needs, provides access to the general curriculum, meets the grade-level standards established by the state, and from which the child receives educational benefit. In order to receive these funds, states must demonstrate that students with disabilities receive special education and related services in accordance with an individualized education program.

INTERRATER RELIABILITY: The extent to which two or more individuals (coders or raters) agree. Interrater reliability addresses the consistency of the implementation of a rating system and is an important feature with certain psychological measures.

INTERSCORER RELIABILITY: The degree of consistency among different persons scoring data on the same performance.

INTOXICATION: A state in which a person's normal capacity to act or reason is inhibited by alcohol or drugs.

K

KLEPTOMANIA: The irresistible urge to steal items that one really does not need and usually have little value. It's a serious mental health disorder that can result in criminal penalties.

L

LDs: Learning disabilities that affect one's academic performance, such as reading, mathematics, and spelling.

LIFE THREATENING: Causing fear or anxiety by threatening great harm; "a dangerous operation"; "a grave situation"; "a grave illness"; "grievous bodily harm"; "a serious wound"; "a serious turn of events"; "a severe case of pneumonia"; "a life-threatening disease."

M

MAJOR DEPRESSIVE DISORDER: Major depressive disorder affects how one feels, thinks and behaves. Depression can lead to a variety of emotional and physical problems. The individual may have trouble doing normal day-to-day activities, and depression may make you feel as if life isn't worth living. It is chronic and is differentiated from dysthymia (q.v.).

MALINGERING: The intentional production of false or grossly exaggerated physical or psychological symptoms, motivated by external incentives such as avoiding military duty, avoiding work, obtaining financial compensation, evading criminal prosecution, or obtaining drugs.

MANIA: A state of abnormally elevated or irritable mood, arousal, and/or energy levels. In a sense, it is the opposite of depression.

MEDICAL ECONOMIST: A medical economist performs in-depth analysis, conducts research and creates reports for the purpose of understanding and improving services surrounding various areas of health care. Forensic economists may testify as to economic damages and expected earnings of decedents.

MENTAL STATUS EXAMINATION: This is a structured manner of observing and describing a patient's current state of mind, under the domains of appearance, attitude, behavior, mood and affect, speech, thought process, thought content, perception, cognition, insight, and judgment. It allows the clinician to make an accurate diagnosis and formulation, which is required for coherent treatment planning.

METABOLIC DERANGEMENTS: A metabolic disorder or derangement occurs when abnormal chemical reactions in one's body disrupt the metabolic process.

METHODOLOGICAL RIGOR: Commitment to a specific process in research that will produce an outcome that is factual and complete.

METHODOLOGY: A body of practices, procedures, and rules used by those who work in a discipline or engage in an inquiry; a set of working methods.

MISATTRIBUTION: Symptoms or impairments that preceded, postdated, or were otherwise unrelated to the index injury, but are fraudulently or mistakenly attributed to that injury. In forensic personal injury settings, exaggeration of existing symptoms is generally more frequent than pure malingering of totally nonexistent illnesses or injuries. Other syndromes commonly seen in a personal injury context include the somatoform disorders and factitious disorder. Note that these do *not* represent conscious malingering and *are* considered bona fide mental disorders: hence, if they can be attributed to the index injury, they may represent additional compensable psychological disabilities in and of themselves.

MIXED SUBSTANCE ABUSE: Otherwise known as polysubstance abuse. The simultaneous use of more than one form of illicit substance (i.e., cocaine and marijuana, etc.).

MONOMANIA: Pathological obsession with one idea or subject. Intense concentration on or exaggerated enthusiasm for a single subject or idea.

MULTIPLE PERSONALITY DISORDER (MPD): Rare condition indicated by the absence of a clear and comprehensive identity. In most cases, two or more independent and distinct personality systems develop in the same individual. Each personality may alternately inhabit the person's conscious awareness to the exclusion of the others, but one is usually dominant. The various personalities typically differ from one another in outlook, temperament, and body language and might assume different first names. The condition is generally viewed as resulting from dissociative mental processes—that is, the splitting off from conscious awareness and control of thoughts, feelings, memories, and other mental components in response to situations that are painful, disturbing, or somehow unacceptable to the person experiencing them. Treatment is aimed at integrating the disparate personalities back into a single and unified personality (see "Dissociative Identity Disorder" above).

MUSCLE RIGIDITY: Muscle rigidity is an alteration of muscle tone in which the muscles are in an involuntary state of continual tension. Muscle rigidity can be a manifestation of neurological damage (basal ganglia diseases) or a side effect of certain medications. Muscle rigidity is the continuous, tonic contraction of the skeletal muscles, often more marked in the flexor muscles than extensors.

N

NARCISSISTIC: Characterized by self-admiration: excessive self-admiration and self-centeredness, inordinate fascination with oneself; excessive self-love; vanity.

NARCISSISTIC PERSONALITY DISORDER: A disorder involving excessive preoccupation with issues of personal adequacy, power, and prestige.

NEUROCOGNITIVE DISORDERS: A reduction or impairment of cognitive function in certain areas of the brain, but particularly when physical changes can be seen to have occurred in the brain, such as after neurological illness, mental illness, drug use, or brain injury.

NEURODEGENERATIVE DEMENTIA: A multifaceted cognitive impairment that is usually progressive, and always involves "functional" impairments. Individuals affected are unable to engage in everyday activities such as spoken and written communication, grooming, preparing meals, driving, and leisure activities. The neurodegenerative dementias are progressive and irreversible due to deterioration of brain cells and their interconnections. There are four major types of neurodegenerative dementias-Alzheimer's dementia (AD), vascular dementia (VaD), Lewy body dementia (LBD), and frontotemporal lobar dementia (FTD).

NEURODEVELOPMENT: Comprises the processes that generate, shape, and reshape the nervous system, from the earliest stages of embryogenesis to the final years of life.

NEUROIMAGING: Includes the use of various techniques to either directly or indirectly image the structure, function/pharmacology of the brain.

NEUROLOGICAL IMPAIRMENT: Refers to a broad group of disorders in which the central nervous system does not function properly and leads to some form of physical or mental problems. The central nervous system is made up of the brain and the spinal cord. A neurological impairment, which affects the brain or spinal cord, can affect a wide range of different capabilities, from motor skills to memory.

NEUROLOGICAL TRAUMAS: Direct physical injury to the brain or spinal cord.

NEUROTRANSMITTER FUNCTIONING: Neurotransmitters function by changing the permeability of the cell membrane to various ions such as sodium and potassium. If an excess of sodium ions flow into the nerve cell, an impulse is generated. If an excess of potassium ions flow out, the impulse is inhibited. Sometimes the receptor cell receives a number of different messages at the same time, which may cancel one another out. By their effects on the receiving cells, neurotransmitters coordinate behavior. The number and kind of neurotransmitter molecules received by the receptor cell, as well as the type of receptor, determines whether the effect will be to stimulate or to inhibit. Many psychiatrically prescribed medications exert their effects through their influence on neurotransmitters.

NO CHILD LEFT BEHIND ACT: The No Child Left Behind Act (NCLB) of 2001 furthered the Elementary and Secondary Education Act of 1965 to include stricter regulations about how federal monies could be used and provided assistance to schools with students with low socioeconomic status. The purpose of NCLB is to close achievement gaps with a combination of accountability, flexibility, and choice. The NCLB requires statewide reading and mathematics tests each year for students grades 3 through 8. Each state was charged with achieving academic proficiency for all students within 12 years, and districts were to document progress towards that goal each year. The NCLB enables public school choice for pupils, and required heightened qualifications for classroom teaching.

NONORGANIC BRAIN SYNDROMES: Brain syndromes that are not due to medical etiology, but are a result of external factors, such as head trauma.

NUTRITIONAL DEFICIENCIES: Any deficiency of the nutrients that are required to sustain human life. A state where an individual's intake of nutrients is insufficient for the body's normal functioning. The body needs a regular intake of many nutrients such as calcium and phosphorus for bones and protein for muscles and energy.

O

OBJECTIVE MEASURE: Those measures that are not dependent primarily on the judgment of the examiner. Such measures typically involve the use of instrumentation and are expressed in real numbers.

OBJECTIVE PERSONALITY TESTING: Assessment methods that use a restricted response format (ordinal scale ratings or true/false questions), and which contain extensively tested validity scales to determine whether the person taking the test is responding truthfully. The Minnesota Multiphasic Personality Inventory (MMPI) is a well-known objective personality test.

OPEN-ENDED INTERVIEW: An open-ended interview is designed to encourage full, meaningful answers using the subject's own knowledge and/or feelings. It is the opposite of a *closed-ended interview*, which encourages short or single-word answers.

ORGANIC BRAIN DISORDER: A general term used to describe decreased mental function due to a medical disease, other than a psychiatric illness.

P

PAIN DISORDER: The essential feature of this condition is chronic pain that causes significant distress or impairment in social, occupational, or other important areas of functioning, and in which psychological factors are judged to play a significant role in the onset, severity, exacerbation, or maintenance of the pain. The pain is not intentionally produced or feigned as malingering or factitious disorder, but rather expresses, represents, or disguises an unconscious need, fear, or somatization disorder.

PAIN INVENTORIES: A method used to provide information on the intensity of pain (the sensory dimension) as well as the degree to which pain interferes with function (the reactive dimension), as well as to ask questions about pain relief, pain quality, and the patient's perception of the cause of pain.

PARANOID IDEATION: An exaggerated, sometimes grandiose, belief or suspicion, usually not of a delusional nature, that one is being harassed, persecuted, or treated unfairly, or beliefs involving general suspiciousness about others' motives or intent.

PARANOID PERSONALITY DISORDER: A psychiatric diagnosis characterized by paranoia and a pervasive, long-standing suspiciousness and generalized mistrust of others. Those with the condition are hypersensitive, are easily slighted, and habitually relate to the world by vigilant scanning of the environment for clues or suggestions to validate their prejudicial ideas or biases. Paranoid individuals are eager observers. They believe that they are in danger and look for signs and threats of that danger, disregarding any facts. They tend to be guarded and suspicious and have quite constricted emotional lives. Their incapacity for meaningful emotional involvement and the general pattern of isolated withdrawal often lend a quality of isolation to their life experience.

PARAPHILIC SEXUAL BEHAVIOR: A biomedical term used to describe sexual arousal to objects, situations, or individuals that are not part of normative stimulation and that may cause distress or serious problems for the paraphiliac or persons associated with him or her. A paraphilia involves sexual arousal and gratification toward sexual behavior that is atypical and extreme.

PATHOGNOMONIC: Specifically distinctive or characteristic of a disease or pathologic condition; denoting a sign or symptom on which a diagnosis can be made.

PATHOPHYSIOLOGICAL DEMENTIA: The functional changes associated with or resulting from disease or injury to the brain.

PEDOPHILIA: A paraphilia in which a person has intense and recurrent sexual urges toward and fantasies about prepubescent children and on which feelings they have either acted or which cause distress or interpersonal difficulty.

PERSONALITY DISORDER: A personality disorder is a type of mental illness in which one has trouble perceiving and relating to situations and to people. There are many specific types of personality disorders. In general, having a personality disorder denotes a rigid and unhealthy pattern of thinking and behaving no matter what the situation. This leads to significant problems and limitations in relationships, social encounters, work, and school.

PERSONALITY STRUCTURE: The basic psychological components or traits of an individual's personality and how they combine together to produce that individual's particular behavioral tendencies in certain situations.

PERSONALITY TESTING: Common personality tests consist of a large number of items, where respondents must rate the applicability of each item to themselves. Projective tests, such as the Thematic Apperception Test (TAT) and the Rorshcach Ink Blots are another form of personality test which attempt to assess personality indirectly. These tests aim to describe aspects of an individual's character that remain stable throughout that person's lifetime, the individual's character pattern of behavior, thoughts, and feelings. Some tests attempt to identify specific characteristics, while others attempt to identify personality as a whole.

PHALLOMETRY: A type of plethysmography that measures changes in blood flow in the penis. Phallometry is typically employed in order to determine the degree of sexual arousal occasioned by exposure to various stimuli.

PLETHYSMOGRAPHY: The measurement of blood flow in or through a bodily organ.

Polysubstance Abuse: Physical dependence on at least three substances that have been classified as habit forming, but without any one of the substances having greater importance or influence than the others. The concept does not include caffeine or nicotine.

Postconcussion Syndrome (PCS): A set of symptoms that an individual may experience for weeks, months, or occasionally up to a year or more after a concussion—a mild form of traumatic brain injury. PCS may also occur in moderate and severe cases of traumatic brain injury.

Post Hoc Assessment: A method of determining whether one event is asserted to be the cause of a later event simply by virtue of it having happened earlier.

Postpartum Depression: A form of clinical depression which can affect women after childbirth. Postpartum depression occurs in women after they have carried a child, usually in the first few months, and may last up to several months or even a year. Symptoms include sadness, fatigue, changes in sleeping and eating patterns, reduced libido, crying episodes, anxiety, and irritability.

Postpartum Psychosis: While it is the most extreme form of postpartum mood disorders, postpartum psychosis is also one of the rarest of the disorder. Usually described as a period when a woman loses touch with reality, the disorder occurs in women who have recently given birth. It affects between one and two per 1,000 women who have given birth.

Posttraumatic Stress Disorder (PTSD): A severe anxiety disorder that can develop after exposure to any event that results in psychological trauma. This event may involve the threat of death to oneself or to someone else, or to one's own or someone else's physical, sexual, or psychological integrity, overwhelming the individual's ability to cope. As an effect of psychological trauma, PTSD is less frequent and more enduring than the more commonly seen acute stress response.

Preexisting Disorders: Disorders that existed prior to the onset of a current condition and that may be affecting that specific condition.

Projective Personality Testing: A test in which the individual offers responses to ambiguous scenes, words, or images. This type of test emerged from the psychoanalytic school of thought, which suggested that people have unconscious thoughts or urges. These projective tests were intended to uncover such unconscious desires that are hidden from conscious awareness. The best-known projective psychological test is the Rorschach Inkblot Test.

PROTOCOL-DRIVEN INTERVIEWS: Interviews that are based on a specific set of criteria, usually with the aim of maintaining a consistent standard or uniformity.

PSEUDO-DEMENTIA: A syndrome seen in older people in which they exhibit symptoms consistent with dementia but the cause is a preexisting psychiatric illness (commonly a depression) rather than a degenerative one.

PSYCHOACTIVE CHEMICAL: A chemical substance that crosses the blood-brain barrier and acts primarily upon the central nervous system where it affects brain function, resulting in changes in perception, mood, consciousness, cognition, and behavior. These drugs may be used recreationally, to purposefully alter one's consciousness for ritual or spiritual purposes, as a tool for studying or augmenting the mind, or therapeutically as medication. These medications can be classed as tranquilizers, antidepressants, stimulants, and sedatives.

PSYCHOLOGICAL AUTOPSY: Psychological autopsy (PA) is often used to assist medical examiners in death classifications, particularly when there is some doubt as to whether or not a decedent committed suicide.

PSYCHOLOGICAL TRAUMA: A type of damage to the psyche that occurs as a result of a traumatic event. Psychological trauma may accompany physical trauma or exist independently of it. Typical causes of psychological trauma include exposure to sexual abuse, bullying, domestic violence, and alcoholism—particularly when this exposure occurs during childhood. Catastrophic events such as earthquakes and volcanic eruptions, war or other mass violence can also cause psychological trauma. Long-term exposure to situations such as extreme poverty or milder forms of abuse, such as verbal abuse, can be traumatic (though verbal abuse can also potentially be traumatic as a single event).

PSYCHOMETRIC ASSESSMENT: There are two types of psychometric assessments—ability or aptitude tests and work styles questionnaires (personality/motivation/emotional intelligence). Ability or aptitude tests provide information on a person's ability to perform certain tasks and their potential to learn and understand new information and tasks. Work style questionnaires or inventories are concerned with how you typically behave, such as the way you relate to others or the way you approach and solve problems. They generally explore personality characteristics relevant to the world of work.

PSYCHOMETRICS: The field of study concerned with the theory and technique of educational and psychological measurement, which includes the measurement of knowledge, abilities, attitudes, and personality traits. The field is primarily concerned with the construction and validation of measurement instruments, such as questionnaires, tests, and personality assessments.

PSYCHOMETRIC TESTING: Any standardized procedure for measuring sensitivity or memory or intelligence or aptitude or personality, etc.

PSYCHOPATHOLOGY: The study of mental illness; mental distress; and abnormal, maladaptive behavior. The term is most commonly used within the field of psychiatry and clinical psychology where pathology refers to disease processes.

PSYCHOSEXUAL HISTORY: Designed for use with individuals referred for psychological or forensic evaluation following allegations of sexual abuse. The clinician will find that it is very comprehensive and addresses several broad areas of life history: physical features, health information, personality styles, parental and family history, childhood/adolescent development history, education history, work history (adult only), substance abuse history, sex history, marital history (adult only), childhood/adolescent behavioral history, adult behavioral history, treatment history, and allegation information.

PSYCHOTROPIC MEDICATION: A chemical compound that crosses the blood–brain barrier and acts primarily upon the central nervous system where it affects brain function, resulting in changes in perception, mood, consciousness, cognition, and behavior.

PYROMANIA: A deliberate impulse to start fires to relieve tension, typically including feelings of gratification or relief afterward. Pyromaniacs start fires to induce euphoria, and often fixate on institutions of fire control like fire stations and firefighters. They may also be set due to a need to express crisis in one's life.

Q

QUANTITATIVE ANALYSIS: Determination of the relative amounts of the components of a substance.

R

REHABILITATION CONSULTANT: A professional who provides assistance to people in obtaining the best possible drug or alcohol treatment, drawing opon that professional's wider range of experience. Rehabilitation consultants provide both profit and nonprofit services to individuals in need.

RELIABLE MEASURE: The consistency of a set of measurements or of a measuring instrument, often used to describe a test.

S

SCHIZOPHRENIA: A group of severe brain disorders in which people interpret reality abnormally. Schizophrenia may result in some combination of hallucinations, delusions, and disordered thinking and behavior. The ability of people with schizophrenia to function normally and to care for themselves tends to deteriorate over time.

SECONDARY GAIN: Secondary gain can be a component of any disease, but is an external motivator. If an individual's disease allows him/her to miss work, gains him/her sympathy, or avoids a jail sentence, these would be examples of secondary gain. These may, but need not be, recognized by the individual. If he/she is deliberately exaggerating symptoms for personal gain, then he/she is malingering. However, secondary gain may simply be an unconscious psychological component of symptoms and other disorders.

SLEEP APNEA: A common disorder in which one has one or more pauses in breathing or shallow breaths during sleep activity. Breathing pauses can last from a few seconds to minutes. They often occur 5 to 30 times or more an hour. Typically, normal breathing then starts again, sometimes with a loud snort or choking sound. Sleep apnea is usually a chronic (ongoing) condition that disrupts one's sleep and may cause psychological effects.

SOCIAL SCIENCE: The study of human society and of individual relationships in and to society.

Sociopathic Traits: Most obvious traits of a sociopath predominantly have a hint of antisocial behavior, which begins in early childhood. Some of the most prominent traits include: manipulative, charming in nature, pathological lying, lacking remorse, lacking emotional expression, being unreliable and egomaniacal.

Sociopathy: A pervasive pattern of disregard for, and violation of, the rights of others that begins in childhood or early adolescence and continues into adulthood; this term is often used interchangeably with the term *psychopathy*.

Sodium Amytal Interview: During an Amytal interview, the physician administers small amounts of Sodium Amytal, a sedative, through the veins every few minutes. The procedure usually takes about an hour. The patient is drowsy and slurred of speech, but awake—the so-called "twilight state" for the duration of the interview. Intravenous Amytal causes a feeling of relaxation, warmth, and closeness to the interviewer; while in this state, the patient is questioned (see also "Sodium Pentothal Interview" below).

Sodium Pentothal Interview: A process used to procure vital information from patients in the practice of forensic interrogation. It involves administering Sodium Thiopental, a short-acting barbiturate that makes patients more compliant to interrogative pressure during an interviewing (see also "Sodium Amytal Interview" above).

Somatic Feigning: A condition in which a person acts as if he or she has an illness by deliberately producing, feigning, or exaggerating symptoms.

Somatization Disorder: This involves a history of multiple unexplained physical symptoms and complaints, beginning before age 30, and often traced to childhood and adolescence, considered to be bodily expressions of psychological issues.

Somatoform Disorders: The common feature of the *somatoform disorders* is the presence of subjective physical symptoms that suggest a medical illness or syndrome, but are not fully explainable by, or attributable to, a general medical condition, substance abuse, or other type of mental disorder.

Standard Objective Measure: A measurement in which all research and practice relevant to a particular variable can be conducted in uniform terms.

STATISTICAL PREVALENCE: A statistic of primary interest in public health because it identifies the level of burden of disease or health-related events on the population and health care system. Prevalence represents new and preexisting cases alive on a certain date, in contrast to incidence which reflects new cases of a condition diagnosed during a given period of time.

SUBSTANCE ABUSE: The overindulgence in and dependence on an addictive substance, especially alcohol or a narcotic drug.

SUNDOWNING: The time of day can significantly affect those over 60 years of age who may be less clear and more symptomatic by the afternoon and evening. The effect of this particular form of delirium occurs due to the decrease in available light when the sun sets, producing decreased sensory stimulation and thus leading to confusion or even paranoia in elderly persons.

T

TENDER YEARS DOCTRINE: Advocating for mothers as the primary nurturers initially of infants and later expanded to include all children, became the standard utilized by the courts in custody matters.

TRANSSEXUALISM: Self-identification with one sex by an individual who has the external genitalia and secondary sexual characteristics of the other sex. Early in life, such an individual adopts the behavior characteristics of the opposite sex.

TRANSVESTISM: The practice of cross-dressing, which is wearing clothing traditionally associated with the opposite sex and doing so for the purpose of sexual arousal.

TRAUMATIC BRAIN INJURY (TBI): Occurs when a sudden trauma causes damage to the brain. The damage can be focal—confined to one area of the brain—or diffuse—involving more than one area of the brain. TBI can result from a *closed head injury* or a *penetrating head injury*. A closed injury occurs when the head suddenly and violently hits an object but the object does not break through the skull. A penetrating injury occurs when an object pierces the skull and enters brain tissue.

TRAUMATIC DEMENTIA: Caused by head trauma. Symptoms vary depending on which part of the brain was damaged by the injury (i.e., poor coordination, slurred speech, long-term memory problems, etc.).

TRIANGULATE: Most commonly used to express a situation in which one family member will not communicate directly with another family member, but will communicate with a third family member, forcing the third family member to then be part of the triangle.

V

VALIDITY: Validity refers to the degree to which a study accurately reflects or assesses the specific concept that the researcher is attempting to measure.

VIOLENCE RISK EVALUATIONS: Used for assistance in sentencing, treating, and/or identifying potentially violent offenders for future violent acts.

VOYEURISM: The sexual interest in or practice of spying on people engaged in intimate behaviors, such as undressing, sexual activity, or other activity usually considered to be of a private nature.

APPENDIX B

Legal Glossary

A

ABUSE: The infliction of some combination of physical, emotional, or sexual maltreatment upon another individual.

ACTUS REUS: The specific physical act that a defendant must have committed in order to be found guilty of a crime (see "Mens Rea").

ADJUDICATION: The court's final determination in a legal disputed matter.

ADMISSIBILITY: The extent to which a court will permit a particular item into evidence for consideration by a judge or jury (see "Relevance").

AFFIRMATION: An appellate court's conclusion that a lower court's decision is allowed to stand.

AGENCY: The status of being authorized to act—or being considered as authorized to act—for another entity; for example, this may serve to extend criminal or civil liability to an employer for an employee's improper actions.

AGGRAVATION: Circumstances surrounding the defendant's commission of a crime that may enhance the criminal penalties applied during sentencing (see "Mitigation").

ANNULMENT: A determination that a marriage never existed due to—for example—the intoxication, low intellectual functioning, or minority of one of the parties (see "Divorce").

APPEAL: An attempt by a party subjected to a losing criminal or civil adjudication to have that decision overturned by a higher court.

APPEAL, INTERLOCUTORY: An attempt by a party disadvantaged by a court's ruling in a criminal or civil proceeding to have that ruling overturned—during the course of the proceedings—by a higher court.

APPELLATE COURT: A higher court responsible for reviewing the decisions of a trial court or lower appellate court (see "Affirmation" and "Remand").

ARRAIGNMENT: The process by which one is formally accused of a crime (see "Indictment").

ARREST: The act of taking an individual into police custody for allegedly criminal behavior.

ASSAULT: A legally proscribed action causing another party to believe that he or she may be subjected to harmful or offensive contact (see "Battery").

ATTORNEY–CLIENT PRIVILEGE: The protected status of communications between a lawyer and the persons he or she represents; disclosure of these communications cannot be compelled, due to the legal system's recognition of the importance of a client's ability to consult confidentially with counsel (see "Privilege").

AUTOMATISM: The status of acting without conscious thought or recognition; this is sometimes asserted as a defense—with highly variable success based upon jurisdiction and fact patterns—on the part of persons accused of committing crimes while, for example, sleepwalking.

AUTOPSY, PSYCHOLOGICAL: A procedure whereby a mental health professional attempts to determine—based upon collateral contact and a review of available records—a deceased individual's legally relevant state of mind at a given point in the past.

B

BAIL: The proffer of money or other property in order to secure a defendant's release from pretrial incarceration; such funds are forfeited if the defendant does not return for hearings and trial as specified by the court.

BATTERY: A legally proscribed action causing undesired harmful or offensive contact (see "Assault").

BEYOND A REASONABLE DOUBT: Proven to an extent that seemingly affords little if any possibility of error; required for conviction in criminal matters (see "Clear and Convincing Evidence," "Preponderance of the Evidence," and "Standard of Proof").

BIFURCATION: A split legal determination in criminal matters, in which the court first takes up the notion of factual guilt or innocence, and then—if necessary—considers the issue of a potential lack of responsibility based upon mental health factors (see "Insanity Defense").

BURDEN OF PROOF: The responsibility for establishing that there is sufficient evidence for a criminal conviction or a finding of civil liability; this burden is typically ascribed to criminal prosecutors and civil plaintiffs (see "Standard of Proof").

C

CAPACITY: The ability to meet and maintain a level of behavioral and mental functioning that is sufficient to meet a defined legal standard.

CAPACITY, TESTAMENTARY: The ability to execute a valid will for devising one's personal possessions or other property; this is typically predicated upon knowing the nature of a bequest and the extent of one's property, being able to identify those naturally expected to receive such property, and being able to devise a rational plan for distribution.

CAPACITY, TESTIMONIAL: The ability to function competently as a witness in legal proceedings; typically such capacity is presumed and local rules for its determination vary widely from jurisdiction to jurisdiction.

CASE LAW: Presumptively binding legal principles that are established on the basis of prior appellate court decisions (see "Precedent").

CAUSATION ANALYSIS: The existence of a reasonable connection between the misfeasance, malfeasance, or nonfeasance of the defendant and the injury or damage suffered by the plaintiff. In a lawsuit in which negligence is alleged, the harm suffered by the plaintiff must be proved to result directly from the negligence of the defendant; causation must be demonstrated.

CERTIFICATION: A judicial determination that a juvenile defendant should be tried criminally as an adult (see "Waiver").

CHARACTER: Evidence of a criminal defendant's personality or behavioral inclinations under various circumstances; if a character witness is employed to speak to positive aspects of a defendant's character, this typically enables prosecutors to produce evidence of negative aspects in rebuttal.

CHATTEL: Property; historically, this refers to the once prevalent view of the courts that fathers essentially stood in a position of ownership with regard to their offspring.

CIVIL COMMITMENT: The process of compelling an individual to undergo inpatient or outpatient mental health treatment, in light of such factors as dangerousness to self or others, amenability to treatment, the likely efficacy of treatment, and the likelihood that the proposed setting for treatment is the least intrusive or confining option available (see "Least Restrictive Alternative").

CLEAR AND CONVINCING EVIDENCE: Proven to an extent that appears unambiguous and reasonably compelling (see "Beyond a Reasonable Doubt," "Preponderance of the Evidence," and "Standard of Proof").

COERCION: The use of force or threats—either physical or mental— to influence an individual's behavior; having been subjected to such tactics may serve to reduce the victim's liability for his or her own criminally or civilly inappropriate actions.

COMMUNITY SERVICE: A sentence consisting of the obligation to work for little or no compensation in support of the public good.

COMPETENCE RESTORATION: The process by which a defendant found incompetent to stand trial can attain competency through a court-ordered combination of treatment and education.

COMPETENCE TO BE EXECUTED: Necessary for subjection to the death penalty, this forensic status typically requires comprehension of the implications of this penalty and the reasons for which it is being applied.

COMPETENCE TO STAND TRIAL: A threshold determination before a defendant can be subjected to further criminal proceedings, this forensic status typically requires comprehension of the nature and consequences of such proceedings and the ability to participate rationally in one's own defense.

CONFESSION: A statement on the part of an individual that he or she has committed a criminal offense.

CONFESSION, FALSE: A phenomenon by which persons not guilty of a crime may nonetheless offer a confession, perhaps as the result of some combination of coercion, dependent personality, and desire for notoriety.

CONFIDENTIALITY: The general expectation that a party receiving information will not disclose that information, its source, or the circumstances under which it was obtained (see "Privilege").

CONFLICT OF INTEREST: The presence of competing or otherwise incompatible obligations or opportunities; typically invoked to limit the questionably appropriate provision of professional services.

CONSERVATORSHIP: Court-ordered imposition of the oversight of one's financial and other property interests due to adjudicated incapacity (see "Curatorship" and "Guardianship").

CONTIGENT FEE: An arrangement by which payment of fees is predicated upon a positive outcome for the client; while acceptable under circumstances for the provision of legal services, this is invariably deemed inappropriate for the provision of expert witness services.

CONTINUANCE: A delay of legal proceedings due to a formally asserted hardship or impracticality.

CONTRACT: A noncoerced agreement between two parties reflecting an offer, an acceptance, and a meeting of the minds concerning the particulars.

CONVICTION: The state of having been found guilty of a criminal offense.

CROSS-EXAMINATION: Counsel's initial elicitation of evidence, during deposition or trial, from the opposing side's witness in a criminal or civil case (see "Direct Examination").

CURATORSHIP: A legally recognized obligation to oversee another person's financial matters, based upon his or her specific and competently proffered request.

CUSTODY: A legally ordained obligation to provide care and support for another individual, based upon his or her minority, physical disability, or mental incapacity.

D

DAMAGES: The nature of the harm occasioned by a civil defendant's allegedly inappropriate personal or professional conduct; this term is also used to refer to the financial penalties imposed on the basis of such harm (see "Tort Law").

DEATH PENALTY: A criminal sentence involving deprivation of life; reserved for the most heinous transgressions such as murder or treason.

DEFENDANT: A person legally accused of having violated criminal law or of having failed to meet civil standards for personal or professional conduct.

DEPARTURE, DOWNWARD: A reduction in criminal sentencing in consideration of the defendant's mental disability or other relevant circumstances of the crime in question.

DEPARTURE, UPWARD: An enhancement in criminal sentencing due to the egregiousness of the crime in question, perhaps including its impact upon those harmed by the defendant's actions (see "Victim Impact Statement").

DEPOSITION: The taking of evidence from a witness prior to the occurrence of an actual criminal or civil trial; this is often conducted to obtain a sense of the potency of the evidence and the likely persuasiveness of the witness himself or herself.

DETERRENCE, GENERAL: The extent to which a criminal penalty is likely to discourage or prevent similar violations on the part of other persons made aware of the penalty in question.

DETERRENCE, SPECIFIC: The extent to which a criminal penalty is likely to discourage or prevent further violations on the part of the individual convicted.

DIMINISHED CAPACITY: A legally relevant diminution of a defendant's cognitive or other psychiatrically related functioning; in some jurisdictions, this condition may function as a defense to criminal behavior or as the basis for a decreased sentence upon conviction.

DIRECT EXAMINATION: Counsel's initial elicitation of evidence, during deposition or trial, from his or her own witness in a criminal or civil case (see "Cross-Examination").

DISABILITY: A lack of legally defined capacity as the result of a specified mental or physical condition.

DISCRIMINATION: Legally proscribed actions regarding another party based upon such considerations as race, gender, age, religion, culture, national origin, disability, or socioeconomic status.

DISPOSITION: The ultimate outcome of criminal or civil proceedings (see "Adjudication").

DIVERSION: A court's determination that a criminal defendant's actions merit some other resolution short of incarceration— for example, the imposition of a fine or a stint of community service.

DIVORCE: Legal dissolution of a marriage, either due to a party's inappropriate actions or due to a party's articulated desire to abandon the union.

DOCKET: A list of legal matters currently before an appellate or trial court for its consideration.

DUE PROCESS: The appropriate conduct of a legal matter, both substantive (concerning essential fairness) and procedural (concerning faithful adherence to codified rules).

E

EGGSHELL CLIENT: A plaintiff particularly susceptible to harm as a result of a defendant's inappropriate actions; such plaintiffs are viewed as no less deserving of compensation (see "Damages" and "Preexisting Condition").

EVIDENCE: Information offered in support of legal arguments in a criminal or civil matter.

EXPERT WITNESS: An individual whose knowledge, skill, education, training, or experience are considered sufficient for providing special assistance to the trier of fact, such that he or she is allowed to offer opinions on various issues before the court.

EXPLOITATION: Undue advantage taken of another individual, typically in light of the latter's minority or his or her physical or mental disability (see "Abuse").

EXTREME EMOTIONAL DISTURBANCE: A state of mind reflecting a temporary loss of control due to provocation; this may be employed in some jurisdictions as a form of mental health defense or otherwise for the reduction of a criminal sentence (see "Insanity Defense" and "Mitigation").

F

FELONY: A serious criminal offense, typically punishable by imprisonment for one or more years or the imposition of a substantial fine (see "Misdemeanor").

FINDER OF FACT: The role of a judge or jury in determining whether a factual allegation has actually been proven (see "Burden of Proof").

FINE: A financial penalty levied by the court as a result of civil or criminal proceedings.

FITNESS FOR DUTY: The capability to engage safely and effectively in a particular line of work.

FORESEEABLE FUTURE: A statutorily prescribed period of time during which an event may or may not occur.

G

GUARDIANSHIP: Court-ordered imposition of the oversight of one's personal care and circumstances, due to adjudicated incapacity (see "Conservatorship" and "Curatorship").

GUILTY: A legal verdict that an individual has committed a criminal act.

GUILTY BUT MENTALLY ILL: A legal verdict that an individual is criminally responsible for a criminal act, but that he or she is or was subject to a mental condition that merits ongoing treatment.

H

HABEAS CORPUS: A court order compelling determination of the appropriateness of an individual's current circumstances of confinement (see "Writ").

HABILITATION: The process of cure or other alleviation of symptoms or deficits due to treatment (see "Civil Commitment").

HARASSMENT: The criminally or civilly actionable infliction of threats or other forms of annoyance; such transgressions may be verbal, physical, or sexual in nature.

HOLDING: The briefly stated core of a judicial opinion in a given case, describing the court's general interpretation of the primary legal issue being disputed.

I

IMMUNITY: Circumstances under which one cannot be convicted of a crime or held civilly liable, occasionally provided in exchange for one's testimony concerning another's alleged wrongdoing.

IMPAIRMENT: A state of diminished mental capacity; this may result in a lack or diminution of criminal responsibility or civil liability.

INCARCERATION: Confinement in a jail upon being accused of a crime, or confinement in a jail or a prison upon being convicted of a crime.

INDICTMENT: A formal accusation that one has committed a crime (see "Arraignment").

INEFFECTIVE ASSISTANCE OF COUNSEL: Failure of an attorney to provide a sufficient level of criminal representation; when this has been established, the result for the defendant may be a new trial or other postconviction relief.

INFORMED CONSENT: Competently granting permission for being subjected to a medical or psychological procedure, upon having been provided with sufficient knowledge concerning that procedure, delivered in suitably accessible language with an opportunity to obtain answers to one's additional questions.

INNOCENT: The status of lacking responsibility for an alleged criminal offense; this may be due to a finding of insanity or due to a determination that the accused person simply did not commit the act in question.

INSANITY DEFENSE: The status of lacking responsibility for what would otherwise be deemed criminal behavior due to the presence at the time of the alleged offense of mental retardation, psychosis, or some other debilitating psychiatric condition.

INTERROGATION: The process of questioning an individual concerning his or her possible involvement in a criminal matter; if this process is conducted subsequent to arrest, the person being questioned is entitled to various warnings concerning his or her legal rights in this context.

INTERROGATORIES: A series of highly specific questions, posed in writing to a witness in the early stages of a civil matter; counsel may ultimately advise the witness to refrain from answering certain of these questions if they are irrelevant or otherwise exceed the scope of proper inquiry.

INTOXICATION, INVOLUNTARY: Being under the influence of drugs or alcohol as the result of coerced ingestion of such substances, or ingestion of those substances without an understanding of their potential effects; this mental state may in some jurisdictions result in a successful insanity defense.

INTOXICATION, VOLUNTARY: Being under the influence of drugs or alcohol as the result of willful, noncoerced ingestion of such substances with an understanding of their potential effects; this mental state is typically unlikely to result in an insanity defense, but may be relevant when it comes to establish that the defendant was incapable of forming the specific intent necessary for criminal liability.

Irresistible Impulse Test: A form of sanity determination in which a defendant may not have to bear criminal responsibility if his or her ability to refrain from illegal conduct was overborne by a qualified mental condition.

J

Jurisdiction: The geographic area within which—or the subject matter concerning which—a particular court is deemed qualified to conduct criminal or civil proceedings.

Juvenile: A minor child accused of a criminal offense, when the offense in question is not one for which trial in the adult criminal justice system is deemed appropriate or necessary.

K

Knowingly: The status of having acted with an understanding of the nature of one's conduct and the harm that such conduct might potentially cause.

L

Least Restrictive Alternative: In civil commitment proceedings, the form of intervention deemed to be the most minimally confining while still achieving the necessary goals of imposed treatment.

Liability: Exposure to the consequences of having violated either criminal law or civil standards for personal or professional conduct.

Licensure: Formal recognition of the right to practice one's profession in a given jurisdiction, typically following upon some combination of written examination, oral examination, or certification that one is suitably licensed in another jurisdiction that adheres to similar standards for enabling professional practice.

Living Will: A document by which an individual can direct health care professionals regarding certain aspects of his or her medical care—up to and including the withholding of life support procedures—in the event that he or she is subsequently deemed incapable of providing competent direction in this regard.

LOCALITY RULE: The process of setting the standard for appropriate professional practice at the level typically observed in one's own geographical area (see "Malpractice," "National Standard," and "Negligence").

LUCID INTERVAL: Relevant to legal proceedings in which the validity of a will is being contested, that window of time in which a typically mentally disabled individual may have been competent to arrange for subsequent distribution of his or her personal possessions or other property.

M

MALPRACTICE: The failure to provide services at a requisite level of professional competency (see "Locality Rule," "National Standard," and "Negligence").

MENS REA: The specific mental state that a defendant must have been experiencing in order to be found guilty of a crime (see "Actus Reus").

MISDEMEANOR: A criminal offense typically punishable by imprisonment for less than one year or the imposition of a fine (see "Felony").

MITIGATION: The introduction of evidence to assert that a defendant's admittedly criminal actions should qualify for a lesser penalty due to the presence of extenuating circumstances; mental illness is a condition frequently invoked in this context (see "Aggravation").

MOTIVE: The apparent reason for which a criminal offense has been committed.

N

NATIONAL STANDARD: The process of gauging the appropriateness of one's practices at the level typically observed in the country-wide professional community (see "Locality Rule," "Malpractice," and "Negligence").

NEGLECT: A criminally or civilly inappropriate failure to provide care for another individual.

NEGLIGENCE: A criminally or civilly inappropriate failure to act as would a reasonable person in a given situation (see "Malpractice").

O

OATH: A formal statement of the truthfulness of one's assertions (see "Perjury").

P

PARENS PATRIAE: The state's presumed obligation to act as would a parent in providing care for citizens with physical or mental disabilities (see "Police Power").

PAROLE: Release from incarceration prior to the expiration of a criminal sentence, conditioned upon the avoidance of specifically proscribed behaviors.

PERJURY: The proffer of deliberately untruthful information in the context of criminal proceedings (see "Oath"); such activity is typically subject to criminal sanctions.

PERPETRATOR: An individual convicted of a criminal offense (see "Defendant").

PETITION: A formalized attempt to obtain the court's involvement in a matter allegedly requiring intervention (see "Conservatorship" and "Guardianship").

PLAINTIFF: A party to a civil proceeding seeking redress for alleged harm (see "Defendant").

POLICE POWER: The state's presumed obligation to intervene in cases of alleged disability for the protection of other citizens (see "Parens Patriae").

POSTCONVICTION PROCEEDINGS: Attempts by a criminal defendant to obtain alteration or reconsideration of a sentence (see "Appeal").

PRECEDENT: The legal notion that prior appellate court decisions constitute binding guidance for future rulings on the same issues.

PREEXISTING CONDITION: The presence of a physical or mental disorder or other susceptibility to harm that was in effect prior to the occurrence of the injury currently serving as the focus of legal action (see "Damages" and "Eggshell Client").

PREPONDERANCE OF THE EVIDENCE: Proven to an extent that is even slightly more convincing than the arguments offered to the contrary (see "Beyond a Reasonable Doubt," "Clear and Convincing," and "Standard of Proof").

PRESENTENCE EVALUATION: A collation of interview data, legal records, mental reports, and other information that is proffered to the court in order to assist in the determination of appropriate criminal penalties.

PRIVILEGE: The right to bar from admission into legal or quasi-legal proceedings certain information or the circumstances under which such information was obtained; this is typically acknowl-edged—with various exceptions—regarding communications be-tween attorneys and clients, between doctors and patients, and between spouses (see "Confidential").

PRO SE: Undertaking to represent oneself or otherwise to seek a particular result from the court without representation by legal counsel.

PROBATION: Conditional release from post-adjudicative incarcera-tion; maintenance of this status is dependent upon compliance with specific court-imposed conditions that typically include such factors as avoidance of reoffending, refraining from alcohol or drug use, and remaining in contact with court authorities.

PROSECUTOR: An officer of the court charged with seeking the appropriate penalty for a defendant's alleged criminal transgressions.

PROVOCATION: A circumstance determined to be sufficiently upset-ting to a criminal or civil defendant as to provide a full or partial explanation or excuse for otherwise actionable behavior (see "Extreme Emotional Disturbance" and "Mitigation").

PROXIMATE CAUSE: Sufficient contribution to harm as to incur civil liability (see "Tort Law").

R

REASONABLE ACCOMMODATION: The codified obligation of certain employers and government entities to alter job or other require-ments in a practicable fashion, in order to enable optimal partici-pation by persons with disabilities.

REASONABLE DEGREE OF CERTAINTY: That level of confidence in one's own opinion deemed necessary by various courts for the proffer of expert witness testimony.

REBUTTAL: The process of proffering evidence for the specific pur-pose of countering the assertions of a legal opponent's witnesses.

RECIDIVISM: The relapse of a criminal defendant into behaviors that formed the basis for a prior conviction.

REGULATION: A legal rule promulgated by an administrative agency, typically in support of codified laws enacted by a legisla-tive body (see "Statute").

Rehabilitation: The process of reversing actionable behavioral tendencies previously exhibited by persons convicted of a crime.

Release: A signed document authorizing the proffer of sensitive information (see "Confidentiality" and "Privilege").

Relevance: Sufficient utility for the tasks of a judge or jury for facts or assertions to be considered formally in the context of legal proceedings (see "Admissibility" and "Evidence").

Remand: When a higher court determines that a lower court must reconsider the latter's ruling in a criminal or civil matter (see "Appeal").

Respondent: An individual who has become the subject of civil proceedings (see "Conservatorship" and "Guardianship").

Restitution: Moneys ordered payable by a civil or criminal court in order to compensate the victim of a physical, emotional, or other injury (see "Damages").

Revocation: The court's dismissal of an order or any other dissolution of previously prescribed conditions.

Ripeness: Reflecting the court's recognition that all necessary circumstances have come to pass for a legal action to be instituted.

S

Sentence: Punishment applied by a court in light of a criminal conviction (see "Community Service," "Fine," and "Restitution").

Sentencing, Determinate: The process of fixing a specific criminal penalty at the time that judgment is rendered.

Sentencing, Indeterminate: The process of fixing a criminal penalty that may vary in its length or other aspects based upon such factors as the defendant's adherence to institutional rules and progress in prescribed treatment.

Sexually Violent Predator: A sexual offender who has been adjudicated as presenting a substantial risk of committing similar acts in the future.

Spoliation: The willful destruction of evidence; this is considered particularly egregious when the court has specifically requested production of the evidence in question.

Stalking: The statutorily proscribed act of following, contacting, or otherwise impermissibly menacing another individual, typically occasioning reasonable fear of harm.

STANDARD OF PRACTICE: The inferred level of competency typically expected in the pursuit of a particular profession (see "Malpractice"). "Standard of Care," a similar concept, refers to the care expected to be rendered to a patient or client by a similarly trained and situated professional.

STANDARD OF PROOF: The degree to which a party must establish the existence of certain facts or circumstances in order to prevail in a legal proceeding (see "Beyond a Reasonable Doubt," "Preponderance of the Evidence," and "Clear and Convincing Evidence").

STATUTE: Codified legal guidance, instituted by a state or federal legislative body, the violation of which may result in criminal proceedings (see "Regulation").

SUBPOENA: A legal document directing that a witness appear in court, perhaps in order to produce a specified item of evidence; a subpoena may be overridden or "quashed" at the court's discretion if the document in question is premature, overreaching, or otherwise inappropriate.

SUBSTITUTED JUDGMENT: The legal process whereby a court will assume or delegate decision making for an individual, due to that individual's relevant physical or mental incapacity and—under certain circumstances—previously expressed wishes.

SUPPRESSION: The court's act of preventing a defendant's alleged confession into evidence in a criminal trial, due to irregularities in obtaining the defendant's statement or concern regarding his or her competency to provide it.

T

TENDER YEARS DOCTRINE: The largely discredited presumption that sole or primary custody should be awarded to a child's mother as opposed to the child's father, due to the unique importance of the former's nurturance during early childhood.

TESTATOR: A person undertaking to leave personal possessions or other property upon his or her demise to another party or parties.

TESTIMONY: The rendering—typically sworn—of a witness' statements during a trial or deposition.

THIRD PARTY: An entity—other than that suing or being sued—with some relevant relationship to the legal matter at issue; for example, an insurer who may be financially liable for a civil defendant's improper actions.

TORT LAW: That body of legal guidance establishing a party's obligations to other persons under certain circumstances, with non-criminal penalties for inadequate compliance that often include providing financial compensation to injured parties; liability typically relies upon the presence of a duty, a breach of that duty, harm to a victim as a result of that breach, and sufficient contribution to that harm by the breach in question (see "Damages" and "Proximate Cause").

TRANSFER HEARING: Legal proceedings during which a court determines whether a juvenile defendant should be tried as an adult (see "Waiver").

TRIAL: The forum in which opposing legal perspectives are formally aired, resulting in the rendering of a decision by a judge or jury.

TRIER OF FACT: The role of the judge or jury in determining whether certain events or situations occurred or existed at a given time; this is distinct from determining if an applicable legal standard has been met.

TRIER OF LAW: The role of the judge in determining whether an applicable standard has been met.

U

ULTIMATE ISSUE: The actual legal matter that a court is attempting to determine; some jurisdictions maintain that expert witnesses should be prevented from addressing such matters directly— for example, that they should be allowed to opine on the presence or absence of relevant mental conditions and abilities, but not on the presence of absence of "competency" or "capacity."

UNDUE INFLUENCE: Impermissible interference with an individual's attempt to execute a will or otherwise distribute his or her personal possessions or other property.

V

VERDICT: A legal determination that an accused party either has or has not committed a criminal act or has displayed a civilly actionable lapse in personal or professional conduct.

Victim Impact Statement: A description, prepared in anticipation of sentencing, of the ways in which a criminal defendant's actions may have affected those harmed by the offense in question.

Violation: A breach of statutory, regulatory, or case law that may render an individual subject to criminal prosecution.

Visitation: An individual's court-sanctioned opportunity to spend time with a minor child, during or subsequent to divorce or child custody proceedings, typically pursuant to a schedule and in some cases subject to third party supervision.

Voluntary: Performed or committed as the product of an individual's sufficiently informed free will.

W

Waiver: The process by which a juvenile defendant may be tried as an adult, typically based upon a statutorily defined list of factors such as maturity, the seriousness of the crime, and the likelihood that the defendant would benefit from treatment options available under either adult or juvenile circumstances of incarceration (see "Transfer Hearing").

Will: A document stating which of an individual's possessions shall be distributed to whom upon the individual's demise.

Writ: A court order directing or enabling a party to act in a prescribed fashion.

APPENDIX C

Compendium of Cited Psychological Tests

A

Abel Assessment of Sexual Interest (AASI)
Achenbach System of Empirically Based Assessment (ASEBA)
Acute-2007
Addiction Acknowledgment Scale (AAS)
Addiction Potential Scale (APS)
Adult Functional Adaptive Behavioral Scale
Alcohol Problems Scale
Assessment of Consent Capacity for Treatment (ACCT)

B

Behavior Assessment System for Children (BASC-2)
Bender Gestalt Test
Brief Psychiatric Rating Scale (BPRS)

C

Classification of Violence Risk (COVR)
Community Competency Scale
Competence to Stand Trial Assessment Instrument (CSTAI)
Competency Assessment Interview (CAI)
Competency Assessment to Stand Trial for Defendants with Mental Retardation (CAST-MR)

Competency Interview Schedule (CIS)
Competency Screening Test (CST)
Competency to Consent to Treatment Instrument (CCTI)
Computerized Axial Tomography (CAT)
Comprehension of Miranda Rights (CMR)
Comprehension of Miranda Rights—Recognition (CMR-R)
Comprehension of Miranda Vocabulary (CMV)
Curriculum Based Assessments (CBA)
Curriculum Based Measurements (CBM)
Custody History Questionnaire

D

Danger Assessment
Decision-Making Instrument for Guardianship
Detailed Assessment of Posttraumatic Stress (DAPS)
Differential Ability Scales (DAS-II)
Direct Assessment of Functional Status

E

Employee Risk Assessment (ERA-20)
Evaluation of Competency to Stand Trial—Revised (ECST-R)

F

Fitness Interview Test—Revised (FIT-R)
Function of Rights in Interrogation (FRI)

G

Georgia Court Competency Test (GCCT)
Gray Oral Reading Tests (GORT-4)
Gudjonsson Suggestibility Scale

H

Hare Psychopathy Checklist—Revised (PCL-R)
Hare Psychopathy Checklist—Screening Version (PCL-SV)
Hare Psychopathy Checklist—Youth Version (PCL-YV)
HCR-20 Assessing Risk for Violence (HCR-20: Version 2)

N

Nelson Denny Reading Test

O

Overt Aggression Scale

P

Parents Questionnaire
Peabody Picture Vocabulary Test (PPVT-4)
Penile Plethysmography (PPG)
Penile Tumescence Testing (PTT)
Personal History Questionnaire
Personality Assessment Inventory (PAI)
Positron Emissions Testing (PET)
Psychological Screening Inventory (PSI)

R

Rapid Risk Assessment for Sex Offense Recidivism (RRASOR)
Repeatable Battery of Neuropsychological Status (RBANS)
Rey 15-Item Memorization Test
Rogers Criminal Responsibility Assessment Scales (R-CRAS).
Rogers Discriminant Function (RDF)
Rorschach Inkblot Technique

S

Scales of Independent Behavior—Revised (SIB-R)
Screening Scale for Pedophilic Interests (SSPI)
Screening Test for the Luria–Nebraska Neuropsychological
   Battery (LNNB-ST)
Sentence Completion Test
Sex Offender Risk Appraisal Guide (SORAG)
Shipley Institute of Living Scale (SILS-2)
Social Responsive Scale (SRS)
Social Skills Intervention Systems (SSIS)
Stable-2007
Stanford-Binet Intelligence Scales (SB-V)
Static-99
Structured Clinical Interview

Stroop Neuropsychological Screening Test
Structured Interview for Competency and Incompetency
    Assessment Testing and Ranking Inventory (SICIATR)
Structured Interview of Reported Symptoms (SIRS-2)
Structured Inventory of Malingered Symptomatology (SIMS)
Substance Abuse Subtle Screening Inventory (SASSI-3)
Symbol Digit Modalities Test

T

Test of Memory Malingering (TOMM)
Thematic Apperception Test (TAT)

V

Validity Indicator Profile (VIP)
Verbal Comprehension Index (VCI)
Vineland Adaptive Behavior Scales (VABS-II)
Violence Risk Appraisal Guide (VRAG)
Violence Risk Assessment-HCR 20

W

Wechsler Abbreviated Scale of Intelligence (WASI)
Wechsler Adult Intelligence (WAIS-IV)
Wechsler Individual Achievement Test (WIAT-III)
Wechsler Intelligence Scale for Children (WISC-IV)
Wechsler Preschool Primary Scale of Intelligence (WPPSI-III)
Wide Range Achievement Test, Fourth Edition (WRAT4)
Woodcock-Johnson Tests of Achievement (W-J-III NU)
Woodcock-Johnson Test of Cognitive Abilities (WJ-III-COG)
Workplace Assessment of Violence Risk (WAVR-21)
Workplace Violence Risk Assessment Checklist

Y

Youth Behavior Checklist

APPENDIX D

Sample Reports

PSYCHIATRIC EVALUATION—JUVENILE DECERTIFICATION

January 15, 2007

John Doe, Esquire
Assistant Public Defender
Anytown, USA

RE: Ms. "A":

Dear Mr. Doe:

Pursuant to your request, I examined your client, a 15-year-old female (birthdate: March 13, 1991), on two separate occasions: initially, on July 7, 2006, and secondly, on August 1, 2006. Each examination lasted about two hours, and both were conducted at the County Jail, where she is currently confined awaiting trial on charges of aggravated assault and possession of an instrument of crime. The purpose of this examination is to determine her mental status and to determine whether she is amenable to treatment in the juvenile system, that is, that she is appropriate for decertification from adult court to juvenile court.

Ms. "A" was told that I am a psychiatrist requested by your office to conduct this examination with respect to the charges against her. She was told that I would be taking notes during the examination and preparing a report that I would send to you. Further, she was told that I would not be treating her and there could be no traditional doctor–patient confidentiality. She was also told that I would likely have to testify in court and that anything she told me could be revealed in that court hearing. Ms. "A" understood the directions and agreed to be examined.

MENTAL STATUS EXAMINATION

Ms. "A" is a 15-plus-year-old, single Hispanic-Italian female who is of short to average height (5'1") and of average weight (135 pounds). She appears to be her stated age and presents her difficulties in a clear and relevant manner, without current hallucinations or delusions. She is well oriented, and her memory is not impaired. She is able to present her history clearly, articulately, and in a logical manner. She does become tearful at times during the examination, especially when talking about the tumultuous background that she has had and about her current incarceration. She also shows flexibility of affect by laughing appropriately and responding to various stimuli in an appropriate manner. She indicates that she had been taking medication in the past, as she had been diagnosed with bipolar disorder, but is currently on no medication.

PAST HISTORY

Past history reveals that Ms. "A" was born and raised in Pennsylvania and had a very disruptive childhood, being sent, at the age of two, into foster care with her year-older sister. She had been returned to her mother, who had drug and alcohol problems, and her biological father had been incarcerated much of her early life. Mother relapsed several times during Ms. "A's" childhood, and Ms. "A" had to be returned to foster care. (Please see Dr. D's very detailed report on her childhood experiences.)

It should be noted that Ms. "A" has one older full sister, age 16. She has several half-siblings, ranging in age from 11 to 3, by various relationships mother had with different men. She states her parents were never married. She denies any serious medical problems, but the hospital records that I had reviewed indicated that at approximately one year of age, Ms. "A" developed a thickening in her lungs, causing her some airway problems. She has had subsequent respiratory difficulties as a result of this condition, but apparently the matter has not been debilitating for her.

From a psychiatric standpoint, Ms. "A" had been diagnosed as having bipolar disorder after her 13th birthday. She was treated with

Seroquel and Tegretol-XR. She isn't certain whether the medication was helpful for her, but she did not take it consistently or regularly. There is also indication that Ms. "A's" mother and brother had been diagnosed with bipolar disorder, and another sibling was diagnosed with attention deficit/hyperactivity disorder (ADHD). Despite her parents' use of illicit drugs and excessive use of alcohol, Ms. "A" states that she has been able to avoid abuse of substances. She states that she did not use alcohol because she did not want to be like her parents and always wanted to maintain some degree of control over her behavior. She does admit to smoking cigarettes and, in fact, had some difficulties in her placement situations because smoking was prohibited and she did so against the rules. She was also caught with matches and a lighter at these facilities, also prohibited items. There is some question in her childhood about her use of fire to burn something at home, but this did not appear to be a pattern of arson or abuse of fire. She did not seem to have a sexual fascination with fire. She had no history of late bedwetting and was not cruel to animals. She did have some fights in school, but usually when she was teased or egged on by others rather than acting as the instigator of the fight. One of those fights in school resulted in her being placed on probation for six months, which she handled well.

Ms. "A" indicates that there were some placements in foster care that were enjoyable for her, and where she wanted to stay. It was at one of those placements that she left as a result of a call from her sister, who was unhappy with her placement in a group home. Ms. "A" believed that she had to rescue her sister, so she left her placement without permission, and she and her sister were runaways, according to the law. She had stayed with her paternal grandfather for several weeks, until she was apprehended.

Educational history reveals that Ms. "A" attended the eighth grade at the time she was apprehended. She apparently was a fairly good student, and her psychological testing, conducted by Dr. D, showed that she had a fairly high IQ—that is, in the upper average range.

CURRENT OFFENSE

Ms. "A" was charged with aggravated assault and possession of an instrument of crime when she and her friend, "J," were en route to a local market when they encountered an acquaintance by the name of

"V." Her friend, "J," said she wanted "V's" cell phone and asked "V" to use it. When it was given to her she ran, in order to keep the phone. "V" ran after Ms. "A" and her friend, "J," and Ms. "A" was trapped in a dead-end alley; when she was accosted by "V" and "V's" sister, "N," Ms. "A" said she picked up a board in an attempt to defend herself, but was grabbed by "V's" sister, "N," from behind, and was punched by "N" with a blade that caused serious cuts and puncture wounds in Ms. "A's" back and arms. It should be noted that I did observe scars from these puncture wounds from the previous assault on her by "N."

The fight was broken up by two males and Ms. "A" returned to "J's" home, and then to Ms. "A's" aunt's house. She had taken the kitchen knife from her father's home in order to protect herself in case there were further altercations with "V" and "N." Ms. "A" then went to "V's" home and ran to "N," stabbing her in the back, causing the knife blade to break from the force of the attack. Ms. "A" left "V's" home and ran to her father's house. The state police were called and took Ms. "A" into custody. She initially went to the hospital for treatment of her wounds. That occurred on the day she was incarcerated on June 15, 2006.

It was shortly after her incarceration that I was asked to examine Ms. "A," which I did, and determined that because of her history of bipolar disorder and the need for decertification assessment, that psychological testing was required. Dr. D saw her on two occasions, on July 12 and July 13, 2006. I then consulted with him and returned to reevaluate Ms. "A" on August 1, 2006, for another two hours, going over the materials that I had reviewed, and the consultation that I had with Dr. D.

Records Reviewed

In addition to my examination of Ms. "A," I also reviewed the following records that you provided:

1. State Police Department records, dated 12-23-03 and 2-9-04.
2. State Police Department records, dated 6-15-06.
3. County Juvenile Probation Department case history, dated 10-4-06.
4. Court of Common Pleas County Juvenile Dependency document, dated 4-29-92.

5. Records from Local Hospital Center, dated 2004.
6. Records from the Catholic Social Agency, Foster Placement, Health and Education information, dated 1993.
7. Health Bureau Immunization records, dated 1991.
8. Community Health Service records, dated 1991.
9. Records from the County Office of Children and Youth Services.
10. Records from the Local Mentor Program.
11. Records from Educare.
12. A copy of Ms. "A's" psychiatric evaluation conducted by Dr. Smith, dated 2-9-05, in which he had diagnosed her as having bipolar disorder and recommended medication.
13. Records from Youth House, dated 1-13-04 to 4-27-04.
14. Records from her school district on her education.
15. Records from Local Hospital for 1992 and 1993.
16. Records from Boys and Girls Club Family and Youth Intervention Programs for the years 1997 and 1998.
17. Permanency Hearing Determinations and Order, dated 10-13-05.
18. Court Order Pursuant to Petition for Review of Disposition and Placement, dated 4-2-96.
19. Complete education file from Ms. "A's" high school and her local school district.
20. County Prison records, dated 6-19-06 to 11-22-06.
21. A copy of the psychological report of Dr. D, dated 1-12-07, in which he confirms the diagnosis of bipolar disorder and recommends that Ms. "A" continue with medication, treatment, and that she is, in his opinion, with a reasonable degree of psychological certainty, amenable to treatment in the juvenile system.

SUMMARY AND CONCLUSIONS, WITH RECOMMENDATION

Based on my two examinations of Ms. "A" and review of all of the aforementioned records, the following are my opinions, given with a reasonable degree of medical certainty:

Ms. "A" is a 15-year-old female who has had a very tumultuous and disturbed upbringing, having two parents involved in criminal behavior and drug and alcohol abuse. She has been placed in foster care on several occasions and has had some difficulty in her behavior, having one period of probation for fighting in school and having some concern about firesetting when she was younger. She has also had some minor infractions since her incarceration, but nothing major. Dr. D has described these minor infractions in his report.

It is my opinion, to a reasonable degree of medical certainty, that as a result of Ms. "A's" bipolar disorder and her personality difficulties plus her disturbed background, that she acted impulsively, although she did have time to reflect on her behavior. Clearly, her behavior is affected by her bipolar disorder as well as the circumstances of her life.

In the statute regarding the factors affecting decertification, it is clear that despite the severity of the attack on "N," Ms. "A" does possess the characteristics amenable to treatment in the juvenile system. She has a treatable mental condition and she has shown remorse for her impulsive violent behavior toward "N." She will require further treatment, with medication, and her treatment should begin in a secure environment, which is available in the juvenile system. She has shown the ability to adjust in various circumstances of confinement and it is expected that she will do so at this time as well. She has over five years until she is 21 and, in my opinion, that is sufficient time for her to receive the treatment that will stabilize her condition. She requires education in order to succeed in life, and she has the ability to handle that education as well.

Ms. "A" has not had a semblance of stability in her brief life of 15 years, and it is recommended that stability will be extremely helpful for her over the next several years. She should be in one place, in a therapeutic environment, not a punitive environment, in order for her to reemerge into society at the age of 21, with safety in the community. She has been able to avoid drugs and alcohol despite the environment in which she has been raised, and she has also avoided intimate contact with males, having no sexual experiences. There are many reasons for this, one of which is that she has mistrust for males, and that would need to be explored in therapy as well.

I have reviewed Dr. D's recommendations, and I agree with all of them, and it is my opinion, with a reasonable degree of medical certainty, that this 15-year-old female with a diagnosis of bipolar disorder, if properly treated within the juvenile system, will emerge as a constructive, productive citizen. She deserves the opportunity to have stability in her life, with consistency, treatment, education, and an opportunity for success in the future.

Should further records become available, I would be pleased to review them and prepare an addendum to this report, if necessary.

Yours very sincerely,

Z, MD
Clinical Professor of Forensic Psychiatry
XXX University
Board Certified in Psychiatry
and Forensic Psychiatry

PSYCHOLOGICAL EVALUATION—
JUVENILE DECERTIFICATION

NAME:	Ms. "A"
DATE OF BIRTH:	3/13/91
DATES OF EVALUATION:	7/12/06 and 7/13/06
DATE OF REPORT:	1/12/07
REFERRED BY:	John Doe, Esq., Assistant Public Defender

TECHNIQUES USED

House-Tree-Person, Kinetic Family Drawing, Bender Visual-Motor Gestalt Test with Recall, Rorschach Technique, Adult Sentence Completion Test, Thematic Apperception Test (TAT) (Selected Cards), Beck Depression Inventory (BDI), Beck Suicide Inventory (BSI), Beck Anxiety Inventory (BAI), Beck Hopelessness Scale (BHS), Wechsler Abbreviated Scale of Intelligence (WASI), Jesness Behavior Checklist, Minnesota Multiphasic Personality Inventory-A (MMPI-A), Aggression Questionnaire (AQ), HCR-20 Violence Risk Assessment, conversation with former guardian, Jane Doe, Esq., on 11/23/06, Mr. Robert Smith from SPORE on 12/13/06, Ms. Mary White from the County Office of Children and Youth Services on 12/15/06, review of background information, and clinical interview.

DOCUMENTS REVIEWED

- Cover letter from John Doe, Esq., dated 6/29/06.
- State Police Department records, dated 12/23/03 and 2/9/04.
- State Police Department records, dated 6/15/06.
- County Juvenile Probation Department case history as of 10/4/06.
- Court of Common Pleas, County Juvenile Dependency document dated 4/29/92.
- Records from Local Hospital Center, dated 2004.
- Records from the Catholic Social Agency, Foster Placement, Health and Education Information, dated 1993.
- Health Bureau Immunization records, dated 1991.
- Community Health Service records, dated 1991.

- Records from the County Office of Children and Youth Services.
- Information from the Local Mentor Program.
- Records from Educare.
- Psychiatric evaluation, dated 2/9/05.
- Records from Youth House, dated 1/13/04 to 4/27/04.
- Educational records from School District.
- Records from Local Hospital for the years 1992 and 1993. Boys and Girls Club Family and Youth Intervention Programs for the years 1997 and 1998.
- Permanency hearing determinations and order, dated 10/13/05.
- Court order pursuant to petition for review of disposition and placement, dated 4/2/96.
- Complete education file from high school, and other local School Districts.
- County Prison records, dated 6/19/06 to 11/22/06.

BACKGROUND INFORMATION AND CLINICAL OBSERVATIONS

Ms. "A" is a 15 $^3/_4$-year-old, single, biracial female who is half Hispanic and half Italian. She has shoulder-length, brown hair, and brown eyes, and appears to be her stated age and gender. Ms. "A" stands 5'1" in height, weighs approximately 135 lbs., and was neat and appropriately groomed for the interview. She was dressed in a tan prison smock as per the regulations for the Department of Corrections. Ms. "A" is currently incarcerated in the County Prison as of 6/16/06 on charges of aggravated assault and possession of an instrument of crime. She is currently awaiting a disposition on decertification. Prior to her incarceration, she was residing in a rented apartment with her father and paternal aunt.

Ms. "A" was referred for a psychological evaluation by her criminal defense attorney, John Doe, Esq., in order to provide a mental status, and also to aid in determining whether or not she is amenable to treatment and rehabilitation in the juvenile system. This evaluation was, therefore, intended to be used as evidence in a decertification hearing.

During the initial interview session, Ms. "A" presented herself as a pleasant young lady who was polite and congenial with this examiner. She made excellent eye contact, articulated clearly, and produced test protocols of sufficient quality and length to permit interpretation. Ms. "A" possesses no body tattoos or body piercings, other than one piercing in each ear. The ornaments have been removed due to her incarceration. She does have several scars on her body, which include one that is curved and is one-half centimeter in length under her left eye. She also has another scar that is a quarter centimeter in length on her right upper arm. She possesses puncture wound on her right lower back, punctures under each breast, and a scar that is a quarter centimeter in length on her right temple. She also has a small puncture wound on the top of her head, all of which were verified by the documents reviewed.

During the initial interview session, Ms. "A" was informed of the basic tenet of this evaluation and that anything that she conveyed to me during the course of the assessment would not be kept confidential as in the case of a traditional doctor/patient relationship. She was further informed that the results of the assessment would be incorporated into a written report and forwarded to her criminal defense attorney. Ms. "A" acknowledged her understanding of the evaluation and signed a written consent form, granting me permission to release this information to the aforementioned party.

It was on 7/12/06 that Ms. "A" provided me with the following rendition of her life:

Ms. "A" was born to both biological parents on 3/13/91 in Pennsylvania. She is the youngest of two children born to Mr. B and Ms. C. She has one biological sister who is age 16. She also has several half-siblings who include brothers, E, age 11, F, age 10, G, age 4, and H, age 3. These offspring are from her mother's various relationships with other men. Ms. "A" claims that her parents were never formally married. She denies any medical complications at the time of her birth and equally denies any delays with her developmental milestones. However, when reviewing early records from the local hospital, it is indicated that when Ms. "A" was approximately one year of age, she did develop a central peribronchial thickening consistent with airway disease. This was situated in the left upper lobe area of her lung. It is not clear, however, how this condition was treated or rectified. This condition suggests that she may also have developed subsequent respiratory difficulties as a result, although this was not reported in any medical reports. Aside from this condition, Ms. "A" reports no other medical difficulties during her early upbringing.

Ms. "A" reports that her parents were only together until she was 6 years of age. Her father was never formally employed because he was in and out of prison on charges of illicit substances, auto theft, etc. Ms. "A's" father worked mostly labor jobs when he was employed. Her mother also worked at a sewing facility, but experienced an accident there while working on a machine. Apparently, one of her pant-legs became caught in a mechanism and disabled her leg. She has since been awarded full disability, commencing in 1999.

Ms. "A" claims that both of her parents were involved heavily with illicit substance abuse. Early reports indicate that Ms."A's" biological father had a history of both juvenile and adult criminal activity and was documented on the ranks of juvenile, as well as adult probation, in the local County. These offenses involved theft, receiving stolen property, substance abuse (mostly alcohol), and possession of an unlicensed firearm. Ms. "A's" biological mother has a juvenile history as well. Her mother was heavily involved in heroin and alcohol use and was involved with several paramours who also possessed juvenile histories.

Ms. "A's" family of origin was also involved with the County Office of Children and Youth Services, who eventually intervened because of a report that was made, and indicated, that Ms. "A" was being neglected. The agency eventually intervened and removed Ms. "A" and her sister at one and two years of age due to illicit drugs in the home, as well as neglectful circumstances. Both Ms. "A" and her sister were placed in foster care for a brief period of time and later returned to their mother's care. Their mother later voluntarily placed both children back into foster care through the County Office of Children and Youth Services. It was around this time that Ms. "A" contends that her father was also incarcerated in the state correctional institute.

At the age of six, Ms. "A" recalls that she returned to her mother's care. Her parents had physically separated by this time. Her mother appeared to be in a period of sobriety. She had previously been heavily involved with crack cocaine. Ms. "A" lived with her mother from ages 6 to 12. During this time, she attended public school on a regular basis. She had initially been in a preschool at a church and later went on to attend kindergarten to fourth grade at the local elementary school. She then went on to fifth grade at the local middle school and transferred to sixth grade at another middle school.

The family apparently resided in Pennsylvania for a while. Ms. "A's" mother had a paramour by the name of M, with whom she is reportedly still residing. Apparently, Ms. "A" reports that she and her sister suspected that their mother was still involved with illicit substance use and, on one occasion, actually found drug paraphernalia in the home. By this time, her mother had given birth to her younger brothers. Ms. "A" recalls that her mother would sometimes disappear for hours at a time. Her mother's paramour was also heavily involved with crack cocaine and worked at a general temporary agency at the time. Despite this tumultuous environment, Ms. "A" denies any physical, sexual, or psychological abuse perpetrated upon her or her siblings.

Ms. "A" does report that, at the age of 12, her mother admitted to her that she had become reinvolved with illicit substance use and contacted the County Office of Children and Youth Services on her own accord. As a result, the agency removed Ms. "A" and her sister once again from her mother's care. Ms. "A" was sent back into foster care with a woman by the name of "Jane." Ms. "A" was in foster care for approximately 1 year. These records were reviewed in detail, which verify Ms. "A's" rendition. Ms. "A" claims that she turned 13 years of age while in foster placement, but up to that point, however, she had experienced no behavioral problems or academic difficulties. She was angry with her mother for not caring for her properly and had a great deal of trust issues with authority. She got along well with her foster mother, Jane. Ms. "A" considered Jane to be a second mother to her. She still maintained visits with her biological mother on a regular basis under the supervision of the Office of Children and Youth.

Ms. "A" claims that her mother attempted to rehabilitate herself and, after being discharged, attended AA (Alcoholic Anonymous) and NA (Narcotic Anonymous) meetings. Ms. "A" returned home at the age of 13 to reside with her biological mother. Her mother had discontinued illicit substance use altogether, but continued to use alcohol frequently. The family subsequently relocated to a small apartment in town, which was a big adjustment for Ms. "A" since she had experienced so much disruption with her environment.

During this time, she claims that she became involved in a fight at school with another female youth. Apparently, some other girls were egging her on and Ms. "A" started to fight with one of the females who was her same age. Apparently, they were teasing each other and they exchanged statements about each other's mothers. When the other girl called Ms. "A's" mother a "whore" because she had so many children, Ms. "A" lost control of herself and grabbed the other girl's hair. She was subsequently charged with aggravated assault. As a result, she was placed on juvenile probation for a period of 6 months. She reportedly did well with probationary supervision. These records were reviewed in detail. I also had an opportunity to speak with Ms. "A's" probation officer, Mr. Robert Smith, who confirmed these facts for me. Ms. "A" also went to a juvenile camp for one weekend, which she found to be a very educational placement. Camp helped her while on probation and she only violated on one occasion with a late curfew. She had also smoked cigarettes for which she received house arrest for one month. She claims, however, that she received no other probationary violations. Once again, this information was verified through collateral sources.

During this time, Ms. "A" began attending high school. During her academic years, her grades were "A's" and "B's" with an occasional "C" in math. Once again, these records were reviewed, which verify Ms. "A's" performance. Ms. "A" proudly explains that during this time, she had no involvement with any illicit drug or alcohol use and only smoked cigarettes on occasion.

It was around this time that Ms. "A" also became interested in males and claims that she kissed a boy once in the eighth grade. She was not involved in any petting or sexual activity. She claims that she remained with her mother on Maple Street and attended seventh grade at the local junior high school. Unfortunately, Ms. "A's" mother relapsed on illicit drug use and Ms. "A" was consequently placed back in foster care. At this point, all of her mother's children had been placed in foster care. Ms. "A" was placed in a separate foster home from her siblings. She was in a foster home with a woman by the name of Sally who was located in Pennsylvania. It was during this time that she was attending high school for the eighth and ninth grades.

Ms. "A" indicates that the many placements outside of her natural environment have hurt her due to the frequent disruptions with friendships and being separated from her siblings and her family of origin. All of this time, Ms. "A" claims that she hadn't had any visits with her biological father, who apparently was in and out of state incarceration. Ms. "A" recalls that she remained in placement with Sally for one year. During this time, she turned 14 years of age.

She did well in school, both academically and behaviorally and seemed to straighten out her life. She was transferred to another foster home because she and Sally were not getting along too well together. Ms. "A" informs me that Sally was an older woman in her 60s and had less tolerance for unruly adolescent behaviors. Consequently, Ms. "A" was sent to a foster home in western Pennsylvania with a woman by the name of Kim where she remained for a period of six weeks. She claims that she was removed from that facility, however, because this particular foster home was said to have been infested with fleas. Other sources indicate that there were other problems that pertained to Ms. "A's" transfer, however, they were not elaborated on. Ms. "A" subsequently went to another foster home in Pennsylvania under the care of a woman by the name of Kathy, where she remained for one year. During this time she reached the age of 15 years. She claims that this was a positive placement for her and that she enjoyed living with Kathy.

During this time, Ms. "A" received a call from her sister who said that the foster agency who they were involved with wanted to place her in a group home because she didn't like the foster home that she was in. Ms. "A's" sister didn't want to go to a group home. Consequently, Ms. "A" ran away from her foster placement to "rescue" her sister and take her to her father's home. Ms. "A's" father had apparently been released from incarceration by this time and was residing in a single apartment. Consequently, Ms. "A" left the foster home without permission and was, consequently, reported as a "runaway," which commenced on 3/3/06. Ms. "A" remained on the run from March of 2006 until June of 2006 with a period of placement in the interim.

During this time, Ms. "A" had rented a room from a friend. Her sister had money from her job, which allowed Ms. "A" to afford the rent. Her father and paternal grandfather also helped her, knowing quite well that Ms. "A" was on the run from foster care. She claims that her father did contact the Office of Children and Youth Services to notify them, but she and her sister would elude their father and the agency and, consequently, manipulated the paternal grandfather, who remained silent about their whereabouts. Ms. "A" stated in retrospect that she really hated this decision, however, because she truly liked living in foster care with Kathy. She really didn't want to be on runaway status and had preferred to be situated; however, she felt the need to come to her sister's aid because she didn't feel that her sister should be placed in a group home. She had also been slated to return to her biological mother's home around the same time, which raises the question of whether or not Ms. "A" unconsciously wanted to avoid being returned to her mother's home. She also doesn't feel that the County Office of Children and Youth Services searched very hard for her anyway, which, in part, allowed her to remain on runaway status as long as she did.

Ms. "A" informs me that two months into her runaway status, she spent the majority of time at her paternal grandfather's home and on the streets. She recalls that she just hung out and didn't do much of anything. During this period of time, she claims that she had thoughts about turning herself in and did talk to her mother about it, but decided against it. Her mother had suggested that she consider negotiating with the County Office of Children and Youth Services, but Ms. "A" feared being remanded to a group home and was, consequently, reluctant to even contact the agency for fear of negative reprisal. Ms. "A's" aunt contacted the police, who then contacted Ms. Z, a caseworker with the County Office of Children and Youth Services' and informed the police of Ms. "A's" whereabouts. The police reportedly came to the paternal grandfather's home and returned Ms. "A" to the foster care system. Ms. "A" claims that her paternal grandfather was at work at the time that the police arrived at his home.

The police reportedly took Ms. "A" to the Government Center and eventually to the Office of Children and Youth Services, who, in turn, sent her to a residential center in eastern Pennsylvania, where she was placed for one week. Ms. "A" ran away from that facility, however, and returned to her hometown. She was on the run once again for a 1-month period of time. She apparently had a dentist appointment and was transported by a driver to the dentist's office. The driver reportedly fell asleep in the waiting room and Ms. "A" took advantage of the opportunity to abscond. She ran down the street until she saw a taxicab and flagged it down. The taxi driver allowed Ms. "A" to use his phone to call a friend who came and retrieved her. Her girlfriend took her to her paternal grandfather's home where she remained once again until 6/16/06. On 5/15/06, Ms. "A" went to the paternal grandfather's house and her paternal aunt's house. She basically hung out there and attended church. She was running the streets for some of the time until she was eventually taken into custody; however, she informs me that the entire time that she was on the run, she was not involved with any trouble with the law.

It was on 6/15/06 that Ms. "A" and her sister got into an argument over the fact that the sister had revealed private information about Ms. "A" to other people. Ms. "A" went to her friend's house and went for a walk to the store with her. While they were walking to the grocery market, the two chatted about Ms. "A's" circumstance. She claims that they had been en route to the market to buy candy. Once at the market, they each bought some candy and were en route to J's house via Seventh Street when they passed a female's home by the name of V. Apparently, Ms. "A's" friend, J, knew this young lady from school. V was seated on her front porch, talking on her cell phone. At that point, J whispered to Ms. "A," "I want that cell phone," intimating that she planned to steal it from V. Ms. "A" said to her, "You're crazy!" J subsequently walked up to V and asked her to borrow her cell phone. When V gave it to J, she took it and ran from her. Ms. "A" claims that she also started running as well, mostly to avoid questioning about the incident. The two girls ran into an alleyway, at which point Ms. "A" stopped to see where J had gone. She then learned that she had run into a dead end. Apparently, the victim, V, came around the corner and approached Ms. "A" with her sister, who had accompanied her. V asked for her cell phone back, at which point Ms. "A" responded, "I don't have it." A fight ensued and Ms. "A" picked up a board in an attempt to defend herself. V's sister, N, held her from behind and was punching her, but, apparently, she also had a blade in between her fingers in which she inflicted cuts and punctures on Ms. "A." Ms. "A" showed me that she had sustained several puncture wounds from this altercation. Two male bystanders on the street intervened and broke up the fight. V's father consequently came down to the scene and took N and V back to their home. The two men subsequently walked Ms. "A" to J's home. J, took Ms. "A" to her aunt's home. Ms. "A's" father subsequently called the aunt, and J took Ms. "A" and her sister to V's house to show her parents the violent wounds that N inflicted on Ms. "A." Ms. "A" claims that before they left her father's home, she grabbed a kitchen knife and put it in her pocket because she anticipated a potential altercation. While at V and N's home, Ms. "A" claims that she impulsively ran up to N and literally stabbed her in the back.

The knife blade actually broke off in her back from the force of the stabbing. Ms. "A" subsequently ran to her father's house. It was her father who later called the State Police. The police arrived and took Ms. "A" to the hospital. Ms. "A" claims that she didn't really want to stab N, but her sister, F, "egged her on." Ms. "A" also claimed that she was so angry and charged up over what had occurred that she lost control of herself. Apparently, the police arrived and interviewed Ms. "A" at police headquarters. At that point, she signed the *Miranda* warning without an attorney present. Ms. "A" was brought before a magistrate and remanded to the county prison, where she remains as of this writing.

I had an opportunity to review the voluminous amount of information with regard to Ms. "A's" various placements and involvement with the County Office of Children and Youth Services, several hospital units, and the Office of Juvenile Probation. Police reports indicate that the victim in this matter, Ms. N, was classified as a Class I trauma patient at the hospital as a result of the stab wound incurred during the altercation. As a result, she was transferred to the operating room at the local Hospital Center where her wounds were repaired. Further psychiatric records indicate that while Ms. "A" was in placement, she had been diagnosed as bipolar disorder type I, manic with psychosis, intermittent explosive disorder, and oppositional defiant disorder. She had been placed on psychotropic medication, which included Seroquel, 200 mg, 1 tab., p.o., b.i.d., and Tegretol-XR, 200 mg, p.o., b.i.d. She apparently responded well to this regimen and stabilized in a relatively short period of time.

There is also indication in the records that suggest that Ms. "A" had a fascination with fire and played with matches during the time that she was attending the hospital school in 2004 and 2005. It was further indicated that she attempted to pass a book of matches to peers while at the lunch table. She also had passed her medication tablets to two peers during her stay at this facility. She was often found with lighters and matches on her person, which was against regulations. This has to do with the fact that she smoked cigarettes, however, there had also been ongoing concern about a preoccupation with fire, which Ms. "A" didn't necessarily deny during the interview. She admitted that, when she was very young, she engaged in burning covers and papers on a wall while at her mother's home, but denies using fire in any other medium. She had also possessed illegal contraband, such as cigarettes, cigars, and matches while in the Mentor Program.

Additional records from the juvenile probation office indicate that there was a great deal of fighting within the biological home between members of Ms. "A's" family of origin. She was reported as being much different when in foster placement, particularly when she could view herself in a "positive light." She clearly became very frustrated with her mother and her mother's behaviors and the frequent physical relocations, which soured Ms. "A." She was reported to have initially been placed in foster care on 1/13/94, due to her mother's neglect.

It is reported that Ms. "A's" family of origin has a history of bipolar disorder with her mother and brother, along with another sibling, who is diagnosed with attention deficit/hyperactivity disorder.

MENTAL STATUS

During the clinical interview, Ms. "A" presented herself as being alert and responsive and oriented in time, place, and person. Her mood and affect were congruous and appropriate. She was devoid of any psychotic ideation interfering with her primary or secondary thought processes. She denied any hallucinations or delusions and equally denied any suicidal or homicidal ideation. There was a subtle air of depression with her demeanor, particularly when talking about her family of origin and her history of multiple relocations and place-ments. She is also very unhappy about the fact that her parents both have a strong history of criminal activity and illicit substance use, which, obviously, has been a major source of distress to her. She has no history of physical, sexual, or psychological abuse and is not sexually active.

There is no other reported history of mental illness with her family of origin other than that which is indicated with Ms. "A's" mother and brother. She also has another sibling who is reported to be diagnosed with attention deficit/hyperactivity disorder, combined type. Ms. "A" denies any history of illicit drug or alcohol use herself, although she does admit to smoking cigarettes. She also does admit that both of her parents have a history of heavy illicit drug abuse. Her mother has a history of heroin, crack cocaine, and alcohol abuse, and her father has a history of marijuana and primarily alcohol abuse. Ms. "A" is negative for any other history of criminal activity prior to the instant offense, other than one assault several years earlier between her and her girlfriend. There is no history of other criminal activities other than being reported as a runaway.

Ms. "A" does have a history of mental health treatment in which she saw numerous counselors and family therapists while in placement. There is no indication of how she fared in treatment other than the fact that treatment was often disrupted because of her many relocations.

Prior to her incarceration, Ms. "A" was maintained on a regimen of psychotropic medication, which is reflective of treatment for bipolar illness. This regimen involves Seroquel, 200 mg, 1 tab., b.i.d., and Tegretol-XR, 200 mg, 1 tab., b.i.d. Ms."A" reported to me at the time of the assessment that, since being incarcerated, she was not maintained on any medication whatsoever.

A review of the records from the Department of Corrections indicates that Ms. "A" has adjusted fairly well to incarceration. She has only received a few misconduct reports over minor incidents. One infraction included tearing her underwear into pieces in order to use the elastic band as a hair tie. The other infraction was for breaking off the tooth of a comb in order to hold open her nose piercing to avoid its closure. She was also found to be in possession of unauthorized correspondence from another inmate, which consisted of a written letter.

Aside from the aforementioned, there were no other reported incidences of misconduct involving Ms. "A."

Ms. "A" does have a history of being quite active athletically. She enjoys swimming, playing basketball, biking, dancing/singing, and fishing. She also enjoys animals and utilizing the Internet to research various topics and current issues. She is reported to be a relatively hard worker and can be a conscientious student when she wants to be.

COGNITIVE AND INTELLECTUAL FUNCTIONING

On 7/13/06, Ms. "A" was administered the Wechsler Abbreviated Scale of Intelligence (WASI). She produced a verbal score of 112 and a performance score of 99, yielding a full scale IQ score of 107. This score places her in the average range of intellectual functioning on the Wechsler scales. The 13-point difference between her verbal and performance score (with verbal > performance) is indicative of some depression, as well as denotes some problem with concentration. This involves primarily visual spatial reasoning. Ms. "A's" greatest strengths were evidenced on subtest areas of similarities, which measures logical abstractive (categorical) reasoning. She also had a high average score in general vocabulary and on tasks measuring spacial conceptualization. Her lowest strengths appear in the area of matrix reasoning, which measures visual spatial reasoning, visual organization, and an analysis of parts with a whole. These scores are commensurate with previous intelligence scores obtained in January of 2005 through the school district. School records also indicate that Ms. "A" has a learning disability with weaknesses in the area of mathematical problem solving skills, written expression, vocabulary, and encoding skills.

Overall, Ms. "A" does have a good, strong, average IQ with some possible attention deficit aspects, which may or may not be an artifact of her bipolar disorder.

On the Bender Visual-Motor Gestalt test, Ms. "A" produced designs that fell well into the normal range. There was some chaotic placement of her figures, which indicates impulsiveness, however, aside from this, there were no angulation or rotation difficulties. There was some slight heavy pencil emphasis on two designs that involved dots, although no gross embellishments were noted.

On the Bender recall, Ms. "A" was able to recall eight out of the nine designs from immediate memory, suggesting that she has excellent immediate recall. Once again, there was some heavy pencil emphasis and some slight angulation on several of her figures, however, no major rotations or embellishments were noted.

Overall, there are no indications that would suggest any major learning impairments, nor were there any neurological deficits noted. Overall, there were no indications of any major impediments existing with her higher executive functioning.

PERSONALITY DYNAMICS

Ms. "A" is a very interesting young adolescent female who truly has a number of positive qualities. She can present as a bright, affable young lady who appeals to others when she is on an even keel. Unfortunately, Ms. "A" had very little choice of the environment in which she was raised, which was laden with illicit drug abuse, neglect, turmoil, and inconsistency. This young lady, unfortunately, never really had much of a chance in that she was born to two parents who had criminal histories and maintained criminal activities throughout her lifetime. She only made it to the age of one or two before needing to be placed in foster care due to what was deemed to be neglect in an unfit household. This was followed by a cascade of tumultuous placements and interruptions in the bonding process, which no doubt had a major impact on the course of Ms. "A's" life. For example, some of her fire-setting behaviors seemed to pertain to the disruption of her placement in the natural environment, as well as her feeling of loss of control. Even though there has been no further preoccupation with fire reported, she still laments over the loss of her natural environment and has acted-out by running away from her various placements.

Surprisingly, this young lady has avoided illicit substance use and has not engaged in any alcohol use whatsoever. When asked specifically how she was able to successfully avoid alcohol use, she stated quite frankly that she didn't want to end up the same way that her parents had as a result of their substance use. She does use tobacco products, however, she has managed to maintain her abstinence with any sexual activity, which is, again, quite admirable when one considers her environment and what she has been exposed to. Unfortunately, the greatest detriment with this young lady is her mental illness, which caused her to be highly volatile at times and in this most recent incident, inflammatory. She is burdened with a bipolar disorder I, manic type, with psychotic features. Her behaviors are also consistent with intermittent explosive disorder, which has been evidenced and documented at least twice during the course of her young life.

The results of the psychological test indicate that this is a bright, intuitive young lady who, when stable, does quite well in society. There is quite a bit of underlying hostility that exists with her, however. She perceives herself as having gotten a "raw deal" regarding her family of origin. This has clearly contributed to a substantial amount of stress and depression. She is in denial of her anxiety and depression, in which she reports a very low level on the Beck scales. There is also no indication of suicidal behavior. She actually has very little degree of hopelessness and attempts to remain as optimistic as possible.

As a result of her experiences, there is indication that Ms. "A" has difficulty trusting authority and more important, trusting males in general. In fact, this is one of the reasons that she has avoided becoming involved intimately with any males up to this point. There is indication that she views herself as being susceptible to negative influence by others. In many respects, she is distraught over the events that have occurred over the past several years and, in many ways, wishes that she could start her life over.

Ms. "A" still maintains hope for a cohesive family life, although much of her dreams in this regard have been shattered. She doesn't have a very good self-image nor self-esteem as a female and may be struggling with some issues related to her sexual identity. There is indication that she does have a flair for creativity and has a lot of energy, although this energy may be part of her illness that spirals out of hand from time to time, particularly when she is provoked. There are some oppositional qualities with Ms. "A" that clearly exist with a potential for her to escalate into anger outbursts very rapidly.

On the Minnesota Multiphasic Personality Inventory-A (MMPI-A), Ms."A" produced a profile that suggests that she was extremely defensive in answering the test questions. Consequently, it was determined that she is somewhat biased to underreporting psycho-pathology and her condition may be underestimated due to her de-fensiveness. There is indication that she is protective in many ways with regard to her sexual identity and also has a strong propensity towards manic-type behaviors. There is no indication that suggests that she has a strong potential for antisocial personality character-istics, and that the majority of her behaviors has more to do with her mental illness than it has to do with any antisocial condition. This is not to say that she wouldn't be prone towards engaging in antisocial acts during periods of expansive mood, which has certainly been the case in the past, as well as with the instant offense.

As a result of her scores on the Jesness Behavior Checklist and the HCR-20 Violence Risk Assessment, there is indication that Ms. "A" has the propensity to act out violently on occasion, specifically when provoked. Her behaviors may be quite lethal, as with the instant offense. Overall, her general score on the HCR-20 is a 26 out of 40, indicating that she is a moderate to high risk for violent acting-out behaviors. This score suggests that, due to her poor interpersonal skills, her anger and the destabilizing effect of her environment with her family of origin causes her to be at a significant risk. This is despite the fact that her profile on the Aggression Questionnaire (AQ) suggests a low level of anger and hostility. This is something that can very easily spiral quickly to the point where she acts out in aggressive, erratic fashion. Once again, this is most likely to occur in tandem with her bipolar illness and is more situation specific than it is behavior that would occur on a regular basis.

FACTORS AFFECTING DECERTIFICATION

Pursuant to Act 43 Pa C.S.A. §§ 6302, Factors Affecting Decertification, the impact of Ms. "A's" offense on the victim/victims was severe. It is my understanding that the stab wounds that were incurred by the victim were in a rather serious location of the torso and the victim needed to be transported to the Valley Hospital and undergo immediate surgery. The impact of the offense on the community was equally severe in that it raises the level of vigilance and also serves as a threat to the community at large. The threat to the safety of the general public is, in this respect, of significance as well. The nature and circumstances of the offense, despite being a result of provocation initially, are still considered severe because Ms. "A" had adequate time to calm down and think about her actions, which she failed to do. It should be noted, once again, that this behavior was likely fueled in part by her bipolar illness. The degree of her culpability is clear and she certainly is aware of her responsibility and is remorseful for her actions. She did express remorse and concern for the victim during the clinical interview.

It is in my professional opinion that the adequacy and duration of dispositional alternatives available in the juvenile system are such that Ms. "A" may benefit from them substantially. She is clearly amenable to treatment, supervision, and rehabilitation in the juvenile system long before the age of 21. She is presently 15½ years of age, which leaves her with a good 5½ years in which to achieve those goals. In my conversation with Mr. Robert Smith of County SPORE on 12/13/06, he informed me that Ms. "A" had done quite well when under supervision with him and was cooperative and amenable to his leads and directives. Her mental capacity is excellent with a good strong IQ that is documented within the average range of intelligence. There is also enough level of maturity with Ms. "A" to suggest that she would be responsive to various treatment interventions within the juvenile system. Based on the records that were reviewed, in past placements, Ms. "A" had done fairly well and has responded positively to treatment, both pharmacologically, as well as through counseling.

With regard to the degree of criminal sophistication, there was not very much time for Ms. "A" to plan her assault, although she did have thoughts and actions to suggest that her behaviors constituted a substantial risk. She has only one previous history of a minor assault in which she pulled a girl's hair one year prior. Therefore, the extent of prior delinquent history is relatively insignificant. There is indication that she was successful in her attempts to rehabilitate, but, once again, this recent incident is very likely to have been greatly affected by her serious mental illness, namely her bipolar illness, as well as her disrupted living situation.

It is my opinion, within a reasonable degree of psychological certainty, that Ms. "A" is therefore amenable to treatment and rehabilitation in the juvenile system and that she will likely remain a good candidate for treatment throughout the course of her probationary period.

In order to aid in the development of future treatment and placement, the aforementioned impressions and following recommendations are all offered within a reasonable degree of psychological certainty:

RECOMMENDATIONS

1. I strongly recommend that Ms. "A" be considered for decertification in the juvenile system and that she be considered for a secure placement in a facility that will address her impulsive, aggressive behaviors, as well as her bipolar illness. She clearly needs to be under psychiatric care and maintained on a psychotropic regimen of medication that will stabilize her moods. This will be the core ingredient to her partial success in treatment for her illness. A secure placement will also be necessary in order to ensure that she will not run away from such a facility. She also needs to undergo individual psychotherapy in order to learn how to deal appropriately with

psychosocial stressors and reduce the tension from circumstances that contribute to escalation of her anger and manic behaviors. Such a program may also help her to develop her social skills and also to deal with her many issues regarding her family of origin.

2. Subsequent to placement in a secure program, I would strongly recommend that she be considered for outpatient treatment and possibly group psychotherapy. Therapy should address issues stemming from her family of origin, as well as anger management, stress reduction, and interpersonal relationships. There is also the aspect of her depression, which she tends to deny. This needs to be addressed in great detail. I would also recommend that Ms. "A" follow-up with a psychiatrist on an outpatient basis and that her regular medication compliance should be mandatory, along with submitting to regular therapeutic serum levels to ensure that her medication is within a therapeutic range. Her compliance with treatment is essential in order for her to fully rehabilitate. I would also recommend that she continue with family therapy on an outpatient basis in order to address the issues surrounding her disenchantment with her parents and the traumas that she sustained as a child.

3. It is not clear, depending on the age that Ms. "A" will be once she is released from prison, whether or not she should return to the care of either of her biological parents. Hopefully, one of the two of these individuals will have stabilized their environment and will be able to provide a secure and salubrious setting to which Ms. "A" can return. She clearly needs to work through issues with her family of origin, although, if it is deemed at any point that these are not viable alternatives, she should consider either independent living, or perhaps finish out her youth until the age of 21 in foster placement. This is certainly a tenuous issue since Ms. "A" has been in numerous placements as long as she has been in her biological parents' care and my guess is that she is tired of being in the system. Despite this, however, she needs to be in a placement where she can continue to rehabilitate and make improvement since this will be optimal in allowing her to go on with her life in a productive fashion.

4. I would strongly urge that, wherever Ms. "A" is placed, she continue with her education and obtain her high school

diploma. She is a good candidate for higher education and will likely do well and should be encouraged to pursue this avenue. If she is not college bound, then I would strongly recommend that she become involved in a Vo-Tech program or some type of job skills training so that she could develop a skill for herself. This will aid her in the future with securing a career. Regardless of the direction, she should be encouraged to engage in productive activity and do the best that she can in the best interest of her complete rehabilitation.

5. It goes without saying that Ms. "A" will likely remain in the ranks of juvenile probation until the age of 21. She should certainly adhere to all of the directives set forth by the Office of Juvenile Probation and remain mindful of the stipulations of her probation in the best interest of her full rehabilitation.

Unless the above recommendations are strongly considered, future behavioral and/or emotional problems are very likely.

Respectfully submitted,

D, PhD, ABPP
Board Certified in Clinical Psychology
American Board of Professional Psychology

PRELIMINARY REPORT ON PSYCHOLOGY BOARD COMPLAINT BY MS. B AGAINST A, PhD

February 8, 2009

DATABASE

In preparing this preliminary report, we have reviewed materials including but not limited to the following:

1. Record of B, including treatment notes by Dr. A and others and various cards and letters to and from Dr. A
2. Complaint, related documents and responses
3. Chronology of treatment
4. Chronology of hospitalizations
5. Medical summaries of charts
6. "Professional input" (including materials from Drs. 1, 2, 3, and 4, and Mses. 5, 6, 7, and 8)
7. Listing of actions in education, consultation, and remediation undertaken by Dr. A, some done before the complaint
8. Corrections and rebuttals to various documents by Dr. A
9. Summaries of various documents
10. Communications by and to various attorneys in the case
11. Consultation notes prepared by Dr. A regarding various consultations
12. Ms. B's diary notes

Depositions of:

A, PhD
Ms. B, Vols. I and II
C, MD
D

QUALIFICATIONS

The qualifications of F, MD, are set forth in a curriculum vitae submitted separately. In addition, Dr. F has served as an expert or consulting witness in over 250 cases involving boundary issues throughout the United States and in Canada. Furthermore, Dr. F's articles in peer-reviewed professional journals are considered essential and are some of the most often and widely cited in this area.

The qualifications of G, PhD, are set forth in a curriculum vitae submitted separately. In addition, Dr. G has served as an expert or consulting witness in approximately 25 cases involving boundary violations. Furthermore, Dr. G has served as an author or coauthor of 35 peer-reviewed articles addressing issues specific to the standard of practice for psychologists conducting psychotherapy.

FORENSIC QUESTION

At the request of Attorney H we were asked: What could be concluded about the particular difficulties presented by a patient such as Ms. B in her treatment by Dr. A? What are the implications of those issues for sanctions for Dr. A? What contextual issues were missed or overlooked in the board investigation? What evidentiary deficits appear in the assessment of the care by Dr. A by subsequent treaters of Ms. B?

CONCLUSIONS

Based on our review of the above materials and our own training and experience, it is Dr. F's professional opinion to a reasonable degree of medical certainty and Dr. G's professional opinion to a reasonable degree of psychological certainty that Ms. B presented extraordinary difficulties to treatment by anyone for reasons discussed subsequently; that Dr. A actively sought consultation and input from a number of highly reputable sources during the treatment, some of which consults were blocked or refused; that, although Ms. B blames her entire difficulties on Dr. A, both Ms. B's underlying mental health issues before, during, and after her treatment with Dr. A account parsimoniously for her current problems; that Ms. B's experiences with past treaters such as J, PhD, and with subsequent treaters reveal the same issues and conflicts; that the years of success in Ms. B's treatment by Dr. A indicate that useful care was being proffered; that after the inclusion of Dr. C in the treatment team, and after a series of ill-advised and highly atypical consultations with the patient present, the relationship deteriorated; that appropriate referrals took place, refuting any claims of abandonment; that somehow the interventions that Dr. A attempted are clearly being misunderstood or misrepresented as though they were sexualized boundary violations without basis; and that appropriate, valid sanctions that are case specific would require only some remedial education on personality disorders, boundary issues, and rejection of inappropriate consultations. Note that it apparently takes five treaters to deal with this patient at present.

Supporting data for these conclusions now follow.

SUPPORTING DATA

For coherence, supporting data are presented under a series of headings.

PROBLEMS WITH CONTEXT

As noted repeatedly in peer-reviewed articles on the subject of boundaries, the single most important factor in determining whether a boundary event is a crossing (relatively harmless) or a violation (exploitative and presumptively harmful) is the matter of context. Indeed, it is only necessary to note the *abstracts* of two significant articles in this area (attached), appearing in the peer-reviewed official journal of the American Psychiatric Association, to discover the importance of this essential element, without even needing to go to the full content.

The centrality of context is so probative in assessing a boundary issue that the identical behavior may, in one context, represent a problematic boundary violation and, in another, a harmless crossing; once again, the former are characterized by an intent to exploit. These critical distinctions may be lost in a kind of false syllogism frequently encountered in boundary-related litigation concerning a particular behavior: for example, boundary-violating predators send cards and gifts; this therapist sent cards and gifts; therefore this therapist is a boundary violator. In our extensive experience with such cases, this violation of elementary logic is surprisingly common among fact finders.

In the instant case, several crossings occurred, including, but not limited to, meeting outside the office, cards and gifts, and limited hand holding. Had they occurred in a progressive manner without the patient's urgent requests or exigencies of space (no office space available so meet in a public place) as part of a predatory sequence by a therapist intent on exploiting the patient, they would indeed be considered ominous harbingers of a possible sexual exploitation and thus problematic in themselves. But nothing of that sort occurred here. In context, with a particular kind of patient, they likely represented attempts to reach a highly demanding patient and avert another hospitalization. A related contextual factor was the recommendation from one consultant that Dr. A strive for a more "relational" mode of therapy. Note for completeness of context assessment that Dr. A never hugged Ms. B despite significant pressure to do so and at least one alleged threatened "hug by force"; and the overwhelming majority of sessions were kept to 50 minutes barring emergencies. These two boundary areas are commonly violated in cases of actual boundary problems.

Some events, which would be problematic in other contexts, are simply irrelevant. Exploitative therapists may unexpectedly meet with a victim on a weekend to take advantage of the absence of others. In this case, however, Saturday treatment hours were part of the usual routine (itself an important context), which the patient well understood.

Diagnosis and Its Implications

Ms. B's diagnosis—and perhaps more importantly, her clinical condition—are vital aspects of understanding this case and complaint. Note at the outset that it is unethical for us to give an *independent* diagnosis without a personal examination. In this case, other diagnosticians who *have* directly examined Ms. B have identified highly relevant diagnostic features that we will provisionally accept. A problem arises from the outset.

Ask any knowledgeable clinician blind, what is the most likely diagnosis for a patient who: struggles with mood swings, overdosing, difficulty tolerating boundaries and limit-setting; practices self-cutting; develops intense transferences to therapists; is dramatically and excessively oversensitive to minimal slights (e.g., suicidal ideation in reaction to email responses perceived as too short); is prone to distortion and misperception of factual content; makes efforts to control the therapy; has brief psychotic or prepsychotic episodes; uses dissociation as a defense mechanism; externalizes responsibility by blaming others and treats feelings as though they were external realities (i.e., "I feel" becomes "It is")? Only one diagnosis out of the entire diagnostic system would fit: borderline personality disorder (BPD). However, these patients are notoriously difficult to treat; for example, the galley of an article on such patients in the Harvard Mental Health Letter (attached) begins:

Borderline personality disorder is one of the most challenging psychiatric disorders to treat. . . . The disorder consists of three major components: an unstable sense of self, impulsive thoughts and behaviors, and sudden shifts of mood. The result is a maelstrom of symptoms. Patients with borderline personality disorder may become suddenly depressed, irritable, anxious, or enraged for no apparent reason. They provoke conflict, even while fearing abandonment. They engage in self-destructive habits such as self-mutilation or substance abuse, and are at higher than average risk for suicide. . . . [P]atients are unable to interpret or control their own emotions, *and may misunderstand and overreact to what other people say or do.* (p. x) [Emphasis added]

As a result of these difficulties this diagnosis is associated, understandably, with some stigma. As an illustration, attention is drawn to the fact that in a significant number of Ms. B's records, Axis II of the diagnostic system (on which BPD would be listed) is frequently described as "deferred" (that is, to be addressed later, though it never is). In another group of records, the Axis II is given as "Cluster B"—another diagnostic subgrouping that would also contain BPD. Finally, later charts actually state BPD as an Axis II diagnosis.

The factor of concern for stigma and the wish to avoid seeming to blame the patient account for an avoidance of the BPD diagnosis by some therapists; however, this self-blinding may leave treaters ill-equipped to deal constructively with the challenges presented by such individuals or to understand, appropriately and in context, another therapist's actions and difficulties. Although we cannot supply an *independent* diagnosis, the theoretical application of the official BPD criteria from the *Diagnostic and Statistical Manual* (DSM-IV-TR) may represent a useful exercise in the instant case.

General points: A pervasive pattern of instability of interpersonal relationship, self-image and affects, and marked impulsivity beginning in early adulthood and present in a variety of contexts, as indicated by five (or more) of the following:

1. Frantic efforts to avoid real or imagined abandonment. Note that Ms. B's diary reveals a constant preoccupation with whether A will leave her or be driven away.

2. A pattern of intense and unstable interpersonal relationships characterized by alternating between extremes of idealization and devaluation. While this arguably also applies to her husband, Ms. B shows this in multiple diary entries indicating her idealization of Dr. A, now presenting as devaluation in the form of blaming the latter for all her problems. More rapid alternations occurred during treatment when Ms. B would become preoccupied with a single comment from Dr. A and feel the relationship to be utterly compromised ("How could A say that?"), only to return to a working alliance with continued work.

3. Identity disturbance: markedly and persistently unstable self-image or sense of self. In this case, the matter went beyond "Who am I?" as the diary reveals, to her uncertain sexual orientation: Is she a lesbian or not? Note that this particular confusion is common in patients with BPD.

4. Impulsivity in at least two areas that are potentially self-damaging (suicidal impulses are separated out into criterion 5: e.g., spending, sex, substance abuse, reckless driving, binge eating). Although the best example here is death threats against Dr. A and others (self-damaging as they bring one to police attention, as here), this issue is better located under the next category.

5. Recurrent suicidal behaviors, gestures, or threats or self-mutilating behavior. Of course, the case is replete with examples of this criterion in both its aspects; it is the major trigger for recurrent hospitalizations.

6. Affective instability due to marked reactivity of mood (e.g., intense episodic dysphoria, irritability, or anxiety usually lasting a few hours and only rarely more than a few days). The records reveal countless examples of rapid mood swings, sometimes within minutes, approached pharmacologically by traditional and novel mood stabilizer medications; Seroquel appeared particularly helpful.

7. Chronic feelings of emptiness. Ms. B's diary reveals self-reports of this kind of existential experience, sometimes as feeling nothing or numb.

8. Inappropriate intense anger or difficulty controlling anger (e.g., frequent displays of temper, constant anger, recurrent physical fights). The record contains many examples of Ms. B's fury at Ms. K, Dr. A, and others when she is not given the license she demands or when limits are set on her. Hitting her husband, making death threats against Dr. A and others and overdosing itself would be examples here of a control problem (note in passing that these death threats—an extremely serious symptom connoting significant pathology—appear almost ignored or discounted as serious when subsequent treaters attempt to assess the patient's risk and condition and the need for flexible responses). Some of the recorded episodes of dissociation may also be responses to rage.

9. Transient stress-related paranoid ideation or severe dissociative symptoms. This category includes the so-called "micropsychoses" that historically made this entity so hard to understand and taxonomize, especially because, as is commonly the case, the psychotic material emerged only in the transference, thus leaving clinicians, attorneys, and fact finders baffled to make sense of a patient seemingly intact otherwise. The film, *Fatal Attraction,* captures this well: The lead actress plays an editor in a New York publishing house—a highly competitive and demanding job—but the character undergoes a serious, murderous psychotic decompensation in the context of the relationship with the male protagonist—a relationship that she both misinterprets and experiences as abandoning. The micropsychotic content in Ms. B includes seeing blood dripping down shower walls and fearing to see Dr. A's face as "horrifying and disfigured" [diary note of 7/8/99]. This distortion of the therapist's face or person is one of the most common psychotic phenomena in BPD since it relates to psychosis in the transference.

The dissociation mentioned (a trancelike state that represents a "tuning out" of external reality for relief from overwhelming feeling) is important in other ways because the person usually has amnesia for what happened during the dissociated state. Thus, when Ms. B vehemently dismisses the reality of her witnessed behavior (e.g., Dr. A describing her approaching Dr. A with arms outstretched as though to force a hug), it does not necessarily mean that Ms. B is lying; it may also mean that she was in a dissociated (trance) state when she behaved in that way, and thus it is not accessible to her memory (without, say, hypnosis).

The above listing represents the "official" diagnostic criteria for BPD. In our forensic experience three additional factors cause problems for treaters and confuse and baffle fact finders. The first is high intelligence, some obsessive tendencies (e.g., rumination) and articulateness in the patient with BPD. Both treaters and subsequent fact finders often cannot fully grasp that such a marked departure from reality can occur with someone so intelligent and otherwise oriented and intact: The patient does not *seem* crazy, so that when the patient devalues or blames the previous therapist for ruining her life, the claim is plausible and even persuasive. *Note that none of the subsequent treaters sought input, previous records or any information from Dr. A.* So a serious deviation from the standard of care by otherwise apparently competent subsequent treating clinicians might be explained (though, regrettably, not excused) by the patient's persuasiveness: "Don't talk to her, she ruined my life and abused me; take my word for it." Uncharacteristically, the subsequent treaters may have taken this on faith.

The second is the issue of "splitting," a complex but important and often clinically dominant factor in assessment of the patient and the treater. In the simplest possible terms, patients with BPD typically use a form of management of intense emotions by dividing the world into "good guys and bad guys," wherein the good feelings are attributed to one person or set of persons and the bad, disavowed feelings are attributed to another set. This phenomenon is also referred to as "all-or-none thinking." An example here would be that Dr. A is bad, abusive, and caused all her problems while her current treaters are good (earlier, Ms. K was bad and Dr. A was good). Having five treaters at present at one time may, in fact, prevent some splitting, but even that breaks down, as Ms. B's overdose in front of one of her subsequent treaters suggests.

The forensic point here is that all negative feelings are "dumped" on the person or group who constitute the down side of the split—in the case of the instant litigation, Dr. A. Since the patient believes the validity of her own defense mechanism, the negative view may convince others. Because this is not an individual clinical phenomenon—rather, a social field phenomenon—it took some time for the profession itself to appreciate this phenomenon and its dynamic origins.

The third factor is boundary confusion in the patient completely independent of the therapist. A peer-reviewed article (attached) in the official journal of the American Psychiatric Association puts it this way:

Under stress, patients with borderline personality disorder may lose sight of the me–thee boundary and . . . may induce similar confusion in therapists. This confusion may derive from patients' own boundary-blurring interpersonal manner. If the therapist colludes in such boundary confusion, reciprocal perceptions of both the real therapist and the real patient may be powerfully influenced and distorted by the intense affects, longings and wishes common in patients with borderline personality disorder. (p. x)

Strict adherence to boundaries is recommended here, but note that Dr. A was getting directly opposite advice from her trusted colleague and consultant, Dr. C.

SIGNIFICANT DATA OMISSIONS

To review, the omission of relevant data from Dr. A's treatment that might clarify the views of the subsequent treaters who ignored those data has been mentioned above, as has the curious indifference of evaluators to Ms. B's history of death threats to Dr. A and others as indices of the severity of her disturbance. An additional omission is the fact that Ms. B was noncompliant with her prescribed Seroquel during the key summer of 1999. Seroquel acts not only as a nighttime sedative and mood stabilizer but also as an antipsychotic, an effect that would aid Ms. B in avoiding distorting or misinterpreting experiences in the real world. This significant vulnerability appears also avoided in assessment of Ms. B's capacity to appreciate objectively what Dr. A was actually trying to accomplish, and Dr. A's attempts to deal with Ms. B.

SOME SIGNIFICANT BOUNDARY CROSSINGS AND AVOIDANCE OF SAME

The main trouble in this case appears to flow from the Scott Peck quotation offered to Ms. B with alleged motives of caring and encouragement. Ms. B apparently leaped to the conclusion that Dr. A was in love with her and that therefore therapy could not continue (an example of "I *feel* this, therefore it IS this"). Ms. B allegedly showed the card with a complete and utter absence of any context to her friend who pronounced it a valentine. Ms. B unbendingly refused to accept any explanations from Dr. A as to the actual purpose and meaning of the card ("I *feel* it means this, therefore it DOES mean this"). The final breakdown of the relationship flows indirectly from this card.

Clearly with patients like Ms. B sending this kind of card was a technical mistake; such patients are often incapable of taking the other person's perspective and hold tenaciously to their own (mis)perceptions. Given that many cards and the plant gift were handled appropriately by Ms. B, suggesting that this card might also be managed, this error seems minor and not deserving of extensive re-education or other extensive sanctions against Dr. A.

On the patient's request, music was played on one or two occasions. Since patients with BPD, because of their troubled history, often have difficulty taking seriously verbal interactions from others (as in the discussion about the meaning of the card) the use of music and, in some cases, expressive art, may offer a way of reaching the patient. In context, the music may have been helpful or soothing to the patient; in any case, there is not a scintilla of evidence that it exploited her.

Note for contrast that offers to hug the patient, dance with the patient, and the like were resisted appropriately and the 50-minute time was adhered to almost all the time.

A final comment might be relevant from a peer-reviewed journal:

> In the case examples [in the attached article on boundary problems], the patient was often either a professional or someone sophisticated, trained or experienced in psychology, psychiatry, or psychotherapy. Often they were extremely intelligent and articulate; in several of the cases the patients were more articulate than the therapist and—consequently—more convincing in telling the story of their complaint. Patients with personality disorders, perhaps in particular those with borderline personality disorder, are distinguished from other forms of psychopathology by the possibility of successful, high functioning outside intense relationships; indeed, the decompensations in the cases were limited to the transference relationships.

The patients' high functioning concealed primitive dynamics that were largely missed by the therapists; the high functioning also allowed the patients, within litigation and outside the transference-bound relationship, to present their cases persuasively, despite the "craziness" of some of the content. Of course, the transference itself and its mismanagement may have brought out regressive trends not present in the patient's outside lives. (p. x)

The relevance of this analysis to the present case is self-evident.

CONCLUSION

It should be understood that this report proffers an opinion that is preliminary and is based on materials made available to us thus far (see list at the head of this report). This preliminary opinion may be modified as discovery continues.

On the whole and in context, Dr. A's treatment of this extraordinarily difficult patient broadly comported with the standard of care—for psychotherapists in general, and specifically for psychologists practicing in this jurisdiction; Dr. A resisted a number of pitfalls into which others have fallen, only to misjudge the effect of a card quoting an author the patient respected and admired. Confusing consultations in unusual format may have introduced problematic elements into the treatment and Dr. A's vision of the therapy; but on her own Dr. A showed diligence in seeking input from recognized experts. This difficult patient thwarted some of these laudable efforts. The record also documents Dr. A's diligent efforts to understand this patient and those like her—efforts initiated even before the claims and litigation began and continued after.

An appropriate remedial regimen offered by the board and suited to the actual problems in this case would include some instruction on special problems with boundary issues in personality-disordered patients and encouragement to trust her instincts when a consultation seems ill advised and to reject it.

Thank you for thinking of us in requesting this consultation; please let us know if you have any questions about the foregoing.

Very truly yours,
F, MD
G, PhD

Author Index

Subject Index

competency to consent to,
503–518
employment discrimination
and harassment
assessment prognosis for,
321
ethical guidelines on,
562–563
involuntary, 8–9 (*see also*
Civil commitment
assessments)
juvenile delinquent, 234
length of, 8
malpractice cases due to,
543–566, 654–655
medication as, 8–9, 82, 86, 98,
159, 268–269, 290, 404
negligent use of, 551–552,
554–555
noncompliance with, 354
personal injury case
assessment
recommendations for,
289–291
of sex offenders, 98
for trial incompetence, 8
Treatment consent competency
assessments:
communication of
assessment results,
512–518
data collection for, 507–511
data interpretation for,
511–512
ethical issues in, 507
focus and scope of, 506
informed consent in, 504,
505, 507, 514
overview of, 503–504
physiological assessments in,
516
preparing for, 505–507
psychological testing in,
508–511, 516
records review in, 514–515
referrals for, 505–506
third-party information in,
506–507, 514–515
timing of, 506
Trial competence:
amnesia and, 4–5
basis for raising issue of, 4
communication of
assessment results, 18–19
competence assessment
instruments, 14–17
data collection for, 12–18
data interpretation for, 18

decisional competence and, 7
defined, 3–4
ethical issues related to, 10
guilty pleas and, 5, 6
insanity defense and, 6
involuntary medication for,
8–9
juvenile decertification
assessment consideration
of, 231–232, 247
postconviction assessment
of, 219
preparing for assessment of,
9–11
restoration of, 79–92
standard of proof for, 7–8
treatment length after
incompetence finding, 8
waiving counsel and, 6–7
Trop v. Dulles (1958), 50

Understanding of Treatment
Disclosures, 509–510
U.S. v. Allen (1997), 189
U.S. v. Booker (2005), 66, 172
U.S. v. Brawner (1972), 125
U.S. v. Charters (1987), 8
U.S. v. Comstock (2010), 220
U.S. v. Denny-Schaffer (1993),
135
U.S. v. Duhon (2000), 7, 8
U.S. v. Marble (1991), 6
U.S. v. McBroom (1998), 181
U.S. v. Raineri (1980), 189

Validity Indicator Profile (VIP),
41, 130, 131, 162, 669
Verbal Comprehension Index
(VCI), 37
Victims. *See also* Plaintiffs
juvenile decertification
assessment consideration
of, 240
sentencing assessment
consideration of, 66
sex offender assessment
consideration of, 106, 111
violence risk to (*see* Violence
risk assessments)
Video/audio recordings:
of child abuse and neglect
assessments, 371, 372
of death penalty defendant
assessments, 158
of depositions, 640
forensic practices using, 631
of *Miranda* rights waivers,
34–35

of personal injury case
plaintiffs, 283, 285
of treatment consent
competency assessments,
507
Vignette methods, 511
Vineland Adaptive Behavior
Scales, 58, 429
Vineland Adaptive Behavior
Scales-II, 179
Violence, domestic. *See* Adult
abuse and neglect
assessments; Child abuse
and neglect assessments
Violence Risk Appraisal Guide
(VRAG), 61–62, 238,
341–342
Violence risk assessments. *See
also* Risk assessments
of AIDS encephalitis, 353
in Americans with
Disabilities Act
assessments, 462, 467,
474–475
of available means, 345
civil commitment
assessments as, 99–100,
103–104, 105, 107–108, 111,
479–499
clinical method of, 335–336,
343
communication of
assessment results,
354–356
data collection for, 337–343
data interpretation for,
343–354
in death penalty cases, 150,
156, 157, 162, 163, 164
of dementia, 352
of demographic
characteristics, 354
of electrolyte imbalance and
hypoxia, 353
of endocrine disorders,
353–354
of epilepsy, 353
in fitness for duty
assessments, 572, 582, 588
of history of violence/
impulsive behavior,
345–346
of intent, 345
in juvenile decertification
assessments, 241–242,
247–248
of mental retardation, 348,
352